2013

revised 34th edition

Howard J. Curtis

Contents

Introduction 4
Acknowledgements 6
Abbreviations 6
A Guide to the Location of Operational Bases in the UK 11
British Military Aircraft Registrations 12
British Military Aircraft Markings 14
Civil Registered Aircraft in UK Military Service 109
RAF Maintenance/Support Command Cross Reference 112
RN Landing Platform and Shore Station code-letters 115
Ships' Numeric Code-Deck Letters Analysis 115
RN Code-Squadron-Base-Aircraft Cross-check 116
Royal Air Force Squadron Markings 117
UK Military Aircraft Code Decode 122
Historic Aircraft in Overseas Markings 125
Irish Military Aircraft Markings 144
Overseas Military Aircraft Markings 145
US Military Aircraft Markings 204
UK-based USAF/Navy Aircraft 204
European-based USAF Aircraft 206
European-based US Navy/US Army Aircraft 207
US-based USAF Aircraft 210
US-based USN/USMC Aircraft 231
US-based US Coast Guard Aircraft 234
US Government Aircraft 234
Military Aviation Sites on the Internet 235

Photographs by Howard J Curtis (HJC) unless otherwise credited

This 34th edition published 2013

ISBN 978 0 7110 3761 8

Published by Ian Allan Publishing

an imprint of Ian Allan Publishing Ltd, Hersham, Surrey KT12 4RG.

Printed in England

Front cover: Michael Brazier / aviation-images.com

Back cover: Michael Brazier / aviation-images.com

Introduction

This 34th annual edition of *abc Military Aircraft Markings*, follows the pattern of previous years and lists in alphabetical and numerical order the aircraft that carry a United Kingdom military registration and which are normally based, or might be seen, in the UK. It also includes airworthy and current RAF/RN/Army aircraft that are based permanently or temporarily overseas. The term 'aircraft' used here covers powered, manned aeroplanes, helicopters, airships and gliders as well as target drones. Included are all the current Royal Air Force, Royal Navy, Army Air Corps, Ministry of Defence, QinetiQ - operated, manufacturers' test aircraft and civilian-owned aircraft with military markings or operated for the Ministry of Defence.

Aircraft withdrawn from operational use but which are retained in the UK for ground training purposes or otherwise preserved by the Services and in the numerous museums or collections are listed. The registrations of some incomplete aircraft have been included, such as the cockpit sections of machines displayed by the RAF, aircraft used by airfield fire sections and for service battle damage repair training (BDRT), together with significant parts of aircraft held by preservation groups and societies. Where only part of the aircraft fuselage remains, the abbreviation <ff> for front fuselage/cockpit section or <rf> for rear fuselage, is shown after the type. Many of these aircraft are allocated, and sometimes wear, a secondary identity, such as an RAF 'M' maintenance number; these numbers are listed against those aircraft to which they have been allocated.

A registration 'missing' from a sequence is either because it was never issued as it formed part of a 'black-out block' or because the aircraft has been written off, scrapped, sold abroad or allocated an alternative marking. Aircraft used as targets on MoD ranges to which access is restricted, and UK military aircraft that have been permanently grounded overseas and unlikely to return to Britain have generally been omitted. With the appearance of some military-registered UAVs, drones and small target aircraft at public events, these have now been included if they are likely to be seen.

In the main, the registrations listed are those markings presently displayed on the aircraft. Where an aircraft carries a false registration it is quoted in *italic type*. Very often these registrations are carried by replicas, that are denoted by <R> after the type. The manufacturer and aircraft type are given, together with recent alternative, previous, secondary or civil identity shown in round brackets. Complete records of multiple previous identities are only included where space permits. The operating unit and its based location, along with any known unit and code markings, in square brackets, are given as accurately as possible. Where aircraft carry special or commemorative markings, a $ indicates this. Unit markings are normally carried boldly on the sides of the fuselage or on the aircraft's tail. In the case of RAF, RN and AAC machines currently in service, they are usually one or two letters or numbers, while the RN also continues to use a well-established system of three-figure codes between 000 and 999 often with a two-letter deck code on the tail, denoting the aircraft's operational base. RN squadrons, units and bases are allocated blocks of numbers from which individual aircraft codes are issued. To help identification of RN bases and landing platforms on ships, a list of tail-letter codes with their appropriate name, helicopter code number, ship pennant number and type of vessel, is included; as is a helicopter code number/ships' tail-letter code grid cross-reference.

Code changes, for example when aircraft move between units and therefore the markings currently painted on a particular aircraft, might not be those shown in this edition because of subsequent events. Aircraft still under manufacture or not yet delivered to the Service, such as Eurofighter Typhoons and Airbus A400Ms are listed under their allocated registration numbers. Likewise there are a number of newly built aircraft for overseas air arms that carry British registrations for their UK test and delivery flights. The airframes which will not appear in the next edition because of sale, accident, etc., have their fates, where known, shown in italic type in the *locations* column.

The Irish Army Air Corps fleet is listed, together with the registrations of other overseas air arms whose aircraft might be seen visiting the UK from time to time. The registration numbers are as usually presented on the individual machine or as they are normally identified. Where possible, the aircraft's base and operating unit have been shown.

USAF, US Army and US Navy aircraft based in the UK and in Western Europe, and types that regularly visit the UK from the USA, are each listed in separate sections by aircraft type. The serial number actually displayed on the aircraft is shown in full, with additional Fiscal Year (FY) or full serial information also provided. Where appropriate, details of the operating wing, squadron allocation and base are added. The USAF is, like the RAF, in a continuing period of change, resulting in the adoption of new unit titles, squadron and equipment changes and the closure of bases. Only details that concern changes effected by February 2013 are shown.

Veteran and vintage aircraft which carry overseas military markings but which are based in the UK or regularly visit from mainland Europe, have been separately listed, showing their principal means of identification. The growing list of aircraft in government or military service, often under contract to private operating companies, which carry civil registrations has again been included at the end of the respective country.

With the use of the Internet now very well established as a rich source of information, the section listing a selection of military aviation 'world wide web' sites, has again been updated this year and 'Military Aircraft Markings' now has its own web site. Although only a few of these sites provide details of aircraft registrations and markings, they do give interesting insights into air arms and their operating units, aircraft, museums and a broad range of associated topics.

Information shown is believed to be correct at 28 February 2013.

Acknowledgements

The compiler wishes to thank the many people who have taken the trouble to send comments, additions, deletions and other useful information since the publication of the previous edition of Military Aircraft Markings. In particular the following individuals: Phil Adkin, Dave Arkle, Allan Barley, Lee Barton, Colin Boyd, Glyn Coney, Patrick Dirksen, Bob Dunn, Ray Fitton, Matt Hallam, Willy Henderickx, Billy McNally, Frank Mink, Ian Poxon, Norman Roberson, Mark Rourke, Paul Rushton, Mark Rourke, Mike Screech, Kev Slade, Glenn Stanley, Dave Taylor, David Thompson, Steve Tydeman & Tony Wood.

The 2013 edition has also relied upon the printed publications and/or associated internet web-sites as follows: Aerodata Quantum+, 'Aeroplane' magazine, Airfields Yahoo! Group, 'Air Forces Monthly' magazine, BAEG Yahoo! Group, Bones' Aviation Page, Breizh Spotting Team, Andy Carney/British Military Aviation Lists, CAA G-INFO Web Site, the late, lamented 'Classic Aircraft' magazine, 'Combat Aircraft' magazine, Delta Reflex, Fighter Control, 'FlyPast' magazine, Joe Baugher's Home Page, Brian Pickering/'Military Aviation Review', Mil Spotters' Forum, NAMAR Yahoo! Group, RAF Leeming Yahoo! Group, RAF Shawbury Yahoo! Group, 'Scramble' magazine, Souairport e-mail group, Target Lock web site, Tom McGhee/UK Serials Resource Centre, USMil Google Group, Vintage British Military Jets Yahoo! Group, Mick Boulanger & Mark Ray/Wolverhampton Aviation Group and 'Wrecks & Relics'.

HJC
February 2013

Abbreviations

$	Aircraft in special markings
AAC	Army Air Corps
ACC	Air Combat Command
ACCGS	Air Cadets Central Gliding School
ACS	Air Control Squadron
ACTS	Air Control Training Squadron
ACW	Air Control Wing
AD&StA	Aberdeen, Dundee & St Andrews
AEF	Air Experience Flight
AESS	Air Engineering & Survival School
AEW	Airborne Early Warning
AF	Arméflyget (Army Air Battalion)
AFB	Air Force Base
AFD	Air Fleet Department
AFRC	Air Force Reserve Command
AFSC	Air Force Systems Command
AFSK	Armeflygskolan (Army Flying School)
AG	Airlift Group
AGA	Academia General del Aire (General Air Academy)
AkG	Aufklärüngsgeschwader (Reconnaissance Wing)
AMC	Air Mobility Command
AMD-BA	Avions Marcel Dassault-Breguet Aviation
AMF	Aircraft Maintenance Flight
AMG	Aircraft Maintenance Group
AMIF	Aircraft Maintenance Instruction Flight
AMW	Air Mobility Wing
ANG	Air National Guard
APS	Aircraft Preservation Society
ARS	Air Refueling Squadron
ARW	Air Refueling Wing
AS	Airlift Squadron/Air Squadron
ASF	Aircraft Servicing Flight
AS&RU	Aircraft Salvage and Repair Unit
ATC	Air Training Corps
ATCC	Air Traffic Control Centre
AVDEF	Aviation Defence Service
Avn	Aviation
AW	AgustaWestland/Airlift Wing/Armstrong Whitworth Aircraft
AWC	Air Warfare Centre
BAC	British Aircraft Corporation
BAe	British Aerospace
BAPC	British Aviation Preservation Council
BATUS	British Army Training Unit Suffield
BBMF	Battle of Britain Memorial Flight

BDRF Battle Damage Repair Flight
BDRT Battle Damage Repair Training
Be Beech
Bf Bayerische Flugzeugwerke
BG Bomber Group
BGA British Gliding & Soaring Association
bk black (squadron colours and markings)
bl blue (squadron colours and markings)
BNFL British Nuclear Fuels Ltd
BP Boulton & Paul
br brown (squadron colours and markings)
BS Bomber Squadron
B-V Boeing-Vertol
BW Bomber Wing
CAARP Co-operative des Ateliers Air de la Région Parisienne
CAC Commonwealth Aircraft Corporation
CARG Cotswold Aircraft Restoration Group
CASA Construcciones Aeronautics SA
Cav Cavalry
CC County Council
CCF Combined Cadet Force/Canadian Car & Foundry Company
CDE Chemical Defence Establishment
CEAM Centre d'Expérimentation Aériennes Militaires (Military Air Experimental Centre)
CEPA Centre d'Expérimentation Pratique de l'Aéronautique Navale
CFS Central Flying School
CGMF Central Glider Maintenance Flight
CHFMU Centre d'Instruction des Equipages d'Hélicoptères
CIEH Commando Helicopter Force Maintenance Unit
CinC Commander in Chief
CinCLANT Commander in Chief Atlantic
CLV Centrum Leteckeho Vycviku (Air Training Centre)
CMU Central Maintenance Unit
Co Company
COMALAT Commandement de l'Aviation Légère de l'Armée de Terre
Comp Composite with
CT College of Technology
CTE Central Training Establishment
CV Chance-Vought
D-BA Daimler-Benz Aerospace
D-BD Dassault-Breguet Dornier
D&G Dumfries and Galloway
DCAE Defence College of Aeronautical Engineering
DE&S Defence Equipment and Support
DEFTS Defence Elementary Flying Training School
DEODS Defence Explosives Ordnance Disposal School
Det Detachment
DFTDC Defence Fire Training and Development Centre
DGA Délégation Générale de l'Armement
DH de Havilland
DHC de Havilland Canada
DHFS Defence Helicopter Flying School
DLMW Dywizjon Lotniczy Marynarki Wojennej
DMS Defence Movements School
DS&TL Defence Science & Technology Laboratory
DSAE Defence School of Aeronautical Engineering
DSEME Defence School of Electro-Mechanical Engineering
DSG Defence Support Group
DSMarE Defence School of Marine Engineering
DSEME Defence School of Electro-Mechanical Engineering
DTI Department of Trade and Industry
EA Escadron Aérien (Air Squadron)
EAAT Escadrille Avions de l'Armée de Terre
EAC Ecole de l'Aviation de Chasse (Fighter Aviation School)
EALAT Ecole de l'Aviation Légère de l'Armée de Terre
EAP European Aircraft Project
EAT Ecole de l'Aviation de Transport (Transport Aviation School)
EC Escadre de Chasse (Fighter Wing)
ECG Electronic Combat Group
ECM Electronic Counter Measures
ECS Electronic Countermeasures Squadron
EDA Escadre de Detection Aéroportée (Air Detection Wing)
EdC Escadron de Convoyage
EDCA Escadron de Détection et de Control Aéroportée (Airborne Detection & Control Sqn)
EE English Electric/Escadrille Electronique
EEA Escadron Electronique Aéroporté
EFA Ecole Franco Allemande
EFTS Elementary Flying Training School
EH Escadron d'Helicoptères (Helicopter Flight)
EHADT Escadrille Helicoptères de l'Armée de Terre
EHI European Helicopter Industries
EKW Eidgenössiches Konstruktionswerkstätte
el Eskadra Lotnicza (Air Sqn)
EL Escadre de Liaison (Liaison Wing)
elt Eskadra Lotnictwa Taktycznego (Tactical Air Squadron)
eltr Eskadra Lotnictwa Transportowego (Air Transport Squadron)
EMA East Midlands Airport
EMVO Elementaire Militaire Vlieg Opleiding (Elementary Flying Training)
ENOSA Ecole des Navigateurs Operationales Systemes d'Armees (Navigation School)
EoN Elliot's of Newbury
EPAA Ecole de Pilotage Elementaire de l'Armée de l'Air (Air Force Elementary Flying School)
EPE Ecole de Pilotage Elementaire (Elementary Flying School)
EPNER Ecole du Personnel Navigant d'Essais et de Reception
ER Escadre de Reconnaissance (Reconnaissance Wing)
ERS Escadron de Reconnaissance Stratégique (Strategic Reconnaissance Squadron)
ES Escadrille de Servitude
ESAM Ecole Supérieur d'Application du Matériel
Esc Escuadron (Squadron)
Esk Eskadrille (Squadron)
Eslla Escuadrilla (Squadron)
Esq Esquadra (Squadron)
ET Escadre de Transport (Transport Squadron)
ETE Escadron de Transport et Entrainment (Transport Training Squadron)
ETEC Escadron de Transport d'Entrainement et de Calibration (Transport Training & Calibration Sqn)

ETED Escadron de Transformation des Equipages Mirage 2000D
ETL Escadron de Transport Légère (Light Transport Squadron)
ETO Escadron de Transition Operationnelle
ETOM Escadron de Transport Outre Mer (Overseas Transport Squadron)
ETPS Empire Test Pilots' School
ETR Escadron de Tranformation Rafale
ETS Engineering Training School
EVAA Ecole de Voltige de l'Armée de l'Air (French Air Force Aerobatics School)
FAA Fleet Air Arm/Federal Aviation Administration
FBS Flugbereitschaftstaffel
FBW Fly-by-wire
FC Forskokcentralen (Flight Centre)
FE Further Education
FETC Fire and Emergency Training Centre
ff Front fuselage
FG Fighter Group
FH Fairchild-Hiller
FI Falkland Islands
FJWOEU Fast Jet & Guided Weapon Operational Evaluation Unit
FLO Forsvarets Logistikk Organisasjon (Defence Logistics Organisation)
FlSt Flieger Staffel (Flight Squadron)
Flt Flight
FMA Fabrica Militar de Aviones
FMT Flotila Militara de Transport (Transport Regiment)
FMV Forsvarets Materielwerk
FRADU Fleet Requirements and Air Direction Unit
FS Fighter Squadron
FSAIU Flight Safety & Accident Investigation Unit
FSCTE Fire Services Central Training Establishment
FTS Flying Training School
FTW Flying Training Wing
Fw Focke Wulf
FW Fighter Wing/Foster Wickner
FWTS Fixed Wing Test Squadron
FY Fiscal Year
GAF Government Aircraft Factory
GAFFTC German Air Force Flight Training Centre
GAL General Aircraft Ltd
GAM Groupe Aerien Mixte (Composite Air Group)
GAM/STAT Groupement Aéromobile/Section Technique de l'Armée de Terre
gd gold (squadron colours and markings)
GD General Dynamics
GDSH Gazelle Depth Support Hub
GHL Groupe d'Helicopteres Legeres (Light Helicopter Group)
GI Ground Instruction/Groupement d'Instruction (Instructional Group)
gn green (squadron colours and markings)
GRD Gruppe fur Rustunggdienste (Group for Service Preparation)
GRV Groupe de Ravitaillement en Vol (Air Refuelling Group)
GT Grupo de Transporte (Transport Wing)
GTT Grupo de Transporte de Tropos (Troop Carrier Wing)
gy grey (squadron colours and markings)
H&W Hereford and Worcester
HAF Historic Aircraft Flight
HAT&ES Heavy Aircraft Test & Evaluation Squadron
HC Helicopter Combat Support Squadron
HF Historic Flying Ltd
HFUS Heeresfliegerunterstützungsstaffel
HFVAS Heeresfliegerverbindungs/ Aufklärungsstaffel
HFVS Heeresfliegerversuchstaffel
HFWS Heeresflieger Waffenschule (Army Air Weapons School)
Hkp.Bat Helikopter Bataljon (Helicopter Battalion)
HMA Helicopter Maritime Attack
HMF Harrier Maintenance Flight/Helicopter Maintenance Flight
HMS Her Majesty's Ship
HP Handley-Page
HPAC SAM Harrier Platform Availability Contract and Service and Aircraft Maintenance
HQ Headquarters
HS Hawker Siddeley
HSG Hubschraubergeschwader
IAF Israeli Air Force
IAP International Airport
INTA Instituto Nacional de Tecnica Aerospacial
IOW Isle Of Wight
IWM Imperial War Museum
JARTS Joint Aircraft Recovery & Transportation Sqn
JATE Joint Air Transport Establishment
JbG Jagdbombergeschwader (Fighter Bomber Wing)
JFACTSU Joint Forward Air Control Training & Standards Unit
JG Jagdgeschwader (Fighter Wing)
JHC Joint Helicopter Command
JHF Joint Helicopter Force
KHR Kampfhubschrauberregiment
Kridlo Wing
lbvr letka Bitevnich Vrtulníkú (Attack Helicopter Squadron)
Letka Squadron
LTG Lufttransportgeschwader (Air Transport Wing)
LTO Transportna en Letalska Transportni Oddelek
LTSF Long Term Storage Flight
LTV Ling-Temco-Vought
LVG Luftwaffen Versorgungs Geschwader (Air Force Maintenance Wing)/Luft Verkehrs Gesellschaft
LZO Letecky Zku ební Odbor (Aviation Test Department)
m multi-coloured (squadron colours and markings)
MAPK Mira Anachestisis Pantos Kerou (All Weather Interception Sqn)
MASD Marine Air Support Detachment
MBB Messerschmitt Bolkow-Blohm
MCAS Marine Corps Air Station
McD McDonnell Douglas
MDMF Merlin Depth Maintenance Facilities
Med Medical
MFG Marine Flieger Geschwader (Naval Air Wing)
MH Max Holste
MI Maritime Interdiction
MIB Military Intelligence Battalion
MiG Mikoyan — Gurevich
Mod Modified

MoD	Ministry of Defence
MR	Maritime Reconnaissance
MRH	Multi-role Helikopters
M&RU	Marketing & Recruitment Unit
MS	Morane-Saulnier
MTHR	Mittlerer Transporthubschrauber Regiment (Medium Transport Helicopter Regiment)
MTM	Mira Taktikis Metaforon (Tactical Transport Sqn)
NA	North American
NACDS	Naval Air Command Driving School
NAEW&CF	NATO Airborne Early Warning & Control Force
NAF	Naval Air Facility
NAS	Naval Air Squadron (UK)/Naval Air Station (US)
NATO	North Atlantic Treaty Organisation
NAWC	Naval Air Warfare Center
NAWC-AD	Naval Air Warfare Center Aircraft Division
NBC	Nuclear, Biological and Chemical
NE	North-East
NFATS	Naval Force Aircraft Test Squadron
NI	Northern Ireland
NTOCU	National Tornado Operational Conversion Unit
NYARC	North Yorks Aircraft Restoration Centre
OCU	Operational Conversion Unit
OEU	Operational Evaluation Unit
OFMC	Old Flying Machine Company
OGMA	Oficinas Gerais de Material Aeronautico
or	orange (squadron colours and markings)
OSAC	Operational Support Airlift Command
OSBL	Oddelek Sholskih Bojni Letal (Training & Combat School)
OVH Kmp	Observations-Helicopter Kompagni
PAT	Priority Air Transport Detachment
PBN	Pilatus Britten-Norman
PDSH	Puma Depth Support Hub
PLM	Pulk Lotnictwa Mysliwskiego (Fighter Regiment)
pr	purple (squadron colours and markings)
PVH Kmp	Panservaerns-Helicopter Kompagni
r	red (squadron colours and markings)
R	Replica
RAeS	Royal Aeronautical Society
RAF	Royal Aircraft Factory/Royal Air Force
RAFC	Royal Air Force College
RAFM	Royal Air Force Museum
RAFGSA	Royal Air Force Gliding and Soaring Association
RE	Royal Engineers
Regt	Regiment
REME	Royal Electrical & Mechanical Engineers
rf	Rear fuselage
RFA	Royal Fleet Auxiliary
RHC	Régiment d'Helicoptères de Combat
RHFS	Régiment d'Helicoptères des Forces Spéciales
RJAF	Royal Jordanian Air Force
RM	Royal Marines
RMB	Royal Marines Base
RN	Royal Navy
RNAS	Royal Naval Air Station
RNGSA	Royal Navy Gliding and Soaring Association
RQS	Rescue Squadron
R-R	Rolls-Royce
RS	Reid & Sigrist/Reconnaissance Squadron
RSV	Reparto Sperimentale Volo (Experimental Flight School)
RTP	Reduction To Produce
RW	Reconnaissance Wing

SA Scottish Aviation
SAAB Svenska Aeroplan Aktieboleg
SAH School of Aircraft Handling
SAL Scottish Aviation Limited
SAR Search and Rescue
Saro Saunders-Roe
SARTU Search and Rescue Training Unit
SCW Strategic Communications Wing
SEAE School of Electrical & Aeronautical Engineering
SEPECAT Société Européenne de Production de l'avion Ecole de Combat et d'Appui Tactique
SFDO School of Flight Deck Operations
SHAPE Supreme Headquarters Allied Powers Europe
si silver (squadron colours and markings)
SIET Section d'Instruction et d'Etude du Tir
SKAMG Sea King Aircraft Maintenance Group
SKTU Sea King Training Unit
Skv Skvadron (Squadron)
SLK Stíhacie Letecké Kridlo (Fighter Air Wing)
slt stíhací letka (Fighter Squadron)
SLV School Licht Vliegwezen (Flying School)
Sm Smaldeel (Squadron)
smdl Smisena Dopravní Letka
SNCAN Société Nationale de Constructions Aéronautiques du Nord
SOF Special Operations Flightproximate
SOG Special Operations Group
SOS Special Operations Squadron
SoTT School of Technical Training
SOW Special Operations Wing
SPAD Société Pour les Appareils Deperdussin
SPP Strojirny Prvni Petilesky
Sqn Squadron
Sz.D.REB 'Szentgyörgyi Deszö' Harcászati Repülö Bázis
TA Territorial Army
TAP Transporten Avio Polk (Air Transport Regiment)
TCF Training Consolidation Flight
TEF Tornado Engineering Flight
TFC The Fighter Collection
TGp Test Groep
TIARA Tornado Integrated Avionics Research Aircraft
TL Taktická Letka (Tactical Squadron)
TMF Tornado Maintenance Flight
TMTS Trade Management Training School
TOCU Typhoon Operational Conversion Unit
tpzlt taktická a prúzkumná letka (Tactical & Reconnaissance Squadron)
TS Test Squadron
TsAGI Tsentral'ny Aerogidrodinamicheski Instut (Central Aero & Hydrodynamics Institute)
TsLw Technische Schule der Luftwaffe (Luftwaffe Technical School)
TW Test Wing
UAS University Air Squadron
UAV Unmanned Air Vehicle
Uberwg Uberwachunggeschwader (Surveillance Wing)
UK United Kingdom
UKAEA United Kingdom Atomic Energy Authority
US United States
USAF United States Air Force
USAFE United States Air Forces in Europe
USAREUR US Army Europe
USCGS US Coast Guard Station
USEUCOM United States European Command
USMC United States Marine Corps
USN United States Navy
NWTSPM United States Navy Test Pilots School
VAAC Vectored thrust Advanced Aircraft flight Control
VFW Vereinigte Flugtechnische Werke
VGS Volunteer Gliding Squadron
VLA Vojenska Letecka Akademia
vlt vycviková letka (Training Squadron)
VMGR Marine Aerial Refuelling/Transport Squadron
VMGRT Marine Aerial Refuelling/Transport Training Squadron
VQ Fleet Air Reconnaissance Squadron
VR Fleet Logistic Support Squadron
VrK Vrtulnikové Letecké Kridlo
VS Vickers-Supermarine
VSD Vegyes Szàllitorepülö Dandàr (Aircraft Transport Brigade)
w white (squadron colours and markings)
Wg Wing
WHL Westland Helicopters Ltd
WLT Weapons Loading Training
WRS Weather Reconnaissance Squadron
WS Westland
WSK Wytwornia Sprzetu Kominikacyjnego
WTD Wehrtechnische Dienstelle (Technical Support Unit)
WW2 World War II
y yellow (squadron colours and markings)
zDL základna Dopravního Letectva (Air Transport Base)
zL základna Letectva
zSL základna Speciálního Letectva (Training Air Base)
zTL základna Taktického Letectva (Tactical Air Base)
zVrL základna Vrtulníkového Letectva (Helicopter Air Base)

A Guide to the Location of Operational Military Bases in the UK

This section is to assist the reader to locate the places in the United Kingdom where operational military aircraft (including helicopters and gliders) are based.

The alphabetical order listing gives each location in relation to its county and to its nearest classified road(s) (*by* means adjoining; *of* means close to), together with its approximate direction and mileage from the centre of a nearby major town or city. Some civil airports are included where active military units are also based, but **excluded** are MoD sites with non-operational aircraft (eg *gate guardians*), the bases of privately-owned civil aircraft that wear military markings and museums. For GPS users, Latitude and Longitude are also listed.

User	*Base name*	*County/Region*	*Location [Lat./long.]*	*Distance/direction from (town)*
Army	Abingdon	Oxfordshire	W by B4017, W of A34 [N51°41'16"W001°18'58"]	5m SSW of Oxford
Army	Aldergrove/Belfast Airport	Co Antrim	W by A26 [N54°39'27"W006°12'578"]	13m W of Belfast
RM	Arbroath	Angus	E of A933 [N56°34'51"W002°36'55"]	2m NW of Arbroath
RAF	Barkston Heath	Lincolnshire	W by B6404, S of A153 [N52°57'46"W000°33'38"]	5m NNE of Grantham
RAF	Benson	Oxfordshire	E by A423 [N51°36'55"W001°05'45"]	1m NE of Wallingford
QinetiQ/ RAF	Boscombe Down	Wiltshire	S by A303, W of A338 [N51°09'12"W001°45'04"]	6m N of Salisbury
RAF	Boulmer	Northumberland	E of B1339 [N55°24'43"W001°35'37"]	4m E of Alnwick
RAF	Brize Norton	Oxfordshire	W of A4095 [N51°45'00"W001°35'01"]	5m SW of Witney
Marshall	Cambridge Airport/ Teversham	Cambridgeshire	S by A1303 [N52°12'18"E000°10'30"]	2m E of Cambridge
RM/RAF	Chivenor	Devon	S of A361 [N51°05'14"W004°09'01"]	4m WNW of Barnstaple
RAF	Church Fenton	North Yorkshire	S of B1223 [N53°50'04"W001°11'43"]	7m WNW of Selby
Army	Colerne	Wiltshire	S of A420, [N51°26'30"W002°16'46"]	E of Fosse Way 5m NE of Bath
RAF	Coningsby	Lincolnshire	S of A153, W by B1192 [N53°05'35"W000°10'00"]	10m NW of Boston
DCAE	Cosford	Shropshire	W of A41, N of A464 [N52°38'25"W002°18'20"]	9m WNW of Wolverhampton
RAF	Cranwell	Lincolnshire	N by A17, S by B1429 [N53°01'49"W000°29'00"]	5m WNW of Sleaford
RN	Culdrose	Cornwall	E by A3083 [N50°05'08"W005°15'17"]	1m SE of Helston
Army	Dishforth	North Yorkshire	E by A1 [N54°08'14"W001°25'13"]	4m E of Ripon
USAF	Fairford	Gloucestershire	S of A417 [N51°41'01"W001°47'24"]	9m ESE of Cirencester
RN	Fleetlands	Hampshire	E by A32 [N50°50'06"W001°10'07"]	2m SE of Fareham
RAF	Halton	Buckinghamshire	N of A4011, S of B4544 [N51°47'28"W000°44'11"]	4m ESE of Aylesbury
RAF	Henlow	Bedfordshire	E of A600, W of A6001 [N52°01'10"W000°18'06"]	1m SW of Henlow
Army	Hullavington	Wiltshire	W of A429 [N51°31'47"W002°08'14"]	1m N of M4 jn 17
RAF	Kenley	Greater London	W of A22 [N51°18'20"W000°05'37"]	1m W of Warlingham
RAF	Kirknewton	Lothian	E by B7031, N by A70 [N55°52'32"W003°24'04"]	8m SW of Edinburgh
USAF	Lakenheath	Suffolk	W by A1065 [N52°24'33"E000°33'40"]	8m W of Thetford
RAF/Army	Leconfield (Normandy Barracks)	East Riding of Yorkshire	E by A164 [N53°52'39"W000°26'08"]	2m N of Beverley

RAF	Leeming	North Yorkshire	E by A1 [N54°17'33"W001°32'07"]	5m SW of Northallerton
RAF	Leuchars	Fife	E of A919 [N56°22'28"W002°51'50"]	7m SE of Dundee
RAF	Linton-on-Ouse	North Yorkshire	E of B6265 [N54°02'57"W001°15'12"]	10m NW of York
RAF	Lossiemouth	Grampian	W of B9135, S of B9040 [N57°42'22"W003°20'20"]	4m N of Elgin
RAF	Marham	Norfolk	N by A1122 [N52°38'54"E000°33'02"]	6m W of Swaffham
Army	Middle Wallop	Hampshire	S by A343 [N51°08'35"W001°34'14"]	6m SW of Andover
USAF	Mildenhall	Suffolk	S by A1101 [N52°21'42"E000°29'12"]	9m NNE of Newmarket
RAF	Northolt	Greater London	N by A40 [N51°33'11"W000°25'06"]	3m E of M40 jn 1
RAF	Odiham	Hampshire	E of A32 [N51°14'03"W000°56'34"]	2m S of M3 jn 5
RN	Predannack	Cornwall	W by A3083 [N50°00'07"W005°13'54"]	7m S of Helston
RAF	Scampton	Lincolnshire	W by A15 [N53°18'28"W000°33'04"]	6m N of Lincoln
RAF	Shawbury	Shropshire	W of B5063 [N52°47'53"W002°40'05"]	7m NNE of Shrewsbury
RAF	Syerston	Nottinghamshire	W by A46 [N53°01'22"W000°54'47"]	5m SW of Newark
RAF	Ternhill	Shropshire	SW by A41 [N52°52'24"W002°31'54"]	3m SW of Market Drayton
RAF/Army	Topcliffe	North Yorkshire	E of A167, W of A168 [N54°12'20"W001°22'55"]	3m SW of Thirsk
RAF	Valley	Gwynedd	S of A5 on Anglesey [N53°14'53"W004°32'06"]	5m SE of Holyhead
RAF	Waddington	Lincolnshire	E by A607, W by A15 [N53°09'58"W000°31'26"]	5m S of Lincoln
Army/RAF	Wattisham	Suffolk	N of B1078 [N52°07'38"E000°57'21"]	5m SSW of Stowmarket
RAF	Woodvale	Merseyside	W by A565 [N53°34'56"W003°03'24"]	5m SSW of Southport
RAF	Wyton	Cambridgeshire	E of A141, N of B1090 [N52°21'25"W000°06'28"]	3m NE of Huntingdon
RN	Yeovilton	Somerset	S by B3151, S of A303 [N51°00'30"W002°38'43"]	5m N of Yeovil

British Military Aircraft Registrations

The Committee of Imperial Defence through its Air Committee introduced a standardised system of numbering aircraft in November 1912. The Air Department of the Admiralty was allocated the first batch 1-200 and used these to cover aircraft already in use and those on order. The Army was issued with the next block from 201-800, which included the number 304 which was given to the Cody Biplane now preserved in the Science Museum. By the outbreak of World War I, the Royal Navy was on its second batch of registrations 801-1600 and this system continued with alternating allocations between the Army and Navy until 1916 when number 10000, a Royal Flying Corps BE2C, was reached.

It was decided not to continue with five digit numbers but instead to start again from 1, prefixing RFC aircraft with the letter A and RNAS aircraft with the prefix N. The RFC allocations commenced with A1 an FE2D and before the end of the year had reached A9999 an Armstrong Whitworth FK8. The next group commenced with B1 and continued in logical sequence through the C, D, E and F prefixes. G was used on a limited basis to identify captured German aircraft, while H was the last block of wartime-ordered aircraft. To avoid confusion I was not used, so the new post-war machines were allocated registrations in the J range. A further minor change was made in the numbering system in August 1929 when it was decided to maintain four numerals after the prefix letter, thus omitting numbers 1 to 999. The new K series therefore commenced at K1000, which was allocated to an AW Atlas.

The Naval N prefix was not used in such a logical way. Blocks of numbers were allocated for specific types of aircraft such as seaplanes or flying-boats. By the late 1920s the sequence had largely been used up and a new series using the prefix S was commenced. In 1930 separate naval allocations were stopped and subsequent registrations were issued in the 'military' range which had by this time reached the K series. A further change in the pattern of allocations came in the L range. Commencing with L7272 numbers were issued in blocks with smaller blocks of registrations between not used. These were known as 'black-out blocks'. As M had already been used as a suffix for Maintenance Command instructional airframes it was not used as a prefix. Although N had previously been used for naval aircraft it was used again for registrations allocated from 1937.

With the build-up to World War II, the rate of allocations quickly accelerated and the prefix R was being used when war was declared. The letters O and Q were not allotted, nor was S, which had been used up to S1865 for naval aircraft before integration into the RAF series. By 1940 the registration Z9999 had been reached, as part of a black-out block, with the letters U and Y not used to avoid confusion.

The option to recommence registration allocation at A1000 was not taken up; instead it was decided to use an alphabetical two-letter prefix with three numerals running from 100 to 999. Thus, AA100 was allocated to a Blenheim IV and this two-letter, three-numeral registration system which started in 1940 continues today. The letters C, I, O, Q, U and Y were, with the exception of NC, not used. For various reasons the following letter combinations were not issued: DA, DB, DH, EA, GA to GZ, HA, HT, JE, JH, JJ, KR to KT, MR, NW, NZ, SA to SK, SV, TN, TR and VE. The first post-war registrations issued were in the VP range while the end of the WZs had been reached by the Korean War.

In January 1952 a civil servant at the then Air Ministry penned a memo to his superiors alerting them to the fact that a new military aircraft registration system would soon have to be devised. With allocations accelerating to accommodate a NATO response to the Korean War and a perceived Soviet threat building, he estimated that the end of the ZZs would quickly be reached. However, more than five decades later the allocations are only in the ZKs and at the present rate are unlikely to reach ZZ999 until the end of this century!

Military aircraft registrations are allocated by Defence Equipment and Support, where the Military Aircraft Register is maintained. It should be pointed out that strictly the register places a space before the last three digits of the registration and, contrary to popular opinion, refers to them as 'registrations', not serials.

A change in policy in 2003 resulted in the use of the first 99 digits in the ZK sequence (ZK001 to ZK099), following on from ZJ999. The first of these, ZK001 to ZK004, were allocated to AgustaWestland Merlins. There is also a growing trend for 'out-of-sequence' registration numbers to be issued. At first this was to a manufacturer's prototype or development aircraft. However, following the Boeing C-17 Globemasters leased and subsequently purchased from Boeing (ZZ171-ZZ178), more allocations have been noted.

Since 2002 there has also been a new official policy concerning the use of military registration numbers on some types of UAV. 'Where a UAV is of modular construction the nationality and registration mark shall be applied to the fuselage of the vehicle or on the assembly forming the main part of the fuselage. To prevent the high usage of numbers for target drones which are eventually destroyed, a single registration mark (prefix) should be issued relating to the UAV type. The agency or service operating the target drone will be responsible for the identification of each individual UAV covered by that registration mark by adding a suffix.' This has resulted in the use of the same registration on a number of UAVs and drones with numbers following it - hence the appearance of ZZ420/001 etc. on Banshee drones. Aircraft using this system are denoted in the text by an asterisk (*).

Note: The compiler will be pleased to receive comments, corrections and further information for inclusion in subsequent editions of *Military Aircraft Markings* and the monthly up-date of additions and amendments. Please send your information to Military Aircraft Markings, Ian Allan Publishing Ltd, Riverdene Business Park, Molesey Road, Hersham, Surrey, KT12 4RG or by e-mail to admin@aviation-links.co.uk.

British Military Aircraft Markings

A serial in *italics* denotes that it is not the genuine marking for that airframe.

Notes	Serial	Type (code/other identity)	Owner/operator location or fate
	46	VS361 Spitfire LF IX <R> (*MH486*/BAPC 206) [FT-E]	RAF Museum, Hendon
	168	Sopwith Tabloid Scout <R> (G-BFDE)	RAF Museum, Hendon
	304	Cody Biplane (BAPC 62)	Science Museum, South Kensington
	347	RAF BE2c <R> (G-AWYI)	Privately owned, Sywell
	687	RAF BE2b <R> (BAPC 181)	RAF Museum, Hendon
	2345	Vickers FB5 Gunbus <R> (G-ATVP)	RAF Museum, Hendon
	2699	RAF BE2c	Imperial War Museum, Duxford
	2783	RAF BE2b <R>	Boscombe Down Aviation Collection, Old Sarum
	3066	Caudron GIII (G-AETA/9203M)	RAF Museum, Hendon
	5964	DH2 <R> (BAPC 112)	Privately owned, Stretton on Dunsmore
	5964	DH2 <R> (G-BFVH)	Privately owned, Wickenby
	6232	RAF BE2c <R> (BAPC 41)	Yorkshire Air Museum, stored Elvington
	8359	Short 184 <ff>	FAA Museum, RNAS Yeovilton
	9917	Sopwith Pup (G-EBKY/N5180)	The Shuttleworth Collection, Old Warden
	A301	Morane BB (frame)	RAF Museum Reserve Collection, Stafford
	A653	Sopwith Pup <R> (*A7317*/BAPC 179)	Privately owned, Stow Maries, Essex
	A1452	Vickers FB5 Gunbus <R>	Privately owned, Sywell
	A1742	Bristol Scout D <R> (BAPC 38)	Privately owned, Old Warden
	A3930	RAF RE8 <R> (ZK-TVC)	RAF Museum, Hendon
	A6526	RAF FE2b <R>	RAF Museum, Hendon
	A7288	Bristol F2b Fighter <R>	Bristol Aero Collection, Filton
	A7317	Sopwith Pup <R> (BAPC 179)	*Repainted as A653*
	A8226	Sopwith 1½ Strutter <R> (G-BIDW)	RAF Museum, Hendon
	B595	RAF SE5a <R> (G-BUOD) [W]	Privately owned, Defford
	B619	Sopwith 1½ Strutter <R>	RAF Manston History Museum
	B2458	Sopwith 1F.1 Camel <R> (G-BPOB/*F542*) [R]	Privately owned, Booker
	B5539	Sopwith 1F.1 Camel <R>	Privately owned, Booker
	B5577	Sopwith 1F.1 Camel <R> (*D3419*/BAPC 59) [W]	Montrose Air Station Heritage Centre
	B6401	Sopwith 1F.1 Camel <R> (G-AWYY/C1701)	FAA Museum, stored RNAS Yeovilton
	B7270	Sopwith 1F.1 Camel <R> (G-BFCZ)	Brooklands Museum, Weybridge
	C1904	RAF SE5a <R> (G-PFAP) [Z]	Privately owned, Castle Bytham, Lincs
	C3009	Currie Wot (G-BFWD)	Privately owned, Dunkeswell
	C3011	Phoenix Currie Super Wot (G-SWOT) [S]	Privately owned,
	C3988	Sopwith 5F.1 Dolphin (comp D5329)	RAF Museum, Hendon
	C4451	Avro 504J <R> (BAPC 210)	Solent Sky, Southampton
	C4918	Bristol M1C <R> (G-BWJM)	The Shuttleworth Collection, Old Warden
	C4994	Bristol M1C <R> (G-BLWM)	RAF Museum, Hendon
	C5430	RAF SE5a <R> (G-CCXG) [V]	Privately owned, Wrexham
	C6468	RAF SE5a <R> (G-CEKL) [A]	Privately owned, RAF Halton
	C8996	RAF SE5a (G-ECAE/A2-25)	Privately owned, Milden
	C9533	RAF SE5a <R> (G-BUWE) [M]	Privately owned, Boscombe Down
	D276	RAF SE5a <R> (BAPC 208) [A]	Prince's Mead Shopping Centre, Farnborough
	D5649	Airco DH9	Imperial War Museum, Duxford
	D7560	Avro 504K	Science Museum, South Kensington
	D8096	Bristol F2b Fighter (G-AEPH) [D]	The Shuttleworth Collection, Old Warden
	E449	Avro 504K (G-EBJE/9205M)	RAF Museum, Hendon
	E2466	Bristol F2b Fighter (BAPC 165) [I]	RAF Museum, Hendon
	E2581	Bristol F2b Fighter [13]	Imperial War Museum, Duxford

Serial	*Type (code/other identity)*	*Owner/operator location or fate*	*Notes*
E3273	Avro 504K (H5199/BK892/3118M/ G-ACNB/G-ADEV)	The Shuttleworth Collection, Old Warden	
E6655	Sopwith 7F.1 Snipe <R> [B]	RAF Museum, Hendon	
E8894	Airco DH9 (G-CDLI)	Aero Vintage, Westfield, Sussex	
F141	RAF SE5a <R> (G-SEVA) [G]	Privately owned, Boscombe Down	
F235	RAF SE5a <R> (G-BMDB) [B]	Privately owned, Boscombe Down	
F904	RAF SE5a (G-EBIA)	The Shuttleworth Collection, Old Warden	
F904	RAF SE5a <R>	Aeroventure, Doncaster	
F938	RAF SE5a (G-EBIC/9208M)	RAF Museum, Hendon	
F943	RAF SE5a <R> (G-BIHF) [S]	Privately owned, White Waltham	
F943	RAF SE5a <R> (G-BKDT)	Yorkshire Air Museum, Elvington	
F1010	Airco DH9A [C]	RAF Museum, Hendon	
F3556	RAF RE8	Imperial War Museum, Duxford	
F5447	RAF SE5a <R> (G-BKER) [N]	Privately owned, Bridge of Weir	
F5459	RAF SE5a <R> (G-INNY) [Y]	Privately owned, North Coates	
F5475	RAF SE5a <R> (BAPC 250)	Brooklands Museum, Weybridge	
F6314	Sopwith 1F.1 Camel (9206M) [B]	RAF Museum, Hendon	
F8010	RAF SE5a <R> (G-BDWJ) [Z]	Privately owned, Langport, Somerset	
F8614	Vickers FB27A Vimy IV <R> (G-AWAU)	RAF Museum, Hendon	
H1968	Avro 504K <R> (BAPC 42)	Yorkshire Air Museum, stored Elvington	
H5199	Avro 504K (BK892/3118M/G-ACNB/G-ADEV)	*Repainted as E3273, 2012*	
J7326	DH53 Humming Bird (G-EBQP)	Mosquito Aircraft Museum, London Colney	
J7904	Gloster Gamecock <R>	Jet Age Museum, Gloucester	
J8067	Westland Pterodactyl 1a	Science Museum, South Kensington	
J9941	Hawker Hart 2 (G-ABMR)	RAF Museum, Hendon	
K1786	Hawker Tomtit (G-AFTA)	The Shuttleworth Collection, Old Warden	
K2046	Isaacs Fury II (G-AYJY)	Privately owned, Little Rissington	
K2048	Isaacs Fury II (G-BZNW)	Privately owned, Linton-on-Ouse	
K2050	Isaacs Fury II (G-ASCM)	Privately owned, Enstone	
K2059	Isaacs Fury II (G-PFAR)	Privately owned, Netherthorpe	
K2060	Isaacs Fury II (G-BKZM)	Privately owned stored, Limetree, Ireland	
K2075	Isaacs Fury II (G-BEER)	Privately owned, Combrook, Warks	
K2227	Bristol 105 Bulldog IIA (G-ABBB)	RAF Museum, Hendon	
K2567	DH82A Tiger Moth (DE306/7035M/G-MOTH)	Privately owned, Tadlow	
K2572	DH82A Tiger Moth (NM129/G-AOZH)	Privately owned, Wanborough, Wilts	
K2585	DH82A Tiger Moth II (T6818/G-ANKT)	The Shuttleworth Collection, Old Warden	
K2587	DH82A Tiger Moth <R> (G-BJAP)	Privately owned, Shobdon	
K3241	Avro 621 Tutor (K3215/G-AHSA)	The Shuttleworth Collection, Old Warden	
K3661	Hawker Nimrod II (G-BURZ) [562]	Aero Vintage, Duxford	
K3731	Isaacs Fury <R> (G-RODI)	Privately owned, Hailsham	
K4232	Avro 671 Rota I (SE-AZB)	RAF Museum, Hendon	
K4259	DH82A Tiger Moth (G-ANMO) [71]	Privately owned, Sywell	
K4972	Hawker Hart Trainer IIA (1764M)	RAF Museum, Hendon	
K5054	Supermarine Spitfire <R> (BAPC 190/*EN398*)	Privately owned, Hawkinge	
K5054	Supermarine Spitfire <R> (BAPC 214)	Tangmere Military Aviation Museum	
K5054	Supermarine Spitfire <R> (G-BRDV)	Privately owned, Kent	
K5054	Supermarine Spitfire <R>	Kent Battle of Britain Museum, Hawkinge	
K5054	Supermarine Spitfire <R>	Southampton Airport, on display	
K5409	Hawker Hind	Vintage Flyers, Cotswold Airport	
K5414	Hawker Hind (G-AENP/BAPC 78) [XV]	The Shuttleworth Collection, Old Warden	
K5462	Hawker Hind	Vintage Flyers, Cotswold Airport	
K5554	Hawker Hind	Vintage Flyers, Cotswold Airport	
K5600	Hawker Audax I (2015M/G-BVVI)	Aero Vintage, Westfield, Sussex	
K5673	Isaacs Fury II (G-BZAS)	Privately owned, Morpeth	
K5673	Hawker Fury I <R> (BAPC 249)	Brooklands Museum, Weybridge	
K5674	Hawker Fury I (G-CBZP)	Historic Aircraft Collection Ltd, Goodwood	

Notes	Serial	Type (code/other identity)	Owner/operator location or fate
	K6035	Westland Wallace II (2361M)	RAF Museum, Hendon
	K6618	Hawker Hind	Vintage Flyers, Cotswold Airport
	K6833	Hawker Hind	Vintage Flyers, Cotswold Airport
	K7271	Hawker Fury II <R> (BAPC 148)	Shropshire Wartime Aircraft Recovery Grp Mus, Sleap
	K7271	Isaacs Fury II <R> (G-CCKV)	Privately owned, Roche, Cornwall
	K7985	Gloster Gladiator I (L8032/G-AMRK)	The Shuttleworth Collection, Old Warden
	K8042	Gloster Gladiator II (8372M)	RAF Museum, Hendon
	K8203	Hawker Demon I (G-BTVE/2292M)	Demon Displays, Hatch
	K8303	Isaacs Fury II (G-BWWN) [D]	Privately owned, RAF Henlow
	K9926	VS300 Spitfire I <R> (BAPC 217) [JH-C]	RAF Bentley Priory, on display
	K9942	VS300 Spitfire I (8383M) [SD-D]	RAF Museum, Cosford
	K9998	VS300 Spitfire I <R> [QJ-K]	RAF Biggin Hill, on display
	L1067	VS300 Spitfire I <R> (BAPC 227) [XT-D]	Edinburgh Airport, on display
	L1592	Hawker Hurricane I [KW-Z]	Science Museum, South Kensington
	L1639	Hawker Hurricane I	Cambridge Fighter & Bomber Society, Little Gransden
	L1679	Hawker Hurricane I <R> (BAPC 241) [JX-G]	Tangmere Military Aviation Museum
	L1684	Hawker Hurricane I <R> (BAPC 219)	RAF Northolt, on display
	L2301	VS Walrus I (G-AIZG)	FAA Museum, RNAS Yeovilton
	L2940	Blackburn Skua I	FAA Museum, RNAS Yeovilton
	L5343	Fairey Battle I	RAF Museum, Hendon
	L6906	Miles M14A Magister I (G-AKKY/T9841/BAPC 44)	Museum of Berkshire Aviation, Woodley
	L7005	Boulton Paul P82 Defiant I <R> [PS-B]	Boulton Paul Association, Wolverhampton
	L7181	Hawker Hind (G-CBLK)	Aero Vintage, Duxford
	L7191	Hawker Hind	Vintage Flyers, Cotswold Airport
	L7775	Vickers Wellington B IC <ff>	Lincolnshire Avn Heritage Centre, E Kirkby
	L8756	Bristol 149 Bolingbroke IVT (RCAF 10001) [XD-E]	RAF Museum, Hendon
	N248	Supermarine S6A (*S1596*)	Solent Sky, Southampton
	N500	Sopwith LC-1T Triplane <R> (G-PENY/G-BWRA)	Privately owned, Yarcombe, Devon/RNAS Yeovilton
	N546	Wright Quadruplane 1 <R> (BAPC 164)	Solent Sky, Southampton
	N1671	Boulton Paul P82 Defiant I (8370M) [EW-D]	RAF Museum, Hendon
	N1854	Fairey Fulmar II (G-AIBE)	FAA Museum, RNAS Yeovilton
	N2078	Sopwith Baby (8214/8215)	FAA Museum, stored RNAS Yeovilton
	N2532	Hawker Hurricane I <R> (BAPC 272) [GZ-H]	Kent Battle of Britain Museum, Hawkinge
	N2980	Vickers Wellington IA [R]	Brooklands Museum, Weybridge
	N3194	VS300 Spitfire I <R> (BAPC 220) [GR-Z]	Privately owned, Hixon, Staffs
	N3200	VS300 Spitfire IA (G-CFGJ) (fuselage)	The Aircraft Restoration Company, Duxford
	N3289	VS300 Spitfire I <R> (BAPC 65) [DW-K]	Kent Battle of Britain Museum, Hawkinge
	N3290	VS300 Spitfire I <R> [AI-H]	Privately owned, St Mawgan
	N3310	VS361 Spitfire IX [A] <R>	Privately owned, Abingdon
	N3313	VS300 Spitfire I <R> (*MH314*/BAPC 69) [KL-B]	Kent Battle of Britain Museum, Hawkinge
	N3378	Boulton Paul P82 Defiant I	Boulton Paul Association, Wolverhampton
	N3788	Miles M14A Magister I (V1075/G-AKPF)	Privately owned, Leicester
	N4389	Fairey Albacore (N4172) [4M]	FAA Museum, stored RNAS Yeovilton
	N4877	Avro 652A Anson I (G-AMDA) [MK-V]	Imperial War Museum, Duxford
	N5137	DH82A Tiger Moth (N6638/G-BNDW)	Caernarfon Air World
	N5177	Sopwith 1½ Strutter <R>	Privately owned, Sedgensworth, Hants
	N5182	Sopwith Pup <R> (G-APUP/9213M)	RAF Museum, Hendon
	N5195	Sopwith Pup (G-ABOX)	Museum of Army Flying, Middle Wallop
	N5199	Sopwith Pup <R> (G-BZND)	Privately owned, Yarcombe, Devon
	N5459	Sopwith Triplane <R> (BAPC 111)	FAA Museum, stored RNAS Yeovilton
	N5518	Gloster Sea Gladiator	FAA Museum, RNAS Yeovilton
	N5628	Gloster Gladiator II	RAF Museum, Hendon
	N5719	Gloster Gladiator II (G-CBHO)	Privately owned, Dursley, Glos
	N5903	Gloster Gladiator II (*N2276*/G-GLAD)	The Fighter Collection, Duxford
	N5912	Sopwith Triplane (8385M)	RAF Museum, Hendon

Serial	Type (code/other identity)	Owner/operator location or fate	Notes
N5914	Gloster Gladiator II	Jet Age Museum, Dursley, Glos (on rebuild)	
N6290	Sopwith Triplane <R> (G-BOCK)	The Shuttleworth Collection, Old Warden	
N6452	Sopwith Pup <R> (G-BIAU)	FAA Museum, RNAS Yeovilton	
N6466	DH82A Tiger Moth (G-ANKZ)	Privately owned, Compton Abbas	
N6473	DH82A Tiger Moth (F-GTBO)	Privately owned, Orbigny, France	
N6537	DH82A Tiger Moth (G-AOHY)	Privately owned, Wickenby	
N6635	DH82A Tiger Moth (comp G-APAO & G-APAP) [25]	Imperial War Museum, Duxford	
N6720	DH82A Tiger Moth (G-BYTN/7014M) [VX]	Privately owned, Wickenby	
N6797	DH82A Tiger Moth (G-ANEH)	Privately owned, Swyncombe	
N6812	Sopwith 2F.1 Camel	Imperial War Museum, Duxford	
N6847	DH82A Tiger Moth (G-APAL)	Privately owned, Great Casterton, Rutland	
N6965	DH82A Tiger Moth (G-AJTW) [FL-J]	Privately owned, Tibenham	
N7033	Noorduyn AT-16 Harvard IIB (FX442)	Kent Battle of Britain Museum, Hawkinge	
N9191	DH82A Tiger Moth (G-ALND)	Privately owned, Pontypool	
N9192	DH82A Tiger Moth (G-DHZF) [RCO-N]	Privately owned, Sywell	
N9389	DH82A Tiger Moth (G-ANJA)	Privately owned, Thruxton	
N9899	Supermarine Southampton I (fuselage)	RAF Museum, Hendon	
P1344	HP52 Hampden I (9175M) [PL-K]	RAF Museum Restoration Centre, Cosford	
P2617	Hawker Hurricane I (8373M) [AF-F]	RAF Museum, Hendon	
P2725	Hawker Hurricane I (wreck)	Imperial War Museum, Lambeth	
P2725	Hawker Hurricane I <R> (BAPC 68) [TM-B]	Privately owned, Delabole, Cornwall	
P2793	Hawker Hurricane I <R> (BAPC 236) [SD-M]	Eden Camp Theme Park, Malton, North Yorkshire	
P2902	Hawker Hurricane I (G-ROBT) [DX-R]	Privately owned, Milden	
P2921	Hawker Hurricane I <R> (BAPC 273) [GZ-L]	Kent Battle of Britain Museum, Hawkinge	
P2921	Hawker Hurricane I <R> [GZ-L]	RAF Biggin Hill, on display	
P2954	Hawker Hurricane I <R> (BAPC 267) [WX-E]	Imperial War Museum, Duxford	
P2970	Hawker Hurricane I <R> (BAPC 291) [US-X]	Battle of Britain Memorial, Capel le Ferne, Kent	
P3059	Hawker Hurricane I <R> (BAPC 64) [SD-N]	Kent Battle of Britain Museum, Hawkinge	
P3144	Hawker Hurricane I <R> [CZ-B]	*Repainted as V6555*	
P3175	Hawker Hurricane I (wreck)	RAF Museum, Hendon	
P3179	Hawker Hurricane I <ff>	Tangmere Military Aviation Museum	
P3208	Hawker Hurricane I <R> (BAPC 63/*L1592*) [SD-T]	Kent Battle of Britain Museum, Hawkinge	
P3386	Hawker Hurricane I <R> (BAPC 218) [FT-A]	RAF Bentley Priory, on display	
P3395	Hawker Hurricane IV (KX829)[JX-B]	Thinktank, Birmingham	
P3398	Supermarine Aircraft Spitfire 26 (G-CEPL)	Privately owned, Thurrock	
P3554	Hawker Hurricane I (composite)	The Air Defence Collection, Salisbury	
P3679	Hawker Hurricane I <R> (BAPC 278) [GZ-K]	Kent Battle of Britain Museum, Hawkinge	
P3708	Hawker Hurricane I	Norfolk & Suffolk Avn Museum, Flixton (on rebuild)	
P3873	Hawker Hurricane I <R> (BAPC 265) [YO-H]	Yorkshire Air Museum, Elvington	
P3901	Hawker Hurricane I <R> [RF-E]	Battle of Britain Bunker, Uxbridge	
P4139	Fairey Swordfish II (HS618) [5H]	FAA Museum, RNAS Yeovilton	
P6382	Miles M14A Hawk Trainer 3 (G-AJRS) [C]	The Shuttleworth Collection, Old Warden	
P7350	VS329 Spitfire IIA (G-AWIJ) [EB-G]	RAF BBMF, Coningsby	
P7370	VS329 Spitfire II <R> [ZP-A]	Battle of Britain Experience, Canterbury	
P7540	VS329 Spitfire IIA [DU-W]	Dumfries & Galloway Avn Mus, Ripon (on rebuild)	
P7666	VS329 Spitfire II <R> [EB-Z]	RAF High Wycombe, on display	
P7819	VS329 Spitfire IIA (G-TCHZ)	Privately owned, Exeter	
P7966	VS329 Spitfire II <R> [D-B]	Manx Aviation & Military Museum, Ronaldsway	
P8088	VS329 Spitfire IIA (G-CGRM) [NK-K]	Privately owned, Oxon	
P8140	VS329 Spitfire II <R> (*P9390*/BAPC 71) [ZF-K]	Norfolk & Suffolk Avn Museum, Flixton	
P8208	VS329 Spitfire IIB (G-RRFF)	Privately owned, Oxon	
P8448	VS329 Spitfire II <R> (BAPC 225) [UM-D]	RAF Cranwell, on display	
P9373	VS300 Spitfire IA (G-CFGN) (wreck)	Privately owned, Duxford	
P9374	VS300 Spitfire IA (G-MKIA) [J]	Privately owned, Duxford	
P9398	Supermarine Aircraft Spitfire 26 (G-CEPL) [KL-B]	Privately owned, Audley End	
P9444	VS300 Spitfire IA [RN-D]	Science Museum, South Kensington	

Notes	Serial	Type (code/other identity)	Owner/operator location or fate
	P9637	Supermarine Aircraft Spitfire 26 (G-RORB) [GR-B]	Privately owned, Perth
	R1914	Miles M14A Magister (G-AHUJ)	Privately owned, Strathallan
	R3821	Bristol 149 Bolingbroke IVT (G-BPIV/*Z5722*)	Blenheim(Duxford) Ltd, Duxford (on rebuild)
	R4118	Hawker Hurricane I (G-HUPW) [UP-W]	Privately owned, Didcot, Oxon
	R4229	VS300 Spitfire I <R> [GN-J]	Alexandra Park, Windsor
	R4922	DH82A Tiger Moth II (G-APAO)	Privately owned, Henlow
	R4959	DH82A Tiger Moth II (G-ARAZ) [59]	Privately owned, Temple Bruer, Lincs
	R5136	DH82A Tiger Moth II (G-APAP)	Privately owned, Henlow
	R5172	DH82A Tiger Moth II (G-AOIS) [FIJE]	Privately owned, Breighton
	R5246	DH82A Tiger Moth II (G-AMIV) [40]	Privately owned, Germany
	R5868	Avro 683 Lancaster I (7325M) [PO-S]	RAF Museum, Hendon
	R6690	VS300 Spitfire I <R> (BAPC 254) [PR-A]	Yorkshire Air Museum, Elvington
	R6775	VS300 Spitfire I <R> (BAPC 299) [YT-J]	Battle of Britain Memorial, Capel le Ferne, Kent
	R6904	VS300 Spitfire I <R> [BT-K]	Privately owned, Cornwall
	R6915	VS300 Spitfire I	Imperial War Museum, Duxford
	R9125	Westland Lysander III (8377M)[LX-L]	RAF Museum, Hendon
	S1287	Fairey Flycatcher <R> (G-BEYB)	FAA Museum, stored RNAS Yeovilton
	S1579	Hawker Nimrod I <R> (G-BBVO) [571]	Privately owned, stored Felixkirk
	S1581	Hawker Nimrod I (G-BWWK) [573]	The Fighter Collection, Duxford
	S1595	Supermarine S6B [1]	Science Museum, South Kensington
	S1615	Isaacs Fury II (G-BMEU)	Privately owned, stored Netherthorpe
	T5298	Bristol 156 Beaufighter I (4552M) <ff>	Midland Air Museum, Coventry
	T5424	DH82A Tiger Moth II (G-AJOA)	Privately owned, Swindon
	T5854	DH82A Tiger Moth II (G-ANKK)	Privately owned, Baxterley
	T5879	DH82A Tiger Moth II (G-AXBW) [RUC-W]	Privately owned, Frensham
	T6296	DH82A Tiger Moth II (8387M)	RAF Museum, Hendon
	T6562	DH82A Tiger Moth II (G-ANTE)	Privately owned, Sywell
	T6953	DH82A Tiger Moth II (G-ANNI)	Privately owned, Tisted, Hants
	T6991	DH82A Tiger Moth II (DE694/HB-UPY)	Privately owned, Lausanne, Switzerland
	T7230	DH82A Tiger Moth II (G-AFVE)	Privately owned, Mazowiecke, Poland
	T7281	DH82A Tiger Moth II (G-ARTL)	Privately owned, Egton, nr Whitby
	T7793	DH82A Tiger Moth II (G-ANKV)	Privately owned, Wickenby
	T7842	DH82A Tiger Moth II (G-AMTF)	Privately owned, Westfield, Surrey
	T7909	DH82A Tiger Moth II (G-ANON)	Privately owned, Sherburn-in-Elmet
	T7997	DH82A Tiger Moth II (NL750/G-AHUF)	Privately owned, Wickenby
	T8191	DH82A Tiger Moth II (G-BWMK)	Privately owned, stored Sleap
	T9707	Miles M14A Magister I (G-AKKR/8378M/T9708)	Museum of Army Flying, Middle Wallop
	T9738	Miles M14A Magister I (G-AKAT)	Privately owned, Breighton
	V3388	Airspeed AS10 Oxford I (G-AHTW)	Imperial War Museum, Duxford
	V6028	Bristol 149 Bolingbroke IVT (G-MKIV) [GB-D] <rf>	The Aircraft Restoration Co, stored Duxford
	V6555	Hawker Hurricane I (*P3144*) <R> [DT-A]	Battle of Britain Experience, Canterbury
	V6799	Hawker Hurricane I <R> (BAPC 72/*V7767*) [SD-X]	Jet Age Museum, stored Gloucester
	V7313	Hawker Hurricane I <R> [US-F]	Privately owned, North Weald, on display
	V7350	Hawker Hurricane I (fuselage)	Brenzett Aeronautical Museum
	V7467	Hawker Hurricane I <R> (BAPC 223) [LE-D]	RAF High Wycombe, on display
	V7467	Hawker Hurricane I <R> (BAPC 288) [LE-D]	Wonderland Pleasure Park, Farnsfield, Notts
	V7497	Hawker Hurricane I (G-HRLI)	Hawker Restorations, Milden
	V9367	Westland Lysander IIIA (G-AZWT) [MA-B]	The Shuttleworth Collection, Old Warden
	V9673	Westland Lysander IIIA (V9300/G-LIZY) [MA-J]	Imperial War Museum, Duxford
	V9723	Westland Lysander IIIA (V9546/OO-SOT) [MA-D]	SABENA Old Timers, Brussels, Belgium

Serial	*Type (code/other identity)*	*Owner/operator location or fate*	*Notes*
V9312	Westland Lysander IIIA (G-CCOM)	The Aircraft Restoration Co, Duxford	
W1048	HP59 Halifax II (8465M) [TL-S]	RAF Museum, Hendon	
W2068	Avro 652A Anson I (9261M/VH-ASM) [68]	RAF Museum, Hendon	
W2718	VS Walrus I (G-RNLI)	Privately owned, Audley End	
W3644	VS349 Spitfire V <R> [QV-J]	Privately owned, Lake Fairhaven, Lancs	
W3850	VS349 Spitfire V <R> [PR-A]	Privately owned, Cheshire	
W4041	Gloster E28/39	Science Museum, South Kensington	
W4041	Gloster E28/39 <R>	Jet Age Museum, Gloucester	
W4050	DH98 Mosquito	Mosquito Aircraft Museum, London Colney	
W5856	Fairey Swordfish II (G-BMGC) [A2A]	RN Historic Flight, Yeovilton	
W9385	DH87B Hornet Moth (G-ADND) [YG-L,3]	Privately owned, Hullavington	
X4178	VS300 Spitfire I <R> [EB-K]	Imperial War Museum, Duxford	
X4276	VS300 Spitfire I (G-CDGU)	Privately owned, Sandown	
X4474	VS509 Spitfire T9 (PV202/*H-98*/G-CCCA) [QV-I]	Historic Flying Ltd, Duxford	
X4590	VS300 Spitfire I (8384M) [PR-F]	RAF Museum, Hendon	
X4650	VS300 Spitfire I (G-CGUK) [KL-A]	Privately owned, Biggin Hill	
X4683	Jurca MJ10 Spitfire (G-CDPM) [EB-N]	Privately owned, Fishburn	
X7688	Bristol 156 Beaufighter I (3858M/G-DINT)	Privately owned, Hatch	
Z1206	Vickers Wellington IV (fuselage)	Privately owned, Kenilworth	
Z2033	Fairey Firefly I (G-ASTL) [275/N]	FAA Museum, RNAS Yeovilton	
Z2315	Hawker Hurricane IIA [JU-E]	Imperial War Museum, Duxford	
Z2389	Hawker Hurricane IIA [XR-T]	Brooklands Museum, Weybridge	
Z3427	Hawker Hurricane IIC <R> (BAPC 205) [AV-R]	RAF Museum, Hendon	
Z5140	Hawker Hurricane XIIA (*Z7381*/G-HURI) [HA-C]	Historic Aircraft Collection, Duxford	
Z5207	Hawker Hurricane IIB (G-BYDL)	Privately owned, Thruxton	
Z5252	Hawker Hurricane IIB (G-BWHA/Z5053) [GO-B]	Privately owned, Milden	
Z7015	Hawker Sea Hurricane IB (G-BKTH) [7-L]	The Shuttleworth Collection, Old Warden	
Z7197	Percival P30 Proctor III (G-AKZN/8380M)	RAF Museum Reserve Collection, Stafford	
Z7258	DH89A Dragon Rapide (NR786/G-AHGD)	Privately owned, Membury (wreck)	
AB196	Supermarine Aircraft Spitfire 26 (G-CCGH)	Privately owned, Hawarden	
AB550	VS349 Spitfire VB <R> (BAPC 230/*AA908*) [GE-P]	Eden Camp Theme Park, Malton, North Yorkshire	
AB910	VS349 Spitfire VB (G-AISU) [MD-E]	RAF BBMF, Coningsby	
AD540	VS349 Spitfire VB (wreck)	Kennet Aviation, Tollerton (on rebuild)	
AE436	HP52 Hampden I [PL-J] (parts)	Lincolnshire Avn Heritage Centre, E Kirkby	
AE977	Hawker Sea Hurricane X (N33TF) [LE-D]	Privately owned, Biggin Hill	
AL246	Grumman Martlet I	FAA Museum, RNAS Yeovilton	
AP506	Cierva C30A (G-ACWM) (wreck)	The Helicopter Museum, Weston-super-Mare	
AP507	Cierva C30A (G-ACWP) [KX-P]	Science Museum, South Kensington	
AR213	VS300 Spitfire IA (*K9853*/G-AIST) [JZ-E]	Privately owned, Duxford	
AR501	VS349 Spitfire LF VC (G-AWII/*AR4474*) [NN-A]	The Shuttleworth Collection, Old Warden	
AV511	EHI-101 Merlin <R> [511]	SFDO, RNAS Culdrose	
BB803	DH82A Tiger Moth (G-ADWJ) [75]	Privately owned, Henstridge	
BB807	DH82A Tiger Moth (G-ADWO)	Solent Sky, Southampton	
BD713	Hawker Hurricane IIB	Privately owned, Taunton	
BE505	Hawker Hurricane IIB (RCAF 5403/G-HHII) [XP-L]	Hangar 11 Collection, North Weald	
BL614	VS349 Spitfire VB (4354M) [ZD-F]	RAF Museum, Hendon	
BL655	VS349 Spitfire VB (wreck)	Lincolnshire Avn Heritage Centre, East Kirkby	
BL735	Supermarine Aircraft Spitfire 26 (G-HABT) [BT-A]	Privately owned, North Coates	
BL924	VS349 Spitfire VB <R> (BAPC 242) [AZ-G]	Tangmere Military Aviation Museum	
BL927	Supermarine Aircraft Spitfire 26 (G-CGWI) [YH-I]	Privately owned, Perth	
BM361	VS349 Spitfire VB <R> (BAPC 269) [XR-C]	RAF Lakenheath, on display	

Notes	*Serial*	*Type (code/other identity)*	*Owner/operator location or fate*
	BM481	VS349 Spitfire VB <R> [YO-T] (also wears *PK651*/RAO-B)	Thornaby Aerodrome Memorial
	BM539	VS349 Spitfire LF VB (G-CGBI)	Privately owned, Hastings
	BM597	VS349 Spitfire LF VB (5718M/G-MKVB) [JH-C]	Historic Aircraft Collection, Duxford
	BN230	Hawker Hurricane IIC (LF751/5466M) [FT-A]	RAF Manston, Memorial Pavilion
	BP926	VS353 Spitfire PR IV (G-PRIV)	Privately owned, Newport Pagnell
	BS239	VS361 Spitfire IX <R> (BAPC 222) [5R-E]	Battle of Britain Bunker, Uxbridge
	BS410	VS361 Spitfire IXC (G-TCHI)	Airframe Assemblies Ltd, Sandown
	BS435	VS361 Spitfire IX <R> [FY-F]	Privately owned, Lytham St Annes
	BW853	Hawker Hurricane XIIA (G-BRKE) (fuselage)	Privately owned, Cotswold Airport
	DD931	Bristol 152 Beaufort VIII (9131M) [L]	RAF Museum, Hendon
	DE208	DH82A Tiger Moth II (G-AGYU)	Privately owned, Treswell, Notts
	DE470	DH82A Tiger Moth II (G-ANMY) [16]	Privately owned, Garford, Oxon
	DE623	DH82A Tiger Moth II (G-ANFI)	Privately owned, Cardiff
	DE673	DH82A Tiger Moth II (6948M/G-ADNZ)	Privately owned, Tibenham
	DE992	DH82A Tiger Moth II (G-AXXV)	Privately owned, Upavon
	DF112	DH82A Tiger Moth II (G-ANRM)	Privately owned, Clacton/Duxford
	DF128	DH82A Tiger Moth II (G-AOJJ) [RCO-U]	Privately owned, White Waltham
	DF155	DH82A Tiger Moth II (G-ANFV)	*Crashed 13 August 2012, Shempston Farm, Lossiemouth*
	DF198	DH82A Tiger Moth II (G-BBRB)	Privately owned, Biggin Hill
	DG202	Gloster F9/40 (5758M)	RAF Museum, Hendon
	DG590	Miles M2H Hawk Major (8379M/G-ADMW)	RAF Museum Reserve Collection, Stafford
	DP872	Fairey Barracuda II <ff>	FAA Museum, Kiltech Vehicle Protection, Newcastle
	DR348	Hawker Hurricane I (composite) (P7317/G-HITT)	Privately owned, Milden
	DV372	Avro 683 Lancaster I <ff>	Imperial War Museum, Duxford
	DZ313	DH98 Mosquito B IV <R>	Privately owned, Little Rissington
	EB518	Airspeed AS10 Oxford V	Privately owned, Kenilworth
	EE416	Gloster Meteor F3 <ff>	Martin Baker Aircraft, Chalgrove, fire section
	EE425	Gloster Meteor F3 <ff>	Jet Age Museum, stored Gloucester
	EE531	Gloster Meteor F4 (7090M)	Midland Air Museum, Coventry
	EE549	Gloster Meteor F4 (7008M) [A]	Tangmere Military Aviation Museum
	EF545	VS349 Spitfire LF VC (G-CDGY)	Aero Vintage, Rye
	EJ693	Hawker Tempest V (N7027E) [SA-J]	Privately owned, Booker
	EJ922	Hawker Typhoon IB <ff>	Privately owned, Hawkinge
	EM720	DH82A Tiger Moth II (G-AXAN)	Privately owned, Treswell, Notts
	EM840	DH82A Tiger Moth II (G-ANBY)	Assault Glider Trust, Shawbury
	EN179	VS361 Spitfire F IX (G-TCHO)	Privately owned, Exeter
	EN224	VS366 Spitfire F XII (G-FXII)	Privately owned, Newport Pagnell
	EN398	VS361 Spitfire F IX <R> (BAPC 184) [JE-J]	Privately owned, Tonbridge, Kent
	EN398	VS361 Spitfire F IX <R> [JE-J]	Shropshire Wartime Aircraft Recovery Grp Mus, Sleap
	EN526	VS361 Spitfire IX <R> (*MH777*/BAPC 221) [SZ-G]	*Repainted as MH314*
	EN961	Isaacs Spitfire <R> (G-CGIK) [SD-X]	Privately owned,
	EP120	VS349 Spitfire LF VB (5377M/8070M/G-LFVB) [AE-A]	The Fighter Collection, Duxford
	EP122	VS349 Spitfire F VB	Privately owned, Sandown
	EV771	Fairchild UC-61 Argus <R> (BAPC.294)	Thorpe Camp Preservation Group, Lincs
	EX976	NA AT-6D Harvard III (FAP 1657)	FAA Museum, RNAS Yeovilton
	FE695	Noorduyn AT-16 Harvard IIB (G-BTXI) [94]	The Fighter Collection, Duxford
	FE788	CCF Harvard IV (MM54137/G-CTKL)	Privately owned, Biggin Hill
	FE905	Noorduyn AT-16 Harvard IIB (LN-BNM)	RAF Museum, Hendon
	FJ992	Boeing-Stearman PT-17 Kaydet (OO-JEH) [44]	Privately owned, Wevelgem, Belgium
	FK338	Fairchild 24W-41 Argus I (G-AJOZ)	Yorkshire Air Museum, Elvington
	FL586	Douglas C-47B Dakota (OO-SMA) [AI-N] (fuselage)	WWII Remembrance Museum, Handcross, W Sussex

Serial	Type (code/other identity)	Owner/operator location or fate	Notes
FR886	Piper L-4J Cub (G-BDMS)	Privately owned, Old Sarum	
FS628	Fairchild Argus 2 (43-14601/G-AIZE)	RAF Museum, Cosford	
FS728	Noorduyn AT-16 Harvard IIB (D-FRCP)	Privately owned, Gelnhausen, Germany	
FT118	Noorduyn AT-16 Harvard IIB (G-BZHL)	Privately owned, Wickenby	
FT323	NA AT-6D Harvard III (FAP 1513/G-CCOY)	Privately owned, Bruntingthorpe	
FT391	Noorduyn AT-16 Harvard IIB (G-AZBN)	Privately owned, Goodwood	
FX301	NA AT-6D Harvard III (EX915/G-TXAN) [FD-NQ]	*Repainted in US marks as 51970, May 2012*	
FX322	Noorduyn AT-16 Harvard IIB <ff>	Privately owned, Doncaster	
FX760	Curtiss P-40N Kittyhawk IV (A29-556/9150M) [GA-?]	RAF Museum, Hendon	
FZ626	Douglas Dakota III (KN566/G-AMPO) [YS-DH]	RAF Brize Norton, for display	
HB275	Beech C-45 Expeditor II (RCAF 2324/G-BKGM)	Privately owned, Exeter	
HB751	Fairchild Argus III (G-BCBL)	Privately owned, Woolsery, Devon	
HG691	DH89A Dragon Rapide (G-AIYR)	Privately owned, Clacton/Duxford	
HH268	GAL48 Hotspur II (HH379/BAPC 261) [H]	Museum of Army Flying, Middle Wallop	
HJ711	DH98 Mosquito NF II [VI-C]	Night-Fighter Preservation Tm, Elvington	
HM580	Cierva C-30A (G-ACUU) [KX-K]	Imperial War Museum, Duxford	
HS503	Fairey Swordfish IV (BAPC 108)	RAF Museum Reserve Collection, Stafford	
IR206	Eurofighter Typhoon F2 <R> [IR]	RAF M&RU, Bottesford	
IR808	B-V Chinook HC2 <R>	RAF M&RU, Bottesford	
JF343	Supermarine Aircraft Spitfire 26 (G-CCZP) [JW-P]	*Sold as N343FJ, July 2012*	
JG668	VS359 Spitfire LF VIIIC (A58-441/G-CFGA)	Privately owned, Haverfordwest	
JP843	Hawker Typhoon IB [Y]	Privately owned, Shrewsbury	
JR505	Hawker Typhoon IB <ff>	Midland Air Museum, Coventry	
JV482	Grumman Wildcat V	Ulster Aviation Society, Long Kesh	
JV579	Grumman FM-2 Wildcat (N4845V/G-RUMW) [F]	The Fighter Collection, Duxford	
JV928	Consolidated PBY-5A Catalina (N423RS) [Y]	Super Catalina Restoration, North Weald	
KB889	Avro 683 Lancaster B X (G-LANC) [NA-I]	Imperial War Museum, Duxford	
KB976	Avro 683 Lancaster B X <ff>	Brooklands Museum, Weybridge	
KB976	Avro 683 Lancaster B X (G-BCOH) <rf>	Aeroventure, Doncaster	
KB994	Avro 683 Lancaster B X (G-BVBP) <ff>	Privately owned,	
KD345	Goodyear FG-1D Corsair (88297/G-FGID) [130-A]	The Fighter Collection, Duxford	
KD431	CV Corsair IV [E2-M]	FAA Museum, RNAS Yeovilton	
KE209	Grumman Hellcat II	FAA Museum, RNAS Yeovilton	
KE418	Hawker Tempest <rf>	*Currently not known*	
KF183	Noorduyn AT-16 Harvard IIB [3]	MoD/AFD/QinetiQ, Boscombe Down	
KF388	Noorduyn AT-16 Harvard IIB (composite)	Bournemouth Aviation Museum	
KF435	Noorduyn AT-16 Harvard IIB <ff>	Privately owned, Swindon	
KF532	Noorduyn AT-16 Harvard IIB <ff>	Newark Air Museum, Winthorpe	
KF584	CCF T-6J Texan (G-RAIX) [RAI-X]	Privately owned, Lee-on-Solent	
KF729	CCF T-6J Texan (G-BJST)	Privately owned, Duxford	
KF741	Noorduyn AT-16 Harvard IIB <ff>	Privately owned, Kenilworth	
KG374	Douglas Dakota IV (KP208) [YS-DM]	Merville Barracks, Colchester, on display	
KG651	Douglas Dakota III (G-AMHJ)	Assault Glider Trust, Shawbury	
KJ351	Airspeed AS58 Horsa II (TL659/BAPC 80) [23]	Museum of Army Flying, Middle Wallop	
KJ994	Douglas Dakota III (F-AZTE)	Dakota et Cie, La Ferté Alais, France	
KK116	Douglas Dakota IV (G-AMPY)	Classic Air Force, Coventry	
KK995	Sikorsky Hoverfly I [E]	RAF Museum, Hendon	
KL216	Republic P-47D Thunderbolt (45-49295/9212M) [RS-L]	RAF Museum, Hendon	
KN353	Douglas Dakota IV (G-AMYJ)	Yorkshire Air Museum, Elvington	
KN645	Douglas Dakota IV (*KG374*/8355M)	RAF Museum, Cosford	
KN751	Consolidated Liberator C VI (IAF HE807) [F]	RAF Museum, Hendon	

Notes	*Serial*	*Type (code/other identity)*	*Owner/operator location or fate*
	KZ191	Hawker Hurricane IV (frame only)	Privately owned, East Garston, Bucks
	LA198	VS356 Spitfire F21 (7118M) [RAI-G]	Kelvingrove Art Gallery & Museum, Glasgow
	LA226	VS356 Spitfire F21 (7119M)	RAF Museum Reserve Collection, Stafford
	LA255	VS356 Spitfire F21 (6490M)	RAF, Leuchars
	LA543	VS474 Seafire F46 <ff>	The Air Defence Collection, Salisbury
	LA546	VS474 Seafire F46 (G-CFZJ)	Privately owned, Colchester
	LA564	VS474 Seafire F46 (G-FRSX)	Kennet Aviation, North Weald
	LB264	Taylorcraft Plus D (G-AIXA)	RAF Museum, Hendon
	LB294	Taylorcraft Plus D (G-AHWJ)	Saywell Heritage Centre, Worthing
	LB312	Taylorcraft Plus D (*HH982*/G-AHXE)	Privately owned, Netheravon
	LB323	Taylorcraft Plus D (G-AHSD)	Privately owned, Old Buckenham
	LB367	Taylorcraft Plus D (G-AHGZ)	Privately owned, Henstridge
	LB375	Taylorcraft Plus D (G-AHGW)	Privately owned, Coventry
	LF363	Hawker Hurricane IIC [YB-W]	RAF BBMF, Coningsby
	LF738	Hawker Hurricane IIC (5405M) [UH-A]	RAF Museum, Cosford
	LF789	DH82 Queen Bee (K3584/BAPC 186) [R2-K]	Mosquito Aircraft Museum, London Colney
	LF858	DH82 Queen Bee (G-BLUZ)	Privately owned, Henlow
	LH291	Airspeed AS51 Horsa I <R> (BAPC 279)	Assault Glider Trust, RAF Shawbury
	LS326	Fairey Swordfish II (G-AJVH) [L2]	RN Historic Flight, Yeovilton
	LV907	HP59 Halifax III (HR792) [NP-F] (marked *NP763* [H7-N] on port side)	Yorkshire Air Museum, Elvington
	LZ551	DH100 Vampire	FAA Museum, RNAS Yeovilton
	LZ766	Percival P34 Proctor III (G-ALCK)	Imperial War Museum, Duxford
	LZ842	VS361 Spitfire F IX (G-CGZU) [EF-D]	Privately owned, Biggin Hill
	LZ844	VS349 Spitfire F VC [UP-X]	Vintage Flyers, Cotswold Airport
	MA764	VS361 Spitfire F IX (G-MCDB)	Privately owned, Bentwaters
	MB293	VS357 Seafire IIC (G-CFGI) (wreck)	Privately owned, Duxford
	MD338	VS359 Spitfire LF VIII	Privately owned, Sandown
	MF628	Vickers Wellington T10 (9210M)	RAF Museum Restoration Centre, Cosford
	MH314	VS361 Spitfire IX <R> (*EN526*/BAPC 221) [SZ-G]	RAF Northolt, on display
	MH415	VS361 Spitfire IX <R> (*MJ751*/BAPC 209) [DU-V]	The Aircraft Restoration Co, Duxford
	MH434	VS361 Spitfire LF IXB (G-ASJV) [ZD-B]	The Old Flying Machine Company, Duxford
	MJ627	VS509 Spitfire T9 (G-BMSB) [9G-P]	Privately owned, RAF Waddington
	MJ832	VS361 Spitfire IX <R> (*L1096*/BAPC 229) [DN-Y]	RAF Digby, on display
	MK356	VS361 Spitfire LF IXC (5690M) [UF-Q]	RAF BBMF, Coningsby
	MK356	VS361 Spitfire LF IXC <R> [2I-V]	Kent Battle of Britain Museum, Hawkinge
	MK356	VS361 Spitfire LF IXC (BAPC 289) <R>	RAF Cosford, on display
	MK805	VS361 Spitfire IX <R> [SH]	Privately owned, Oulton Broad, Suffolk
	MK912	VS361 Spitfire LF IXC (G-BRRA) [SH-L]	Privately owned, Biggin Hill
	ML407	VS509 Spitfire T9 (G-LFIX) [OU-V]	Privately owned, Bentwaters
	ML411	VS361 Spitfire LF IXE (G-CBNU)	Privately owned, Ashford, Kent
	ML427	VS361 Spitfire IX (6457M) [HK-A]	Thinktank, Birmingham
	ML796	Short S25 Sunderland V [NS-F]	Imperial War Museum, Duxford
	ML824	Short S25 Sunderland V [NS-Z]	RAF Museum, Hendon
	MN235	Hawker Typhoon IB	RAF Museum, Hendon
	MP425	Airspeed AS10 Oxford I (G-AITB) [G]	RAF Museum, Hendon
	MS902	Miles M25 Martinet TT1 (TF-SHC)	Museum of Berkshire Aviation, Woodley
	MT182	Auster J/1 Autocrat (G-AJDY)	Privately owned, Spanhoe
	MT197	Auster IV (G-ANHS)	Privately owned, Spanhoe
	MT255	Auster IV (G-ANHU)	Privately owned, Wickenby
	MT438	Auster III (G-AREI)	Privately owned, Eggesford
	MT818	VS502 Spitfire T8 (G-AIDN)	Privately owned, Booker
	MT847	VS379 Spitfire FR XIVE (6960M) [AX-H]	Museum of Science & Industry, Manchester
	MT928	VS359 Spitfire HF VIIIC (D-FEUR/MV154/*AR654*)[ZX-M]	Privately owned, Bremgarten, Germany

Serial	Type (code/other identity)	Owner/operator location or fate	Notes
MV268	VS379 Spitfire FR XIVE (MV293/G-SPIT) [JE-J]	The Fighter Collection, Duxford	
MW401	Hawker Tempest II (IAF HA604/G-PEST)	Privately owned, Wickenby	
MW404	Hawker Tempest II (IAF HA557)	*Sold to the US, May 2012*	
MW763	Hawker Tempest II (IAF HA586/G-TEMT) [HF-A]	Privately owned, Wickenby	
MW810	Hawker Tempest II (IAF HA591) <ff>	Privately owned, Bentwaters	
NF370	Fairey Swordfish III [NH-L]	Imperial War Museum, Duxford	
NF389	Fairey Swordfish III [D]	RN Historic Flight, Yeovilton	
NH238	VS361 Spitfire LF IXE (G-MKIX) [D-A]	Privately owned, stored Greenham Common	
NJ633	Auster 5D (G-AKXP)	Privately owned, Old Sarum	
NJ673	Auster 5D (G-AOCR)	Privately owned, Shenington, Oxon	
NJ695	Auster AOP5 (G-AJXV)	Privately owned, Newark	
NJ703	Auster AOP5 (G-AKPI)	*Repainted as TJ207, March 2012*	
NJ719	Auster AOP5 (TW385/G-ANFU)	North-East Aircraft Museum, Usworth	
NJ728	Auster AOP5 (G-AIKE)	Privately owned, Wickenby	
NJ889	Auster AOP3 (G-AHLK)	Privately owned, Leicester East	
NL750	DH82A Tiger Moth II (T7997/G-AOBH)	Privately owned, Eaglescott	
NL985	DH82A Tiger Moth I (7015M/G-BWIK)	Privately owned, Sywell	
NM138	DH82A Tiger Moth I (G-ANEW) [44]	Privately owned, Henstridge	
NM181	DH82A Tiger Moth I (G-AZGZ)	Privately owned, Rush Green	
NP294	Percival P31 Proctor IV [TB-M]	Lincolnshire Avn Heritage Centre, E Kirkby	
NV778	Hawker Tempest TT5 (8386M)	RAF Museum, Hendon	
NX534	Auster III (G-BUDL)	Privately owned, Spanhoe	
NX611	Avro 683 Lancaster B VII (8375M/G-ASXX) [DX-C,LE-C]	Lincolnshire Avn Heritage Centre, E Kirkby	
PA474	Avro 683 Lancaster B I [KC-A]	RAF BBMF, Coningsby	
PD685	Slingsby T7 Cadet TX1	Boulton Paul Association, Wolverhampton	
PF179	HS Gnat T1 (XR541/8602M)	Privately owned, Bruntingthorpe	
PK519	VS356 Spitfire F22 [G-SPXX]	Privately owned, Newport Pagnell	
PK624	VS356 Spitfire F22 (8072M)	The Fighter Collection, Duxford	
PK664	VS356 Spitfire F22 (7759M) [V6-B]	RAF Museum Reserve Collection, Stafford	
PK683	VS356 Spitfire F24 (7150M)	Solent Sky, Southampton	
PK724	VS356 Spitfire F24 (7288M)	RAF Museum, Hendon	
PL256	VS361 Spitfire IX <R> [TM-L]	Privately owned, Leicester	
PL279	VS361 Spitfire IX <R> (*N3317*/BAPC 268) [ZF-Z]	Privately owned, St Mawgan	
PL904	VS365 Spitfire PR XI <R> (BAPC 226)	RAF Benson, on display	
PL965	VS365 Spitfire PR XI (G-MKXI) [R]	Hangar 11 Collection, North Weald	
PL983	VS365 Spitfire PR XI (G-PRXI)	Privately owned, Duxford (on rebuild)	
PM631	VS390 Spitfire PR XIX	RAF BBMF, Coningsby	
PM651	VS390 Spitfire PR XIX (7758M) [X]	RAF Museum, Cosford	
PN323	HP Halifax VII <ff>	Imperial War Museum, Duxford	
PP566	Fairey Firefly I <rf>	Privately owned, Newton Abbott, Devon	
PP972	VS358 Seafire LF IIIC (G-BUAR)	Privately owned, Bentwaters	
PR536	Hawker Tempest II (IAF HA457)[OQ-H]	RAF Museum, Hendon	
PS853	VS390 Spitfire PR XIX (G-RRGN) [C]	Rolls-Royce, East Midlands	
PS890	VS390 Spitfire PR XIX (F-AZJS) [UM-E]	Privately owned, Dijon, France	
PS915	VS390 Spitfire PR XIX (7548M/7711M)	RAF BBMF, Coningsby	
PT462	VS509 Spitfire T9 (G-CTIX/N462JC) [SW-A]	Privately owned, Caernarfon/Duxford	
PT462	VS361 Spitfire IX <R> [SW-A]	Privately owned, Moffat, Dumfries & Galloway	
PV303	Supermarine Aircraft Spitfire 26 (G-CCJL) [ON-B]	Privately owned, Barton	
PZ865	Hawker Hurricane IIC (G-AMAU) [EX-S]	RAF BBMF, Duxford (on overhaul)	
QQ100	Agusta A109E Power Elite (G-CFVB)	MoD/AFD/QinetiQ, Boscombe Down	
QQ101	BAe RJ.100 (G-BZAY)	MoD/ETPS, Boscombe Down	
QQ102	BAe RJ.70ER (G-BVRJ)	MoD/AFD/QinetiQ, Boscombe Down	

Notes	*Serial*	*Type (code/other identity)*	*Owner/operator location or fate*
	RA848	Slingsby T7 Cadet TX1	Privately owned, Leeds
	RA854	Slingsby T7 Cadet TX1	Yorkshire Air Museum, Elvington
	RA897	Slingsby T7 Cadet TX1	Newark Air Museum, Winthorpe
	RA905	Slingsby T7 Cadet TX1 (BGA1143)	Trenchard Museum, RAF Halton
	RB142	Supermarine Aircraft Spitfire 26 (G-CEFC) [DW-B]	Privately owned, Basingstoke, Hant
	RB159	VS379 Spitfire F XIV <R> [DW-D]	Privately owned, Delabole, Cornwall
	RD220	Bristol 156 Beaufighter TF X	Royal Scottish Mus'm of Flight, stored E Fortune
	RD253	Bristol 156 Beaufighter TF X (7931M)	RAF Museum, Hendon
	RF398	Avro 694 Lincoln B II (8376M)	RAF Museum, Cosford
	RG333	Miles M38 Messenger IIA (G-AIEK)	Privately owned, Felton, Bristol
	RG904	VS Spitfire <R> [BT-K]	RAF Museum, Cosford
	RH746	Bristol 164 Brigand TF1 (fuselage)	RAF Museum Restoration Centre, Cosford
	RK855	Supermarine Aircraft Spitfire 26 (G-PIXY) [FT-C]	Privately owned, Henstridge
	RL962	DH89A Dominie II (G-AHED)	RAF Museum Reserve Collection, Stafford
	RM169	Percival P31 Proctor IV (SE-CEA) [4-47]	Privately owned, Great Oakley, Essex
	RM221	Percival P31 Proctor IV (G-ANXR)	Privately owned, Biggin Hill
	RM689	VS379 Spitfire F XIV (G-ALGT)	Rolls-Royce, stored East Midlands Airport
	RM694	VS379 Spitfire F XIV (G-DBKL/6640M)	Privately owned, Booker
	RM927	VS379 Spitfire F XIV (G-JNMA)	Privately owned, Sandown
	RN218	Isaacs Spitfire <R> (G-BBJI) [N]	Privately owned, Builth Wells
	RR232	VS361 Spitfire HF IXC (G-BRSF)	Privately owned, Colerne
	RT486	Auster 5 (G-AJGJ)	Privately owned, Lee-on-Solent
	RT520	Auster 5 (G-ALYB)	Aeroventure, Doncaster
	RT610	Auster 5A-160 (G-AKWS)	Privately owned, Shobdon
	RW382	VS361 Spitfire LF XVIE (7245M/8075M/G-PBIX) [3W-P]	Privately owned, Biggin Hill
	RW386	VS361 Spitfire LF XVIE (6944M/SE-BIR) [NG-D]	Privately owned, Angelholm, Sweden
	RW388	VS361 Spitfire LF XVIE (6946M) [U4-U]	Stoke-on-Trent City Museum, Hanley
	RX168	VS358 Seafire L IIIC (IAC 157/G-BWEM)	Privately owned, Exeter
	SL611	VS361 Spitfire LF XVIE	Supermarine Aero Engineering, Stoke-on-Trent
	SL674	VS361 Spitfire LF IX (8392M) [RAS-H]	RAF Museum Reserve Collection, Stafford
	SM520	VS509 Spitfire T9 (*H-99*/G-ILDA) [KJ-I]	Privately owned, Kidlington
	SM845	VS394 Spitfire FR XVIII (G-BUOS)	Privately owned, Duxford (on rebuild)
	SN280	Hawker Tempest V <ff>	Aeroventure, Doncaster
	SX137	VS384 Seafire F XVII	FAA Museum, RNAS Yeovilton
	SX300	VS384 Seafire F XVII (G-RIPH)	Kennet Aviation, North Weald
	SX336	VS384 Seafire F XVII (G-KASX) [105/VL]	Kennet Aviation, Yeovilton
	TA122	DH98 Mosquito FB VI [UP-G]	Mosquito Aircraft Museum, London Colney
	TA634	DH98 Mosquito TT35 (G-AWJV) [8K-K]	Mosquito Aircraft Museum, London Colney
	TA639	DH98 Mosquito TT35 (7806M) [AZ-E]	RAF Museum, Cosford
	TA719	DH98 Mosquito TT35 (G-ASKC)	Imperial War Museum, Duxford
	TA805	VS361 Spitfire HF IX (G-PMNF) [FX-M]	Privately owned, Biggin Hill
	TB382	VS361 Spitfire LF XVIE (*X4277/MK673*)	RAF BBMF, stored Coningsby
	TB675	VS361 Spitfire LF XVIE (RW393/7293M) [4D-V]	RAF Museum Reserve Collection, Stafford
	TB752	VS361 Spitfire LF XVIE (8086M) [KH-Z]	RAF Manston, Memorial Pavilion
	TD248	VS361 Spitfire LF XVIE (7246M/G-OXVI) [CR-S]	Spitfire Limited, Humberside
	TD248	VS361 Spitfire LF XVIE [8Q-T] (fuselage)	Norfolk & Suffolk Avn Mus'm, Flixton
	TD314	VS361 Spitfire LF IX (G-CGYJ) [FX-P]	Privately owned, Biggin Hill
	TE184	VS361 Spitfire LF XVIE (6850M/G-MXVI) [EJC]	Privately owned, Biggin Hill
	TE311	VS361 Spitfire LF XVIE (*MK178*/7241M) [4D-V]	RAF BBMF, Coningsby
	TE462	VS361 Spitfire LF XVIE (7243M)	Royal Scottish Mus'm of Flight, E Fortune
	TE517	VS361 Spitfire LF IXE (G-JGCA) [HL-K]	Privately owned, Biggin Hill
	TE566	VS361 Spitfire LF IXE (VH-IXT)	Vintage Flyers, Cotswold Airport (wreck)
	TG263	Saro SR A1 (G-12-1)	Solent Sky, Southampton
	TG511	HP67 Hastings T5 (8554M) [511]	RAF Museum, Cosford
	TG517	HP67 Hastings T5 [517]	Newark Air Museum, Winthorpe

Serial	Type (code/other identity)	Owner/operator location or fate	Notes
TG528	HP67 Hastings C1A [528,T]	Imperial War Museum, Duxford	
TJ118	DH98 Mosquito TT35 <ff>	Mosquito Aircraft Museum, stored London Colney	
TJ138	DH98 Mosquito B35 (7607M) [VO-L]	RAF Museum, Hendon	
TJ207	Auster AOP5 (NJ703/G-AKPI) [P]	Privately owned, Spanhoe	
TJ343	Auster AOP5 (G-AJXC)	Privately owned, Hook	
TJ398	Auster AOP6 (BAPC 70)	North-East Aircraft Museum, Usworth	
TJ518	Auster J/1 Autocrat (G-AJIH)	Privately owned, Bidford	
TJ534	Auster AOP5 (G-AKSY)	Privately owned, Dunsfold	
TJ569	Auster AOP5 (G-AKOW)	Museum of Army Flying, Middle Wallop	
TJ652	Auster AOP5 (TJ565/G-AMVD)	Privately owned, Hardwick, Norfolk	
TJ672	Auster 5D (G-ANIJ) [TS-D]	Privately owned, Netheravon	
TK718	GAL59 Hamilcar I (fuselage)	The Tank Museum, Bovington	
TK777	GAL59 Hamilcar I (fuselage)	Museum of Army Flying, Middle Wallop	
TP298	VS394 Spitfire FR XVIII [UM-T]	Privately owned, Sandown	
TS291	Slingsby T7 Cadet TX1 (BGA852)	Royal Scottish Museum of Flight, stored Granton	
TS798	Avro 685 York C1 (G-AGNV/*MW100*)	RAF Museum, Cosford	
TW439	Auster AOP5 (G-ANRP)	Privately owned, Wickenby	
TW467	Auster AOP5 (G-ANIE)	Privately owned, Spanhoe	
TW477	Auster AOP5 (OY-EFI)	Privately owned, Ringsted, Denmark	
TW501	Auster AOP5 (G-ALBJ)	Privately owned, Dunkeswell	
TW511	Auster AOP5 (G-APAF)	Privately owned, Chisledon, Wilts	
TW536	Auster AOP6 (7704M/G-BNGE) [TS-V]	Privately owned, Netheravon	
TW591	Auster 6A (G-ARIH) [6]	Privately owned, Eaglescott	
TW641	Beagle A61 Terrier 2 (G-ATDN)	Privately owned, Biggin Hill	
TX213	Avro 652A Anson C19 (G-AWRS)	North-East Aircraft Museum, Usworth	
TX214	Avro 652A Anson C19 (7817M)	RAF Museum, Cosford	
TX226	Avro 652A Anson C19 (7865M)	Classic Air Force, stored Compton Verney	
TX235	Avro 652A Anson C19	Classic Air Force, stored Compton Verney	
TX310	DH89A Dragon Rapide 6 (G-AIDL)	Classic Air Force, Coventry	
VF301	DH100 Vampire F1 (7060M) [RAL-G]	Midland Air Museum, Coventry	
VF512	Auster 6A (G-ARRX) [PF-M]	Privately owned, Popham	
VF516	Beagle A61 Terrier 2 (G-ASMZ)	Privately owned, Eggesford	
VF519	Auster AOP6 (G-ASYN)	Privately owned, Doncaster	
VF526	Auster 6A (G-ARXU) [T]	Privately owned, Netheravon	
VF557	Auster 6A (G-ARHM) [H]	Privately owned, Spanhoe	
VF560	Auster 6A (frame)	Aeroventure, Doncaster	
VF581	Beagle A61 Terrier 1 (G-ARSL) [G]	Privately owned, Eggesford	
VH127	Fairey Firefly TT4 [200/R]	FAA Museum, stored RNAS Yeovilton	
VL348	Avro 652A Anson C19 (G-AVVO)	Newark Air Museum, Winthorpe	
VL349	Avro 652A Anson C19 (G-AWSA) [V7-Q]	Norfolk & Suffolk Avn Mus'm, Flixton	
VM325	Avro 652A Anson C19	Privately owned, Carew Cheriton, Pembrokeshire	
VM360	Avro 652A Anson C19 (G-APHV)	Royal Scottish Mus'm of Flight, E Fortune	
VM684	Slingsby Cadet T2 (BGA791)	*Currently not known*	
VM687	Slingsby T8 Tutor (BGA794)	Privately owned, Lee-on-Solent	
VM791	Slingsby Cadet TX3 (XA312/8876M)	RAF Manston History Museum	
VN485	VS356 Spitfire F24 (7326M)	Imperial War Museum, Duxford	
VN799	EE Canberra T4 (WJ874/G-CDSX)	AIRBASE, Coventry	
VP293	Avro 696 Shackleton T4 [X] <ff>	Shackleton Preservation Trust, Coventry	
VP519	Avro 652A Anson C19 (G-AVVR) <ff>	Aeroventure, Doncaster	
VP952	DH104 Devon C2 (8820M)	RAF Museum, Cosford	
VP955	DH104 Devon C2 (G-DVON)	Privately owned, Little Rissington	
VP957	DH104 Devon C2 (8822M) <ff>	No 1137 Sqn ATC, Belfast	
VP967	DH104 Devon C2 (G-KOOL)	Yorkshire Air Museum, Elvington	
VP975	DH104 Devon C2 [M]	Science Museum, Wroughton	
VP981	DH104 Devon C2 (G-DHDV)	Classic Air Force, Coventry	
VR137	Westland Wyvern TF1	FAA Museum, stored RNAS Yeovilton	
VR192	Percival P40 Prentice T1 (G-APIT)	Privately owned, Cambs	
VR249	Percival P40 Prentice T1 (G-APIY) [FA-EL]	Newark Air Museum, Winthorpe	
VR259	Percival P40 Prentice T1 (G-APJB) [M]	Classic Air Force, Coventry	

Notes	*Serial*	*Type (code/other identity)*	*Owner/operator location or fate*
	VR930	Hawker Sea Fury FB11 (8382M) [110/Q]	RN Historic Flight, Yeovilton
	VS356	Percival P40 Prentice T1 (G-AOLU)	Privately owned, Montrose
	VS562	Avro 652A Anson T21 (8012M)	Privately owned, Market Drayton
	VS610	Percival P40 Prentice T1 (G-AOKL)[K-L]	The Shuttleworth Collection, Old Warden
	VS618	Percival P40 Prentice T1 (G-AOLK)	RAF Museum, Hendon
	VS623	Percival P40 Prentice T1 (G-AOKZ)[KQ-F]	Midland Air Museum, Coventry
	VT812	DH100 Vampire F3 (7200M) [N]	RAF Museum, Hendon
	VT935	Boulton Paul P111A (VT769)	Midland Air Museum, Coventry
	VT987	Auster AOP6 (G-BKXP)	Privately owned, Thruxton
	VV106	Supermarine 510 (7175M)	FAA Museum, stored RNAS Yeovilton
	VV217	DH100 Vampire FB5 (7323M)	Mosquito Aircraft Museum, stored London Colney
	VV400	EoN Olympia 2 (BGA1697)	Privately owned, Rivar Hill, Wilts
	VV401	EoN Olympia 2 (BGA1125) [99]	Privately owned, Ringmer, E Sussex
	VV612	DH112 Venom FB50 (J-1523/*WE402*/G-VENI)	Privately owned, Bournemouth (dismantled)
	VV901	Avro 652A Anson T21	Yorkshire Air Museum, Elvington
	VW453	Gloster Meteor T7 (8703M) [Z]	RAF Innsworth, on display
	VW957	DH103 Sea Hornet NF21 <rf>	Privately owned, Chelmsford
	VW993	Beagle A61 Terrier 2 (G-ASCD)	Yorkshire Air Museum, Elvington
	VX113	Auster AOP6 (G-ARNO) [36]	Privately owned, Stow Maries, Essex
	VX147	Alon A2 Aircoupe (G-AVIL)	Privately owned, Eaglescott
	VX185	EE Canberra B(I)8 (7631M) <ff>	Royal Scottish Mus'm of Flight, E Fortune
	VX250	DH103 Sea Hornet NF21 [48] <rf>	Mosquito Aircraft Museum, London Colney
	VX272	Hawker P.1052 (7174M)	FAA Museum, stored RNAS Yeovilton
	VX275	Slingsby T21B Sedbergh TX1 (8884M/BGA572)	RAF Museum Reserve Collection, Stafford
	VX281	Hawker Sea Fury T20S (G-RNHF) [120/VL]	Naval Aviation Ltd, Yeovilton
	VX573	Vickers Valetta C2 (8389M)	RAF Museum, stored Cosford
	VX580	Vickers Valetta C2 [580]	Norfolk & Suffolk Avn Museum, Flixton
	VX595	WS51 Dragonfly HR1	FAA Museum, stored RNAS Yeovilton
	VX665	Hawker Sea Fury FB11 <rf>	RN Historic Flight, at BAE Systems Brough
	VX926	Auster T7 (G-ASKJ)	Privately owned, Gamlingay, Cambs
	VX927	Auster T7 (G-ASYG)	Privately owned, Wickenby
	VZ193	DH100 Vampire FB5 <ff>	Privately owned, Hooton Park
	VZ345	Hawker Sea Fury T20S	The Fighter Collection, Duxford
	VZ440	Gloster Meteor F8 (WA984) [X]	Tangmere Military Aviation Museum
	VZ477	Gloster Meteor F8 (7741M) <ff>	Midland Air Museum, Coventry
	VZ608	Gloster Meteor FR9	Newark Air Museum, Winthorpe
	VZ634	Gloster Meteor T7 (8657M)	Newark Air Museum, Winthorpe
	VZ638	Gloster Meteor T7 (G-JETM) [HF]	Gatwick Aviation Museum, Charlwood, Surrey
	VZ728	RS4 Desford Trainer (G-AGOS)	Snibston Discovery Park, stored Coalville
	VZ962	WS51 Dragonfly HR1 [904]	*To Malta, 2011*
	WA346	DH100 Vampire FB5	RAF Museum, stored Cosford
	WA473	VS Attacker F1 [102/J]	FAA Museum, RNAS Yeovilton
	WA576	Bristol 171 Sycamore 3 (7900M/G-ALSS)	Dumfries & Galloway Avn Mus, Dumfries
	WA577	Bristol 171 Sycamore 3 (7718M/G-ALST)	North-East Aircraft Museum, Usworth
	WA591	Gloster Meteor T7 (7917M/G-BWMF) [FMK-Q]	Classic Air Force, Coventry
	WA630	Gloster Meteor T7 [69] <ff>	Robertsbridge Aviation Society, Newhaven
	WA634	Gloster Meteor T7/8	RAF Museum, Cosford
	WA638	Gloster Meteor T7(mod)	Martin Baker Aircraft, Chalgrove
	WA662	Gloster Meteor T7	Aeroventure, Doncaster
	WB188	Hawker Hunter F3 (7154M)	Tangmere Military Aviation Museum
	WB188	Hawker Hunter GA11 (WV256/G-BZPB)	Classic Air Force, Newquay
	WB188	Hawker Hunter GA11 (XF300/G-BZPC)	Privately owned, Melksham, Wilts
	WB440	Fairey Firefly AS6 <ff>	Privately owned, Newton Abbott, Devon
	WB491	Avro 706 Ashton 2 (TS897/G-AJJW) <ff>	Newark Air Museum, Winthorpe
	WB555	DHC1 Chipmunk T10 <ff>	Privately owned, Ellerton
	WB556	DHC1 Chipmunk T10 (fuselage) [O-C,P]	Privately owned, Bournemouth
	WB560	DHC1 Chipmunk T10 (comp WG403)	Privately owned, South Molton, Devon
	WB565	DHC1 Chipmunk T10 (G-PVET) [X]	Privately owned, Rendcomb

Serial	*Type (code/other identity)*	*Owner/operator location or fate*	*Notes*
WB569	DHC1 Chipmunk T10 (G-BYSJ) [R]	Privately owned, Cotswold Airport	
WB571	DHC1 Chipmunk T10 (G-AOSF) [34]	Privately owned, Trier, Germany	
WB584	DHC1 Chipmunk T10 (comp WG303/7706M)	Newcastle Aviation Academy	
WB585	DHC1 Chipmunk T10 (G-AOSY) [M]	Privately owned, Audley End	
WB588	DHC1 Chipmunk T10 (G-AOTD) [D]	Privately owned, Old Sarum	
WB615	DHC1 Chipmunk T10 (G-BXIA) [E]	Privately owned, Blackpool	
WB624	DHC1 Chipmunk T10	Newark Air Museum, Winthorpe	
WB626	DHC1 Chipmunk T10 <ff>	Trenchard Museum, RAF Halton	
WB627	DHC1 Chipmunk T10 (9248M) (fuselage) [N]	Dulwich College CCF	
WB654	DHC1 Chipmunk T10 (G-BXGO) [U]	Privately owned, Booker	
WB657	DHC1 Chipmunk T10 [908]	RN Historic Flight, Yeovilton	
WB670	DHC1 Chipmunk T10 (comp WG303)(8361M)	Privately owned, Carlisle	
WB671	DHC1 Chipmunk T10 (G-BWTG) [910]	Privately owned, Teuge, The Netherlands	
WB685	DHC1 Chipmunk T10 (comp WP969/G-ATHC)	Mosquito Aircraft Museum, London Colney	
WB685	DHC1 Chipmunk T10 <rf>	North-East Aircraft Museum, stored Usworth	
WB697	DHC1 Chipmunk T10 (G-BXCT) [95]	Privately owned, Wickenby	
WB702	DHC1 Chipmunk T10 (G-AOFE)	Privately owned, Goodwood	
WB703	DHC1 Chipmunk T10 (G-ARMC)	Privately owned, Compton Abbas	
WB711	DHC1 Chipmunk T10 (G-APPM)	Privately owned, Sywell	
WB726	DHC1 Chipmunk T10 (G-AOSK) [E]	Privately owned, Halton	
WB733	DHC1 Chipmunk T10 (comp WG422)	Aeroventure, Doncaster	
WB763	DHC1 Chipmunk T10 (G-BBMR) [14]	Privately owned, Bicester	
WB922	Slingsby T21B Sedbergh TX1 (BGA4366)	Privately owned, Bicester (under restoration)	
WB924	Slingsby T21B Sedbergh TX1 (BGA3901)	Privately owned, Dunstable	
WB943	Slingsby T21B Sedbergh TX1 (BGA2941)	*Sold to Thailand*	
WB944	Slingsby T21B Sedbergh TX1 (BGA3160)	Privately owned, Bicester	
WB945	Slingsby T21B Sedbergh TX1 (BGA1254)	Privately owned, Lasham	
WB971	Slingsby T21B Sedbergh TX1 (BGA3324)	Privately owned, Felthorpe	
WB975	Slingsby T21B Sedbergh TX1 (BGA3288) [FJB]	Privately owned, Shipdham	
WB980	Slingsby T21B Sedbergh TX1 (BGA3290)	Privately owned, Husbands Bosworth	
WB981	Slingsby T21B Sedbergh TX1 (BGA3238)	Privately owned, Keevil	
WD286	DHC1 Chipmunk T10 (G-BBND)	Privately owned, Little Gransden	
WD292	DHC1 Chipmunk T10 (G-BCRX)	Privately owned, White Waltham	
WD293	DHC1 Chipmunk T10 (7645M) <ff>	Privately owned, St Athan	
WD310	DHC1 Chipmunk T10 (G-BWUN) [B]	Privately owned, Deanland	
WD319	DHC1 Chipmunk T10 (OY-ATF)	Privately owned, Stauning, Denmark	
WD321	DHC1 Chipmunk T10 (G-BDCC)	Boscombe Down Aviation Collection, Old Sarum	
WD325	DHC1 Chipmunk T10 [N]	AAC Historic Aircraft Flight, Middle Wallop	
WD331	DHC1 Chipmunk T10 (G-BXDH)	Privately owned, Farnborough	
WD355	DHC1 Chipmunk T10 (WD335/G-CBAJ)	Privately owned, Eastleigh	
WD363	DHC1 Chipmunk T10 (G-BCIH) [5]	Privately owned, Audley End	
WD370	DHC1 Chipmunk T10 <ff>	No 225 Sqn ATC, Brighton	
WD373	DHC1 Chipmunk T10 (G-BXDI) [12]	Privately owned, Bicester	
WD377	DHC1 Chipmunk T10 <ff>	Privately owned, Lancs	
WD386	DHC1 Chipmunk T10 (comp WD377)	Privately owned, Lisburn, Northern Ireland	
WD388	DHC1 Chipmunk T10 (D-EPAK) [68]	Quax Flieger, Hamm, Germany	
WD390	DHC1 Chipmunk T10 (G-BWNK) [68]	Privately owned, Wickenby	
WD413	Avro 652A Anson T21 (7881M/G-VROE)	Classic Air Force, Coventry	
WD615	Gloster Meteor TT20 (WD646/8189M) [R]	RAF Manston History Museum	
WD686	Gloster Meteor NF11 [S]	Muckleburgh Collection, Weybourne	
WD790	Gloster Meteor NF11 (8743M)<ff>	North-East Aircraft Museum, Usworth	
WD889	Fairey Firefly AS5 (comp VT809)	Privately owned, Newton Abbot, Devon	
WD931	EE Canberra B2 <ff>	RAF Museum, stored Cosford	
WD935	EE Canberra B2 (8440M) <ff>	Aeroventure, Doncaster	
WD954	EE Canberra B2 <ff>	Privately owned, St Mawgan	
WE113	EE Canberra B2 <ff>	Privately owned, Tangmere	
WE122	EE Canberra TT18 [845] <ff>	Blyth Valley Aviation Collection, Walpole, Suffolk	
WE139	EE Canberra PR3 (8369M)	RAF Museum, Hendon	

Notes	Serial	Type (code/other identity)	Owner/operator location or fate
	WE168	EE Canberra PR3 (8049M) <ff>	Norfolk & Suffolk Avn Museum, Flixton
	WE173	EE Canberra PR3 (8740M) <ff>	Robertsbridge Aviation Society, Mayfield
	WE188	EE Canberra T4	Solway Aviation Society, Carlisle
	WE192	EE Canberra T4 <ff>	Blyth Valley Aviation Collection, Walpole, Suffolk
	WE275	DH112 Venom FB50 (J-1601/G-VIDI)	BAE Systems Hawarden, Fire Section
	WE569	Auster T7 (G-ASAJ)	Classic Air Force, Coventry
	WE570	Auster T7 (G-ASBU)	Privately owned, Stonehaven
	WE591	Auster T7 (F-AZTJ)	Privately owned, Toussus-le-Noble, France
	WE600	Auster T7 Antarctic (7602M)	RAF Museum, Cosford
	WE724	Hawker Sea Fury FB11 (VX653/G-BUCM) [062]	The Fighter Collection, Duxford
	WE982	Slingsby T30B Prefect TX1 (8781M)	RAF Museum, stored Cosford
	WE987	Slingsby T30B Prefect TX1 (BGA2517)	Aeroventure, Doncaster
	WE990	Slingsby T30B Prefect TX1 (BGA2583)	Privately owned, stored Beds
	WE992	Slingsby T30B Prefect TX1 (BGA2692)	Privately owned, Hullavington
	WF118	Percival P57 Sea Prince T1 (G-DACA) [569/CU]	Gatwick Aviation Museum, Charlwood, Surrey
	WF122	Percival P57 Sea Prince T1 [575/CU]	Aeroventure, Doncaster
	WF128	Percival P57 Sea Prince T1 (8611M)	Norfolk & Suffolk Avn Museum, Flixton
	WF137	Percival P57 Sea Prince C1	Privately owned, Booker
	WF145	Hawker Sea Hawk F1 <ff>	Privately owned, Newton Abbot, Devon
	WF219	Hawker Sea Hawk F1 <rf>	FAA Museum, stored RNAS Yeovilton
	WF225	Hawker Sea Hawk F1 [CU]	RNAS Culdrose, at main gate
	WF259	Hawker Sea Hawk F2 [171/A]	Royal Scottish Mus'm of Flight, E Fortune
	WF369	Vickers Varsity T1 [F]	Newark Air Museum, Winthorpe
	WF372	Vickers Varsity T1 [A]	Brooklands Museum, Weybridge
	WF408	Vickers Varsity T1 (8395M) <ff>	Privately owned, Ashford, Kent
	WF643	Gloster Meteor F8 [P]	Norfolk & Suffolk Avn Museum, Flixton
	WF784	Gloster Meteor T7 (7895M)	Jet Age Museum, stored Gloucester
	WF825	Gloster Meteor T7 (8359M) [A]	Montrose Air Station Heritage Centre
	WF911	EE Canberra B2 [CO] <ff>	Privately owned, Alveley, Shrops
	WF922	EE Canberra PR3	Midland Air Museum, Coventry
	WG303	DHC1 Chipmunk T10 (8208M) <ff>	Privately owned, Partridge Green, W Sussex
	WG308	DHC1 Chipmunk T10 (G-BYHL) [8]	Privately owned, Syerston
	WG316	DHC1 Chipmunk T10 (G-BCAH)	Privately owned, Church Fenton
	WG321	DHC1 Chipmunk T10 (G-DHCC)	Privately owned, Wevelgem, Belgium
	WG348	DHC1 Chipmunk T10 (G-BBMV)	Privately owned, Biggin Hill
	WG350	DHC1 Chipmunk T10 (G-BPAL)	Privately owned, Cascais, Portugal
	WG362	DHC1 Chipmunk T10 (8437M/8630M/*WX643*) <ff>	No 1094 Sqn ATC, Ely
	WG407	DHC1 Chipmunk T10 (G-BWMX) [67]	Privately owned, Croydon, Cambs
	WG418	DHC1 Chipmunk T10 (8209M/G-ATDY) <ff>	No 1940 Sqn ATC, Levenshulme, Gr Manchester
	WG419	DHC1 Chipmunk T10 (8206M) <ff>	Sywell Aviation Museum
	WG422	DHC1 Chipmunk T10 (8394M/G-BFAX) [16]	Privately owned, Eggesford
	WG432	DHC1 Chipmunk T10 [L]	Museum of Army Flying, Middle Wallop
	WG458	DHC1 Chipmunk T10 (N458BG) [2]	Privately owned, Breighton
	WG465	DHC1 Chipmunk T10 (G-BCEY)	Privately owned, White Waltham
	WG469	DHC1 Chipmunk T10 (G-BWJY) [72]	Privately owned, Sligo, Eire
	WG471	DHC1 Chipmunk T10 (8210M) <ff>	Thameside Aviation Museum, East Tilbury
	WG472	DHC1 Chipmunk T10 (G-AOTY)	Privately owned, Bryngwyn Bach, Clwyd
	WG477	DHC1 Chipmunk T10 (8362M/G-ATDP) <ff>	No 281 Sqn ATC, Birkdale, Merseyside
	WG486	DHC1 Chipmunk T10 [G]	RAF BBMF, Coningsby
	WG498	Slingsby T21B Sedbergh TX1 (BGA3245)	Privately owned, Aston Down
	WG511	Avro 696 Shackleton T4 (fuselage)	Flambards Village Theme Park, Helston
	WG655	Hawker Sea Fury T20 (G-CHFP) [910/GN]	The Fighter Collection, Duxford
	WG719	WS51 Dragonfly HR5 (G-BRMA)	The Helicopter Museum, Weston-super-Mare
	WG724	WS51 Dragonfly HR5 [932]	North-East Aircraft Museum, Usworth
	WG751	WS51 Dragonfly HR5 [710/GJ]	World Naval Base, Chatham
	WG760	EE P1A (7755M)	RAF Museum, Cosford
	WG763	EE P1A (7816M)	Museum of Science & Industry, Manchester

Serial	Type (code/other identity)	Owner/operator location or fate	Notes
WG768	Short SB5 (8005M)	RAF Museum, Cosford	
WG774	BAC 221	Science Museum, at FAA Museum, RNAS Yeovilton	
WG777	Fairey FD2 (7986M)	RAF Museum, Cosford	
WG789	EE Canberra B2/6 <ff>	Norfolk & Suffolk Avn Museum, Flixton	
WH132	Gloster Meteor T7 (7906M) [J]	RAF Leconfield, for display	
WH166	Gloster Meteor T7 (8052M) [A]	Privately owned, Birlingham, Worcs	
WH291	Gloster Meteor F8	Privately owned, Liverpool Airport	
WH301	Gloster Meteor F8 (7930M) [T]	RAF Museum, Hendon	
WH364	Gloster Meteor F8 (8169M)	Jet Age Museum, stored Gloucester	
WH453	Gloster Meteor D16 [L]	Bentwaters Cold War Air Museum	
WH646	EE Canberra T17A <ff>	Midland Air Museum, Coventry	
WH657	EE Canberra B2 <ff>	Brenzett Aeronautical Museum	
WH725	EE Canberra B2	Imperial War Museum, Duxford	
WH734	EE Canberra B2(mod) <ff>	Privately owned, Pershore	
WH739	EE Canberra B2 <ff>	No 2475 Sqn ATC, Ammanford, Dyfed	
WH740	EE Canberra T17 (8762M) [K]	East Midlands Airport Aeropark	
WH773	EE Canberra PR7 (8696M)	Gatwick Aviation Museum, Charlwood, Surrey	
WH775	EE Canberra PR7 (8128M/8868M) <ff>	Privately owned, Welshpool	
WH779	EE Canberra PR7 <ff>	Newark Air Museum, Winthorpe	
WH779	EE Canberra PR7 [BP] <rf>	RAF, stored Shawbury	
WH792	EE Canberra PR7 (WH791/8165M/8176M/8187M)	Newark Air Museum, Winthorpe	
WH798	EE Canberra PR7 (8130M) <ff>	Privately owned, Kesgrave, Suffolk	
WH840	EE Canberra T4 (8350M)	Privately owned, Flixton	
WH846	EE Canberra T4	Yorkshire Air Museum, Elvington	
WH850	EE Canberra T4 <ff>	Privately owned, Narborough	
WH863	EE Canberra T17 (8693M) <ff>	Newark Air Museum, Winthorpe	
WH876	EE Canberra B2(mod) <ff>	Boscombe Down Aviation Collection, Old Sarum	
WH887	EE Canberra TT18 [847] <ff>	Privately owned, Upwood, Cambs	
WH903	EE Canberra B2 <ff>	Yorkshire Air Museum, Elvington	
WH904	EE Canberra T19	Newark Air Museum, Winthorpe	
WH953	EE Canberra B6(mod) <ff>	Blyth Valley Aviation Collection, Walpole, Suffolk	
WH957	EE Canberra E15 (8869M) <ff>	Lincolnshire Avn Heritage Centre, East Kirkby	
WH960	EE Canberra B15 (8344M) <ff>	Rolls-Royce Heritage Trust, Derby	
WH964	EE Canberra E15 (8870M) <ff>	Privately owned, Lewes	
WH984	EE Canberra B15 (8101M) <ff>	City of Norwich Aviation Museum	
WH991	WS51 Dragonfly HR3	Yorkshire Helicopter Preservation Group, Elvington	
WJ231	Hawker Sea Fury FB11 (*WE726*) [115/O]	FAA Museum, RNAS Yeovilton	
WJ306	Slingsby T21B Sedbergh TX1 (BGA3240)	Privately owned, Weston-on-the-Green	
WJ306	Slingsby T21B Sedbergh TX1 (WB957/BGA2720)	Privately owned, Parham Park, Sussex	
WJ358	Auster AOP6 (G-ARYD)	Museum of Army Flying, Middle Wallop	
WJ368	Auster AOP6 (G-ASZX)	Privately owned, Eggesford	
WJ404	Auster AOP6 (G-ASOI)	Privately owned, Bidford-on-Avon, Warks	
WJ476	Vickers Valetta T3 <ff>	North-East Aircraft Museum, Usworth	
WJ565	EE Canberra T17 (8871M) <ff>	Aeroventure, Doncaster	
WJ567	EE Canberra B2 <ff>	Privately owned, Houghton, Cambs	
WJ576	EE Canberra T17 <ff>	Boulton Paul Association, Wolverhampton	
WJ633	EE Canberra T17 <ff>	City of Norwich Aviation Museum	
WJ639	EE Canberra TT18 [39]	North-East Aircraft Museum, Usworth	
WJ677	EE Canberra B2 <ff>	Privately owned, Redruth	
WJ717	EE Canberra TT18 (9052M) <ff>	RAF St Athan, Fire Section	
WJ721	EE Canberra TT18 [21] <ff>	No 2405 Det Flt ATC, Gairloch	
WJ731	EE Canberra B2T [BK] <ff>	Privately owned, Golders Green	
WJ775	EE Canberra B6 (8581M) <ff>	Privately owned, Upwood, Cambs	
WJ821	EE Canberra PR7 (8668M)	Army, Bassingbourn, on display	
WJ865	EE Canberra T4 <ff>	Boscombe Down Aviation Collection, Old Sarum	
WJ880	EE Canberra T4 (8491M) <ff>	Dumfries & Galloway Avn Mus, Dumfries	

Notes	Serial	Type (code/other identity)	Owner/operator location or fate
	WJ903	Vickers Varsity T1 <ff>	Aeroventure, Doncaster
	WJ945	Vickers Varsity T1 (G-BEDV) [21]	Classic Air Force, Newquay
	WJ975	EE Canberra T19 <ff>	Aeroventure, Doncaster
	WJ992	EE Canberra T4	Bournemouth Airport Fire Section
	WK001	Thales Watchkeeper 450 UAV (4X-USC)	Thales, for Army
	WK002	Thales Watchkeeper 450 UAV (4X-USD)	Thales, for Army
	WK003	Thales Watchkeeper 450 UAV	Thales, for Army
	WK004	Thales Watchkeeper 450 UAV	Thales, for Army
	WK005	Thales Watchkeeper 450 UAV	Thales, for Army
	WK006	Thales Watchkeeper 450 UAV	Thales, for Army
	WK007	Thales Watchkeeper 450 UAV	Thales, for Army
	WK008	Thales Watchkeeper 450 UAV	Thales, for Army
	WK009	Thales Watchkeeper 450 UAV	Thales, for Army
	WK010	Thales Watchkeeper 450 UAV	Thales, for Army
	WK011	Thales Watchkeeper 450 UAV	Thales, for Army
	WK012	Thales Watchkeeper 450 UAV	Thales, for Army
	WK013	Thales Watchkeeper 450 UAV	Thales, for Army
	WK014	Thales Watchkeeper 450 UAV	Thales, for Army
	WK015	Thales Watchkeeper 450 UAV	Thales, for Army
	WK016	Thales Watchkeeper 450 UAV	Thales, for Army
	WK017	Thales Watchkeeper 450 UAV	Thales, for Army
	WK018	Thales Watchkeeper 450 UAV	Thales, for Army
	WK019	Thales Watchkeeper 450 UAV	Thales, for Army
	WK020	Thales Watchkeeper 450 UAV	Thales, for Army
	WK021	Thales Watchkeeper 450 UAV	Thales, for Army
	WK022	Thales Watchkeeper 450 UAV	Thales, for Army
	WK023	Thales Watchkeeper 450 UAV	Thales, for Army
	WK024	Thales Watchkeeper 450 UAV	Thales, for Army
	WK025	Thales Watchkeeper 450 UAV	Thales, for Army
	WK026	Thales Watchkeeper 450 UAV	Thales, for Army
	WK027	Thales Watchkeeper 450 UAV	Thales, for Army
	WK028	Thales Watchkeeper 450 UAV	Thales, for Army
	WK029	Thales Watchkeeper 450 UAV	Thales, for Army
	WK030	Thales Watchkeeper 450 UAV	Thales, for Army
	WK031	Thales Watchkeeper 450 UAV	Thales, for Army
	WK032	Thales Watchkeeper 450 UAV	Thales, for Army
	WK033	Thales Watchkeeper 450 UAV	Thales, for Army
	WK034	Thales Watchkeeper 450 UAV	Thales, for Army
	WK035	Thales Watchkeeper 450 UAV	Thales, for Army
	WK036	Thales Watchkeeper 450 UAV	Thales, for Army
	WK037	Thales Watchkeeper 450 UAV	Thales, for Army
	WK038	Thales Watchkeeper 450 UAV	Thales, for Army
	WK039	Thales Watchkeeper 450 UAV	Thales, for Army
	WK040	Thales Watchkeeper 450 UAV	Thales, for Army
	WK060	Thales Watchkeeper 450 UAV	Thales, for Army
	WK102	EE Canberra T17 (8780M) <ff>	Privately owned, Welshpool
	WK118	EE Canberra TT18 [CQ] <ff>	Privately owned, Holt Heath, Worcs
	WK122	EE Canberra TT18 <ff>	Privately owned, Wesham, Lancs
	WK124	EE Canberra TT18 (9093M) [CR]	MoD DFTDC, Manston
	WK126	EE Canberra TT18 (N2138J) [843]	Jet Age Museum, stored Gloucester
	WK127	EE Canberra TT18 (8985M) <ff>	Privately owned, Peterborough
	WK146	EE Canberra B2 <ff>	Gatwick Aviation Museum, Charlwood, Surrey
	WK163	EE Canberra B2/6 (G-BVWC)	AIRBASE, Coventry
	WK198	VS Swift F4 (7428M) (fuselage)	Brooklands Museum, Weybridge
	WK275	VS Swift F4	Privately owned, Thorpe Wood, N Yorks
	WK277	VS Swift FR5 (7719M) [N]	Newark Air Museum, Winthorpe
	WK281	VS Swift FR5 (7712M) [S]	Tangmere Military Aviation Museum
	WK393	DH112 Venom FB1 <ff>	Aeroventure, stored Doncaster

Serial	*Type (code/other identity)*	*Owner/operator location or fate*	*Notes*
WK436	DH112 Venom FB50 (J-1614/G-VENM)	Classic Air Force, Coventry	
WK512	DHC1 Chipmunk T10 (G-BXIM) [A]	Privately owned, South Cerney	
WK514	DHC1 Chipmunk T10 (G-BBMO)	Privately owned, Wellesbourne Mountford	
WK517	DHC1 Chipmunk T10 (G-ULAS)	Privately owned, Denham	
WK518	DHC1 Chipmunk T10 [C]	RAF BBMF, Coningsby	
WK522	DHC1 Chipmunk T10 (G-BCOU)	Privately owned, Duxford	
WK549	DHC1 Chipmunk T10 (G-BTWF)	Privately owned, Sturgate	
WK562	DHC1 Chipmunk T10 (F-AZUR) [91]	Privately owned, La Baule, France	
WK570	DHC1 Chipmunk T10 (8211M) <ff>	No 424 Sqn ATC, Solent Sky, Southampton	
WK576	DHC1 Chipmunk T10 (8357M) <ff>	No 1046 Sqn ATC, Fordhouses, Wolverhampton	
WK577	DHC1 Chipmunk T10 (G-BCYM)	Privately owned, Oaksey Park	
WK584	DHC1 Chipmunk T10 (7556M) <ff>	No 511 Sqn ATC, Ramsey, Cambs	
WK585	DHC1 Chipmunk T10 (9265M/G-BZGA)	Privately owned, Duxford	
WK586	DHC1 Chipmunk T10 (G-BXGX) [V]	Privately owned, Slinfold	
WK590	DHC1 Chipmunk T10 (G-BWVZ) [69]	Privately owned, Spanhoe	
WK608	DHC1 Chipmunk T10 [906]	RN Historic Flight, Yeovilton	
WK609	DHC1 Chipmunk T10 (G-BXDN) [93]	Privately owned, Booker	
WK611	DHC1 Chipmunk T10 (G-ARWB)	Privately owned, Thruxton	
WK620	DHC1 Chipmunk T10 [T] (fuselage)	Privately owned, Twyford, Bucks	
WK622	DHC1 Chipmunk T10 (G-BCZH)	Privately owned, Horsford	
WK624	DHC1 Chipmunk T10 (G-BWHI)	Privately owned, Woodvale	
WK626	DHC1 Chipmunk T10 (8213M) <ff>	Aeroventure, stored Doncaster	
WK628	DHC1 Chipmunk T10 (G-BBMW)	Privately owned, Goodwood	
WK630	DHC1 Chipmunk T10 (G-BXDG)	Privately owned, Felthorpe	
WK633	DHC1 Chipmunk T10 (G-BXEC) [A]	Privately owned, Redhill	
WK635	DHC1 Chipmunk T10 (G-HFRH)	Privately owned, Bicester	
WK638	DHC1 Chipmunk T10 (G-BWJZ) (fuselage)	Privately owned, South Marston, Swindon	
WK640	DHC1 Chipmunk T10 (G-BWUV) [C]	Privately owned	
WK640	OGMA/DHC1 Chipmunk T20 (G-CERD)	Privately owned, Spanhoe	
WK642	DHC1 Chipmunk T10 (G-BXDP) [94]	Privately owned, Kilrush, Eire	
WK654	Gloster Meteor F8 (8092M) [B]	City of Norwich Aviation Museum	
WK800	Gloster Meteor D16 [Z]	Boscombe Down Aviation Collection, Old Sarum	
WK864	Gloster Meteor F8 (WL168/7750M) [C]	Yorkshire Air Museum, Elvington	
WK935	Gloster Meteor Prone Pilot (7869M)	RAF Museum, Cosford	
WK991	Gloster Meteor F8 (7825M)	Imperial War Museum, Duxford	
WL131	Gloster Meteor F8 (7751M) <ff>	Aeroventure, Doncaster	
WL181	Gloster Meteor F8 [X]	North-East Aircraft Museum, Usworth	
WL332	Gloster Meteor T7 [888]	Privately owned, Long Marston	
WL345	Gloster Meteor T7	Gloucester Avn Coll, Gloucester	
WL349	Gloster Meteor T7	Gloucestershire Airport, Staverton, on display	
WL375	Gloster Meteor T7(mod)	Dumfries & Galloway Avn Mus, Dumfries	
WL405	Gloster Meteor T7 <ff>	Privately owned, Parbold, Lancs	
WL419	Gloster Meteor T7(mod)	Martin Baker Aircraft, Chalgrove	
WL505	DH100 Vampire FB9 (7705M/G-FBIX)	*Currently not known*	
WL626	Vickers Varsity T1 (G-BHDD) [P]	East Midlands Airport Aeropark	
WL627	Vickers Varsity T1 (8488M) [D] <ff>	Privately owned, Preston, E Yorkshire	
WL679	Vickers Varsity T1 (9155M)	RAF Museum, Cosford	
WL732	BP P108 Sea Balliol T21	RAF Museum, stored Cosford	
WL795	Avro 696 Shackleton MR2C (8753M) [T]	RAF St Mawgan, on display	
WL798	Avro 696 Shackleton MR2C (8114M) <ff>	Privately owned, Elgin	
WM145	AW Meteor NF11 <ff>	Privately owned, Over Dinsdale, N Yorks	
WM167	AW Meteor NF11 (G-LOSM)	Classic Air Force, Coventry	
WM224	AW Meteor TT20 (*WM311*/8177M) [X]	East Midlands Airport Aeropark	
WM267	AW Meteor NF11 <ff>	City of Norwich Aviation Museum	
WM292	AW Meteor TT20 [841]	FAA Museum, stored RNAS Yeovilton	
WM366	AW Meteor NF13 (4X-FNA) (comp VZ462)	Privately owned, Bruntingthorpe	
WM367	AW Meteor NF13 <ff>	East Midlands Airport Aeropark	
WM571	DH112 Sea Venom FAW21 [VL]	Solent Sky, stored Romsey	

Notes	Serial	Type (code/other identity)	Owner/operator location or fate
	WM729	DH113 Vampire NF10 <ff>	Mosquito Aircraft Museum, stored London Colney
	WM913	Hawker Sea Hawk FB5 (8162M) [456/J]	Newark Air Museum, Winthorpe
	WM961	Hawker Sea Hawk FB5 [J]	Caernarfon Air World
	WM969	Hawker Sea Hawk FB5 [10/Z]	Imperial War Museum, Duxford
	WN105	Hawker Sea Hawk FB3 (WF299/8164M)	Privately owned, Birlingham, Worcs
	WN108	Hawker Sea Hawk FB5 [033]	Ulster Aviation Society, Long Kesh
	WN149	BP P108 Balliol T2 [AT]	Boulton Paul Association, Wolverhampton
	WN411	Fairey Gannet AS1 (fuselage)	Privately owned, Sholing, Hants
	WN493	WS51 Dragonfly HR5	FAA Museum, RNAS Yeovilton
	WN499	WS51 Dragonfly HR5	Aeroventure, Doncaster
	WN516	BP P108 Balliol T2 <ff>	Staffs Aircraft Restoration Team, Baxterley
	WN534	BP P108 Balliol T2 <ff>	Staffs Aircraft Restoration Team, Baxterley
	WN890	Hawker Hunter F2 <ff>	Boscombe Down Aviation Collection, Old Sarum
	WN904	Hawker Hunter F2 (7544M)	Sywell Aviation Museum
	WN907	Hawker Hunter F2 (7416M) <ff>	Robertsbridge Aviation Society, Newhaven
	WN957	Hawker Hunter F5 <ff>	Privately owned, Stockport
	WP185	Hawker Hunter F5 (7583M)	Privately owned, Great Dunmow, Essex
	WP190	Hawker Hunter F5 (7582M/8473M/*WP180*) [K]	Tangmere Military Aviation Museum
	WP255	DH113 Vampire NF10 <ff>	Aeroventure, stored Doncaster
	WP269	EoN Eton TX1 (BGA3214)	Privately owned, stored Keevil
	WP270	EoN Eton TX1 (8598M)	RAF Museum Reserve Collection, Stafford
	WP308	Percival P57 Sea Prince T1 (G-GACA) [572/CU]	Gatwick Aviation Museum, Charlwood, Surrey
	WP313	Percival P57 Sea Prince T1 [568/CU]	FAA Museum, stored RNAS Yeovilton
	WP314	Percival P57 Sea Prince T1 (8634M) [573/CU]	Privately owned, Carlisle Airport
	WP321	Percival P57 Sea Prince T1 (G-BRFC) [750/CU]	Privately owned, St Athan
	WP772	DHC1 Chipmunk T10 [Q] (wreck)	RAF Manston History Museum
	WP784	DHC1 Chipmunk T10 <ff>	East Midlands Airport Aeropark
	WP788	DHC1 Chipmunk T10 (G-BCHL)	Privately owned, Sleap
	WP790	DHC1 Chipmunk T10 (G-BBNC) [T]	Mosquito Aircraft Museum, London Colney
	WP795	DHC1 Chipmunk T10 (G-BVZZ) [901]	Privately owned, Lee-on-Solent
	WP800	DHC1 Chipmunk T10 (G-BCXN) [2]	Privately owned, Halton
	WP803	DHC1 Chipmunk T10 (G-HAPY) [G]	Privately owned, Booker
	WP805	DHC1 Chipmunk T10 (G-MAJR) [D]	Privately owned, Lee-on-Solent
	WP808	DHC1 Chipmunk T10 (G-BDEU)	*Damaged beyond repair, 5 January 2012, Prestwick*
	WP809	DHC1 Chipmunk T10 (G-BVTX) [78]	Privately owned, Husbands Bosworth
	WP835	DHC1 Chipmunk T10 (D-ERTY)	Privately owned, Teuge, The Netherlands
	WP840	DHC1 Chipmunk T10 (G-BXDM) [9]	Privately owned, Reims, France
	WP844	DHC1 Chipmunk T10 (G-BWOX) [85]	Privately owned, Shobdon
	WP857	DHC1 Chipmunk T10 (G-BDRJ) [24]	*Repainted in Irish Air Corps markings as 170*
	WP859	DHC1 Chipmunk T10 (G-BXCP) [E]	Privately owned, Fishburn
	WP860	DHC1 Chipmunk T10 (G-BXDA) [6]	Privately owned, Kirknewton
	WP863	DHC1 Chipmunk T10 (8360M/G-ATJI) <ff>	No 1011 Sqn ATC, Boscombe Down
	WP869	DHC1 Chipmunk T10 (8215M) <ff>	Mosquito Aircraft Museum, London Colney
	WP870	DHC1 Chipmunk T10 (G-BCOI) [12]	Privately owned, Rayne Hall Farm, Essex
	WP896	DHC1 Chipmunk T10 (G-BWVY)	Privately owned, RAF Halton
	WP901	DHC1 Chipmunk T10 (G-BWNT) [B]	Privately owned, East Midlands Airport
	WP903	DHC1 Chipmunk T10 (G-BCGC)	Privately owned, Henlow
	WP912	DHC1 Chipmunk T10 (8467M)	RAF Museum, Cosford
	WP921	DHC1 Chipmunk T10 (G-ATJJ) <ff>	Privately owned, Brooklands
	WP925	DHC1 Chipmunk T10 (G-BXHA) [C]	Privately owned, Seppe, The Netherlands
	WP927	DHC1 Chipmunk T10 (8216M/G-ATJK) <ff>	Privately owned, St Neots, Cambs
	WP928	DHC1 Chipmunk T10 (G-BXGM) [D]	Privately owned, Shoreham
	WP929	DHC1 Chipmunk T10 (G-BXCV) [F]	Privately owned, Duxford
	WP930	DHC1 Chipmunk T10 (G-BXHF) [J]	Privately owned, Duxford
	WP962	DHC1 Chipmunk T10 (9287M) [C]	RAF Museum, Hendon
	WP971	DHC1 Chipmunk T10 (G-ATHD)	Privately owned, Denham
	WP977	DHC1 Chipmunk T10 (G-BHRD) <ff>	Privately owned, Yateley, Hants
	WP983	DHC1 Chipmunk T10 (G-BXNN) [B]	Privately owned, Eggesford

Serial	*Type (code/other identity)*	*Owner/operator location or fate*	*Notes*
WP984	DHC1 Chipmunk T10 (G-BWTO) [H]	Privately owned, Little Gransden	
WR360	DH112 Venom FB50 (J-1626/G-DHSS) [K]	Privately owned, Bournemouth (dismantled)	
WR410	DH112 Venom FB50 (J-1539/G-DHUU/*WE410*)	Privately owned, Bournemouth (dismantled)	
WR410	DH112 Venom FB54 (J-1790/G-BLKA) [N]	Mosquito Aircraft Museum, London Colney	
WR421	DH112 Venom FB50 (J-1611/G-DHTT)	Privately owned, Bournemouth (dismantled)	
WR470	DH112 Venom FB50 (J-1542/G-DHVM)	Classic Air Force, Coventry	
WR539	DH112 Venom FB4 (8399M) <ff>	Privately owned, Cantley, Norfolk	
WR960	Avro 696 Shackleton AEW2 (8772M)	Museum of Science & Industry, Manchester	
WR963	Avro 696 Shackleton AEW2 [B-M]	AIRBASE, Coventry	
WR971	Avro 696 Shackleton MR3 (8119M) [Q] (fuselage)	Fenland & W Norfolk Aviation Museum, Wisbech	
WR974	Avro 696 Shackleton MR3 (8117M) [K]	Gatwick Aviation Museum, Charlwood, Surrey	
WR977	Avro 696 Shackleton MR3 (8186M) [B]	Newark Air Museum, Winthorpe	
WR982	Avro 696 Shackleton MR3 (8106M) [J]	Gatwick Aviation Museum, Charlwood, Surrey	
WR985	Avro 696 Shackleton MR3 (8103M) [H]	Privately owned, Long Marston	
WS103	Gloster Meteor T7 [709]	FAA Museum, stored RNAS Yeovilton	
WS692	Gloster Meteor NF12 (7605M) [C]	Newark Air Museum, Winthorpe	
WS726	Gloster Meteor NF14 (7960M) [H]	No 1855 Sqn ATC, Royton, Gr Manchester	
WS739	Gloster Meteor NF14 (7961M)	Newark Air Museum, Winthorpe	
WS760	Gloster Meteor NF14 (7964M)	East Midlands Airport Aeropark	
WS776	Gloster Meteor NF14 (7716M) [K]	Bournemouth Aviation Museum	
WS788	Gloster Meteor NF14 (7967M) [Z]	Yorkshire Air Museum, Elvington	
WS792	Gloster Meteor NF14 (7965M) [K]	Brighouse Bay Caravan Park, Borgue, D&G	
WS807	Gloster Meteor NF14 (7973M) [N]	Jet Age Museum, stored Gloucester	
WS832	Gloster Meteor NF14	Solway Aviation Society, Carlisle	
WS838	Gloster Meteor NF14 [D]	Midland Air Museum, Coventry	
WS843	Gloster Meteor NF14 (7937M) [J]	RAF Museum, Cosford	
WT121	Douglas Skyraider AEW1 [415/CU]	FAA Museum, stored RNAS Yeovilton	
WT205	EE Canberra B15 <ff>	RAF Manston History Museum	
WT308	EE Canberra B(I)6	RN, Predannack Fire School	
WT309	EE Canberra B(I)6 <ff>	Farnborough Air Sciences Trust, Farnborough	
WT319	EE Canberra B(I)6 <ff>	Aeroventure, Doncaster	
WT333	EE Canberra B6(mod) (G-BVXC)	Privately owned, Bruntingthorpe	
WT339	EE Canberra B(I)8 (8198M)	RAF Barkston Heath Fire Section	
WT486	EE Canberra T4 (8102M) <ff>	Privately owned, Newtownards	
WT507	EE Canberra PR7 (8131M/8548M) [44] <ff>	No 384 Sqn ATC, Mansfield	
WT520	EE Canberra PR7 (8094M/8184M) <ff>	No 967 Sqn ATC, Warton	
WT525	EE Canberra T22 [855] <ff>	Privately owned, St Mawgan	
WT532	EE Canberra PR7 (8728M/8890M) <ff>	Bournemouth Aviation Museum	
WT534	EE Canberra PR7 (8549M) [43] <ff>	Privately owned, Upwood	
WT536	EE Canberra PR7 (8063M) <ff>	Privately owned, Shirrell Heath, Hants	
WT555	Hawker Hunter F1 (7499M)	Vanguard Haulage, Greenford, London	
WT569	Hawker Hunter F1 (7491M)	No 2117 Sqn ATC, Kenfig Hill, Mid-Glamorgan	
WT612	Hawker Hunter F1 (7496M)	RAF Henlow, on display	
WT619	Hawker Hunter F1 (7525M)	RAF Museum, stored Cosford	
WT648	Hawker Hunter F1 (7530M) <ff>	Boscombe Down Aviation Collection, Old Sarum	
WT651	Hawker Hunter F1 (7532M) [C]	Newark Air Museum, Winthorpe	
WT660	Hawker Hunter F1 (7421M) [C]	Highland Aviation Museum, Inverness	
WT680	Hawker Hunter F1 (7533M) [J]	Privately owned, Holbeach, Lincs	
WT684	Hawker Hunter F1 (7422M) <ff>	Privately owned, Olney, Bucks	
WT694	Hawker Hunter F1 (7510M)	Caernarfon Air World	
WT711	Hawker Hunter GA11 [833/DD]	Lakes Lightnings, Spark Bridge, Cumbria	
WT720	Hawker Hunter F51 (RDAF E-408/8565M) [B]	Privately owned, North Scarle, Lincs	
WT722	Hawker Hunter T8C (G-BWGN) [878/VL]	Classic Air Force, Newquay	
WT741	Hawker Hunter GA11 [791] <ff>	Privately owned, Doncaster	
WT744	Hawker Hunter GA11 [868/VL]	Privately owned, Ilfracombe	
WT804	Hawker Hunter GA11 [831/DD]	FETC, Moreton-in-Marsh, Glos	

Notes	Serial	Type (code/other identity)	Owner/operator location or fate
	WT806	Hawker Hunter GA11	Privately owned, Bruntingthorpe
	WT859	Supermarine 544 <ff>	Boscombe Down Aviation Collection, Old Sarum
	WT867	Slingsby T31B Cadet TX3	Privately owned, Eaglescott
	WT874	Slingsby T31B Cadet TX3 (BGA1255)	Privately owned, New Milton, Hants
	WT877	Slingsby T31B Cadet TX3	Staffs Aircraft Restoration Team, Baxterley
	WT900	Slingsby T31B Cadet TX3 (BGA3272)	Privately owned, Lee-on-Solent
	WT905	Slingsby T31B Cadet TX3	Privately owned, Keevil
	WT908	Slingsby T31B Cadet TX3 (BGA3487)	Privately owned, Dunstable
	WT910	Slingsby T31B Cadet TX3 (BGA3953)	Privately owned, Llandegla, Denbighshire
	WT914	Slingsby T31B Cadet TX3 (BGA3194) (fuselage)	Privately owned, Tibenham
	WT933	Bristol 171 Sycamore 3 (G-ALSW/7709M)	Newark Air Museum, Winthorpe
	WV106	Douglas Skyraider AEW1 [427/C]	FAA Museum, stored RNAS Yeovilton
	WV198	Sikorsky S55 Whirlwind HAR21 (G-BJWY) [K]	Solway Aviation Society, Carlisle
	WV318	Hawker Hunter T7A (9236M/G-FFOX)	Hunter Flight Academy, RAF Cranwell
	WV322	Hawker Hunter T8C (G-BZSE/9096M) [Y]	Hunter Flying Ltd, North Weald
	WV332	Hawker Hunter F4 (7673M) <ff>	Tangmere Military Aircraft Museum
	WV372	Hawker Hunter T7 (G-BXFI) [R]	Privately owned, North Weald
	WV381	Hawker Hunter GA11 [732] <ff>	Privately owned, Chiltern Park, Wallingford
	WV382	Hawker Hunter GA11 [830/VL]	East Midlands Airport Aeropark
	WV383	Hawker Hunter T7	Farnborough Air Sciences Trust, Farnborough
	WV396	Hawker Hunter T8C (9249M) [91]	RAF Valley, at main gate
	WV486	Percival P56 Provost T1 (7694M) [N-D]	*Scrapped at Thatcham, Berks, 2012*
	WV493	Percival P56 Provost T1 (G-BDYG/7696M) [29]	Royal Scottish Mus'm of Flight, stored E Fortune
	WV499	Percival P56 Provost T1 (G-BZRF/7698M) [P-G]	Privately owned, Westonzoyland, Somerset
	WV514	Percival P56 Provost T51 (G-BLIW) [N-C]	Privately owned, Shoreham
	WV562	Percival P56 Provost T1 (7606M) [P-C]	RAF Museum, Cosford
	WV605	Percival P56 Provost T1 [T-B]	Norfolk & Suffolk Avn Museum, Flixton
	WV606	Percival P56 Provost T1 (7622M)[P-B]	Newark Air Museum, Winthorpe
	WV679	Percival P56 Provost T1 (7615M) [O-J]	Wellesbourne Wartime Museum
	WV705	Percival P66 Pembroke C1 <ff>	Privately owned, Awbridge, Hants
	WV740	Percival P66 Pembroke C1 (G-BNPH)	Privately owned, St Athan
	WV746	Percival P66 Pembroke C1 (8938M)	RAF Museum, Cosford
	WV781	Bristol 171 Sycamore HR12 (G-ALTD/7839M) <ff>	Caernarfon Air World
	WV783	Bristol 171 Sycamore HR12 (G-ALSP/7841M)	RAF Museum, Hendon
	WV787	EE Canberra B2/8 (8799M)	Newark Air Museum, Winthorpe
	WV795	Hawker Sea Hawk FGA6 (8151M)	Privately owned, Dunsfold
	WV797	Hawker Sea Hawk FGA6 (8155M) [491/J]	Midland Air Museum, Coventry
	WV798	Hawker Sea Hawk FGA6 [026/CU]	Classic Air Force, Newquay
	WV838	Hawker Sea Hawk FGA4 [182] <ff>	Norfolk & Suffolk Avn Museum, Flixton
	WV856	Hawker Sea Hawk FGA6 [163]	FAA Museum, RNAS Yeovilton
	WV903	Hawker Sea Hawk FGA4 (8153M) [128] <ff>	*Scrapped, 2013*
	WV903	Hawker Sea Hawk FGA4 (8153M) [C] <rf>	Privately owned, Booker
	WV908	Hawker Sea Hawk FGA6 (8154M) [188/A]	RN Historic Flight, Yeovilton
	WV910	Hawker Sea Hawk FGA6 <ff>	Boscombe Down Aviation Collection, Old Sarum
	WV911	Hawker Sea Hawk FGA4 [115/C]	RN Historic Flight, stored Yeovilton
	WW138	DH112 Sea Venom FAW22 [227/Z]	FAA Museum, stored RNAS Yeovilton
	WW145	DH112 Sea Venom FAW22 [680/LM]	Royal Scottish Mus'm of Flight, E Fortune
	WW217	DH112 Sea Venom FAW22 [351]	Newark Air Museum, Winthorpe
	WW388	Percival P56 Provost T1 (7616M) [O-F]	Privately owned, stored Hinstock, Shrops
	WW421	Percival P56 Provost T1 (WW450/G-BZRE/7689M) [P-B]	Bournemouth Aviation Museum
	WW442	Percival P56 Provost T1 (7618M) [N]	Gatwick Aviation Museum, Charlwood, Surrey
	WW444	Percival P56 Provost T1 [D]	Privately owned, Brownhills, Staffs
	WW447	Percival P56 Provost T1 [F]	Privately owned, Shoreham
	WW453	Percival P56 Provost T1 (G-TMKI) [W-S]	Privately owned, Westonzoyland, Somerset
	WW654	Hawker Hunter GA11 [834/DD]	Privately owned, Ford, W Sussex
	WW664	Hawker Hunter F4 <ff>	Privately owned, Norfolk

Serial	*Type (code/other identity)*	*Owner/operator location or fate*	*Notes*
WX788	DH112 Venom NF3	Privately owned, Storwood, Yorkshire	
WX853	DH112 Venom NF3 (7443M)	Mosquito Aircraft Museum, stored London Colney	
WX905	DH112 Venom NF3 (7458M)	Newark Air Museum, Winthorpe	
WZ425	DH115 Vampire T11	Privately owned, Birlingham, Worcs	
WZ450	DH115 Vampire T11 <ff>	Privately owned, Corscombe, Dorset	
WZ507	DH115 Vampire T11 (G-VTII) [74]	Privately owned, North Weald	
WZ515	DH115 Vampire T11 [60]	Solway Aviation Society, Carlisle	
WZ518	DH115 Vampire T11 [B]	North-East Aircraft Museum, Usworth	
WZ549	DH115 Vampire T11 (8118M) [F]	Ulster Aviation Society, Long Kesh	
WZ553	DH115 Vampire T11 (G-DHYY) <ff>	Privately owned, Stockton, Warks	
WZ557	DH115 Vampire T11	Privately owned, Over Dinsdale, N Yorks	
WZ572	DH115 Vampire T11 (8124M) [65] <ff>	Privately owned, Sholing, Hants	
WZ581	DH115 Vampire T11 <ff>	The Vampire Collection, Hemel Hempstead	
WZ584	DH115 Vampire T11 (G-BZRC) [K]	Privately owned, Cantley, Norfolk	
WZ589	DH115 Vampire T11 [19]	Privately owned, Rochester	
WZ589	DH115 Vampire T55 (U-1230/LN-DHZ)	Privately owned, Norway	
WZ590	DH115 Vampire T11 [49]	Imperial War Museum, Duxford	
WZ662	Auster AOP9 (G-BKVK)	Privately owned, Eggesford	
WZ706	Auster AOP9 (7851M/G-BURR)	Privately owned, Eggesford	
WZ711	Auster AOP9/Beagle E3 (G-AVHT)	Privately owned, Spanhoe	
WZ721	Auster AOP9	Museum of Army Flying, Middle Wallop	
WZ724	Auster AOP9 (7432M)	AAC Middle Wallop, at main gate	
WZ729	Auster AOP9 (G-BXON)	Privately owned, Newark-on-Trent	
WZ736	Avro 707A (7868M)	Museum of Science & Industry, Manchester	
WZ744	Avro 707C (7932M)	RAF Museum, Cosford	
WZ753	Slingsby T38 Grasshopper TX1	Solent Sky, Southampton	
WZ755	Slingsby T38 Grasshopper TX1 (BGA3481)	Boulton Paul Association, Wolverhampton	
WZ757	Slingsby T38 Grasshopper TX1 (comp XK820)	Privately owned, Kirton-in-Lindsey, Lincs	
WZ767	Slingsby T38 Grasshopper TX1	North-East Aircraft Museum, stored Usworth	
WZ772	Slingsby T38 Grasshopper TX1	Trenchard Museum, RAF Halton	
WZ773	Slingsby T38 Grasshopper TX1	Edinburgh Academy	
WZ784	Slingsby T38 Grasshopper TX1	Privately owned, stored Southend	
WZ791	Slingsby T38 Grasshopper TX1 (8944M)	RAF Museum, Hendon	
WZ793	Slingsby T38 Grasshopper TX1	Privately owned, Keevil	
WZ796	Slingsby T38 Grasshopper TX1	Privately owned, stored Aston Down	
WZ798	Slingsby T38 Grasshopper TX1	Privately owned, stored Hullavington	
WZ816	Slingsby T38 Grasshopper TX1 (BGA3979)	Privately owned, Redhill	
WZ818	Slingsby T38 Grasshopper TX1 (BGA4361)	Privately owned, Nympsfield	
WZ819	Slingsby T38 Grasshopper TX1 (BGA3498)	Privately owned, Halton	
WZ820	Slingsby T38 Grasshopper TX1	Sywell Aviation Museum	
WZ822	Slingsby T38 Grasshopper TX1	Aeroventure, stored Doncaster	
WZ824	Slingsby T38 Grasshopper TX1	Solway Aviation Society, Carlisle	
WZ826	Vickers Valiant B(K)1 (XD826/7872M) <ff>	Privately owned, Rayleigh, Essex	
WZ828	Slingsby T38 Grasshopper TX1 (BGA4421)	Privately owned, Hullavington	
WZ831	Slingsby T38 Grasshopper TX1	Privately owned, stored Nympsfield, Glos	
WZ846	DHC1 Chipmunk T10 (G-BCSC/8439M)	No 2427 Sqn ATC, Biggin Hill	
WZ847	DHC1 Chipmunk T10 (G-CPMK) [F]	Privately owned, Sleap	
WZ868	DHC1 Chipmunk T10 (WG322/G-ARMF)	Privately owned, Cotswold Airport	
WZ869	DHC1 Chipmunk T10 (8019M) <ff>	Privately owned, Leicester	
WZ872	DHC1 Chipmunk T10 (G-BZGB) [E]	Privately owned, Blackpool	
WZ876	DHC1 Chipmunk T10 (G-BBWN) <ff>	Privately owned, Yateley, Hants	
WZ879	DHC1 Chipmunk T10 (G-BWUT) [X]	Privately owned, Duxford	
WZ882	DHC1 Chipmunk T10 (G-BXGP) [K]	Privately owned, Eaglescott	
XA109	DH115 Sea Vampire T22	Montrose Air Station Heritage Centre	
XA127	DH115 Sea Vampire T22 <ff>	FAA Museum, RNAS Yeovilton	
XA129	DH115 Sea Vampire T22	FAA Museum, stored RNAS Yeovilton	
XA225	Slingsby T38 Grasshopper TX1	Privately owned, Keevil	

Notes	*Serial*	*Type (code/other identity)*	*Owner/operator location or fate*
	XA226	Slingsby T38 Grasshopper TX1	Norfolk & Suffolk Avn Museum, Flixton
	XA228	Slingsby T38 Grasshopper TX1	Royal Scottish Mus'm of Flight, stored Granton
	XA230	Slingsby T38 Grasshopper TX1 (BGA4098)	Privately owned, Henlow
	XA231	Slingsby T38 Grasshopper TX1 (8888M)	RAF Manston History Museum
	XA240	Slingsby T38 Grasshopper TX1 (BGA4556)	Privately owned, Portmoak, Perth & Kinross
	XA241	Slingsby T38 Grasshopper TX1	Shuttleworth Collection, Old Warden
	XA243	Slingsby T38 Grasshopper TX1 (8886M)	Privately owned, Gransden Lodge, Cambs
	XA244	Slingsby T38 Grasshopper TX1	Privately owned, Keevil
	XA282	Slingsby T31B Cadet TX3	Caernarfon Air World
	XA289	Slingsby T31B Cadet TX3	Privately owned, Eaglescott
	XA290	Slingsby T31B Cadet TX3	Privately owned, Portmoak, Perth & Kinross
	XA293	Slingsby T31B Cadet TX3 <ff>	Privately owned, Breighton
	XA295	Slingsby T31B Cadet TX3 (BGA3336)	Privately owned, Aston Down
	XA302	Slingsby T31B Cadet TX3 (BGA3786)	RAF Museum, Hendon
	XA310	Slingsby T31B Cadet TX3 (BGA4963)	Privately owned, Hullavington
	XA459	Fairey Gannet ECM6 [E]	Privately owned, White Waltham
	XA460	Fairey Gannet ECM6 [768/BY]	Ulster Aviation Society, Long Kesh
	XA466	Fairey Gannet COD4 [777/LM]	FAA Museum, stored RNAS Yeovilton
	XA508	Fairey Gannet T2 [627/GN]	FAA Museum, at Midland Air Museum, Coventry
	XA564	Gloster Javelin FAW1 (7464M)	RAF Museum, Cosford
	XA634	Gloster Javelin FAW4 (7641M)	RAF Leeming, on display
	XA699	Gloster Javelin FAW5 (7809M)	Midland Air Museum, Coventry
	XA847	EE P1B (8371M)	Privately owned, Stowmarket, Suffolk
	XA862	WS55 Whirlwind HAR1 (G-AMJT) <ff>	Yorkshire Helicopter Preservation Group, Elvington
	XA864	WS55 Whirlwind HAR1	FAA Museum, stored RNAS Yeovilton
	XA870	WS55 Whirlwind HAR1 [911]	Aeroventure, Doncaster
	XA880	DH104 Devon C2 (G-BVXR)	Privately owned, Little Rissington
	XA893	Avro 698 Vulcan B1 (8591M) <ff>	RAF Museum, Cosford
	XA903	Avro 698 Vulcan B1 <ff>	Privately owned, Stoneykirk, D&G
	XA917	HP80 Victor B1 (7827M) <ff>	Privately owned, Cupar, Fife
	XB259	Blackburn B101 Beverley C1 (G-AOAI)	Fort Paull Armoury
	XB261	Blackburn B101 Beverley C1 <ff>	Newark Air Museum, Winthorpe
	XB446	Grumman TBM-3 Avenger ECM6B	FAA Museum, Yeovilton
	XB480	Hiller HT1 [537]	FAA Museum, stored RNAS Yeovilton
	XB812	Canadair CL-13 Sabre F4 (9227M) [U]	RAF Museum, Cosford
	XD145	Saro SR53	RAF Museum, Cosford
	XD163	WS55 Whirlwind HAR10 (8645M) [X]	The Helicopter Museum, Weston-super-Mare
	XD165	WS55 Whirlwind HAR10 (8673M)	Caernarfon Airfield Fire Section
	XD215	VS Scimitar F1 <ff>	Privately owned, Cheltenham
	XD235	VS Scimitar F1 <ff>	Privately owned, Olney, Bucks
	XD317	VS Scimitar F1 [112/R]	FAA Museum, RNAS Yeovilton
	XD332	VS Scimitar F1 [194/C]	Solent Sky, stored Romsey
	XD375	DH115 Vampire T11 (7887M)	Privately owned, Elland, W Yorks
	XD377	DH115 Vampire T11 (8203M) <ff>	Aeroventure, stored Doncaster
	XD425	DH115 Vampire T11 <ff>	Privately owned, Newcastle
	XD434	DH115 Vampire T11 [25]	Fenland & W Norfolk Aviation Museum, Wisbech
	XD445	DH115 Vampire T11 [51]	Privately owned, Abbots Bromley
	XD447	DH115 Vampire T11 [50]	East Midlands Airport Aeropark
	XD452	DH115 Vampire T11 (7990M) [66] <ff>	Privately owned, Dursley, Glos
	XD459	DH115 Vampire T11 [63] <ff>	East Midlands Airport Aeropark
	XD506	DH115 Vampire T11 (7983M)	Jet Age Museum, stored Gloucester
	XD515	DH115 Vampire T11 (7998M/*XM515*)	RAF Museum Restoration Centre, Cosford
	XD534	DH115 Vampire T11 [41]	East Midlands Airport Aeropark
	XD542	DH115 Vampire T11 (7604M) [N]	Montrose Air Station Heritage Centre
	XD547	DH115 Vampire T11 [Z] (composite)	Privately owned, Cantley, Norfolk
	XD593	DH115 Vampire T11	Newark Air Museum, Winthorpe
	XD595	DH115 Vampire T11 <ff>	Privately owned, Glentham, Lincs
	XD596	DH115 Vampire T11 (7939M)	Solent Sky, Southampton

Serial	Type (code/other identity)	Owner/operator location or fate	Notes
XD599	DH115 Vampire T11 [A] <ff>	Sywell Aviation Museum	
XD602	DH115 Vampire T11 (7737M) <ff>	*Sold to Germany, November 2011*	
XD616	DH115 Vampire T11 [56]	Mosquito Aircraft Museum, stored Gloucester	
XD622	DH115 Vampire T11 (8160M)	No 2214 Sqn ATC, Usworth	
XD624	DH115 Vampire T11	Privately owned, Hooton Park	
XD626	DH115 Vampire T11 [Q]	Midland Air Museum, stored Coventry	
XD674	Hunting Jet Provost T1 (7570M)	RAF Museum, Cosford	
XD693	Hunting Jet Provost T1 (XM129/G-AOBU) [Z-Q]	Kennet Aviation, North Weald	
XD816	Vickers Valiant B(K)1 <ff>	Brooklands Museum, Weybridge	
XD818	Vickers Valiant B(K)1 (7894M)	RAF Museum, Cosford	
XD857	Vickers Valiant B(K)1 <ff>	Norfolk & Suffolk Aviation Museum, Flixton	
XD875	Vickers Valiant B(K)1 <ff>	Highland Aviation Museum, Inverness	
XE317	Bristol 171 Sycamore HR14 (G-AMWO) [S-N]	Aeroventure, stored Doncaster	
XE339	Hawker Sea Hawk FGA6 (8156M) [149] <ff>	Privately owned, Glos	
XE339	Hawker Sea Hawk FGA6 (8156M) [E] <rf>	Privately owned, Booker	
XE340	Hawker Sea Hawk FGA6 [131/Z]	FAA Museum, stored RNAS Yeovilton	
XE364	Hawker Sea Hawk FGA6 (G-JETH) (comp WM983) [485/J]	Gatwick Aviation Museum, Charlwood, Surrey	
XE368	Hawker Sea Hawk FGA6 [200/J]	Privately owned, Barrow-in-Furness	
XE521	Fairey Rotodyne Y (parts)	The Helicopter Museum, Weston-super-Mare	
XE584	Hawker Hunter FGA9 <ff>	Privately owned, Hooton Park	
XE597	Hawker Hunter FGA9 (8874M) <ff>	Privately owned, Bromsgrove	
XE601	Hawker Hunter FGA9 (G-ETPS)	*Sold to Canada, March 2012*	
XE606	Hawker Hunter F6A (*XJ673*/8841M)	RAF, Barkston Heath	
XE624	Hawker Hunter FGA9 (8875M) [G]	Privately owned, Wickenby	
XE627	Hawker Hunter F6A [T]	Imperial War Museum, Duxford	
XE643	Hawker Hunter FGA9 (8586M) <ff>	RAF M&RU, Aldergrove	
XE650	Hawker Hunter FGA9 (G-9-449) <ff>	Farnborough Air Sciences Trust, Farnborough	
XE664	Hawker Hunter F4 <ff>	Jet Age Museum, stored Gloucester	
XE665	Hawker Hunter T8C (G-BWGM) [876/VL]	Vintage Flyers, Cotswold Airport	
XE668	Hawker Hunter GA11 [832/DD]	Hamburger Hill Paintball, Marksbury, Somerset	
XE670	Hawker Hunter F4 (7762M/8585M) <ff>	RAF Museum, Cosford	
XE683	Hawker Hunter F51 (RDAF E-409) [G]	City of Norwich Aviation Museum	
XE685	Hawker Hunter GA11 (G-GAII) [861/VL]	Hawker Hunter Aviation, Scampton	
XE689	Hawker Hunter GA11 (G-BWGK) <ff>	Privately owned, Cotswold Airport	
XE707	Hawker Hunter GA11 (N707XE) [863]	Bentwaters Cold War Museum	
XE786	Slingsby T31B Cadet TX3 (BGA4033)	Privately owned, Arbroath	
XE793	Slingsby T31B Cadet TX3 (8666M)	Privately owned, Tamworth	
XE799	Slingsby T31B Cadet TX3 (8943M) [R]	Privately owned, Abbots Bromley	
XE802	Slingsby T31B Cadet TX3 (BGA5283)	Privately owned, Shipdham	
XE849	DH115 Vampire T11 (7928M) [V3]	Privately owned, Barton	
XE852	DH115 Vampire T11 [H]	No 2247 Sqn ATC, Hawarden	
XE855	DH115 Vampire T11	Midland Air Museum, stored Coventry	
XE856	DH115 Vampire T11 (G-DUSK) [V]	Bournemouth Aviation Museum	
XE864	DH115 Vampire T11(comp XD435) <ff>	Privately owned, Ingatstone, Essex	
XE872	DH115 Vampire T11 [62]	Midland Air Museum, Coventry	
XE874	DH115 Vampire T11 (8582M)	Paintball Commando, Birkin, W Yorks	
XE897	DH115 Vampire T11 (XD403)	Privately owned, Errol, Tayside	
XE921	DH115 Vampire T11 [64] <ff>	Privately owned, St Mawgan	
XE935	DH115 Vampire T11	Aeroventure, Doncaster	
XE946	DH115 Vampire T11 (7473M) <ff>	RAF Cranwell Aviation Heritage Centre	
XE956	DH115 Vampire T11 (G-OBLN)	De Havilland Aviation, stored Rochester	
XE979	DH115 Vampire T11 [54]	Privately owned, Cantley, Norfolk	
XE982	DH115 Vampire T11 (7564M) [01]	Privately owned, Weston, Eire	
XE985	DH115 Vampire T11 (*WZ476*)	Privately owned, New Inn, Torfaen	
XE993	DH115 Vampire T11 (8161M) <ff>	Privately owned, Staffs	
XE998	DH115 Vampire T11 (*U-1215)*	*Painted in Swiss markings*	
XF113	VS Swift F7 [19] <ff>	Boscombe Down Aviation Collection, Old Sarum	

Notes	*Serial*	*Type (code/other identity)*	*Owner/operator location or fate*
	XF114	VS Swift F7 (G-SWIF)	Solent Sky, stored Romsey
	XF314	Hawker Hunter F51 (RDAF E-412) [N]	Brooklands Museum, Weybridge
	XF321	Hawker Hunter T7 <ff>	Privately owned, Welshpool
	XF321	Hawker Hunter T7 <rf>	Phoenix Aviation, Bruntingthorpe
	XF375	Hawker Hunter F6A (8736M/G-BUEZ) [05]	Boscombe Down Aviation Collection, Old Sarum
	XF382	Hawker Hunter F6A [15]	Midland Air Museum, Coventry
	XF383	Hawker Hunter F6 (8706M) <ff>	Gloster Aviation Club, Gloucester
	XF418	Hawker Hunter F51 (RDAF E-430)	Gatwick Aviation Museum, Charlwood, Surrey
	XF506	Hawker Hunter F4 (WT746/7770M) [A]	Dumfries & Galloway Avn Mus, Dumfries
	XF509	Hawker Hunter F6 (8708M)	Fort Paull Armoury
	XF522	Hawker Hunter F6 <ff>	Herts & Bucks ATC Wing, RAF Halton
	XF526	Hawker Hunter F6 (8679M) [78/E]	Privately owned, Birlingham, Worcs
	XF527	Hawker Hunter F6 (8680M)	RAF Halton, on display
	XF545	Percival P56 Provost T1 (7957M) [O-K]	Privately owned, Bucklebury, Berks
	XF597	Percival P56 Provost T1 (G-BKFW) [AH]	Privately owned, Brimpton, Berks
	XF603	Percival P56 Provost T1 (G-KAPW)	Shuttleworth Collection, Old Warden
	XF690	Percival P56 Provost T1 (8041M/G-MOOS)	Kennet Aviation, Yeovilton
	XF708	Avro 716 Shackleton MR3 [C]	Imperial War Museum, Duxford
	XF785	Bristol 173 (7648M/G-ALBN)	Bristol Aero Collection, stored Filton
	XF836	Percival P56 Provost T1 (8043M/G-AWRY) [JG]	Privately owned, Brimpton, Berks
	XF926	Bristol 188 (8368M)	RAF Museum, Cosford
	XF940	Hawker Hunter F4 <ff>	Privately owned, Kew Stoke, Somerset
	XF994	Hawker Hunter T8C (G-CGHU) [873/VL]	Hawker Hunter Aviation, Scampton
	XF995	Hawker Hunter T8B (G-BZSF/9237M) [K]	Hawker Hunter Aviation, Scampton
	XG154	Hawker Hunter FGA9 (8863M) [54]	RAF Museum, Hendon
	XG160	Hawker Hunter F6A (8831M/G-BWAF) [U]	Bournemouth Aviation Museum
	XG164	Hawker Hunter F6 (8681M)	Privately owned, Wellington, Somerset
	XG168	Hawker Hunter F6A (XG172/8832M) [10]	City of Norwich Aviation Museum
	XG190	Hawker Hunter F51 (RDAF E-425) [C]	Solway Aviation Society, Carlisle
	XG193	Hawker Hunter FGA9 (XG297) (comp with WT741) <ff>	Aeroventure, Doncaster
	XG194	Hawker Hunter FGA9 (8839M)	Wattisham Airfield Museum
	XG194	Hawker Hunter PR11 (WT723/G-PRII) [N]	Hunter Flying Ltd, St Athan
	XG195	Hawker Hunter FGA9 <ff>	Privately owned, Lewes
	XG196	Hawker Hunter F6A (8702M) [31]	Army, Mytchett, Surrey, on display
	XG209	Hawker Hunter F6 (8709M) <ff>	Privately owned, Kingston-on-Thames
	XG210	Hawker Hunter F6	Privately owned, Beck Row, Suffolk
	XG225	Hawker Hunter F6A (8713M)	DSAE Cosford, at main gate
	XG226	Hawker Hunter F6A (8800M) <ff>	RAF Manston History Museum
	XG252	Hawker Hunter FGA9 (8840M) [U]	*To France*
	XG254	Hawker Hunter FGA9 (8881M) [A]	Norfolk & Suffolk Avn Museum, Flixton
	XG274	Hawker Hunter F6 (8710M) [71]	Privately owned, Newmarket
	XG290	Hawker Hunter F6 (8711M) <ff>	Boscombe Down Aviation Collection, Old Sarum
	XG290	Hawker Hunter T7 (comp XL578 & XL586)	Privately owned, Kirkstead, Lincs
	XG297	Hawker Hunter FGA9 <ff>	Aeroventure, Doncaster
	XG325	EE Lightning F1 <ff>	Privately owned, Norfolk
	XG329	EE Lightning F1 (8050M)	Privately owned, Flixton
	XG331	EE Lightning F1 <ff>	Privately owned, Glos
	XG337	EE Lightning F1 (8056M) [M]	RAF Museum, Cosford
	XG452	Bristol 192 Belvedere HC1 (7997M/G-BRMB)	The Helicopter Museum, Weston-super-Mare
	XG454	Bristol 192 Belvedere HC1 (8366M)	Museum of Science & Industry, Manchester
	XG462	Bristol 192 Belvedere HC1 <ff>	The Helicopter Museum, stored Weston-super-Mare
	XG474	Bristol 192 Belvedere HC1 (8367M) [O]	RAF Museum, Hendon
	XG502	Bristol 171 Sycamore HR14	Museum of Army Flying, Middle Wallop
	XG518	Bristol 171 Sycamore HR14 (8009M) [S-E]	Norfolk & Suffolk Avn Museum, Flixton
	XG523	Bristol 171 Sycamore HR14 <ff> [V]	Norfolk & Suffolk Avn Museum, Flixton
	XG574	WS55 Whirlwind HAR3 [752/PO]	FAA Museum, stored RNAS Yeovilton
	XG588	WS55 Whirlwind HAR3 (G-BAMH/VR-BEP)	East Midlands Airport Aeropark
	XG592	WS55 Whirlwind HAS7 [54]	*Task Force* Adventure Park, Cowbridge, S Glam

Serial	*Type (code/other identity)*	*Owner/operator location or fate*	*Notes*
XG594	WS55 Whirlwind HAS7 [517]	FAA Museum, stored Yeovilton	
XG596	WS55 Whirlwind HAS7 [66]	The Helicopter Museum, Weston-super-Mare	
XG613	DH112 Sea Venom FAW21	*Sold to Poland, January 2013*	
XG629	DH112 Sea Venom FAW22	Privately owned, Stone, Staffs	
XG680	DH112 Sea Venom FAW22 [438]	North-East Aircraft Museum, Usworth	
XG692	DH112 Sea Venom FAW22 [668/LM]	Privately owned, Stockport	
XG730	DH112 Sea Venom FAW22 [499/A]	Mosquito Aircraft Museum, London Colney	
XG736	DH112 Sea Venom FAW22	Privately owned, East Midlands	
XG737	DH112 Sea Venom FAW22 [220/Z]	East Midlands Airport Aeropark	
XG743	DH115 Sea Vampire T22 [597/LM]	Privately owned, Ripon	
XG797	Fairey Gannet ECM6 [277]	Imperial War Museum, Duxford	
XG831	Fairey Gannet ECM6 [396]	Davidstow Airfield & Cornwall At War Museum	
XG882	Fairey Gannet T5 (8754M) [771/LM]	Privately owned, Errol, Tayside	
XG883	Fairey Gannet T5 [773/BY]	FAA Museum, at Museum of Berkshire Aviation, Woodley	
XG900	Short SC1	Science Museum, South Kensington	
XG905	Short SC1	Ulster Folk & Transport Mus, Holywood, Co Down	
XH131	EE Canberra PR9	Ulster Aviation Society, Long Kesh	
XH134	EE Canberra PR9 (G-OMHD)	Privately owned, Cotswold Airport	
XH135	EE Canberra PR9	Privately owned, Cotswold Airport	
XH136	EE Canberra PR9 (8782M) [W] <ff>	Privately owned, Ashford, Kent	
XH165	EE Canberra PR9 <ff>	Blyth Valley Aviation Collection, Walpole	
XH168	EE Canberra PR9	RAF Marham Fire Section	
XH169	EE Canberra PR9	RAF Marham, on display	
XH170	EE Canberra PR9 (8739M)	RAF Wyton, on display	
XH171	EE Canberra PR9 (8746M) [U]	RAF Museum, Cosford	
XH174	EE Canberra PR9 <ff>	Privately owned, Leicester	
XH175	EE Canberra PR9 <ff>	Privately owned, Bewdley, Worcs	
XH177	EE Canberra PR9 <ff>	Newark Air Museum, Winthorpe	
XH278	DH115 Vampire T11 (8595M/7866M) [42]	Yorkshire Air Museum, Elvington	
XH313	DH115 Vampire T11 (G-BZRD) [E]	Tangmere Military Aviation Museum	
XH318	DH115 Vampire T11 (7761M) [64]	Privately owned, Sholing, Hants	
XH328	DH115 Vampire T11 <ff>	Privately owned, Cantley, Norfolk	
XH330	DH115 Vampire T11 [73]	Privately owned, Camberley, Surrey	
XH537	Avro 698 Vulcan B2MRR (8749M) <ff>	Privately owned, Bournemouth	
XH558	Avro 698 Vulcan B2 (G-VLCN)	Vulcan To The Sky Trust, Doncaster Sheffield Airport	
XH560	Avro 698 Vulcan K2 <ff>	Privately owned, Foulness	
XH563	Avro 698 Vulcan B2MRR <ff>	Privately owned, Over Dinsdale, N Yorks	
XH584	EE Canberra T4 (G-27-374) <ff>	Aeroventure, Doncaster	
XH592	HP80 Victor B1A (8429M) <ff>	Phoenix Aviation, Bruntingthorpe	
XH648	HP80 Victor K1A	Imperial War Museum, Duxford	
XH669	HP80 Victor K2 (9092M) <ff>	Privately owned, Foulness	
XH670	HP80 Victor SR2 <ff>	Privately owned, Foulness	
XH672	HP80 Victor K2 (9242M)	RAF Museum, Cosford	
XH673	HP80 Victor K2 (8911M)	RAF Marham, on display	
XH767	Gloster Javelin FAW9 (7955M) [L]	Yorkshire Air Museum, Elvington	
XH783	Gloster Javelin FAW7 (7798M) <ff>	Privately owned, Catford	
XH837	Gloster Javelin FAW7 (8032M) <ff>	Caernarfon Air World	
XH892	Gloster Javelin FAW9R (7982M) [J]	Norfolk & Suffolk Avn Museum, Flixton	
XH897	Gloster Javelin FAW9	Imperial War Museum, Duxford	
XH903	Gloster Javelin FAW9 (7938M)	Gloucester Airport, on display	
XH992	Gloster Javelin FAW8 (7829M) [P]	Newark Air Museum, Winthorpe	
XJ314	RR Thrust Measuring Rig	Science Museum, South Kensington	
XJ380	Bristol 171 Sycamore HR14 (8628M)	Boscombe Down Aviation Collection, Old Sarum	
XJ389	Fairey Jet Gyrodyne (XD759/G-AJJP)	Museum of Berkshire Aviation, Woodley	
XJ398	WS55 Whirlwind HAR10 (XD768/G-BDBZ)	Aeroventure, Doncaster	
XJ435	WS55 Whirlwind HAR10 (XD804/8671M) [V]	RAF Manston History Museum, spares use	
XJ476	DH110 Sea Vixen FAW1 <ff>	Boscombe Down Aviation Collection, Old Sarum	

Notes	Serial	Type (code/other identity)	Owner/operator location or fate
	XJ481	DH110 Sea Vixen FAW1 [VL]	FAA Museum, stored RNAS Yeovilton
	XJ482	DH110 Sea Vixen FAW1 [713/VL]	Norfolk & Suffolk Avn Museum, Flixton
	XJ488	DH110 Sea Vixen FAW1 <ff>	Robertsbridge Aviation Society, Mayfield
	XJ494	DH110 Sea Vixen FAW2 [121/E]	Privately owned, Bruntingthorpe
	XJ560	DH110 Sea Vixen FAW2 (8142M) [243/H]	Newark Air Museum, Winthorpe
	XJ565	DH110 Sea Vixen FAW2 [127/E]	Mosquito Aircraft Museum, London Colney
	XJ571	DH110 Sea Vixen FAW2 (8140M) [242/R]	Solent Sky, Southampton
	XJ575	DH110 Sea Vixen FAW2 <ff> [SAH-13]	Wellesbourne Wartime Museum
	XJ579	DH110 Sea Vixen FAW2 <ff>	Midland Air Museum, Coventry
	XJ580	DH110 Sea Vixen FAW2 [131/E]	Tangmere Military Aviation Museum
	XJ714	Hawker Hunter FR10 (comp XG226)	East Midlands Airport Aeropark
	XJ723	WS55 Whirlwind HAR10	Privately owned, Newcastle upon Tyne
	XJ726	WS55 Whirlwind HAR10	Caernarfon Air World
	XJ727	WS55 Whirlwind HAR10 (8661M) [L]	Privately owned, Ramsgate
	XJ758	WS55 Whirlwind HAR10 (8464M) <ff>	Privately owned, Welshpool
	XJ771	DH115 Vampire T55 (U-1215/G-HELV)	Classic Air Force, Coventry
	XJ772	DH115 Vampire T11 [H]	Mosquito Aircraft Museum, London Colney
	XJ823	Avro 698 Vulcan B2A	Solway Aviation Society, Carlisle
	XJ824	Avro 698 Vulcan B2A	Imperial War Museum, Duxford
	XJ917	Bristol 171 Sycamore HR14 [H-S]	Bristol Sycamore Group, stored Filton
	XJ918	Bristol 171 Sycamore HR14 (8190M)	RAF Museum, Cosford
	XK416	Auster AOP9 (7855M/G-AYUA)	Privately owned, Widmerpool
	XK417	Auster AOP9 (G-AVXY)	Privately owned, Messingham, Lincs
	XK418	Auster AOP9 (7976M)	93rd Bomb Group Museum, Hardwick, Norfolk
	XK421	Auster AOP9 (8365M) (frame)	Privately owned, South Molton, Devon
	XK488	Blackburn NA39 Buccaneer S1	FAA Museum, stored RNAS Yeovilton
	XK526	Blackburn NA39 Buccaneer S2 (8648M)	RAF Honington, at main gate
	XK527	Blackburn NA39 Buccaneer S2D (8818M) <ff>	Privately owned, North Wales
	XK532	Blackburn NA39 Buccaneer S1 (8867M) [632/LM]	Highland Aviation Museum, Inverness
	XK533	Blackburn NA39 Buccaneer S1 <ff>	Royal Scottish Mus'm of Flight, stored Granton
	XK590	DH115 Vampire T11 [V]	Wellesbourne Wartime Museum
	XK623	DH115 Vampire T11 (*G-VAMP*) [56]	Caernarfon Air World
	XK624	DH115 Vampire T11 [32]	Norfolk & Suffolk Avn Museum, Flixton
	XK625	DH115 Vampire T11 [14]	Brenzett Aeronautical Museum
	XK627	DH115 Vampire T11 <ff>	Davidstow Airfield & Cornwall At War Museum
	XK632	DH115 Vampire T11 <ff>	Privately owned, Greenford, London
	XK637	DH115 Vampire T11 [56]	Privately owned, Gr Manchester
	XK695	DH106 Comet C2(RC) (G-AMXH/9164M) <ff>	Mosquito Aircraft Museum, London Colney
	XK699	DH106 Comet C2 (7971M) [699]	RAF Lyneham on display
	XK724	Folland Gnat F1 (7715M)	RAF Museum, Cosford
	XK740	Folland Gnat F1 (8396M)	Solent Sky, Southampton
	XK776	ML Utility 1	Museum of Army Flying, Middle Wallop
	XK789	Slingsby T38 Grasshopper TX1	Midland Air Museum, stored Coventry
	XK790	Slingsby T38 Grasshopper TX1	Privately owned, stored Husbands Bosworth
	XK819	Slingsby T38 Grasshopper TX1	Privately owned, Breighton
	XK822	Slingsby T38 Grasshopper TX1	Privately owned, Partridge Green, W Sussex
	XK885	Percival P66 Pembroke C1 (8452M/N46EA)	Gatwick Aviation Museum, Charlwood, Surrey
	XK895	DH104 Sea Devon C20 (G-SDEV) [19/CU]	Classic Air Force, Coventry
	XK907	WS55 Whirlwind HAS7	Midland Air Museum, stored Coventry
	XK911	WS55 Whirlwind HAS7 [519/PO]	Privately owned, stored Dagenham
	XK936	WS55 Whirlwind HAS7 [62]	Imperial War Museum, Duxford
	XK940	WS55 Whirlwind HAS7 (G-AYXT) [911]	The Helicopter Museum, Weston-super-Mare
	XK970	WS55 Whirlwind HAR10 (8789M)	Army, Bramley, Hants
	XL149	Blackburn B101 Beverley C1 (7988M) <ff>	Aeroventure, Doncaster
	XL160	HP80 Victor K2 (8910M) <ff>	Norfolk & Suffolk Avn Museum, Flixton
	XL164	HP80 Victor K2 (9215M) <ff>	Gatwick Aviation Museum, Charlwood, Surrey
	XL190	HP80 Victor K2 (9216M) <ff>	RAF Manston History Museum

Serial	Type (code/other identity)	Owner/operator location or fate	Notes
XL231	HP80 Victor K2	Yorkshire Air Museum, Elvington	
XL318	Avro 698 Vulcan B2 (8733M)	RAF Museum, Hendon	
XL319	Avro 698 Vulcan B2	North-East Aircraft Museum, Usworth	
XL360	Avro 698 Vulcan B2A	Midland Air Museum, Coventry	
XL388	Avro 698 Vulcan B2 <ff>	Aeroventure, Doncaster	
XL426	Avro 698 Vulcan B2 (G-VJET)	Vulcan Restoration Trust, Southend	
XL445	Avro 698 Vulcan K2 (8811M) <ff>	Norfolk & Suffolk Avn Museum, Flixton	
XL449	Fairey Gannet AEW3 <ff>	Privately owned, Camberley, Surrey	
XL472	Fairey Gannet AEW3 [044/R]	Gatwick Aviation Museum, Charlwood, Surrey	
XL497	Fairey Gannet AEW3 [041/R]	Dumfries & Galloway Avn Mus, Dumfries	
XL500	Fairey Gannet AEW3 (G-KAEW) [CU]	Hunter Flying Ltd, St Athan	
XL502	Fairey Gannet AEW3 (8610M/G-BMYP)	Yorkshire Air Museum, Elvington	
XL503	Fairey Gannet AEW3 [070/E]	FAA Museum, RNAS Yeovilton	
XL563	Hawker Hunter T7 (9218M)	Privately owned, Southmoor, Oxon	
XL564	Hawker Hunter T7 <ff>	Privately owned, Tilehurst, Berks	
XL565	Hawker Hunter T7 (parts of WT745) [Y]	Privately owned, Bruntingthorpe	
XL568	Hawker Hunter T7A (9224M) [X]	RAF Museum, Cosford	
XL569	Hawker Hunter T7 (8833M)	East Midlands Airport Aeropark	
XL571	Hawker Hunter T7 (XL572/8834M/G-HNTR) [V]	Yorkshire Air Museum, Elvington	
XL573	Hawker Hunter T7 (G-BVGH)	Hunter Flying Ltd, St Athan	
XL577	Hawker Hunter T7 (G-BXKF/8676M) [V]	Privately owned, Cotswold Airport	
XL580	Hawker Hunter T8M [723]	FAA Museum, RNAS Yeovilton	
XL586	Hawker Hunter T7 (comp XL578)	Action Park, Wickford, Essex	
XL587	Hawker Hunter T7 (8807M/G-HPUX) [Z]	Hawker Hunter Aviation, stored Scampton	
XL591	Hawker Hunter T7	Gatwick Aviation Museum, Charlwood, Surrey	
XL592	Hawker Hunter T7 (8836M) [Y]	Privately owned, Booker	
XL601	Hawker Hunter T7 (G-BZSR) [874/VL]	Classic Fighters, Brustem, Belgium	
XL602	Hawker Hunter T8M (G-BWFT)	Hunter Flying Ltd, St Athan	
XL609	Hawker Hunter T7 <ff>	Lakes Lightnings, Spark Bridge, Cumbria	
XL612	Hawker Hunter T7 [2]	Privately owned, Swansea	
XL618	Hawker Hunter T7 (8892M)	Caernarfon Air World	
XL621	Hawker Hunter T7 (G-BNCX)	Privately owned, Dunsfold	
XL623	Hawker Hunter T7 (8770M)	The Planets Leisure Centre, Woking	
XL629	EE Lightning T4	MoD/QinetiQ Boscombe Down, at main gate	
XL703	SAL Pioneer CC1 (8034M) [Z]	RAF Museum, Cosford	
XL714	DH82A Tiger Moth II (T6099/G-AOGR)	Privately owned, Boughton, Lincs	
XL738	Saro Skeeter AOP12 (7860M)	Privately owned, Storwood, Yorkshire	
XL739	Saro Skeeter AOP12	AAC, stored Wattisham	
XL762	Saro Skeeter AOP12 (8017M)	Royal Scottish Mus'm of Flight, E Fortune	
XL763	Saro Skeeter AOP12	Privately owned, Storwood, Yorkshire	
XL764	Saro Skeeter AOP12 (7940M) [J]	Newark Air Museum, Winthorpe	
XL765	Saro Skeeter AOP12	Privately owned, Melksham, Wilts	
XL767	Saro Skeeter AOP12 <ff>	The Helicopter Museum, Weston-super-Mare	
XL770	Saro Skeeter AOP12 (8046M)	Solent Sky, Southampton	
XL809	Saro Skeeter AOP12 (G-BLIX)	Privately owned, Wilden, Beds	
XL811	Saro Skeeter AOP12	The Helicopter Museum, Weston-super-Mare	
XL812	Saro Skeeter AOP12 (G-SARO)	AAC Historic Aircraft Flight, stored Middle Wallop	
XL813	Saro Skeeter AOP12	Museum of Army Flying, Middle Wallop	
XL814	Saro Skeeter AOP12	AAC Historic Aircraft Flight, Middle Wallop	
XL824	Bristol 171 Sycamore HR14 (8021M)	RAF Museum Reserve Collection, Stafford	
XL829	Bristol 171 Sycamore HR14	The Helicopter Museum, Weston-super-Mare	
XL840	WS55 Whirlwind HAS7	Privately owned, Bawtry	
XL853	WS55 Whirlwind HAS7 [PO]	FAA Museum, stored RNAS Yeovilton	
XL875	WS55 Whirlwind HAR9	Perth Technical College	
XL929	Percival P66 Pembroke C1 (G-BNPU)	Classic Air Force, stored Compton Verney	
XL954	Percival P66 Pembroke C1 (9042M/N4234C/G-BXES)	Classic Air Force, Coventry	
XL993	SAL Twin Pioneer CC1 (8388M)	RAF Museum, Cosford	
XM135	BAC Lightning F1 [B]	Imperial War Museum, Duxford	

Notes	*Serial*	*Type (code/other identity)*	*Owner/operator location or fate*
	XM144	BAC Lightning F1 (8417M) <ff>	Lakes Lightnings, Spark Bridge, Cumbria
	XM169	BAC Lightning F1A (8422M) <ff>	Highland Aviation Museum, Inverness
	XM172	BAC Lightning F1A (8427M)	Lakes Lightnings, Spark Bridge, Cumbria
	XM173	BAC Lightning F1A (8414M) [A]	Privately owned, Dodington, Glos
	XM191	BAC Lightning F1A (7854M/8590M) <ff>	Privately owned, North Scarle
	XM192	BAC Lightning F1A (8413M) [K]	Thorpe Camp Preservation Group, Lincs
	XM223	DH104 Devon C2 (G-BWWC) [J]	Classic Air Force, stored Compton Verney
	XM279	EE Canberra B(I)8 <ff>	Privately owned, Flixton
	XM300	WS58 Wessex HAS1	Privately owned, Nantgarw, Rhondda
	XM328	WS58 Wessex HAS3 [653/PO]	The Helicopter Museum, Weston-super-Mare
	XM330	WS58 Wessex HAS1	The Helicopter Museum, Weston-super-Mare
	XM350	Hunting Jet Provost T3A (9036M) [89]	Aeroventure, Doncaster
	XM351	Hunting Jet Provost T3 (8078M) [Y]	RAF Museum, Cosford
	XM355	Hunting Jet Provost T3 (8229M)	Newcastle Aviation Academy
	XM358	Hunting Jet Provost T3A (8987M) [53]	Privately owned, Newbridge, Powys
	XM362	Hunting Jet Provost T3 (8230M)	DSAE, No 1 SoTT, Cosford
	XM365	Hunting Jet Provost T3A (G-BXBH) [37]	Privately owned, Bruntingthorpe
	XM369	Hunting Jet Provost T3 (8084M) [C]	*Sold to The Netherlands*
	XM373	Hunting Jet Provost T3 (7726M) [2] <ff>	Yorkshire Air Museum, Elvington
	XM383	Hunting Jet Provost T3A [90]	Newark Air Museum, Winthorpe
	XM402	Hunting Jet Provost T3 (8055AM) [18]	Fenland & W Norfolk Aviation Museum, Wisbech
	XM404	Hunting Jet Provost T3 (8055BM)	FETC, Moreton-in-Marsh, Glos
	XM409	Hunting Jet Provost T3 (8082M) <ff>	Air Scouts, Guernsey Airport
	XM410	Hunting Jet Provost T3 (8054AM) [B]	Privately owned, Gillingham, Kent
	XM411	Hunting Jet Provost T3 (8434M) <ff>	Aeroventure, Doncaster
	XM412	Hunting Jet Provost T3A (9011M) [41]	Privately owned, Balado Bridge, Scotland
	XM414	Hunting Jet Provost T3A (8996M)	Ulster Aviation Society, Long Kesh
	XM417	Hunting Jet Provost T3 (8054BM) [D] <ff>	Privately owned, Cannock
	XM419	Hunting Jet Provost T3A (8990M) [102]	Newcastle Aviation Academy
	XM425	Hunting Jet Provost T3A (8995M) [88]	Privately owned, Longton, Staffs
	XM463	Hunting Jet Provost T3A [38] (fuselage)	RAF Museum, Hendon
	XM468	Hunting Jet Provost T3 (8081M) <ff>	Privately owned, Terrington St Clement, Norfolk
	XM473	Hunting Jet Provost T3A (8974M/*G-TINY*)	Privately owned, Wethersfield
	XM474	Hunting Jet Provost T3 (8121M) <ff>	No 2517 Sqn ATC, Levenshulme
	XM479	Hunting Jet Provost T3A (G-BVEZ)	Privately owned, Newcastle
	XM480	Hunting Jet Provost T3 (8080M)	4x4 Car Centre, Chesterfield
	XM496	Bristol 253 Britannia C1 (EL-WXA) [496]	Britannia Preservation Society, Cotswold Airport
	XM497	Bristol 175 Britannia 312F (G-AOVF) [497]	RAF Museum, Cosford
	XM529	Saro Skeeter AOP12 (7979M/G-BDNS)	Privately owned, Handforth
	XM553	Saro Skeeter AOP12 (G-AWSV)	Yorkshire Air Museum, Elvington
	XM555	Saro Skeeter AOP12 (8027M)	RAF Museum Reserve Collection, Stafford
	XM557	Saro Skeeter AOP12 <ff>	The Helicopter Museum, Weston-super-Mare
	XM569	Avro 698 Vulcan B2 <ff>	Jet Age Museum, stored Gloucester
	XM575	Avro 698 Vulcan B2A (G-BLMC)	East Midlands Airport Aeropark
	XM594	Avro 698 Vulcan B2	Newark Air Museum, Winthorpe
	XM597	Avro 698 Vulcan B2	Royal Scottish Mus'm of Flight, E Fortune
	XM598	Avro 698 Vulcan B2 (8778M)	RAF Museum, Cosford
	XM602	Avro 698 Vulcan B2 (8771M) <ff>	Manchester Museum of Science & Industry, stored
	XM603	Avro 698 Vulcan B2	Avro Aircraft Heritage Society, Woodford
	XM607	Avro 698 Vulcan B2 (8779M)	RAF Waddington, on display
	XM612	Avro 698 Vulcan B2	City of Norwich Aviation Museum
	XM651	Saro Skeeter AOP12 (XM561/7980M)	Aeroventure, Doncaster
	XM652	Avro 698 Vulcan B2 <ff>	Privately owned, Welshpool
	XM655	Avro 698 Vulcan B2 (G-VULC)	Privately owned, Wellesbourne Mountford
	XM685	WS55 Whirlwind HAS7 (G-AYZJ) [513/PO]	Newark Air Museum, Winthorpe
	XM692	HS Gnat T1 <ff>	Privately owned, Welshpool
	XM693	HS Gnat T1 (7891M)	BAE Systems Hamble, on display
	XM697	HS Gnat T1 (G-NAAT)	Reynard Garden Centre, Carluke, S Lanarkshire
	XM708	HS Gnat T1 (8573M)	Privately owned, Lytham St Annes
	XM715	HP80 Victor K2	Cold War Jets Collection, Bruntingthorpe

Serial	Type (code/other identity)	Owner/operator location or fate	Notes
XM717	HP80 Victor K2 <ff>	RAF Museum, Hendon	
XM819	Lancashire EP9 Prospector (G-APXW)	Museum of Army Flying, Middle Wallop	
XM833	WS58 Wessex HAS3	North-East Aircraft Museum, Usworth	
XN126	WS55 Whirlwind HAR10 (8655M) [S]	Pinewood Studios, Elstree	
XN137	Hunting Jet Provost T3 <ff>	Privately owned, Little Addington, Notts	
XN156	Slingsby T21B Sedbergh TX1 (BGA3250)	Privately owned, Portmoak	
XN157	Slingsby T21B Sedbergh TX1 (BGA3255)	Privately owned, stored Long Mynd	
XN185	Slingsby T21B Sedbergh TX1 (8942M/BGA4077)	RAF Museum Reserve Collection, Stafford	
XN186	Slingsby T21B Sedbergh TX1 (BGA3905) [HFG]	Privately owned, Watton	
XN187	Slingsby T21B Sedbergh TX1 (BGA3903)	Privately owned, Halton	
XN198	Slingsby T31B Cadet TX3	Privately owned, Bodmin	
XN238	Slingsby T31B Cadet TX3 <ff>	Aeroventure, Doncaster	
XN239	Slingsby T31B Cadet TX3 (8889M) [G]	Imperial War Museum, Duxford	
XN246	Slingsby T31B Cadet TX3	Solent Sky, Southampton	
XN258	WS55 Whirlwind HAR9 [589/CU]	North-East Aircraft Museum, Usworth	
XN297	WS55 Whirlwind HAR9 (XN311) [12]	Privately owned, Hull	
XN298	WS55 Whirlwind HAR9 [810/LS]	Privately owned	
XN299	WS55 Whirlwind HAS7 [758]	Tangmere Military Aviation Museum	
XN304	WS55 Whirlwind HAS7 [WW/B]	Norfolk & Suffolk Avn Museum, Flixton	
XN332	Saro P531 (G-APNV) [759]	FAA Museum, stored RNAS Yeovilton	
XN334	Saro P531	FAA Museum, stored RNAS Yeovilton	
XN341	Saro Skeeter AOP12 (8022M)	Stondon Transport Mus & Garden Centre, Beds	
XN344	Saro Skeeter AOP12 (8018M)	Science Museum, South Kensington	
XN345	Saro Skeeter AOP12 <ff>	The Helicopter Museum, Weston-super-Mare	
XN351	Saro Skeeter AOP12 (G-BKSC)	Privately owned, Ipswich	
XN380	WS55 Whirlwind HAS7	RAF Manston History Museum	
XN385	WS55 Whirlwind HAS7	Battleground Paintball, Yarm, Cleveland	
XN386	WS55 Whirlwind HAR9 [435/ED]	Aeroventure, Doncaster	
XN412	Auster AOP9	Auster 9 Group, Melton Mowbray	
XN437	Auster AOP9 (G-AXWA)	Privately owned, North Weald	
XN441	Auster AOP9 (G-BGKT)	Privately owned, Exeter	
XN458	Hunting Jet Provost T3 (8234M/*XN594*)	Privately owned, Northallerton	
XN459	Hunting Jet Provost T3A (G-BWOT)	Transair(UK) Ltd, North Weald	
XN462	Hunting Jet Provost T3A [17]	FAA Museum, stored RNAS Yeovilton	
XN466	Hunting Jet Provost T3A [29] <ff>	No 1005 Sqn ATC, Radcliffe, Gr Manchester	
XN492	Hunting Jet Provost T3 (8079M) <ff>	No 2434 Sqn ATC, Linton-on-Ouse	
XN493	Hunting Jet Provost T3 (XN137) <ff>	Privately owned, Camberley	
XN494	Hunting Jet Provost T3A (9012M) [43]	Gatwick Aviation Museum, Charlwood, Surrey	
XN500	Hunting Jet Provost T3A	Norfolk & Suffolk Avn Museum, Flixton	
XN503	Hunting Jet Provost T3 <ff>	Boscombe Down Aviation Collection, Old Sarum	
XN508	Hunting Jet Provost T3A <ff>	MoD/DSG, St Athan	
XN511	Hunting Jet Provost T3 [64] <ff>	Aeroventure, Doncaster	
XN549	Hunting Jet Provost T3 (8235M) <ff>	Privately owned, Warrington	
XN551	Hunting Jet Provost T3A (8984M)	Privately owned, Felton Common, Bristol	
XN554	Hunting Jet Provost T3 (8436M) [K]	Gunsmoke Paintball, Hadleigh, Suffolk	
XN573	Hunting Jet Provost T3 [E] <ff>	Newark Air Museum, Winthorpe	
XN579	Hunting Jet Provost T3A (9137M) [14]	Gunsmoke Paintball, Hadleigh, Suffolk	
XN582	Hunting Jet Provost T3A (8957M) [95,H]	Privately owned, Bruntingthorpe	
XN584	Hunting Jet Provost T3A (9014M) [E]	Phoenix Aviation, Bruntingthorpe	
XN586	Hunting Jet Provost T3A (9039M) [91,S]	Brooklands Technical College	
XN589	Hunting Jet Provost T3A (9143M) [46]	RAF Linton-on-Ouse, on display	
XN597	Hunting Jet Provost T3 (7984M) <ff>	Privately owned, Market Drayton, Shrops	
XN607	Hunting Jet Provost T3 <ff>	Highland Aviation Museum, Inverness	
XN623	Hunting Jet Provost T3 (XN632/8352M)	Privately owned, Birlingham, Worcs	
XN629	Hunting Jet Provost T3A (G-BVEG/G-KNOT) [49]	Bentwaters Cold War Museum	
XN634	Hunting Jet Provost T3A <ff>	Privately owned, Blackpool	
XN634	Hunting Jet Provost T3A [53] <rf>	BAE Systems Warton Fire Section	

Notes	*Serial*	*Type (code/other identity)*	*Owner/operator location or fate*
	XN637	Hunting Jet Provost T3 (G-BKOU) [03]	Privately owned, North Weald
	XN647	DH110 Sea Vixen FAW2 <ff>	Privately owned, Steventon, Oxon
	XN650	DH110 Sea Vixen FAW2 [456] <ff>	Privately owned, Norfolk
	XN651	DH110 Sea Vixen FAW2 <ff>	Privately owned, Olney, Bucks
	XN685	DH110 Sea Vixen FAW2 (8173M) [703/VL]	Midland Air Museum, Coventry
	XN696	DH110 Sea Vixen FAW2 [751] <ff>	North-East Aircraft Museum, Usworth
	XN714	Hunting H126	RAF Museum, Cosford
	XN726	EE Lightning F2A (8545M) <ff>	Boscombe Down Aviation Collection, Old Sarum
	XN728	EE Lightning F2A (8546M) <ff>	Privately owned, Lincoln
	XN774	EE Lightning F2A (8551M) <ff>	Privately owned, Boston
	XN776	EE Lightning F2A (8535M) [C]	Royal Scottish Mus'm of Flight, E Fortune
	XN795	EE Lightning F2A <ff>	Privately owned, Rayleigh, Essex
	XN819	AW660 Argosy C1 (8205M) <ff>	Newark Air Museum, Winthorpe
	XN923	HS Buccaneer S1 [13]	Gatwick Aviation Museum, Charlwood, Surrey
	XN928	HS Buccaneer S1 (8179M) <ff>	Privately owned, Gravesend
	XN957	HS Buccaneer S1 [630/LM]	FAA Museum, RNAS Yeovilton
	XN964	HS Buccaneer S1 [118/V]	Newark Air Museum, Winthorpe
	XN967	HS Buccaneer S1 [233] <ff>	City of Norwich Aviation Museum
	XN972	HS Buccaneer S1 (8183M/XN962) <ff>	RAF Museum, Cosford
	XN974	HS Buccaneer S2A	Yorkshire Air Museum, Elvington
	XN979	HS Buccaneer S2 <ff>	Aeroventure, Doncaster
	XN981	HS Buccaneer S2B (fuselage)	Privately owned, Errol
	XN983	HS Buccaneer S2B <ff>	Fenland & W Norfolk Aviation Museum, Wisbech
	XP110	WS58 Wessex HAS3 (A2636)	DSMarE AESS, *HMS Sultan*, Gosport
	XP137	WS58 Wessex HAS3 [11/DD]	RN, Predannack Fire School
	XP142	WS58 Wessex HAS3	FAA Museum, RNAS Yeovilton
	XP150	WS58 Wessex HAS3 [LS]	FETC, Moreton-in-Marsh, Glos
	XP165	WS Scout AH1	The Helicopter Museum, Weston-super-Mare
	XP190	WS Scout AH1	Aeroventure, Doncaster
	XP191	WS Scout AH1	Privately owned, Prenton, The Wirral
	XP226	Fairey Gannet AEW3	Newark Air Museum, Winthorpe
	XP241	Auster AOP9 (G-CEHR)	Privately owned, Eggesford
	XP242	Auster AOP9 (G-BUCI)	AAC Historic Aircraft Flight, Middle Wallop
	XP244	Auster AOP9 (7864M/*M7922*)	Privately owned, Stretton on Dunsmore
	XP248	Auster AOP9 (7863M/WZ679)	Privately owned, Coventry
	XP254	Auster AOP11 (G-ASCC)	Privately owned, Cambs
	XP279	Auster AOP9 (G-BWKK)	Privately owned, Popham
	XP280	Auster AOP9	Snibston Discovery Park, Coalville
	XP281	Auster AOP9	Imperial War Museum, Duxford
	XP286	Auster AOP9	Privately owned, South Molton, Devon
	XP299	WS55 Whirlwind HAR10 (8726M)	RAF Museum, Hendon
	XP328	WS55 Whirlwind HAR10 (G-BKHC)	Privately owned, Tattershall Thorpe (wreck)
	XP329	WS55 Whirlwind HAR10 (8791M) [V]	Privately owned, Tattershall Thorpe (wreck)
	XP330	WS55 Whirlwind HAR10	CAA Fire School, Durham/Tees Valley
	XP344	WS55 Whirlwind HAR10 (8764M) [H723]	RAF North Luffenham Training Area
	XP345	WS55 Whirlwind HAR10 (8792M) [N]	Yorkshire Helicopter Preservation Group, Doncaster
	XP346	WS55 Whirlwind HAR10 (8793M)	Privately owned, Long Marston
	XP350	WS55 Whirlwind HAR10	Privately owned, Bassetts Pole, Staffs
	XP351	WS55 Whirlwind HAR10 (8672M) [Z]	Gatwick Aviation Museum, Charlwood, Surrey
	XP355	WS55 Whirlwind HAR10 (8463M/G-BEBC)	City of Norwich Aviation Museum
	XP360	WS55 Whirlwind HAR10 [V]	Privately owned, Bicton, nr Leominster
	XP398	WS55 Whirlwind HAR10 (8794M)	Gatwick Aviation Museum, Charlwood, Surrey
	XP404	WS55 Whirlwind HAR10 (8682M)	The Helicopter Museum, Weston-super-Mare
	XP411	AW660 Argosy C1 (8442M) [C]	RAF Museum, Cosford
	XP454	Slingsby T38 Grasshopper TX1	Privately owned, Sywell
	XP459	Slingsby T38 Grasshopper TX1	Privately owned, stored Nayland, Suffolk
	XP463	Slingsby T38 Grasshopper TX1 (BGA4372)	Privately owned, Lasham
	XP488	Slingsby T38 Grasshopper TX1	Privately owned, Keevil
	XP490	Slingsby T38 Grasshopper TX1 (BGA4552)	Privately owned, stored Watton

Serial	*Type (code/other identity)*	*Owner/operator location or fate*	*Notes*
XP492	Slingsby T38 Grasshopper TX1 (BGA3480)	Privately owned, Gallows Hill, Dorset	
XP493	Slingsby T38 Grasshopper TX1	Privately owned, stored Aston Down	
XP494	Slingsby T38 Grasshopper TX1	Privately owned, Wolverhampton	
XP502	HS Gnat T1 (8576M)	*Repainted as XR540, 2012*	
XP505	HS Gnat T1	Science Museum, Wroughton	
XP516	HS Gnat T1 (8580M) [16]	Farnborough Air Sciences Trust, Farnborough	
XP540	HS Gnat T1 (8608M) [62]	Privately owned, North Weald	
XP542	HS Gnat T1 (8575M)	Solent Sky, Hamble	
XP556	Hunting Jet Provost T4 (9027M) [B]	RAF Cranwell Aviation Heritage Centre	
XP557	Hunting Jet Provost T4 (8494M) [72]	Dumfries & Galloway Avn Mus, Dumfries	
XP558	Hunting Jet Provost T4 (8627M) <ff>	Privately owned, Stoneykirk, D&G	
XP558	Hunting Jet Provost T4 (8627M)[20] <rf>	Privately owned, Sproughton	
XP563	Hunting Jet Provost T4 (9028M) [C]	Privately owned, Sproughton	
XP568	Hunting Jet Provost T4	East Midlands Airport Aeropark	
XP573	Hunting Jet Provost T4 (8236M) [19]	Jersey Airport Fire Section	
XP585	Hunting Jet Provost T4 (8407M) [24]	NE Wales Institute, Wrexham	
XP627	Hunting Jet Provost T4	North-East Aircraft Museum, stored Usworth	
XP629	Hunting Jet Provost T4 (9026M) [P]	Gunsmoke Paintball, Hadleigh, Suffolk	
XP640	Hunting Jet Provost T4 (8501M) [M]	Yorkshire Air Museum, Elvington	
XP642	Hunting Jet Provost T4 <ff>	Privately owned, Welshpool	
XP672	Hunting Jet Provost T4 (8458M/G-RAFI) [03]	Privately owned, Bruntingthorpe	
XP680	Hunting Jet Provost T4 (8460M)	FETC, Moreton-in-Marsh, Glos	
XP686	Hunting Jet Provost T4 (8401M/8502M) [G]	Gunsmoke Paintball, Hadleigh, Suffolk	
XP701	BAC Lightning F3 (8924M) <ff>	Robertsbridge Aviation Society, Mayfield	
XP703	BAC Lightning F3 <ff>	Lightning Preservation Group, Bruntingthorpe	
XP706	BAC Lightning F3 (8925M)	Aeroventure, Doncaster	
XP743	BAC Lightning F3 <ff>	Wattisham Airfield Museum	
XP745	BAC Lightning F3 (8453M) <ff>	Vanguard Haulage, Greenford, London	
XP757	BAC Lightning F3 <ff>	Privately owned, Boston, Lincs	
XP765	BAC Lightning F6 (XS897) [A]	Lakes Lightnings, RAF Coningsby	
XP820	DHC2 Beaver AL1	AAC Historic Aircraft Flight, Middle Wallop	
XP821	DHC2 Beaver AL1 [MCO]	Museum of Army Flying, Middle Wallop	
XP822	DHC2 Beaver AL1	Museum of Army Flying, Middle Wallop	
XP831	Hawker P.1127 (8406M)	Science Museum, South Kensington	
XP841	Handley-Page HP115	FAA Museum, RNAS Yeovilton	
XP847	WS Scout AH1	Museum of Army Flying, Middle Wallop	
XP848	WS Scout AH1	DSEME Arborfield, on display	
XP853	WS Scout AH1	Privately owned, Sutton, Surrey	
XP854	WS Scout AH1 (7898M/TAD 043)	Mayhem Paintball, Abridge, Essex	
XP855	WS Scout AH1	DSEME SEAE, Arborfield	
XP883	WS Scout AH1	Privately owned, Bruntingthorpe	
XP884	WS Scout AH1	AAC, stored Middle Wallop	
XP885	WS Scout AH1	AAC Wattisham, instructional use	
XP886	WS Scout AH1	The Helicopter Museum, Weston-super-Mare	
XP888	WS Scout AH1	Privately owned, Sproughton	
XP890	WS Scout AH1 [G] (fuselage)	Privately owned, Ipswich	
XP893	WS Scout AH1	AAC Middle Wallop, BDRT	
XP895	WS Scout AH1	Privately owned, Woodley, Berks	
XP899	WS Scout AH1 [D]	DSEME SEAE, Arborfield	
XP900	WS Scout AH1	AAC Wattisham, instructional use	
XP902	WS Scout AH1 <ff>	Aeroventure, Doncaster	
XP905	WS Scout AH1	Privately owned, stored Sproughton	
XP907	WS Scout AH1 (G-SROE)	Privately owned, Wattisham	
XP910	WS Scout AH1	Museum of Army Flying, Middle Wallop	
XP924	DH110 Sea Vixen D3 (G-CVIX) [134/E]	Privately owned, Bournemouth	
XP925	DH110 Sea Vixen FAW2 [752] <ff>	No 1268 Sqn ATC, Haslemere, Surrey	
XP980	Hawker P.1127	FAA Museum, RNAS Yeovilton	
XP984	Hawker P.1127	Brooklands Museum, Weybridge	
XR220	BAC TSR2 (7933M)	RAF Museum, Cosford	

Notes	*Serial*	*Type (code/other identity)*	*Owner/operator location or fate*
	XR222	BAC TSR2	Imperial War Museum, Duxford
	XR232	Sud Alouette AH2 (F-WEIP)	Museum of Army Flying, Middle Wallop
	XR239	Auster AOP9	Privately owned, Stretton on Dunsmore
	XR240	Auster AOP9 (G-BDFH)	Privately owned, Yeovilton
	XR241	Auster AOP9 (G-AXRR)	Privately owned, Eggesford
	XR244	Auster AOP9	AAC Historic Aircraft Flight, Middle Wallop
	XR246	Auster AOP9 (7862M/G-AZBU)	Privately owned, Melton Mowbray
	XR267	Auster AOP9 (G-BJXR)	Privately owned, Hucknall
	XR271	Auster AOP9	Royal Artillery Experience, Woolwich
	XR346	Northrop Shelduck D1 (comp XW578)	Bournemouth Aviation Museum
	XR371	SC5 Belfast C1	RAF Museum, Cosford
	XR379	Sud Alouette AH2	AAC Historic Aircraft Flight, Middle Wallop
	XR453	WS55 Whirlwind HAR10 (8873M) [A]	RAF Odiham, on gate
	XR458	WS55 Whirlwind HAR10 (8662M) [H]	*Currently not known*
	XR485	WS55 Whirlwind HAR10 [Q]	Norfolk & Suffolk Avn Museum, Flixton
	XR486	WS55 Whirlwind HCC12 (8727M/G-RWWW)	The Helicopter Museum, Weston-super-Mare
	XR498	WS58 Wessex HC2 (9342M) [X]	DSMarE AESS, *HMS Sultan*, Gosport
	XR501	WS58 Wessex HC2	Army, Keogh Barracks, Aldershot, instructional use
	XR502	WS58 Wessex HC2 (G-CCUP) [Z]	*Sold as N486KA, January 2013*
	XR503	WS58 Wessex HC2	MoD DFTDC, Manston
	XR506	WS58 Wessex HC2 (9343M) [V]	*Privately owned, Thorpe Wood, N Yorks*
	XR516	WS58 Wessex HC2 (9319M) [V]	RAF Shawbury, on display
	XR517	WS58 Wessex HC2 [N]	Ulster Aviation Society, Long Kesh
	XR518	WS58 Wessex HC2	DSMarE AESS, *HMS Sultan*, Gosport
	XR523	WS58 Wessex HC2 [M]	RN *HMS Raleigh*, Torpoint, instructional use
	XR525	WS58 Wessex HC2 [G]	RAF Museum, Cosford
	XR526	WS58 Wessex HC2 (8147M)	The Helicopter Museum, Weston-super-Mare
	XR528	WS58 Wessex HC2	Privately owned, Little Rissington (GI use)
	XR529	WS58 Wessex HC2 (9268M) [E]	RAF Aldergrove, on display
	XR534	HS Gnat T1 (8578M) [65]	Newark Air Museum, Winthorpe
	XR537	HS Gnat T1 (8642M/G-NATY)	Privately owned, Bournemouth
	XR538	HS Gnat T1 (8621M/G-RORI) [01]	Heritage Aircraft Trust, North Weald
	XR540	HS Gnat T1 (XP502/8576M)	Privately owned, Cotswold Airport
	XR571	HS Gnat T1 (8493M)	RAF *Red Arrows*, Scampton, on display
	XR574	HS Gnat T1 (8631M) [72]	Trenchard Museum, Halton
	XR595	WS Scout AH1 (G-BWHU) [M]	Privately owned, North Weald
	XR601	WS Scout AH1	Army Whittington Barracks, Lichfield, on display
	XR627	WS Scout AH1 [X]	Privately owned, Storwood, Yorkshire
	XR628	WS Scout AH1	Privately owned, Ipswich
	XR629	WS Scout AH1 (fuselage)	Privately owned, Ipswich
	XR635	WS Scout AH1	Midland Air Museum, Coventry
	XR650	Hunting Jet Provost T4 (8459M) [28]	Boscombe Down Aviation Collection, Old Sarum
	XR654	Hunting Jet Provost T4 <ff>	Privately owned, Chester
	XR658	Hunting Jet Provost T4 (8192M)	Deeside College, Connah's Quay, Clwyd
	XR662	Hunting Jet Provost T4 (8410M) [25]	Boulton Paul Association, Wolverhampton
	XR673	Hunting Jet Provost T4 (G-BXLO/9032M) [L]	Privately owned, Church Fenton
	XR681	Hunting Jet Provost T4 (8588M) <ff>	Robertsbridge Aviation Society, Mayfield
	XR700	Hunting Jet Provost T4 (8589M) <ff>	RAF Aldergrove
	XR713	BAC Lightning F3 (8935M) [C]	RAF Leuchars, on display
	XR718	BAC Lightning F6 (8932M) [DA]	Privately owned, Over Dinsdale, N Yorks
	XR724	BAC Lightning F6 (G-BTSY)	The Lightning Association, Binbrook
	XR725	BAC Lightning F6	Privately owned, Binbrook
	XR726	BAC Lightning F6 <ff>	Privately owned, Harrogate
	XR728	BAC Lightning F6 [JS]	Lightning Preservation Grp, Bruntingthorpe
	XR747	BAC Lightning F6 <ff>	Privately owned, Cubert, Cornwall
	XR749	BAC Lightning F3 (8934M) [DA]	Privately owned, Peterhead
	XR751	BAC Lightning F3 <ff>	Privately owned, Thorpe Wood, N Yorks
	XR753	BAC Lightning F6 (8969M) [XI]	RAF Coningsby on display
	XR753	BAC Lightning F53 (ZF578) [A]	Tangmere Military Aviation Museum
	XR754	BAC Lightning F6 (8972M) <ff>	Aeroventure, Doncaster

Serial	Type (code/other identity)	Owner/operator location or fate	Notes
XR755	BAC Lightning F6	Privately owned, Callington, Cornwall	
XR757	BAC Lightning F6 <ff>	RAF Scampton Historical Museum	
XR759	BAC Lightning F6 <ff>	Privately owned, Haxey, Lincs	
XR770	BAC Lightning F6 [AA]	RAF Waddington, for display	
XR771	BAC Lightning F6 [BF]	Midland Air Museum, Coventry	
XR806	BAC VC10 C1K (9285M) <ff>	RAF Brize Norton, BDRT	
XR808	BAC VC10 C1K [R] $	RAF No 101 Sqn, Brize Norton	
XR810	BAC VC10 C1K <ff>	Privately owned, Crondall, Hants	
XR944	Wallis WA116 (G-ATTB)	Privately owned, Reymerston Hall, Norfolk	
XR977	HS Gnat T1 (8640M) [3]	RAF Museum, Cosford	
XR991	HS Gnat T1 (8624M/XS102/G-MOUR)	Heritage Aircraft Trust, North Weald	
XR993	HS Gnat T1 (8620M/XP534/G-BVPP)	Privately owned, Bruntingthorpe	
XS100	HS Gnat T1 (8561M) <ff>	Privately owned, London SW3	
XS100	HS Gnat T1 (8561M) <rf>	Privately owned, Fyfield, Essex	
XS104	HS Gnat T1 (8604M/G-FRCE)	Privately owned, North Weald	
XS111	HS Gnat T1 (8618M/XP504/G-TIMM)	Heritage Aircraft Trust, North Weald	
XS149	WS58 Wessex HAS3 [661/GL]	The Helicopter Museum, Weston-super-Mare	
XS176	Hunting Jet Provost T4 (8514M) <ff>	Highland Aviation Museum, Inverness	
XS177	Hunting Jet Provost T4 (9044M) [N]	Privately owned, Binbrook	
XS179	Hunting Jet Provost T4 (8237M) [20]	Museum of Science & Industry, stored Manchester	
XS180	Hunting Jet Provost T4 (*8238M*/8338M) [21]	MoD, Boscombe Down	
XS181	Hunting Jet Provost T4 (9033M) <ff>	Lakes Lightnings, Spark Bridge, Cumbria	
XS183	Hunting Jet Provost T4 <ff>	Privately owned, Plymouth	
XS186	Hunting Jet Provost T4 (8408M) [M]	Metheringham Airfield Visitors Centre	
XS209	Hunting Jet Provost T4 (8409M)	Solway Aviation Society, Carlisle	
XS216	Hunting Jet Provost T4 <ff>	Aeroventure, Doncaster	
XS218	Hunting Jet Provost T4 (8508M) <ff>	No 447 Sqn ATC, Henley-on-Thames, Berks	
XS231	BAC Jet Provost T5 (G-ATAJ)	Boscombe Down Aviation Collection, Old Sarum	
XS235	DH106 Comet 4C (G-CPDA)	Cold War Jets Collection, Bruntingthorpe	
XS238	Auster AOP9 (TAD 200)	Newark Air Museum, stored Winthorpe	
XS416	BAC Lightning T5	Privately owned, New York, Lincs	
XS417	BAC Lightning T5 [DZ]	Newark Air Museum, Winthorpe	
XS420	BAC Lightning T5	Lakes Lightnings, FAST, Farnborough	
XS421	BAC Lightning T5 <ff>	Privately owned, Foulness	
XS456	BAC Lightning T5 [DX]	Skegness Water Leisure Park	
XS457	BAC Lightning T5 <ff>	Privately owned, Binbrook	
XS458	BAC Lightning T5 [T]	T5 Projects, Cranfield	
XS459	BAC Lightning T5 [AW]	Fenland & W Norfolk Aviation Museum, Wisbech	
XS463	WS Wasp HAS1 (XT431)	Gatwick Aviation Museum, Charlwood, Surrey	
XS481	WS58 Wessex HU5	Aeroventure, Doncaster	
XS482	WS58 Wessex HU5	RAF Manston History Museum	
XS486	WS58 Wessex HU5 (9272M) [524/CU,F]	The Helicopter Museum, Weston-super-Mare	
XS488	WS58 Wessex HU5 (9056M) [F]	DSMarE AESS, *HMS Sultan*, Gosport	
XS489	WS58 Wessex HU5 [R]	Privately owned, Westerham, Kent	
XS493	WS58 Wessex HU5	Vector Aerospace, stored Fleetlands	
XS496	WS58 Wessex HU5 [625/PO]	*Scrapped, 2012*	
XS507	WS58 Wessex HU5	RAF Benson, for display	
XS508	WS58 Wessex HU5	FAA Museum, stored RNAS Yeovilton	
XS510	WS58 Wessex HU5 [626/PO]	No 1414 Sqn ATC, Crowborough, Sussex	
XS511	WS58 Wessex HU5 [M]	Tangmere Military Aircraft Museum	
XS513	WS58 Wessex HU5	RNAS Yeovilton Fire Section	
XS514	WS58 Wessex HU5 (A2740) [L/PO]	DSMarE AESS, *HMS Sultan*, Gosport	
XS515	WS58 Wessex HU5 [N]	Army, Keogh Barracks, Aldershot, instructional use	
XS516	WS58 Wessex HU5 [Q]	Privately owned, Redruth, Cornwall	
XS520	WS58 Wessex HU5 [F]	RN, Predannack Fire School	
XS522	WS58 Wessex HU5 [ZL]	Blackball Paintball, Truro, Cornwall	
XS527	WS Wasp HAS1	FAA Museum, stored RNAS Yeovilton	
XS529	WS Wasp HAS1	Privately owned, Redruth, Cornwall	
XS539	WS Wasp HAS1 [435]	Vector Aerospace Fleetlands Apprentice School	

Notes	Serial	Type (code/other identity)	Owner/operator location or fate
	XS567	WS Wasp HAS1 [434/E]	Imperial War Museum, Duxford
	XS568	WS Wasp HAS1 (A2715) [441]	DSMarE AESS, *HMS Sultan*, Gosport
	XS570	WS Wasp HAS1 [445/P]	MSS Holdings, Kirkham, Lancs
	XS574	Northrop Shelduck D1 <R>	FAA Museum, stored RNAS Yeovilton
	XS576	DH110 Sea Vixen FAW2 [125/E]	Imperial War Museum, Duxford
	XS587	DH110 Sea Vixen FAW(TT)2 (8828M/G-VIXN)	Gatwick Aviation Museum, Charlwood, Surrey
	XS590	DH110 Sea Vixen FAW2 [131/E]	FAA Museum, RNAS Yeovilton
	XS596	HS Andover C1(PR)	MoD, Boscombe Down (wfu)
	XS598	HS Andover C1 (fuselage)	FETC, Moreton-in-Marsh, Glos
	XS606	HS Andover C1	*Sold to Nigeria, 2013*
	XS639	HS Andover E3A (9241M)	RAF Museum, Cosford
	XS641	HS Andover C1PR (9198M) (fuselage)	Privately owned, Sandbach, Cheshire
	XS643	HS Andover E3A (9278M) <ff>	Privately owned, Stock, Essex
	XS646	HS Andover C1 (mod)	MoD, Boscombe Down (wfu)
	XS651	Slingsby T45 Swallow TX1 (BGA1211)	Privately owned, Keevil
	XS652	Slingsby T45 Swallow TX1 (BGA1107)	Privately owned, Chipping, Lancs
	XS674	WS58 Wessex HC2 [R]	Privately owned, Biggin Hill
	XS695	HS Kestrel FGA1	RAF Museum Restoration Centre, Cosford
	XS709	HS125 Dominie T1 [M]	RAF Museum, Cosford
	XS710	HS125 Dominie T1 (9259M) [O]	RAF Cranwell Fire Section
	XS711	HS125 Dominie T1 (fuselage)	*Scrapped, October 2012*
	XS713	HS125 Dominie T1 [C]	RAF Shawbury Fire Section
	XS714	HS125 Dominie T1 (9246M) [P]	MoD DFTDC, Manston
	XS726	HS125 Dominie T1 (9273M) [T]	Privately owned, Sproughton
	XS727	HS125 Dominie T1 [D]	RAF Cranwell (wfu)
	XS733	HS125 Dominie T1 (9276M) [Q]	Privately owned, Sproughton
	XS734	HS125 Dominie T1 (9260M) [N]	Privately owned, Sproughton
	XS735	HS125 Dominie T1 (9264M) [R]	Absolute Adventure, Craig-y-nos, Powys
	XS736	HS125 Dominie T1 [S]	MoD Winterbourne Gunner, Wilts
	XS738	HS125 Dominie T1 (9274M) [U]	RN, Predannack Fire School
	XS743	Beagle B206Z	MoD/ETPS, Boscombe Down
	XS765	Beagle B206 Basset CC1 (G-BSET)	MoD, QinetiQ, Boscombe Down (spares use)
	XS770	Beagle B206 Basset CC1 (G-HRHI)	MoD, QinetiQ, Boscombe Down (spares use)
	XS790	HS748 Andover CC2 <ff>	Boscombe Down Aviation Collection, Old Sarum
	XS791	HS748 Andover CC2 (fuselage)	Privately owned, Stock, Essex
	XS863	WS58 Wessex HAS1 [304/R]	Imperial War Museum, Duxford
	XS876	WS58 Wessex HAS1 [523/PO]	*Sold to Greece, September 2012*
	XS885	WS58 Wessex HAS1 [512/DD]	RN, Predannack Fire School
	XS886	WS58 Wessex HAS1 [527/CU]	Privately owned, Ditchling, E Sussex
	XS887	WS58 Wessex HAS1 [403/FI]	Aeroventure, Doncaster
	XS888	WS58 Wessex HAS1 [521]	Guernsey Airport Fire Section
	XS898	BAC Lightning F6 <ff>	Privately owned, Lavendon, Bucks
	XS899	BAC Lightning F6 <ff>	Privately owned, Binbrook
	XS903	BAC Lightning F6 [BA]	Yorkshire Air Museum, Elvington
	XS904	BAC Lightning F6 [BQ]	Lightning Preservation Grp, Bruntingthorpe
	XS919	BAC Lightning F6	Privately owned, stored Dinton Wilts
	XS922	BAC Lightning F6 (8973M) <ff>	Lakes Lightnings, Spark Bridge, Cumbria
	XS923	BAC Lightning F6 <ff>	Privately owned, Welshpool
	XS925	BAC Lightning F6 (8961M) [BA]	RAF Museum, Hendon
	XS928	BAC Lightning F6 [AD]	BAE Systems Warton, on display
	XS932	BAC Lightning F6 <ff>	Privately owned, Walcott, Lincs
	XS933	BAC Lightning F6 <ff>	Privately owned, Farnham
	XS933	BAC Lightning F53 (ZF594) [BF]	North-East Aircraft Museum, Usworth
	XS936	BAC Lightning F6	Castle Motors, Liskeard, Cornwall
	XT108	Agusta-Bell 47G-3 Sioux AH1 [U]	Museum of Army Flying, Middle Wallop
	XT123	WS Sioux AH1 (XT827) [D]	AAC Middle Wallop, at main gate
	XT131	Agusta-Bell 47G-3 Sioux AH1 [B]	AAC Historic Aircraft Flight, Middle Wallop
	XT140	Agusta-Bell 47G-3 Sioux AH1	Perth Technical College
	XT141	Agusta-Bell 47G-3 Sioux AH1	Privately owned, Newcastle

Serial	*Type (code/other identity)*	*Owner/operator location or fate*	*Notes*
XT150	Agusta-Bell 47G-3 Sioux AH1 (7883M) [R]	Privately owned, Aeroventure, Doncaster	
XT151	WS Sioux AH1	Museum of Army Flying, stored Middle Wallop	
XT176	WS Sioux AH1 [U]	FAA Museum, stored RNAS Yeovilton	
XT190	WS Sioux AH1	The Helicopter Museum, Weston-super-Mare	
XT200	WS Sioux AH1 [F]	Newark Air Museum, Winthorpe	
XT208	WS Sioux AH1 (wreck)	Blessingbourne Museum, Fivemiletown, Co Tyrone, NI	
XT223	WS Sioux AH1 (G-XTUN)	Privately owned, Sherburn-in-Elmet	
XT236	WS Sioux AH1 (frame only)	Aeroventure, Doncaster	
XT242	WS Sioux AH1 (composite) [12]	Aeroventure, Doncaster	
XT257	WS58 Wessex HAS3 (8719M)	Bournemouth Aviation Museum	
XT277	HS Buccaneer S2A (8853M) <ff>	Privately owned, Welshpool	
XT280	HS Buccaneer S2A <ff>	Dumfries & Galloway Avn Mus, Dumfries	
XT284	HS Buccaneer S2A (8855M) <ff>	Privately owned, Felixstowe	
XT288	HS Buccaneer S2B (9134M)	Royal Scottish Museum of Flight, stored E Fortune	
XT420	WS Wasp HAS1 (G-CBUI) [606]	Privately owned, Lee-on-Solent	
XT427	WS Wasp HAS1 [606]	FAA Museum, stored RNAS Yeovilton	
XT434	WS Wasp HAS1 (G-CGGK) [455]	Privately owned, Breighton	
XT435	WS Wasp HAS1 (NZ3907/G-RIMM) [430]	Privately owned, Badwell Green, Suffolk	
XT437	WS Wasp HAS1 [423]	Boscombe Down Aviation Collection, Old Sarum	
XT439	WS Wasp HAS1 [605]	Privately owned, Hemel Hempstead	
XT443	WS Wasp HAS1 [422/AU]	The Helicopter Museum, Weston-super-Mare	
XT453	WS58 Wessex HU5 (A2756) [B/PO]	DSMarE AESS, *HMS Sultan*, Gosport	
XT455	WS58 Wessex HU5 (A2654) [U]	DSMarE AESS, *HMS Sultan*, Gosport	
XT456	WS58 Wessex HU5 (8941M) [XZ]	RAF Aldergrove, BDRT	
XT458	WS58 Wessex HU5 (A2768) [P/VL]	RNAS Yeovilton, for display	
XT466	WS58 Wessex HU5 (A2617/8921M) [XV]	Army Whittington Barracks, Lichfield, on display	
XT467	WS58 Wessex HU5 (8922M) [BF]	Gunsmoke Paintball, Hadleigh, Suffolk	
XT469	WS58 Wessex HU5 (8920M)	Privately owned, Bowgreave, Lancs	
XT472	WS58 Wessex HU5 [XC]	The Helicopter Museum, Weston-super-Mare	
XT480	WS58 Wessex HU5 [468/RG]	Rednal Paintball, Shropshire	
XT482	WS58 Wessex HU5 [ZM/VL]	FAA Museum, RNAS Yeovilton	
XT484	WS58 Wessex HU5 (A2742) [H]	DSMarE AESS, *HMS Sultan*, Gosport	
XT485	WS58 Wessex HU5 (A2680)	DSMarE, stored *HMS Sultan*, Gosport	
XT486	WS58 Wessex HU5 (8919M)	Dumfries & Galloway Avn Mus, Dumfries	
XT550	WS Sioux AH1 [D]	AAC, stored Middle Wallop	
XT575	Vickers Viscount 837 <ff>	Brooklands Museum, Weybridge	
XT581	Northrop Shelduck D1	Imperial War Museum, Duxford	
XT583	Northrop Shelduck D1	Royal Artillery Experience, Woolwich	
XT596	McD F-4K Phantom FG1	FAA Museum, RNAS Yeovilton	
XT597	McD F-4K Phantom FG1	Privately owned, Boscombe Down	
XT601	WS58 Wessex HC2 (9277M) (composite)	RAF Odiham, BDRT	
XT604	WS58 Wessex HC2	East Midlands Airport Aeropark	
XT617	WS Scout AH1	AAC Wattisham, on display	
XT621	WS Scout AH1	Defence Academy of the UK, Shrivenham	
XT623	WS Scout AH1	DSEME SEAE, Arborfield	
XT626	WS Scout AH1 [Q]	AAC Historic Aircraft Flt, Middle Wallop	
XT630	WS Scout AH1 (G-BXRL) [X]	Privately owned, Bruntingthorpe	
XT631	WS Scout AH1 [D]	Privately owned, Ipswich	
XT633	WS Scout AH1	DSEME SEAE, Arborfield	
XT634	WS Scout AH1 (G-BYRX) [T]	Privately owned, Tollerton	
XT638	WS Scout AH1 [N]	AAC Middle Wallop, at gate	
XT640	WS Scout AH1	Privately owned, Sproughton	
XT643	WS Scout AH1 [Z]	Army, Thorpe Camp, East Wretham	
XT672	WS58 Wessex HC2 [WE]	RAF Stafford, on display	
XT681	WS58 Wessex HC2 (9279M) [U] <ff>	Privately owned, Wallingford, Oxon	
XT761	WS58 Wessex HU5	DSMarE AESS, *HMS Sultan*, Gosport	
XT762	WS58 Wessex HU5	Hamburger Hill Paintball, Marksbury, Somerset	
XT765	WS58 Wessex HU5 [J]	FAA Museum, RNAS Yeovilton	
XT769	WS58 Wessex HU5 [823]	FAA Museum, RNAS Yeovilton	
XT771	WS58 Wessex HU5 [620/PO]	DSMarE AESS, *HMS Sultan*, Gosport	

Notes	Serial	Type (code/other identity)	Owner/operator location or fate
	XT773	WS58 Wessex HU5 (9123M)	RAF Shawbury Fire Section
	XT778	WS Wasp HAS1 [430]	FAA Museum, stored RNAS Yeovilton
	XT780	WS Wasp HAS1 [636]	Fareham Tertiary College, Hants
	XT787	WS Wasp HAS1 (NZ3905/G-KAXT)	Privately owned, Middle Wallop
	XT788	WS Wasp HAS1 (G-BMIR) [474]	Aeroventure, Doncaster
	XT793	WS Wasp HAS1 (G-BZPP) [456]	Privately owned, Lee-on-Solent
	XT863	McD F-4K Phantom FG1 <ff>	Privately owned, Cowes, IOW
	XT864	McD F-4K Phantom FG1 (8998M/*XT684*) [BJ]	RAF Leuchars on display
	XT891	McD F-4M Phantom FGR2 (9136M) [P]	RAF Coningsby, at main gate
	XT903	McD F-4M Phantom FGR2 <ff>	RAF Museum Restoration Centre, Cosford
	XT905	McD F-4M Phantom FGR2 (9286M) [P]	RAF North Luffenham Training Area
	XT907	McD F-4M Phantom FGR2 (9151M) [W]	DEODS, Chattenden, Kent
	XT914	McD F-4M Phantom FGR2 (9269M) [Z]	Wattisham Station Heritage Museum
	XV101	BAC VC10 K1 [S]	*Scrapped at Bruntingthorpe, May 2012*
	XV102	BAC VC10 C1K [T]	*Scrapped at Bruntingthorpe, May 2012*
	XV104	BAC VC10 C1K [U]	Privately owned, Bruntingthorpe
	XV105	BAC VC10 C1K [V]	*Scrapped at Bruntingthorpe, May 2012*
	XV106	BAC VC10 C1K [W]	Privately owned, Bruntingthorpe
	XV107	BAC VC10 C1K [X]	*Scrapped at Bruntingthorpe, May 2012*
	XV108	BAC VC10 C1K [Y]	Privately owned, Bruntingthorpe
	XV109	BAC VC10 C1K <ff>	Privately owned, Bruntingthorpe
	XV118	WS Scout AH1 (9141M)	Kennet Aviation, North Weald
	XV122	WS Scout AH1 [D]	Defence Academy of the UK, Shrivenham
	XV123	WS Scout AH1	RAF Shawbury, on display
	XV127	WS Scout AH1	Museum of Army Flying, Middle Wallop
	XV130	WS Scout AH1 (G-BWJW) [R]	Privately owned, Lee-on-Solent
	XV131	WS Scout AH1 [Y]	AAC 70 Aircraft Workshops, Middle Wallop, BDRT
	XV136	WS Scout AH1 [X]	AAC Netheravon, on display
	XV137	WS Scout AH1 (G-CRUM)	Privately owned, Chiseldon, Wilts
	XV137	WS Scout AH1 (XV139)	Aeroventure, stored Doncaster
	XV138	WS Scout AH1 (G-SASM)	Privately owned, Lee-on-Solent
	XV141	WS Scout AH1	REME Museum, Arborfield
	XV148	HS Nimrod MR1(mod) <ff>	Privately owned, Malmesbury
	XV161	HS Buccaneer S2B (9117M) <ff>	Dundonald Aviation Centre
	XV165	HS Buccaneer S2B <ff>	Privately owned, Ashford, Kent
	XV168	HS Buccaneer S2B [AF]	BAE Systems Brough, on display
	XV177	Lockheed C-130K Hercules C3A [177]	RAF No 47 Sqn, Brize Norton
	XV188	Lockheed C-130K Hercules C3A [188]	RAF No 47 Sqn, Brize Norton
	XV196	Lockheed C-130K Hercules C1 [196]	RAF No 47 Sqn, Brize Norton
	XV197	Lockheed C-130K Hercules C3 [197]	Privately owned, Hixon, Staffs
	XV200	Lockheed C-130K Hercules C1 [200]	RAF No 47 Sqn, Brize Norton
	XV201	Lockheed C-130K Hercules C1K <ff>	Marshalls, Cambridge
	XV202	Lockheed C-130K Hercules C3 [202]	RAF Museum, Cosford
	XV208	Lockheed C-130K Hercules W2	Marshalls, Cambridge (wfu)
	XV209	Lockheed C-130K Hercules C3A [209]	RAF No 47 Sqn, Brize Norton
	XV212	Lockheed C-130K Hercules C3 [212]	*Scrapped at Cambridge, May 2012*
	XV214	Lockheed C-130K Hercules C3A [214]	RAF No 47 Sqn, Brize Norton
	XV217	Lockheed C-130K Hercules C3	Privately owned, Hixon, Staffs
	XV220	Lockheed C-130K Hercules C3	Privately owned, Hixon, Staffs
	XV221	Lockheed C-130K Hercules C3 [221]	Privately owned, Bruntingthorpe
	XV226	HS Nimrod MR2 $	Cold War Jets Collection, Bruntingthorpe
	XV229	HS Nimrod MR2 [29]	MoD DFTDC, Manston
	XV231	HS Nimrod MR2 [31]	Aviation Viewing Park, Manchester
	XV232	HS Nimrod MR2 [32]	AIRBASE, Coventry
	XV235	HS Nimrod MR2 [35] <ff>	Privately owned, RAF Scampton
	XV240	HS Nimrod MR2 [40] <ff>	Spey Bay Salvage, Dallachy, Moray
	XV241	HS Nimrod MR2 [41] <ff>	Royal Scottish Mus'm of Flight, E Fortune
	XV244	HS Nimrod MR2 [44] <ff>	Morayavia, RAF Kinloss
	XV249	HS Nimrod R1 $	RAF Museum, Cosford

Serial	Type (code/other identity)	Owner/operator location or fate	Notes
XV250	HS Nimrod MR2 [50]	Yorkshire Air Museum, Elvington	
XV252	HS Nimrod MR2 [52] <ff>	Privately owned, Cullen, Moray	
XV254	HS Nimrod MR2 [54] <ff>	Highland Aviation Museum, Inverness	
XV255	HS Nimrod MR2 [55]	City of Norwich Aviation Museum	
XV259	BAe Nimrod AEW3 <ff>	Privately owned,	
XV263	BAe Nimrod AEW3P (8967M) <ff>	BAE Systems, Brough	
XV263	BAe Nimrod AEW3P (8967M) <rf>	MoD/BAE Systems, Woodford	
XV268	DHC2 Beaver AL1 (G-BVER)	Privately owned, Cumbernauld	
XV277	HS P.1127(RAF)	Royal Scottish Mus'm of Flight, E Fortune	
XV279	HS P.1127(RAF) (8566M)	RAF Wittering	
XV280	HS P.1127(RAF) <ff>	RNAS Yeovilton Fire Section	
XV294	Lockheed C-130K Hercules C3 [294]	*Scrapped at Cambridge, 23 February 2012*	
XV295	Lockheed C-130K Hercules C1 [295]	RAF No 47 Sqn, Brize Norton	
XV301	Lockheed C-130K Hercules C3 [301]	Privately owned, Bruntingthorpe	
XV302	Lockheed C-130K Hercules C3 [302]	Marshalls, Cambridge, fatigue test airframe	
XV303	Lockheed C-130K Hercules C3A [303]	RAF No 47 Sqn, Brize Norton	
XV304	Lockheed C-130K Hercules C3A	RAF Brize Norton, instructional use	
XV305	Lockheed C-130K Hercules C3 $	Privately owned, Hixon, Staffs	
XV307	Lockheed C-130K Hercules C3 (G-52-40) [307]	MoD/Marshalls, stored Cambridge, for disposal	
XV328	BAC Lightning T5 <ff>	Phoenix Aviation, Bruntingthorpe	
XV333	HS Buccaneer S2B [234/H]	FAA Museum, RNAS Yeovilton	
XV344	HS Buccaneer S2C	QinetiQ Farnborough, on display	
XV350	HS Buccaneer S2B	East Midlands Airport Aeropark	
XV352	HS Buccaneer S2B <ff>	RAF Manston History Museum	
XV359	HS Buccaneer S2B [035/R]	Privately owned, Topsham, Devon	
XV361	HS Buccaneer S2B	Ulster Aviation Society, Long Kesh	
XV370	Sikorsky SH-3D (A2682) [260]	DSMarE AESS, *HMS Sultan*, Gosport	
XV371	WS61 Sea King HAS1(DB) [61/DD]	SFDO, RNAS Culdrose	
XV372	WS61 Sea King HAS1	RAF, St Mawgan, instructional use	
XV383	Northrop MQM-57A/3 (fuselage)	Privately owned, Wimborne, Dorset	
XV401	McD F-4M Phantom FGR2 [I]	Privately owned, Boscombe Down	
XV402	McD F-4M Phantom FGR2 <ff>	Privately owned, Kent	
XV406	McD F-4M Phantom FGR2 (9098M) [CK]	Solway Aviation Society, Carlisle	
XV408	McD F-4M Phantom FGR2 (9165M) [Z]	Tangmere Military Aviation Museum	
XV411	McD F-4M Phantom FGR2 (9103M) [L]	MoD DFTDC, Manston	
XV415	McD F-4M Phantom FGR2 (9163M) [E]	RAF Boulmer, on display	
XV424	McD F-4M Phantom FGR2 (9152M) [I]	RAF Museum, Hendon	
XV426	McD F-4M Phantom FGR2 <ff>	City of Norwich Aviation Museum	
XV426	McD F-4M Phantom FGR2 [P] <rf>	RAF Coningsby, BDRT	
XV460	McD F-4M Phantom FGR2 <ff>	No 2214 Sqn ATC, Usworth	
XV474	McD F-4M Phantom FGR2 [T]	The Old Flying Machine Company, Duxford	
XV490	McD F-4M Phantom FGR2 [R] <ff>	Newark Air Museum, Winthorpe	
XV497	McD F-4M Phantom FGR2 (9295M) [D]	Privately owned, Bentwaters	
XV499	McD F-4M Phantom FGR2	RAF Leeming, WLT	
XV581	McD F-4K Phantom FG1 (9070M) <ff>	No 2481 Sqn ATC, Bridge of Don	
XV582	McD F-4K Phantom FG1 (9066M) [M]	RAF Leuchars, on display	
XV586	McD F-4K Phantom FG1 (9067M) [AJ]	Privately owned, RNAS Yeovilton	
XV591	McD F-4K Phantom FG1 [013] <ff>	RAF Museum, Cosford	
XV625	WS Wasp HAS1 (A2649) [471]	DSMarE AESS, *HMS Sultan*, Gosport	
XV631	WS Wasp HAS1 (fuselage)	Farnborough Air Sciences Trust, Farnborough	
XV642	WS61 Sea King HAS2A (A2614) [259]	DSMarE AESS, *HMS Sultan*, Gosport	
XV643	WS61 Sea King HAS6 [262]	DSAE, No 1 SoTT, Cosford	
XV647	WS61 Sea King HU5 [28]	MoD/Vector Aerospace, Fleetlands	
XV648	WS61 Sea King HU5 [18/CU]	RN No 771 NAS, Culdrose	
XV649	WS61 Sea King ASaC7 [180]	RN No 849 NAS, Culdrose	
XV651	WS61 Sea King HU5	MoD/AFD/QinetiQ, Boscombe Down	
XV653	WS61 Sea King HAS6 (9326M) [63/CU]	DSAE, No 1 SoTT, Cosford	
XV654	WS61 Sea King HAS6 [05/DD] (wreck)	SFDO, RNAS Culdrose	
XV655	WS61 Sea King HAS6 [270/N]	DSMarE AESS, *HMS Sultan*, Gosport	
XV656	WS61 Sea King ASaC7 [185]	RN No 849 NAS, Culdrose	

Notes	*Serial*	*Type (code/other identity)*	*Owner/operator location or fate*
	XV657	WS61 Sea King HAS5 (*ZA135*) [32/DD]	SFDO, RNAS Culdrose
	XV659	WS61 Sea King HAS6 (9324M) [62/CU]	DSAE, No 1 SoTT, Cosford
	XV660	WS61 Sea King HAS6 [69/N]	DSMarE AESS, *HMS Sultan*, Gosport
	XV661	WS61 Sea King HU5 [26]	RN No 771 NAS, Culdrose
	XV663	WS61 Sea King HAS6	National Maritime Museum Cornwall, Falmouth
	XV664	WS61 Sea King ASaC7 [190]	RN No 849 NAS, Culdrose
	XV665	WS61 Sea King HAS6 [507/CU]	DSMarE AESS, *HMS Sultan*, Gosport
	XV666	WS61 Sea King HU5 [21]	MoD/Vector Aerospace, Fleetlands
	XV670	WS61 Sea King HU5 [17]	MoD/Vector Aerospace, Fleetlands
	XV671	WS61 Sea King ASaC7 [183]	RN No 849 NAS, Culdrose
	XV672	WS61 Sea King ASaC7 [187]	RN No 857 NAS, Culdrose
	XV673	WS61 Sea King HU5 [27/CU]	RN No 771 NAS, Culdrose
	XV675	WS61 Sea King HAS6 [701/PW]	DSMarE AESS, *HMS Sultan*, Gosport
	XV676	WS61 Sea King HC6 [ZE]	DSMarE, stored *HMS Sultan*, Gosport
	XV677	WS61 Sea King HAS6 [269]	Aeroventure, Doncaster
	XV696	WS61 Sea King HAS6 [267/L]	DSMarE AESS, *HMS Sultan*, Gosport
	XV697	WS61 Sea King ASaC7 [181]	RN No 849 NAS, Culdrose
	XV699	WS61 Sea King HU5 [823/PW]	RN No 771 NAS, Prestwick
	XV700	WS61 Sea King HC6 [ZC]	DSMarE, stored *HMS Sultan*, Gosport
	XV701	WS61 Sea King HAS6 [268/N,64]	DSAE, No 1 SoTT, Cosford
	XV703	WS61 Sea King HC6 [ZD]	DSMarE, stored *HMS Sultan*, Gosport
	XV705	WS61 Sea King HU5 [29]	RN No 771 NAS, Culdrose
	XV706	WS61 Sea King HAS6 (9344M) [017/L]	RN ETS, Culdrose
	XV707	WS61 Sea King ASaC7 [184]	MoD/AFD/QinetiQ, Boscombe Down
	XV708	WS61 Sea King HAS6 [501/CU]	DSMarE AESS, *HMS Sultan*, Gosport
	XV709	WS61 Sea King HAS6 (9303M) [263]	RAF Valley, instructional use
	XV711	WS61 Sea King HAS6 [15/CW]	DSMarE AESS, *HMS Sultan*, Gosport
	XV712	WS61 Sea King HAS6 [66]	Imperial War Museum, Duxford
	XV713	WS61 Sea King HAS6 (A2646) [018/L]	DSMarE AESS, *HMS Sultan*, Gosport
	XV714	WS61 Sea King ASaC7 [188]	RN No 849 NAS, Culdrose
	XV720	WS58 Wessex HC2 (A2701)	Privately owned, Hixon, Staffs
	XV722	WS58 Wessex HC2 (8805M) [WH]	Privately owned, Badgers Mount, Kent
	XV724	WS58 Wessex HC2	DSMarE AESS, *HMS Sultan*, Gosport
	XV725	WS58 Wessex HC2 [C]	MoD DFTDC, Manston
	XV726	WS58 Wessex HC2 [J]	Privately owned, Biggin Hill
	XV728	WS58 Wessex HC2 [A]	Newark Air Museum, Winthorpe
	XV731	WS58 Wessex HC2 [Y]	Privately owned, Badgers Mount, Kent
	XV732	WS58 Wessex HCC4	RAF Museum, Hendon
	XV733	WS58 Wessex HCC4	The Helicopter Museum, Weston-super-Mare
	XV741	HS Harrier GR3 (A2608) [41/DD]	*Currently not known*
	XV744	HS Harrier GR3 (9167M) [3K]	Defence Academy of the UK, Shrivenham
	XV748	HS Harrier GR3 [3D]	Yorkshire Air Museum, Elvington
	XV751	HS Harrier GR3	Gatwick Aviation Museum, Charlwood
	XV752	HS Harrier GR3 (9075M) [B]	Aeroventure, Doncaster
	XV753	HS Harrier GR3 (9078M) [53/DD]	RN, Predannack Fire School
	XV755	HS Harrier GR3 [M]	RNAS Yeovilton Fire Section
	XV759	HS Harrier GR3 [O] <ff>	Privately owned, Hitchin, Herts
	XV760	HS Harrier GR3 <ff>	Solent Sky, Southampton
	XV779	HS Harrier GR3 (8931M)	Harrier Heritage Centre, RAF Wittering
	XV783	HS Harrier GR3 [83/DD]	Privately owned, Sproughton
	XV784	HS Harrier GR3 (8909M) <ff>	Boscombe Down Aviation Collection, Old Sarum
	XV786	HS Harrier GR3 <ff>	RNAS Culdrose Fire Section
	XV786	HS Harrier GR3 [S] <rf>	RN, Predannack Fire School
	XV798	HS Harrier GR1(mod)	The Helicopter Museum, Weston-super-Mare
	XV804	HS Harrier GR3 (9280M) [O]	RAF North Luffenham Training Area
	XV806	HS Harrier GR3 <ff>	Privately owned, Worksop
	XV808	HS Harrier GR3 (9076M/A2687) [08/DD]	*Currently not known*
	XV810	HS Harrier GR3 (9038M) [K]	Privately owned, Bruntingthorpe
	XV814	DH106 Comet 4 (G-APDF) <ff>	Privately owned, Chipping Campden
	XV863	HS Buccaneer S2B (9115M/9139M/9145M) [S]	Privately owned, Weston, Eire

Serial	Type (code/other identity)	Owner/operator location or fate	Notes
XV864	HS Buccaneer S2B (9234M)	MoD DFTDC, Manston	
XV865	HS Buccaneer S2B (9226M)	Imperial War Museum, Duxford	
XV867	HS Buccaneer S2B <ff>	Highland Aviation Museum, Inverness	
XW175	HS Harrier T4(VAAC)	MoD, Boscombe Down (wfu)	
XW198	WS Puma HC1	RAF Benson (wfu)	
XW199	WS Puma HC2	MoD/Eurocopter, Brasov, Romania (conversion)	
XW200	WS Puma HC1 (wreck)	RAF, stored Shawbury	
XW201	WS Puma HC1	RAF Benson, BDRT	
XW202	WS Puma HC1	RAF, stored Shawbury	
XW204	WS Puma HC2	MoD/Eurocopter, Brasov, Romania (conversion)	
XW206	WS Puma HC1	RAF, stored Shawbury	
XW207	WS Puma HC1	RAF, stored Shawbury	
XW208	WS Puma HC1	RAF, stored Shawbury	
XW209	WS Puma HC2	MoD/Eurocopter, Brasov, Romania (conversion)	
XW210	WS Puma HC1 (comp XW215)	RAF Benson (wfu)	
XW212	WS Puma HC2	MoD/Eurocopter, Brasov, Romania (conversion)	
XW213	WS Puma HC1	RAF Benson (wfu)	
XW214	WS Puma HC2	MoD/Eurocopter, Brasov, Romania (conversion)	
XW216	WS Puma HC2 (F-ZWDD)	MoD/AFD/QinetiQ, Boscombe Down	
XW217	WS Puma HC2	MoD/Eurocopter, Brasov, Romania (conversion)	
XW218	WS Puma HC1 (wreck)	RAF, stored Shawbury (for disposal)	
XW219	WS Puma HC2	MoD/Eurocopter, Brasov, Romania (conversion)	
XW220	WS Puma HC2	MoD/Eurocopter, Brasov, Romania (conversion)	
XW222	WS Puma HC1	RAF Benson (wfu)	
XW223	WS Puma HC1	RAF Benson (wfu)	
XW224	WS Puma HC2	MoD/Eurocopter, Brasov, Romania (conversion)	
XW226	WS Puma HC1	RAF Benson (wfu)	
XW227	WS Puma HC1	Privately owned, Colsterworth, Leics	
XW229	WS Puma HC2	MoD/Eurocopter, Brasov, Romania (conversion)	
XW231	WS Puma HC2	MoD/Eurocopter, Brasov, Romania (conversion)	
XW232	WS Puma HC2 (F-ZWDE)	MoD/Eurocopter, Marseilles, France	
XW235	WS Puma HC2	MoD/Eurocopter, Brasov, Romania (conversion)	
XW236	WS Puma HC1	RAF Benson (wfu)	
XW237	WS Puma HC2	MoD/Eurocopter, Brasov, Romania (conversion)	
XW241	Sud SA330E Puma	Farnborough Air Sciences Trust, Farnborough	
XW264	HS Harrier T2 <ff>	Jet Age Museum, stored Gloucester	
XW265	HS Harrier T4A (9258M) <ff>	No 2345 Sqn ATC, RAF Leuchars	
XW265	HS Harrier T4A (9258M) <rf>	DSG, St Athan	
XW267	HS Harrier T4 (9263M) [SA]	Territorial Army, Toton, Notts	
XW268	HS Harrier T4N	City of Norwich Aviation Museum	
XW269	HS Harrier T4 [TB]	Caernarfon Air World	
XW270	HS Harrier T4 (fuselage)	Coventry University, instructional use	
XW271	HS Harrier T4 [71/DD]	Privately owned, Sproughton	
XW272	HS Harrier T4 (8783M) (fuselage) (comp XV281)	Privately owned, Cannock, Staffs	
XW276	Aérospatiale SA341 Gazelle (F-ZWRI)	Newark Air Museum, Winthorpe	
XW281	WS Scout AH1 (G-BYNZ) [T]	Privately owned, Wembury, Devon	
XW283	WS Scout AH1 [U]	Privately owned, Plymouth	
XW289	BAC Jet Provost T5A (G-BVXT/G-JPVA) [73]	Kennet Aviation, Yeovilton	
XW290	BAC Jet Provost T5A (9199M) [41,MA]	DSAE, Cosford (wfu)	
XW293	BAC Jet Provost T5 (G-BWCS) [Z]	Privately owned, Bournemouth	
XW299	BAC Jet Provost T5A (9146M) [60,MB]	DSAE, Cosford (wfu)	
XW301	BAC Jet Provost T5A (9147M) [63,MC]	DSAE, Cosford (wfu)	
XW303	BAC Jet Provost T5A (9119M) [127]	RAF Halton	
XW304	BAC Jet Provost T5 (9172M) [MD]	Privately owned, Eye, Suffolk	
XW309	BAC Jet Provost T5 (9179M) [V,ME]	Hartlepool College of Further Education	
XW311	BAC Jet Provost T5 (9180M) [W,MF]	Privately owned, North Weald	
XW315	BAC Jet Provost T5A <ff>	Privately owned, Preston	
XW318	BAC Jet Provost T5A (9190M) [78,MG]	DSAE, Cosford (wfu)	

Notes	Serial	Type (code/other identity)	Owner/operator location or fate
	XW320	BAC Jet Provost T5A (9015M) [71]	DSAE, No 1 SoTT, Cosford
	XW321	BAC Jet Provost T5A (9154M) [62,MH]	DSAE, No 1 SoTT, Cosford
	XW323	BAC Jet Provost T5A (9166M) [86]	RAF Museum, Hendon
	XW324	BAC Jet Provost T5 (G-BWSG) [U]	Privately owned, East Midlands
	XW325	BAC Jet Provost T5B (G-BWGF) [E]	Privately owned, Carlisle
	XW327	BAC Jet Provost T5A (9130M) [62]	DSAE, No 1 SoTT, Cosford
	XW328	BAC Jet Provost T5A (9177M) [75,MI]	DSAE, No 1 SoTT, Cosford
	XW330	BAC Jet Provost T5A (9195M) [82,MJ]	DSAE, No 1 SoTT, Cosford
	XW333	BAC Jet Provost T5A (G-BVTC)	Global Aviation, Humberside
	XW353	BAC Jet Provost T5A (9090M) [3]	RAF Cranwell, on display
	XW354	BAC Jet Provost T5A (XW355/G-JPTV)	Privately owned, Church Fenton
	XW358	BAC Jet Provost T5A (9181M) [59,MK]	DSAE, Cosford (wfu)
	XW360	BAC Jet Provost T5A (9153M) [61,ML]	DSAE, Cosford (wfu)
	XW361	BAC Jet Provost T5A (9192M) [81,MM]	DSAE, Cosford (wfu)
	XW363	BAC Jet Provost T5A [36]	Dumfries & Galloway Avn Mus, Dumfries
	XW364	BAC Jet Provost T5A (9188M) [35,MN]	RAF Halton
	XW367	BAC Jet Provost T5A (9193M) [64,MO]	DSAE, No 1 SoTT, Cosford
	XW370	BAC Jet Provost T5A (9196M) [72,MP]	DSAE, No 1 SoTT, Cosford
	XW375	BAC Jet Provost T5A (9149M) [52]	DSAE, No 1 SoTT, Cosford
	XW404	BAC Jet Provost T5A (9049M) [77]	Hartlepool FE College
	XW405	BAC Jet Provost T5A (9187M) [J,MQ]	Hartlepool FE College
	XW409	BAC Jet Provost T5A (9047M)	Privately owned, Hawarden
	XW410	BAC Jet Provost T5A (9125M) [80,MR]	DSAE, Cosford (wfu)
	XW416	BAC Jet Provost T5A (9191M) [84,MS]	DSAE, No 1 SoTT, Cosford
	XW418	BAC Jet Provost T5A (9173M) [MT]	DSAE, No 1 SoTT, Cosford
	XW419	BAC Jet Provost T5A (9120M) [125]	Privately owned, Bournemouth
	XW420	BAC Jet Provost T5A (9194M) [83,MU]	DSAE, Cosford (wfu)
	XW422	BAC Jet Provost T5A (G-BWEB) [3]	Privately owned, Cotswold Airport
	XW423	BAC Jet Provost T5A (G-BWUW) [14]	Deeside College, Connah's Quay, Clwyd
	XW425	BAC Jet Provost T5A (9200M) [H,MV]	DSAE, Cosford (wfu)
	XW430	BAC Jet Provost T5A (9176M) [77,MW]	DSAE, No 1 SoTT, Cosford
	XW432	BAC Jet Provost T5A (9127M) [76,MX]	DSAE, No 1 SoTT, Cosford
	XW433	BAC Jet Provost T5A (G-JPRO)	Classic Air Force, Coventry
	XW434	BAC Jet Provost T5A (9091M) [78,MY]	DSAE, Cosford (wfu)
	XW436	BAC Jet Provost T5A (9148M) [68]	DSAE, No 1 SoTT, Cosford
	XW530	HS Buccaneer S2B [530]	Buccaneer Service Station, Elgin
	XW541	HS Buccaneer S2B (8858M) <ff>	Privately owned, Lavendon, Bucks
	XW544	HS Buccaneer S2B (8857M) [O]	Privately owned, Bruntingthorpe
	XW547	HS Buccaneer S2B (9095M/9169M) [R]	RAF Museum, Hendon
	XW550	HS Buccaneer S2B <ff>	Privately owned, West Horndon, Essex
	XW560	SEPECAT Jaguar S <ff>	Boscombe Down Aviation Collection, Old Sarum
	XW563	SEPECAT Jaguar S (*XX822*/8563M)	County Hall, Norwich, on display
	XW566	SEPECAT Jaguar B	Farnborough Air Sciences Trust, Farnborough
	XW612	WS Scout AH1 (G-BXRR)	Privately owned, North Weald
	XW613	WS Scout AH1 (G-BXRS)	Privately owned, New Milton, Hants
	XW616	WS Scout AH1	AAC Dishforth, instructional use
	XW630	HS Harrier GR3	RNAS Yeovilton, Fire Section
	XW635	Beagle D5/180 (G-AWSW)	Privately owned, Spanhoe
	XW664	HS Nimrod R1	East Midlands Airport Aeropark
	XW666	HS Nimrod R1 <ff>	Aeroventure, Doncaster
	XW763	HS Harrier GR3 (9002M/9041M) <ff>	Privately owned, Wigston, Leics
	XW768	HS Harrier GR3 (9072M) [N]	MoD DFTDC, Manston
	XW784	Mitchell-Procter Kittiwake I (G-BBRN) [VL]	Privately owned, RNAS Yeovilton
	XW795	WS Scout AH1	Blessingbourne Museum, Fivemiletown, Co Tyrone, NI
	XW796	WS Scout AH1	Gunsmoke Paintball, Hadleigh, Suffolk
	XW838	WS Lynx (TAD 009)	DSEME SEAE, Arborfield
	XW839	WS Lynx	The Helicopter Museum, Weston-super-Mare
	XW844	WS Gazelle AH1	Vector Aerospace Fleetlands Apprentice School
	XW846	WS Gazelle AH1	AAC No 665 Sqn/5 Regt, Aldergrove
	XW847	WS Gazelle AH1	AAC MPSU, Middle Wallop

Serial	Type (code/other identity)	Owner/operator location or fate	Notes
XW848	WS Gazelle AH1 [D]	Privately owned, Stapleford Tawney	
XW849	WS Gazelle AH1 <ff>	AAC MPSU, Middle Wallop	
XW851	WS Gazelle AH1	Privately owned, Durham	
XW852	WS Gazelle HCC4 (9331M)	DSAE, No 1 SoTT, Cosford	
XW854	WS Gazelle HT2 (G-TIZZ) [46/CU]	*Sold to Russia, December 2012*	
XW855	WS Gazelle HCC4	RAF Museum, Hendon	
XW858	WS Gazelle HT3 (G-ONNE) [C]	Privately owned, Steeple Bumstead, Cambs	
XW860	WS Gazelle HT2 (TAD 021)	DSEME SEAE, Arborfield	
XW862	WS Gazelle HT3 (G-CBKC) [D]	Privately owned, Fowlmere	
XW863	WS Gazelle HT2 (TAD 022)	Privately owned, Fairoaks	
XW864	WS Gazelle HT2 [54/CU]	FAA Museum, stored RNAS Yeovilton	
XW865	WS Gazelle AH1 [5C]	AAC No 29 Flt, BATUS, Suffield, Canada	
XW870	WS Gazelle HT3 (9299M) [F]	MoD DFTDC, Manston	
XW888	WS Gazelle AH1 (TAD 017)	DSEME SEAE, Arborfield	
XW889	WS Gazelle AH1 (TAD 018)	*Currently not known*	
XW890	WS Gazelle HT2	RNAS Yeovilton, on display	
XW892	WS Gazelle AH1 (G-CGJX/9292M) [C]	Privately owned, Babcary, Somerset	
XW897	WS Gazelle AH1	DSAE, No 1 SoTT, Cosford	
XW899	WS Gazelle AH1 [Z]	DSAE, No 1 SoTT, Cosford	
XW900	WS Gazelle AH1 (TAD 900)	Army, Bramley, Hants	
XW902	WS Gazelle HT3 (G-CGJY) [H]	Privately owned, Hurstbourne Tarrant, Hants	
XW904	WS Gazelle AH1 [H]	AAC MPSU, Middle Wallop	
XW906	WS Gazelle HT3 [J]	QinetiQ Boscombe Down, Apprentice School	
XW908	WS Gazelle AH1 [A]	QinetiQ, Boscombe Down (spares use)	
XW909	WS Gazelle AH1	Privately owned, Stapleford Tawney	
XW912	WS Gazelle AH1 (TAD 019)	DSEME SEAE, Arborfield	
XW913	WS Gazelle AH1	Privately owned, Stapleford Tawney	
XW917	HS Harrier GR3 (8975M)	NATS Air Traffic Control Centre, Swanwick	
XW922	HS Harrier GR3 (8885M)	MoD DFTDC, Manston	
XW923	HS Harrier GR3 (8724M) <ff>	Harrier Heritage Centre, Wittering	
XW924	HS Harrier GR3 (9073M) [G]	RAF Coningsby, preserved	
XW927	HS Harrier T4 <ff>	Privately owned, South Molton, Devon	
XW934	HS Harrier T4 [Y]	Farnborough Air Sciences Trust, Farnborough	
XW994	Northrop Chukar D1	FAA Museum, stored RNAS Yeovilton	
XW999	Northrop Chukar D1	Davidstow Airfield & Cornwall At War Museum	
XX108	SEPECAT Jaguar GR1(mod)	Imperial War Museum, Duxford	
XX109	SEPECAT Jaguar GR1 (8918M) [GH]	City of Norwich Aviation Museum	
XX110	SEPECAT Jaguar GR1 (8955M) [EP]	DSAE, No 1 SoTT, Cosford	
XX110	SEPECAT Jaguar GR1 <R> (BAPC 169)	DSAE, No 1 SoTT, Cosford	
XX112	SEPECAT Jaguar GR3A [EA]	DSAE, No 1 SoTT, Cosford	
XX115	SEPECAT Jaguar GR1 (8821M) (fuselage)	DSAE, No 1 SoTT, Cosford	
XX116	SEPECAT Jaguar GR3A [EO]	MoD DFTDC, Manston	
XX117	SEPECAT Jaguar GR3A [ES]	DSAE, No 1 SoTT, Cosford	
XX119	SEPECAT Jaguar GR3A (8898M) [AI]$	DSAE, No 1 SoTT, Cosford	
XX121	SEPECAT Jaguar GR1 [EQ]	Privately owned, Charlwood, Surrey	
XX139	SEPECAT Jaguar T4 [PT]	Privately owned, Sproughton	
XX140	SEPECAT Jaguar T2 (9008M) <ff>	Privately owned, Chesterfield	
XX141	SEPECAT Jaguar T2A (9297M) [Y]	DCAE, TCF, RAFC Cranwell	
XX144	SEPECAT Jaguar T2A [U]	Privately owned, Sproughton	
XX145	SEPECAT Jaguar T2A	Privately owned, Bruntingthorpe	
XX146	SEPECAT Jaguar T4 [GT]	Privately owned, Sproughton	
XX150	SEPECAT Jaguar T4 [FY]	Privately owned, Bentwaters	
XX153	WS Lynx AH1 (9320M)	Museum of Army Flying, Middle Wallop	
XX154	HS Hawk T1	MoD/ETPS, Boscombe Down	
XX156	HS Hawk T1 [156]	RAF No 4 FTS/208(R) Sqn, Valley	
XX157	HS Hawk T1A $	RN FRADU, Culdrose	
XX158	HS Hawk T1A [158]	RAF No 4 FTS/208(R) Sqn, Valley	
XX159	HS Hawk T1A $	RN FRADU, Culdrose	
XX160	HS Hawk T1 [160]	RN, stored Shawbury	

Notes	Serial	Type (code/other identity)	Owner/operator location or fate
	XX161	HS Hawk T1W [161]	RAF, stored Shawbury
	XX162	HS Hawk T1	RAF Centre of Aviation Medicine, Boscombe Down
	XX165	HS Hawk T1 [165]	RN, stored Shawbury
	XX167	HS Hawk T1W [167]	RAF, stored Shawbury
	XX168	HS Hawk T1 [168]	RN, stored Shawbury
	XX169	HS Hawk T1 [169]	RN, stored Shawbury
	XX170	HS Hawk T1 [170]	RN FRADU, Culdrose
	XX171	HS Hawk T1 [171]	RAF, stored Shawbury
	XX172	HS Hawk T1 [172]	RN, stored Shawbury
	XX173	HS Hawk T1	RN, stored Shawbury
	XX174	HS Hawk T1 [174]	RAF, stored Shawbury
	XX175	HS Hawk T1 [175]	RAF, stored Shawbury
	XX176	HS Hawk T1W [176]	RAF, stored Shawbury
	XX177	HS Hawk T1	RAF *Red Arrows*, Scampton
	XX178	HS Hawk T1W [178]	RAF, stored Shawbury
	XX181	HS Hawk T1W [181]	RAF, stored Shawbury
	XX184	HS Hawk T1 [CQ]	RAF No 100 Sqn, Leeming
	XX185	HS Hawk T1 [185]	RAF, stored Shawbury
	XX187	HS Hawk T1A [187]	RAF No 4 FTS/208(R) Sqn, Valley
	XX188	HS Hawk T1A [188]	RAF No 4 FTS/208(R) Sqn, Valley
	XX189	HS Hawk T1A [CR]	RAF No 100 Sqn, Leeming
	XX190	HS Hawk T1A [CN]	RAF, stored Shawbury
	XX191	HS Hawk T1A [191]	RAF, stored Shawbury
	XX194	HS Hawk T1A [194]	RAF No 4 FTS/208(R) Sqn, Valley
	XX195	HS Hawk T1W [195]	RAF, stored Shawbury
	XX198	HS Hawk T1A [CG]	RAF No 100 Sqn, Leeming
	XX199	HS Hawk T1A [199]	RAF No 4 FTS/208(R) Sqn, Valley
	XX200	HS Hawk T1A [200]	RAF No 100 Sqn, Leeming
	XX201	HS Hawk T1A	RAF No 4 FTS/208(R) Sqn, Valley
	XX202	HS Hawk T1A [CF]	RAF No 100 Sqn, Leeming
	XX203	HS Hawk T1A [CC]	RAF No 100 Sqn, Leeming
	XX204	HS Hawk T1A [204]	RAF No 4 FTS/208(R) Sqn, Valley
	XX205	HS Hawk T1A $	RN FRADU, Culdrose
	XX217	HS Hawk T1A [217]	RN FRADU, Culdrose
	XX218	HS Hawk T1A [218]	RAF No 4 FTS/208(R) Sqn, Valley
	XX219	HS Hawk T1A	RAF *Red Arrows*, Scampton
	XX220	HS Hawk T1A [220]	RAF, stored Shawbury
	XX221	HS Hawk T1A [221]	RN FRADU, Culdrose (on repair)
	XX222	HS Hawk T1A [CI]	RAF, stored Shawbury
	XX223	HS Hawk T1 <ff>	Privately owned, Charlwood, Surrey
	XX224	HS Hawk T1W [224]	RAF, stored Shawbury
	XX225	HS Hawk T1 [225]	RN, stored Shawbury
	XX226	HS Hawk T1 [226]	RN, stored Shawbury
	XX227	HS Hawk T1 <R> (*XX226*/BAPC 152)	RAF M&RU, Bottesford
	XX227	HS Hawk T1A	RAF *Red Arrows*, Scampton
	XX228	HS Hawk T1A [CG]	RAF, stored Shawbury
	XX230	HS Hawk T1A $	RAF No 4 FTS/208(R) Sqn, Valley
	XX231	HS Hawk T1W [213]	RAF, stored Shawbury
	XX232	HS Hawk T1 [232]	RAF, stored Shawbury
	XX234	HS Hawk T1 [234]	RAF, stored Shawbury
	XX235	HS Hawk T1W [235]	RAF, stored Shawbury
	XX236	HS Hawk T1W [CP]	RAF No 100 Sqn, Leeming
	XX237	HS Hawk T1	RAF, stored Shawbury
	XX238	HS Hawk T1 [238]	RAF, stored Shawbury
	XX239	HS Hawk T1W [239]	RAF, stored Shawbury
	XX240	HS Hawk T1 [240]	RN FRADU, Culdrose
	XX242	HS Hawk T1	RAF *Red Arrows*, Scampton
	XX244	HS Hawk T1	RAF *Red Arrows*, Scampton
	XX245	HS Hawk T1	RAF *Red Arrows*, Scampton
	XX246	HS Hawk T1A [95-Y] $	RAF No 100 Sqn, Leeming

Serial	Type (code/other identity)	Owner/operator location or fate	Notes
XX247	HS Hawk T1A [247]	RAF, stored Shawbury	
XX248	HS Hawk T1A [CJ]	RAF, stored Shawbury	
XX250	HS Hawk T1 [250]	RAF No 4 FTS/208(R) Sqn, Valley	
XX253	HS Hawk T1A	RAF Scampton, on display	
XX254	HS Hawk T1A <ff>	*Scrapped at St Athan*	
XX254	HS Hawk T1A	*Scrapped*	
XX254	HS Hawk T1A <R>	Privately owned, Marlow, Bucks	
XX255	HS Hawk T1A [CL]	RAF No 100 Sqn, Leeming	
XX256	HS Hawk T1A [256]	RAF No 4 FTS/208(R) Sqn, Valley	
XX257	HS Hawk T1A (fuselage)	Privately owned, Charlwood, Surrey	
XX258	HS Hawk T1A [CE]	RAF No 100 Sqn, Leeming	
XX260	HS Hawk T1A	RAF, stored Shawbury	
XX261	HS Hawk T1A $	RN FRADU, Culdrose	
XX263	HS Hawk T1A	RAF *Red Arrows*, Scampton	
XX264	HS Hawk T1A	RAF *Red Arrows*, Scampton	
XX265	HS Hawk T1A [265]	RAF, stored Shawbury	
XX266	HS Hawk T1A	RAF *Red Arrows*, Scampton	
XX278	HS Hawk T1A $	RAF No 4 FTS/208(R) Sqn, Valley	
XX280	HS Hawk T1A [CM]	RAF No 100 Sqn, Leeming	
XX281	HS Hawk T1A	RN FRADU, Culdrose	
XX283	HS Hawk T1W [283]	RAF No 4 FTS/208(R) Sqn, Valley	
XX284	HS Hawk T1A [CA]	RAF, stored Shawbury	
XX285	HS Hawk T1A [CB]	RAF No 100 Sqn, Leeming	
XX286	HS Hawk T1A [286]	RAF, stored Shawbury	
XX287	HS Hawk T1A [287]	RAF No 4 FTS/208(R) Sqn, Valley	
XX289	HS Hawk T1A [CO]	RAF, stored Shawbury	
XX290	HS Hawk T1W [CU]	RAF, stored Shawbury	
XX292	HS Hawk T1	RAF, stored Shawbury	
XX294	HS Hawk T1	RAF, stored Shawbury	
XX295	HS Hawk T1W [295]	RAF, stored Shawbury	
XX296	HS Hawk T1 [296]	RAF, stored Shawbury	
XX299	HS Hawk T1W [299]	RAF, stored Shawbury	
XX301	HS Hawk T1A $	RN FRADU, Culdrose	
XX303	HS Hawk T1A	RN FRADU, Culdrose	
XX304	HS Hawk T1A <rf>	Cardiff International Airport Fire Section	
XX306	HS Hawk T1A	RAF, stored Shawbury	
XX307	HS Hawk T1 [307]	RAF, stored Shawbury	
XX308	HS Hawk T1	RAF *Red Arrows*, Scampton	
XX308	HS Hawk T1 <R> (*XX263*/BAPC 171)	RAF M&RU, Bottesford	
XX309	HS Hawk T1	RAF, stored Shawbury	
XX310	HS Hawk T1W [310]	RAF, stored Shawbury	
XX311	HS Hawk T1	RAF *Red Arrows*, Scampton	
XX312	HS Hawk T1W	RAF, stored Shawbury	
XX313	HS Hawk T1W [313]	RAF, stored Shawbury	
XX314	HS Hawk T1W [314]	RAF, stored Shawbury	
XX315	HS Hawk T1A [315]	RAF No 4 FTS/208(R) Sqn, Valley	
XX316	HS Hawk T1A [316]	RN FRADU, Culdrose	
XX317	HS Hawk T1A [317]	RAF No 4 FTS/208(R) Sqn, Valley	
XX318	HS Hawk T1A [95-Y] $	RAF No 100 Sqn, Leeming	
XX319	HS Hawk T1A	RAF *Red Arrows*, Scampton	
XX320	HS Hawk T1A <ff>	RAF Scampton Historical Aviation Museum	
XX321	HS Hawk T1A [CI]	RAF No 100 Sqn, Leeming	
XX322	HS Hawk T1A	RAF *Red Arrows*, Scampton	
XX323	HS Hawk T1A	RAF *Red Arrows*, Scampton	
XX324	HS Hawk T1A	RAF No 4 FTS/208(R) Sqn, Valley	
XX325	HS Hawk T1A	RAF *Red Arrows*, Scampton	
XX326	HS Hawk T1A <ff>	MoD/DSG, St Athan	
XX326	HS Hawk T1A	MoD/BAE Systems, Brough (on rebuild)	
XX327	HS Hawk T1	RAF Centre of Aviation Medicine, Boscombe Down	
XX329	HS Hawk T1A [CJ]	RAF No 100 Sqn, Leeming	

Notes	*Serial*	*Type (code/other identity)*	*Owner/operator location or fate*
	XX330	HS Hawk T1A [330]	RN FRADU, Culdrose
	XX331	HS Hawk T1A [331]	RN, stored Shawbury
	XX332	HS Hawk T1A [CD]	RAF No 100 Sqn, Leeming
	XX335	HS Hawk T1A [335]	RAF, stored Shawbury
	XX337	HS Hawk T1A	RN FRADU, Culdrose
	XX338	HS Hawk T1	RAF No 4 FTS/208(R) Sqn, Valley
	XX339	HS Hawk T1A [CK]	RAF No 100 Sqn, Leeming
	XX341	HS Hawk T1 ASTRA	MoD/ETPS, Boscombe Down
	XX342	HS Hawk T1 [2]	MoD/ETPS, Boscombe Down
	XX343	HS Hawk T1 [3] (fuselage)	Boscombe Down Aviation Collection, Old Sarum
	XX345	HS Hawk T1A [CE]	RAF, stored Shawbury
	XX346	HS Hawk T1A [CH]	RAF No 100 Sqn, Leeming
	XX348	HS Hawk T1A [348]	RAF Leeming, RTP
	XX349	HS Hawk T1W	RAF Valley (for display)
	XX350	HS Hawk T1A [350]	RAF, stored Shawbury
	XX351	HS Hawk T1A	RAF, stored Shawbury
	XX371	WS Gazelle AH1 (G-CHLU)	Privately owned, Stapleford Tawney
	XX372	WS Gazelle AH1	MoD/QinetiQ, Boscombe Down
	XX375	WS Gazelle AH1	Privately owned, Shepherds Bush
	XX378	WS Gazelle AH1 [Q]	AAC, stored Shawbury
	XX379	WS Gazelle AH1 [Y]	AAC, stored Shawbury
	XX380	WS Gazelle AH1 [A]	Wattisham Airfield Museum
	XX381	WS Gazelle AH1	Privately owned, Welbeck
	XX383	WS Gazelle AH1 [D]	Privately owned, Stapleford Tawney
	XX384	WS Gazelle AH1	AAC Dishforth, instructional use
	XX386	WS Gazelle AH1	Privately owned, Stapleford Tawney
	XX387	WS Gazelle AH1 (TAD 014)	Privately owned, stored Cranfield
	XX392	WS Gazelle AH1	Army, Middle Wallop, preserved
	XX394	WS Gazelle AH1 [X]	Privately owned, Stapleford Tawney
	XX396	WS Gazelle HT3 (8718M) [N]	DCAE, TCF, RAFC Cranwell
	XX398	WS Gazelle AH1	Privately owned, Stapleford Tawney
	XX399	WS Gazelle AH1 [B]	AAC, stored Shawbury
	XX403	WS Gazelle AH1 [U]	AAC, stored Shawbury
	XX405	WS Gazelle AH1	AAC No 667 Sqn/7 Rgt, Middle Wallop
	XX406	WS Gazelle HT3 (G-CBSH) [P]	Privately owned, Rochester
	XX409	WS Gazelle AH1	Privately owned, Stapleford Tawney
	XX411	WS Gazelle AH1 [X]	Aeroventure, Doncaster
	XX411	WS Gazelle AH1 <rf>	FAA Museum, RNAS Yeovilton
	XX412	WS Gazelle AH1 [B]	DSAE, No 1 SoTT, Cosford
	XX414	WS Gazelle AH1 [V]	Privately owned, Badgers Mount, Kent
	XX416	WS Gazelle AH1	Privately owned, Stapleford Tawney
	XX418	WS Gazelle AH1	Privately owned, Hurstbourne Tarrant, Hants
	XX419	WS Gazelle AH1	AAC MPSU, Middle Wallop
	XX431	WS Gazelle HT2 (9300M) [43/CU]	RAF Shawbury, for display
	XX433	WS Gazelle AH1 <ff>	Privately owned, Hurstbourne Tarrant, Hants
	XX435	WS Gazelle AH1 (fuselage)	QinetiQ, Boscombe Down (spares use)
	XX436	WS Gazelle AH1 (G-ZZLE)	Privately owned, Yorkshire
	XX437	WS Gazelle AH1	Privately owned, Stapleford Tawney
	XX438	WS Gazelle AH1 [F]	Privately owned, Stapleford Tawney
	XX439	WS Gazelle AH1 (G-CHLW)	Privately owned, Stapleford Tawney
	XX440	WS Gazelle AH1 (G-BCHN/G-CHBJ)	Privately owned, Stapleford Tawney
	XX442	WS Gazelle AH1 [E]	AAC, stored Shawbury
	XX443	WS Gazelle AH1 [Y]	DSMarE, *stored HMS Sultan*, Gosport
	XX444	WS Gazelle AH1	Wattisham Airfield Museum
	XX445	WS Gazelle AH1 [T]	Privately owned, Stapleford Tawney
	XX447	WS Gazelle AH1 [D1]	AAC, stored Shawbury
	XX449	WS Gazelle AH1	MoD/QinetiQ, Boscombe Down
	XX453	WS Gazelle AH1	MoD/QinetiQ, Boscombe Down
	XX454	WS Gazelle AH1 (TAD 023) (fuselage)	DSEME SEAE, Arborfield
	XX455	WS Gazelle AH1	Privately owned, Stapleford Tawney

Serial	Type (code/other identity)	Owner/operator location or fate	Notes
XX456	WS Gazelle AH1	Privately owned, Stapleford Tawney	
XX457	WS Gazelle AH1 (TAD 001)	East Midlands Airport Aeropark	
XX460	WS Gazelle AH1	AAC, stored Shawbury	
XX462	WS Gazelle AH1 [W]	Privately owned, Stapleford Tawney	
XX466	HS Hunter T66B/T7	Guernsey Airport Fire Section	
XX467	HS Hunter T66B/T7 (XL605/G-TVII) [86]	Privately owned, Bruntingthorpe	
XX477	HP137 Jetstream T1 (G-AXXS/8462M) <ff>	Aeroventure, Doncaster	
XX478	HP137 Jetstream T2 (G-AXXT) [564/CU]	Privately owned, Sproughton	
XX479	HP137 Jetstream T2 (G-AXUR)	RN, Predannack Fire School	
XX481	HP137 Jetstream T2 (G-AXUP) [560/CU]	Privately owned, Sproughton	
XX482	SA Jetstream T1 [J]	Privately owned, Hixon, Staffs	
XX483	SA Jetstream T2 [562] <ff>	Dumfries & Galloway Avn Mus, Dumfries	
XX486	SA Jetstream T2 [567/CU]	Privately owned, Sproughton	
XX487	SA Jetstream T2 [568/CU]	Barry Technical College, instructional use	
XX491	SA Jetstream T1 [K]	Northbrook College, Shoreham, instructional use	
XX492	SA Jetstream T1 [A]	Newark Air Museum, Winthorpe	
XX494	SA Jetstream T1 [B]	Privately owned, Bruntingthorpe	
XX495	SA Jetstream T1 [C]	Bedford College, instructional use	
XX496	SA Jetstream T1 [D]	RAF Museum, Cosford	
XX499	SA Jetstream T1 [G]	Brooklands Museum, Weybridge	
XX500	SA Jetstream T1 [H]	Privately owned, Pinewood Studios	
XX510	WS Lynx HAS2 [69/DD]	SFDO, RNAS Culdrose	
XX513	SA Bulldog T1 (G-KKKK) [10]	Privately owned, Meppershall	
XX515	SA Bulldog T1 (G-CBBC) [4]	Privately owned, Blackbushe	
XX518	SA Bulldog T1 (G-UDOG) [S]	Privately owned, Ursel, Belgium	
XX520	SA Bulldog T1 (9288M) [A]	No 172 Sqn ATC, Haywards Heath	
XX521	SA Bulldog T1 (G-CBEH) [H]	Privately owned, Charney Bassett, Oxon	
XX522	SA Bulldog T1 (G-DAWG) [06]	Privately owned, Blackpool	
XX524	SA Bulldog T1 (G-DDOG) [04]	Privately owned, Malaga, Spain	
XX525	SA Bulldog T1 (G-CBJJ) [03]	Privately owned, Kortrijk, Belgium	
XX528	SA Bulldog T1 (G-BZON) [D]	Privately owned, Earls Colne	
XX530	SA Bulldog T1 (XX637/9197M) [F]	No 2175 Sqn ATC, RAF Kinloss	
XX534	SA Bulldog T1 (G-EDAV) [B]	Privately owned, Tollerton	
XX537	SA Bulldog T1 (G-CBCB) [C]	Privately owned, RAF Halton	
XX538	SA Bulldog T1 (G-TDOG) [O]	Privately owned, Shobdon	
XX539	SA Bulldog T1 [L]	Privately owned, Derbyshire	
XX543	SA Bulldog T1 (G-CBAB) [F]	Privately owned, Duxford	
XX546	SA Bulldog T1 (G-WINI) [03]	Privately owned, Conington	
XX549	SA Bulldog T1 (G-CBID) [6]	Privately owned, White Waltham	
XX550	SA Bulldog T1 (G-CBBL) [Z]	Privately owned, Abbeyshrule, Eire	
XX551	SA Bulldog T1 (G-BZDP) [E]	Privately owned, Boscombe Down	
XX554	SA Bulldog T1 (G-BZMD) [09]	Privately owned, Wellesbourne Mountford	
XX557	SA Bulldog T1	Privately owned, stored Fort Paull, Yorks	
XX561	SA Bulldog T1 (G-BZEP) [7]	Privately owned, Biggin Hill	
XX611	SA Bulldog T1 (G-CBDK) [7]	Privately owned, Coventry	
XX612	SA Bulldog T1 (G-BZXC) [A,03]	Ayr College, instructional use	
XX614	SA Bulldog T1 (G-GGRR) [V]	Privately owned, Enstone	
XX619	SA Bulldog T1 (G-CBBW) [T]	Privately owned, Coventry	
XX621	SA Bulldog T1 (G-CBEF) [H]	Privately owned, Leicester	
XX622	SA Bulldog T1 (G-CBGX) [B]	Privately owned, Shoreham	
XX623	SA Bulldog T1 [M]	Privately owned, Hurstbourne Tarrant, Hants	
XX624	SA Bulldog T1 (G-KDOG) [E]	Privately owned, Ursel, Belgium	
XX626	SA Bulldog T1 (9290M/G-CDVV) [W,02]	Privately owned, Abbots Bromley, Staffs	
XX628	SA Bulldog T1 (G-CBFU) [9]	Privately owned, Faversham	
XX629	SA Bulldog T1 (G-BZXZ) [V]	Privately owned, Wellesbourne Mountford	
XX630	SA Bulldog T1 (G-SIJW) [5]	Privately owned, Cranfield	
XX631	SA Bulldog T1 (G-BZXS) [W]	Privately owned, Sligo, Eire	
XX633	SA Bulldog T1 [X]	Privately owned, Diseworth, Leics	
XX634	SA Bulldog T1 [T]	Newark Air Museum, Winthorpe	
XX636	SA Bulldog T1 (G-CBFP) [Y]	Privately owned, Empringham, Rutland	

Notes	Serial	Type (code/other identity)	Owner/operator location or fate
	XX638	SA Bulldog T1 (G-DOGG)	Privately owned, Hurstbourne Tarrant, Hants
	XX639	SA Bulldog T1 (F-AZTF) [D]	Privately owned, La Baule, France
	XX654	SA Bulldog T1 [3]	RAF Museum, Cosford
	XX655	SA Bulldog T1 (9294M) [V] <ff>	Aeroventure, Doncaster
	XX656	SA Bulldog T1 [C]	Privately owned, Derbyshire
	XX658	SA Bulldog T1 (G-BZPS) [07]	Privately owned, Wellesbourne Mountford
	XX659	SA Bulldog T1 [E]	Privately owned, Derbyshire
	XX664	SA Bulldog T1 (F-AZTV) [04]	Privately owned, Pontoise, France
	XX665	SA Bulldog T1 (9289M)	No 2409 Sqn ATC, Halton
	XX667	SA Bulldog T1 (G-BZFN) [16]	Privately owned, Ronaldsway, IoM
	XX668	SA Bulldog T1 (G-CBAN) [1]	Privately owned, St Athan
	XX669	SA Bulldog T1 (8997M) [B]	Aeroventure, Doncaster
	XX671	SA Bulldog T1 [D]	Privately owned, Diseworth, Leics
	XX687	SA Bulldog T1 [F]	Barry Technical College, Cardiff Airport
	XX690	SA Bulldog T1 [A]	Privately owned, Strathaven, S Lanarks
	XX692	SA Bulldog T1 (G-BZMH) [A]	Privately owned, Wellesbourne Mountford
	XX693	SA Bulldog T1 (G-BZML) [07]	Privately owned, Elmsett
	XX694	SA Bulldog T1 (G-CBBS) [E]	Privately owned, Newcastle
	XX695	SA Bulldog T1 (G-CBBT)	Privately owned, Fishburn
	XX698	SA Bulldog T1 (G-BZME) [9]	Privately owned, Breighton
	XX699	SA Bulldog T1 (G-CBCV) [F]	*To Australia, 28 February 2012*
	XX700	SA Bulldog T1 (G-CBEK) [17]	Privately owned, Blackbushe
	XX702	SA Bulldog T1 (G-CBCR) [π]	Privately owned, Egginton
	XX704	SA122 Bulldog (G-BCUV/G-112)	Privately owned, Bournemouth
	XX705	SA Bulldog T1 [5]	QinetiQ Boscombe Down, Apprentice School
	XX707	SA Bulldog T1 (G-CBDS) [4]	Privately owned, Caernarfon
	XX711	SA Bulldog T1 (G-CBBU) [X]	Privately owned, stored Fishburn
	XX720	SEPECAT Jaguar GR3A [FL]	Privately owned, Sproughton
	XX722	SEPECAT Jaguar GR1 (9252M) <ff>	RAF St Athan, instructional use
	XX723	SEPECAT Jaguar GR3A [EU]	DSAE, No 1 SoTT, Cosford
	XX724	SEPECAT Jaguar GR3A [EC]	DSAE, No 1 SoTT, Cosford
	XX725	SEPECAT Jaguar GR3A [T]	DSAE, No 1 SoTT, Cosford
	XX726	SEPECAT Jaguar GR1 (8947M) [EB]	DSAE, No 1 SoTT, Cosford
	XX727	SEPECAT Jaguar GR1 (8951M) [ER]	DSAE, No 1 SoTT, Cosford
	XX729	SEPECAT Jaguar GR3A [EL]	DSAE, No 1 SoTT, Cosford
	XX733	SEPECAT Jaguar GR1B [EB] (wreck)	Privately owned, Faygate
	XX734	SEPECAT Jaguar GR1 (8816M)	Gatwick Aviation Museum, Charlwood
	XX736	SEPECAT Jaguar GR1 (9110M) <ff>	Aeroventure, Doncaster
	XX738	SEPECAT Jaguar GR3A [ED]	DSAE, No 1 SoTT, Cosford
	XX739	SEPECAT Jaguar GR1 (8902M) [I]	RAF Syerston, instructional use
	XX741	SEPECAT Jaguar GR1A [04]	Bentwaters Cold War Museum
	XX743	SEPECAT Jaguar GR1 (8949M) [EG]	DSAE, No 1 SoTT, Cosford
	XX744	SEPECAT Jaguar GR1 (9251M)	Mayhem Paintball, Abridge, Essex
	XX745	SEPECAT Jaguar GR1A <ff>	No 1350 Sqn ATC, Fareham
	XX746	SEPECAT Jaguar GR1 (8895M) [S]	DSAE, No 1 SoTT, Cosford
	XX747	SEPECAT Jaguar GR1 (8903M)	DCAE, TCF, RAFC Cranwell
	XX748	SEPECAT Jaguar GR3A [EG]	DSAE, No 1 SoTT, Cosford
	XX751	SEPECAT Jaguar GR1 (8937M) [10]	RAF Syerston, instructional use
	XX752	SEPECAT Jaguar GR3A [EK]	DSAE, No 1 SoTT, Cosford
	XX753	SEPECAT Jaguar GR1 (9087M) <ff>	Newark Air Museum, Winthorpe
	XX756	SEPECAT Jaguar GR1 (8899M) [W]	DSAE, No 1 SoTT, Cosford
	XX757	SEPECAT Jaguar GR1 (8948M) [CU]	*Sold to Brazil, February 2012*
	XX761	SEPECAT Jaguar GR1 (8600M) <ff>	Boscombe Down Aviation Collection, Old Sarum
	XX763	SEPECAT Jaguar GR1 (9009M)	Bournemouth Aviation Museum
	XX764	SEPECAT Jaguar GR1 (9010M)	Privately owned, Woodmancote, W Sussex
	XX765	SEPECAT Jaguar ACT	RAF Museum, Cosford
	XX766	SEPECAT Jaguar GR3A [EF]	DSAE, No 1 SoTT, Cosford
	XX767	SEPECAT Jaguar GR3A [FK]	DSAE, No 1 SoTT, Cosford
	XX818	SEPECAT Jaguar GR1 (8945M) [DE]	DSAE, No 1 SoTT, Cosford
	XX819	SEPECAT Jaguar GR1 (8923M) [CE]	DSAE, No 1 SoTT, Cosford

Serial	Type (code/other identity)	Owner/operator location or fate	Notes
XX821	SEPECAT Jaguar GR1 (8896M) [P]	DSAE, No 1 SoTT, Cosford	
XX824	SEPECAT Jaguar GR1 (9019M) [AD]	DSAE, No 1 SoTT, Cosford	
XX825	SEPECAT Jaguar GR1 (9020M) [BN]	DSAE, No 1 SoTT, Cosford	
XX826	SEPECAT Jaguar GR1 (9021M) <ff>	Privately owned, Shropshire	
XX829	SEPECAT Jaguar T2A [GZ]	Newark Air Museum, Winthorpe	
XX830	SEPECAT Jaguar T2 <ff>	City of Norwich Aviation Museum	
XX832	SEPECAT Jaguar T2A [EZ]	Privately owned, Bentwaters	
XX833	SEPECAT Jaguar T2B	DSAE, No 1 SoTT, Cosford	
XX835	SEPECAT Jaguar T4 [EX]	DSAE, No 1 SoTT, Cosford	
XX836	SEPECAT Jaguar T2A [X]	Privately owned, Sproughton	
XX837	SEPECAT Jaguar T2 (8978M) [Z]	DSAE, No 1 SoTT, Cosford	
XX838	SEPECAT Jaguar T4 [FZ]	Privately owned, Bentwaters	
XX840	SEPECAT Jaguar T4 [EY]	DSAE, No 1 SoTT, Cosford	
XX841	SEPECAT Jaguar T4	Privately owned, Tunbridge Wells	
XX842	SEPECAT Jaguar T2A [FX]	Privately owned, Bentwaters	
XX845	SEPECAT Jaguar T4 [EV]	RN, Predannack Fire School	
XX847	SEPECAT Jaguar T4 [EZ]	DSAE, No 1 SoTT, Cosford	
XX885	HS Buccaneer S2B (9225M/G-HHAA)	Hawker Hunter Aviation, Scampton	
XX888	HS Buccaneer S2B <ff>	Privately owned, Barnstaple	
XX889	HS Buccaneer S2B [T]	Blackburn Buccaneer Society, Bruntingthorpe	
XX892	HS Buccaneer S2B <ff>	Blue Sky Experiences, Methven, Perth & Kinross	
XX894	HS Buccaneer S2B [020/R]	Buccaneer Supporters Club, Bruntingthorpe	
XX897	HS Buccaneer S2B(mod)	*Sold to Ireland, August 2012*	
XX899	HS Buccaneer S2B <ff>	Midland Air Museum, Coventry	
XX900	HS Buccaneer S2B [900]	Cold War Jets Collection, Bruntingthorpe	
XX901	HS Buccaneer S2B	Yorkshire Air Museum, Elvington	
XX907	WS Lynx AH1	Privately owned, Stoke-on-Trent	
XX910	WS Lynx HAS2	The Helicopter Museum, Weston-super-Mare	
XX914	BAC VC10/1103 (8777M) <rf>	RAF Defence Movements School, Brize Norton	
XX919	BAC 1-11/402AP (PI-C1121) <ff>	Boscombe Down Aviation Collection, Old Sarum	
XX946	Panavia Tornado (P02) (8883M)	RAF Museum, Cosford	
XX947	Panavia Tornado (P03) (8797M)	Shoreham Airport, on display	
XX958	SEPECAT Jaguar GR1 (9022M) [BK]	DSAE, No 1 SoTT, Cosford	
XX959	SEPECAT Jaguar GR1 (8953M) [CJ]	DSAE, No 1 SoTT, Cosford	
XX965	SEPECAT Jaguar GR1A (9254M) [C]	DSAE, No 1 SoTT, Cosford	
XX967	SEPECAT Jaguar GR1 (9006M) [AC]	DSAE, No 1 SoTT, Cosford	
XX968	SEPECAT Jaguar GR1 (9007M) [AJ]	DSAE, No 1 SoTT, Cosford	
XX969	SEPECAT Jaguar GR1 (8897M) [01]	DSAE, No 1 SoTT, Cosford	
XX970	SEPECAT Jaguar GR3A [EH]	DSAE, No 1 SoTT, Cosford	
XX974	SEPECAT Jaguar GR3 [FE]	*Sold to The Netherlands*	
XX975	SEPECAT Jaguar GR1 (8905M) [07]	DSAE, No 1 SoTT, Cosford	
XX976	SEPECAT Jaguar GR1 (8906M) [BD]	DSAE, No 1 SoTT, Cosford	
XX977	SEPECAT Jaguar GR1 (9132M) [DL,05] <rf>	Privately owned, Sproughton	
XX979	SEPECAT Jaguar GR1A (9306M) <ff>	Air Defence Radar Museum, Neatishead	
XZ103	SEPECAT Jaguar GR3A [EF]	DSAE, No 1 SoTT, Cosford	
XZ104	SEPECAT Jaguar GR3A [FM]	DSAE, No 1 SoTT, Cosford	
XZ106	SEPECAT Jaguar GR3A [FD,FW]	RAF Manston History Museum	
XZ107	SEPECAT Jaguar GR3A [FH]	Privately owned, Bentwaters	
XZ109	SEPECAT Jaguar GR3A [EN]	DSAE, No 1 SoTT, Cosford	
XZ112	SEPECAT Jaguar GR3A [GW]	DSAE, No 1 SoTT, Cosford	
XZ113	SEPECAT Jaguar GR3 [FD]	Privately owned, Bentwaters	
XZ114	SEPECAT Jaguar GR3 [EO]	DSAE, No 1 SoTT, Cosford	
XZ115	SEPECAT Jaguar GR3 [ER]	DSAE, No 1 SoTT, Cosford	
XZ117	SEPECAT Jaguar GR3 [ES]	DSAE, No 1 SoTT, Cosford	
XZ118	SEPECAT Jaguar GR3	*Scrapped, 2012*	
XZ119	SEPECAT Jaguar GR1A (9266M) [FG]	Royal Scottish Mus'm of Flight, E Fortune	
XZ130	HS Harrier GR3 (9079M) [A]	No 1034 Sqn ATC, Tolworth, Surrey	
XZ131	HS Harrier GR3 (9174M) <ff>	Privately owned, Spark Bridge, Cumbria	
XZ132	HS Harrier GR3 (9168M) [C]	DCAE, TCF, RAFC Cranwell	

Notes	Serial	Type (code/other identity)	Owner/operator location or fate
	XZ133	HS Harrier GR3 [10]	Imperial War Museum, Duxford
	XZ138	HS Harrier GR3 (9040M) <ff>	RAFC Cranwell, Trenchard Hall
	XZ145	HS Harrier T4 [45/DD]	Privately owned, Sproughton
	XZ146	HS Harrier T4 (9281M) [S]	Harrier Heritage Centre, Wittering
	XZ166	WS Lynx HAS2 <ff>	Farnborough Air Sciences Trust, Farnborough
	XZ170	WS Lynx AH9	DSEME SEAE, Arborfield
	XZ171	WS Lynx AH7	Army, Salisbury Plain
	XZ172	WS Lynx AH7	DSEME SEAE, Arborfield
	XZ173	WS Lynx AH7 <ff>	Privately owned, Hixon, Staffs
	XZ174	WS Lynx AH7 <ff>	Defence Coll of Policing, Gosport, instructional use
	XZ175	WS Lynx AH7	Warfighters R6 Centre, Barby, Northants
	XZ176	WS Lynx AH7	AAC No 1 Regt, Gütersloh
	XZ177	WS Lynx AH7	AAC No 9 Regt, Dishforth
	XZ178	WS Lynx AH7 <ff>	Privately owned,
	XZ179	WS Lynx AH7	MoD/Vector Aerospace, Fleetlands
	XZ180	WS Lynx AH7	MoD/Vector Aerospace, Fleetlands
	XZ181	WS Lynx AH1	AAC Middle Wallop Fire Section
	XZ182	WS Lynx AH7 [Z]	AAC No 671 Sqn/7 Regt, Middle Wallop
	XZ183	WS Lynx AH7 <ff>	MoD St Athan, instructional use
	XZ184	WS Lynx AH7	MoD/Vector Aerospace, Fleetlands
	XZ185	WS Lynx AH7	AAC No 1 Regt, Gütersloh
	XZ187	WS Lynx AH7	DSEME SEAE, Arborfield
	XZ188	WS Lynx AH7	DSEME SEAE, Arborfield
	XZ190	WS Lynx AH7 <ff>	AAC MPSU, Middle Wallop
	XZ191	WS Lynx AH7 [A]	AAC No 9 Regt, Dishforth
	XZ192	WS Lynx AH7	AAC No 9 Regt, Dishforth
	XZ193	WS Lynx AH7 <ff>	Privately owned,
	XZ194	WS Lynx AH7 [V]	AAC MPSU, Middle Wallop
	XZ195	WS Lynx AH7 <ff>	Privately owned, Hixon, Staffs
	XZ196	WS Lynx AH7 [T]	AAC No 671 Sqn/7 Regt, Middle Wallop
	XZ197	WS Lynx AH7 <ff>	*To Gütersloh for instructional use, 2012*
	XZ198	WS Lynx AH7 <ff>	*Currently not known*
	XZ203	WS Lynx AH7 [F]	Army, Salisbury Plain
	XZ205	WS Lynx AH7 <ff>	*Destroyed, Leavesden, November 2012*
	XZ206	WS Lynx AH7 <ff>	Privately owned, Hixon, Staffs
	XZ207	WS Lynx AH7 <rf>	DSEME SEAE, Arborfield
	XZ208	WS Lynx AH7	AAC No 671 Sqn/7 Regt, Middle Wallop
	XZ209	WS Lynx AH7 <ff>	MoD JARTS, Boscombe Down
	XZ211	WS Lynx AH7	AAC No 1 Regt, Gütersloh
	XZ212	WS Lynx AH7 [X]	AAC Middle Wallop, GI use
	XZ213	WS Lynx AH1 (TAD 213)	Vector Aerospace Fleetlands Apprentice School
	XZ214	WS Lynx AH7	MoD/Vector Aerospace, Fleetlands
	XZ215	WS Lynx AH7	MoD DFTDC, Manston
	XZ216	WS Lynx AH7	DSEME SEAE, Arborfield
	XZ217	WS Lynx AH7	Privately owned,
	XZ218	WS Lynx AH7	Warfighters R6 Centre, Barby, Northants
	XZ219	WS Lynx AH7 <ff>	Army, Bramley, Hants
	XZ220	WS Lynx AH7 [U]	*Destroyed, Leavesden, November 2012*
	XZ221	WS Lynx AH7 [Z]	AAC No 9 Rgt, Dishforth
	XZ222	WS Lynx AH7	AAC No 657 Sqn, Odiham
	XZ228	WS Lynx HAS3GMS [313]	RN Historic Flight, stored Yeovilton
	XZ229	WS Lynx HAS3GMS [360/MC]	Privately owned, Hixon, Staffs
	XZ230	WS Lynx HAS3GMS <ff>	Privately owned,
	XZ232	WS Lynx HAS3GMS [634]	RN No 702 NAS, Yeovilton
	XZ233	WS Lynx HAS3S [635] $	RN Historic Flight, stored Yeovilton
	XZ234	WS Lynx HAS3S [630]	RN MPSU, Middle Wallop
	XZ235	WS Lynx HAS3S(ICE) [630]	Privately owned, Hixon, Staffs
	XZ236	WS Lynx HMA8 [LST-1]	RN ETS, Yeovilton, GI use
	XZ237	WS Lynx HAS3S [631]	RN Lynx RTP, Yeovilton
	XZ238	WS Lynx HAS3S(ICE) [633]	RN No 702 NAS, Yeovilton

Serial	Type (code/other identity)	Owner/operator location or fate	Notes
XZ239	WS Lynx HAS3GMS [633]	Privately owned, Hixon, Staffs	
XZ245	WS Lynx HAS3GMS [630]	RN GDSH, Middle Wallop	
XZ246	WS Lynx HAS3S(ICE) [434/EE]	MoD/Vector Aerospace, stored Fleetlands	
XZ248	WS Lynx HAS3S [666]	SFDO, RNAS Culdrose	
XZ250	WS Lynx HAS3S [426/PO] $	RN, Portland, Dorset, on display	
XZ252	WS Lynx HAS3S	Privately owned, Hixon, Staffs	
XZ254	WS Lynx HAS3S	Privately owned, Hixon, Staffs	
XZ255	WS Lynx HMA8SRU [313]	RN No 815 NAS, MI Flt, Yeovilton	
XZ257	WS Lynx HAS3S <ff>	Privately owned, Hixon, Staffs	
XZ287	BAe Nimrod AEW3 (9140M) (fuselage)	RAF TSW, Stafford	
XZ290	WS Gazelle AH1	AAC MPSU, Middle Wallop	
XZ291	WS Gazelle AH1	Privately owned, Stapleford Tawney	
XZ292	WS Gazelle AH1	Privately owned, Stapleford Tawney	
XZ294	WS Gazelle AH1 [X]	AAC, stored Shawbury	
XZ295	WS Gazelle AH1	AAC, stored Shawbury	
XZ296	WS Gazelle AH1 [V]	Privately owned, Stapleford Tawney	
XZ298	WS Gazelle AH1 <ff>	AAC Middle Wallop, GI use	
XZ303	WS Gazelle AH1	AAC, stored Shawbury	
XZ304	WS Gazelle AH1	Privately owned, Stapleford Tawney	
XZ305	WS Gazelle AH1 (TAD 020)	DSMarE AESS *HMS Sultan*, Gosport	
XZ307	WS Gazelle AH1 (G-CHBN)	Privately owned, Stapleford Tawney	
XZ308	WS Gazelle AH1	QinetiQ, Boscombe Down (spares use)	
XZ311	WS Gazelle AH1 [U]	AAC, stored Shawbury	
XZ312	WS Gazelle AH1	RAF Henlow, instructional use	
XZ313	WS Gazelle AH1 <ff>	Privately owned, Shotton, Durham	
XZ314	WS Gazelle AH1 [A]	Privately owned, Stapleford Tawney	
XZ315	WS Gazelle AH1 <ff>	Privately owned, Babcary, Somerset	
XZ316	WS Gazelle AH1 [B]	DSEME SEAE, Arborfield	
XZ318	WS Gazelle AH1 (fuselage)	Tong Paintball Park, Shropshire	
XZ320	WS Gazelle AH1	AAC No 665 Sqn/5 Regt, Aldergrove	
XZ322	WS Gazelle AH1 (9283M) [N]	DSAE, No 1 SoTT, Cosford	
XZ323	WS Gazelle AH1	AAC, stored Shawbury	
XZ324	WS Gazelle AH1	Privately owned, Stapleford Tawney	
XZ325	WS Gazelle AH1 [T]	DSEME SEAE, Arborfield	
XZ326	WS Gazelle AH1	AAC No 665 Sqn/5 Regt, Aldergrove	
XZ327	WS Gazelle AH1	AAC Middle Wallop (recruiting aid)	
XZ328	WS Gazelle AH1 [C]	AAC, stored Shawbury	
XZ329	WS Gazelle AH1 (G-BZYD) [J]	Privately owned, East Garston, Bucks	
XZ330	WS Gazelle AH1 [Y]	AAC Wattisham, instructional use	
XZ331	WS Gazelle AH1 [D]	AAC, stored Shawbury	
XZ332	WS Gazelle AH1 [O]	DSEME SEAE, Arborfield	
XZ333	WS Gazelle AH1 [A]	REME Museum, Arborfield	
XZ334	WS Gazelle AH1	AAC No 665 Sqn/5 Regt, Aldergrove	
XZ335	WS Gazelle AH1	North-East Aircraft Museum, stored Usworth	
XZ337	WS Gazelle AH1 [Z]	AAC, stored Shawbury	
XZ338	WS Gazelle AH1 [Y]	Privately owned, Stapleford Tawney	
XZ340	WS Gazelle AH1	AAC No 29 Flt, BATUS, Suffield, Canada	
XZ341	WS Gazelle AH1	AAC, Middle Wallop	
XZ342	WS Gazelle AH1	AAC No 8 Flt, Credenhill	
XZ343	WS Gazelle AH1	AAC, stored Shawbury	
XZ344	WS Gazelle AH1 [Y]	Privately owned, Stapleford Tawney	
XZ345	WS Gazelle AH1 [M]	AAC No 671 Sqn/7 Regt, Middle Wallop	
XZ345	Aérospatiale SA341G Gazelle (G-SFTA) [T]	North-East Aircraft Museum, Usworth	
XZ346	WS Gazelle AH1	AAC Netheravon, at main gate	
XZ347	WS Gazelle AH1	Privately owned, Hurstbourne Tarrant, Hants	
XZ349	WS Gazelle AH1	AAC, stored Shawbury	
XZ356	SEPECAT Jaguar GR3A [FU]	Privately owned, Welshpool	
XZ358	SEPECAT Jaguar GR1A (9262M) [L]	DCAE, TCF, RAFC Cranwell	
XZ360	SEPECAT Jaguar GR3 [FN]	Privately owned, Bentwaters	
XZ363	SEPECAT Jaguar GR1A <R> (*XX824*/BAPC 151) [A]	RAF M&RU, Bottesford	

Notes	Serial	Type (code/other identity)	Owner/operator location or fate
	XZ364	SEPECAT Jaguar GR3A <ff>	Privately owned, Tunbridge Wells
	XZ366	SEPECAT Jaguar GR3A [FC]	Privately owned, Bentwaters
	XZ367	SEPECAT Jaguar GR3 [GP]	DSAE, No 1 SoTT, Cosford
	XZ368	SEPECAT Jaguar GR1 [8900M] [E]	DSAE, No 1 SoTT, Cosford
	XZ369	SEPECAT Jaguar GR3A [EU]	Privately owned, Bentwaters
	XZ370	SEPECAT Jaguar GR1 (9004M) [JB]	DSAE, No 1 SoTT, Cosford
	XZ371	SEPECAT Jaguar GR1 (8907M) [AP]	DSAE, No 1 SoTT, Cosford
	XZ372	SEPECAT Jaguar GR3 [FV]	Aberdeen Airport, on display
	XZ374	SEPECAT Jaguar GR1 (9005M) [JC]	DSAE, stored Cosford
	XZ375	SEPECAT Jaguar GR1A (9255M) <ff>	City of Norwich Aviation Museum
	XZ377	SEPECAT Jaguar GR3A [EP]	DSAE, No 1 SoTT, Cosford
	XZ378	SEPECAT Jaguar GR1A [EP]	Privately owned, Topsham, Devon
	XZ382	SEPECAT Jaguar GR1 (8908M)	Cold War Jets Collection, Bruntingthorpe
	XZ383	SEPECAT Jaguar GR1 (8901M) [AF]	DSAE, No 1 SoTT, Cosford
	XZ384	SEPECAT Jaguar GR1 (8954M) [BC]	DSAE, No 1 SoTT, Cosford
	XZ385	SEPECAT Jaguar GR3A [FT]	Privately owned, Bentwaters
	XZ389	SEPECAT Jaguar GR1 (8946M) [BL]	DSAE, No 1 SoTT, Cosford
	XZ390	SEPECAT Jaguar GR1 (9003M) [DM]	DSAE, No 1 SoTT, Cosford
	XZ391	SEPECAT Jaguar GR3A [ET]	DSAE, No 1 SoTT, Cosford
	XZ392	SEPECAT Jaguar GR3A [EM]	DSAE, No 1 SoTT, Cosford
	XZ394	SEPECAT Jaguar GR3 [FG]	Privately owned, Bentwaters
	XZ396	SEPECAT Jaguar GR3A [EQ]	Privately owned, Bentwaters
	XZ398	SEPECAT Jaguar GR3A [EQ]	DSAE, No 1 SoTT, Cosford
	XZ399	SEPECAT Jaguar GR3A [EJ]	DSAE, No 1 SoTT, Cosford
	XZ400	SEPECAT Jaguar GR3A [FQ]	Privately owned, Bentwaters
	XZ431	HS Buccaneer S2B (9233M) <ff>	Privately owned, Market Drayton, Shropshire
	XZ440	BAe Sea Harrier FA2 [40/DD]	SFDO, RNAS Culdrose
	XZ455	BAe Sea Harrier FA2 [001] (wreck)	Privately owned, Thorpe Wood, N Yorks
	XZ457	BAe Sea Harrier FA2 [104/VL]	Boscombe Down Aviation Collection, Old Sarum
	XZ459	BAe Sea Harrier FA2 [126]	Privately owned, Sussex
	XZ492	BAe Sea Harrier FA2 (wreck)	Privately owned, Faygate
	XZ493	BAe Sea Harrier FRS1 (comp XV760) [001/N]	FAA Museum, RNAS Yeovilton
	XZ493	BAe Sea Harrier FRS1 <ff>	RN Yeovilton, Fire Section
	XZ494	BAe Sea Harrier FA2 [128]	Privately owned, Wedmore, Somerset
	XZ497	BAe Sea Harrier FA2 [126]	Privately owned, Charlwood
	XZ499	BAe Sea Harrier FA2 [003]	FAA Museum, RNAS Yeovilton
	XZ559	Slingsby T61F Venture T2 (G-BUEK)	Privately owned, Tibenham
	XZ570	WS61 Sea King HAS5(mod)	RN, Predannack Fire School
	XZ574	WS61 Sea King HAS6	FAA Museum, RNAS Yeovilton
	XZ575	WS61 Sea King HU5	MoD/AFD/QinetiQ, Boscombe Down
	XZ576	WS61 Sea King HAS6	DSMarE AESS, *HMS Sultan*, Gosport
	XZ578	WS61 Sea King HU5 [30]	RN No 771 NAS, Culdrose
	XZ579	WS61 Sea King HAS6 [707/PW]	DSMarE AESS, *HMS Sultan*, Gosport
	XZ580	WS61 Sea King HC6 [ZB]	DSMarE AESS, *HMS Sultan*, Gosport
	XZ581	WS61 Sea King HAS6 [69/CU]	DSMarE AESS, *HMS Sultan*, Gosport
	XZ585	WS61 Sea King HAR3 [A]	RAF No 202 Sqn, D Flt, Lossiemouth
	XZ586	WS61 Sea King HAR3 [B]	RAF No 202 Sqn, D Flt, Lossiemouth
	XZ587	WS61 Sea King HAR3 [C]	RAF SKAMG, RNAS Yeovilton
	XZ588	WS61 Sea King HAR3 [D]	RAF SKAMG, RNAS Yeovilton
	XZ589	WS61 Sea King HAR3 [E] $	RAF No 22 Sqn, C Flt/No 203(R) Sqn, Valley
	XZ590	WS61 Sea King HAR3 [F]	RAF No 202 Sqn, A Flt, Boulmer
	XZ591	WS61 Sea King HAR3 [G]	MoD/Vector Aerospace, Fleetlands
	XZ592	WS61 Sea King HAR3 [H]	RAF No 202 Sqn, E Flt, Leconfield
	XZ593	WS61 Sea King HAR3 [I]	RAF No 22 Sqn, C Flt/No 203(R) Sqn, Valley
	XZ594	WS61 Sea King HAR3	MoD/Vector Aerospace, Fleetlands
	XZ595	WS61 Sea King HAR3 [K]	RAF No 1564 Flt, Mount Pleasant, FI
	XZ596	WS61 Sea King HAR3 [L]	RAF No 202 Sqn, A Flt, Boulmer
	XZ597	WS61 Sea King HAR3 [M]	RAF No 1564 Flt, Mount Pleasant, FI
	XZ598	WS61 Sea King HAR3 [N]	RAF SKAMG, RNAS Yeovilton
	XZ599	WS61 Sea King HAR3 [P]	RAF No 202 Sqn, E Flt, Leconfield

Serial	*Type (code/other identity)*	*Owner/operator location or fate*	*Notes*
XZ605	WS Lynx AH7 [L]	AAC No 671 Sqn/7 Regt, Middle Wallop	
XZ606	WS Lynx AH7	MoD/Vector Aerospace, Fleetlands	
XZ607	WS Lynx AH7	DSEME SEAE, Arborfield	
XZ608	WS Lynx AH7	AAC No 657 Sqn, Odiham	
XZ609	WS Lynx AH7	AAC No 1 Regt, Gütersloh	
XZ611	WS Lynx AH7 <ff>	Privately owned, Hixon, Staffs	
XZ612	WS Lynx AH7	AAC No 9 Regt, Dishforth	
XZ613	WS Lynx AH7 [F]	AAC Stockwell Hall, Middle Wallop	
XZ615	WS Lynx AH7 <ff>	Privately owned,	
XZ616	WS Lynx AH7	MoD/Vector Aerospace, Fleetlands	
XZ617	WS Lynx AH7	AAC MPSU, Middle Wallop	
XZ630	Panavia Tornado GR1 (8976M)	RAF Halton, on display	
XZ631	Panavia Tornado GR1	Yorkshire Air Museum, Elvington	
XZ641	WS Lynx AH7 [A]	AAC No 671 Sqn/7 Regt, Middle Wallop	
XZ642	WS Lynx AH7	AAC No 667 Sqn/7 Regt, Middle Wallop	
XZ643	WS Lynx AH7 [C]	AAC No 671 Sqn/7 Regt, Middle Wallop	
XZ645	WS Lynx AH7	AAC No 9 Regt, Dishforth	
XZ646	WS Lynx AH7 <ff>	MoD JARTS, Boscombe Down	
XZ646	WS Lynx AH7 (really XZ649)	Bristol University, instructional use	
XZ647	WS Lynx AH7 <ff>	*Currently not known*	
XZ648	WS Lynx AH7 <ff>	Privately owned,	
XZ651	WS Lynx AH7	MoD/Vector Aerospace, Fleetlands	
XZ652	WS Lynx AH7 [A,W]	AAC No 671 Sqn/7 Regt, Middle Wallop	
XZ653	WS Lynx AH7	MoD/Vector Aerospace, Fleetlands	
XZ654	WS Lynx AH7	AAC No 9 Regt, Dishforth	
XZ655	WS Lynx AH7 <ff>	Privately owned,	
XZ661	WS Lynx AH7 [V]	Army, Bramley, Hants	
XZ663	WS Lynx AH7 <ff>	Privately owned, Hixon, Staffs	
XZ664	WS Lynx AH7	Warfighters R6 Centre, Barby, Northants	
XZ665	WS Lynx AH7	Warfighters R6 Centre, Barby, Northants	
XZ666	WS Lynx AH7	DSEME SEAE, Arborfield	
XZ669	WS Lynx AH7 [I]	AAC No 671 Sqn/7 Regt, Middle Wallop	
XZ670	WS Lynx AH7	AAC No 9 Regt, Dishforth	
XZ671	WS Lynx AH7 <ff>	AgustaWestland, Yeovil, instructional use	
XZ672	WS Lynx AH7 <ff>	AAC Middle Wallop, instructional use	
XZ673	WS Lynx AH7	AAC No 1 Regt, Gütersloh	
XZ674	WS Lynx AH7	MoD/Vector Aerospace, Fleetlands	
XZ675	WS Lynx AH7 [H]	Museum of Army Flying, Middle Wallop	
XZ676	WS Lynx AH7 [N]	AAC MPSU, Middle Wallop	
XZ677	WS Lynx AH7	AAC MPSU, Middle Wallop	
XZ678	WS Lynx AH7	AAC No 9 Regt, Dishforth	
XZ679	WS Lynx AH7 [W]	AAC No 1 Regt, Gütersloh	
XZ680	WS Lynx AH7 <ff>	Privately owned, Hixon, Staffs	
XZ689	WS Lynx HMA8SRU [306]	RN No 815 NAS, HQ Flt, Yeovilton	
XZ690	WS Lynx HMA8SRU [300/LA]	RN No 815 NAS, *Lancaster* Flt, Yeovilton	
XZ691	WS Lynx HMA8SRU [304]	RN No 815 NAS, *Westminster* Flt, Yeovilton	
XZ692	WS Lynx HMA8SRU [641] $	MoD/Vector Aerospace, Fleetlands	
XZ693	WS Lynx HAS3S [311]	Privately owned, Hixon, Staffs	
XZ696	WS Lynx HAS3GMS [633]	Privately owned, Hixon, Staffs	
XZ697	WS Lynx HMA8SRU [316]	RN No 815 NAS, MI Flt, Yeovilton	
XZ698	WS Lynx HMA8SRU [642]	RN No 702 NAS, Yeovilton	
XZ699	WS Lynx HAS2	FAA Museum, stored RNAS Yeovilton	
XZ719	WS Lynx HMA8SRU [316]	RN No 702 NAS, Yeovilton	
XZ720	WS Lynx HAS3GMS [410/GC]	FAA Museum, Yeovilton	
XZ721	WS Lynx HAS3GMS [322]	Privately owned, Hixon, Staffs	
XZ722	WS Lynx HMA8SRU [645]$	MoD/Vector Aerospace, Fleetlands	
XZ723	WS Lynx HMA8SRU [474/RM]	RN No 815 NAS, *Richmond* Flt, Yeovilton	
XZ725	WS Lynx HMA8SRU	RN No 815 NAS, HQ Flt, Yeovilton	
XZ726	WS Lynx HMA8SRU [671]	RN No 702 NAS, Yeovilton	
XZ727	WS Lynx HAS3S [634]	RN MPSU, Middle Wallop	

Notes	Serial	Type (code/other identity)	Owner/operator location or fate
	XZ728	WS Lynx HMA8 [326/AW]	RNAS Yeovilton, on display
	XZ729	WS Lynx HMA8SRU [451/DA]	RN No 815 NAS, *Daring* Flt, Yeovilton
	XZ730	WS Lynx HAS3S	Privately owned, Hixon, Staffs
	XZ731	WS Lynx HMA8SRU [302]	RN No 702 NAS, Yeovilton
	XZ732	WS Lynx HMA8SRU [641]	RN No 702 NAS, Yeovilton
	XZ733	WS Lynx HAS3GMS [305]	Privately owned, Hixon, Staffs
	XZ735	WS Lynx HAS3GMS [404]	MoD/Vector Aerospace, stored Fleetlands
	XZ736	WS Lynx HMA8SRU [322/AS]	RN No 815 NAS, HQ Flt, Yeovilton
	XZ791	Northrop Shelduck D1	Davidstow Airfield & Cornwall At War Museum
	XZ795	Northrop Shelduck D1	Museum of Army Flying, Middle Wallop
	XZ920	WS61 Sea King HU5 [707/PW]	MoD/Vector Aerospace, Fleetlands
	XZ921	WS61 Sea King HAS6 [269/N]	DSMarE, stored *HMS Sultan*, Gosport
	XZ922	WS61 Sea King HC6 [ZA]	DSMarE AESS, *HMS Sultan*, Gosport
	XZ930	WS Gazelle HT3 (A2713) [Q]	DSMarE AESS, *HMS Sultan*, Gosport
	XZ934	WS Gazelle HT3 (G-CBSI) [U]	Privately owned, Babcary, Somerset
	XZ935	WS Gazelle HCC4	DSEME SEAE, Arborfield
	XZ936	WS Gazelle HT2 [6]	MoD/ETPS, Boscombe Down
	XZ936	WS Gazelle HT3 (XZ933/G-CGJZ)	Privately owned, Hurstbourne Tarrant, Hants
	XZ939	WS Gazelle HT2 [9]	MoD/ETPS, Boscombe Down
	XZ941	WS Gazelle HT2 (9301M) [B]	DSAE, No 1 SoTT, Cosford
	XZ964	BAe Harrier GR3 [D]	Royal Engineers Museum, Chatham
	XZ966	BAe Harrier GR3 (9221M) [G]	MoD DFTDC, Manston
	XZ968	BAe Harrier GR3 (9222M) [3G]	Muckleborough Collection, Weybourne
	XZ969	BAe Harrier GR3 [69/DD]	RN, Predannack Fire School
	XZ971	BAe Harrier GR3 (9219M)	HQ DSDA, Donnington, Shropshire, on display
	XZ987	BAe Harrier GR3 (9185M) [C]	RAF Stafford, at main gate
	XZ990	BAe Harrier GR3 <ff>	*Currently not known*
	XZ990	BAe Harrier GR3 <rf>	RAF Wittering, derelict
	XZ991	BAe Harrier GR3 (9162M) [3A]	DSAE, No 1 SoTT, Cosford
	XZ993	BAe Harrier GR3 (9240M) <ff>	Privately owned, Welshpool
	XZ994	BAe Harrier GR3 (9170M) [U]	RAF Defence Movements School, Brize Norton
	XZ995	BAe Harrier GR3 (9220M/G-CBGK) [3G]	Privately owned, Dunboyne, Eire
	XZ996	BAe Harrier GR3 [96/DD]	Privately owned, Sproughton
	XZ997	BAe Harrier GR3 (9122M) [V]	RAF Museum, Hendon
	ZA101	BAe Hawk 100 (G-HAWK)	BAE Systems Warton, Overseas Customer Training Centre
	ZA105	WS61 Sea King HAR3	RAF No 22 Sqn, C Flt/No 203(R) Sqn, Valley
	ZA110	BAe Jetstream T2 (F-BTMI) [563/CU]	Aberdeen Airport
	ZA111	BAe Jetstream T2 (9Q-CTC) [565/CU]	SFDO, RNAS Culdrose
	ZA126	WS61 Sea King ASaC7 [191]	MoD/Vector Aerospace, Fleetlands
	ZA127	WS61 Sea King HAS6 [509/CU]	DSMarE, stored *HMS Sultan*, Gosport
	ZA128	WS61 Sea King HAS6 [010]	DSAE, No 1 SoTT, Cosford
	ZA130	WS61 Sea King HU5 [19]	RN No 771 NAS, Prestwick
	ZA131	WS61 Sea King HAS6 [271/N]	DSAE, No 1 SoTT, Cosford
	ZA133	WS61 Sea King HAS6 [831/CU]	MoD/Vector Aerospace, Fleetlands, GI use
	ZA134	WS61 Sea King HU5 [25]	RN No 771 NAS, Prestwick
	ZA135	WS61 Sea King HAS6	Privately owned, Hixon, Staffs
	ZA136	WS61 Sea King HAS6 [018]	DSMarE, AESS, *HMS Sultan*, Gosport (wreck)
	ZA137	WS61 Sea King HU5 [20]	RN No 771 NAS, Culdrose
	ZA144	BAe VC10 K2 (G-ARVC) <ff>	MoD JARTS, Boscombe Down
	ZA147	BAe VC10 K3 (5H-MMT) [F]	RAF No 101 Sqn, Brize Norton
	ZA148	BAe VC10 K3 (5Y-ADA) [G]	RAF No 101 Sqn, Brize Norton
	ZA149	BAe VC10 K3 (5X-UVJ) [H]	RAF No 101 Sqn, Brize Norton
	ZA150	BAe VC10 K3 (5H-MOG) [J]	RAF No 101 Sqn, Brize Norton
	ZA166	WS61 Sea King HU5 [16/CU]	RN No 771 NAS, Culdrose
	ZA167	WS61 Sea King HU5 [22/CU]	RN No 771 NAS, Culdrose
	ZA168	WS61 Sea King HAS6 [830/CU]	DSMarE, AESS, *HMS Sultan*, Gosport
	ZA169	WS61 Sea King HAS6 [515/CW]	DSAE, No 1 SoTT, Cosford
	ZA170	WS61 Sea King HAS5	DSMarE, AESS, *HMS Sultan*, Gosport

Serial	Type (code/other identity)	Owner/operator location or fate	Notes
ZA175	BAe Sea Harrier FA2	Norfolk & Suffolk Avn Museum, Flixton	
ZA176	BAe Sea Harrier FA2 [126/R]	Newark Air Museum, Winthorpe	
ZA195	BAe Sea Harrier FA2	Tangmere Military Aviation Museum	
ZA209	Short MATS-B	Museum of Army Flying, Middle Wallop	
ZA220	Short MATS-B	Privately owned, Awbridge, Hants	
ZA250	BAe Harrier T52 (G-VTOL)	Brooklands Museum, Weybridge	
ZA254	Panavia Tornado F2 (9253M) (fuselage)	*Scrapped*	
ZA267	Panavia Tornado F2 (9284M)	RAF Marham, instructional use	
ZA291	WS61 Sea King HC4 [N]	RN No 848 NAS, Yeovilton	
ZA292	WS61 Sea King HC4 [WU]	MoD/AgustaWestland, Yeovil	
ZA293	WS61 Sea King HC4 [A]	RN No 845 NAS, Yeovilton	
ZA295	WS61 Sea King HC4 [U]	RN No 846 NAS, Yeovilton	
ZA296	WS61 Sea King HC4 [Q]	RN No 846 NAS, Yeovilton	
ZA297	WS61 Sea King HC4 [W]	RN No 845 NAS, Yeovilton	
ZA298	WS61 Sea King HC4 (G-BJNM) [Y]	RN No 845 NAS, Yeovilton	
ZA299	WS61 Sea King HC4 [D]	MoD/Vector Aerospace, Fleetlands	
ZA310	WS61 Sea King HC4 [B]	RN No 848 NAS, Yeovilton	
ZA312	WS61 Sea King HC4 [E]	RN No 845 NAS, Yeovilton	
ZA313	WS61 Sea King HC4 [M]	RN No 845 NAS, Yeovilton	
ZA314	WS61 Sea King HC4 [WT]	RN No 848 NAS, Yeovilton	
ZA319	Panavia Tornado GR1 (9315M)	DSDA, Arncott, Oxon, on display	
ZA320	Panavia Tornado GR1 (9314M) [TAW]	DSAE, No 1 SoTT, Cosford	
ZA323	Panavia Tornado GR1 [TAZ]	DSAE, No 1 SoTT, Cosford	
ZA325	Panavia Tornado GR1 <ff>	RAF Manston History Museum	
ZA325	Panavia Tornado GR1 [TAX] <rf>	RAF, stored Shawbury	
ZA326	Panavia Tornado GR1P	MoD, Boscombe Down (wfu)	
ZA327	Panavia Tornado GR1 <ff>	BAE Systems, Warton	
ZA328	Panavia Tornado GR1	Marsh Lane Technical School, Preston	
ZA353	Panavia Tornado GR1 [B-53]	Privately owned, Thorpe Wood, N Yorks	
ZA354	Panavia Tornado GR1	Yorkshire Air Museum, Elvington	
ZA355	Panavia Tornado GR1 (9310M) [TAA]	RAF, stored Lossiemouth	
ZA356	Panavia Tornado GR1 <ff>	RAF Tornado Maintenance School, Marham	
ZA357	Panavia Tornado GR1 [TTV]	DSAE, No 1 SoTT, Cosford	
ZA359	Panavia Tornado GR1	BAE Systems Warton, Overseas Customer Training Centre	
ZA360	Panavia Tornado GR1 (9318M) <ff>	RAF Marham, instructional use	
ZA361	Panavia Tornado GR1 [TD]	Privately owned, New York, Lincs	
ZA362	Panavia Tornado GR1 [AJ-F]	Highland Aviation Museum, Inverness	
ZA365	Panavia Tornado GR4 [001]	RAF Lossiemouth Wing	
ZA367	Panavia Tornado GR4 [002,KC-N]	RAF Leeming, RTP	
ZA369	Panavia Tornado GR4A [003]	RAF CMU, Marham	
ZA370	Panavia Tornado GR4A [004]	RAF CMU, Marham	
ZA371	Panavia Tornado GR4A [005]	RAF Marham Wing	
ZA372	Panavia Tornado GR4A [006]	RAF CMU, Marham	
ZA373	Panavia Tornado GR4A [007,H]	RAF Lossiemouth Wing	
ZA375	Panavia Tornado GR1 (9335M) [AJ-W]	RAF Marham, Fire Section	
ZA393	Panavia Tornado GR4 [008]	RAF, stored Marham	
ZA395	Panavia Tornado GR4A [009]	RAF Lossiemouth Wing	
ZA398	Panavia Tornado GR4A $	RAF No 2 Sqn, Marham	
ZA399	Panavia Tornado GR1 (9316M) [AJ-C]	DSAE, No 1 SoTT, Cosford	
ZA400	Panavia Tornado GR4A [011]	RAF TEF, Lossiemouth	
ZA401	Panavia Tornado GR4A [012] $	RAF Lossiemouth Wing	
ZA402	Panavia Tornado GR4A	MoD/BAE Systems, Warton	
ZA404	Panavia Tornado GR4A [013]	RAF Lossiemouth Wing	
ZA405	Panavia Tornado GR4A [014]	RAF Lossiemouth Wing	
ZA406	Panavia Tornado GR4 [015]	RAF TEF, Lossiemouth	
ZA407	Panavia Tornado GR1 (9336M) [AJ-N]	RAF Marham, on display	
ZA409	Panavia Tornado GR1 [VII]	RAF Lossiemouth (wfu)	
ZA410	Panavia Tornado GR4 [016]	RAF Lossiemouth Wing	
ZA411	Panavia Tornado GR1	MoD/BAE Systems, Warton	

Notes	*Serial*	*Type (code/other identity)*	*Owner/operator location or fate*
	ZA412	Panavia Tornado GR4 [017]	RAF TEF, Lossiemouth
	ZA446	Panavia Tornado GR4 [018]	RAF Leeming, RTP
	ZA447	Panavia Tornado GR4 [EB-R]	RAF Marham Wing
	ZA449	Panavia Tornado GR4 [020]	RAF Marham Wing
	ZA450	Panavia Tornado GR1 (9317M) [TH]	DSAE, No 1 SoTT, Cosford
	ZA452	Panavia Tornado GR4 [021]	RAF Marham Wing
	ZA453	Panavia Tornado GR4 [022]	RAF TEF, Lossiemouth
	ZA456	Panavia Tornado GR4 [023]	RAF Marham Wing
	ZA457	Panavia Tornado GR1 [AJ-J]	RAF Museum, Hendon
	ZA458	Panavia Tornado GR4 [024]	RAF Marham Wing
	ZA459	Panavia Tornado GR4 [F] $	RAF CMU, Marham
	ZA461	Panavia Tornado GR4 [026]	RAF Lossiemouth Wing
	ZA462	Panavia Tornado GR4 [027]	RAF Marham Wing
	ZA463	Panavia Tornado GR4 [028]	RAF Lossiemouth Wing
	ZA465	Panavia Tornado GR1 [FF]	Imperial War Museum, Duxford
	ZA469	Panavia Tornado GR4 [029] $	RAF CMU, Marham
	ZA470	Panavia Tornado GR4	RAF Leeming, for scrapping
	ZA472	Panavia Tornado GR4 [031]	RAF Marham Wing
	ZA473	Panavia Tornado GR4 [032]	RAF Marham Wing
	ZA474	Panavia Tornado GR1 (9312M)	RAF, stored Lossiemouth
	ZA475	Panavia Tornado GR1 (9311M) [AJ-G]	RAF Lossiemouth, on display
	ZA492	Panavia Tornado GR4 [033]	RAF TEF, Lossiemouth
	ZA541	Panavia Tornado GR4 [034]	RAF Lossiemouth Wing
	ZA542	Panavia Tornado GR4 [035]	RAF TEF, Lossiemouth
	ZA543	Panavia Tornado GR4 [036]	RAF TEF, Lossiemouth
	ZA544	Panavia Tornado GR4 [037]	RAF Leeming, RTP
	ZA546	Panavia Tornado GR4 [038]	RAF Lossiemouth Wing
	ZA547	Panavia Tornado GR4 [039] $	RAF Lossiemouth Wing
	ZA548	Panavia Tornado GR4 [040]	RAF Marham Wing
	ZA549	Panavia Tornado GR4 [041]	RAF Tornado Maintenance School, Marham
	ZA550	Panavia Tornado GR4 [042]	RAF TEF, Lossiemouth
	ZA551	Panavia Tornado GR4 [043]	RAF Marham Wing
	ZA552	Panavia Tornado GR4 [044]	RAF Leeming, RTP
	ZA553	Panavia Tornado GR4 [045]	RAF Lossiemouth Wing
	ZA554	Panavia Tornado GR4 [046]	RAF Lossiemouth Wing
	ZA556	Panavia Tornado GR4 [047]	RAF CMU, Marham
	ZA556	Panavia Tornado GR1 <R> (*ZA368*/BAPC 155) [Z]	RAF M&RU, Bottesford
	ZA557	Panavia Tornado GR4 [048]	RAF TEF, Lossiemouth
	ZA559	Panavia Tornado GR4 [049]	RAF Lossiemouth Wing
	ZA560	Panavia Tornado GR4 [050]	RAF TEF, Lossiemouth
	ZA562	Panavia Tornado GR4 [051]	RAF Lossiemouth Wing
	ZA563	Panavia Tornado GR4	RAF Leeming, for scrapping
	ZA564	Panavia Tornado GR4 $	RAF TEF, Lossiemouth
	ZA585	Panavia Tornado GR4 [054]	RAF Lossiemouth Wing
	ZA587	Panavia Tornado GR4 [055]	RAF Marham Wing
	ZA588	Panavia Tornado GR4 [056]	RAF TEF, Lossiemouth
	ZA589	Panavia Tornado GR4 [057]	RAF TEF, Lossiemouth
	ZA591	Panavia Tornado GR4 [058]	RAF CMU, Marham
	ZA592	Panavia Tornado GR4 [059]	RAF AWC/FJWOEU/No 41(R) Sqn, Coningsby
	ZA594	Panavia Tornado GR4 [060]	RAF CMU, Marham
	ZA595	Panavia Tornado GR4 [061]	RAF Marham Wing
	ZA597	Panavia Tornado GR4 [063]	RAF Marham Wing
	ZA598	Panavia Tornado GR4 [064]	RAF TEF, Lossiemouth
	ZA600	Panavia Tornado GR4 [EB-G] $	RAF AWC/FJWOEU/No 41(R) Sqn, Coningsby
	ZA601	Panavia Tornado GR4 [EB-B]	RAF AWC/FJWOEU/No 41(R) Sqn, Coningsby
	ZA602	Panavia Tornado GR4 [067]	RAF CMU, stored Marham
	ZA604	Panavia Tornado GR4 [068]	RAF TEF, Lossiemouth
	ZA606	Panavia Tornado GR4 [069]	RAF TEF, Lossiemouth
	ZA607	Panavia Tornado GR4 [070]	RAF Marham Wing

Serial	Type (code/other identity)	Owner/operator location or fate	Notes
ZA608	Panavia Tornado GR4	RAF Leeming, RTP	
ZA609	Panavia Tornado GR4 [072]	RAF TEF, Lossiemouth	
ZA611	Panavia Tornado GR4 [073]	RAF TEF, Lossiemouth	
ZA612	Panavia Tornado GR4 [IV]	MoD/BAE Systems, Warton	
ZA613	Panavia Tornado GR4 [075]	RAF Marham Wing	
ZA614	Panavia Tornado GR4 [EB-Z] $	RAF AWC/FJWOEU/No 41(R) Sqn, Coningsby	
ZA630	Slingsby T61F Venture T2 (G-BUGL)	Privately owned, Tibenham	
ZA634	Slingsby T61F Venture T2 (G-BUHA) [C]	Privately owned, Saltby, Leics	
ZA652	Slingsby T61F Venture T2 (G-BUDC)	Privately owned, Enstone	
ZA670	B-V Chinook HC4 (N37010) [AA]	MoD/Vector Aerospace, Fleetlands (conversion)	
ZA671	B-V Chinook HC2 (N37011) [AB]	*Crashed 7 April 2012, Yuma, USA*	
ZA674	B-V Chinook HC2 (N37019) [AD]	RAF Odiham Wing	
ZA675	B-V Chinook HC2 (N37020) [AE]	RAF Odiham Wing	
ZA677	B-V Chinook HC4 (N37022) [AF]	MoD/AFD/QinetiQ, Boscombe Down	
ZA678	B-V Chinook HC1 (N37023/9229M) [EZ] (wreck)	RAF Odiham, BDRT	
ZA679	B-V Chinook HC2 (N37025) [AG]	RAF Odiham Wing	
ZA680	B-V Chinook HC2 (N37026) [AH]	MoD/Vector Aerospace, Fleetlands	
ZA681	B-V Chinook HC2 (N37027) [AI]	RAF Odiham Wing	
ZA682	B-V Chinook HC2 (N37029) [AJ]	RAF Odiham Wing	
ZA683	B-V Chinook HC4 (N37030) [AK]	RAF Odiham Wing	
ZA684	B-V Chinook HC2 (N37031) [AL]	RAF Odiham Wing	
ZA704	B-V Chinook HC2 (N37033)	RAF Odiham Wing	
ZA705	B-V Chinook HC2 (N37035) [AN]	RAF Odiham Wing	
ZA707	B-V Chinook HC2 (N37040) [AO]	RAF Odiham Wing	
ZA708	B-V Chinook HC2 (N37042) [AP]	MoD/Vector Aerospace, Fleetlands	
ZA710	B-V Chinook HC2 (N37044) [AR]	MoD/Vector Aerospace, Fleetlands	
ZA711	B-V Chinook HC4 (N37046) $	RAF Odiham Wing	
ZA712	B-V Chinook HC2 (N37047) [AT]	RAF Odiham Wing	
ZA713	B-V Chinook HC2 (N37048)	RAF Odiham Wing	
ZA714	B-V Chinook HC4 (N37051) [AV] $	MoD/Vector Aerospace, Fleetlands (conversion)	
ZA717	B-V Chinook HC1 (N37056/9238M) (wreck)	RAFC Cranwell, instructional use	
ZA718	B-V Chinook HC4 (N37058) [BN]	RAF Odiham Wing	
ZA720	B-V Chinook HC2 (N37060) [AW]	RAF Odiham Wing	
ZA726	WS Gazelle AH1 [F1]	Privately owned, Stapleford Tawney	
ZA728	WS Gazelle AH1 [E]	Privately owned, Stapleford Tawney	
ZA729	WS Gazelle AH1	AAC Wattisham, BDRT	
ZA731	WS Gazelle AH1	AAC No 29 Flt, BATUS, Suffield, Canada	
ZA733	WS Gazelle AH1 (G-CHBR)	Privately owned, Stapleford Tawney	
ZA735	WS Gazelle AH1	DSEME SEAE, Arborfield	
ZA736	WS Gazelle AH1	AAC No 29 Flt, BATUS, Suffield, Canada	
ZA737	WS Gazelle AH1	Museum of Army Flying, Middle Wallop	
ZA766	WS Gazelle AH1	AAC No 665 Sqn/5 Regt, Aldergrove	
ZA768	WS Gazelle AH1 [F] (wreck)	MoD/Vector Aerospace, stored Fleetlands	
ZA769	WS Gazelle AH1 [K]	DSEME SEAE, Arborfield	
ZA771	WS Gazelle AH1	DSAE, No 1 SoTT, Cosford	
ZA772	WS Gazelle AH1	AAC No 667 Sqn, 7 Rgt, Middle Wallop	
ZA773	WS Gazelle AH1 [F]	AAC, stored Shawbury	
ZA774	WS Gazelle AH1	Privately owned, Babcary, Somerset	
ZA775	WS Gazelle AH1	AAC, stored Shawbury	
ZA776	WS Gazelle AH1 [F]	Privately owned, Stapleford Tawney	
ZA804	WS Gazelle HT3	Privately owned, Solstice Park, Amesbury, Wilts	
ZA935	WS Puma HC2	MoD/Eurocopter, Brasov, Romania (conversion)	
ZA936	WS Puma HC2	MoD/Eurocopter, Brasov, Romania (conversion)	
ZA937	WS Puma HC1	RAF Benson (wfu)	
ZA939	WS Puma HC2	MoD/Eurocopter, Brasov, Romania (conversion)	
ZA940	WS Puma HC2	MoD/Eurocopter, Brasov, Romania (conversion)	
ZA947	Douglas Dakota C3	RAF BBMF, Coningsby	
ZB500	WS Lynx 800 (G-LYNX/ZA500)	The Helicopter Museum, Weston-super-Mare	

Notes	Serial	Type (code/other identity)	Owner/operator location or fate
	ZB506	WS61 Sea King Mk 4X	MoD/AFD/QinetiQ, Boscombe Down
	ZB507	WS61 Sea King HC4 [F]	RN No 848 NAS, Yeovilton
	ZB601	BAe Harrier T4 (fuselage)	RNAS Yeovilton, Fire Section
	ZB603	BAe Harrier T8 [T03/DD]	SFDO, RNAS Culdrose
	ZB604	BAe Harrier T8 [722]	FAA Museum, stored RNAS Yeovilton
	ZB615	SEPECAT Jaguar T2A	DCAE, TCF, RAFC Cranwell
	ZB625	WS Gazelle HT3 [N]	MoD/AFD/QinetiQ, Boscombe Down
	ZB627	WS Gazelle HT3 (G-CBSK) [A]	Privately owned, Hurstbourne Tarrant, Hants
	ZB646	WS Gazelle HT2 (G-CBGZ) [59/CU]	Privately owned, Knebworth
	ZB647	WS Gazelle HT2 (G-CBSF) [40]	Privately owned, Redhill
	ZB665	WS Gazelle AH1	AAC, stored Shawbury
	ZB667	WS Gazelle AH1	AAC No 665 Sqn/5 Regt, Aldergrove
	ZB668	WS Gazelle AH1 (TAD 015)	DSEME SEAE, Arborfield
	ZB669	WS Gazelle AH1	AAC No 665 Sqn/5 Regt, Aldergrove
	ZB670	WS Gazelle AH1	AAC Dishforth, on display
	ZB671	WS Gazelle AH1	AAC No 29 Flt, BATUS, Suffield, Canada
	ZB672	WS Gazelle AH1	Army Training Regiment, Winchester
	ZB673	WS Gazelle AH1 [P]	Privately owned, Stapleford Tawney
	ZB674	WS Gazelle AH1	AAC No 665 Sqn/5 Regt, Aldergrove
	ZB677	WS Gazelle AH1 [5B]	AAC MPSU, Middle Wallop
	ZB678	WS Gazelle AH1	AAC MPSU, Middle Wallop
	ZB679	WS Gazelle AH1	AAC MPSU, Middle Wallop
	ZB682	WS Gazelle AH1	AAC, stored Dishforth
	ZB683	WS Gazelle AH1	AAC No 665 Sqn/5 Regt, Aldergrove
	ZB684	WS Gazelle AH1	RAF Defence Movements School, Brize Norton
	ZB686	WS Gazelle AH1 <ff>	The Helicopter Museum, Weston-super-Mare
	ZB688	WS Gazelle AH1 (G-CHMF)	Privately owned, Stapleford Tawney
	ZB689	WS Gazelle AH1	AAC No 665 Sqn/5 Regt, Aldergrove
	ZB690	WS Gazelle AH1	MoD, stored Shawbury
	ZB691	WS Gazelle AH1 [S]	AAC No 671 Sqn/7 Regt, Middle Wallop
	ZB692	WS Gazelle AH1 [Y]	AAC No 671 Sqn/7 Regt, Middle Wallop
	ZB693	WS Gazelle AH1	AAC No 671 Sqn/7 Regt, Middle Wallop
	ZD230	BAC Super VC10 K4 (G-ASGA) <ff>	Privately owned, Crondall, Hants
	ZD240	BAC Super VC10 K4 (G-ASGL) <ff>	Privately owned, Crondall, Hants
	ZD241	BAC Super VC10 K4 (G-ASGM) [N]	RAF No 1312 Flt, Mount Pleasant, FI
	ZD249	WS Lynx HAS3S [631]	RN No 702 NAS, Yeovilton
	ZD250	WS Lynx HAS3S [636]	RAF Henlow, instructional use
	ZD252	WS Lynx HMA8SRU [321/WL]	RN No 815 NAS, MI Flt, Yeovilton
	ZD254	WS Lynx HAS3S [306]	DSMarE AESS, *HMS Sultan*, Gosport
	ZD255	WS Lynx HAS3GMS [635]	RN No 702 NAS, Yeovilton
	ZD257	WS Lynx HMA8SRU [642]	RN No 815 NAS, *Lancaster* Flt, Yeovilton
	ZD258	WS Lynx HMA8SRU [303/MR]	RN No 815 NAS, HQ Flt, Yeovilton
	ZD259	WS Lynx HMA8SRU [304/IR]	RN No 815 NAS, HQ Flt, Yeovilton
	ZD260	WS Lynx HMA8SRU [315]	MoD/Vector Aerospace, Fleetlands
	ZD261	WS Lynx HMA8SRU [444]	RN No 815 NAS, *Montrose* Flt, Yeovilton
	ZD262	WS Lynx HMA8SRU [301]	MoD/Vector Aerospace, Fleetlands
	ZD263	WS Lynx HAS3S [632]	RN No 702 NAS, Yeovilton
	ZD264	WS Lynx HAS3GMS [407]	Privately owned, Hixon, Staffs
	ZD265	WS Lynx HMA8SRU [644]	MoD/Vector Aerospace, Fleetlands
	ZD266	WS Lynx HMA8SRU [643]	RN No 702 NAS, Yeovilton
	ZD267	WS Lynx HMA8 (comp XZ672) [LST-2]	RN ETS, Yeovilton, GI use
	ZD268	WS Lynx HMA8SRU [365/AY]	RN No 815 NAS, *Argyll* Flt, Yeovilton
	ZD272	WS Lynx AH7 [W]	AAC MPSU, Middle Wallop
	ZD273	WS Lynx AH7 <ff>	AAC MPSU, Middle Wallop
	ZD274	WS Lynx AH7 [E]	MoD/Vector Aerospace, Fleetlands
	ZD276	WS Lynx AH7	Mayhem Paintball, Abridge, Essex
	ZD277	WS Lynx AH7 [U]	AAC No 9 Regt, Dishforth
	ZD278	WS Lynx AH7 [F]	AAC No 671 Sqn/7 Regt, Middle Wallop
	ZD279	WS Lynx AH7 <ff>	Privately owned,

Serial	Type (code/other identity)	Owner/operator location or fate	Notes
ZD280	WS Lynx AH7	AAC No 9 Regt, Dishforth	
ZD281	WS Lynx AH7 [K]	MoD/Vector Aerospace, Fleetlands, GI use	
ZD282	WS Lynx AH7	AAC No 9 Regt, Dishforth	
ZD283	WS Lynx AH7 <ff>	Privately owned, Hixon, Staffs	
ZD283	WS Lynx AH7 (ZD273)	AAC Middle Wallop, instructional use	
ZD284	WS Lynx AH7 [K]	AAC No 671 Sqn/7 Regt, Middle Wallop	
ZD285	WS Lynx AH7	MoD/AFD/QinetiQ, Boscombe Down	
ZD318	BAe Harrier GR7A	Harrier Heritage Centre, Wittering	
ZD320	BAe Harrier GR9 [21]	*Sold to the USA, 2012*	
ZD321	BAe Harrier GR9 [02]	*Sold to the USA, 2012*	
ZD327	BAe Harrier GR9 [08A,SH-M]	*Sold to the USA, 2012*	
ZD328	BAe Harrier GR9 [09]	*Sold to the USA, 2012*	
ZD329	BAe Harrier GR9A [10]	*Sold to the USA, 2012*	
ZD330	BAe Harrier GR9 $	*Sold to the USA, 2012*	
ZD346	BAe Harrier GR9 [13]	*Sold to the USA, 2012*	
ZD347	BAe Harrier GR9A [14]	*Sold to the USA, 2012*	
ZD348	BAe Harrier GR9A [15A]	*Sold to the USA, 2012*	
ZD351	BAe Harrier GR9A $	*Sold to the USA, 2012*	
ZD352	BAe Harrier GR9 [19]	*Sold to the USA, 2012*	
ZD353	BAe Harrier GR5 (fuselage)	Privately owned, Sproughton	
ZD354	BAe Harrier GR9 [21]	*Sold to the USA, 2012*	
ZD375	BAe Harrier GR9 [23]	*Sold to the USA, 2012*	
ZD376	BAe Harrier GR7A [24A]	*Sold to the USA, December 2011*	
ZD378	BAe Harrier GR9A [26A]	*Sold to the USA, 2012*	
ZD379	BAe Harrier GR9 [27]	*Sold to the USA, 2012*	
ZD401	BAe Harrier GR9 [30]	*Sold to the USA, 2012*	
ZD402	BAe Harrier GR9 [31]	*Sold to the USA, 2012*	
ZD403	BAe Harrier GR9 [32,JX-B]	*Sold to the USA, 2012*	
ZD404	BAe Harrier GR7A [33A]	*Sold to the USA, December 2011*	
ZD405	BAe Harrier GR9 [34]	*Sold to the USA, 2012*	
ZD406	BAe Harrier GR9 $	*Sold to the USA, 2012*	
ZD407	BAe Harrier GR7 [36]	*Sold to the USA, December 2011*	
ZD409	BAe Harrier GR9 [38]	*Sold to the USA, 2012*	
ZD410	BAe Harrier GR9 $	*Sold to the USA, 2012*	
ZD411	BAe Harrier GR7 [40]	*Sold to the USA, 2012*	
ZD412	BAe Harrier GR5 (fuselage)	Privately owned, Sproughton	
ZD431	BAe Harrier GR7A [43A]	*Sold to the USA, 2012*	
ZD433	BAe Harrier GR9A [45A]	FAA Museum, stored RNAS Yeovilton	
ZD435	BAe Harrier GR9 [47]	*Sold to the USA, 2012*	
ZD436	BAe Harrier GR9A [48A]	*Sold to the USA, 2012*	
ZD437	BAe Harrier GR9 [EB-J]	*Sold to the USA, 2012*	
ZD438	BAe Harrier GR9 [50]	*Sold to the USA, 2012*	
ZD461	BAe Harrier GR9A [51A]	Imperial War Museum, Duxford	
ZD462	BAe Harrier GR7 (9302M) [52]	Privately owned, Malmesbury, Wilts	
ZD463	BAe Harrier GR7 [53]	*Sold to the USA, 2012*	
ZD465	BAe Harrier GR9 [55]	DSMarE AESS, *HMS Sultan*, Gosport	
ZD466	BAe Harrier GR7 [56]	*Sold to the USA, 2012*	
ZD467	BAe Harrier GR9A [57A]	*Sold to the USA, 2012*	
ZD468	BAe Harrier GR9 [58]	*Sold to the USA, 2012*	
ZD469	BAe Harrier GR7A	RAF Wittering, on display	
ZD470	BAe Harrier GR9 [60]	*Sold to the USA, 2012*	
ZD476	WS61 Sea King HC4 [WZ]	RN No 846 NAS, Yeovilton	
ZD477	WS61 Sea King HC4 [E]	DSMarE, stored *HMS Sultan*, Gosport	
ZD478	WS61 Sea King HC4 [J]	Privately owned, Hixon, Staffs	
ZD479	WS61 Sea King HC4 [WQ]	MoD/AFD/QinetiQ, Boscombe Down	
ZD480	WS61 Sea King HC4 [J]	RN 845 NAS, Yeovilton	
ZD559	WS Lynx AH5X	MoD, Boscombe Down (wfu)	
ZD560	WS Lynx AH7	MoD, Boscombe Down (wfu)	
ZD565	WS Lynx HMA8SRU [314]	RN No 815 NAS, MI Flt, Yeovilton	
ZD566	WS Lynx HMA8SRU	RN No 702 NAS, Yeovilton	

Notes	Serial	Type (code/other identity)	Owner/operator location or fate
	ZD574	B-V Chinook HC4 (N37077) [DB]	RAF Odiham Wing
	ZD575	B-V Chinook HC4 (N37078) [DC]	RAF Odiham Wing
	ZD578	BAe Sea Harrier FA2 [000,122]	RNAS Yeovilton, at main gate
	ZD579	BAe Sea Harrier FA2 [79/DD]	SFDO, RNAS Culdrose
	ZD580	BAe Sea Harrier FA2 [710]	Privately owned, Cheshire
	ZD581	BAe Sea Harrier FA2 [124]	RN, Predannack Fire School
	ZD582	BAe Sea Harrier FA2 [002/N]	Privately owned, Banbury, Oxon
	ZD607	BAe Sea Harrier FA2	RN, stored Bicester
	ZD610	BAe Sea Harrier FA2 [714,002/N]	Privately owned, Bruntingthorpe
	ZD611	BAe Sea Harrier FA2	RNAS Culdrose Fire Section
	ZD612	BAe Sea Harrier FA2	Privately owned, Topsham, Devon
	ZD613	BAe Sea Harrier FA2 [127/R]	Privately owned, Cross Green, Leeds
	ZD614	BAe Sea Harrier FA2 [122/R]	Privately owned, Sproughton
	ZD620	BAe 125 CC3	RAF No 32(The Royal) Sqn, Northolt
	ZD621	BAe 125 CC3	RAF No 32(The Royal) Sqn, Northolt
	ZD625	WS61 Sea King HC4 [P]	DSMarE, stored *HMS Sultan*, Gosport
	ZD626	WS61 Sea King HC4 [S]	RN No 846 NAS, Yeovilton
	ZD627	WS61 Sea King HC4 [WO]	MoD/Vector Aerospace, Fleetlands
	ZD630	WS61 Sea King HAS6 [012/L]	DSMarE, AESS, *HMS Sultan*, Gosport
	ZD631	WS61 Sea King HAS6 [66] (fuselage)	Privately owned, St Agnes, Cornwall
	ZD633	WS61 Sea King HAS6 [014/L]	DSMarE, stored *HMS Sultan*, Gosport
	ZD634	WS61 Sea King HAS6 [503]	DSMarE, stored *HMS Sultan*, Gosport
	ZD636	WS61 Sea King ASaC7 [182/CU]	RN No 857 NAS, Culdrose
	ZD637	WS61 Sea King HAS6 [700/PW]	DSMarE, AESS, *HMS Sultan*, Gosport
	ZD667	BAe Harrier GR3 (9201M) [67/DD]	Privately owned, Bentwaters
	ZD703	BAe 125 CC3	RAF No 32(The Royal) Sqn, Northolt
	ZD704	BAe 125 CC3	RAF No 32(The Royal) Sqn, Northolt
	ZD707	Panavia Tornado GR4 [077]	RAF Lossiemouth Wing
	ZD708	Panavia Tornado GR4	RAF Leeming, for scrapping
	ZD709	Panavia Tornado GR4 [078]	RAF, stored Lossiemouth
	ZD710	Panavia Tornado GR1 <ff>	Privately owned, Ruthin, Denbighshire
	ZD711	Panavia Tornado GR4 [079]	RAF Lossiemouth Wing
	ZD712	Panavia Tornado GR4 [080] $	RAF TEF, Lossiemouth
	ZD713	Panavia Tornado GR4 [081]	RAF Marham Wing
	ZD714	Panavia Tornado GR4 [082]	RAF Lossiemouth Wing
	ZD715	Panavia Tornado GR4 [083]	RAF Marham, WLT
	ZD716	Panavia Tornado GR4 [084]	RAF TEF, Lossiemouth
	ZD719	Panavia Tornado GR4 [085]	RAF CMU, Marham
	ZD720	Panavia Tornado GR4 [086]	RAF Marham Wing
	ZD739	Panavia Tornado GR4 [087]	RAF Marham Wing
	ZD740	Panavia Tornado GR4 [088]	RAF AWC/FJWOEU/No 41(R) Sqn, Coningsby
	ZD741	Panavia Tornado GR4 [089]	RAF CMU, Marham
	ZD742	Panavia Tornado GR4 [090]	RAF Lossiemouth Wing
	ZD743	Panavia Tornado GR4 [091]	*Crashed 3 July 2012, Moray Firth*
	ZD744	Panavia Tornado GR4 [092]	RAF Lossiemouth Wing
	ZD745	Panavia Tornado GR4 [093]	RAF Lossiemouth Wing
	ZD746	Panavia Tornado GR4 [094]	RAF Lossiemouth Wing
	ZD747	Panavia Tornado GR4 [095]	RAF Marham Wing
	ZD748	Panavia Tornado GR4 [096] $	RAF Lossiemouth Wing
	ZD749	Panavia Tornado GR4 [097]	RAF Lossiemouth Wing
	ZD788	Panavia Tornado GR4 [098]	MoD/AFD/QinetiQ, Boscombe Down
	ZD790	Panavia Tornado GR4 [099]	RAF TEF, Lossiemouth
	ZD792	Panavia Tornado GR4 [100] $	RAF Marham Wing
	ZD793	Panavia Tornado GR4 [101]	RAF Lossiemouth, WLT
	ZD810	Panavia Tornado GR4 [102]	RAF TEF, Lossiemouth
	ZD811	Panavia Tornado GR4 [103]	RAF Lossiemouth Wing
	ZD812	Panavia Tornado GR4 [104]	*Crashed 3 July 2012, Moray Firth*
	ZD842	Panavia Tornado GR4 [105]	RAF CMU, Marham
	ZD843	Panavia Tornado GR4 [106]	RAF CMU, Marham
	ZD844	Panavia Tornado GR4 [107]	RAF Lossiemouth Wing

Serial	Type (code/other identity)	Owner/operator location or fate	Notes
ZD847	Panavia Tornado GR4 [108]	RAF AWC/FJWOEU/No 41(R) Sqn, Coningsby	
ZD848	Panavia Tornado GR4 [109]	RAF Marham Wing	
ZD849	Panavia Tornado GR4 [110]	RAF, stored Marham	
ZD850	Panavia Tornado GR4 [111]	RAF Leeming, RTP	
ZD851	Panavia Tornado GR4 [112]	RAF, stored Lossiemouth	
ZD890	Panavia Tornado GR4 [113]	RAF TEF, Lossiemouth	
ZD892	Panavia Tornado GR4 [TG]	RAF Leeming, RTP	
ZD895	Panavia Tornado GR4 [115]	RAF Marham Wing	
ZD899	Panavia Tornado F2	MoD, Boscombe Down, spares use	
ZD902	Panavia Tornado F2A(TIARA)	MoD/AFD/QinetiQ, Boscombe Down	
ZD906	Panavia Tornado F2 (comp ZE294) <ff>	RAF Leuchars, BDRT	
ZD932	Panavia Tornado F2 (comp ZE255) (9308M) (fuselage)	Privately owned, Thorpe Wood, N Yorks	
ZD934	Panavia Tornado F2 (comp ZE786) <ff>	*Scrapped at Leeming*	
ZD936	Panavia Tornado F2 (comp ZE251) <ff>	Boscombe Down Aviation Collection, Old Sarum	
ZD938	Panavia Tornado F2 (comp ZE295) <ff>	Aeroventure, Doncaster	
ZD939	Panavia Tornado F2 (comp ZE292) <ff>	DSAE Cosford, instructional use	
ZD948	Lockheed TriStar KC1 (G-BFCA)	RAF No 216 Sqn, Brize Norton	
ZD949	Lockheed TriStar K1 (G-BFCB)	MoD/Marshalls, stored Cambridge	
ZD950	Lockheed TriStar KC1 (G-BFCC)	RAF No 216 Sqn, Brize Norton	
ZD951	Lockheed TriStar K1 (G-BFCD)	RAF No 216 Sqn, Brize Norton	
ZD952	Lockheed TriStar KC1 (G-BFCE)	RAF No 216 Sqn, Brize Norton	
ZD953	Lockheed TriStar KC1 (G-BFCF)	RAF No 216 Sqn, Brize Norton	
ZD980	B-V Chinook HC2 (N37082) [DD]	RAF No 1310 Flt, Kandahar, Afghanistan	
ZD981	B-V Chinook HC4 (N37083)	RAF Odiham Wing	
ZD982	B-V Chinook HC4 (N37085) [DF]	MoD/Vector Aerospace, Fleetlands (conversion)	
ZD983	B-V Chinook HC2 (N37086) [DG]	RAF Odiham Wing	
ZD984	B-V Chinook HC4 (N37088) [DH]	RAF Odiham Wing	
ZD990	BAe Harrier T8 [T90/DD]	SFDO, RNAS Culdrose	
ZD992	BAe Harrier T8 [724] (fuselage)	Privately owned, Gr Manchester	
ZD993	BAe Harrier T8 [723/VL]	MoD, Boscombe Down (spares use)	
ZD996	Panavia Tornado GR4A [EB-B]	RAF Leeming, RTP	
ZE116	Panavia Tornado GR4A [116]	RAF Marham Wing	
ZE163	Panavia Tornado F3 (comp ZG753) [HY]	*Scrapped at Leeming*	
ZE164	Panavia Tornado F3 [HO]	*Scrapped at Leeming*	
ZE165	Panavia Tornado F3 [GE]	RAF, stored Shawbury	
ZE168	Panavia Tornado F3 [HH]	*Scrapped at Leeming*	
ZE201	Panavia Tornado F3 [HU]	*Scrapped at Leeming*	
ZE203	Panavia Tornado F3 [GA]	RAF Leeming, RTP	
ZE204	Panavia Tornado F3 [FC]	RAF, stored Shawbury	
ZE256	Panavia Tornado F3 [DZ] (wears ZE248 on port side)	Privately owned, Thorpe Wood, N Yorks	
ZE288	Panavia Tornado F3 (comp ZD940) [HA] $	RAF Leeming, RTP	
ZE338	Panavia Tornado F3 [GJ]	RAF Leeming, RTP	
ZE340	Panavia Tornado F3 (*ZE758*/9298M) [GO]	DSAE, No 1 SoTT, Cosford	
ZE341	Panavia Tornado F3 [HI]	*Scrapped at Leeming*	
ZE342	Panavia Tornado F3 [HP]	RAF Leeming, RTP	
ZE350	McD F-4J(UK) Phantom (9080M) <ff>	Privately owned, Shrewsbury	
ZE352	McD F-4J(UK) Phantom (9086M) <ff>	Privately owned, Hooton Park	
ZE360	McD F-4J(UK) Phantom (9059M) [O]	MoD DFTDC, Manston	
ZE368	WS61 Sea King HAR3 [R]	RAF SKAMG, RNAS Yeovilton	
ZE369	WS61 Sea King HAR3 [S]	RAF No 22 Sqn, C Flt/No 203(R) Sqn, Valley	
ZE370	WS61 Sea King HAR3 [T]	MoD/Vector Aerospace, Fleetlands	
ZE375	WS Lynx AH9A	AAC No 667 Sqn/7 Regt, Middle Wallop	
ZE376	WS Lynx AH9A	MoD/Vector Aerospace, Fleetlands	
ZE378	WS Lynx AH7	AAC No 657 Sqn, Odiham	
ZE379	WS Lynx AH7	AAC Dishforth, BDRT	
ZE380	WS Lynx AH9A	AAC No 657 Sqn, Odiham	
ZE381	WS Lynx AH7 [X]	DSEME SEAE, Arborfield	
ZE395	BAe 125 CC3	RAF No 32(The Royal) Sqn, Northolt	

Notes	Serial	Type (code/other identity)	Owner/operator location or fate
	ZE396	BAe 125 CC3	RAF No 32(The Royal) Sqn, Northolt
	ZE410	Agusta A109A (AE-334)	Museum of Army Flying, stored Middle Wallop
	ZE411	Agusta A109A (AE-331)	*Repainted as AE-331, 2012*
	ZE412	Agusta A109A	DSEME SEAE, Arborfield
	ZE413	Agusta A109A	Army Whittington Barracks, Lichfield, GI use
	ZE416	Agusta A109E Power Elite (G-ESLH)	MoD/ETPS, Boscombe Down
	ZE418	WS61 Sea King ASaC7 [186]	RN No 857 NAS, Culdrose
	ZE420	WS61 Sea King ASaC7 [189]	RN No 849 NAS, Culdrose
	ZE422	WS61 Sea King ASaC7 [192]	RN No 849 NAS, Culdrose
	ZE425	WS61 Sea King HC4 [WR]	RN No 848 NAS, Yeovilton
	ZE426	WS61 Sea King HC4 [WX]	DSMarE, stored *HMS Sultan*, Gosport
	ZE427	WS61 Sea King HC4 [K]	MoD/AgustaWestland, Yeovil
	ZE428	WS61 Sea King HC4 [H]	MoD/AgustaWestland, Yeovil
	ZE432	BAC 1-11/479FU (DQ-FBV)	MoD, Boscombe Down Apprentice School
	ZE433	BAC 1-11/479FU (DQ-FBQ)	MoD, Boscombe Down (wfu)
	ZE449	SA330L Puma HC1 (9017M/PA-12)	RAF, stored Shawbury (wreck)
	ZE477	WS Lynx 3	The Helicopter Museum, Weston-super-Mare
	ZE495	Grob G103 Viking T1 (BGA3000) [VA]	RAF No 625 VGS, Hullavington
	ZE496	Grob G103 Viking T1 (BGA3001) [VB]	RAF No 662 VGS, Arbroarth
	ZE498	Grob G103 Viking T1 (BGA3003) [VC]	RAF CGMF, stored Syerston
	ZE499	Grob G103 Viking T1 (BGA3004) [VD]	RAF ACCGS/No 643 VGS, Syerston
	ZE502	Grob G103 Viking T1 (BGA3007) [VF]	RAF No 614 VGS, Wethersfield
	ZE503	Grob G103 Viking T1 (BGA3008) [VG]	RAF ACCGS/No 643 VGS, Syerston
	ZE504	Grob G103 Viking T1 (BGA3009) [VH]	RAF ACCGS/No 643 VGS, Syerston
	ZE520	Grob G103 Viking T1 (BGA3010) [VJ]	RAF No 661 VGS, Kirknewton
	ZE521	Grob G103 Viking T1 (BGA3011) [VK]	RAF CGMF, Syerston
	ZE522	Grob G103 Viking T1 (BGA3012) [VL]	RAF No 625 VGS, Hullavington
	ZE524	Grob G103 Viking T1 (BGA3014) [VM]	RAF ACCGS/No 643 VGS, Syerston
	ZE526	Grob G103 Viking T1 (BGA3016) [VN]	RAF No 626 VGS, Predannack
	ZE527	Grob G103 Viking T1 (BGA3017) [VP]	RAF No 626 VGS, Predannack
	ZE528	Grob G103 Viking T1 (BGA3018) [VQ]	RAF No 661 VGS, Kirknewton
	ZE529	Grob G103 Viking T1 (BGA3019) (comp ZE655) [VR]	RAF ACCGS/No 643 VGS, Syerston
	ZE530	Grob G103 Viking T1 (BGA3020) [VS]	RAF No 625 VGS, Hullavington
	ZE531	Grob G103 Viking T1 (BGA3021) [VT]	RAF CGMF, stored Syerston
	ZE532	Grob G103 Viking T1 (BGA3022) [VU]	RAF CGMF, Syerston
	ZE533	Grob G103 Viking T1 (BGA3023) [VV]	RAF No 661 VGS, Kirknewton
	ZE550	Grob G103 Viking T1 (BGA3025) [VX]	RAF CGMF, Syerston (damaged)
	ZE551	Grob G103 Viking T1 (BGA3026) [VY]	RAF No 614 VGS, Wethersfield
	ZE552	Grob G103 Viking T1 (BGA3027) [VZ]	RAF CGMF, Syerston
	ZE553	Grob G103 Viking T1 (BGA3028) [WA]	RAF CGMF, Syerston
	ZE554	Grob G103 Viking T1 (BGA3029) [WB]	RAF No 615 VGS, Kenley
	ZE555	Grob G103 Viking T1 (BGA3030) [WC]	RAF CGMF, Syerston
	ZE556	Grob G103 Viking T1 (BGA3031) <ff>	RAF CGMF, stored Syerston
	ZE557	Grob G103 Viking T1 (BGA3032) [WE]	RAF CGMF, stored Syerston
	ZE558	Grob G103 Viking T1 (BGA3033) [WF]	RAF No 615 VGS, Kenley
	ZE559	Grob G103 Viking T1 (BGA3034) [WG]	RAF ACCGS/No 643 VGS, Syerston
	ZE560	Grob G103 Viking T1 (BGA3035) [WH]	RAF ACCGS/No 643 VGS, Syerston
	ZE561	Grob G103 Viking T1 (BGA3036) [WJ]	RAF CGMF, Syerston
	ZE562	Grob G103 Viking T1 (BGA3037) [WK]	RAF ACCGS/No 643 VGS, Syerston
	ZE563	Grob G103 Viking T1 (BGA3038) [WL]	RAF No 615 VGS, Kenley
	ZE564	Grob G103 Viking T1 (BGA3039) [WN]	RAF No 622 VGS, Upavon
	ZE584	Grob G103 Viking T1 (BGA3040) [WP]	RAF CGMF, stored Syerston
	ZE585	Grob G103 Viking T1 (BGA3041) [WQ]	RAF No 614 VGS, Wethersfield
	ZE586	Grob G103 Viking T1 (BGA3042) [WR]	RAF No 661 VGS, Kirknewton
	ZE587	Grob G103 Viking T1 (BGA3043) [WS]	RAF No 622 VGS, Upavon
	ZE590	Grob G103 Viking T1 (BGA3046) [WT]	RAF ACCGS/No 643 VGS, Syerston
	ZE591	Grob G103 Viking T1 (BGA3047) [WU]	RAF CGMF, Syerston
	ZE592	Grob G103 Viking T1 (BGA3048) <ff>	RAFGSA, stored Henlow
	ZE593	Grob G103 Viking T1 (BGA3049) [WW]	RAF No 615 VGS, Kenley

Serial	Type (code/other identity)	Owner/operator location or fate	Notes
ZE594	Grob G103 Viking T1 (BGA3050) [WX]	RAF No 662 VGS, Arbroath	
ZE595	Grob G103 Viking T1 (BGA3051) [WY]	RAF No 661 VGS, Kirknewton	
ZE600	Grob G103 Viking T1 (BGA3052) [WZ]	RAF No 615 VGS, Kenley	
ZE601	Grob G103 Viking T1 (BGA3053) [XA]	RAF CGMF, stored Syerston	
ZE602	Grob G103 Viking T1 (BGA3054) [XB]	RAF CGMF, Syerston	
ZE603	Grob G103 Viking T1 (BGA3055) [XC]	RAF No 614 VGS, Wethersfield	
ZE604	Grob G103 Viking T1 (BGA3056) [XD]	RAF No 621 VGS, Hullavington	
ZE605	Grob G103 Viking T1 (BGA3057) [XE]	RAF ACCGS/No 643 VGS, Syerston	
ZE606	Grob G103 Viking T1 (BGA3058) [XF]	RAF No 614 VGS, Wethersfield	
ZE607	Grob G103 Viking T1 (BGA3059) [XG]	RAF No 622 VGS, Upavon	
ZE608	Grob G103 Viking T1 (BGA3060) [XH]	RAF CGMF, Syerston	
ZE609	Grob G103 Viking T1 (BGA3061) [XJ]	RAF ACCGS/No 643 VGS, Syerston	
ZE610	Grob G103 Viking T1 (BGA3062) [XK]	RAF CGMF, stored Syerston	
ZE611	Grob G103 Viking T1 (BGA3063) [XL]	RAF No 626 VGS, Predannack	
ZE613	Grob G103 Viking T1 (BGA3065) [XM]	RAF No 621 VGS, Hullavington	
ZE614	Grob G103 Viking T1 (BGA3066) [XN]	RAF CGMF, Syerston	
ZE625	Grob G103 Viking T1 (BGA3067) [XP]	RAF ACCGS/No 643 VGS, Syerston	
ZE626	Grob G103 Viking T1 (BGA3068) [XQ]	RAF CGMF, stored Syerston	
ZE627	Grob G103 Viking T1 (BGA3069) [XR]	RAF ACCGS/No 643 VGS, Syerston	
ZE628	Grob G103 Viking T1 (BGA3070) [XS]	RAF No 622 VGS, Upavon	
ZE629	Grob G103 Viking T1 (BGA3071) [XT]	RAF No 662 VGS, Arbroath	
ZE630	Grob G103 Viking T1 (BGA3072) [XU]	RAF No 662 VGS, Arbroath	
ZE631	Grob G103 Viking T1 (BGA3073) [XV]	RAF No 626 VGS, Predannack	
ZE632	Grob G103 Viking T1 (BGA3074) [XW]	RAF No 662 VGS, Arbroath	
ZE633	Grob G103 Viking T1 (BGA3075) [XX]	RAF CGMF, Syerston	
ZE636	Grob G103 Viking T1 (BGA3078) [XZ]	RAF CGMF, Syerston	
ZE637	Grob G103 Viking T1 (BGA3079) [YA]	RAF No 615 VGS, Kenley	
ZE650	Grob G103 Viking T1 (BGA3080) [YB]	RAF ACCGS/No 643 VGS, Syerston	
ZE651	Grob G103 Viking T1 (BGA3081) [YC]	RAF No 621 VGS, Hullavington	
ZE652	Grob G103 Viking T1 (BGA3082) [YD]	RAF ACCGS/No 643 VGS, Syerston	
ZE653	Grob G103 Viking T1 (BGA3083) [YE]	RAF No 625 VGS, Hullavington	
ZE656	Grob G103 Viking T1 (BGA3086) [YH]	RAF ACCGS/No 643 VGS, Syerston	
ZE657	Grob G103 Viking T1 (BGA3087) [YJ]	RAF CGMF, stored Syerston	
ZE658	Grob G103 Viking T1 (BGA3088) [YK]	RAF CGMF, stored Syerston	
ZE677	Grob G103 Viking T1 (BGA3090) [YM]	RAF CGMF, Syerston	
ZE678	Grob G103 Viking T1 (BGA3091) [YN]	RAF ACCGS/No 643 VGS, Syerston	
ZE679	Grob G103 Viking T1 (BGA3092) [YP]	RAF CGMF, Syerston	
ZE680	Grob G103 Viking T1 (BGA3093) [YQ]	RAF ACCGS/No 643 VGS, Syerston	
ZE681	Grob G103 Viking T1 (BGA3094) <ff>	RAF Hullavington	
ZE682	Grob G103 Viking T1 (BGA3095) [YS]	RAF CGMF, stored Syerston	
ZE683	Grob G103 Viking T1 (BGA3096) [YT]	RAF ACCGS/No 643 VGS, Syerston	
ZE684	Grob G103 Viking T1 (BGA3097) [YU]	RAF ACCGS/No 643 VGS, Syerston	
ZE685	Grob G103 Viking T1 (BGA3098) [YV]	RAF No 614 VGS, Wethersfield	
ZE686	Grob G103 Viking T1 (BGA3099) <ff>	RAF Museum, Hendon	
ZE690	BAe Sea Harrier FA2 [90/DD]	SFDO, RNAS Culdrose	
ZE691	BAe Sea Harrier FA2 [710]	Classic Autos, Winsford, Cheshire	
ZE692	BAe Sea Harrier FA2 [92/DD]	SFDO, RNAS Culdrose	
ZE693	BAe Sea Harrier FA2 [717]	Privately owned, Sproughton	
ZE694	BAe Sea Harrier FA2 [004]	Midland Air Museum, Coventry	
ZE695	BAe Sea Harrier FA2	*Scrapped, 2012*	
ZE697	BAe Sea Harrier FA2 [006]	Privately owned, Binbrook	
ZE698	BAe Sea Harrier FA2 [001]	Privately owned, Charlwood	
ZE700	BAe 146 CC2 (G-6-021)	RAF No 32(The Royal) Sqn, Northolt	
ZE701	BAe 146 CC2 (G-6-029)	RAF No 32(The Royal) Sqn, Northolt	
ZE704	Lockheed TriStar C2 (N508PA)	RAF No 216 Sqn, Brize Norton	
ZE705	Lockheed TriStar C2 (N509PA)	RAF No 216 Sqn, Brize Norton	
ZE706	Lockheed TriStar C2A (N503PA)	RAF No 216 Sqn, Brize Norton	
ZE707	BAe 146 C3	RAF No 32(The Royal) Sqn, Afghanistan	
ZE708	BAe 146 C3	RAF No 32(The Royal) Sqn, Afghanistan	
ZE734	Panavia Tornado F3 [JU]$	*Scrapped at Leeming*	

Notes	Serial	Type (code/other identity)	Owner/operator location or fate
	ZE737	Panavia Tornado F3 [GK]	RAF Leeming, RTP
	ZE760	Panavia Tornado F3 (MM7206) [AP]	RAF Coningsby, on display
	ZE763	Panavia Tornado F3 [HD]	*Scrapped at Leeming, January 2013*
	ZE788	Panavia Tornado F3 [HV]	RAF Leeming, RTP
	ZE790	Panavia Tornado F3 [HC]	RAF Leeming, RTP
	ZE791	Panavia Tornado F3 $	RAF Leeming, RTP
	ZE794	Panavia Tornado F3 [FL]	RAF Leeming, RTP
	ZE810	Panavia Tornado F3 [GG]	*Scrapped at Leeming*
	ZE831	Panavia Tornado F3 [GN]	*Scrapped at Leeming*
	ZE834	Panavia Tornado F3 [HA]	*Scrapped at Leeming*
	ZE838	Panavia Tornado F3 [GH]	*Scrapped at Leeming*
	ZE887	Panavia Tornado F3 [GF] $	RAF Museum, Hendon
	ZE934	Panavia Tornado F3 [TA]	Royal Scottish Mus'm of Flight, E Fortune
	ZE936	Panavia Tornado F3 [HE]	*Scrapped at Leeming*
	ZE961	Panavia Tornado F3 [HB]	RAF Leeming, RTP
	ZE965	Panavia Tornado F3 [HZ]	*Scrapped at Leeming*
	ZE966	Panavia Tornado F3 [VT]	Museum of Science & Industry, stored Manchester
	ZE967	Panavia Tornado F3 [UT]	RAF Leuchars, at main gate
	ZE968	Panavia Tornado F3	*Scrapped at Leeming*
	ZE983	Panavia Tornado F3 [HL]	*Scrapped at Leeming*
	ZF115	WS61 Sea King HC4 [R,WV]	RN No 848 NAS, Yeovilton
	ZF116	WS61 Sea King HC4 [WP]	RN No 845 NAS, Yeovilton
	ZF117	WS61 Sea King HC4 [X]	MoD/Vector Aerospace, Fleetlands
	ZF118	WS61 Sea King HC4 [O]	RN No 845 NAS, Yeovilton
	ZF119	WS61 Sea King HC4 [WY]	RN No 848 NAS, Yeovilton
	ZF120	WS61 Sea King HC4 [Z]	RN No 846 NAS, Yeovilton
	ZF121	WS61 Sea King HC4 [T]	DSMarE, stored *HMS Sultan*, Gosport
	ZF122	WS61 Sea King HC4 [V]	RN No 845 NAS, Yeovilton
	ZF123	WS61 Sea King HC4 [WW]	DSMarE, stored *HMS Sultan*, Gosport
	ZF124	WS61 Sea King HC4 [L]	RN No 848 *HMS Sultan*, Gosport
	ZF135	Shorts Tucano T1 [135]	RAF No 1 FTS, Linton-on-Ouse
	ZF137	Shorts Tucano T1 [137]	RAF, stored Linton-on-Ouse
	ZF139	Shorts Tucano T1 [139]	RAF No 1 FTS, Linton-on-Ouse
	ZF140	Shorts Tucano T1 [140]	RAF No 1 FTS, Linton-on-Ouse
	ZF142	Shorts Tucano T1 [142]	RAF No 1 FTS, Linton-on-Ouse
	ZF143	Shorts Tucano T1 [143]	RAF No 1 FTS, Linton-on-Ouse
	ZF144	Shorts Tucano T1 [144]	RAF No 1 FTS, Linton-on-Ouse
	ZF145	Shorts Tucano T1 [145]	RAF No 1 FTS, Linton-on-Ouse
	ZF160	Shorts Tucano T1 [160]	RAF, stored Shawbury
	ZF161	Shorts Tucano T1 [161]	RAF, stored Shawbury
	ZF163	Shorts Tucano T1 [163]	RAF, stored Shawbury
	ZF166	Shorts Tucano T1 [166]	RAF, stored Shawbury
	ZF167	Shorts Tucano T1 (fuselage)	Shorts, Belfast
	ZF169	Shorts Tucano T1 [169]	RAF, stored Linton-on-Ouse
	ZF170	Shorts Tucano T1 [MP-A]	RAF, stored Linton-on-Ouse
	ZF171	Shorts Tucano T1 [171]	RAF No 1 FTS, Linton-on-Ouse
	ZF172	Shorts Tucano T1 [MP-D]	RAF No 1 FTS, Linton-on-Ouse
	ZF202	Shorts Tucano T1 [202]	RAF Linton-on-Ouse, on display
	ZF203	Shorts Tucano T1 [203]	RAF, stored Shawbury
	ZF204	Shorts Tucano T1 [204]	RAF No 1 FTS, Linton-on-Ouse
	ZF205	Shorts Tucano T1 [205]	RAF No 1 FTS/*72(R) Sqn*, Linton-on-Ouse
	ZF209	Shorts Tucano T1 [209]	*Scrapped*
	ZF210	Shorts Tucano T1 [210]	RAF No 1 FTS, Linton-on-Ouse
	ZF211	Shorts Tucano T1 [211]	RAF, stored Shawbury
	ZF212	Shorts Tucano T1 [212]	RAF, stored Shawbury
	ZF239	Shorts Tucano T1 [239,MP-T]	RAF No 1 FTS, Linton-on-Ouse
	ZF240	Shorts Tucano T1 [240]	RAF No 1 FTS, Linton-on-Ouse
	ZF242	Shorts Tucano T1 [242]	RAF, stored Shawbury
	ZF243	Shorts Tucano T1	RAF No 1 FTS, Linton-on-Ouse

Serial	Type (code/other identity)	Owner/operator location or fate	Notes
ZF244	Shorts Tucano T1 [244]	RAF, stored Linton-on-Ouse	
ZF263	Shorts Tucano T1 [263]	RAF, stored Shawbury	
ZF264	Shorts Tucano T1 [MP-Q]	RAF No 1 FTS, Linton-on-Ouse	
ZF267	Shorts Tucano T1 [267]	Privately owned, Norwich	
ZF268	Shorts Tucano T1 [268]	RAF, stored Shawbury	
ZF269	Shorts Tucano T1 $	RAF No 1 FTS, Linton-on-Ouse	
ZF286	Shorts Tucano T1 [286]	RAF, stored Shawbury	
ZF287	Shorts Tucano T1 [287]	RAF No 1 FTS/*72(R) Sqn*, Linton-on-Ouse	
ZF288	Shorts Tucano T1 [288]	RAF, stored Shawbury	
ZF289	Shorts Tucano T1 [289]	RAF No 1 FTS, Linton-on-Ouse	
ZF290	Shorts Tucano T1 [290]	RAF No 1 FTS, Linton-on-Ouse	
ZF291	Shorts Tucano T1 [291]	RAF, stored Linton-on-Ouse	
ZF292	Shorts Tucano T1 [292]	RAF, stored Linton-on-Ouse	
ZF293	Shorts Tucano T1 [293]	RAF No 1 FTS, Linton-on-Ouse	
ZF294	Shorts Tucano T1 [294]	RAF, stored Linton-on-Ouse	
ZF295	Shorts Tucano T1 [295] $	RAF No 1 FTS/*72(R) Sqn*, Linton-on-Ouse	
ZF315	Shorts Tucano T1 [315]	RAF, stored Shawbury	
ZF317	Shorts Tucano T1 [317]	RAF No 1 FTS, Linton-on-Ouse	
ZF318	Shorts Tucano T1 [318] $	RAF, stored Shawbury	
ZF319	Shorts Tucano T1 [319]	RAF, stored Linton-on-Ouse	
ZF338	Shorts Tucano T1 [338,MP-W]	RAF, stored Linton-on-Ouse	
ZF339	Shorts Tucano T1 [339]	RAF No 1 FTS/*72(R) Sqn*, Linton-on-Ouse	
ZF341	Shorts Tucano T1 [341]	RAF, stored Linton-on-Ouse	
ZF342	Shorts Tucano T1 [342]	RAF, stored Linton-on-Ouse	
ZF343	Shorts Tucano T1 [343]	RAF No 1 FTS/*72(R) Sqn*, Linton-on-Ouse	
ZF345	Shorts Tucano T1 [345]	RAF, stored Shawbury	
ZF347	Shorts Tucano T1 [347]	RAF No 1 FTS, Linton-on-Ouse	
ZF348	Shorts Tucano T1 [348]	RAF, stored Linton-on-Ouse	
ZF349	Shorts Tucano T1 [349]	RAF Linton-on-Ouse (wreck)	
ZF350	Shorts Tucano T1 [350]	RAF, stored Shawbury	
ZF372	Shorts Tucano T1 [372]	RAF, stored Shawbury	
ZF374	Shorts Tucano T1 $	RAF No 1 FTS, Linton-on-Ouse	
ZF376	Shorts Tucano T1 [376]	RAF, stored Shawbury	
ZF377	Shorts Tucano T1 [377]	RAF No 1 FTS, Linton-on-Ouse	
ZF378	Shorts Tucano T1 [378] $	RAF No 1 FTS, Linton-on-Ouse	
ZF379	Shorts Tucano T1 [379]	RAF No 1 FTS, Linton-on-Ouse	
ZF380	Shorts Tucano T1 [380]	RAF, stored Shawbury	
ZF405	Shorts Tucano T1 [405]	RAF, stored Shawbury	
ZF406	Shorts Tucano T1 [406]	RAF No 1 FTS, Linton-on-Ouse	
ZF407	Shorts Tucano T1 [407]	RAF No 1 FTS, Linton-on-Ouse	
ZF408	Shorts Tucano T1 [408]	RAF, stored Shawbury	
ZF409	Shorts Tucano T1 [409]	RAF Church Fenton, for scrapping	
ZF410	Shorts Tucano T1 [410]	RAF, stored Shawbury	
ZF412	Shorts Tucano T1 [412]	RAF, stored Shawbury	
ZF414	Shorts Tucano T1 [414]	RAF, stored Shawbury	
ZF416	Shorts Tucano T1 [416]	RAF, stored Shawbury	
ZF417	Shorts Tucano T1 [417]	RAF No 1 FTS, Linton-on-Ouse	
ZF418	Shorts Tucano T1 [418]	RAF, stored Shawbury	
ZF446	Shorts Tucano T1 [446]	RAF, stored Shawbury	
ZF447	Shorts Tucano T1 [447]	RAF, stored Shawbury	
ZF448	Shorts Tucano T1 [448]	RAF No 1 FTS/*72(R) Sqn*, Linton-on-Ouse	
ZF449	Shorts Tucano T1 [449]	RAF, stored Shawbury	
ZF483	Shorts Tucano T1 [483]	RAF, stored Shawbury	
ZF484	Shorts Tucano T1 [484]	RAF, stored Shawbury	
ZF485	Shorts Tucano T1 (G-BULU) [485]	RAF, stored Linton-on-Ouse	
ZF486	Shorts Tucano T1 [486]	RAF, stored Shawbury	
ZF487	Shorts Tucano T1 [487]	RAF, stored Shawbury	
ZF488	Shorts Tucano T1 [488]	RAF, stored Shawbury	
ZF489	Shorts Tucano T1 [489]	RAF No 1 FTS, Linton-on-Ouse	
ZF490	Shorts Tucano T1 [490]	RAF, stored Shawbury	

Notes	*Serial*	*Type (code/other identity)*	*Owner/operator location or fate*
	ZF491	Shorts Tucano T1 [491]	RAF No 1 FTS, Linton-on-Ouse
	ZF492	Shorts Tucano T1 [492]	RAF, stored Shawbury
	ZF510	Shorts Tucano T1 [510]	MoD/AFD/QinetiQ, Boscombe Down
	ZF511	Shorts Tucano T1 [511]	MoD/AFD/QinetiQ, Boscombe Down
	ZF512	Shorts Tucano T1 [512]	RAF No 1 FTS/*72(R) Sqn*, Linton-on-Ouse
	ZF513	Shorts Tucano T1 [513]	RAF, stored Shawbury
	ZF514	Shorts Tucano T1 [514]	RAF, stored Shawbury
	ZF515	Shorts Tucano T1 [515]	RAF, stored Linton-on-Ouse
	ZF516	Shorts Tucano T1 [516]	RAF, stored Shawbury
	ZF534	BAe EAP	RAF Museum, Cosford
	ZF537	WS Lynx AH9A	RM No 847 NAS, Yeovilton
	ZF538	WS Lynx AH9A	RM No 847 NAS, Yeovilton
	ZF539	WS Lynx AH9A	MoD/Vector Aerospace, Fleetlands
	ZF540	WS Lynx AH9A	MoD/AgustaWestland, Yeovil
	ZF557	WS Lynx HMA8SRU [453/DM]	RN No 815 NAS, *Diamond* Flt, Yeovilton
	ZF558	WS Lynx HMA8SRU [411/EN]	RN No 815 NAS, *Edinburgh* Flt, Yeovilton
	ZF560	WS Lynx HMA8SRU [455]	RN No 815 NAS, *Dragon* Flt, Yeovilton
	ZF562	WS Lynx HMA8SRU [301]	RN No 815 NAS, HQ Flt, Yeovilton
	ZF563	WS Lynx HMA8SRU [303]	MoD/Vector Aerospace, Fleetlands
	ZF573	PBN 2T Islander CC2 (G-SRAY)	RAF Northolt Station Flight
	ZF579	BAC Lightning F53	Gatwick Aviation Museum, Charlwood
	ZF580	BAC Lightning F53	BAE Systems Samlesbury, at main gate
	ZF581	BAC Lightning F53	Cold War Jets Museum, Bentwaters
	ZF582	BAC Lightning F53 <ff>	Bournemouth Aviation Museum
	ZF583	BAC Lightning F53	Solway Aviation Society, Carlisle
	ZF584	BAC Lightning F53	Dumfries & Galloway Avn Mus, Dumfries
	ZF587	BAC Lightning F53 <ff>	Lashenden Air Warfare Museum, Headcorn
	ZF588	BAC Lightning F53 [L]	East Midlands Airport Aeropark
	ZF590	BAC Lightning F53 <ff>	Privately owned, Upwood, Cambs
	ZF595	BAC Lightning T55 (fuselage)	Privately owned, Binbrook
	ZF596	BAC Lightning T55 <ff>	Lakes Lightnings, Spark Bridge, Cumbria
	ZF622	Piper PA-31 Navajo Chieftain 350 (N3548Y)	MoD/AFD/QinetiQ, Boscombe Down
	ZF641	EHI-101 [PP1]	SFDO, RNAS Culdrose
	ZF649	EHI-101 Merlin (A2714) [PP5]	DSMarE AESS, *HMS Sultan*, Gosport
	ZG101	EHI-101 (mock-up) [GB]	AgustaWestland, Yeovil
	ZG347	Northrop Chukar D2	Davidstow Airfield & Cornwall At War Museum
	ZG471	BAe Harrier GR7 [61A]	*Sold to the USA, December 2011*
	ZG472	BAe Harrier GR9A [62]	*Sold to the USA, 2012*
	ZG474	BAe Harrier GR9 [64]	*Sold to the USA, 2012*
	ZG477	BAe Harrier GR9 $	RAF Museum, Cosford
	ZG478	BAe Harrier GR9 (fuselage)	Privately owned, Sproughton
	ZG479	BAe Harrier GR9A [69A]	*Sold to the USA, 2012*
	ZG480	BAe Harrier GR9 [70]	*Sold to the USA, 2012*
	ZG500	BAe Harrier GR9 [71]	*Sold to the USA, 2012*
	ZG501	BAe Harrier GR9 [EB-Q]	*Sold to the USA, 2012*
	ZG502	BAe Harrier GR9 $	*Sold to the USA, 2012*
	ZG503	BAe Harrier GR9 [EB-Z]	*Sold to the USA, December 2011*
	ZG504	BAe Harrier GR9A [75A]	*Sold to the USA, 2012*
	ZG505	BAe Harrier GR9 [76]	*Sold to the USA, 2012*
	ZG506	BAe Harrier GR9A $	*Sold to the USA, 2012*
	ZG507	BAe Harrier GR9 [78]	*Sold to the USA, 2012*
	ZG508	BAe Harrier GR9 [79]	*Sold to the USA, 2012*
	ZG509	BAe Harrier GR7 [80]	Privately owned, Sproughton
	ZG511	BAe Harrier GR9A [82A]	*Sold to the USA, 2012*
	ZG530	BAe Harrier GR9 [84]	*Sold to the USA, 2012*
	ZG531	BAe Harrier GR9 [85]	*Sold to the USA, 2012*
	ZG631	Northrop Chukar D2	Farnborough Air Sciences Trust, Farnborough
	ZG705	Panavia Tornado GR4A [118]	RAF Marham Wing
	ZG706	Panavia Tornado GR1A [E]	MoD/DSG, stored St Athan

Serial	Type (code/other identity)	Owner/operator location or fate	Notes
ZG707	Panavia Tornado GR4A [EB-Z]	RAF Lossiemouth Wing	
ZG709	Panavia Tornado GR4A [120]	RAF, stored Lossiemouth	
ZG712	Panavia Tornado GR4A [122]	RAF Lossiemouth Wing	
ZG713	Panavia Tornado GR4A [123]	RAF Marham Wing	
ZG714	Panavia Tornado GR4A [124]	RAF TEF, Lossiemouth	
ZG726	Panavia Tornado GR4A [125]	RAF Leeming, RTP	
ZG727	Panavia Tornado GR4A [126]	RAF, stored Lossiemouth	
ZG729	Panavia Tornado GR4A [127]	RAF Lossiemouth Wing	
ZG750	Panavia Tornado GR4 [128]	RAF Lossiemouth Wing	
ZG752	Panavia Tornado GR4 [129]	RAF Lossiemouth Wing	
ZG754	Panavia Tornado GR4 [130]	RAF Lossiemouth Wing	
ZG756	Panavia Tornado GR4 [131]	RAF Lossiemouth Wing	
ZG769	Panavia Tornado GR4	RAF Leeming, for scrapping	
ZG771	Panavia Tornado GR4 [133]	RAF Lossiemouth Wing	
ZG773	Panavia Tornado GR4	MoD/BAE Systems, Warton	
ZG774	Panavia Tornado F3 [HM]	RAF Leeming, RTP	
ZG775	Panavia Tornado GR4 [134]	RAF Marham Wing	
ZG777	Panavia Tornado GR4 [EB-Q]	RAF AWC/FJWOEU/No 41(R) Sqn, Coningsby	
ZG779	Panavia Tornado GR4 [136]	RAF CMU, Marham	
ZG780	Panavia Tornado F3	*Scrapped at Leeming, January 2013*	
ZG791	Panavia Tornado GR4 [137]	RAF Lossiemouth Wing	
ZG794	Panavia Tornado GR4 [TN]	RAF Leeming, for scrapping	
ZG816	WS61 Sea King HAS6 [014/L]	DSMarE, stored *HMS Sultan*, Gosport	
ZG817	WS61 Sea King HAS6 [702/PW]	DSMarE AESS, *HMS Sultan*, Gosport	
ZG818	WS61 Sea King HAS6 [707/PW]	DSMarE AESS, *HMS Sultan*, Gosport	
ZG819	WS61 Sea King HAS6 [265/N]	DSMarE AESS, *HMS Sultan*, Gosport	
ZG820	WS61 Sea King HC4 [I]	RN No 848 NAS, Yeovilton	
ZG821	WS61 Sea King HC4 [G]	MoD/Vector Aerospace, Fleetlands	
ZG822	WS61 Sea King HC4 [WS]	DSMarE, stored *HMS Sultan*, Gosport	
ZG844	PBN 2T Islander AL1 (G-BLNE)	AAC, stored Shawbury	
ZG845	PBN 2T Islander AL1 (G-BLNT)	AAC No 651 Sqn/5 Regt, Aldergrove	
ZG846	PBN 2T Islander AL1 (G-BLNU)	AAC No 651 Sqn/5 Regt, Aldergrove	
ZG847	PBN 2T Islander AL1 (G-BLNV)	AAC, stored Shawbury	
ZG848	PBN 2T Islander AL1 (G-BLNY)	AAC No 651 Sqn/5 Regt, Aldergrove	
ZG857	BAe Harrier GR9 [EB-Z]	*Sold to the USA, 2012*	
ZG858	BAe Harrier GR9 $	*Sold to the USA, 2012*	
ZG859	BAe Harrier GR9A [91A]	*Sold to the USA, 2012*	
ZG860	BAe Harrier GR9	*Sold to the USA, 2012*	
ZG862	BAe Harrier GR9 [94]	*Sold to the USA, 2012*	
ZG875	WS61 Sea King HAS6 [013/L]	DSMarE, stored *HMS Sultan*, Gosport (damaged)	
ZG884	WS Lynx AH9A	MoD/AgustaWestland, Yeovil	
ZG885	WS Lynx AH9A	RM No 847 NAS, Yeovilton	
ZG886	WS Lynx AH9A	AAC No 667 Sqn/7 Regt, Middle Wallop	
ZG887	WS Lynx AH9A	AAC No 1 Regt, Gütersloh	
ZG888	WS Lynx AH9A	AAC No 1 Regt, Gütersloh	
ZG889	WS Lynx AH9A	RM No 847 NAS, Yeovilton	
ZG914	WS Lynx AH9A	MoD/AgustaWestland, Yeovil	
ZG915	WS Lynx AH9A	RM No 847 NAS, Yeovilton	
ZG916	WS Lynx AH9A	AAC No 1 Regt, Gütersloh	
ZG917	WS Lynx AH9A	MoD/Vector Aerospace, Fleetlands	
ZG918	WS Lynx AH9A	AAC No 657 Sqn, Odiham	
ZG919	WS Lynx AH9A	RM No 847 NAS, Yeovilton	
ZG920	WS Lynx AH9A	AAC No 1 Regt, Gütersloh	
ZG921	WS Lynx AH9A	RM No 847 NAS, Yeovilton	
ZG922	WS Lynx AH9	Privately owned, Staverton, instructional use	
ZG923	WS Lynx AH9A	RM No 847 NAS, Yeovilton	
ZG969	Pilatus PC-9 (HB-HQE)	BAE Systems Warton (wfu)	
ZG989	PBN 2T Islander ASTOR (G-DLRA)	AAC, stored Shawbury	
ZG993	PBN 2T Islander AL1 (G-BOMD)	AAC, stored Shawbury	
ZG994	PBN 2T Islander AL1 (G-BPLN) (fuselage)	Britten-Norman, stored Bembridge	

Notes	Serial	Type (code/other identity)	Owner/operator location or fate
	ZG995	PBN 2T Defender AL1 (G-SURV)	AAC No 651 Sqn/5 Regt, Aldergrove
	ZG996	PBN 2T Defender AL2 (G-BWPR)	AAC No 651 Sqn/5 Regt, Aldergrove
	ZG997	PBN 2T Defender AL2 (G-BWPV)	AAC No 651 Sqn/5 Regt, Aldergrove
	ZG998	PBN 2T Defender AL1 (G-BWPX)	AAC No 651 Sqn/5 Regt, Aldergrove
	ZH001	PBN 2T Defender AL2 (G-CEIO)	AAC No 651 Sqn/5 Regt, Aldergrove
	ZH002	PBN 2T Defender AL2 (G-CEIP)	AAC No 651 Sqn/5 Regt, Aldergrove
	ZH003	PBN 2T Defender AL2 (G-CEIR)	AAC No 651 Sqn/5 Regt, Aldergrove
	ZH004	PBN 2T Defender T3 (G-BWPO)	AAC No 651 Sqn/5 Regt, Aldergrove
	ZH005	PBN 2T Defender AL2 (G-CGVB)	AAC No 651 Sqn/5 Regt, Aldergrove
	ZH101	Boeing E-3D Sentry AEW1 [01]	RAF No 8 Sqn, Waddington
	ZH102	Boeing E-3D Sentry AEW1 [02]	RAF No 8 Sqn, Waddington
	ZH103	Boeing E-3D Sentry AEW1 [03]	RAF No 8 Sqn, Waddington
	ZH104	Boeing E-3D Sentry AEW1 [04]	RAF No 8 Sqn, Waddington
	ZH105	Boeing E-3D Sentry AEW1 [05]	RAF, stored Waddington
	ZH106	Boeing E-3D Sentry AEW1 [06]	RAF No 8 Sqn, Waddington
	ZH107	Boeing E-3D Sentry AEW1 [07]	RAF No 8 Sqn, Waddington
	ZH115	Grob G109B Vigilant T1 [TA]	RAF ACCGS/No 644 VGS, Syerston
	ZH116	Grob G109B Vigilant T1 [TB]	RAF No 618 VGS, Odiham
	ZH117	Grob G109B Vigilant T1 [TC]	RAF No 642 VGS, Linton-on-Ouse
	ZH118	Grob G109B Vigilant T1 [TD]	RAF No 664 VGS, Newtownards
	ZH119	Grob G109B Vigilant T1 [TE]	RAF No 632 VGS, Ternhill
	ZH120	Grob G109B Vigilant T1 [TF]	RAF ACCGS/No 644 VGS, Syerston
	ZH121	Grob G109B Vigilant T1 [TG]	RAF No 642 VGS, Linton-on-Ouse
	ZH122	Grob G109B Vigilant T1 [TH]	RAF No 616 VGS, Henlow
	ZH123	Grob G109B Vigilant T1 [TJ]	RAF No 637 VGS, Little Rissington
	ZH124	Grob G109B Vigilant T1 [TK]	RAF No 631 VGS, Woodvale
	ZH125	Grob G109B Vigilant T1 [TL]	RAF ACCGS/No 644 VGS, Syerston
	ZH126	Grob G109B Vigilant T1 (D-KGRA) [TM]	RAF No 613 VGS, Halton
	ZH127	Grob G109B Vigilant T1 (D-KEEC) [TN]	RAF CGMF, Syerston
	ZH128	Grob G109B Vigilant T1 [TP]	RAF No 632 VGS, Ternhill
	ZH129	Grob G109B Vigilant T1 [TQ]	RAF No 632 VGS, Ternhill
	ZH139	BAe Harrier GR7 <R> (BAPC 191/*ZD472*)	RAF M&RU, Bottesford (wfu)
	ZH144	Grob G109B Vigilant T1 [TR]	RAF No 635 VGS, Topcliffe
	ZH145	Grob G109B Vigilant T1 [TS]	RAF No 624 VGS, Chivenor RMB
	ZH146	Grob G109B Vigilant T1 [TT]	RAF No 642 VGS, Linton-on-Ouse
	ZH147	Grob G109B Vigilant T1 [TU]	RAF No 613 VGS, Halton
	ZH148	Grob G109B Vigilant T1 [TV]	RAF ACCGS/No 644 VGS, Syerston
	ZH184	Grob G109B Vigilant T1 [TW]	RAF No 632 VGS, Ternhill
	ZH185	Grob G109B Vigilant T1 [TX]	RAF No 633 VGS, Cosford
	ZH186	Grob G109B Vigilant T1 [TY]	RAF ACCGS/No 644 VGS, Syerston
	ZH187	Grob G109B Vigilant T1 [TZ]	RAF No 664 VGS, Newtownards
	ZH188	Grob G109B Vigilant T1 [UA]	RAF No 633 VGS, Cosford
	ZH189	Grob G109B Vigilant T1 [UB]	RAF No 636 VGS, Swansea
	ZH190	Grob G109B Vigilant T1 [UC]	RAF No 645 VGS, Topcliffe
	ZH191	Grob G109B Vigilant T1 [UD]	RAF No 613 VGS, Halton
	ZH192	Grob G109B Vigilant T1 [UE]	RAF No 633 VGS, Cosford
	ZH193	Grob G109B Vigilant T1 [UF]	RAF No 631 VGS, Woodvale
	ZH194	Grob G109B Vigilant T1 [UG]	RAF No 633 VGS, Cosford
	ZH195	Grob G109B Vigilant T1 [UH]	RAF No 624 VGS, Chivenor RMB
	ZH196	Grob G109B Vigilant T1 [UJ]	RAF No 663 VGS, Kinloss
	ZH197	Grob G109B Vigilant T1 [UK]	RAF No 618 VGS, Odiham
	ZH200	BAe Hawk 200	Loughborough University
	ZH205	Grob G109B Vigilant T1 [UL]	RAF ACCGS/No 644 VGS, Syerston
	ZH206	Grob G109B Vigilant T1 [UM]	RAF No 631 VGS, Woodvale
	ZH207	Grob G109B Vigilant T1 [UN]	RAF No 612 VGS, Abingdon
	ZH208	Grob G109B Vigilant T1 [UP]	RAF No 645 VGS, Topcliffe
	ZH209	Grob G109B Vigilant T1 [UQ]	RAF No 634 VGS, St Athan
	ZH211	Grob G109B Vigilant T1 [UR]	RAF No 616 VGS, Henlow
	ZH247	Grob G109B Vigilant T1 [US]	RAF No 616 VGS, Henlow

Serial	Type (code/other identity)	Owner/operator location or fate	Notes
ZH248	Grob G109B Vigilant T1 [UT]	RAF No 618 VGS, Odiham	
ZH249	Grob G109B Vigilant T1 [UU]	RAF No 636 VGS, Swansea	
ZH257	B-V CH-47C Chinook (9217M) (fuselage)	RAF Odiham, BDRT	
ZH263	Grob G109B Vigilant T1 [UV]	RAF ACCGS/No 644 VGS, Syerston	
ZH264	Grob G109B Vigilant T1 [UW]	RAF CGMF, Syerston	
ZH265	Grob G109B Vigilant T1 [UX]	RAF No 618 VGS, Odiham	
ZH266	Grob G109B Vigilant T1 [UY]	RAF No 612 VGS, Abingdon	
ZH267	Grob G109B Vigilant T1 [UZ]	RAF No 635 VGS, Topcliffe	
ZH268	Grob G109B Vigilant T1 [SA]	RAF No 612 VGS, Abingdon	
ZH269	Grob G109B Vigilant T1 [SB]	RAF No 663 VGS, Kinloss	
ZH270	Grob G109B Vigilant T1 [SC]	RAF CGMF, Syerston	
ZH271	Grob G109B Vigilant T1 [SD]	RAF No 637 VGS, Little Rissington	
ZH278	Grob G109B Vigilant T1 (D-KAIS) [SF]	RAF No 616 VGS, Henlow	
ZH279	Grob G109B Vigilant T1 (D-KNPS) [SG]	RAF No 664 VGS, Newtownards	
ZH536	PBN 2T Islander CC2 (G-BSAH)	RAF Northolt Station Flight	
ZH537	PBN 2T Islander CC2 (G-SELX)	RAF Northolt Station Flight	
ZH540	WS61 Sea King HAR3A	RAF No 22 Sqn, A Flt, Chivenor RMB	
ZH541	WS61 Sea King HAR3A [V]	RAF No 22 Sqn, A Flt, Chivenor RMB	
ZH542	WS61 Sea King HAR3A [W]	MOD/Vector Airspace, Fleetlands	
ZH543	WS61 Sea King HAR3A [X]	RAF SKAMG, RNAS Yeovilton	
ZH544	WS61 Sea King HAR3A	RAF No 22 Sqn, B Flt, Wattisham	
ZH545	WS61 Sea King HAR3A $	RAF No 22 Sqn, B Flt, Wattisham	
ZH552	Panavia Tornado F3 [HW]	RAF Leeming, RTP	
ZH553	Panavia Tornado F3 [RT]	RAF, stored Shawbury	
ZH554	Panavia Tornado F3 [HX,JU-C]	RAF Leeming, RTP	
ZH555	Panavia Tornado F3 [PT]	*Scrapped at Leeming*	
ZH588	Eurofighter Typhoon (DA2)	RAF Museum, Hendon	
ZH590	Eurofighter Typhoon (DA4)	Imperial War Museum, Duxford	
ZH654	BAe Harrier T10 <ff>	RAF, Cottesmore	
ZH655	BAe Harrier T10 <ff>	Privately owned, Bentwaters	
ZH657	BAe Harrier T12 [105]	*Sold to the USA, 2012*	
ZH658	BAe Harrier T10 [fuselage]	Privately owned, Sproughton	
ZH659	BAe Harrier T12 [107]	*Sold to the USA, 2012*	
ZH660	BAe Harrier T12 [108]	*Sold to the USA, 2012*	
ZH661	BAe Harrier T12 [109]	*Sold to the USA, 2012*	
ZH662	BAe Harrier T10 [110]	*Sold to the USA, 2012*	
ZH663	BAe Harrier T12 [111]	*Sold to the USA, 2012*	
ZH664	BAe Harrier T12 [112]	*Sold to the USA, 2012*	
ZH665	BAe Harrier T12A [113]	*Sold to the USA, 2012*	
ZH763	BAC 1-11/539GL (G-BGKE)	MOD Boscombe Down (wfu)	
ZH775	B-V Chinook HC2 (N7424J) [HB]	RAF Odiham Wing	
ZH776	B-V Chinook HC2 (N7424L) [HC]	RAF Odiham Wing	
ZH777	B-V Chinook HC2 (N7424M) [HE]	RAF Odiham Wing	
ZH796	BAe Sea Harrier FA2 [001/L]	SFDO, RNAS Culdrose	
ZH797	BAe Sea Harrier FA2 [97/DD]	SFDO, RNAS Culdrose	
ZH798	BAe Sea Harrier FA2 [98/DD]	SFDO, RNAS Culdrose	
ZH799	BAe Sea Harrier FA2 [730]	Privately owned, Tunbridge Wells	
ZH800	BAe Sea Harrier FA2 (ZH801) [123]	RNAS Culdrose	
ZH801	BAe Sea Harrier FA2 (ZH800) [001]	RNAS Culdrose	
ZH802	BAe Sea Harrier FA2 [02/DD]	SFDO, RNAS Culdrose	
ZH803	BAe Sea Harrier FA2 [03/DD]	SFDO, RNAS Culdrose	
ZH804	BAe Sea Harrier FA2 [003/L]	RN, stored Culdrose	
ZH806	BAe Sea Harrier FA2 [007]	Privately owned, Bentwaters	
ZH807	BAe Sea Harrier FA2 <ff>	Privately owned, Thorpe Wood, N Yorks	
ZH810	BAe Sea Harrier FA2 [125]	Privately owned, Sproughton	
ZH811	BAe Sea Harrier FA2 [002/L]	RN, stored Culdrose	
ZH812	BAe Sea Harrier FA2 [005/L]	Privately owned, Bentwaters	
ZH813	BAe Sea Harrier FA2 [13/DD]	SFDO, RNAS Culdrose	
ZH814	Bell 212HP AH1 (G-BGMH)	AAC No 7 Flt, Brunei	
ZH815	Bell 212HP AH1 (G-BGCZ)	AAC No 7 Flt, Brunei	

Notes	Serial	Type (code/other identity)	Owner/operator location or fate
	ZH816	Bell 212HP AH1 (G-BGMG)	AAC No 7 Flt, Brunei
	ZH821	EHI-101 Merlin HM1	AgustaWestland, Yeovil, Fire Section
	ZH822	EHI-101 Merlin HM1	RN, stored Shawbury
	ZH823	EHI-101 Merlin HM1	RN, stored Shawbury
	ZH824	EHI-101 Merlin HM1 [65]	RN No 814 NAS, Culdrose
	ZH825	EHI-101 Merlin HM1 [583]	RN, stored Shawbury
	ZH826	EHI-101 Merlin HM2	MoD/AFD/QinetiQ, Boscombe Down
	ZH827	EHI-101 Merlin HM1 [14]	RN No 820 NAS, Culdrose
	ZH828	EHI-101 Merlin HM2 [65/CU]	MoD/AgustaWestland, Yeovil (conversion)
	ZH829	EHI-101 Merlin HM2 [CU]	MoD/AFD/QinetiQ, Boscombe Down
	ZH830	EHI-101 Merlin HM1	MoD/AFD/QinetiQ, Boscombe Down
	ZH831	EHI-101 Merlin HM2	MoD/AFD/QinetiQ, Boscombe Down
	ZH832	EHI-101 Merlin HM2	MoD/AgustaWestland, Yeovil
	ZH833	EHI-101 Merlin HM2 [85]	MoD/AgustaWestland, Yeovil (conversion)
	ZH834	EHI-101 Merlin HM2 [86]	MoD/AgustaWestland, Yeovil (conversion)
	ZH835	EHI-101 Merlin HM1 [87/CU]	RN No 824 NAS, Culdrose
	ZH836	EHI-101 Merlin HM1	RN No 829 NAS, Culdrose
	ZH837	EHI-101 Merlin HM2 [503/LA]	MoD/AgustaWestland, Yeovil (conversion)
	ZH838	EHI-101 Merlin HM1 [86]	RN No 820 NAS, Culdrose
	ZH839	EHI-101 Merlin HM1 [11]	RN No 820 NAS, Culdrose
	ZH840	EHI-101 Merlin HM1 [67]	RN No 814 NAS, Culdrose
	ZH841	EHI-101 Merlin HM1 [502]	RN No 829 NAS, Culdrose
	ZH842	EHI-101 Merlin HM1 [88/CU]	MoD/AgustaWestland, Yeovil
	ZH843	EHI-101 Merlin HM2	MoD/AgustaWestland, Yeovil
	ZH845	EHI-101 Merlin HM2	MoD/AgustaWestland, Yeovil (conversion)
	ZH846	EHI-101 Merlin HM1 [13/CU]	RN MDMF, Culdrose
	ZH847	EHI-101 Merlin HM1 [67]	RN No 814 NAS, Culdrose
	ZH848	EHI-101 Merlin HM1	RN No 829 NAS, Culdrose
	ZH849	EHI-101 Merlin HM1 [12]	RN No 820 NAS, Culdrose
	ZH850	EHI-101 Merlin HM2 [12]	MoD/AgustaWestland, Yeovil (conversion)
	ZH851	EHI-101 Merlin HM1 [66]	RN No 814 NAS, Culdrose
	ZH852	EHI-101 Merlin HM1	RN No 829 NAS, Culdrose
	ZH853	EHI-101 Merlin HM2 [68]	MoD/AgustaWestland, Yeovil (conversion)
	ZH854	EHI-101 Merlin HM1 [84]	RN No 824 NAS, Culdrose
	ZH855	EHI-101 Merlin HM1 [12]	RN No 820 NAS, Culdrose
	ZH856	EHI-101 Merlin HM2 [82]	MoD/AgustaWestland, Yeovil (conversion)
	ZH857	EHI-101 Merlin HM1 [70]	MoD/AgustaWestland, Yeovil (conversion)
	ZH858	EHI-101 Merlin HM1	RN No 820 NAS, Culdrose
	ZH860	EHI-101 Merlin HM1 [68] $	RN No 814 NAS, Culdrose
	ZH861	EHI-101 Merlin HM1 [81]	RN No 824 NAS, Culdrose
	ZH862	EHI-101 Merlin HM2	MoD/AgustaWestland, Yeovil (conversion)
	ZH863	EHI-101 Merlin HM1	RN MDMF, Culdrose
	ZH864	EHI-101 Merlin HM2 [17]	MoD/AgustaWestland, Yeovil (conversion)
	ZH865	Lockheed C-130J-30 Hercules C4 (N130JA) [865]	RAF No 24 Sqn/No 30 Sqn/No 47 Sqn, Brize Norton
	ZH866	Lockheed C-130J-30 Hercules C4 (N130JE) [866]	LMTAS, Marietta, USA
	ZH867	Lockheed C-130J-30 Hercules C4 (N130JJ) [867]	RAF No 24 Sqn/No 30 Sqn/No 47 Sqn, Brize Norton
	ZH868	Lockheed C-130J-30 Hercules C4 (N130JN) [868]	RAF No 24 Sqn/No 30 Sqn/No 47 Sqn, Brize Norton
	ZH869	Lockheed C-130J-30 Hercules C4 (N130JV) [869]	RAF No 24 Sqn/No 30 Sqn/No 47 Sqn, Brize Norton
	ZH870	Lockheed C-130J-30 Hercules C4 (N78235) [870]	RAF No 24 Sqn/No 30 Sqn/No 47 Sqn, Brize Norton
	ZH871	Lockheed C-130J-30 Hercules C4 (N73238) [871]	RAF No 24 Sqn/No 30 Sqn/No 47 Sqn, Brize Norton
	ZH872	Lockheed C-130J-30 Hercules C4 (N4249Y) [872]	RAF No 24 Sqn/No 30 Sqn/No 47 Sqn, Brize Norton
	ZH873	Lockheed C-130J-30 Hercules C4 (N4242N) [873]	RAF No 24 Sqn/No 30 Sqn/No 47 Sqn, Brize Norton

Serial	Type (code/other identity)	Owner/operator location or fate	Notes
ZH874	Lockheed C-130J-30 Hercules C4 (N41030) [874]	RAF No 24 Sqn/No 30 Sqn/No 47 Sqn, Brize Norton	
ZH875	Lockheed C-130J-30 Hercules C4 (N4099R) [875]	RAF No 24 Sqn/No 30 Sqn/No 47 Sqn, Brize Norton	
ZH877	Lockheed C-130J-30 Hercules C4 (N4081M) [877]	RAF No 24 Sqn/No 30 Sqn/No 47 Sqn, Brize Norton	
ZH878	Lockheed C-130J-30 Hercules C4 (N73232) [878]	RAF No 24 Sqn/No 30 Sqn/No 47 Sqn, Brize Norton	
ZH879	Lockheed C-130J-30 Hercules C4 (N4080M) [879]	RAF No 24 Sqn/No 30 Sqn/No 47 Sqn, Brize Norton	
ZH880	Lockheed C-130J Hercules C5 (N73238) [880]	RAF No 24 Sqn/No 30 Sqn/No 47 Sqn, Brize Norton	
ZH881	Lockheed C-130J Hercules C5 (N4081M) [881]	RAF No 24 Sqn/No 30 Sqn/No 47 Sqn, Brize Norton	
ZH882	Lockheed C-130J Hercules C5 (N4099R) [882]	RAF No 1312 Flt, Mount Pleasant, FI	
ZH883	Lockheed C-130J Hercules C5 (N4242N) [883]	RAF No 24 Sqn/No 30 Sqn/No 47 Sqn, Brize Norton	
ZH884	Lockheed C-130J Hercules C5 (N4249Y) [884]	RAF No 24 Sqn/No 30 Sqn/No 47 Sqn, Brize Norton	
ZH885	Lockheed C-130J Hercules C5 (N41030) [885]	RAF No 24 Sqn/No 30 Sqn/No 47 Sqn, Brize Norton	
ZH886	Lockheed C-130J Hercules C5 (N73235) [886]	RAF No 24 Sqn/No 30 Sqn/No 47 Sqn, Brize Norton	
ZH887	Lockheed C-130J Hercules C5 (N4187W) [887]	RAF No 24 Sqn/No 30 Sqn/No 47 Sqn, Brize Norton	
ZH888	Lockheed C-130J Hercules C5 (N4187) [888]	RAF No 24 Sqn/No 30 Sqn/No 47 Sqn, Brize Norton	
ZH889	Lockheed C-130J Hercules C5 (N4099R) [889]	RAF No 24 Sqn/No 30 Sqn/No 47 Sqn, Brize Norton	
ZH890	Grob G109B Vigilant T1 [SE]	RAF No 613 VGS, Halton	
ZH891	B-V Chinook HC2A (N20075) [HF]	RAF Odiham Wing	
ZH892	B-V Chinook HC2A (N2019V) [HG]	RAF Odiham Wing	
ZH893	B-V Chinook HC2A (N2025L) [HH]	MoD/Vector Aerospace, Fleetlands	
ZH894	B-V Chinook HC2A (N2026E) [HI]	RAF Odiham Wing	
ZH895	B-V Chinook HC2A (N2034K) [HJ] $	RAF Odiham Wing	
ZH896	B-V Chinook HC2A (N2038G) [HK]	RAF Odiham Wing	
ZH897	B-V Chinook HC3R (N2045G)	RAF Odiham Wing	
ZH898	B-V Chinook HC3R (N2057Q)	RAF Odiham Wing	
ZH899	B-V Chinook HC3R (N2057R)	RAF Odiham Wing	
ZH900	B-V Chinook HC3R (N2060H)	RAF Odiham Wing	
ZH901	B-V Chinook HC3R (N2060M)	RAF Odiham Wing	
ZH902	B-V Chinook HC3R (N2064W)	MoD/Vector Aerospace, Fleetlands	
ZH903	B-V Chinook HC3R (N20671) [HR]	RAF Odiham Wing	
ZH904	B-V Chinook HC3R (N2083K)	RAF Odiham Wing	
ZH917	Panavia Tornado IDS (RSAF 6631)	MoD/BAE Systems, Warton	
ZJ100	BAe Hawk 102D	MoD/BAE Systems, stored Warton	
ZJ117	EHI-101 Merlin HC3	MoD/AgustaWestland, Yeovil	
ZJ118	EHI-101 Merlin HC3 [B]	RAF No 1419 Flt, Kandahar, Afghanistan	
ZJ119	EHI-101 Merlin HC3 [C]	RAF MDMF, RNAS Culdrose	
ZJ120	EHI-101 Merlin HC3 [D]	RAF No 1419 Flt, Kandahar, Afghanistan	
ZJ121	EHI-101 Merlin HC3 [E]	RAF No 28 Sqn/No 78 Sqn, Benson	
ZJ122	EHI-101 Merlin HC3 [F]	RAF No 28 Sqn/No 78 Sqn, Benson	
ZJ123	EHI-101 Merlin HC3 [G]	RAF MDMF, RNAS Culdrose	
ZJ124	EHI-101 Merlin HC3 [H]	RAF MDMF, RNAS Culdrose	
ZJ125	EHI-101 Merlin HC3 [J]	RAF No 1419 Flt, Kandahar, Afghanistan	
ZJ126	EHI-101 Merlin HC3 [K]	MoD/AgustaWestland, Yeovil	
ZJ127	EHI-101 Merlin HC3 [L]	RAF No 1419 Flt, Kandahar, Afghanistan	
ZJ128	EHI-101 Merlin HC3 [M]	RAF MDMF, RNAS Culdrose	
ZJ129	EHI-101 Merlin HC3 [N]	RAF No 1419 Flt, Kandahar, Afghanistan	
ZJ130	EHI-101 Merlin HC3 [O]	RAF No 28 Sqn/No 78 Sqn, Benson	
ZJ131	EHI-101 Merlin HC3 [P]	RAF No 28 Sqn/No 78 Sqn, Benson	
ZJ132	EHI-101 Merlin HC3 [Q]	RAF No 28 Sqn/No 78 Sqn, Benson	
ZJ133	EHI-101 Merlin HC3 [R]	RAF No 28 Sqn/No 78 Sqn, Benson	
ZJ134	EHI-101 Merlin HC3 [S]	RAF No 28 Sqn/No 78 Sqn, Benson	
ZJ135	EHI-101 Merlin HC3 [T]	RAF No 28 Sqn/No 78 Sqn, Benson	
ZJ136	EHI-101 Merlin HC3 [U]	RAF No 28 Sqn/No 78 Sqn, Benson	
ZJ137	EHI-101 Merlin HC3 [W]	RAF No 1419 Flt, Kandahar, Afghanistan	
ZJ138	EHI-101 Merlin HC3 [X]	DSMarE, stored *HMS Sultan*, Gosport	

Notes	Serial	Type (code/other identity)	Owner/operator location or fate
	ZJ164	AS365N-2 Dauphin 2 (G-BTLC)	RN/Bond Helicopters, Newquay
	ZJ165	AS365N-2 Dauphin 2 (G-NTOO)	RN/Bond Helicopters, Newquay
	ZJ166	WAH-64 Apache AH1 (N9219G)	AAC No 673 Sqn/7 Regt, Middle Wallop
	ZJ167	WAH-64 Apache AH1 (N3266B)	AAC No 673 Sqn/7 Regt, Middle Wallop
	ZJ168	WAH-64 Apache AH1 (N3123T)	AAC No 3 Regt, Wattisham
	ZJ169	WAH-64 Apache AH1 (N3114H)	AAC No 4 Regt, Wattisham
	ZJ170	WAH-64 Apache AH1 (N3065U)	AAC No 673 Sqn/7 Regt, Middle Wallop
	ZJ171	WAH-64 Apache AH1 (N3266T)	AAC No 4 Regt, Wattisham
	ZJ172	WAH-64 Apache AH1	AAC, stored Wattisham
	ZJ173	WAH-64 Apache AH1 (N3266W)	AAC No 3 Regt, Wattisham
	ZJ174	WAH-64 Apache AH1	AAC No 4 Regt, Wattisham
	ZJ175	WAH-64 Apache AH1 (N3218V)	AAC No 673 Sqn/7 Regt, Middle Wallop
	ZJ176	WAH-64 Apache AH1	AAC No 4 Regt, Wattisham
	ZJ177	WAH-64 Apache AH1	AAC, stored Wattisham (damaged)
	ZJ178	WAH-64 Apache AH1	AAC No 4 Regt, Wattisham
	ZJ179	WAH-64 Apache AH1	AAC No 3 Regt, Wattisham
	ZJ180	WAH-64 Apache AH1	AAC No 673 Sqn/7 Regt, Middle Wallop
	ZJ181	WAH-64 Apache AH1	AAC No 4 Regt, Wattisham
	ZJ182	WAH-64 Apache AH1	AAC No 4 Regt, Wattisham
	ZJ183	WAH-64 Apache AH1	AAC No 4 Regt, Wattisham
	ZJ184	WAH-64 Apache AH1	AAC No 4 Regt, Wattisham
	ZJ185	WAH-64 Apache AH1	AAC No 3 Regt, Wattisham
	ZJ186	WAH-64 Apache AH1	AAC No 3 Regt, Wattisham
	ZJ187	WAH-64 Apache AH1	AAC No 3 Regt, Wattisham
	ZJ188	WAH-64 Apache AH1	AAC No 3 Regt, Wattisham
	ZJ189	WAH-64 Apache AH1	AAC No 673 Sqn/7 Regt, Middle Wallop
	ZJ190	WAH-64 Apache AH1	AAC No 3 Regt, Wattisham
	ZJ191	WAH-64 Apache AH1	AAC No 4 Regt, Wattisham
	ZJ192	WAH-64 Apache AH1	AAC No 673 Sqn/7 Regt, Middle Wallop
	ZJ193	WAH-64 Apache AH1	AAC No 3 Regt, Wattisham
	ZJ194	WAH-64 Apache AH1	AAC No 3 Regt, Wattisham
	ZJ195	WAH-64 Apache AH1	AAC No 3 Regt, Wattisham
	ZJ196	WAH-64 Apache AH1	AAC No 4 Regt, Wattisham
	ZJ197	WAH-64 Apache AH1	AAC No 3 Regt, Wattisham
	ZJ198	WAH-64 Apache AH1	AAC No 673 Sqn/7 Regt, Middle Wallop
	ZJ199	WAH-64 Apache AH1	AAC No 3 Regt, Wattisham
	ZJ200	WAH-64 Apache AH1	AAC No 4 Regt, Wattisham
	ZJ202	WAH-64 Apache AH1	AAC No 3 Regt, Wattisham
	ZJ203	WAH-64 Apache AH1	AAC No 3 Regt, Wattisham
	ZJ204	WAH-64 Apache AH1	AAC No 3 Regt, Wattisham
	ZJ205	WAH-64 Apache AH1	AAC No 3 Regt, Wattisham
	ZJ206	WAH-64 Apache AH1	AAC No 673 Sqn/7 Regt, Middle Wallop
	ZJ207	WAH-64 Apache AH1	AAC No 4 Regt, Wattisham
	ZJ208	WAH-64 Apache AH1	AAC No 3 Regt, Wattisham
	ZJ209	WAH-64 Apache AH1	AAC No 3 Regt, Wattisham
	ZJ210	WAH-64 Apache AH1	AAC No 4 Regt, Wattisham
	ZJ211	WAH-64 Apache AH1	AAC No 3 Regt, Wattisham
	ZJ212	WAH-64 Apache AH1	AAC No 673 Sqn/7 Regt, Middle Wallop
	ZJ213	WAH-64 Apache AH1	AAC No 673 Sqn/7 Regt, Middle Wallop
	ZJ214	WAH-64 Apache AH1	AAC No 673 Sqn/7 Regt, Middle Wallop
	ZJ215	WAH-64 Apache AH1	AAC No 3 Regt, Wattisham
	ZJ216	WAH-64 Apache AH1	AAC No 3 Regt, Wattisham
	ZJ217	WAH-64 Apache AH1	AAC No 4 Regt, Wattisham
	ZJ218	WAH-64 Apache AH1	AAC No 4 Regt, Wattisham
	ZJ219	WAH-64 Apache AH1	AAC No 673 Sqn/7 Regt, Middle Wallop
	ZJ220	WAH-64 Apache AH1	AAC No 673 Sqn/7 Regt, Middle Wallop
	ZJ221	WAH-64 Apache AH1	AAC No 4 Regt, Wattisham
	ZJ222	WAH-64 Apache AH1	AAC No 4 Regt, Wattisham
	ZJ223	WAH-64 Apache AH1	AAC No 673 Sqn/7 Regt, Middle Wallop
	ZJ224	WAH-64 Apache AH1	AAC No 3 Regt, Wattisham

Serial	Type (code/other identity)	Owner/operator location or fate	Notes
ZJ225	WAH-64 Apache AH1	AAC No 3 Regt, Wattisham	
ZJ226	WAH-64 Apache AH1	AAC No 673 Sqn/7 Regt, Middle Wallop	
ZJ227	WAH-64 Apache AH1	AAC, stored Wattisham	
ZJ228	WAH-64 Apache AH1	AAC No 4 Regt, Wattisham	
ZJ229	WAH-64 Apache AH1	AAC No 4 Regt, Wattisham	
ZJ230	WAH-64 Apache AH1	AAC No 4 Regt, Wattisham	
ZJ231	WAH-64 Apache AH1	MoD/AgustaWestland, Yeovil	
ZJ232	WAH-64 Apache AH1	AAC No 4 Regt, Wattisham	
ZJ233	WAH-64 Apache AH1	AAC No 4 Regt, Wattisham	
ZJ234	Bell 412EP Griffin HT1 (G-BWZR) [S]	DHFS No 60(R) Sqn, RAF Shawbury	
ZJ235	Bell 412EP Griffin HT1 (G-BXBF) [I]	DHFS No 60(R) Sqn, RAF Shawbury	
ZJ236	Bell 412EP Griffin HT1 (G-BXBE) [X]	DHFS No 60(R) Sqn, RAF Shawbury	
ZJ237	Bell 412EP Griffin HT1 (G-BXFF) [T]	DHFS No 60(R) Sqn, RAF Shawbury	
ZJ238	Bell 412EP Griffin HT1 (G-BXHC) [Y]	DHFS No 60(R) Sqn, RAF Shawbury	
ZJ239	Bell 412EP Griffin HT1 (G-BXFH) [R]	DHFS No 60(R) Sqn/SARTU, RAF Valley	
ZJ240	Bell 412EP Griffin HT1 (G-BXIR) [U] $	DHFS No 60(R) Sqn, RAF Shawbury	
ZJ241	Bell 412EP Griffin HT1 (G-BXIS) [L]	DHFS No 60(R) Sqn, RAF Shawbury	
ZJ242	Bell 412EP Griffin HT1 (G-BXDK) [E]	DHFS No 60(R) Sqn, RAF Shawbury	
ZJ243	AS350BA Squirrel HT2 (G-BWZS) [43]	School of Army Aviation/No 670 Sqn, Middle Wallop	
ZJ244	AS350BA Squirrel HT2 (G-BXMD) [44]	School of Army Aviation/No 670 Sqn, Middle Wallop	
ZJ245	AS350BA Squirrel HT2 (G-BXME) [45]	School of Army Aviation/No 670 Sqn, Middle Wallop	
ZJ246	AS350BA Squirrel HT2 (G-BXMJ) [46]	School of Army Aviation/No 670 Sqn, Middle Wallop	
ZJ248	AS350BA Squirrel HT2 (G-BXNE) [48]	School of Army Aviation/No 670 Sqn, Middle Wallop	
ZJ249	AS350BA Squirrel HT2 (G-BXNJ) [49]	School of Army Aviation/No 670 Sqn, Middle Wallop	
ZJ250	AS350BA Squirrel HT2 (G-BXNY) [50]	School of Army Aviation/No 670 Sqn, Middle Wallop	
ZJ251	AS350BA Squirrel HT2 (G-BXOG) [51]	DHFS, RAF Shawbury	
ZJ252	AS350BA Squirrel HT2 (G-BXOK) [52]	School of Army Aviation/No 670 Sqn, Middle Wallop	
ZJ253	AS350BA Squirrel HT2 (G-BXPG) [53]	School of Army Aviation/No 670 Sqn, Middle Wallop	
ZJ254	AS350BA Squirrel HT2 (G-BXPJ) [54]	School of Army Aviation/No 670 Sqn, Middle Wallop	
ZJ255	AS350BB Squirrel HT1 (G-BXAG) [55]	DHFS, RAF Shawbury	
ZJ256	AS350BB Squirrel HT1 (G-BXCE) [56]	DHFS, RAF Shawbury	
ZJ257	AS350BB Squirrel HT1 (G-BXDJ) [57]	DHFS, RAF Shawbury	
ZJ258	AS350BB Squirrel HT1 (G-BXEO) [58]	RAF Shawbury (wreck)	
ZJ260	AS350BB Squirrel HT1 (G-BXGB) [60]	DHFS, RAF Shawbury	
ZJ261	AS350BB Squirrel HT1 (G-BXGJ) [61]	DHFS, RAF Shawbury	
ZJ262	AS350BB Squirrel HT1 (G-BXHB) [62]	DHFS, RAF Shawbury	
ZJ264	AS350BB Squirrel HT1 (G-BXHW) [64]	DHFS, RAF Shawbury	
ZJ265	AS350BB Squirrel HT1 (G-BXHX) [65]	DHFS, RAF Shawbury	
ZJ266	AS350BB Squirrel HT1 (G-BXIL) [66]	DHFS, RAF Shawbury	
ZJ267	AS350BB Squirrel HT1 (G-BXIP) [67]	DHFS, RAF Shawbury	
ZJ268	AS350BB Squirrel HT1 (G-BXJE) [68]	DHFS, RAF Shawbury	
ZJ269	AS350BB Squirrel HT1 (G-BXJN) [69]	DHFS, RAF Shawbury	
ZJ270	AS350BB Squirrel HT1 (G-BXJR) [70]	DHFS, RAF Shawbury	
ZJ271	AS350BB Squirrel HT1 (G-BXKE) [71]	DHFS, RAF Shawbury	
ZJ272	AS350BB Squirrel HT1 (G-BXKN) [72]	DHFS, RAF Shawbury	
ZJ273	AS350BB Squirrel HT1 (G-BXKP) [73]	DHFS, RAF Shawbury	
ZJ274	AS350BB Squirrel HT1 (G-BXKR) [74]	DHFS, RAF Shawbury	
ZJ275	AS350BB Squirrel HT1 (G-BXLB) [75]	DHFS, RAF Shawbury	
ZJ276	AS350BB Squirrel HT1 (G-BXLE) [76]	RAF Shawbury (wreck)	
ZJ277	AS350BB Squirrel HT1 (G-BXLH) [77]	DHFS, RAF Shawbury	
ZJ278	AS350BB Squirrel HT1 (G-BXMB) [78]	DHFS, RAF Shawbury	
ZJ279	AS350BB Squirrel HT1 (G-BXMC) [79]	DHFS, RAF Shawbury	
ZJ280	AS350BB Squirrel HT1 (G-BXMI) [80]	DHFS, RAF Shawbury	
ZJ369	GEC Phoenix UAV	Defence Academy of the UK, Shrivenham	
ZJ385	GEC Phoenix UAV	Muckleburgh Collection, Weybourne, Norfolk	
ZJ449	GEC Phoenix UAV	REME Museum, Arborfield	
ZJ452	GEC Phoenix UAV	Science Museum, Wroughton	
ZJ489	GAF Jindivik 800 (A92-809)	*Currently not known*	
ZJ493	GAF Jindivik 800 (A92-814)	RAF Stafford	
ZJ496	GAF Jindivik 900 (A92-901)	Farnborough Air Sciences Trust, Farnborough	

Notes	Serial	Type (code/other identity)	Owner/operator location or fate
	ZJ515	BAE Systems Nimrod MRA4 (XV258) <ff>	Cranfield University, instructional use
	ZJ645	D-BD Alpha Jet (98+62) [45]	MoD/AFD/QinetiQ, Boscombe Down
	ZJ646	D-BD Alpha Jet (98+55) [46]	MoD/AFD/QinetiQ, Boscombe Down
	ZJ647	D-BD Alpha Jet (98+71) [47]	MoD/AFD/QinetiQ, Boscombe Down
	ZJ648	D-BD Alpha Jet (98+09) [48]	MoD/AFD/QinetiQ, Boscombe Down
	ZJ649	D-BD Alpha Jet (98+73) [49]	MoD/ETPS, Boscombe Down
	ZJ650	D-BD Alpha Jet (98+35)	MoD/QinetiQ, stored Boscombe Down
	ZJ651	D-BD Alpha Jet (41+42) [51]	MoD/ETPS, Boscombe Down
	ZJ652	D-BD Alpha Jet (41+09)	MoD/QinetiQ Boscombe Down, spares use
	ZJ653	D-BD Alpha Jet (40+22)	MoD/QinetiQ Boscombe Down, spares use
	ZJ654	D-BD Alpha Jet (41+02)	MoD/QinetiQ Boscombe Down, spares use
	ZJ655	D-BD Alpha Jet (41+19)	MoD/QinetiQ Boscombe Down, spares use
	ZJ656	D-BD Alpha Jet (41+40)	MoD/QinetiQ Boscombe Down, spares use
	ZJ690	Bombardier Sentinel R1 (C-GJRG)	RAF No 5 Sqn, Waddington
	ZJ691	Bombardier Sentinel R1 (C-FZVM)	RAF No 5 Sqn, Waddington
	ZJ692	Bombardier Sentinel R1 (C-FZWW)	RAF No 5 Sqn, Waddington
	ZJ693	Bombardier Sentinel R1 (C-FZXC)	RAF No 5 Sqn, Waddington
	ZJ694	Bombardier Sentinel R1 (C-FZYL)	RAF No 5 Sqn, Waddington
	ZJ699	Eurofighter Typhoon (PT001)	MoD/BAE Systems, Warton
	ZJ700	Eurofighter Typhoon (PS002)	MoD/BAE Systems, Warton
	ZJ703	Bell 412EP Griffin HAR2 (G-CBST) [*Spades*, 3]	DHFS No 60(R) Sqn, RAF Shawbury
	ZJ704	Bell 412EP Griffin HAR2 (G-CBWT) [*Clubs*,4]	RAF No 84 Sqn, Akrotiri
	ZJ705	Bell 412EP Griffin HAR2 (G-CBXL) [*Hearts*,5]	RAF No 84 Sqn, Akrotiri
	ZJ706	Bell 412EP Griffin HAR2 (G-CBYR) [*Diamonds*,6]	RAF No 84 Sqn, Akrotiri
	ZJ707	Bell 412EP Griffin HT1 (G-CBUB) [O]	DHFS No 60(R) Sqn, RAF Shawbury
	ZJ708	Bell 412EP Griffin HT1 (G-CBVP) [K]	DHFS No 60(R) Sqn, RAF Shawbury
	ZJ780	AS365N-3 Dauphin II (G-CEXT)	AAC No 8 Flt, Credenhill
	ZJ781	AS365N-3 Dauphin II (G-CEXU)	AAC No 8 Flt, Credenhill
	ZJ782	AS365N-3 Dauphin II (G-CEXV)	AAC No 8 Flt, Credenhill
	ZJ783	AS365N-3 Dauphin II (G-CEXW)	AAC No 8 Flt, Credenhill
	ZJ785	AS365N-3 Dauphin II (G-CFFW)	AAC No 8 Flt, Credenhill
	ZJ800	Eurofighter Typhoon T3 [BC]	RAF No 29(R) Sqn, Coningsby
	ZJ801	Eurofighter Typhoon T3 [BJ]	RAF No 29(R) Sqn, Coningsby
	ZJ802	Eurofighter Typhoon T3 [QO-B]	RAF No 3 Sqn, Coningsby
	ZJ803	Eurofighter Typhoon T3 [BA]	RAF No 29(R) Sqn, Coningsby
	ZJ804	Eurofighter Typhoon T3 [BM]	RAF No 29(R) Sqn, Coningsby
	ZJ805	Eurofighter Typhoon T3 [BD]	RAF TMF, Coningsby
	ZJ806	Eurofighter Typhoon T3 [BE]	RAF No 29(R) Sqn, Coningsby
	ZJ807	Eurofighter Typhoon T3 [BF]	RAF No 29(R) Sqn, Coningsby
	ZJ808	Eurofighter Typhoon T3 [DW]	RAF No 11 Sqn, Coningsby
	ZJ809	Eurofighter Typhoon T3 [EY]	RAF No 6 Sqn, Leuchars
	ZJ810	Eurofighter Typhoon T3 [BI]	RAF TMF, Coningsby
	ZJ811	Eurofighter Typhoon T3 [BP]	RAF No 29(R) Sqn, Coningsby
	ZJ812	Eurofighter Typhoon T3 [BK]	RAF No 29(R) Sqn, Coningsby
	ZJ813	Eurofighter Typhoon T3 [BL]	RAF No 29(R) Sqn, Coningsby
	ZJ814	Eurofighter Typhoon T3 [BH]	RAF No 29(R) Sqn, Coningsby
	ZJ815	Eurofighter Typhoon T3 [BN]	RAF No 29(R) Sqn, Coningsby
	ZJ910	Eurofighter Typhoon FGR4 [BV]	RAF No 29(R) Sqn, Coningsby
	ZJ911	Eurofighter Typhoon FGR4 [BZ]	RAF No 29(R) Sqn, Coningsby
	ZJ912	Eurofighter Typhoon FGR4 [AB]	RAF No 17(R) Sqn, Coningsby
	ZJ913	Eurofighter Typhoon FGR4 [QO-M]	RAF TMF, Coningsby
	ZJ914	Eurofighter Typhoon FGR4 [DS]	RAF No 11 Sqn, Coningsby
	ZJ915	Eurofighter Typhoon FGR4 [BY]	RAF No 29(R) Sqn, Coningsby
	ZJ916	Eurofighter Typhoon FGR4 [QO-S]	RAF No 3 Sqn, Coningsby
	ZJ917	Eurofighter Typhoon FGR4 [QO-G]	RAF No 3 Sqn, Coningsby
	ZJ918	Eurofighter Typhoon FGR4 [QO-L]	RAF No 3 Sqn, Coningsby
	ZJ919	Eurofighter Typhoon FGR4 [DC]	RAF TMF, Coningsby
	ZJ920	Eurofighter Typhoon FGR4 [QO-A]	RAF No 3 Sqn, Coningsby
	ZJ921	Eurofighter Typhoon FGR4 [QO-H]	RAF No 3 Sqn, Coningsby

Serial	Type (code/other identity)	Owner/operator location or fate	Notes
ZJ922	Eurofighter Typhoon FGR4 [QO-C]	RAF TMF, Coningsby	
ZJ923	Eurofighter Typhoon FGR4 [DM]	RAF No 11 Sqn, Coningsby	
ZJ924	Eurofighter Typhoon FGR4 [DD]	RAF No 11 Sqn, Coningsby	
ZJ925	Eurofighter Typhoon FGR4 [QO-R]	RAF No 3 Sqn, Coningsby	
ZJ926	Eurofighter Typhoon FGR4 [QO-Y]	RAF No 3 Sqn, Coningsby	
ZJ927	Eurofighter Typhoon FGR4 [AE]	RAF No 17(R) Sqn, Coningsby	
ZJ928	Eurofighter Typhoon FGR4 [BX]	RAF No 29(R) Sqn, Coningsby	
ZJ929	Eurofighter Typhoon FGR4 [DL]	RAF No 3 Sqn, Coningsby	
ZJ930	Eurofighter Typhoon FGR4 [AA]	RAF No 17(R) Sqn, Coningsby	
ZJ931	Eurofighter Typhoon FGR4 [DA]	RAF No 11 Sqn, Coningsby	
ZJ932	Eurofighter Typhoon FGR4 [DB]	RAF TMF, Coningsby	
ZJ933	Eurofighter Typhoon FGR4 [DF]	RAF No 11 Sqn, Coningsby	
ZJ934	Eurofighter Typhoon FGR4 [QO-T]	RAF No 3 Sqn, Coningsby	
ZJ935	Eurofighter Typhoon FGR4 [DJ]	RAF No 11 Sqn, Coningsby	
ZJ936	Eurofighter Typhoon FGR4 [QO-C] $	RAF No 3 Sqn, Coningsby	
ZJ937	Eurofighter Typhoon FGR4 [QO-W]	RAF No 3 Sqn, Coningsby	
ZJ938	Eurofighter Typhoon FGR4	MoD/BAE Systems, Warton	
ZJ939	Eurofighter Typhoon FGR4 [DX]	RAF No 11 Sqn, Coningsby	
ZJ940	Eurofighter Typhoon FGR4	RAF, stored Coningsby	
ZJ941	Eurofighter Typhoon FGR4 [QO-J]	RAF No 3 Sqn, Coningsby	
ZJ942	Eurofighter Typhoon FGR4 [DH]	RAF No 11 Sqn, Coningsby	
ZJ943	Eurofighter Typhoon FGR4 [DK]	RAF, stored Coningsby (wreck)	
ZJ944	Eurofighter Typhoon FGR4 [F]	RAF No 1435 Flt, Mount Pleasant, FI	
ZJ945	Eurofighter Typhoon FGR4	RAF, stored Coningsby	
ZJ946	Eurofighter Typhoon FGR4 [AG]	RAF No 17(R) Sqn, Coningsby	
ZJ947	Eurofighter Typhoon FGR4 [AH]	RAF No 17(R) Sqn, Coningsby	
ZJ948	Eurofighter Typhoon FGR4	RAF, stored Coningsby	
ZJ949	Eurofighter Typhoon FGR4 [H]	RAF No 1435 Flt, Mount Pleasant, FI	
ZJ950	Eurofighter Typhoon FGR4 [C]	RAF No 1435 Flt, Mount Pleasant, FI	
ZJ951	BAE Systems Hawk 120D	MoD/BAE Systems, Warton	
ZJ954	SA330H Puma HC2 (SAAF 144)	MoD/Eurocopter, Marseilles, France (conversion)	
ZJ955	SA330H Puma HC2 (SAAF 148)	MoD/Eurocopter, Brasov, Romania (conversion)	
ZJ956	SA330H Puma HC2 (SAAF 172)	MoD/Eurocopter, Brasov, Romania (conversion)	
ZJ957	SA330H Puma HC2 (SAAF 169)	MoD/Eurocopter, Marseilles, France (conversion)	
ZJ958	SA330H Puma (SAAF 173)	DE&S, stored Bicester	
ZJ959	SA330H Puma (SAAF 184)	DE&S, stored Bicester	
ZJ960	Grob G109B Vigilant T1 (D-KSMU) [SH]	RAF ACCGS/No 644 VGS, Syerston	
ZJ961	Grob G109B Vigilant T1 (D-KLCW) [SJ]	RAF No 637 VGS, Little Rissington	
ZJ962	Grob G109B Vigilant T1 (D-KBEU) [SK]	RAF No 634 VGS, St Athan	
ZJ963	Grob G109B Vigilant T1 (D-KMSN) [SL]	RAF CGMF, Syerston	
ZJ964	Bell 212HP AH2 (G-BJGV) [D]	AAC No 25 Flt, Kenya	
ZJ966	Bell 212HP AH2 (G-BJJO) [C]	AAC No 25 Flt, Kenya	
ZJ967	Grob G109B Vigilant T1 (G-DEWS) [SM]	RAF CGMF, Syerston	
ZJ968	Grob G109B Vigilant T1 (N109BT) [SN]	RAF No 631 VGS, Woodvale	
ZJ969	Bell 212HP AH1 (G-BGLJ) [K]	AAC No 25 Flt, Kenya	
ZJ990	EHI-101 Merlin HC3A (M-501) [AA]	RAF No 28 Sqn/No 78 Sqn, Benson	
ZJ992	EHI-101 Merlin HC3A (M-503) [AB]	RAF MDMF, RNAS Culdrose	
ZJ994	EHI-101 Merlin HC3A (M-505) [AC]	RAF No 28 Sqn/No 78 Sqn, Benson	
ZJ995	EHI-101 Merlin HC3A (M-506) [AD]	RAF No 28 Sqn/No 78 Sqn, Benson	
ZJ998	EHI-101 Merlin HC3A (M-509) [AE]	RAF No 28 Sqn/No 78 Sqn, Benson	
ZK001	EHI-101 Merlin HC3A (M-511) [AF]	RAF No 28 Sqn/No 78 Sqn, Benson	
ZK005	Grob G109B Vigilant T1 (OH-797) [SP]	RAF No 645 VGS, Topcliffe	
ZK010	BAE Systems Hawk T2 [A]	RAF No 4 FTS/4(R) Sqn, Valley	
ZK011	BAE Systems Hawk T2 [B]	RAF No 4 FTS/4(R) Sqn, Valley	
ZK012	BAE Systems Hawk T2 [C]	RAF No 4 FTS/4(R) Sqn, Valley	
ZK013	BAE Systems Hawk T2	RAF No 4 FTS/4(R) Sqn, Valley	
ZK014	BAE Systems Hawk T2 [E]	RAF No 4 FTS/4(R) Sqn, Valley	
ZK015	BAE Systems Hawk T2	RAF No 4 FTS/4(R) Sqn, Valley	
ZK016	BAE Systems Hawk T2	RAF No 4 FTS/4(R) Sqn, Valley	

Notes	Serial	Type (code/other identity)	Owner/operator location or fate
	ZK017	BAE Systems Hawk T2	RAF No 4 FTS/4(R) Sqn, Valley
	ZK018	BAE Systems Hawk T2 [I] $	RAF No 4 FTS/4(R) Sqn, Valley
	ZK019	BAE Systems Hawk T2	RAF No 4 FTS/4(R) Sqn, Valley
	ZK020	BAE Systems Hawk T2 [K] $	RAF No 4 FTS/4(R) Sqn, Valley
	ZK021	BAE Systems Hawk T2 [L]	RAF No 4 FTS/4(R) Sqn, Valley
	ZK022	BAE Systems Hawk T2 [M]	RAF No 4 FTS/4(R) Sqn, Valley
	ZK023	BAE Systems Hawk T2	RAF No 4 FTS/4(R) Sqn, Valley
	ZK024	BAE Systems Hawk T2 [O]	RAF No 4 FTS/4(R) Sqn, Valley
	ZK025	BAE Systems Hawk T2 [P]	RAF No 4 FTS/4(R) Sqn, Valley
	ZK026	BAE Systems Hawk T2 [Q]	RAF No 4 FTS/4(R) Sqn, Valley
	ZK027	BAE Systems Hawk T2 [R]	RAF No 4 FTS/4(R) Sqn, Valley
	ZK028	BAE Systems Hawk T2 [S]	RAF No 4 FTS/4(R) Sqn, Valley
	ZK029	BAE Systems Hawk T2 [T]	RAF No 4 FTS/4(R) Sqn, Valley
	ZK030	BAE Systems Hawk T2	RAF No 4 FTS/4(R) Sqn, Valley
	ZK031	BAE Systems Hawk T2 [V]	RAF No 4 FTS/4(R) Sqn, Valley
	ZK032	BAE Systems Hawk T2 [W]	RAF No 4 FTS/4(R) Sqn, Valley
	ZK033	BAE Systems Hawk T2 [X]	RAF No 4 FTS/4(R) Sqn, Valley
	ZK034	BAE Systems Hawk T2 [Y]	RAF No 4 FTS/4(R) Sqn, Valley
	ZK035	BAE Systems Hawk T2	RAF No 4 FTS/4(R) Sqn, Valley
	ZK036	BAE Systems Hawk T2	RAF No 4 FTS/4(R) Sqn, Valley
	ZK037	BAE Systems Hawk T2 [AB]	RAF No 4 FTS/4(R) Sqn, Valley
	ZK045	BAE Systems Hawk T2	*Not taken up*
	ZK046	BAE Systems Hawk T2	*Not taken up*
	ZK047	BAE Systems Hawk T2	*Not taken up*
	ZK048	BAE Systems Hawk T2	*Not taken up*
	ZK049	BAE Systems Hawk T2	*Not taken up*
	ZK050	BAE Systems Hawk T2	*Not taken up*
	ZK051	BAE Systems Hawk T2	*Not taken up*
	ZK052	BAE Systems Hawk T2	*Not taken up*
	ZK053	BAE Systems Hawk T2	*Not taken up*
	ZK054	BAE Systems Hawk T2	*Not taken up*
	ZK055	BAE Systems Hawk T2	*Not taken up*
	ZK056	BAE Systems Hawk T2	*Not taken up*
	ZK057	BAE Systems Hawk T2	*Not taken up*
	ZK058	BAE Systems Hawk T2	*Not taken up*
	ZK059	BAE Systems Hawk T2	*Not taken up*
	ZK067	Bell 212HP AH3 (G-BFER) [B]	AAC JHC/No 7 Regt, Middle Wallop
	ZK085	Eurofighter EF2000B Typhoon	BAe Systems, for R Saudi AF
	ZK086	Eurofighter EF2000B Typhoon	BAe Systems, for R Saudi AF
	ZK087	Eurofighter EF2000B Typhoon	BAe Systems, for R Saudi AF
	ZK088	Eurofighter EF2000B Typhoon	BAe Systems, for R Saudi AF
	ZK089	Eurofighter EF2000B Typhoon	BAe Systems, for R Saudi AF
	ZK090	Eurofighter EF2000B Typhoon	BAe Systems, for R Saudi AF
	ZK113	Panavia Tornado IDS (RSAF 6606)	MoD/BAE Systems, Warton
	ZK114	M2370 UAV	QinetiQ
	ZK119	Pilatus PC-9 (HB-HQU/RSAF 2204)	*Returned to R Saudi AF as 2204*
	ZK150*	Lockheed Martin Desert Hawk 3 UAV	Army 47 Regt Royal Artillery, Thorney Island
	ZK155*	Honeywell T-Hawk UAV	Army 32 Regt Royal Artillery, Larkhill
	ZK184	AgustaWestland Super Lynx Mk.130	*To Algeria as AN10, 31 January 2012*
	ZK205	Grob G109B Vigilant T1 (D-KBRU) [SS]	RAF No 624 VGS, Chivenor RMB
	ZK206	Bell 212EP AH2 (G-CFXE) [A]	AAC JHC/No 7 Regt, Middle Wallop
	ZK210	BAE Systems Mantis UAV	MoD/BAE Systems, Warton
	ZK300	Eurofighter Typhoon FGR4 [DG]	RAF No 11 Sqn, Coningsby
	ZK301	Eurofighter Typhoon FGR4 [D]	RAF No 1435 Flt, Mount Pleasant, FI
	ZK302	Eurofighter Typhoon FGR4 [EA]	RAF No 6 Sqn, Leuchars
	ZK303	Eurofighter Typhoon T3 [AX]	MoD/BAE Systems, Warton
	ZK304	Eurofighter Typhoon FGR4 [EB]	RAF No 6 Sqn, Leuchars
	ZK305	Eurofighter Typhoon FGR4 [DE]	RAF No 11 Sqn, Coningsby
	ZK306	Eurofighter Typhoon FGR4 [BT]	RAF No 29(R) Sqn, Coningsby
	ZK307	Eurofighter Typhoon FGR4 [BU]	RAF No 29(R) Sqn, Coningsby

Serial	Type (code/other identity)	Owner/operator location or fate	Notes
ZK308	Eurofighter Typhoon FGR4 [BW]	RAF No 29(R) Sqn, Coningsby	
ZK309	Eurofighter Typhoon FGR4 [QO-P]	RAF No 3 Sqn, Coningsby	
ZK310	Eurofighter Typhoon FGR4 [EL]	RAF TMF, Coningsby	
ZK311	Eurofighter Typhoon FGR4 [EK]	RAF No 6 Sqn, Leuchars	
ZK312	Eurofighter Typhoon FGR4 [EM]	RAF No 6 Sqn, Leuchars	
ZK313	Eurofighter Typhoon FGR4 [EN]	RAF No 6 Sqn, Leuchars	
ZK314	Eurofighter Typhoon FGR4 [EO]	RAF No 6 Sqn, Leuchars	
ZK315	Eurofighter Typhoon FGR4	MoD/BAE Systems, Warton	
ZK316	Eurofighter Typhoon FGR4 [FA]	RAF No 1 Sqn, Leuchars	
ZK317	Eurofighter Typhoon FGR4 [ES]	RAF No 6 Sqn, Leuchars	
ZK318	Eurofighter Typhoon FGR4 [ET]	RAF No 6 Sqn, Leuchars	
ZK319	Eurofighter Typhoon FGR4 [QO-D]	RAF No 3 Sqn, Coningsby	
ZK320	Eurofighter Typhoon FGR4 [EV]	RAF No 6 Sqn, Leuchars	
ZK321	Eurofighter Typhoon FGR4 [EU]	RAF No 6 Sqn, Leuchars	
ZK322	Eurofighter Typhoon FGR4 [BR]	RAF No 29(R) Sqn, Coningsby	
ZK323	Eurofighter Typhoon FGR4 [DN]	RAF No 11 Sqn, Coningsby	
ZK324	Eurofighter Typhoon FGR4 [EI]	RAF No 6 Sqn, Leuchars	
ZK325	Eurofighter Typhoon FGR4 [EQ]	RAF No 16 Sqn, Leuchars	
ZK326	Eurofighter Typhoon FGR4 [FB]	RAF No 1 Sqn, Leuchars	
ZK327	Eurofighter Typhoon FGR4 [EJ]	RAF No 6 Sqn, Leuchars	
ZK328	Eurofighter Typhoon FGR4 [BS]	RAF No 29(R) Sqn, Coningsby	
ZK329	Eurofighter Typhoon FGR4	RAF No 3 Sqn, Coningsby	
ZK330	Eurofighter Typhoon FGR4 [EZ]	RAF No 6 Sqn, Leuchars	
ZK331	Eurofighter Typhoon FGR4 [EE]	RAF No 6 Sqn, Leuchars	
ZK332	Eurofighter Typhoon FGR4 [AI]	RAF No 17(R) Sqn, Coningsby	
ZK333	Eurofighter Typhoon FGR4 [EH]	RAF No 6 Sqn, Leuchars	
ZK334	Eurofighter Typhoon FGR4 [EC]	RAF No 6 Sqn, Leuchars	
ZK335	Eurofighter Typhoon FGR4	RAF No 1 Sqn, Leuchars	
ZK336	Eurofighter Typhoon FGR4 [FD]	RAF No 1 Sqn, Leuchars	
ZK337	Eurofighter Typhoon FGR4 [FE]	RAF No 1 Sqn, Leuchars	
ZK338	Eurofighter Typhoon FGR4	RAF No 1 Sqn, Leuchars	
ZK339	Eurofighter Typhoon FGR4	RAF No 1 Sqn, Leuchars	
ZK340	Eurofighter Typhoon FGR4	RAF No 1 Sqn, Leuchars	
ZK341	Eurofighter Typhoon FGR4	RAF No 1 Sqn, Leuchars	
ZK342	Eurofighter Typhoon FGR4	RAF No 6 Sqn, Leuchars	
ZK343	Eurofighter Typhoon FGR4	RAF TMF, Coningsby	
ZK344	Eurofighter Typhoon FGR4	RAF TMF, Coningsby	
ZK345	Eurofighter Typhoon FGR4	MoD/BAE Systems, Warton	
ZK346	Eurofighter Typhoon FGR4	MoD/BAE Systems, Warton	
ZK347	Eurofighter Typhoon FGR4	DE&S/BAE Systems, Warton, for RAF	
ZK348	Eurofighter Typhoon FGR4	DE&S/BAE Systems, Warton, for RAF	
ZK349	Eurofighter Typhoon FGR4	DE&S/BAE Systems, Warton, for RAF	
ZK350	Eurofighter Typhoon FGR4	DE&S/BAE Systems, Warton, for RAF	
ZK351	Eurofighter Typhoon FGR4	DE&S/BAE Systems, Warton, for RAF	
ZK352	Eurofighter Typhoon FGR4	DE&S/BAE Systems, Warton, for RAF	
ZK353	Eurofighter Typhoon FGR4	DE&S/BAE Systems, Warton, for RAF	
ZK354	Eurofighter Typhoon FGR4	DE&S/BAE Systems, Warton, for RAF	
ZK355	Eurofighter Typhoon FGR4	DE&S/BAE Systems, Warton, for RAF	
ZK356	Eurofighter Typhoon FGR4	DE&S/BAE Systems, Warton, for RAF	
ZK357	Eurofighter Typhoon FGR4	DE&S/BAE Systems, Warton, for RAF	
ZK358	Eurofighter Typhoon FGR4	DE&S/BAE Systems, Warton, for RAF	
ZK359	Eurofighter Typhoon FGR4	DE&S/BAE Systems, Warton, for RAF	
ZK360	Eurofighter Typhoon FGR4	DE&S/BAE Systems, Warton, for RAF	
ZK379	Eurofighter Typhoon T3 [BB]	RAF No 29(R) Sqn, Coningsby	
ZK380	Eurofighter Typhoon T3 [BG]	RAF No 1 Sqn, Leuchars	
ZK381	Eurofighter Typhoon T3 [EX]	RAF No 6 Sqn, Leuchars	
ZK382	Eurofighter Typhoon T3	RAF TMF, Coningsby	
ZK383	Eurofighter Typhoon T3	DE&S/BAE Systems, Warton, for RAF	
ZK384	Eurofighter Typhoon T3	DE&S/BAE Systems, Warton, for RAF	
ZK450	Beech King Air B200 (G-RAFJ) [J]	SERCO/RAF No 3 FTS/45(R) Sqn, Cranwell	

Notes	Serial	Type (code/other identity)	Owner/operator location or fate
	ZK451	Beech King Air B200 (G-RAFK) [K]	SERCO/RAF No 3 FTS/45(R) Sqn, Cranwell
	ZK452	Beech King Air B200 (G-RAFL) [L]	SERCO/RAF No 3 FTS/45(R) Sqn, Cranwell
	ZK453	Beech King Air B200 (G-RAFM) [M]	SERCO/RAF No 3 FTS/45(R) Sqn, Cranwell
	ZK454	Beech King Air B200 (G-RAFN) [N]	SERCO/RAF No 3 FTS/45(R) Sqn, Cranwell
	ZK455	Beech King Air B200 (G-RAFO) [O]	SERCO/RAF No 3 FTS/45(R) Sqn, Cranwell
	ZK456	Beech King Air B200 (G-RAFP) [P]	SERCO/RAF No 3 FTS/45(R) Sqn, Cranwell
	ZK457	Beech King Air B200 (G-ROWN)	MoD/Foreign & Commonwealth Office, Afghanistan
	ZK458	Hawker Beechcraft King Air B200GT (G-RAFD) [D]	SERCO/RAF No 3 FTS/45(R) Sqn, Cranwell
	ZK459	Hawker Beechcraft King Air B200GT (G-RAFX) [X]	SERCO/RAF No 3 FTS/45(R) Sqn, Cranwell
	ZK460	Hawker Beechcraft King Air B200GT (G-RAFU) [U]	SERCO/RAF No 3 FTS/45(R) Sqn, Cranwell
	ZK501	Elbit Hermes 450 UAV	Army 32 Regt Royal Artillery, Larkhill
	ZK502	Elbit Hermes 450 UAV	Army 32 Regt Royal Artillery, Larkhill
	ZK503	Elbit Hermes 450 UAV	Army 32 Regt Royal Artillery, Larkhill
	ZK504	Elbit Hermes 450 UAV	Army 32 Regt Royal Artillery, Larkhill
	ZK505	Elbit Hermes 450 UAV	Army 32 Regt Royal Artillery, Larkhill
	ZK506	Elbit Hermes 450 UAV	Army 32 Regt Royal Artillery, Larkhill
	ZK507	Elbit Hermes 450 UAV	Army 32 Regt Royal Artillery, Larkhill
	ZK508	Elbit Hermes 450 UAV	Army 32 Regt Royal Artillery, Larkhill
	ZK509	Elbit Hermes 450 UAV	Army 32 Regt Royal Artillery, Larkhill
	ZK510	Elbit Hermes 450 UAV	Army 32 Regt Royal Artillery, Larkhill
	ZK511	Elbit Hermes 450 UAV	Army 32 Regt Royal Artillery, Larkhill
	ZK512	Elbit Hermes 450 UAV	Army 32 Regt Royal Artillery, Larkhill
	ZK513	Elbit Hermes 450 UAV	Army 32 Regt Royal Artillery, Larkhill
	ZK514	Elbit Hermes 450 UAV	Army 32 Regt Royal Artillery, Larkhill
	ZK515	Elbit Hermes 450 UAV	Army 32 Regt Royal Artillery, Larkhill
	ZK516	Elbit Hermes 450 UAV	Army 32 Regt Royal Artillery, Larkhill
	ZK517	Elbit Hermes 450 UAV	Army 32 Regt Royal Artillery, Larkhill
	ZK518	Elbit Hermes 450 UAV	Army 32 Regt Royal Artillery, Larkhill
	ZK519	Elbit Hermes 450 UAV	Army 32 Regt Royal Artillery, Larkhill
	ZK520	Elbit Hermes 450 UAV	Army 32 Regt Royal Artillery, Larkhill
	ZK521	Elbit Hermes 450 UAV	Army 32 Regt Royal Artillery, Larkhill
	ZK522	Elbit Hermes 450 UAV	Army 32 Regt Royal Artillery, Larkhill
	ZK523	Elbit Hermes 450 UAV	Army 32 Regt Royal Artillery, Larkhill
	ZK524	Elbit Hermes 450 UAV	Army 32 Regt Royal Artillery, Larkhill
	ZK525	Elbit Hermes 450 UAV	Army 32 Regt Royal Artillery, Larkhill
	ZK531	BAe Hawk T53 (LL-5306)	MoD/BAE Systems, Warton
	ZK532	BAe Hawk T53 (LL-5315)	MoD/BAE Systems, Warton
	ZK533	BAe Hawk T53 (LL-5317)	Aircraft Maintenance Training Academy, Doncaster
	ZK534	BAe Hawk T53 (LL-5319)	Privately owned, Bentwaters
	ZK535	BAe Hawk T53 (LL-5320)	Aircraft Maintenance Training Academy, Doncaster
	ZK550	Boeing Chinook HC6 [N701UK]	Boeing, for RAF
	ZK551	Boeing Chinook HC6 [N702UK]	Boeing, for RAF
	ZK552	Boeing Chinook HC6 [N703UK]	Boeing, for RAF
	ZK553	Boeing Chinook HC6 [N700UK]	Boeing, for RAF
	ZK554	Boeing Chinook HC6 [N705UK]	Boeing, for RAF
	ZK555	Boeing Chinook HC6 [N706UK]	Boeing, for RAF
	ZK556	Boeing Chinook HC6 [N707UK]	Boeing, for RAF
	ZK557	Boeing Chinook HC6 [N708UK]	Boeing, for RAF
	ZK558	Boeing Chinook HC6 [N709UK]	Boeing, for RAF
	ZK559	Boeing Chinook HC6 [N710UK]	Boeing, for RAF
	ZK560	Boeing Chinook HC6 [N711UK]	Boeing, for RAF
	ZK561	Boeing Chinook HC6 [N712UK]	Boeing, for RAF
	ZK562	Boeing Chinook HC6 [N713UK]	Boeing, for RAF
	ZK563	Boeing Chinook HC6 [N714UK]	Boeing, for RAF
	ZM135	Lockheed Martin F-35B Lightning II (BK-1)	RAF/LMTAS, Eglin AFB, Florida
	ZM136	Lockheed Martin F-35B Lightning II (BK-2)	RAF/LMTAS, Eglin AFB, Florida

Serial	Type (code/other identity)	Owner/operator location or fate	Notes
ZM137	Lockheed Martin F-35B Lightning II	Reservation for RAF/RN	
ZM138	Lockheed Martin F-35B Lightning II	Reservation for RAF/RN	
ZM139	Lockheed Martin F-35B Lightning II	Reservation for RAF/RN	
ZM140	Lockheed Martin F-35B Lightning II	Reservation for RAF/RN	
ZM141	Lockheed Martin F-35B Lightning II	Reservation for RAF/RN	
ZM142	Lockheed Martin F-35B Lightning II	Reservation for RAF/RN	
ZM143	Lockheed Martin F-35B Lightning II	Reservation for RAF/RN	
ZM144	Lockheed Martin F-35B Lightning II	Reservation for RAF/RN	
ZM145	Lockheed Martin F-35B Lightning II	Reservation for RAF/RN	
ZM146	Lockheed Martin F-35B Lightning II	Reservation for RAF/RN	
ZM147	Lockheed Martin F-35B Lightning II	Reservation for RAF/RN	
ZM148	Lockheed Martin F-35B Lightning II	Reservation for RAF/RN	
ZM149	Lockheed Martin F-35B Lightning II	Reservation for RAF/RN	
ZM150	Lockheed Martin F-35B Lightning II	Reservation for RAF/RN	
ZM151	Lockheed Martin F-35B Lightning II	Reservation for RAF/RN	
ZM152	Lockheed Martin F-35B Lightning II	Reservation for RAF/RN	
ZM153	Lockheed Martin F-35B Lightning II	Reservation for RAF/RN	
ZM154	Lockheed Martin F-35B Lightning II	Reservation for RAF/RN	
ZM155	Lockheed Martin F-35B Lightning II	Reservation for RAF/RN	
ZM156	Lockheed Martin F-35B Lightning II	Reservation for RAF/RN	
ZM157	Lockheed Martin F-35B Lightning II	Reservation for RAF/RN	
ZM158	Lockheed Martin F-35B Lightning II	Reservation for RAF/RN	
ZM159	Lockheed Martin F-35B Lightning II	Reservation for RAF/RN	
ZM160	Lockheed Martin F-35B Lightning II	Reservation for RAF/RN	
ZM161	Lockheed Martin F-35B Lightning II	Reservation for RAF/RN	
ZM162	Lockheed Martin F-35B Lightning II	Reservation for RAF/RN	
ZM163	Lockheed Martin F-35B Lightning II	Reservation for RAF/RN	
ZM164	Lockheed Martin F-35B Lightning II	Reservation for RAF/RN	
ZM165	Lockheed Martin F-35B Lightning II	Reservation for RAF/RN	
ZM166	Lockheed Martin F-35B Lightning II	Reservation for RAF/RN	
ZM167	Lockheed Martin F-35B Lightning II	Reservation for RAF/RN	
ZM168	Lockheed Martin F-35B Lightning II	Reservation for RAF/RN	
ZM169	Lockheed Martin F-35B Lightning II	Reservation for RAF/RN	
ZM170	Lockheed Martin F-35B Lightning II	Reservation for RAF/RN	
ZM171	Lockheed Martin F-35B Lightning II	Reservation for RAF/RN	
ZM172	Lockheed Martin F-35B Lightning II	Reservation for RAF/RN	
ZM173	Lockheed Martin F-35B Lightning II	Reservation for RAF/RN	
ZM174	Lockheed Martin F-35B Lightning II	Reservation for RAF/RN	
ZM175	Lockheed Martin F-35B Lightning II	Reservation for RAF/RN	
ZM176	Lockheed Martin F-35B Lightning II	Reservation for RAF/RN	
ZM177	Lockheed Martin F-35B Lightning II	Reservation for RAF/RN	
ZM178	Lockheed Martin F-35B Lightning II	Reservation for RAF/RN	
ZM179	Lockheed Martin F-35B Lightning II	Reservation for RAF/RN	
ZM180	Lockheed Martin F-35B Lightning II	Reservation for RAF/RN	
ZM181	Lockheed Martin F-35B Lightning II	Reservation for RAF/RN	
ZM182	Lockheed Martin F-35B Lightning II	Reservation for RAF/RN	
ZM183	Lockheed Martin F-35B Lightning II	Reservation for RAF/RN	
ZM184	Lockheed Martin F-35B Lightning II	Reservation for RAF/RN	
ZM185	Lockheed Martin F-35B Lightning II	Reservation for RAF/RN	
ZM186	Lockheed Martin F-35B Lightning II	Reservation for RAF/RN	
ZM187	Lockheed Martin F-35B Lightning II	Reservation for RAF/RN	
ZM188	Lockheed Martin F-35B Lightning II	Reservation for RAF/RN	
ZM189	Lockheed Martin F-35B Lightning II	Reservation for RAF/RN	
ZM190	Lockheed Martin F-35B Lightning II	Reservation for RAF/RN	
ZM191	Lockheed Martin F-35B Lightning II	Reservation for RAF/RN	
ZM192	Lockheed Martin F-35B Lightning II	Reservation for RAF/RN	
ZM193	Lockheed Martin F-35B Lightning II	Reservation for RAF/RN	
ZM194	Lockheed Martin F-35B Lightning II	Reservation for RAF/RN	
ZM195	Lockheed Martin F-35B Lightning II	Reservation for RAF/RN	
ZM196	Lockheed Martin F-35B Lightning II	Reservation for RAF/RN	

Notes	Serial	Type (code/other identity)	Owner/operator location or fate
	ZM197	Lockheed Martin F-35B Lightning II	Reservation for RAF/RN
	ZM198	Lockheed Martin F-35B Lightning II	Reservation for RAF/RN
	ZM199	Lockheed Martin F-35B Lightning II	Reservation for RAF/RN
	ZM200	Lockheed Martin F-35B Lightning II	Reservation for RAF/RN
	ZM400	Airbus A400M Atlas C1	Airbus Military, for RAF
	ZM401	Airbus A400M Atlas C1	Airbus Military, for RAF
	ZM402	Airbus A400M Atlas C1	Reservation for RAF
	ZM403	Airbus A400M Atlas C1	Reservation for RAF
	ZM404	Airbus A400M Atlas C1	Reservation for RAF
	ZM405	Airbus A400M Atlas C1	Reservation for RAF
	ZM406	Airbus A400M Atlas C1	Reservation for RAF
	ZM407	Airbus A400M Atlas C1	Reservation for RAF
	ZM408	Airbus A400M Atlas C1	Reservation for RAF
	ZM409	Airbus A400M Atlas C1	Reservation for RAF
	ZM410	Airbus A400M Atlas C1	Reservation for RAF
	ZM411	Airbus A400M Atlas C1	Reservation for RAF
	ZM412	Airbus A400M Atlas C1	Reservation for RAF
	ZM413	Airbus A400M Atlas C1	Reservation for RAF
	ZM414	Airbus A400M Atlas C1	Reservation for RAF
	ZM415	Airbus A400M Atlas C1	Reservation for RAF
	ZM416	Airbus A400M Atlas C1	Reservation for RAF
	ZM417	Airbus A400M Atlas C1	Reservation for RAF
	ZM418	Airbus A400M Atlas C1	Reservation for RAF
	ZM419	Airbus A400M Atlas C1	Reservation for RAF
	ZM420	Airbus A400M Atlas C1	Reservation for RAF
	ZM421	Airbus A400M Atlas C1	Reservation for RAF
	ZR283	AgustaWestland AW139 (G-FBHA)	FBS Helicopters/RAF DHFS, Valley
	ZR322	Agusta A109E Power Elite (G-CDVC)	RAF No 32(The Royal) Sqn, Northolt
	ZR323	Agusta A109E Power Elite (G-CDVE)	RAF No 32(The Royal) Sqn, Northolt
	ZR324	Agusta A109E Power (G-EMHB)	DHFS, RAF Shawbury
	ZR325	Agusta A109E Power (G-BZEI)	DHFS, RAF Shawbury
	ZR326	AgustaWestland AW139 (G-CFUO) [F]	*To G-CFUO, 11 May 2012*
	ZR327	AgustaWestland AW139 (G-CFVD) [B]	*To G-CFVD, 11 May 2012*
	ZR328	AgustaWestland AW101 Mk.610	AgustaWestland, for Algeria
	ZR329	AgustaWestland AW101 Mk.610	AgustaWestland, for Algeria
	ZR330	AgustaWestland AW101 Mk.610	AgustaWestland, for Algeria
	ZR331	AgustaWestland AW101 Mk.610	AgustaWestland, for Algeria
	ZR332	AgustaWestland AW101 Mk.610	AgustaWestland, for Algeria
	ZR334	AgustaWestland AW101 Mk.640	AgustaWestland, for Saudi Arabia
	ZR335	AgustaWestland AW101 Mk.640	AgustaWestland, for Saudi Arabia
	ZR336	AgustaWestland AW101 Mk.643	AgustaWestland, for Turkmenistan
	ZR337	AgustaWestland AW101 Mk.643	*To Turkmenistan as ES-Z715, 20 June 2012*
	ZR338	AgustaWestland AW101 Mk.641	*To India as ZW-4301, 17 December 2012*
	ZR339	AgustaWestland AW101 Mk.641	AgustaWestland, for India as ZW-4302
	ZR340	AgustaWestland AW101 Mk.641	*To India as ZW-4303, 28 December 2012*
	ZR341	AgustaWestland AW101 Mk.641	*To India as ZW-4304, 21 December 2012*
	ZR342	AgustaWestland AW101 Mk.641	AgustaWestland, for India as ZW-4305
	ZR343	AgustaWestland AW101 Mk.641	AgustaWestland, for India as ZW-4306
	ZR344	AgustaWestland AW101 Mk.641	AgustaWestland, for India as ZW-4307
	ZR345	AgustaWestland AW101 Mk.641	AgustaWestland, for India as ZW-4308
	ZR346	AgustaWestland AW101 Mk.641	AgustaWestland, for India as ZW-4309
	ZR347	AgustaWestland AW101 Mk.641	AgustaWestland, for India as ZW-4310
	ZR348	AgustaWestland AW101 Mk.641	AgustaWestland, for India as ZW-4311
	ZR349	AgustaWestland AW101 Mk.641	AgustaWestland, for India as ZW-4312
	ZS782	WS WG25 Sharpeye	The Helicopter Museum, Weston-super-Mare
	ZT800	WS Super Lynx Mk 300	MoD/AgustaWestland, Yeovil

Serial	Type (code/other identity)	Owner/operator location or fate	Notes
ZZ171	Boeing C-17A Globemaster III (00-201/N171UK)	RAF No 99 Sqn, Brize Norton	
ZZ172	Boeing C-17A Globemaster III (00-202/N172UK)	RAF No 99 Sqn, Brize Norton	
ZZ173	Boeing C-17A Globemaster III (00-203/N173UK)	RAF No 99 Sqn, Brize Norton	
ZZ174	Boeing C-17A Globemaster III (00-204/N174UK)	RAF No 99 Sqn, Brize Norton	
ZZ175	Boeing C-17A Globemaster III (06-0205/N9500Z)	RAF No 99 Sqn, Brize Norton	
ZZ176	Boeing C-17A Globemaster III (08-0206/N9500B)	RAF No 99 Sqn, Brize Norton	
ZZ177	Boeing C-17A Globemaster III (09-8207/N9500B)	RAF No 99 Sqn, Brize Norton	
ZZ178	Boeing C-17A Globemaster III (12-0208/N9500N)	RAF No 99 Sqn, Brize Norton	
ZZ190	Hawker Hunter F58 (J-4066/G-HHAE)	Hawker Hunter Aviation, Yeovilton	
ZZ191	Hawker Hunter F58 (J-4058/G-HHAD)	Hawker Hunter Aviation, Yeovilton	
ZZ192	Grob G109B Vigilant T1 (D-KLVI) [SQ]	RAF CGMF, Syerston	
ZZ193	Grob G109B Vigilant T1 (D-KBLO) [SR]	RAF CGMF, Syerston	
ZZ194	Hawker Hunter F58 (J-4021/G-HHAC)	Hawker Hunter Aviation, Scampton	
ZZ201	General Atomics Reaper UAV (07-111)	RAF No 39 Sqn, Creech AFB, Nevada, USA	
ZZ202	General Atomics Reaper UAV (07-117)	RAF No 39 Sqn, Creech AFB, Nevada, USA	
ZZ203	General Atomics Reaper UAV (08-133)	RAF No 39 Sqn, Creech AFB, Nevada, USA	
ZZ204	General Atomics Reaper UAV (10-0157)	RAF No 39 Sqn, Creech AFB, Nevada, USA	
ZZ205	General Atomics Reaper UAV (10-0162)	RAF No 39 Sqn, Creech AFB, Nevada, USA	
ZZ206	General Atomics Reaper UAV	General Atomics, for RAF	
ZZ207	General Atomics Reaper UAV	General Atomics, for RAF	
ZZ208	General Atomics Reaper UAV	General Atomics, for RAF	
ZZ209	General Atomics Reaper UAV	General Atomics, for RAF	
ZZ210	General Atomics Reaper UAV	General Atomics, for RAF	
ZZ211	General Atomics Reaper UAV	General Atomics, for RAF	
ZZ212	General Atomics Reaper UAV	General Atomics, for RAF	
ZZ213	General Atomics Reaper UAV	General Atomics, for RAF	
ZZ250	BAE Systems Taranis UAV	BAE Systems, Warton	
ZZ251	BAE Systems HERTI UAV	BAE Systems, Warton	
ZZ252	BAE Systems HERTI UAV	BAE Systems, Warton	
ZZ253	BAE Systems HERTI UAV	BAE Systems, Warton	
ZZ254	BAE Systems HERTI UAV	BAE Systems, Warton	
ZZ330	Airbus A330 Voyager KC2 (MRTT017/G-VYGA)	RAF No 10 Sqn, Brize Norton	
ZZ331	Airbus A330 Voyager KC2 (MRTT018/G-VYGB)	RAF No 10 Sqn, Brize Norton	
ZZ332	Airbus A330 Voyager KC3 (EC-330)	MoD/Cobham, Bournemouth	
ZZ333	Airbus A330 Voyager KC3 (EC-337)	DE&S/Airbus, for RAF	
ZZ334	Airbus A330 Voyager KC3 (MRTT016/EC-335)	DE&S/Airbus, for RAF	
ZZ335	Airbus A330 Voyager KC2/KC3 (EC-338)	Reservation for RAF	
ZZ336	Airbus A330 Voyager (G-VYGG)	Airtanker Ltd, Brize Norton	
ZZ337	Airbus A330 Voyager KC2/KC3	Reservation for RAF	
ZZ338	Airbus A330 Voyager KC2/KC3	Reservation for RAF	
ZZ339	Airbus A330 Voyager KC2/KC3	Reservation for RAF	
ZZ340	Airbus A330 Voyager KC2/KC3	Reservation for RAF	
ZZ341	Airbus A330 Voyager KC2/KC3	Reservation for RAF	
ZZ342	Airbus A330 Voyager KC2/KC3	Reservation for RAF	
ZZ343	Airbus A330 Voyager KC2/KC3	Reservation for RAF	
ZZ349	AgustaWestland AW159 Wildcat	DE&S/AgustaWestland, Yeovil, for RN/AAC	
ZZ350	AgustaWestland AW159 Wildcat	DE&S/AgustaWestland, Yeovil, for RN/AAC	
ZZ351	AgustaWestland AW159 Wildcat	DE&S/AgustaWestland, Yeovil, for RN/AAC	
ZZ352	AgustaWestland AW159 Wildcat	DE&S/AgustaWestland, Yeovil, for RN/AAC	
ZZ353	AgustaWestland AW159 Wildcat	DE&S/AgustaWestland, Yeovil, for RN/AAC	
ZZ354	AgustaWestland AW159 Wildcat	DE&S/AgustaWestland, Yeovil, for RN/AAC	
ZZ355	AgustaWestland AW159 Wildcat	DE&S/AgustaWestland, Yeovil, for RN/AAC	

Notes	Serial	Type (code/other identity)	Owner/operator location or fate
	ZZ356	AgustaWestland AW159 Wildcat	DE&S/AgustaWestland, Yeovil, for RN/AAC
	ZZ357	AgustaWestland AW159 Wildcat	DE&S/AgustaWestland, Yeovil, for RN/AAC
	ZZ358	AgustaWestland AW159 Wildcat	DE&S/AgustaWestland, Yeovil, for RN/AAC
	ZZ359	AgustaWestland AW159 Wildcat	DE&S/AgustaWestland, Yeovil, for RN/AAC
	ZZ360	AgustaWestland AW159 Wildcat	DE&S/AgustaWestland, Yeovil, for RN/AAC
	ZZ361	AgustaWestland AW159 Wildcat	DE&S/AgustaWestland, Yeovil, for RN/AAC
	ZZ362	AgustaWestland AW159 Wildcat	DE&S/AgustaWestland, Yeovil, for RN/AAC
	ZZ363	AgustaWestland AW159 Wildcat	DE&S/AgustaWestland, Yeovil, for RN/AAC
	ZZ364	AgustaWestland AW159 Wildcat	DE&S/AgustaWestland, Yeovil, for RN/AAC
	ZZ365	AgustaWestland AW159 Wildcat	DE&S/AgustaWestland, Yeovil, for RN/AAC
	ZZ366	AgustaWestland AW159 Wildcat	DE&S/AgustaWestland, Yeovil, for RN/AAC
	ZZ367	AgustaWestland AW159 Wildcat	DE&S/AgustaWestland, Yeovil, for RN/AAC
	ZZ368	AgustaWestland AW159 Wildcat	DE&S/AgustaWestland, Yeovil, for RN/AAC
	ZZ369	AgustaWestland AW159 Wildcat	DE&S/AgustaWestland, Yeovil, for RN/AAC
	ZZ370	AgustaWestland AW159 Wildcat	DE&S/AgustaWestland, Yeovil, for RN/AAC
	ZZ371	AgustaWestland AW159 Wildcat	DE&S/AgustaWestland, Yeovil, for RN/AAC
	ZZ372	AgustaWestland AW159 Wildcat	DE&S/AgustaWestland, Yeovil, for RN/AAC
	ZZ373	AgustaWestland AW159 Wildcat	DE&S/AgustaWestland, Yeovil, for RN/AAC
	ZZ374	AgustaWestland AW159 Wildcat	DE&S/AgustaWestland, Yeovil, for RN/AAC
	ZZ375	AgustaWestland AW159 Wildcat HMA2	DE&S/AgustaWestland, Yeovil, for RN
	ZZ376	AgustaWestland AW159 Wildcat HMA2	DE&S/AgustaWestland, Yeovil, for RN
	ZZ377	AgustaWestland AW159 Wildcat HMA2	DE&S/AgustaWestland, Yeovil, for RN
	ZZ378	AgustaWestland AW159 Wildcat HMA2	DE&S/AgustaWestland, Yeovil, for RN
	ZZ379	AgustaWestland AW159 Wildcat HMA2	DE&S/AgustaWestland, Yeovil, for RN
	ZZ380	AgustaWestland AW159 Wildcat HMA2	DE&S/AgustaWestland, Yeovil, for RN
	ZZ381	AgustaWestland AW159 Wildcat HMA2	DE&S/AgustaWestland, Yeovil, for RN
	ZZ382	AgustaWestland AW159 Wildcat AH1	DE&S/AgustaWestland, Yeovil, for AAC
	ZZ383	AgustaWestland AW159 Wildcat AH1	DE&S/AgustaWestland, Yeovil, for AAC
	ZZ384	AgustaWestland AW159 Wildcat AH1	DE&S/AgustaWestland, Yeovil, for AAC
	ZZ385	AgustaWestland AW159 Wildcat AH1	DE&S/AgustaWestland, Yeovil, for AAC
	ZZ386	AgustaWestland AW159 Wildcat AH1	DE&S/AgustaWestland, Yeovil, for AAC
	ZZ387	AgustaWestland AW159 Wildcat AH1	DE&S/AgustaWestland, Yeovil, for AAC
	ZZ388	AgustaWestland AW159 Wildcat AH1	MoD/AgustaWestland, Yeovil
	ZZ389	AgustaWestland AW159 Wildcat AH1	DE&S/AgustaWestland, Yeovil, for AAC
	ZZ390	AgustaWestland AW159 Wildcat AH1	DE&S/AgustaWestland, Yeovil, for AAC
	ZZ391	AgustaWestland AW159 Wildcat AH1	DE&S/AgustaWestland, Yeovil, for AAC
	ZZ392	AgustaWestland AW159 Wildcat AH1	DE&S/AgustaWestland, Yeovil, for AAC
	ZZ393	AgustaWestland AW159 Wildcat AH1	DE&S/AgustaWestland, Yeovil, for AAC
	ZZ394	AgustaWestland AW159 Wildcat AH1	DE&S/AgustaWestland, Yeovil, for AAC
	ZZ395	AgustaWestland AW159 Wildcat AH1	DE&S/AgustaWestland, Yeovil, for AAC
	ZZ396	AgustaWestland AW159 Wildcat HMA2	DE&S/AgustaWestland, Yeovil, for RN
	ZZ397	AgustaWestland AW159 Wildcat HMA2	MoD/AgustaWestland, Yeovil
	ZZ398	AgustaWestland AW159 Wildcat AH1	MoD/AgustaWestland, Yeovil
	ZZ399	AgustaWestland AW159 Wildcat AH1	MoD/AgustaWestland, Yeovil
	ZZ400	AgustaWestland AW159 Wildcat	MoD/AgustaWestland, Yeovil
	ZZ401	AgustaWestland AW159 Wildcat	MoD/AgustaWestland, Yeovil
	ZZ402	AgustaWestland AW159 Wildcat	MoD/AgustaWestland, Yeovil
	ZZ403	AgustaWestland AW159 Wildcat AH1	AAC Wildcat Fielding Team, Yeovilton
	ZZ404	AgustaWestland AW159 Wildcat AH1	MoD/AgustaWestland, Yeovil
	ZZ405	AgustaWestland AW159 Wildcat AH1	AAC Wildcat Fielding Team, Yeovilton
	ZZ406	AgustaWestland AW159 Wildcat AH1	AAC Wildcat Fielding Team, Yeovilton
	ZZ407	AgustaWestland AW159 Wildcat AH1	AAC Wildcat Fielding Team, Yeovilton
	ZZ408	AgustaWestland AW159 Wildcat AH1	AAC Wildcat Fielding Team, Yeovilton
	ZZ409	AgustaWestland AW159 Wildcat AH1	MoD/AgustaWestland, Yeovil
	ZZ410	AgustaWestland AW159 Wildcat AH1	AAC Wildcat Fielding Team, Yeovilton
	ZZ411	AgustaWestland AW159 Wildcat	DE&S/AgustaWestland, Yeovil, for RN/AAC
	ZZ412	AgustaWestland AW159 Wildcat	DE&S/AgustaWestland, Yeovil, for RN/AAC
	ZZ413	AgustaWestland AW159 Wildcat HMA2	DE&S/AgustaWestland, Yeovil, for RN
	ZZ414	AgustaWestland AW159 Wildcat HMA2	DE&S/AgustaWestland, Yeovil, for RN
	ZZ415	AgustaWestland AW159 Wildcat HMA2	DE&S/AgustaWestland, Yeovil, for RN

Serial	Type (code/other identity)	Owner/operator location or fate	Notes
ZZ416	Hawker Beechcraft Shadow R1 (G-JENC)	RAF No 14 Sqn, Waddington	
ZZ417	Hawker Beechcraft Shadow R1 (G-NICY)	RAF No 14 Sqn, Waddington	
ZZ418	Hawker Beechcraft Shadow R1 (G-JIMG)	RAF No 14 Sqn, Waddington	
ZZ419	Hawker Beechcraft Shadow R1 (G-OTCS)	RAF No 14 Sqn, Waddington	
ZZ500	Hawker Beechcraft Avenger T1 (G-MFTA)	RN No 750 NAS, Culdrose	
ZZ501	Hawker Beechcraft Avenger T1 (G-MFTB)	RN No 750 NAS, Culdrose	
ZZ502	Hawker Beechcraft Avenger T1 (G-MFTC)	RN No 750 NAS, Culdrose	
ZZ503	Hawker Beechcraft Avenger T1 (G-MFTD)	RN No 750 NAS, Culdrose	
ZZ504	Hawker Beechcraft Shadow R1 (G-CGUM)	RAF No 14 Sqn, Waddington	
ZZ664	Boeing RC-135W (64-14833)	Boeing, for RAF	
ZZ665	Boeing RC-135W (64-14838)	Boeing, for RAF	
ZZ666	Boeing RC-135W (64-14830)	Boeing, for RAF	

EP120/AE-A is a Spitfire LF VB, appropriately registered as G-LFVB and operated by The Fighter Collection at Duxford. She wears the colours of 402(RCAF) 'City of Winnipeg' Squadron, the same markings that she wore in April 1944.

Texan G-BJST is based at Duxford and wears the false markings KF729. It was originally an Italian Air Force machine.

Lynx HMA8 XZ732 here wears the code 302 of 815 Naval Air Squadron HQ Flight, based at RNAS Yeovilton.

Tucano T1 ZF269 is based with No 1 Flying Training School at RAF Linton-on-Ouse. Painted in red, white and blue markings, this was one of two specially marked aircraft used by the 2012 RAF Tucano Display Team. 2012 also marked the Queen's Diamond Jubilee, as depicted by the crown on the tail.

Scout AH1 XT626 belongs to the Army Historic Aircraft flight, based at Middle Wallop. Funded purely by donations, the Flight was unable to display as a fully constituted air display team during 2012 and this shot shows a rare foray into the air for its Scout.

Hawk T1A XX278 of No 4 Flying Training School based at RAF Valley wore a very attractive red, white and blue scheme for the 2012 Hawk Display Team appearances. Over the year the team raised £10000 for the RAF Benevolent Fund, before bowing out in October 2012. These were likely to have been the last flying displays by a solo RAF Hawk T1.

001 is the code worn by Tornado GR4 ZA365, based at RAF Lossiemouth, the oldest RAF Tornado flying, having first taken to the skies in July 1982. Aircraft are generally operated on a pool basis but this one also wears the 'XV' markings of 15(R) Squadron and was one of several which performed the magnificent role demonstration at air displays in 2012.

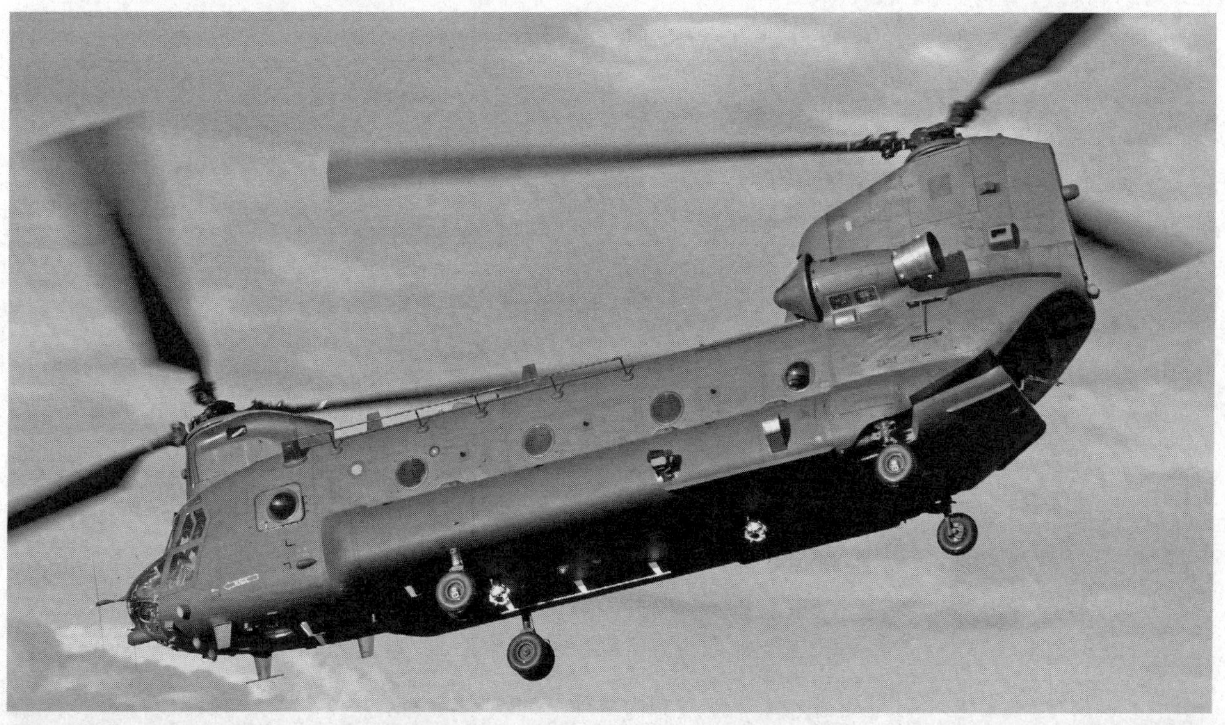

The whip aerials on the nose identify ZA713 as a Chinook HC2, based at RAF Odiham. The HC2 fleet is slowly being converted to HC4 status which includes removal of the whip aerials, one of the few external recognition features distinguishing the two variants.

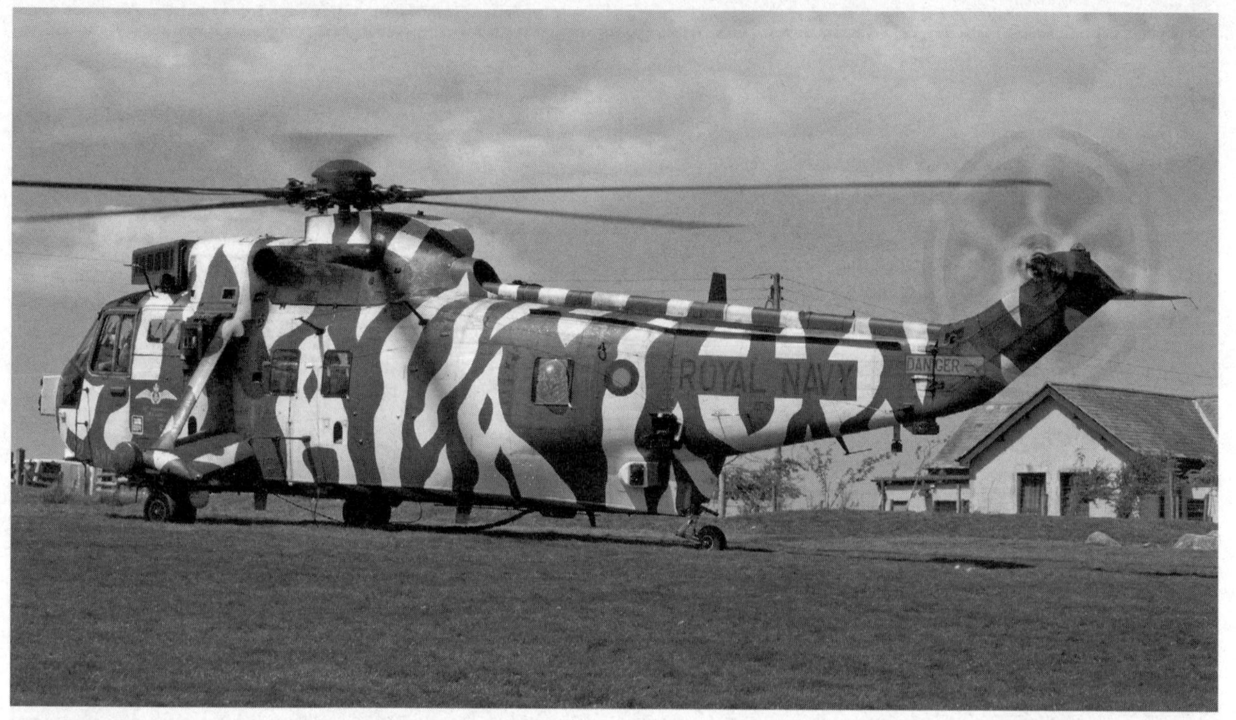

RNAS Yeovilton-based Sea King HC4 ZF115 wears arctic camouflage and still carries special markings commemorating the 40th Anniversary of Sea King in Navy service. It is seen here carrying cables for underlung loads in support of the 2012 'Ten Tors' event.

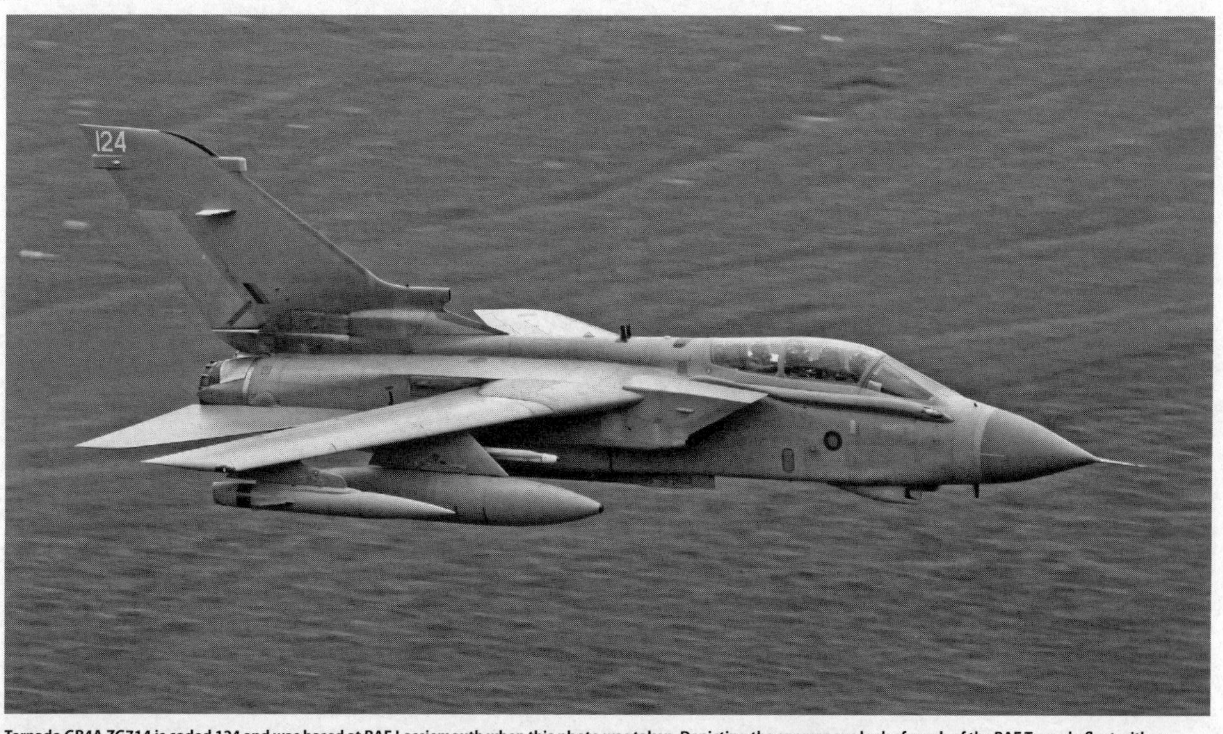

Tornado GR4A ZG714 is coded 124 and was based at RAF Lossiemouth when this photo was taken. Depicting the anonymous look of much of the RAF Tornado fleet with no evident squadron markings, ZG714 is seen here in its element, down low, speeding through the 'Mach Loop' near Cadair Idris.

All 22 of the Army's Lynx AH9 fleet has now been upgraded to AH9A status with the fitting of the CTS800-4N engine used on the Wildcat. ZG919 is an AH9A, which ports wheels rather than the skids seen on the AH7 variant.

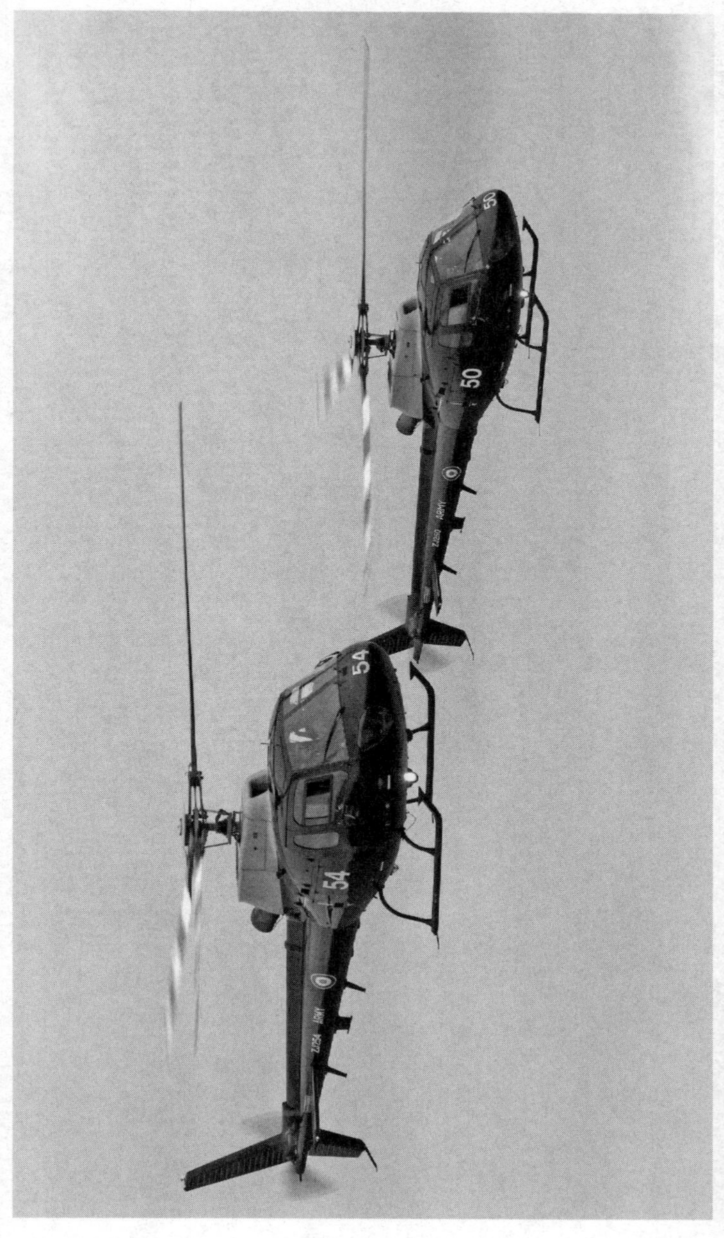

Squirrel HTs ZJ250 and ZJ254 wear the black and yellow markings of the whole Squirrel HT1 and HT2 fleet. The 'Army' titles give this pair away as being based at the School of Army Aviation at Middle Wallop.

Typhoon ZJ935 is coded DJ and flies with No 11 Squadron at RAF Coningsby.

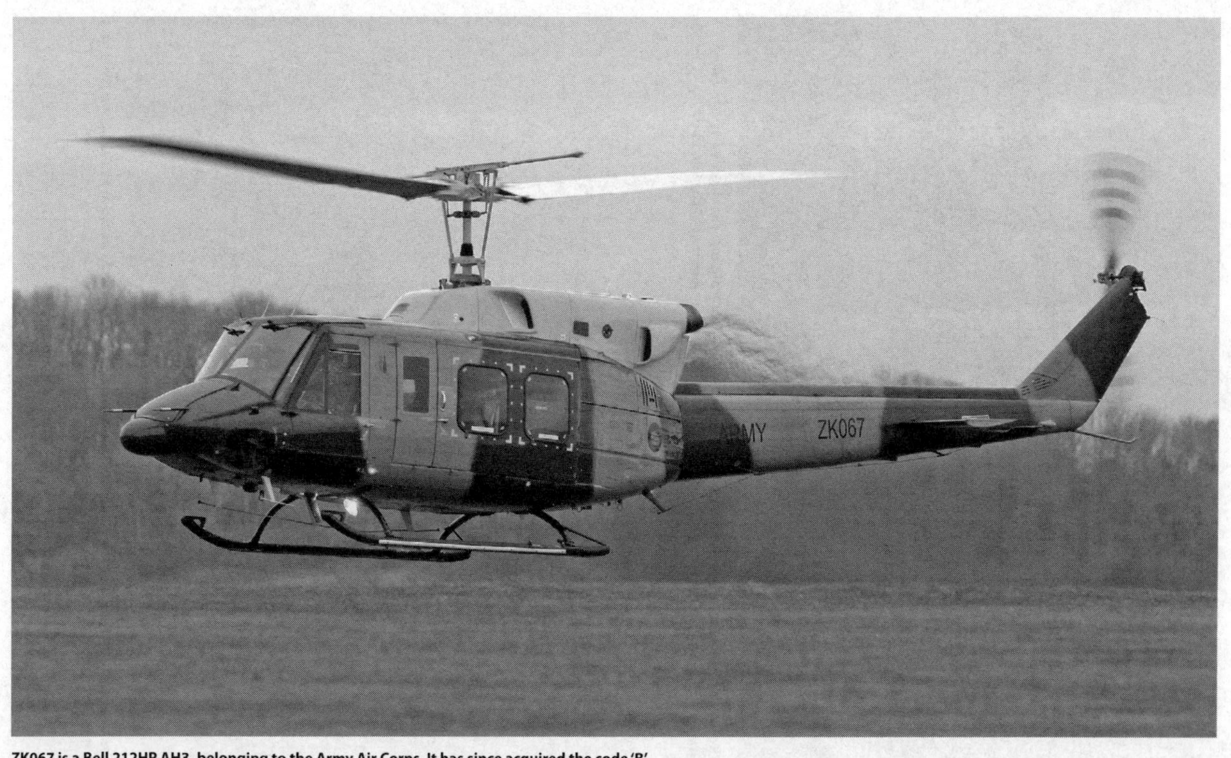

ZK067 is a Bell 212HP AH3, belonging to the Army Air Corps. It has since acquired the code 'B'.

ZK011 is a Hawk T2, operated by No 4(R) Squadron of No 4 Flying Training School, based at RAF Valley. Gradually the whole fleet is acquiring codes and the full, colourful markings of the Squadron.

Typhoon FGR4 ZK330 wears the colours of No 6 Squadron RAF, currently based at RAF Leuchars. Leuchars is due to close in 2013 with the Typhoons moving to Lossiemouth

Serial	Type (code/other identity)	Owner/operator location or fate	Notes
G-BYUA	Grob G.115E Tutor T1	VT Aerospace/No 1 EFTS, Barkston Heath	
G-BYUB	Grob G.115E Tutor T1	VT Aerospace/East Midlands Universities AS/No 16(R) Sqn/ No 115(R) Sqn, Cranwell	
G-BYUC	Grob G.115E Tutor T1	VT Aerospace/East Midlands Universities AS/No 16(R) Sqn/ No 115(R) Sqn, Cranwell	
G-BYUD	Grob G.115E Tutor T1	VT Aerospace/No 1 EFTS, Barkston Heath	
G-BYUE	Grob G.115E Tutor T1	VT Aerospace/East Midlands Universities AS/No 16(R) Sqn/ No 115(R) Sqn, Cranwell	
G-BYUF	Grob G.115E Tutor T1	VT Aerospace/Northumbrian Universities AS, Leeming	
G-BYUG	Grob G.115E Tutor T1	VT Aerospace/Cambridge UAS/University of LondonAS/No 57(R) Sqn, Wyton	
G-BYUH	Grob G.115E Tutor T1	VT Aerospace/Southampton UAS, Boscombe Down	
G-BYUI	Grob G.115E Tutor T1	VT Aerospace/No 1 EFTS, Barkston Heath	
G-BYUJ	Grob G.115E Tutor T1	VT Aerospace/Oxford UAS, Benson	
G-BYUK	Grob G.115E Tutor T1	VT Aerospace/No 1 EFTS, Barkston Heath	
G-BYUL	Grob G.115E Tutor T1	VT Aerospace/No 1 EFTS, Middle Wallop	
G-BYUM	Grob G.115E Tutor T1	VT Aerospace/No 1 EFTS, Barkston Heath	
G-BYUN	Grob G.115E Tutor T1	VT Aerospace/No 1 EFTS, Barkston Heath	
G-BYUO	Grob G.115E Tutor T1	VT Aerospace/Cambridge UAS/University of LondonAS/No 57(R) Sqn, Wyton	
G-BYUP	Grob G.115E Tutor T1	VT Aerospace/East Midlands Universities AS/No 16(R) Sqn/ No 115(R) Sqn, Cranwell	
G-BYUR	Grob G.115E Tutor T1	VT Aerospace/No 1 EFTS, Barkston Heath	
G-BYUS	Grob G.115E Tutor T1	VT Aerospace/Cambridge UAS/University of LondonAS/No 57(R) Sqn, Wyton	
G-BYUU	Grob G.115E Tutor T1	VT Aerospace/Cambridge UAS/University of London AS/No 57(R) Sqn, Wyton	
G-BYUV	Grob G.115E Tutor T1	VT Aerospace/Bristol UAS, Colerne	
G-BYUW	Grob G.115E Tutor T1	VT Aerospace/Cambridge UAS/University of London AS/No 57(R) Sqn, Wyton	
G-BYUX	Grob G.115E Tutor T1	VT Aerospace/No 1 EFTS, Barkston Heath	
G-BYUY	Grob G.115E Tutor T1	VT Aerospace/East Midlands Universities AS/No 16(R) Sqn/ No 115(R) Sqn, Cranwell	
G-BYUZ	Grob G.115E Tutor T1	VT Aerospace/No 1 EFTS, Barkston Heath	
G-BYVA	Grob G.115E Tutor T1	VT Aerospace/No 1 EFTS, Middle Wallop	
G-BYVB	Grob G.115E Tutor T1	VT Aerospace/Oxford UAS, Benson	
G-BYVC	Grob G.115E Tutor T1	VT Aerospace/Cambridge UAS/University of London AS/No 57(R) Sqn, Wyton	
G-BYVD	Grob G.115E Tutor T1	VT Aerospace/No 1 EFTS, Barkston Heath	
G-BYVE	Grob G.115E Tutor T1	VT Aerospace/Cambridge UAS/University of London AS/No 57(R) Sqn, Wyton	
G-BYVF	Grob G.115E Tutor T1	VT Aerospace/RN No 727 NAS, Yeovilton	
G-BYVG	Grob G.115E Tutor T1	VT Aerospace/Cambridge UAS/University of London AS/No 57(R) Sqn, Wyton	
G-BYVH	Grob G.115E Tutor T1	VT Aerospace/No 1 EFTS, Barkston Heath	
G-BYVI	Grob G.115E Tutor T1	VT Aerospace/Cambridge UAS/University of London AS/No 57(R) Sqn, Wyton	
G-BYVJ	Grob G.115E Tutor T1	VT Aerospace/Yorkshire Universities AS, Church Fenton	
G-BYVK	Grob G.115E Tutor T1	VT Aerospace/RN No 727 NAS, Yeovilton	
G-BYVL	Grob G.115E Tutor T1	VT Aerospace/Oxford UAS, Benson	
G-BYVM	Grob G.115E Tutor T1	VT Aerospace/No 1 EFTS, Barkston Heath	
G-BYVO	Grob G.115E Tutor T1	VT Aerospace/No 1 EFTS, Barkston Heath	
G-BYVP	Grob G.115E Tutor T1	VT Aerospace/Cambridge UAS/University of London AS/No 57(R) Sqn, Wyton	
G-BYVR	Grob G.115E Tutor T1	VT Aerospace/East Midlands Universities AS/No 16(R) Sqn/ No 115(R) Sqn, Cranwell	
G-BYVS	Grob G.115E Tutor T1	VT Aerospace/East Midlands Universities AS/No 16(R) Sqn/ No 115(R) Sqn, Cranwell	
G-BYVT	Grob G.115E Tutor T1	VT Aerospace/Cambridge UAS/University of London AS/No 57(R) Sqn, Wyton	
G-BYVU	Grob G.115E Tutor T1	VT Aerospace/No 1 EFTS, Middle Wallop	
G-BYVV	Grob G.115E Tutor T1	VT Aerospace/Northumbrian Universities AS, Leeming	
G-BYVW	Grob G.115E Tutor T1	VT Aerospace/University of Wales AS, St Athan	
G-BYVX	Grob G.115E Tutor T1	VT Aerospace/Yorkshire Universities AS, Church Fenton	
G-BYVY	Grob G.115E Tutor T1	VT Aerospace/No 1 EFTS, Middle Wallop	
G-BYVZ	Grob G.115E Tutor T1	VT Aerospace/No 1 EFTS, Barkston Heath	
G-BYWA	Grob G.115E Tutor T1	VT Aerospace/University of Wales AS, St Athan	
G-BYWB	Grob G.115E Tutor T1	VT Aerospace/East Midlands Universities AS/No 16(R) Sqn/ No 115(R) Sqn, Cranwell	

Notes	Serial	Type (code/other identity)	Owner/operator location or fate
	G-BYWC	Grob G.115E Tutor T1	VT Aerospace/Bristol UAS, Colerne
	G-BYWD	Grob G.115E Tutor T1	VT Aerospace/University of Wales AS, St Athan
	G-BYWE	Grob G.115E Tutor T1	VT Aerospace/Bristol UAS, Colerne
	G-BYWF	Grob G.115E Tutor T1	VT Aerospace/East Midlands Universities AS/No 16(R) Sqn/ No 115(R) Sqn, Cranwell
	G-BYWG	Grob G.115E Tutor T1	VT Aerospace/East Midlands Universities AS/No 16(R) Sqn/ No 115(R) Sqn, Cranwell
	G-BYWH	Grob G.115E Tutor T1	VT Aerospace/Cambridge UAS/University of London AS/No 57(R) Sqn, Wyton
	G-BYWI	Grob G.115E Tutor T1	VT Aerospace/No 1 EFTS, Barkston Heath
	G-BYWJ	Grob G.115E Tutor T1	VT Aerospace/No 1 EFTS, Barkston Heath
	G-BYWK	Grob G.115E Tutor T1	VT Aerospace/Bristol UAS, Colerne
	G-BYWL	Grob G.115E Tutor T1	VT Aerospace/East Midlands Universities AS/No 16(R) Sqn/ No 115(R) Sqn, Cranwell
	G-BYWM	Grob G.115E Tutor T1	VT Aerospace/RN No 727 NAS, Yeovilton
	G-BYWN	Grob G.115E Tutor T1	VT Aerospace/No 1 EFTS, Barkston Heath
	G-BYWO	Grob G.115E Tutor T1	VT Aerospace/Cambridge UAS/University of London AS/No 57(R) Sqn, Wyton
	G-BYWP	Grob G.115E Tutor T1	VT Aerospace/Yorkshire Universities AS, Church Fenton
	G-BYWR	Grob G.115E Tutor T1	VT Aerospace/Cambridge UAS/University of London AS/No 57(R) Sqn, Wyton
	G-BYWS	Grob G.115E Tutor T1	VT Aerospace/No 1 EFTS, Barkston Heath
	G-BYWT	Grob G.115E Tutor T1	VT Aerospace/Northumbrian Universities AS, Leeming
	G-BYWU	Grob G.115E Tutor T1	VT Aerospace/Oxford UAS, Benson
	G-BYWV	Grob G.115E Tutor T1	VT Aerospace/Yorkshire Universities AS, Church Fenton
	G-BYWW	Grob G.115E Tutor T1	VT Aerospace/Southampton UAS, Boscombe Down
	G-BYWX	Grob G.115E Tutor T1	VT Aerospace/Cambridge UAS/University of London AS/No 57(R) Sqn, Wyton
	G-BYWY	Grob G.115E Tutor T1	VT Aerospace/East Midlands Universities AS/No 16(R) Sqn/ No 115(R) Sqn, Cranwell
	G-BYWZ	Grob G.115E Tutor T1	VT Aerospace/East Midlands Universities AS/No 16(R) Sqn/ No 115(R) Sqn, Cranwell
	G-BYXA	Grob G.115E Tutor T1	VT Aerospace/Oxford UAS, Benson
	G-BYXB	Grob G.115E Tutor T1	VT Aerospace/Bristol UAS, Colerne
	G-BYXC	Grob G.115E Tutor T1	VT Aerospace/Oxford UAS, Benson
	G-BYXD	Grob G.115E Tutor T1	VT Aerospace/Southampton UAS, Boscombe Down
	G-BYXE	Grob G.115E Tutor T1	VT Aerospace/Southampton UAS, Boscombe Down
	G-BYXF	Grob G.115E Tutor T1	VT Aerospace/No 1 EFTS, Middle Wallop
	G-BYXG	Grob G.115E Tutor T1	VT Aerospace/Yorkshire Universities AS, Church Fenton
	G-BYXH	Grob G.115E Tutor T1	VT Aerospace/Bristol UAS, Colerne
	G-BYXI	Grob G.115E Tutor T1	VT Aerospace/Southampton UAS, Boscombe Down
	G-BYXJ	Grob G.115E Tutor T1	VT Aerospace/RN No 727 NAS, Yeovilton
	G-BYXK	Grob G.115E Tutor T1	VT Aerospace/RN No 727 NAS, Yeovilton
	G-BYXL	Grob G.115E Tutor T1	VT Aerospace/Oxford UAS, Benson
	G-BYXM	Grob G.115E Tutor T1	VT Aerospace/East Midlands Universities AS/No 16(R) Sqn/ No 115(R) Sqn, Cranwell
	G-BYXN	Grob G.115E Tutor T1	VT Aerospace/East Midlands Universities AS/No 16(R) Sqn/ No 115(R) Sqn, Cranwell
	G-BYXO	Grob G.115E Tutor T1	VT Aerospace/East Midlands Universities AS/No 16(R) Sqn/ No 115(R) Sqn, Cranwell
	G-BYXP	Grob G.115E Tutor T1	VT Aerospace/Cambridge UAS/University of London AS/No 57(R) Sqn, Wyton
	G-BYXS	Grob G.115E Tutor T1	VT Aerospace/RN No 727 NAS, Yeovilton
	G-BYXT	Grob G.115E Tutor T1	VT Aerospace/Cambridge UAS/University of London AS/No 57(R) Sqn, Wyton
	G-BYXX	Grob G.115E Tutor T1	VT Aerospace/No 1 EFTS, Barkston Heath
	G-BYXY	Grob G.115E Tutor T1	VT Aerospace/Cambridge UAS/University of London AS/No 57(R) Sqn, Wyton
	G-BYXZ	Grob G.115E Tutor T1	VT Aerospace/East Midlands Universities AS/No 16(R) Sqn/ No 115(R) Sqn, Cranwell
	G-BYYA	Grob G.115E Tutor T1	VT Aerospace/Northumbrian Universities AS, Leeming
	G-BYYB	Grob G.115E Tutor T1	VT Aerospace/No 1 EFTS, Barkston Heath
	G-CEYO	AS350BB Squirrel HT3 [00]	DHFS, RAF Shawbury
	G-CGKA	Grob G.115E Tutor T1EA	VT Aerospace/No 3 FTS/45(R) Sqn, D Flt, Cranwell
	G-CGKB	Grob G.115E Tutor T1EA	VT Aerospace/No 3 FTS/45(R) Sqn, D Flt, Cranwell
	G-CGKC	Grob G.115E Tutor T1EA	VT Aerospace/No 3 FTS/45(R) Sqn, D Flt, Cranwell
	G-CGKD	Grob G.115E Tutor T1EA	VT Aerospace/University of Birmingham AS, Cosford

Serial	Type (code/other identity)	Owner/operator location or fate	Notes
G-CGKE	Grob G.115E Tutor T1EA	VT Aerospace/University of Birmingham AS, Cosford	
G-CGKF	Grob G.115E Tutor T1EA	VT Aerospace/University of Birmingham AS, Cosford	
G-CGKG	Grob G.115E Tutor T1EA	VT Aerospace/University of Birmingham AS, Cosford	
G-CGKH	Grob G.115E Tutor T1EA	VT Aerospace/University of Birmingham AS, Cosford	
G-CGKI	Grob G.115E Tutor T1EA	VT Aerospace/East of Scotland UAS, Leuchars	
G-CGKJ	Grob G.115E Tutor T1EA	VT Aerospace/East of Scotland UAS, Leuchars	
G-CGKK	Grob G.115E Tutor T1EA	VT Aerospace/East of Scotland UAS, Leuchars	
G-CGKL	Grob G.115E Tutor T1EA	VT Aerospace/East of Scotland UAS, Leuchars	
G-CGKM	Grob G.115E Tutor T1EA	VT Aerospace/East of Scotland UAS, Leuchars	
G-CGKN	Grob G.115E Tutor T1EA	VT Aerospace/Universities of Glasgow & Strathclyde AS, Glasgow	
G-CGKO	Grob G.115E Tutor T1EA	VT Aerospace/Universities of Glasgow & Strathclyde AS,Glasgow	
G-CGKP	Grob G.115E Tutor T1EA	VT Aerospace/Liverpool UAS/Manchester and Salford Universities AS, Woodvale	
G-CGKR	Grob G.115E Tutor T1EA	VT Aerospace/Liverpool UAS/Manchester and Salford Universities AS, Woodvale	
G-CGKS	Grob G.115E Tutor T1EA	VT Aerospace/Liverpool UAS/Manchester and Salford Universities AS, Woodvale	
G-CGKT	Grob G.115E Tutor T1EA	VT Aerospace/Liverpool UAS/Manchester and Salford Universities AS, Woodvale	
G-CGKU	Grob G.115E Tutor T1EA	VT Aerospace/Liverpool UAS/Manchester and Salford Universities AS, Woodvale	
G-CGKV	Grob G.115E Tutor T1EA	VT Aerospace/Liverpool UAS/Manchester and Salford Universities AS, Woodvale	
G-CGKW	Grob G.115E Tutor T1EA	VT Aerospace/Liverpool UAS/Manchester and Salford Universities AS, Woodvale	
G-CGKX	Grob G.115E Tutor T1EA	VT Aerospace/Liverpool UAS/Manchester and Salford Universities AS, Woodvale	
G-DOIT	AS350BB Squirrel HT3 [99]	DHFS, RAF Shawbury	
G-FFRA	Dassault Falcon 20DC (N902FR)	Cobham Leasing Ltd, Bournemouth	
G-FRAD	Dassault Falcon 20E	Cobham Leasing Ltd, Bournemouth	
G-FRAF	Dassault Falcon 20E (N911FR)	Cobham Leasing Ltd, Bournemouth	
G-FRAH	Dassault Falcon 20DC (N900FR)	Cobham Leasing Ltd, Durham/Tees Valley	
G-FRAI	Dassault Falcon 20E (N901FR)	Cobham Leasing Ltd, Bournemouth	
G-FRAJ	Dassault Falcon 20E (N903FR)	Cobham Leasing Ltd, Bournemouth	
G-FRAK	Dassault Falcon 20DC (N905FR)	Cobham Leasing Ltd, Durham/Tees Valley	
G-FRAL	Dassault Falcon 20DC (N904FR)	Cobham Leasing Ltd, Durham/Tees Valley	
G-FRAO	Dassault Falcon 20DC (N906FR)	Cobham Leasing Ltd, Bournemouth	
G-FRAP	Dassault Falcon 20DC (N908FR)	Cobham Leasing Ltd, Bournemouth	
G-FRAR	Dassault Falcon 20DC (N909FR)	Cobham Leasing Ltd, Bournemouth	
G-FRAS	Dassault Falcon 20C (117501)	Cobham Leasing Ltd, Durham/Tees Valley	
G-FRAT	Dassault Falcon 20C (117502)	Cobham Leasing Ltd, Durham/Tees Valley	
G-FRAU	Dassault Falcon 20C (117504)	Cobham Leasing Ltd, Durham/Tees Valley	
G-FRAW	Dassault Falcon 20ECM (117507)	Cobham Leasing Ltd, Durham/Tees Valley	

RAF Maintenance Command/Support Command/Logistics Command 'M' number cross-reference

1764M/K4972
2015M/K5600
2292M/K8203
2361M/K6035
3118M/H5199/(BK892)
3858M/X7688
4354M/BL614
4552M/T5298
5377M/EP120
5405M/LF738
5466M/*BN230*/(LF751)
5690M/MK356
5718M/BM597
5758M/DG202
6457M/ML427
6490M/LA255
6640M/RM694
6850M/TE184
6946M/RW388
6948M/DE673
6960M/MT847
7008M/EE549
7014M/N6720
7015M/NL985
7035M/*K2567*/(DE306)
7060M/VF301
7090M/EE531
7118M/LA198
7119M/LA226
7150M/PK683
7154M/WB188
7174M/VX272
7175M/VV106
7200M/VT812
7241M/TE311/*(MK178)*
7243M/TE462
7245M/RW382
7246M/TD248
7256M/TB752
7257M/TB252
7279M/TB752
7281M/TB252
7288M/PK724
7293M/*TB675*/(RW393)
7323M/VV217
7325M/R5868
7326M/VN485
7362M/475081/(VP546)
7416M/WN907
7421M/WT660
7422M/WT684
7428M/WK198
7432M/WZ724
7438M/*18671*/(WP905)
7443M/WX853
7458M/WX905
7464M/XA564
7470M/XA553
7473M/XE946
7491M/WT569
7496M/WT612
7499M/WT555
7510M/WT694
7525M/WT619
7530M/WT648
7532M/WT651
7533M/WT680
7544M/WN904
7548M/PS915
7556M/WK584
7564M/XE982
7570M/XD674
7582M/WP190
7583M/WP185
7602M/WE600
7605M/WS692
7606M/WV562
7607M/TJ138
7615M/WV679
7616M/WW388
7618M/WW442
7622M/WV606
7631M/VX185
7641M/XA634
7645M/WD293
7648M/XF785
7673M/WV332
7689M/*WW421*/(WW450)
7696M/WV493
7698M/WV499
7704M/TW536
7705M/WL505
7706M/WB584
7709M/WT933
7711M/PS915
7712M/WK281
7715M/XK724
7716M/WS776
7718M/WA577
7719M/WK277
7726M/XM373
7741M/VZ477
7750M/*WK864*/(WL168)
7751M/WL131
7755M/WG760
7758M/PM651
7759M/PK664
7761M/XH318
7762M/XE670
7764M/XH318
7770M/*XF506*/(WT746)
7793M/XG523
7798M/XH783
7806M/TA639
7809M/XA699
7816M/WG763
7817M/TX214
7825M/WK991
7827M/XA917
7829M/XH992
7839M/WV781
7841M/WV783
7851M/WZ706
7854M/XM191
7855M/XK416
7859M/XP283
7860M/XL738
7862M/XR246
7863M/*XP248*
7864M/XP244
7865M/TX226
7866M/XH278
7868M/WZ736
7869M/WK935
7872M/*WZ826*/(XD826)
7881M/WD413
7883M/XT150
7887M/XD375
7891M/XM693
7894M/XD818
7895M/WF784
7898M/XP854
7900M/WA576
7906M/WH132
7917M/WA591
7928M/XE849
7930M/WH301
7931M/RD253
7932M/WZ744
7933M/XR220
7937M/WS843
7938M/XH903
7939M/XD596
7940M/XL764
7955M/XH767
7957M/XF545
7960M/WS726
7961M/WS739
7964M/WS760
7965M/WS792
7967M/WS788
7971M/XK699
7973M/WS807
7979M/XM529
7980M/XM561
7982M/XH892
7983M/XD506
7984M/XN597
7986M/WG777
7988M/XL149
7990M/XD452
7997M/XG452
7998M/*XM515*/(XD515)
8005M/WG768
8009M/XG518
8010M/XG547
8012M/VS562
8017M/XL762
8018M/XN344
8019M/WZ869
8021M/XL824
8022M/XN341
8027M/XM555
8032M/XH837
8034M/XL703
8041M/XF690
8043M/XF836
8046M/XL770
8049M/WE168
8050M/XG329
8052M/WH166
8054AM/XM410
8054BM/XM417
8055AM/XM402
8055BM/XM404
8056M/XG337
8057M/XR243
8063M/WT536
8070M/EP120
8072M/PK624
8073M/TB252
8075M/RW382
8078M/XM351
8080M/XM480
8081M/XM468
8082M/XM409
8086M/TB752
8092M/WK654
8094M/WT520
8097M/XN492
8101M/WH984
8102M/WT486
8103M/WR985
8106M/WR982
8114M/WL798
8117M/WR974
8118M/WZ549
8119M/WR971
8121M/XM474
8124M/WZ572
8128M/WH775
8130M/WH798
8131M/WT507
8140M/XJ571
8142M/XJ560
8147M/XR526
8151M/WV795
8153M/WV903
8154M/WV908
8155M/WV797
8156M/XE339
8158M/XE369
8160M/XD622
8161M/XE993
8162M/WM913
8164M/*WN105*/(WF299)
8165M/WH791
8169M/WH364
8173M/XN685
8176M/WH791
8177M/WM224
8179M/XN928
8183M/*XN972*/(XN962)
8184M/WT520
8186M/WR977
8187M/WH791
8189M/*WD615* (WD646)
8190M/XJ918
8192M/XR658
8198M/WT339
8203M/XD377
8205M/XN819
8206M/WG419
8208M/WG303
8209M/WG418
8210M/WG471

8211M/WK570
8213M/WK626
8215M/WP869
8216M/WP927
8229M/XM355
8230M/XM362
8234M/XN458
8235M/XN549
8236M/XP573
8237M/XS179
8238M/XS180
8338M/XS180
8344M/WH960
8350M/WH840
8352M/XN632
8355M/KN645
8357M/WK576
8359M/WF825
8361M/WB670
8362M/WG477
8364M/WG464
8365M/XK421
8366M/XG454
8367M/XG474
8368M/XF926
8369M/WE139
8370M/N1671
8371M/XA847
8372M/K8042
8373M/P2617
8375M/NX611
8376M/RF398
8377M/R9125
8378M/*T9707*
8379M/DG590
8380M/Z7197
8382M/VR930
8383M/K9942
8384M/X4590
8385M/N5912
8386M/NV778
8387M/T6296
8388M/XL993
8389M/VX573
8392M/SL674
8394M/WG422
8395M/WF408
8396M/XK740
8399M/WR539
8401M/XP686
8406M/XP831
8407M/XP585
8408M/XS186
8409M/XS209
8410M/XR662
8413M/XM192
8414M/XM173
8417M/XM144
8422M/XM169
8427M/XM172
8429M/XH592
8434M/XM411
8436M/XN554
8437M/WG362
8439M/WZ846
8440M/WD935
8442M/XP411
8452M/XK885
8453M/XP745
8458M/XP672
8459M/XR650
8460M/XP680
8462M/XX477
8463M/XP355
8464M/XJ758
8465M/W1048
8466M/L-866
8467M/WP912
8468M/MM5701/(BT474)
8469M/100503
8470M/584219
8471M/701152
8472M/120227/(VN679)
8473M/WP190
8474M/494083
8475M/360043/(PJ876)
8476M/24
8477M/4101/(DG200)
8478M/10639
8479M/730301
8481M/191614
8482M/112372/(VK893)
8483M/420430
8484M/5439
8485M/997
8486M/BAPC 99
8487M/J-1172
8488M/WL627
8491M/WJ880
8493M/XR571
8494M/XP557
8501M/XP640
8502M/XP686
8508M/XS218
8509M/XT141
8514M/XS176
8535M/XN776
8538M/XN781
8545M/XN726
8546M/XN728
8548M/WT507
8549M/WT534
8554M/TG511
8561M/XS100
8563M/*XX822*/(XW563)
8565M/*WT720*/(E-408)
8566M/XV279
8573M/XM708
8575M/XP542
8576M/XP502
8578M/XR534
8581M/WJ775
8582M/XE874
8583M/BAPC 94
8585M/XE670
8586M/XE643
8588M/XR681
8589M/XR700
8590M/XM191
8591M/XA813
8595M/XH278
8598M/WP270
8600M/XX761
8602M/*PF179*/(XR541)
8604M/XS104
8606M/XP530
8608M/XP540
8610M/XL502
8611M/WF128
8618M/*XS111*/(XP504)
8620M/XP534
8621M/XR538
8624M/*XR991*/(XS102)
8627M/XP558
8628M/XJ380
8630M/WG362
8631M/XR574
8633M/3W-17/MK732
8634M/WP314
8640M/XR977
8642M/XR537
8645M/XD163
8648M/XK526
8653M/XS120
8655M/XN126
8656M/XP405
8657M/VZ634
8661M/XJ727
8662M/XR458
8666M/XE793
8668M/WJ821
8671M/XJ435
8672M/XP351
8673M/XD165
8676M/XL577
8679M/XF526
8680M/XF527
8681M/XG164
8682M/XP404
8693M/WH863
8696M/WH773
8702M/XG196
8703M/VW453
8706M/XF383
8708M/XF509
8709M/XG209
8710M/XG274
8711M/XG290
8713M/XG225
8718M/XX396
8719M/XT257
8724M/XW923
8726M/XP299
8727M/XR486
8728M/WT532
8729M/WJ815
8733M/XL318
8736M/XF375
8739M/XH170
8740M/WE173
8741M/XW329
8743M/WD790
8746M/XH171
8749M/XH537
8751M/XT255
8753M/WL795
8762M/WH740
8764M/XP344
8768M/A-522
8769M/A-528
8770M/XL623
8771M/XM602
8772M/WR960
8777M/XX914
8778M/XM598
8779M/XM607
8780M/WK102
8781M/WE982
8782M/XH136
8783M/XW272
8785M/XS642
8789M/XK970
8791M/XP329
8792M/XP345
8793M/XP346
8794M/XP398
8796M/XK943
8797M/XX947
8799M/WV787
8800M/XG226
8805M/XV722
8807M/XL587
8810M/XJ825
8816M/XX734
8818M/XK527
8820M/VP952
8821M/XX115
8822M/VP957
8828M/XS587
8830M/*N-294*/(XF515)
8831M/XG160
8832M/*XG168*/(XG172)
8833M/XL569
8834M/*XL571*
8836M/XL592
8838M/*34037*/(429356)
8839M/XG194
8841M/XE606
8853M/XT277
8855M/XT284
8857M/XW544
8858M/XW541
8863M/XG154
8867M/XK532
8868M/WH775
8869M/WH957
8870M/WH964
8871M/WJ565
8873M/XR453
8874M/XE597
8875M/XE624
8876M/*VM791*/(XA312)
8880M/XF435
8881M/XG254
8883M/XX946
8884M/VX275
8885M/XW922
8886M/XA243
8888M/XA231
8889M/XN239
8890M/WT532
8892M/XL618
8895M/XX746
8896M/XX821
8897M/XX969
8898M/XX119
8899M/XX756
8900M/XZ368
8901M/XZ383
8902M/XX739
8903M/XX747
8905M/XX975
8906M/XX976
8907M/XZ371
8908M/XZ382
8909M/XV784
8910M/XL160
8911M/XH673
8918M/XX109
8919M/XT486

RAF Maintenance Command Cross-Reference

8920M/XT469
8921M/XT466
8922M/XT467
8923M/XX819
8924M/XP701
8925M/XP706
8931M/XV779
8932M/XR718
8934M/XR749
8935M/XR713
8937M/XX751
8938M/WV746
8941M/XT456
8942M/XN185
8943M/XE799
8944M/WZ791
8945M/XX818
8946M/XZ389
8947M/XX726
8949M/XX743
8951M/XX727
8953M/XX959
8954M/XZ384
8955M/XX110
8957M/XN582
8961M/XS925
8967M/XV263
8969M/XR753
8972M/XR754
8973M/XS922
8974M/XM473
8975M/XW917
8976M/XZ630
8978M/XX837
8984M/XN551
8985M/WK127
8986M/XV261
8987M/XM358
8990M/XM419
8995M/XM425
8996M/XM414
8997M/XX669
8998M/XT864
9002M/XW763
9003M/XZ390
9004M/XZ370
9005M/XZ374
9006M/XX967
9007M/XX968
9008M/XX140
9009M/XX763
9010M/XX764
9011M/XM412
9012M/XN494
9014M/XN584
9015M/XW320
9017M/ZE449
9019M/XX824
9020M/XX825
9021M/XX826
9022M/XX958
9026M/XP629
9027M/XP556
9028M/XP563
9032M/XR673
9033M/XS181
9036M/XM350
9038M/XV810
9039M/XN586
9040M/XZ138
9041M/XW763
9042M/XL954
9044M/XS177
9047M/XW409
9048M/XM403
9049M/XW404
9052M/WJ717
9056M/XS488
9059M/ZE360
9066M/XV582
9067M/XV586
9070M/XV581
9072M/XW768
9073M/XW924
9075M/XV752
9076M/XV808
9078M/XV753
9079M/XZ130
9080M/ZE350
9086M/ZE352
9087M/XX753
9090M/XW353
9091M/XW434
9092M/XH669
9093M/WK124
9095M/XW547
9096M/WV322
9098M/XV406
9103M/XV411
9110M/XX736
9111M/XW421
9115M/XV863
9117M/XV161
9119M/XW303
9120M/XW419
9122M/XZ997
9123M/XT773
9125M/XW410
9127M/XW432
9130M/XW327
9131M/*DD931*
9132M/XX977
9133M/*413573*
9134M/XT288
9136M/XT891
9137M/XN579
9139M/XV863
9140M/XZ287
9141M/XV118
9143M/XN589
9145M/XV863
9146M/XW299
9147M/XW301
9148M/XW436
9149M/XW375
9150M/*FX760*
9151M/XT907
9152M/XV424
9153M/XW360
9154M/XW321
9155M/WL679
9162M/XZ991
9163M/XV415
9166M/XW323
9167M/XV744
9168M/XZ132
9169M/XW547
9170M/XZ994
9172M/XW304
9173M/XW418
9174M/XZ131
9175M/P1344
9176M/XW430
9177M/XW328
9179M/XW309
9180M/XW311
9181M/XW358
9185M/XZ987
9187M/XW405
9188M/XW364
9190M/XW318
9191M/XW416
9192M/XW361
9193M/XW367
9194M/XW420
9195M/XW330
9196M/XW370
9197M/*XX530*/(XX637)
9198M/XS641
9199M/XW290
9200M/XW425
9201M/ZD667
9203M/*3066*
9205M/*E449*
9206M/F6314
9207M/8417/18
9208M/F938
9210M/MF628
9211M/733682
9212M/*KL216*/(45-49295)
9213M/N5182
9215M/XL164
9216M/XL190
9217M/ZH257
9218M/XL563
9219M/XZ971
9221M/XZ966
9222M/XZ968
9224M/XL568
9225M/XX885
9226M/XV865
9227M/XB812
9229M/ZA678
9233M/XZ431
9234M/XV864
9236M/WV318
9237M/XF445
9238M/ZA717
9239M/7198/18
9241M/XS639
9242M/XH672
9246M/XS714
9248M/WB627
9249M/WV396
9251M/XX744
9252M/XX722
9254M/XX965
9255M/XZ375
9257M/XX962
9258M/XW265
9259M/XS710
9260M/XS734
9261M/*W2068*
9262M/XZ358
9263M/XW267
9264M/XS735
9265M/WK585
9266M/XZ119
9267M/XW269
9268M/XR529
9269M/XT914
9270M/XZ145
9272M/XS486
9273M/XS726
9274M/XS738
9275M/XS729
9276M/XS733
9277M/XT601
9278M/XS643
9279M/XT681
9280M/XV804
9281M/XZ146
9283M/XZ322
9284M/ZA267
9285M/XR806
9286M/XT905
9287M/WP962
9288M/XX520
9289M/XX665
9290M/XX626
9292M/XW892
9293M/XX830
9294M/XX655
9295M/XV497
9298M/ZE340
9299M/XW870
9300M/XX431
9301M/XZ941
9302M/ZD462
9303M/XV709
9306M/XX979
9308M/ZD932
9310M/ZA355
9311M/ZA475
9312M/ZA474
9314M/ZA320
9315M/ZA319
9316M/ZA399
9317M/ZA450
9318M/ZA360
9319M/XR516
9320M/XX153
9321M/XZ367
9322M/ZB686
9323M/XV643
9324M/XV659
9326M/XV653
9328M/ZD607
9329M/ZD578
9330M/ZB684
9331M/XW852
9332M/XZ935
9335M/ZA375
9336M/ZA407
9337M/ZA774
9338M/ZA325
9339M/ZA323
9340M/XX745
9341M/ZA357
9342M/XR498
9343M/XR506
9344M/XV706

Ships' Numeric Code – Deck Letters Analysis

	0	1	2	3	4	5	6	7	8	9
33									CT	
34									CM	
36						AY	LB			
37			NL			SM				
38										
40					IR					
41		EB	CW	CW		MM				
42		SU			KT	PD	SB			
43					EE	EE				
44					MR					
45		DA	DT	DM		DN			LA	
46			WM							
47					RM					

RN Code - Squadron - Base - Aircraft Cross-check

Deck/Base Code Numbers	*Letters*	*Unit*	*Location*	*Aircraft Type(s)*
010 — 020	CU	820 NAS	Culdrose	Merlin HM1
180 — 190	CU	849 NAS	Culdrose	Sea King ASaC7
180 — 190	CU	854 NAS	Culdrose	Sea King ASaC7
180 — 190	CU	857 NAS	Culdrose	Sea King ASaC7
264 — 274	CU	814 NAS	Culdrose	Merlin HM1
300 — 308	VL	815 NAS	Yeovilton	Lynx HMA8
311 — 316	VL	815 NAS, MI Flight	Yeovilton	Lynx HMA8
321 — 474	*	815 NAS	Yeovilton	Lynx HMA8
500 — 515	CU	829 NAS	Culdrose	Merlin HM1
580 — 588	CU	824 NAS	Culdrose	Merlin HM1
630 — 671	VL	702 NAS	Yeovilton	Lynx HMA8
817 — 831	CU	771 NAS	Culdrose	Sea King HU5/HAS6

*See foregoing separate ships' Deck Letters Analysis
Note that only the 'last two' digits of the Code are worn by some aircraft types, especially helicopters.

RN Landing Platform and Shore Station Code-letters

Code	Deck Letters	Vesel name & Pennant No	Vessel Type & Unit
—	AB	HMS *Albion* (L14)	Assault
—	AS	RFA *Argus* (A135)	Aviation Training ship
365	AY	HMS *Argyll* (F231)	Type 23 (815 NAS)
—	BV	RFA *Black Rover* (A273)	Fleet tanker
—	CB	RFA *Cardigan Bay* (L3009)	Landing ship
348	CM	HMS *Chatham* (F87)	Type 22 (815 NAS)
338	CT	HMS *Campbeltown* (F86)	Type 22 (815 NAS)
—	CU	RNAS Culdrose (HMS *Seahawk*)	
412/3	CW	HMS *Cornwall* (F99)	Type 22 (815 NAS)
451	DA	HMS *Daring* (D32)	Type 45 (815 NAS)
—	DC	HMS *Dumbarton Castle* (P265)	Fishery protection
—	DG	RFA *Diligence* (A132)	Maintenance
453	DM	HMS *Diamond* (D34)	Type 45 (815 NAS)
455	DN	HMS *Dragon* (D35)	Type 45 (815 NAS)
452	DT	HMS *Dauntless* (D33)	Type 45 (815 NAS)
411	EB	HMS *Edinburgh* (D97)	Type 42 (815 NAS)
434/5	EE	HMS *Endurance* (A171)	Ice Patrol (815 NAS)
—	FA	RFA *Fort Austin* (A386)	Support ship
—	FE	RFA *Fort Rosalie* (A385)	Support ship
—	GV	RFA *Gold Rover* (A271)	Fleet tanker
404	IR	HMS *Iron Duke* (F234)	Type 23 (815 NAS)
425	KT	HMS *Kent* (F78)	Type 23 (815 NAS)
—	L	HMS *Illustrious* (R06)	Carrier
457	LA	HMS *Lancaster* (F229)	Type 23 (829 NAS)
366	LB	RFA *Largs Bay* (L3006)	Landing ship
—	LC	HMS *Leeds Castle* (P258)	Fishery protection
—	MB	RFA *Mounts Bay* (L3008)	Landing ship
415	MM	HMS *Monmouth* (F235)	Type 23 (829 NAS)
444	MR	HMS *Montrose* (F236)	Type 23 (815 NAS)
372	NL	HMS *Northumberland* (F238)	Type 23 (829 NAS)
—	O	HMS *Ocean* (L12)	Helicopter carrier
426	PD	HMS *Portland* (F79)	Type 23 (815 NAS)
474	RM	HMS *Richmond* (F239)	Type 23 (815 NAS)
427	SB	HMS *St Albans* (F83)	Type 23 (815 NAS)
375	SM	HMS *Somerset* (F82)	Type 23 (815 NAS)
422	SU	HMS *Sutherland* (F81)	Type 23 (815 NAS)
—	VL	RNAS Yeovilton (HMS *Heron*)	
462	WM	HMS *Westminster* (F237)	Type 23 (829 NAS)
—	—	HMS *Bulwark* (L15)	Assault
—	—	HMS *Defender* (D36)	Type 45
—	—	HMS *Duncan* (D37)	Type 45
—	—	HMS *Protector* (A173)	Ice patrol
—	—	RFA *Fort Victoria* (A387)	Auxiliary Oiler
—	—	RFA *Fort George* (A388)	Auxiliary Oiler
—	—	RFA *Lyme Bay* (L3007)	Landing ship
—	—	RFA *Wave Knight* (A389)	Fleet tanker
—	—	RFA *Wave Ruler* (A390)	Fleet tanker

Royal Air Force Squadron Markings

This table gives brief details of the markings worn by aircraft of RAF squadrons at the beginning of 2012. While this may help to identify the operator of a particular machine, it may not always give the true picture. For example, from time to time aircraft are loaned to other units while others wear squadron marks but are actually operated on a pool basis. Squadron badges are usually located on the front fuselage.

Squadron	*Type(s) operated*	*Base(s)*	*Distinguishing marks & other comments*
No 1 Sqn	Typhoon T3/FGR4	RAF Leuchars	Badge (on tail): A red 1 with yellow wings on a white background, flanked in red. Roundel is flanked by two white chevrons, edged in red. Aircraft are coded F*
No 2 Sqn	Tornado GR4/GR4A	RAF Marham	Badge: A wake knot on a white circular background flanked on either side by black and white triangles. Tail fin has a black stripe with white triangles and the badge repeated on it.
No 3 Sqn	Typhoon T3/FGR4	RAF Coningsby	Badge: A blue cockatrice on a white circular background flanked by two green bars edged with yellow. Tail fin as a green stripe edged with yellow. Aircraft are coded QO-*
No 4(R) Sqn	Hawk T2	RAF Valley	Badge (on nose): A yellow lightning flash on a red background with IV superimposed. Aircraft carry a yellow lightning flash on a red and black background on the tail and this is repeated in bars either side of the roundel on the fuselage. Part of No 4 FTS.
No 5 Sqn	Sentinel R1	RAF Waddington	Badge (on tail): A green maple leaf on a white circle over a red horizontal band.
No 6 Sqn	Typhoon T3/FGR4	RAF Leuchars	Badge (on tail): A red, winged can opener on a blue shield, edged in red. The roundel is flanked by a red zigzag on a blue background. Aircraft are coded E*.
No 7 Sqn	Chinook HC2/HC2A/ HC3R	RAF Odiham	Badge (on tail): A blue badge containing the seven Aircraft pooled with No 18 Sqn and No 27 Sqn.
No 8 Sqn	Sentry AEW1	RAF Waddington	Badge (on tail): A grey, sheathed, Arabian dagger. Aircraft pooled with No 54(R) Sqn.
No 9 Sqn	Tornado GR4/GR4A	RAF Marham	Badge: A green bat on a black circular background, flanked by yellow and green horizontal stripes. The green bat also appears on the tail, edged in yellow.
No 10 Sqn	Voyager KC2/KC3	RAF Brize Norton	No markings worn.
No 11 Sqn	Typhoon T3/FGR4	RAF Coningsby	Badge (on tail): Two eagles in flight on a white shield. The roundel is flanked by yellow and black triangles. Aircraft are coded D*
No 12 Sqn	Tornado GR4/GR4A	RAF Lossiemouth	Roundel is superimposed on a green chevron. Tail fin has a black & white horizontal stripe with the squadron badge, a fox's head on a white circle, in the middle.
No 13 Sqn	Reaper	RAF Waddington	No markings worn.
No 14 Sqn	Shadow R1	RAF Waddington	No markings worn.
No 15(R) Sqn [NTOCU]	Tornado GR4/GR4A	RAF Lossiemouth	Roman numerals XV appear in white on the tail.
No 16(R) Sqn	Tutor	RAF Cranwell	No markings carried. Aircraft pooled with East Midlands UAS and No 115(R) Sqn.

RAF Squadron Markings

Squadron	*Type(s) operated*	*Base(s)*	*Distinguishing marks & other comments*
No 17(R) Test & Evaluation Sqn	Typhoon T3/FGR4	RAF Coningsby	Badge (on tail): A gauntlet on a black and white shield. Roundel is flanked by two white bars which have a pair of jagged black lines running along them horizontally. Aircraft are coded A*.
No 18 Sqn	Chinook HC2/HC2A/ HC3R	RAF Odiham	Badge (on tail): A red winged horse on a black circle. Aircraft pooled with No 7 Sqn and No 27 Sqn.
No 22 Sqn	Sea King HAR3/HAR3A	A Flt: RMB Chivenor B Flt: Wattisham C Flt: RAF Valley	Badge: A black pi symbol in front of a white Maltese cross on a red circle.
No 24 Sqn	Hercules C4/C5	RAF Brize Norton	No squadron markings carried. Aircraft pooled with No 30 Sqn and No 47 Sqn.
No 27 Sqn	Chinook HC2/HC2A/ HC3R	RAF Odiham	Badge (on tail): An dark green elephant on a green circle, flanked by green and dark green stripes. Aircraft pooled with No 7 Sqn and No 18 Sqn.
No 28 Sqn	Merlin HC3/HC3A	RAF Benson	Badge: A winged horse above two white crosses on ared shield. Aircraft pooled with No 78 Sqn.
No 29(R) Sqn [TOCU]	Typhoon T3/FGR4	RAF Coningsby	Badge (on tail): An eagle in flight, preying on a buzzard, with three red Xs across the top. The roundel is flanked by two white bars outlined by a red line, each containing three red Xs. Aircraft are coded B*.
No 30 Sqn	Hercules C4/C5	RAF Brize Norton	No squadron markings carried. Aircraft pooled with No 24 Sqn and No 47 Sqn.
No 31 Sqn	Tornado GR4/GR4A	RAF Marham	Badge: A gold, five-pointed star on a yellow circle flanked by yellow and green checks. The star is repeated on the tail.
No 32(The Royal) Sqn	BAe 125 CC3/146 CC2/ Agusta 109	RAF Northolt	No squadron markings carried but aircraft carry a distinctive livery with a red stripe, edged in blue along the middle of the fuselage and a red tail.
No 33 Sqn	Puma HC2	RAF Benson	Badge: A stag's head.
No 39 Sqn	Predator/Reaper	Nellis AFB Creech AFB	No markings worn
No 41(R) Test & Evaluation Sqn [FJWOEU]	Tornado GR4	RAF Coningsby	Badge: A red, double armed cross, flanked by red and white horizontal stripes. Stripes repeated on tail..
No 45(R) Sqn	Super King Air 200/200GT/Tutor	RAF Cranwell	The King Airs carry a dark blue stripe on the tail superimposed with red diamonds. Part of No 3 FTS.
No 47 Sqn	Hercules C1/C3A/ C4/C5	RAF Brize Norton	No squadron markings usually carried. Aircraft pooled with No 24 Sqn and No 30 Sqn.
No 54(R) Sqn [ISTAR OCU]	Sentry AEW1	RAF Waddington	Based aircraft as required.
No 56(R) Sqn [ISTAR Test & Evaluation Sqn]	Shadow R1/ Sentry AEW1/ Sentinel R1	RAF Waddington	Based aircraft as required.

Squadron	*Type(s) operated*	*Base(s)*	*Distinguishing marks & other comments*
No 57(R) Sqn	Tutor	RAF Wyton	No markings carried. Aircraft pooled with Cambridge UAS and University of London AS.
No 60(R) Sqn	Griffin HT1	RAF Shawbury [DHFS] & RAF Valley [SARTU]	No squadron markings usually carried.
No 72(R) Sqn	Tucano T1	RAF Linton-on-Ouse	Badge: A black swift in flight on a red disk, flanked by blue bars edged with red. The blue bars edged with red also flank the roundel on the fuselage; part of No 1 FTS
No 78 Sqn	Merlin HC3/HC3A	RAF Benson	Badge: A yellow, heraldic tiger with two tails, on a black circle. Aircraft pooled with No 28 Sqn.
No 84 Sqn	Griffin HAR2	RAF Akrotiri	Badge (on tail): A scorpion on a playing card symbol (diamonds, clubs etc). Aircraft carry a vertical light blue stripe through the roundel on the fuselage.
No 99 Sqn	Globemaster III	RAF Brize Norton	Badge (on tail): A black puma leaping.
No 100 Sqn	Hawk T1A	RAF Leeming	Badge (on tail): A skull in front of two bones crossed. Aircraft are usually coded C*. Incorporates the Joint Forward Air Control Training and Standards Unit (JFACTSU).
No 101 Sqn	VC10 C1K/K3	RAF Brize Norton	Badge (on tail): A lion behind a castle turret.
No 115(R) Sqn	Tutor	RAF Cranwell	No markings carried. Aircraft pooled with East Midlands UAS and No 16(R) Sqn.
No 202 Sqn	Sea King HAR3	A Flt: RAF Boulmer D Flt: RAF Lossiemouth E Flt: RAF Leconfield	Badge: A mallard alighting on a white circle.
No 203(R) Sqn	Sea King HAR3	RAF Valley	Badge: A green sea horse on a white circle.
No 206(R) Sqn [HAT&ES]	Hercules C1/C3/C3A/C4 C5	RAF Brize Norton/ Boscombe Down	No squadron markings usually carried.
No 208(R) Sqn	Hawk T1/T1A/T1W	RAF Valley	Badge (on tail): A Sphinx inside a white circle, flanked by flashes of yellow. Aircraft also carry blue and yellow bars either side of the roundel on the fuselage and a blue and yellow chevron on the nose. Part of No 4 FTS.
No 216 Sqn	TriStar K1/KC1/C2/C2A	RAF Brize Norton	Badge (on tail): An eagle in flight with a bomb in its claws.
No 230 Sqn	Puma HC1	RAF Benson	Badge: A tiger in front of a palm tree on a black pentagon.
No 617 Sqn	Tornado GR4/GR4A	RAF Lossiemouth	Badge: Dam breached, flanked on either side by red lightning flashes on a black background. Tail fin is black with a red lightning flash.
No 1312 Flt	VC10 K3/K4 (101 Sqn) Hercules	Mount Pleasant, FI	Badge (on tail): A red Maltese cross on a white circle, flanked by red and white horizontal bars.
No 1419 Flt	Merlin HC3	Afghanistan	No markings carried.
No 1435 Flt	Typhoon FGR4	Mount Pleasant, FI	Badge (on tail): A red Maltese cross on a white circle, flanked by red and white horizontal bars.
No 1564 Flt	Chinook HC2/ Sea King HAR3	Mount Pleasant, FI	No markings known.

University Air Squadrons/Air Experience Flights*

Some UAS aircraft carry squadron badges and markings, usually on the tail. Squadron crests all consist of a white circle surrounded by a blue circle, topped with a red crown and having a yellow scroll beneath. Each differs by the motto on the scroll, the UAS name running around the blue circle & by the contents at the centre and it is the latter which are described below.

* All AEFs come under the administration of local UASs and these are listed here.

UAS	*Base*	*Marks*
Bristol UAS/ No 3 AEF	Colerne	A sailing ship on water.
Cambridge UAS/ No 5 AEF	RAF Wyton	A heraldic lion in front of a red badge. Aircraft pooled with University of London AS
East Midlands Universities AS/ No 7 AEF	RAF Cranwell	A yellow quiver, full of arrows.
East of Scotland UAS/ No 12 AEF	RAF Leuchars	An open book in front of a white diagonal cross edged in blue.
Liverpool UAS	RAF Woodvale	A bird atop an open book, holding a branch in its beak. Aircraft pooled with Manchester and Salford Universities AS
Manchester and Salford Universities AS/ No 10 AEF	RAF Woodvale	A bird of prey with a green snake in its beak. Aircraft pooled with Liverpool UAS
Northumbrian Universities AS/ No 11 AEF	RAF Leeming	A white cross on a blue background.
Oxford UAS/ No 6 AEF	RAF Benson	An open book in front of crossed swords.
Southampton UAS/ No 2 AEF	Boscombe Down	A red stag in front of a stone pillar.
Universities of Glasgow and Strathclyde AS/ No 4 AEF	Glasgow	A bird of prey in flight, holding a branch in its beak, in front of an upright sword.
University of Birmingham AS/ No 8 AEF	DSAE Cosford	A blue griffon with two heads.
University of London AS	RAF Wyton	A globe superimposed over an open book. Aircraft pooled with Cambridge UAS
University of Wales AS/ No 1 AEF	MoD St Athan	A red Welsh dragon in front of an open book, clasping a sword. Some aircraft have the dragon in front of white and green squares.
Yorkshire Universities AS/ No 9 AEF	RAF Church Fenton	An open book in front of a Yorkshire rose with leaves.

Fleet Air Arm Squadron Markings

This table gives brief details of the markings worn by aircraft of FAA squadrons. Squadron badges, when worn, are usually located on the front fuselage. All FAA squadron badges comprise a crown atop a circle edged in gold braid and so the badge details below list only what appears in the circular part.

Squadron	*Type(s) operated*	*Base(s)*	*Distinguishing marks & other comments*
No 702 NAS	Lynx HMA8	RNAS Yeovilton	Badge: A Lynx rearing up in front of a circle comprising alternate dark blue and white sectors.
No 727 NAS	Tutor	RNAS Yeovilton	Badge: The head of Britannia wearing a gold helmet on a background of blue and white waves.
No 750 NAS	Avenger T1	RNAS Culdrose	Badge: A Greek runner bearing a torch & sword on a background of blue and white waves.
No 771 NAS	Sea King HU5/HAS6	RNAS Culdrose & Prestwick	Badge: Three bees on a background of blue and white waves.
No 814 NAS	Merlin HM1	RNAS Culdrose	Badge: A winged tiger mask on a background of dark blue and white waves.
No 815 NAS	Lynx HMA8	RNAS Yeovilton	Badge: A winged, gold harpoon on a background of blue and white waves.
No 820 NAS	Merlin HM1	RNAS Culdrose	Badge: A flying fish on a background of blue and white waves.
No 824 NAS	Merlin HM1	RNAS Culdrose	Badge: A heron on a background of blue and white waves.
No 829 NAS	Merlin HM1	RNAS Culdrose	Badge: A kingfisher hovering on a background of blue and white waves.
No 845 NAS	Sea King HC4	RNAS Yeovilton	Badge: A dragonfly on a background of blue and white waves.
No 846 NAS	Sea King HC4	RNAS Yeovilton	Badge: A swordsman riding a winged horse whilst attacking a serpent on a background of blue and white waves. Aircraft are usually coded V*.
No 847 NAS	Lynx AH7/AH9A	RNAS Yeovilton	Badge: A gold sea lion on a blue background.
No 848 NAS	Sea King HC4	RNAS Yeovilton	Badge: Inside a red circle, a hawk in flight with a torpedo in its claws above white and blue waves. Aircraft are usually coded W*.
No 849 NAS	Sea King ASaC7	RNAS Culdrose	Badge: A winged streak of lightning with an eye in front on a background of blue and white waves.
No 854 NAS	Sea King ASaC7	RNAS Culdrose	Badge: A winged lion in front of a sword.
No 857 NAS	Sea King ASaC7	RNAS Culdrose	Badge: A hand emerging from the waves, clutching a sword aloft.

UK Military Aircraft Code Decode

This section lists the codes worn by some UK military aircraft and, alongside, the Registration of the aircraft currently wearing this code. It should be pointed out that in some cases more than one aircraft wears the same code but the aircraft listed is the one believed to be in service with the unit concerned at the time of going to press. This list will be updated regularly and those with Internet access can download the latest version via the 'Military Aircraft Markings' Web Site, www.militaryaircraftmarkings.co.uk.

ROYAL AIR FORCE

BAC VC10

Code	*Registration*
F	ZA147
G	ZA148
H	ZA149
J	ZA150
N	ZD241
R	XR808

BAE Hawk T1/T2

Code	*Registration*
95-Y	XX246 & XX318
A	ZK010
B	ZK011
C	ZK012
E	ZK014
I	ZK018
K	ZK020
L	ZK021
M	ZK022
O	ZK024
P	ZK025
Q	ZK026
R	ZK027
S	ZK028
T	ZK029
V	ZK031
W	ZK032
X	ZK033
Y	ZK034
AB	ZK037
CB	XX285
CC	XX203
CD	XX332
CE	XX258
CF	XX202
CG	XX198
CH	XX346
CI	XX321
CJ	XX329
CK	XX339
CL	XX255
CM	XX280
CP	XX236
CQ	XX184
CR	XX189

Beech King Air 200

Code	*Registration*
D	ZK458
J	ZK450
K	ZK451
L	ZK452
M	ZK453
N	ZK454
O	ZK455
P	ZK456
U	ZK460
X	ZK459

Bell 412EP Griffin HT1

Code	*Registration*
E	ZJ242
I	ZJ235
K	ZJ708
L	ZJ241
O	ZJ707
R	ZJ239
S	ZJ234
T	ZJ237
U	ZJ240
X	ZJ236
Y	ZJ238

B-V Chinook

Code	*Registration*
AA	ZA670
AB	ZA671
AD	ZA674
AE	ZA675
AF	ZA677
AG	ZA679
AH	ZA680
AI	ZA681
AJ	ZA682
AK	ZA683
AL	ZA684
AN	ZA705
AO	ZA707
AP	ZA708
AR	ZA710
AT	ZA712
AV	ZA714
AW	ZA720
BN	ZA718
DB	ZD574
DC	ZD575
DD	ZD980
DF	ZD982
DG	ZD983
DH	ZD984
HB	ZH775
HC	ZH776
HE	ZH777
HF	ZH891
HG	ZH892
HH	ZH893
HI	ZH894
HJ	ZH895
HK	ZH896
HR	ZH903

EHI-101 Merlin

Code	*Registration*
B	ZJ118
C	ZJ119
D	ZJ120
E	ZJ121
F	ZJ122
G	ZJ123
H	ZJ124
J	ZJ125
K	ZJ126
L	ZJ127
M	ZJ128
N	ZJ129
O	ZJ130
P	ZJ131
Q	ZJ132
R	ZJ133
S	ZJ134
T	ZJ135
U	ZJ136
W	ZJ137
X	ZJ138
AA	ZJ990
AB	ZJ992
AC	ZJ994
AD	ZJ995
AE	ZJ998
AF	ZK001

Eurofighter Typhoon

Code	*Registration*
C	ZJ950
D	ZK301
F	ZJ944
H	ZJ949
AA	ZJ930
AB	ZJ912
AE	ZJ927
AG	ZJ946
AH	ZJ947
AI	ZK332
AX	ZK303
BA	ZJ803
BB	ZK379
BC	ZJ800
BD	ZJ805
BE	ZJ806
BF	ZJ807
BG	ZK380
BH	ZJ814

BI	ZJ810
BJ	ZJ801
BK	ZJ812
BL	ZJ813
BM	ZJ804
BN	ZJ815
BP	ZJ811
BR	ZK322
BS	ZK328
BT	ZK306
BU	ZK307
BV	ZJ910
BW	ZK308
BX	ZJ928
BY	ZJ915
BZ	ZJ911
DA	ZJ931
DB	ZJ932
DC	ZJ919
DD	ZJ924
DE	ZK305
DF	ZJ933
DG	ZK300
DH	ZJ942
DJ	ZJ935
DL	ZJ929
DM	ZJ923
DN	ZK323
DS	ZJ914
DW	ZJ808
DX	ZJ939
EA	ZK302
EB	ZK304
EC	ZK334
EE	ZK331
EH	ZK333
EI	ZK324
EJ	ZK327
EK	ZK311
EL	ZK310
EM	ZK312
EN	ZK313
EO	ZK314
EQ	ZK325
ES	ZK317
ET	ZK318
EU	ZK321
EV	ZK320
EX	ZK381
EY	ZJ809
EZ	ZK330
FA	ZK316
FB	ZK326
FD	ZK336
FE	ZK337
QO-A	ZJ920
QO-B	ZJ802
QO-C	ZJ936
QO-D	ZK319
QO-G	ZJ917
QO-H	ZJ921
QO-J	ZJ941
QO-L	ZJ918
QO-M	ZJ913
QO-P	ZK309
QO-R	ZJ925
QO-S	ZJ916
QO-T	ZJ934
QO-W	ZJ937
QO-Y	ZJ926

Panavia Tornado GR4

Code	*Registration*
001	ZA365
003	ZA369
004	ZA370
005	ZA371
006	ZA372
007	ZA373
008	ZA393
009	ZA395
011	ZA400
012	ZA401
013	ZA404
014	ZA405
015	ZA406
016	ZA410
017	ZA412
020	ZA449
021	ZA452
022	ZA453
023	ZA456
024	ZA458
026	ZA461
027	ZA462
028	ZA463
029	ZA469
031	ZA472
032	ZA473
033	ZA492
034	ZA541
035	ZA542
036	ZA543
038	ZA546
039	ZA547
040	ZA548
041	ZA549
042	ZA550
043	ZA551
045	ZA553
046	ZA554
047	ZA556
048	ZA557
049	ZA559
050	ZA560
051	ZA562
054	ZA585
055	ZA587
056	ZA588
057	ZA589
058	ZA591
059	ZA592
060	ZA594
061	ZA595
062	ZA596
063	ZA597
064	ZA598
067	ZA602
068	ZA604
069	ZA606
070	ZA607
072	ZA609
073	ZA611
075	ZA613
077	ZD707
078	ZD709
079	ZD711
080	ZD712
081	ZD713
082	ZD714
083	ZD715
084	ZD716
085	ZD719
086	ZD720
087	ZD739
088	ZD740
089	ZD741
090	ZD742
092	ZD744
093	ZD745
094	ZD746
095	ZD747
096	ZD748
097	ZD749
098	ZD788
099	ZD790
100	ZD792
101	ZD793
102	ZD810
103	ZD811
105	ZD842
106	ZD843
107	ZD844
108	ZD847
109	ZD848
110	ZD849
112	ZD851
113	ZD890
115	ZD895
116	ZE116
118	ZG705
120	ZG709
122	ZG712
123	ZG713
124	ZG714
126	ZG727
127	ZG719
128	ZG750
129	ZG752
130	ZG754
133	ZG771
134	ZG775
136	ZG779
137	ZG791
F	ZA459
H	ZA373

IV	ZA612
TN	ZG794
EB-B	ZA601
EB-G	ZA600
EB-Q	ZG777
EB-R	ZA447
EB-Z	ZA614
KC-N	ZA367

Shorts Tucano T1

Code	*Registration*
MP-A	ZF170
MP-D	ZF172
MP-Q	ZF264
MP-W	ZF338

WS61 Sea King

Code	*Registration*
A	XZ585
B	XZ586
C	XZ587
D	XZ588
E	XZ589
F	XZ590
G	XZ591
H	XZ592
I	XZ593
K	XZ595
L	XZ596
M	XZ597
N	XZ598
P	XZ599
R	ZE368
S	ZE369
T	ZE370
V	ZH541
X	ZH543

ROYAL NAVY
EHI-101 Merlin

Code	*Registration*
10	ZH827
11	ZH839
12	ZH855
13	ZH846
14	ZH827
17	ZH864
65	ZH828
66	ZH851
67	ZH840
68	ZH860
70	ZH857
81	ZH861
82	ZH856
83	ZH855
84	ZH854
85	ZH833
87	ZH835
88	ZH842
502	ZH841

WS Lynx

Code	*Registration*
300	XZ690
301	ZF562
302	XZ731
303	ZD258
304	XZ691
306	XZ689
313	XZ255
314	ZD565
315	ZD260
316	XZ697
321	ZD252
322	XZ736
332	XZ726
335	ZD252
365	ZD268
410	ZD565
411	ZF558
412	ZF560
444	ZD261
451	XZ729
453	ZF557
455	ZF560
474	XZ723
631	ZD249
632	ZD263
633	XZ238
634	XZ232
635	ZD255
641	XZ732
642	ZD257
643	ZD266
644	ZD265
645	ZD566
671	XZ726

WS61 Sea King

Code	*Registration*
16	ZA166
17	XV670
18	XV648
19	ZA130
20	ZA137
21	XV666
22	ZA167
25	ZA134
26	XV661
27	XV673
28	XV647
29	XV705
30	XZ578
180	XV649
181	XV697
182	ZD636
183	XV671
184	XV707
185	XV656
186	ZE418
187	XV672
188	XV714
189	ZE420
190	XV664
191	ZA126
192	ZE422
707	XZ920
823	XV699
A	ZA293
B	ZA310
D	ZA299
E	ZA312
F	ZB507
G	ZG821
H	ZE428
I	ZG820
J	ZD480
K	ZE427
L	ZF124
M	ZA313
N	ZA291
O	ZF118
Q	ZA296
R	ZF115
S	ZD626
T	ZF121
U	ZA295
V	ZF122
W	ZA297
X	ZF117
Y	ZA298
Z	ZF120
WP	ZF116
WR	ZE425
WT	ZA314
WU	ZA292
WV	ZF115
WY	ZF119
WZ	ZD476

ARMY AIR CORPS
WS Gazelle AH1

Code	*Registration*
M	XZ345
S	ZB691
Y	ZB692

WS Lynx AH7

Code	*Registration*
A	XZ641
C	XZ643
E	ZD274
F	ZD278
H	XZ675
I	XZ669
K	ZD284
L	XZ605
M	XZ345
S	ZB691
T	XZ196
U	ZD277
V	XZ194
W	ZD272 & XZ652
Z	XZ182

Historic Aircraft in Overseas Markings

Some *historic, classic and warbird* aircraft carry the markings of overseas air arms and can be seen in the UK, mainly preserved in museums and collections or taking part in air shows.

Serial	*Type (code/other identity)*	*Owner/operator location or fate*	*Notes*
AFGHANISTAN			
-	Hawker Afghan Hind (BAPC 82)	RAF Museum, Cosford	
ARGENTINA			
-	Bell UH-1H Iroquois (AE-406/*998-8888*) [Z]	RAF Valley, instructional use	
0729	Beech T-34C Turbo Mentor	FAA Museum, stored RNAS Yeovilton	
0767	Aermacchi MB339AA	Rolls-Royce Heritage Trust, stored Derby	
A-515	FMA IA58 Pucara (ZD485)	RAF Museum, Cosford	
A-517	FMA IA58 Pucara (G-BLRP)	Privately owned, Channel Islands	
A-522	FMA IA58 Pucara (8768M)	FAA Museum, at NE Aircraft Museum, Usworth	
A-528	FMA IA58 Pucara (8769M)	Norfolk & Suffolk Avn Museum, Flixton	
A-533	FMA IA58 Pucara (ZD486) <ff>	Privately owned, Cheltenham	
A-549	FMA IA58 Pucara (ZD487)	Imperial War Museum, Duxford	
AE-331	Agusta A109A (ZE411)	FAA Museum, RNAS Yeovilton	
AE-409	Bell UH-1H Iroquois [656]	Museum of Army Flying, Middle Wallop	
AE-422	Bell UH-1H Iroquois	FAA Museum, stored RNAS Yeovilton	
AUSTRALIA			
369	Hawker Fury ISS (F-AZXL) [D]	Privately owned, Avignon, France	
A2-4	Supermarine Seagull V (VH-ALB)	RAF Museum, Hendon	
A11-301	Auster J/5G (G-ARKG) [931-NW]	Privately owned, Spanhoe	
A16-199	Lockheed Hudson IIIA (G-BEOX) [SF-R]	RAF Museum, Hendon	
A17-48	DH82A Tiger Moth (G-BPHR)	Privately owned, Wanborough, Wilts	
A19-144	Bristol 156 Beaufighter XIc (JM135/A8-324)	The Fighter Collection, Duxford	
A92-255	GAF Jindivik 102	DPA/QinetiQ, Boscombe Down, apprentice use	
A92-664	GAF Jindivik 103A	Boscombe Down Aviation Collection, Old Sarum	
A92-708	GAF Jindivik 203B	Bristol Aero Collection, stored Filton	
A92-908	GAF Jindivik 900 (ZJ503)	No 2445 Sqn ATC, Llanbedr	
N6-766	DH115 Sea Vampire T22 (XG766/G-VYPO) [808]	*Sold to South Africa, 2012*	
WH589	Hawker Fury ISS (F-AZXJ) [115-NW]	Privately owned, Dijon, France	
BELGIUM			
A-41	SA318C Alouette II	The Helicopter Museum, Weston-super-Mare	
FT-36	Lockheed T-33A Shooting Star	Dumfries & Galloway Avn Mus, Dumfries	
H-50	Noorduyn AT-16 Harvard IIB (OO-DAF)	Privately owned, Brasschaat, Belgium	
HD-75	Hanriot HD1 (G-AFDX)	RAF Museum, Hendon	
IF-68	Hawker Hunter F6 <ff>	Privately owned, Kings Lynn	
L-44	Piper L-18C Super Cub (OO-SPQ)	Royal Aéro Para Club de Spa, Belgium	
L-47	Piper L-18C Super Cub (OO-SPG)	Aeroclub Brasschaat VZW, Brasschaat, Belgium	
L-156	Piper L-18C Super Cub (OO-LGB)	*Repainted as OL-L49*	
OL-L49	Piper L-18C Super Cub (L-156/OO-LGB)	Aeroclub Brasschaat VZW, Brasschaat, Belgium	
V-4	SNCAN Stampe SV-4B (OO-EIR)	Antwerp Stampe Centre, Antwerp-Deurne, Belgium	
V-18	SNCAN Stampe SV-4B (OO-GWD)	Antwerp Stampe Centre, Antwerp-Deurne, Belgium	
V-29	SNCAN Stampe SV-4B (OO-GWB)	Antwerp Stampe Centre, Antwerp-Deurne, Belgium	
V-66	SNCAN Stampe SV-4C (OO-GWA)	Antwerp Stampe Centre, Antwerp-Deurne, Belgium	
BOLIVIA			
FAB184	SIAI-Marchetti SF.260W (G-SIAI)	Privately owned, Booker	
BRAZIL			
1317	Embraer T-27 Tucano	Shorts, Belfast (engine test bed)	
BURKINA FASO			
BF8431	SIAI-Marchetti SF.260 (G-NRRA) [31]	Privately owned, Oaksey Park	

Notes	Serial	Type (code/other identity)	Owner/operator location or fate
	CANADA		
	-	Lockheed T-33A Shooting Star (17473)	Midland Air Museum, Coventry
	622	Piasecki HUP-3 Retriever (51-16622/N6699D)	The Helicopter Museum, Weston-super-Mare
	920	VS Stranraer (CF-BXO) [Q-N]	RAF Museum, Hendon
	3091	NA81 Harvard II (3019/G-CPPM)	Beech Restorations, Bruntingthorpe
	3349	NA64 Yale (G-BYNF)	Privately owned, Duxford
	5487	Hawker Hurricane II (G-CBOE)	Privately owned, Thruxton
	9041	Bristol 149 Bolingbroke IV <ff>	Manx Aviation Museum, Ronaldsway
	9048	Bristol 149 Bolingbroke IV <ff>	Bristol Aero Collection, Cotswold Airport
	9048	Bristol 149 Bolingbroke IV <rf>	Bristol Aero Collection, stored Filton
	9754	Consolidated PBY-5A Catalina (VP-BPS) [P]	Privately owned, Lee-on-Solent
	9893	Bristol 149 Bolingbroke IVT	Imperial War Museum store, Duxford
	9940	Bristol 149 Bolingbroke IVT	Royal Scottish Mus'm of Flight, E Fortune
	15195	Fairchild PT-19A Cornell	RAF Museum Reserve Collection, Stafford
	16693	Auster J/1N Alpha (G-BLPG) [693]	Privately owned, Clacton
	18393	Avro Canada CF-100 Canuck 4B (G-BCYK)	Imperial War Museum, Duxford
	18671	DHC1 Chipmunk 22 (WP905/7438M/G-BNZC) [671]	The Shuttleworth Collection, Old Warden
	20249	Noorduyn AT-16 Harvard IIB (PH-KLU) [XS-249]	Privately owned, Texel, The Netherlands
	20310	CCF T-6J Texan (G-BSBG) [310]	Privately owned, Tatenhill
	21417	Canadair CT-133 Silver Star	Yorkshire Air Museum, Elvington
	23140	Canadair CL-13 Sabre [AX] <rf>	Midland Air Museum, Coventry
	23380	Canadair CL-13 Sabre <rf>	Privately owned, Haverigg
	FJ777	Boeing-Stearman PT-17D Kaydet (41-8689/G-BIXN)	Privately owned, Rendcomb
	KN448	Douglas Dakota IV <ff>	Science Museum, South Kensington
	CHINA		
	68 r	Nanchang CJ-6A Chujiao (2751219/G-BVVG)	Privately owned, White Waltham
	68 w	Nanchang CJ-6A Chujiao (2632016/G-BXZB)	Privately owned, White Waltham
	61367	Nanchang CJ-6A Chujiao (4532009/G-CGHB) [37]	Privately owned, Headcorn
	61762	Nanchang CJ-6A Chujiao (4532008/G-CGFS) [72]	Privately owned, Seething
	2632016	Nanchang CJ-6A Chujiao (G-BXZB) (also wears *2632019*)	*Repainted as 68 w*
	CZECH REPUBLIC		
	3677	Letov S-103 (MiG-15bisSB) (613677)	Royal Scottish Mus'm of Flight, E Fortune
	3794	Letov S-102 (MiG-15) (623794) (starboard side only, painted in Polish marks as 1972 on port side)	Norfolk & Suffolk Avn Museum, Flixton
	9147	Mil Mi-4	The Helicopter Museum, Weston-super-Mare
	DENMARK		
	A-011	SAAB A-35XD Draken	Privately owned, Westhoughton, Lancs
	AR-107	SAAB S-35XD Draken	Newark Air Museum, Winthorpe
	E-419	Hawker Hunter F51 (G-9-441)	North-East Aircraft Museum, Usworth
	E-420	Hawker Hunter F51 (G-9-442) <ff>	Privately owned, Walton-on-Thames
	E-421	Hawker Hunter F51 (G-9-443)	Brooklands Museum, Weybridge
	E-424	Hawker Hunter F51 (G-9-445)	Aeroventure, Doncaster
	ET-272	Hawker Hunter T7 <ff>	Boulton Paul Association, Wolverhampton
	K-682	Douglas C-47A Skytrain (OY-BPB)	Foreningen For Flyvende Mus, Vaerløse, Denmark
	L-866	Consolidated PBY-6A Catalina (8466M)	RAF Museum, Cosford
	P-129	DHC-1 Chipmunk 22 (OY-ATO)	Privately owned, Roskilde, Denmark
	R-756	Lockheed F-104G Starfighter	Midland Air Museum, Coventry
	S-881	Sikorsky S-55C	The Helicopter Museum, Weston-super-Mare
	S-882	Sikorsky S-55C	Skirmish Paintball, Portishead
	S-886	Sikorsky S-55C	Hamburger Hill Paintball, Marksbury, Somerset
	S-887	Sikorsky S-55C	The Helicopter Museum, Weston-super-Mare
	ECUADOR		
	FAE 259	BAC Strikemaster 80A (G-UPPI) [T59]	Privately owned, St Athan

Serial	Type (code/other identity)	Owner/operator location or fate	Notes
EGYPT			
158	Heliopolis Gomhouria Mk 6	Privately owned, Breighton	
356	Heliopolis Gomhouria Mk 6	Privately owned, Breighton	
764	Mikoyan MiG-21SPS <ff>	Privately owned, Northampton	
773	WS61 Sea King 47 (WA.823)	RNAS Yeovilton Fire Section	
774	WS61 Sea King 47 (WA.822)	Privately owned, Hixon	
775	WS61 Sea King 47 (WA.824)	Privately owned, Hixon	
776	WS61 Sea King 47 (WA.825)	DSMarE AESS, *HMS Sultan*, Gosport	
0446	Mikoyan MiG-21UM <ff>	Thameside Aviation Museum, Tilbury	
7907	Sukhoi Su-7 <ff>	Robertsbridge Aviation Society, Mayfield	
FINLAND			
GA-43	Gloster Gamecock II (G-CGYF)	Privately owned, Dursley, Glos	
GN-101	Folland Gnat F1 (XK741)	Midland Air Museum, Coventry	
VI-3	Valtion Viima 2 (OO-EBL)	Privately owned, Brasschaat, Belgium	
FRANCE			
1/4513	Spad XIII <R> (G-BFYO/*S3398*)	American Air Museum, Duxford	
37	Nord 3400 (G-ZARA) [MAB]	Privately owned, Swanton Morley	
54	SNCAN NC856A Norvigie (G-CGWR) [AOM]	Privately owned, Spanhoe	
67	SNCAN 1101 Noralpha (F-GMCY) [CY]	Privately owned, la Ferté-Alais, France	
70	Dassault Mystère IVA	Midland Air Museum, Coventry	
78	Nord 3202B-1 (G-BIZK)	Privately owned, Norfolk	
79	Dassault Mystère IVA [2-EG]	Norfolk & Suffolk Avn Museum, Flixton	
82	Curtiss H75-C1 Hawk (G-CCVH) [X-881]	The Fighter Collection, Duxford	
82	NA T-28D Fennec (F-AZKG)	Privately owned, Strasbourg, France	
83	Dassault Mystère IVA [8-MS]	Newark Air Museum, Winthorpe	
83	Morane-Saulnier MS733 Alcyon (F-AZKS)	Privately owned, Montlucon, France	
84	Dassault Mystère IVA [8-NF]	Lashenden Air Warfare Museum, Headcorn	
85	Dassault Mystère IVA [8-MV]	Cold War Jets Collection, Bruntingthorpe	
104	MH1521M Broussard (F-GHFG) [307-FG]	Privately owned, Montceau-les-Mines, France	
105	Nord N2501F Noratlas (F-AZVM) [62-SI]	Le Noratlas de Provence, Marseilles, France	
106	MH1521M Broussard (F-GKJT) [33-JT]	Privately owned, Montceau-les-Mines, France	
108	MH1521M Broussard (F-BNEX) [50S9]	Privately owned, Lelystad, The Netherlands	
108	SO1221 Djinn (FR108) [CDL]	The Helicopter Museum, Weston-super-Mare	
121	Dassault Mystère IVA [8-MY]	City of Norwich Aviation Museum	
128	Morane-Saulnier MS733 Alcyon (F-BMMY)	Privately owned, St Cyr, France	
143	Morane-Saulnier MS733 Alcyon (G-MSAL)	Privately owned, Spanhoe	
146	Dassault Mystère IVA [8-MC]	North-East Aircraft Museum, Usworth	
156	SNCAN Stampe SV-4B (G-NIFE)	Privately owned, Gloucester	
157	Morane-SaulnierMS230 Et2 (N230EB) [M-573,01]	Privately owned, Charney Bassett, Oxon	
208	MH1521C1 Broussard (G-YYYY) [IR]	Privately owned, Eggesford	
261	MH1521M Broussard (F-GIBN) [30-QA]	Privately owned, Rotterdam, The Netherlands	
282	Dassault MD311 Flamant (F-AZFX) [316-KY]	Memorial Flt Association, la Ferté-Alais, France	
290	Dewoitine D27 (F-AZJD)	Les Casques de Cuir, la Ferté-Alais, France	
316	MH1521M Broussard (F-GGKR) [315-SN]	Privately owned, Lognes, France	
318	Dassault Mystère IVA [8-NY]	Dumfries & Galloway Avn Mus, Dumfries	
319	Dassault Mystère IVA [8-ND]	Rebel Air Museum, Andrewsfield	
319	Grumman TBM-3E Avenger (HB-RDG) [4F.6]	Privately owned, Lausanne, Switzerland	
354	Morane-Saulnier MS315E-D2 (G-BZNK)	Privately owned, Hemswell	
394	SNCAN Stampe SV-4C (G-BIMO)	Privately owned, White Waltham	
538	Dassault Mirage IIIE [3-QH]	Yorkshire Air Museum, Elvington	
569	Fouga CM170R Magister [F-AZZP]	Privately owned, Le Havre, France	
42157	NA F-100D Super Sabre [11-ML]	North-East Aircraft Museum, Usworth	
54439	Lockheed T-33A Shooting Star (55-4439) [WI]	North-East Aircraft Museum, Usworth	
63938	NA F-100F Super Sabre [11-EZ]	Lashenden Air Warfare Museum, Headcorn	
121748	Grumman F8F-2P Bearcat (F-AZRJ) [5834/P]	*Sold to the USA*	
125716	Douglas AD-4N Skyraider (F-AZFN) [22-DG]	Privately owned, Mélun, France	
127002	Douglas AD-4NA Skyraider (F-AZHK) [20-LN]	Privately owned, Avignon, France	
517692	NA T-28S Fennec (G-TROY) [142]	Privately owned, Duxford	

Notes	*Serial*	*Type (code/other identity)*	*Owner/operator location or fate*
	18-5395	Piper L-18C Super Cub (52-2436/G-CUBJ) [CDG]	Privately owned, Old Warden
	51-7545	NA T-28S Fennec (N14113)	Privately owned, Duxford
	C850	Salmson 2A2 <R>	Barton Aviation Heritage Society, Barton
	MS824	Morane-Saulnier Type N <R> (G-AWBU)	Privately owned, Booker
	N856	SNCAN NC856 (G-CDWE)	Privately owned, Wickenby
	N1977	Nieuport Scout 17/23 <R> (*N1723*/G-BWMJ) [8]	Privately owned, Duxford
	GERMANY		
	-	Fieseler Fi103R-IV (V-1) (BAPC 91)	Lashenden Air Warfare Museum, Headcorn
	-	Fokker Dr1 Dreidekker <R> (BAPC 88)	FAA Museum stored, RNAS Yeovilton
	-	Messerschmitt Bf109 <R> (*6357*/BAPC 74) [6]	Kent Battle of Britain Museum, Hawkinge
	-	Messerschmitt Bf109 <R> [<-]	Battle of Britain Experience, Canterbury
	1	Hispano HA 1.112M1L Buchón (C.4K-31/G-AWHE)	Privately owned, Duxford
	1	Messerschmitt Bf109G <R> (BAPC 240)	Yorkshire Air Museum, Elvington
	3	Messerschmitt Bf109G-10 (D-FDME)	Messerschmitt Stiftung, Manching, Germany
	3	SNCAN 1101 Noralpha (G-BAYV)	Barton Aviation Heritage Society, Barton
	6	Messerschmitt Bf109G-2/Trop (10639/8478M/G-USTV)	RAF Museum, Hendon
	7	Messerschmitt Bf109G-4 (D-FWME)	Messerschmitt Stiftung, Manching, Germany
	8	Focke-Wulf Fw190 <R> (G-WULF)	Privately owned, Halfpenny Green
	9	Focke-Wulf Fw190 <R> (G-CCFW)	Privately owned, Gloucester
	10	Hispano HA 1.112M1L Buchón (C4K-102/G-BWUE)	Historic Flying Ltd, Duxford
	14	Messerschmitt Bf109 <R> (BAPC 67)	Kent Battle of Britain Museum, Hawkinge
	14	Nord 1002 (G-ETME)	Privately owned, White Waltham
	87	Heinkel He111 <R> <ff>	Privately owned, East Kirkby
	139	SNCAN 1101 Noralpha (G-BSMD)	Privately owned, Perth
	152/17	Fokker Dr1 Dreidekker <R> (F-AZPQ)	Les Casques de Cuir, la Ferté-Alais, France
	152/17	Fokker Dr1 Dreidekker <R> (G-BVGZ)	Privately owned, Breighton
	157/18	Fokker D.VIII <R> (BAPC 239)	Norfolk & Suffolk Air Museum, Flixton
	210/16	Fokker EIII (BAPC 56)	Science Museum, South Kensington
	210/16	Fokker EIII <R> (G-CHFS)	Privately owned, Bicester
	403/17	Fokker Dr1 Dreidekker <R> (G-CDXR)	Privately owned, Popham
	416/15	Fokker EIII <R> (G-GSAL)	Privately owned, Aston Down
	422/15	Fokker EIII <R> (G-AVJO)	Privately owned, Booker
	422/15	Fokker EIII <R> (G-FOKR)	Privately owned, Eshott
	425/17	Fokker Dr1 Dreidekker <R> (BAPC 133)	Kent Battle of Britain Museum, Hawkinge
	477/17	Fokker Dr1 Dreidekker <R> (G-FOKK)	Privately owned, Sywell
	556/17	Fokker Dr1 Dreidekker <R> (G-CFHY)	Privately owned, Tibenham
	626/8	Fokker DVII <R> (N6268)	Privately owned, Booker
	764	Mikoyan MiG-21SPS <ff>	Privately owned, Norfolk
	959	Mikoyan MiG-21SPS	Midland Air Museum, Coventry
	1190	Messerschmitt Bf109E-3 [4]	Imperial War Museum, Duxford
	1480	Messerschmitt Bf109 <R> (BAPC 66) [6]	Kent Battle of Britain Museum, Hawkinge
	1801/18	Bowers Fly Baby 1A (G-BNPV)	Privately owned, Chessington
	1803/18	Bowers Fly Baby 1A (G-BUYU)	Privately owned, Chessington
	1983	Messerschmitt Bf109E-3 (G-EMIL)	Privately owned, Colchester
	2100	Focke-Wulf Fw189A-1 (G-BZKY) [V7+1H]	Privately owned, Sandown
	4034	Messerschmitt Bf109E (G-CDTI)	Privately owned,
	4101	Messerschmitt Bf109E-3 (DG200/8477M) [12]	RAF Museum, Hendon
	4477	CASA 1.131E Jungmann (G-RETA) [GD+EG]	The Shuttleworth Collection, Old Warden
	6234	Junkers Ju87R-4 (G-STUK)	Privately owned, Surrey
	7198/18	LVG CVI (G-AANJ/9239M)	RAF Museum Restoration Centre, Cosford
	8417/18	Fokker DVII (9207M)	RAF Museum, Hendon
	12802	Antonov An-2T (D-FOFM)	Historische Flugzeuge, Grossenhain, Germany
	100143	Focke-Achgelis Fa330A-1	Imperial War Museum, Duxford
	100502	Focke-Achgelis Fa330A-1	Privately owned, Millom
	100503	Focke-Achgelis Fa330A-1 (8469M)	RAF Museum, Cosford
	100509	Focke-Achgelis Fa330A-1	Science Museum, stored Wroughton
	100545	Focke-Achgelis Fa330A-1	FAA Museum, stored RNAS Yeovilton

Serial	*Type (code/other identity)*	*Owner/operator location or fate*	*Notes*
100549	Focke-Achgelis Fa330A-1	Lashenden Air Warfare Museum, Headcorn	
110451	Fieseler Fi156D Storch (G-STOR)	Privately owned, Surrey	
112372	Messerschmitt Me262A-2a (AM.51/VK893/8482M) [4]	RAF Museum, Hendon	
120227	Heinkel He162A-2 Salamander (VN679/AM.65/8472M) [2]	RAF Museum, Hendon	
120235	Heinkel He162A-1 Salamander (AM.68)	Imperial War Museum, Duxford	
191316	Messerschmitt Me163B Komet	Science Museum, South Kensington	
191454	Messerschmitt Me163B Komet <R> (BAPC 271)	The Shuttleworth Collection, Old Warden	
191461	Messerschmitt Me163B Komet (191614/8481M) [14]	RAF Museum, Cosford	
191659	Messerschmitt Me163B Komet (8480M) [15]	Royal Scottish Mus'm of Flight, E Fortune	
280020	Flettner Fl282/B-V20 Kolibri (frame only)	Midland Air Museum, Coventry	
360043	Junkers Ju88R-1 (PJ876/8475M) [D5+EV]	RAF Museum, Hendon	
420430	Messerschmitt Me410A-1/U2 (AM.72/8483M) [3U+CC]	RAF Museum, Cosford	
475081	Fieseler Fi156C-7 Storch (VP546/AM.101/7362M) [GM+AK]	RAF Museum, Cosford	
494083	Junkers Ju87D-3 (8474M) [RI+JK]	RAF Museum, Hendon	
584219	Focke-Wulf Fw190F-8/U1 (AM.29/8470M) [38]	RAF Museum, Hendon	
701152	Heinkel He111H-23 (8471M) [NT+SL]	RAF Museum, Hendon	
730301	Messerschmitt Bf110G-4 (AM.34/8479M) [D5+RL]	RAF Museum, Hendon	
733682	Focke-Wulf Fw190A-8/R7 (AM.75/9211M)	RAF Museum, Cosford	
980554	Flug Werk FW190A-8/N (G-FWAB)	Meier Motors, Bremgarten, Germany	
2+1	Focke-Wulf Fw190 <R> (G-SYFW) [7334]	Privately owned, Wickenby	
17+TF	CASA 1.133C Jungmeister (G-BZTJ)	Privately owned, Turweston	
22+35	Lockheed F-104G Starfighter	Privately owned, Bruntingthorpe	
22+57	Lockheed F-104G Starfighter	*Sold to Taiwan, 2013*	
23.02	Albatros B.II <R> (D-EKGH)	Historischer Flugzeugbau, Fürstenwalde, Germany	
28+08	Aero L-39ZO Albatros (142/28+04)	Pinewood Studios, Bucks	
2E+RA	Fieseler Fi-156C-3 Storch (F-AZRA)	Amicale J-B Salis, la Ferté-Alais, France	
4+1	Focke-Wulf Fw190 <R> (G-BSLX)	Privately owned, Norwich	
4V+GH	Amiot AAC1/Ju52 (Port.AF 6316) [9]	*Sold to Poland, 2012*	
6G+ED	Slepcev Storch (G-BZOB) [5447]	Privately owned, Nympsfield	
37+86	McD F-4F Phantom II <ff>	Privately owned, Bruntingthorpe	
58+89	Dornier Do28D-2 Skyservant (D-ICDY)	Privately owned, Uetersen, Germany	
80+39	MBB Bo.105M	Privately owned, Coney Park, Leeds	
80+40	MBB Bo.105M	Privately owned, Coney Park, Leeds	
80+55	MBB Bo.105M	Lufthansa Resource Technical Training, Cotswold Airport	
80+77	MBB Bo.105M	Lufthansa Resource Technical Training, Cotswold Airport	
81+00	MBB Bo.105M (D-HZYR)	The Helicopter Museum, Weston-super-Mare	
96+21	Mil Mi-24D (406)	*Sold to the USA, October 2012*	
96+26	Mil Mi-24D (421)	The Helicopter Museum, Weston-super-Mare	
97+04	Putzer Elster B (G-APVF)	*Sold to France*	
98+14	Sukhoi Su-22M-4	Hawker Hunter Aviation Ltd, stored Scampton	
99+24	NA OV-10B Bronco (F-AZKM)	Privately owned, Montelimar, France	
99+32	NA OV-10B Bronco (G-BZGK)	*Crashed 10 July 2012, Cotswold Airport*	
AZ+JU	CASA 3.52L (F-AZJU)	Amicale J-B Salis, la Ferté-Alais, France	
BU+CC	CASA 1.131E Jungmann (G-BUCC)	Privately owned, Sandown	
CF+HF	Morane-Saulnier MS502 (EI-AUY)	*To Germany, October 2012*	
D5397/17	Albatros DVA <R> (G-BFXL)	FAA Museum, stored RNAS Yeovilton	
D7343/17	Albatros DVA <R> (ZK-TVD)	RAF Museum, Hendon	
DM+BK	Morane-Saulnier MS505 (G-BPHZ)	Historic Aircraft Collection, Duxford	
ES+BH	Messerschmitt Bf108B-2 (D-ESBH)	Messerschmitt Stiftung, Manching, Germany	
FI+S	Morane-Saulnier MS505 (G-BIRW)	Royal Scottish Museum of Flight, E Fortune	
FM+BB	Messerschmitt Bf109G-6 (D-FMBB)	Messerschmitt Stiftung, Manching, Germany	
GM+AI	Fieseler Fi156A Storch (2088/G-STCH)	Privately owned, Old Warden	
LG+03	Bücker Bü133C Jungmeister (G-AEZX)	Privately owned, Milden	
NJ+C11	Nord 1002 (G-ATBG)	Privately owned, Duxford	

Notes	Serial	Type (code/other identity)	Owner/operator location or fate
	NQ+NR	Klemm Kl35D (D-EQXD)	Quax Flieger, Hamm, Germany
	NV+KG	Focke-Wulf Fw44J Stieglitz (D-ENAY)	Quax Flieger, Hamm, Germany
	S4+A07	CASA 1.131E Jungmann (G-BWHP)	Privately owned, Yarcombe, Devon
	S5+B06	CASA 1.131E Jungmann 2000 (G-BSFB)	Privately owned, Old Buckenham
	TP+WX	Heliopolis Gomhouria Mk 6 (G-TPWX)	Privately owned, Swanborough
	GREECE		
	52-6541	Republic F-84F Thunderflash [541]	North-East Aircraft Museum, Usworth
	63-8418	Northrop F-5A <ff>	Martin-Baker Ltd, Chalgrove, Fire Section
	HONG KONG		
	HKG-5	SA128 Bulldog (G-BULL)	Privately owned, Cotswold Airport
	HKG-6	SA128 Bulldog (G-BPCL)	Privately owned, North Weald
	HKG-11	Slingsby T.67M Firefly 200 (G-BYRY)	Privately owned, Antwerp, Belgium
	HKG-13	Slingsby T.67M Firefly 200 (G-BXKW)	Privately owned, St Ghislain, Belgium
	HUNGARY		
	501	Mikoyan MiG-21PF	Imperial War Museum, Duxford
	503	Mikoyan MiG-21SMT (G-BRAM)	RAF Museum, Cosford
	INDIA		
	Q497	EE Canberra T4 (WE191) (fuselage)	Privately owned, Stoneykirk, D&G
	HA561	Hawker Tempest II (MW743)	Privately owned, stored Wickenby
	INDONESIA		
	LL-5313	BAe Hawk T53	BAE Systems, Brough, on display
	IRAQ		
	333	DH115 Vampire T55 <ff>	Aeroventure, stored Doncaster
	ITALY		
	MM5701	Fiat CR42 (BT474/8468M) [13-95]	RAF Museum, Hendon
	MM52801	Fiat G46-3B (G-BBII) [4-97]	*Sold to Italy, September 2012*
	MM53692	CCF T-6G Texan	RAeS Medway Branch, Rochester
	MM53774	Fiat G59-4B (I-MRSV) [181]	Privately owned, Parma, Italy
	MM54099	NA T-6G Texan (G-BRBC) [RR-56]	Privately owned, Chigwell
	MM54532	SIAI-Marchetti SF.260AM (G-ITAF) [70-42]	Privately owned, Leicester
	MM80927	Agusta-Bell AB206A-1 JetRanger [CC-49]	The Helicopter Museum, Weston-super-Mare
	MM81205	Agusta A109A-2 SEM [GF-128]	The Helicopter Museum, Weston-super-Mare
	MM54-2372	Piper L-21B Super Cub	Privately owned, Kesgrave, Suffolk
	JAPAN		
	-	Kawasaki Ki100-1B (8476M/BAPC 83)	RAF Museum, Cosford
	-	Yokosuka MXY 7 Ohka II (BAPC 159)	Imperial War Museum, stored Duxford
	997	Yokosuka MXY 7 Ohka II (8485M/BAPC 98)	Museum of Science & Industry, Manchester
	5439	Mitsubishi Ki46-III (8484M/BAPC 84)	RAF Museum, Cosford
	15-1585	Yokosuka MXY 7 Ohka II (BAPC 58)	Science Museum, at FAA Museum, RNAS Yeovilton
	I-13	Yokosuka MXY 7 Ohka II (8486M/BAPC 99)	RAF Museum, Cosford
	Y2-176	Mitsubishi A6M3-2 Zero (3685) [76]	Imperial War Museum, Duxford
	JORDAN		
	408	SA125 Bulldog (G-BDIN)	Privately owned, Lasham
	KENYA		
	115	Dornier Do28D-2 Skyservant	Privately owned, stored Hibaldstow
	117	Dornier Do28D-2 Skyservant	Privately owned, stored Hibaldstow
	KUWAIT		
	113	BAC Strikemaster 80A (G-CFBK) [K167-113/D]	Privately owned, Bentwaters

Serial	Type (code/other identity)	Owner/operator location or fate	Notes
MYANMAR			
UB441	VS361 Spitfire IX (ML119/G-SDNI)	Privately owned, Sandown	
THE NETHERLANDS			
16-218	Consolidated PBY-5A Catalina (2459/PH-PBY)	Neptune Association, Lelystad, The Netherlands	
174	Fokker S-11 Instructor (E-31/G-BEPV) [K]	Privately owned, Spanhoe	
179	Fokker S-11 Instructor (PH-ACG) [K]	Privately owned, Lelystad, The Netherlands	
197	Fokker S-11 Instructor (PH-GRY) [K]	KLu Historic Flt, Gilze-Rijen, The Netherlands	
204	Lockheed SP-2H Neptune [V]	RAF Museum, Cosford	
A-12	DH82A Tiger Moth (PH-TYG)	Privately owned, Gilze-Rijen, The Netherlands	
B-64	Noorduyn AT-16 Harvard IIB (PH-LSK)	KLu Historic Flt, Gilze-Rijen, The Netherlands	
B-71	Noorduyn AT-16 Harvard IIB (PH-MLM)	KLu Historic Flt, Gilze-Rijen, The Netherlands	
B-118	Noorduyn AT-16 Harvard IIB (PH-IIB)	KLu Historic Flt, Gilze-Rijen, The Netherlands	
B-182	Noorduyn AT-16 Harvard IIB (PH-TBR)	KLu Historic Flt, Gilze-Rijen, The Netherlands	
E-14	Fokker S-11 Instructor (PH-AFS)	Privately owned, Lelystad, The Netherlands	
E-15	Fokker S-11 Instructor (G-BIYU)	Privately owned, Topcliffe	
E-20	Fokker S-11 Instructor (PH-GRB)	Privately owned, Gilze-Rijen, The Netherlands	
E-27	Fokker S-11 Instructor (PH-HOL)	Privately owned, Lelystad, The Netherlands	
E-32	Fokker S-11 Instructor (PH-HOI)	Privately owned, Gilze-Rijen, The Netherlands	
E-39	Fokker S-11 Instructor (PH-HOG)	Privately owned, Lelystad, The Netherlands	
G-29	Beech D18S (PH-KHV)	KLu Historic Flt, Gilze-Rijen, The Netherlands	
MH424	VS361 Spitfire LFIXC (MJ271/H-53)	Privately owned, Duxford	
MK732	VS361 Spitfire LFIXC (8633M/PH-OUQ) [3W-17]	KLu Historic Flt, Gilze-Rijen, The Netherlands	
N-202	Hawker Hunter F6 [10] <ff>	Privately owned, Stockport	
N-250	Hawker Hunter F6 (G-9-185) <ff>	Imperial War Museum, Duxford	
N-268	Hawker Hunter FGA78 (Qatar QA-10)	Yorkshire Air Museum, Elvington	
N-294	Hawker Hunter F6A (XF515/G-KAXF)	Stichting Hawker Hunter Foundation, Leeuwarden, The Netherlands	
N-302	Hawker Hunter T7 (ET-273/G-9-431) <ff>	Aeroventure, Doncaster	
N-315	Hawker Hunter T7 (comp XM121)	Privately owned, Netherley, Aberdeenshire	
N-321	Hawker Hunter T8C (G-BWGL)	Stichting Hawker Hunter Foundation, Leeuwarden, The Netherlands	
N5-149	NA B-25J Mitchell (44-29507/*HD346*/PH-XXV) [232511]	KLu Historic Flt, Gilze-Rijen, The Netherlands	
R-18	Auster III (PH-NGK)	KLu Historic Flt, Gilze-Rijen, The Netherlands	
R-55	Piper L-18C Super Cub (52-2466/G-BLMI)	Privately owned, White Waltham	
R-109	Piper L-21B Super Cub (54-2337/PH-GAZ)	KLu Historic Flt, Gilze-Rijen, The Netherlands	
R-122	Piper L-21B Super Cub (54-2412/PH-PPW)	KLu Historic Flt, Gilze-Rijen, The Netherlands	
R-124	Piper L-21B Super Cub (54-2414/PH-APA)	Privately owned, Eindhoven, The Netherlands	
R-137	Piper L-21B Super Cub (54-2427/PH-PSC)	Privately owned, Gilze-Rijen, The Netherlands	
R-151	Piper L-21B Super Cub (54-2441/G-BIYR)	Privately owned, Yarcombe, Devon	
R-156	Piper L-21B Super Cub (54-2446/G-ROVE)	Privately owned, Headcorn	
R-167	Piper L-21B Super Cub (54-2457/G-LION)	Privately owned, Turweston, Bucks	
R-170	Piper L-21B Super Cub (52-6222/PH-ENJ)	Privately owned, Midden Zealand, The Netherlands	
R-177	Piper L-21B Super Cub (54-2467/PH-KNR)	KLu Historic Flt, Gilze-Rijen, The Netherlands	
R-181	Piper L-21B Super Cub (54-2471/PH-GAU)	Privately owned, Gilze-Rijen, The Netherlands	
R-345	Piper J-3C Cub (PH-UCS)	Privately owned, Hilversum, The Netherlands	
S-9	DHC2 L-20A Beaver (55-4585/PH-DHC)	KLu Historic Flt, Gilze-Rijen, The Netherlands	
NEW ZEALAND			
NZ3909	WS Wasp HAS1 (XT782/G-KANZ)	Kennet Aviation, stored North Weald	
NZ6361	BAC Strikemaster 87 (OJ5/G-BXFP)	*To Malta, 2012*	
NORTH KOREA			
-	WSK Lim-2 (MiG-15) (01420/G-BMZF)	FAA Museum, RNAS Yeovilton	
NORTH VIETNAM			
1211	WSK Lim-5 (MiG-17F) (G-MIGG)	Privately owned, North Weald	

Notes	*Serial*	*Type (code/other identity)*	*Owner/operator location or fate*
	NORWAY		
	163	Fairchild PT-19A Cornell (42-83641/LN-BIF)	Privately owned, Kjeller, Norway
	599	Canadair CT-133AUP Silver Star Mk.3 (133599/NX865SA)	Royal Norwegian Historical Sqn, Ørland, Norway
	848	Piper L-18C Super Cub (LN-ACL) [FA-N]	Privately owned, Norway
	56321	SAAB S91B Safir (G-BKPY)	Newark Air Museum, Winthorpe
	PX-K	DH100 Vampire FB6 (SE-DXS)	Privately owned, Rygge, Norway
	PX-M	DH115 Vampire T55 (LN-DHZ)	Privately owned, Rygge, Norway
	OMAN		
	425	BAC Strikemaster 82A (G-SOAF)	Privately owned, Hawarden
	801	Hawker Hunter T66B <ff>	Privately owned, St Athan
	801	Hawker Hunter T66B <rf>	Privately owned, Hawarden
	853	Hawker Hunter FR10 (XF426)	RAF Museum, Hendon
	POLAND		
	05	WSK SM-2 (Mi-2) (S2-03006)	The Helicopter Museum, Weston-super-Mare
	309	WSK SBLim-2A (MiG-15UTI) <ff>	R Scottish Mus'm of Flight, stored Granton
	458	Mikoyan MiG-23ML (04 red/024003607)	Newark Air Museum, Winthorpe
	618	Mil Mi-8P (10618)	The Helicopter Museum, Weston-super-Mare
	1018	WSK-PZL Mielec TS-11 Iskra (1H-1018/G-ISKA)	Cold War Jets Collection, Bruntingthorpe
	1120	WSK Lim-2 (MiG-15bis)	RAF Museum, Cosford
	1706	WSK-PZL Mielec TS-11 Iskra (1H-0408)	Midland Air Museum, Coventry
	1972	Letov S-102 (MiG-15) (623794) (port side only, painted in Czech marks as 3794 on starboard side)	Norfolk & Suffolk Avn Museum, Flixton
	PORTUGAL		
	85	Isaacs Fury II (G-BTPZ)	Privately owned, Ormskirk
	1350	OGMA/DHC1 Chipmunk T20 (G-CGAO)	Privately owned, Spanhoe
	1360	OGMA/DHC1 Chipmunk T20 (G-BYYU) (fuselage)	Privately owned, Wickenby
	1365	OGMA/DHC1 Chipmunk T20 (G-DHPM)	Privately owned, Sywell
	1367	OGMA/DHC1 Chipmunk T20 (G-UANO)	Privately owned, Sherburn-in-Elmet
	1372	OGMA/DHC1 Chipmunk T20 (HB-TUM)	Privately owned, Switzerland
	1373	OGMA/DHC1 Chipmunk T20 (G-CBJG)	Privately owned, Winwick, Cambs
	1375	OGMA/DHC1 Chipmunk T20 (F-AZJV)	Privately owned, Valenciennes, France
	1377	DHC1 Chipmunk 22 (G-BARS)	Privately owned, Yeovilton
	1741	CCF T-6J Texan (G-HRVD)	Privately owned, Bruntingthorpe
	1747	CCF T-6J Texan (*20385*/G-BGPB)	The Aircraft Restoration Co, Duxford
	1765	CCF T-6J Texan	Privately owned, Cotswold Airport
	3303	MH1521M Broussard (G-CBGL)	Privately owned, Bruntingthorpe
	QATAR		
	QA12	Hawker Hunter FGA78 <ff>	Privately owned, New Inn, Torfaen
	QP30	WS Lynx Mk 28 (G-BFDV/TD 013)	DSEME SEAE, Arborfield
	QP31	WS Lynx Mk 28	Vector Aerospace Fleetlands Apprentice School
	QP32	WS Lynx Mk 28 (TAD 016)	DSEME SEAE, Arborfield
	ROMANIA		
	29	LET L-29 Delfin <ff>	Privately owned, Shropshire
	42	LET L-29 Delfin	Privately owned, Catshill, Worcs
	47	LET L-29 Delfin	Privately owned, Ashton-under-Lyne
	53	LET L-29 Delfin (99954)	Privately owned, Bruntingthorpe
	RUSSIA (& FORMER SOVIET UNION)		
	-	LET L-29S Delfin (491273/YL-PAG)	Privately owned, Breighton
	-	Mil Mi-24D (3532461715415)	Privately owned, Leavesden
	-	Mil Mi-24D (3532464505029)	Midland Air Museum, Coventry
	1 w	SPP Yak C-11 (171314/G-BZMY)	Privately owned, Coventry
	01 y	Yakovlev Yak-52 (9311709/G-YKSZ)	Privately owned, White Waltham

Serial	Type (code/other identity)	Owner/operator location or fate	Notes
03 bl	Yakovlev Yak-55M (910103/RA-01274)	Privately owned, Halfpenny Green	
03 w	Yakovlev Yak-18A (1160403/G-CEIB)	Privately owned, Breighton	
03 w	Yakovlev Yak-52 (899803/G-YAKR)	Privately owned, North Weald	
5 w	Yakovlev Yak-3UA (0470204/D-FYGJ)	Privately owned, Bremgarten, Germany	
06 y	Yakovlev Yak-9UM (HB-RYA)	Flying Fighter Association, Bex, Switzerland	
07 y	WSK SM-1 (Mi-1) (Polish AF 2007)	The Helicopter Museum, Weston-super-Mare	
07 y	Yakovlev Yak-18M (G-BMJY)	Privately owned, East Garston, Bucks	
07 r	Yakovlev Yak-52 (9011107/G-HYAK)	Privately owned, Exeter	
09 y	Yakovlev Yak-52 (9411809/G-BVMU)	Privately owned, Shipdham	
9 w	SPP Yak C-11 (1701139/G-OYAK)	Privately owned, Little Gransden	
10 si	Yakovlev Yak-52 (9111205/G-YAKF)	Privately owned, St Athan	
10 y	Yakovlev Yak-50 (801810/G-BTZB)	Privately owned, Lee-on-Solent	
11 y	SPP Yak C-11 (G-YCII)	Privately owned, Woodchurch, Kent	
12 r	LET L-29 Delfin (194555/ES-YLM/G-DELF)	Privately owned, St Athan	
15 w	SPP Yak C-11 (170103/D-FYAK)	Classic Aviation Company, Hannover, Germany	
20 w	Lavochkin La-11	The Fighter Collection, Duxford	
21 w	Yakovlev Yak-3UA (0470203/G-CDBJ)	Privately owned, Headcorn	
21 w	Yakovlev Yak-9UM (0470403/D-FENK)	Privately owned, Magdeburg, Germany	
23 y	Bell P-39Q Airacobra (44-2911)	Privately owned, Sussex	
23 w	Mikoyan MiG-27D (83712515040)	Privately owned, Hawarden	
26 bl	Yakovlev Yak-52 (9111306/G-BVXK)	Privately owned, White Waltham	
27 w	Yakovlev Yak-3UTI-PW (9/04623/F-AZIM)	Privately owned, la Ferté-Alais, France	
27 r	Yakovlev Yak-52 (9111307/G-YAKX)	Privately owned, Popham	
28 w	Polikarpov Po-2 (0094/G-BSSY)	The Shuttleworth Collection, Old Warden	
31 gy	Yakovlev Yak-52 (9111311/G-YAKV)	Privately owned, Rendcomb	
33 r	Yakovlev Yak-50 (853206/G-YAKZ)	Privately owned, White Waltham	
33 w	Yakovlev Yak-52 (899915/G-YAKH)	Privately owned, White Waltham	
35 r	Sukhoi Su-17M-3 (25102)	Privately owned, Hawarden	
36 w	LET/Yak C-11 (171101/G-KYAK)	Privately owned, North Weald	
36 r	Yakovlev Yak-52 (9111604/G-IUII)	Privately owned, North Weald	
43 bl	Yakovlev Yak-52 (877601/G-BWSV)	Privately owned, North Weald	
48 bl	Yakovlev Yak-52 (9111413/G-CBSN)	Privately owned, Manston	
49 r	Yakovlev Yak-50 (822305/G-YAKU)	Privately owned, Henstridge	
50 bk	Yakovlev Yak-50 (812101/G-CBPM)	Privately owned, High Cross	
50 gy	Yakovlev Yak-52 (9111415/G-CBRW)	Meier Motors, Bremgarten, Germany	
51 r	LET L-29 Delfin (893019/G-BZNT)	Privately owned, St Athan	
51 y	Yakovlev Yak-50 (812004/G-BWYK)	Privately owned, West Meon, Hants	
52 w	Yakovlev Yak C-11 (171312/G-BTZE)	Privately owned, Booker	
52 w	Yakovlev Yak-52 (9612001/G-CCJK)	Privately owned, White Waltham	
52 y	Yakovlev Yak-52 (878202/G-BWVR)	Privately owned, Barton	
54 r	Sukhoi Su-17M (69004)	Privately owned, Hawarden	
55 y	Yakovlev Yak-52 (9111505/G-BVOK)	Privately owned, Shoreham	
61 r	Yakovlev Yak-50 (842710/G-YAKM)	Privately owned, Henstridge	
66 r	Yakovlev Yak-52 (855905/G-YAKN)	Privately owned, Henstridge	
67 r	Yakovlev Yak-52 (822013/G-CBSL)	Privately owned, Church Fenton	
69 r	Hawker Hunter FGA9 (8839M/XG194)	*Repainted as XG194*	
69 bl	Yakovlev Yak-52 (899413/G-XYAK)	Privately owned, Old Buckenham	
69 y	Yakovlev Yak-52 (888712/G-CCSU)	Privately owned, Germany	
71 r	Mikoyan MiG-27K (61912507006)	Newark Air Museum, Winthorpe	
74 w	Yakovlev Yak-52 (877404/G-LAOK) [JA-74, IV-62]	Privately owned, Tollerton	
93 w	Yakovlev Yak-50 (853001/G-JYAK) [R]	Privately owned, North Weald	
100 bl	Yakovlev Yak-52 (866904/G-YAKI)	Privately owned, Popham	
100 w	Yakovlev Yak-3M (0470107/G-CGXG)	Privately owned, Bentwaters	
139 y	Yakovlev Yak-52 (833810/G-BWOD)	Privately owned, Sywell	
526 bk	Mikoyan MiG-29 (2960725887) <ff>	Fenland & West Norfolk Aviation Museum, Wisbech	
1342	Yakovlev Yak-1 (G-BTZD)	Privately owned, Westfield, Sussex	
1870710	Ilyushin Il-2 (G-BZVW)	Privately owned, Wickenby	
1878576	Ilyushin Il-2 (G-BZVX)	Privately owned, Wickenby	
(RK858)	VS361 Spitfire LFIX (G-CGJE)	The Fighter Collection, Duxford	
(SM639)	VS361 Spitfire LFIX	Privately owned, Catfield	

Notes	Serial	Type (code/other identity)	Owner/operator location or fate
	SAUDI ARABIA		
	1104	BAC Strikemaster 80 (G-SMAS)	Privately owned, Hawarden
	1112	BAC Strikemaster 80 (G-FLYY)	Privately owned, Cotswold Airport
	1115	BAC Strikemaster 80A	Global Aviation, Humberside
	1120	BAC Strikemaster 80A (G-RSAF)	Privately owned, Hawarden
	1129	BAC Strikemaster 80A	Global Aviation, Humberside
	1133	BAC Strikemaster 80A (G-BESY)	Imperial War Museum, Duxford
	53-686	BAC Lightning F53 (G-AWON/ZF592)	City of Norwich Aviation Museum
	55-713	BAC Lightning T55 (ZF598) [C]	Midland Air Museum, Coventry
	SINGAPORE		
	311	BAC Strikemaster 84 (G-MXPH)	Privately owned, North Weald
	323	BAC Strikemaster 81 (N21419)	Privately owned, stored Hawarden
	SOUTH AFRICA		
	91	Westland Wasp HAS1 (pod)	Privately owned, Oaksey Park
	92	Westland Wasp HAS1 (G-BYCX)	Privately owned, Babcary, Somerset
	221	DH115 Vampire T55 <ff>	*To South Africa, 2012*
	6130	Lockheed Ventura II (AJ469)	RAF Museum, stored Cosford
	7429	NA AT-6D Harvard III (D-FASS)	Privately owned, Aachen, Germany
	SOUTH VIETNAM		
	24550	Cessna L-19E Bird Dog (G-PDOG) [GP]	Privately owned, Fenland
	SPAIN		
	B.2I-27	CASA 2.111B (He111H-16) (B.2I-103)	Imperial War Museum, stored Duxford
	C.4E-88	Messerschmitt Bf109E	*To Germany*
	E.3B-143	CASA 1.131E Jungmann (G-JUNG)	Privately owned, White Waltham
	E.3B-153	CASA 1.131E Jungmann (G-BPTS) [781-75]	Privately owned, Egginton
	E.3B-350	CASA 1.131E Jungmann (G-BHPL) [05-97]	Privately owned, Henstridge
	(E.3B-369)	CASA 1.131E Jungmann (G-BPDM) [781-32]	Privately owned, Heighington
	(E.3B-379)	CASA 1.131E Jungmann (G-CDJU) [72-36]	Privately owned, Abbeyshrule, Eire
	E.3B-494	CASA 1.131E Jungmann (G-CDLC) [81-47]	Privately owned, Chiseldon
	E.3B-521	CASA 1.131E Jungmann [781-3]	RAF Museum, Hendon
	E.3B-599	CASA 1.131E Jungmann (G-CGTX) [31]	Privately owned, Archerfield, Lothian
	E.18-2	Piper PA-31P Navajo 425 [42-71]	Bentwaters Cold War Museum
	EM-01	DH60G Moth (G-AAOR)	Privately owned, Rendcomb
	ES.1-4	Bücker Bü133C Jungmeister (G-BUTX)	Privately owned, Breighton
	ES.1-16	CASA 1.133L Jungmeister	Privately owned, Stretton, Cheshire
	SWEDEN		
	-	Thulin A/Bleriot XI (SE-XMC)	Privately owned, Loberod, Sweden
	081	CFM 01 Tummelisa <R> (SE-XIL)	Privately owned, Loberod, Sweden
	2542	Fiat CR42 (G-CBLS)	The Fighter Collection, Duxford
	5033	Klemm Kl35D (SE-BPT) [78]	Privately owned, Barkaby, Sweden
	5060	Klemm Kl35D (SE-BPU) [174]	Privately owned, Barkaby, Sweden
	05108	DH60 Moth	Privately owned, Langham
	17239	SAAB B-17A (SE-BYH) [7-J]	Flygvapenmuseum, Linköping, Sweden
	28693	DH100 Vampire FB6 (J-1184/SE-DXY) [9-G]	Scandinavian Historic Flight, Oslo, Norway
	29640	SAAB J-29F [20-08]	Midland Air Museum, Coventry
	29670	SAAB J-29F (SE-DXB) [10-R]	Flygvapenmuseum/F10 Wing, Angelholm, Sweden
	32028	SAAB 32A Lansen (G-BMSG)	Privately owned, Willenhall, Staffs
	34066	Hawker Hunter F58 (J-4089/LN-HNT) [9-G]	*Sold as N337AX, 2012*
	35075	SAAB J-35A Draken [40]	Dumfries & Galloway Aviation Museum
	35515	SAAB J-35F Draken [49]	Airborne Systems, Llangeinor
	37098	SAAB AJSF-37 Viggen (SE-DXN) [52]	Scandinavian Historic Flight, Såtenäs, Sweden
	37918	SAAB AJSH-37 Viggen [57]	Newark Air Museum, Winthorpe
	60140	SAAB 105 (SE-DXG) [140-5]	Flygvapenmuseum/F10 Wing, Angelholm, Sweden
	91130	SAAB S91A Safir (SE-BNN) [10-30]	Privately owned, Barkaby, Sweden

Serial	*Type (code/other identity)*	*Owner/operator location or fate*	*Notes*
SWITZERLAND			
-	DH112 Venom FB54 (J-1758/N203DM)	Grove Technology Park, Wantage, Oxon	
A-10	CASA 1.131E Jungmann (G-BECW)	Privately owned, Rochester	
A-12	Bücker Bu131B Jungmann (G-CCHY)	*Sold to Germany, May 2012*	
A-57	CASA 1.131E Jungmann (G-BECT)	Privately owned, Goodwood	
A-701	Junkers Ju52/3m (HB-HOS)	Ju-Air, Dubendorf, Switzerland	
A-702	Junkers Ju52/3m (HB-HOT)	Ju-Air, Dubendorf, Switzerland	
A-703	Junkers Ju52/3m (HB-HOP)	Ju-Air, Dubendorf, Switzerland	
A-806	Pilatus P3-03 (G-BTLL)	Privately owned, Guist, Norfolk	
A-815	Pilatus P3-03 (HB-RCQ)	Privately owned, Locarno, Switzerland	
A-818	Pilatus P3-03 (HB-RCH)	Privately owned, Ambri, Switzerland	
A-829	Pilatus P3-03 (HB-RCJ)	Privately owned, Locarno, Switzerland	
A-873	Pilatus P3-03 (HB-RCL)	Privately owned, Locarno, Switzerland	
C-552	EKW C-3605 (G-DORN)	Privately owned, Bournemouth	
C-558	EKW C-3605 (G-CCYZ)	Privately owned, Wickenby	
J-1008	DH100 Vampire FB6	Mosquito Aircraft Museum, London Colney	
J-1169	DH100 Vampire FB6	Privately owned, Henley-on-Thames	
J-1172	DH100 Vampire FB6 (8487M)	RAF Museum Reserve Collection, Stafford	
J-1573	DH112 Venom FB50 (G-VICI)	*Sold to Ireland, February 2013*	
J-1605	DH112 Venom FB50 (G-BLID)	Gatwick Aviation Museum, Charlwood, Surrey	
J-1629	DH112 Venom FB50	Privately owned, Shropshire	
J-1632	DH112 Venom FB50 (G-VNOM) <ff>	Privately owned, Cantley, Norfolk	
J-1649	DH112 Venom FB50 <ff>	AIRBASE, Coventry	
J-1704	DH112 Venom FB54	RAF Museum, Cosford	
J-1712	DH112 Venom FB54 <ff>	Privately owned, Connah's Quay, Flintshire	
J-1790	DH112 Venom FB50 (G-BLKA)	Mosquito Aircraft Museum, London Colney	
J-4015	Hawker Hunter F58 (J-4040/HB-RVS)	Privately owned, St Stephan, Switzerland	
J-4021	Hawker Hunter F58 (G-HHAC)	*Repainted as ZZ194, June 2012*	
J-4064	Hawker Hunter F58 (HB-RVQ)	Fliegermuseum Altenrhein, Switzerland	
J-4083	Hawker Hunter F58 (G-EGHH)	Privately owned, St Athan	
J-4086	Hawker Hunter F58 (HB-RVU)	Privately owned, Altenrhein, Switzerland	
J-4201	Hawker Hunter T68 (HB-RVR)	Amici dell'Hunter, Sion, Switzerland	
J-4205	Hawker Hunter T68 (HB-RVP)	Fliegermuseum Altenrhein, Switzerland	
J-4206	Hawker Hunter T68 (HB-RVV)	Fliegermuseum Altenrhein, Switzerland	
U-80	Bücker Bü133D Jungmeister (G-BUKK)	Privately owned, Kirdford, W Sussex	
U-95	Bücker Bü133C Jungmeister (G-BVGP)	Privately owned, Booker	
U-99	Bücker Bü133C Jungmeister (G-AXMT)	Privately owned, Breighton	
U-110	Pilatus P-2 (G-PTWO)	Privately owned, Rochester	
U-1215	DH115 Vampire T11 (XE998)	Solent Sky, Southampton	
V-54	SE3130 Alouette II (G-BVSD)	Privately owned, Glos	
USA			
-	Noorduyn AT-16 Harvard IIB (KLu B-168)	American Air Museum, Duxford	
001	Ryan ST-3KR Recruit (G-BYPY)	Privately owned, Old Warden	
14	Boeing-Stearman A75N-1 Kaydet (G-ISDN)	Privately owned, Oaksey Park	
23	Fairchild PT-23 (N49272)	Privately owned, Sleap	
26	Boeing-Stearman A75N-1 Kaydet (G-BAVO)	Privately owned, Turweston	
27	NA SNJ-7 Texan (90678/G-BRVG)	Privately owned, Rochester	
43	Noorduyn AT-16 Harvard IIB (43-13064/G-AZSC) [SC]	Privately owned, North Weald	
44	Boeing-Stearman D75N-1 Kaydet (42-15852/G-RJAH)	Privately owned, Duxford	
85	WAR P-47 Thunderbolt <R> (G-BTBI)	Privately owned, Perth	
104	Boeing-Stearman PT-13D Kaydet (42-16931/N4712V) [W]	Privately owned, Hardwick, Norfolk	
112	Boeing-Stearman PT-13D Kaydet (42-17397/G-BSWC)	Privately owned, Staverton	
164	Boeing-Stearman PT-13B Kaydet (N60320)	Privately owned, Fenland	
284	Curtiss P-40B Warhawk (41-13297/G-CDWH) [18P]	The Fighter Collection, Duxford	

Notes	Serial	Type (code/other identity)	Owner/operator location or fate
	379	Boeing-Stearman PT-13D Kaydet (42-14865/G-ILLE)	Privately owned, Hohenems, Austria
	399	Boeing-Stearman N2S-5 Kaydet (38495/N67193)	Privately owned, Gelnhausen, Germany
	441	Boeing-Stearman N2S-4 Kaydet (30010/G-BTFG)	Privately owned, Manston
	466	Boeing-Stearman PT-13A Kaydet (37-0089/N731)	Privately owned, Staverton
	540	Piper L-4H Grasshopper (43-29877/G-BCNX)	Privately owned, Monewden
	560	Bell UH-1H Iroquois (73-22077/G-HUEY)	Privately owned, North Weald
	578	Boeing-Stearman N2S-5 Kaydet (N1364V)	Privately owned, North Weald
	586	Boeing-Stearman N2S-3 Kaydet (07874/N74650)	Privately owned, Popham
	628	Beech D17S (44-67761/N18V)	Privately owned, stored East Garston, Bucks
	669	Boeing-Stearman A75N-1 Kaydet (37869/G-CCXA)	Privately owned, Old Buckenham
	671	Boeing-Stearman PT-13D Kaydet (61181/G-CGPY)	Privately owned, Staverton
	699	Boeing-Stearman N2S-3 Kaydet (38233/G-CCXB)	Privately owned, Goodwood
	716	Boeing-Stearman PT-13D Kaydet (42-17553/N1731B)	Privately owned, Compton Abbas
	718	Boeing-Stearman PT-13D Kaydet (42-17555/N5345N)	Privately owned, Tibenham
	744	Boeing-Stearman A75N-1 Kaydet (42-16532/OO-USN)	Privately owned, Wevelgem, Belgium
	805	Boeing-Stearman PT-17 Kaydet (42-17642/N3922B)	Privately owned, Tibenham
	854	Ryan PT-22 Recruit (41-20854/G-BTBH)	Privately owned, Old Warden
	855	Ryan PT-22 Recruit (41-15510/N56421)	Privately owned, Sleap
	897	Aeronca 11AC Chief (G-BJEV) [E]	Privately owned, English Bicknor, Glos
	985	Boeing-Stearman PT-13D Kaydet (42-16930/OO-OPS)	Privately owned, Antwerp, Belgium
	1102	Boeing-Stearman N2S-5 Kaydet (G-AZLE) [102]	Privately owned, Tongham
	1164	Beech D18S (G-BKGL)	The Aircraft Restoration Co, Duxford
	1180	Boeing-Stearman N2S-3 Kaydet (3403/G-BRSK)	Privately owned, Morley
	3072	NA T-6G Texan (49-3072/G-TEXN) [72]	Privately owned, Shoreham
	3397	Boeing-Stearman N2S-3 Kaydet (G-OBEE) [174]	Privately owned, Old Buckenham
	3403	Boeing-Stearman N2S-3 Kaydet (N75TQ) [180]	Privately owned, Tibenham
	3583	Piper L-4B Grasshopper (45-0583/G-FINT) [44-D]	Privately owned, Redhill
	4406	Naval Aircraft Factory N3N-3 (G-ONAF) [12]	Privately owned, Sandown
	6136	Boeing-Stearman A75N-1 Kaydet (42-16136/G-BRUJ) [205]	Privately owned, Liverpool
	6171	NA F-86D Sabre (51-6171)	North-East Aircraft Museum, Usworth
	6771	Republic F-84F Thunderstreak (BAF FU-6)	RAF Museum, stored Cosford
	7797	Aeronca L-16A Grasshopper (47-0797/G-BFAF)	Privately owned, Finmere
	8084	NA AT-6D Texan (42-85068/G-KAMY)	Kennet Aviation, North Weald
	8178	NA F-86A Sabre (48-0178/G-SABR) [FU-178]	Golden Apple Operations/ARC, Duxford
	8242	NA F-86A Sabre (48-0242) [FU-242]	Midland Air Museum, Coventry
	01532	Northrop F-5E Tiger II <R>	RAF Alconbury on display
	02538	Fairchild PT-19B (N33870)	Privately owned, Mendlesham, Suffolk
	07539	Boeing-Stearman N2S-3 Kaydet (N63590) [143]	Privately owned, Billericay
	14286	Lockheed T-33A Shooting Star (51-4286)	American Air Museum, Duxford
	0-14419	Lockheed T-33A Shooting Star (51-4419)	Midland Air Museum, Coventry
	14863	NA AT-6D Harvard III (41-33908/G-BGOR)	Privately owned, Rednal
	15154	Bell OH-58A Kiowa (70-15154)	Defence Academy of the UK, Shrivenham
	15372	Piper L-18C Super Cub (51-15372/N123SA) [372-A]	Privately owned, Anwick, Lincs
	15979	Hughes OH-6A Cayuse (69-15979)	RAF Mildenhall, instructional use
	15990	Bell AH-1F Hueycobra (70-15990)	Museum of Army Flying, Middle Wallop
	16011	Hughes OH-6A Cayuse (69-16011/G-OHGA)	Privately owned, Wesham, Lancs
	16037	Piper J-3C Cub 65 (G-BSFD)	Privately owned, Sleap
	16445	Bell AH-1F Hueycobra (69-16445)	Defence Academy of the UK, Shrivenham
	16506	Hughes OH-6A Cayuse (67-16506)	The Helicopter Museum, Weston-super-Mare
	16544	NA AT-6A Texan (41-16544/N13FY) [FY]	Privately owned, Hilversum, The Netherlands
	16579	Bell UH-1H Iroquois (66-16579)	The Helicopter Museum, Weston-super-Mare
	16718	Lockheed T-33A Shooting Star (51-6718)	City of Norwich Aviation Museum

Serial	*Type (code/other identity)*	*Owner/operator location or fate*	*Notes*
17962	Lockheed SR-71A Blackbird (61-7962)	American Air Museum, Duxford	
18263	Boeing-Stearman PT-17 Kaydet (41-8263/N38940) [822]	Privately owned, Tibenham	
19252	Lockheed T-33A Shooting Star (51-9252)	Tangmere Military Aviation Museum	
21509	Bell UH-1H Iroquois (72-21509/G-UHIH)	Privately owned, Wesham, Lancs	
21605	Bell UH-1H Iroquois (72-21605)	American Air Museum, Duxford	
24538	Kaman HH-43F Huskie (62-4535)	Midland Air Museum, Coventry	
24541	Cessna L-19E Bird Dog (N134TT)	Privately owned, Cotswold Airport	
24568	Cessna L-19E Bird Dog (LN-WNO)	Army Aviation Norway, Kjeller, Norway	
24582	Cessna L-19E Bird Dog (G-VDOG)	Privately owned, Stockbridge, Hants	
28521	CCF T-6J Texan(G-TVIJ) [TA-521]	Privately owned, Woodchurch, Kent	
30274	Piper AE-1 Cub Cruiser (N203SA)	Privately owned, Nangis, France	
30861	NA TB-25J Mitchell (44-30861/N9089Z)	Privately owned, Booker	
31145	Piper L-4B Grasshopper (43-1145/G-BBLH) [26-G]	Privately owned, Biggin Hill	
31171	NA B-25J Mitchell (44-31171/N7614C)	American Air Museum, Duxford	
31430	Piper L-4B Grasshopper (43-1430/G-BHVV)	Privately owned, Perranporth	
31952	Aeronca O-58B Defender (G-BRPR)	Privately owned, Belchamp Water	
34037	NA TB-25N Mitchell (44-29366/N9115Z/8838M)	RAF Museum, Hendon	
37414	McD F-4C Phantom II (63-7414)	Midland Air Museum, stored Coventry	
39624	Wag Aero Sport Trainer (G-BVMH) [39-D]	Privately owned, Temple Bruer	
40467	Grumman F6F-5K Hellcat (80141/G-BTCC) [19]	The Fighter Collection, Duxford	
41386	Thomas-Morse S4 Scout <R> (G-MJTD)	Privately owned, Lutterworth	
42165	NA F-100D Super Sabre (54-2165) [VM]	American Air Museum, Duxford	
42196	NA F-100D Super Sabre (54-2196)	Norfolk & Suffolk Avn Museum, Flixton	
43517	Boeing-Stearman N2S-5 Kaydet (G-NZSS) [227]	Privately owned, Woodchurch, Kent	
46214	Grumman TBM-3E Avenger (69327/CF-KCG) [X-3]	American Air Museum, Duxford	
51970	NA AT-6D Texan (41-33888/G-TXAN) [V-970]	Privately owned, Thruxton	
54433	Lockheed T-33A Shooting Star (55-4433) [TR-433]	Norfolk & Suffolk Avn Museum, Flixton	
54884	Piper L-4J Grasshopper (45-4884/N61787) [57-D]	Privately owned, Sywell	
56498	Douglas C-54Q Skymaster (N44914)	Privately owned, stored North Weald	
60312	McD F-101F Voodoo (56-0312)	Midland Air Museum, Coventry	
60344	Ryan Navion (N4956C)	Privately owned, Earls Colne	
60689	Boeing B-52D Stratofortress (56-0689)	American Air Museum, Duxford	
63000	NA F-100D Super Sabre (54-2212) [FW-000]	USAF Croughton, Oxon, at gate	
63319	NA F-100D Super Sabre (54-2269) [FW-319]	RAF Lakenheath, on display	
66692	Lockheed U-2CT (56-6692)	American Air Museum, Duxford	
70270	McD F-101B Voodoo (57-270) (fuselage)	Midland Air Museum, Coventry	
80105	Replica SE5a <R> (PH-WWI/G-CCBN) [19]	Privately owned, Thruxton	
80995	Cessna 337D Super Skymaster (F-BRPQ)	Privately owned, Strasbourg, France	
82062	DHC U-6A Beaver (58-2062)	Midland Air Museum, Coventry	
85061	NA SNJ-5 Texan (G-CHIA) [61]	Privately owned, Duxford	
88690	Grumman FM-2 Wildcat (N49JC) [F-2]	The Shuttleworth Collection, Old Warden	
93542	CCF T-6J Harvard IV (G-BRLV) [LTA-542]	Privately owned, North Weald	
96995	CV F4U-4 Corsair (OE-EAS) [BR-37]	Flying Bulls, Salzburg, Austria	
111836	NA AT-6C Harvard IIA (41-33262/G-TSIX) [JZ-6]	Privately owned, Church Fenton	
111989	Cessna L-19A Bird Dog (51-11989/N33600)	Museum of Army Flying, Middle Wallop	
114700	NA T-6G Texan (51-14700/G-TOMC)	Privately owned, Netherthorpe	
115042	NA T-6G Texan (51-15042/G-BGHU) [TA-042]	Privately owned, Headcorn	
115227	NA T-6G Texan (51-15227/G-BKRA)	Privately owned, Staverton	
115302	Piper L-18C Super Cub (51-15302/G-BJTP) [TP]	Privately owned, Defford	
115373	Piper L-18C Super Cub (51-15373/G-AYPM) [A-373]	Privately owned, Leicester	
115684	Piper L-21A Super Cub (51-15684/G-BKVM) [DC]	Privately owned, Strubby	
121714	Grumman F8F-2P Bearcat (G-RUMM) [201-B]	The Fighter Collection, Duxford	
124143	Douglas AD-4NA Skyraider (F-AZDP) [205-RM]	Amicale J-B Salis, la Ferté-Alais, France	
124485	Boeing B-17G Flying Fortress (44-85784/G-BEDF)[DF-A]	B-17 Preservation Ltd, Duxford	

Notes	*Serial*	*Type (code/other identity)*	*Owner/operator location or fate*
	124541	CV F4U-5NL Corsair (F-AZYS) [16-WF]	Privately owned, Avignon, France
	124724	CV F4U-5NL Corsair (F-AZEG) [22]	Les Casques de Cuir, la Ferté-Alais, France
	126922	Douglas AD-4NA Skyraider (G-RADR) [503-H]	Kennet Aviation, North Weald
	134076	NA AT-6D Texan (41-34671/F-AZSC) [TA076]	Privately owned, Yvetot, France
	138179	NA T-28A Trojan (OE-ESA) [BA]	The Flying Bulls, Salzburg, Austria
	138266	NA T-28B Trojan (HB-RCT) [266-CT]	Jet Alpine Fighter, Sion, Switzerland
	138343	NA T-28B Trojan (N343NA) [212]	Privately owned, Antwerp, Belgium
	140547	NA T-28C Trojan (F-AZHN) [IF-28]	Privately owned, Toussus le Noble, France
	140566	NA T-28C Trojan (N556EB) [252]	Privately owned, la Ferté-Alais, France
	146289	NA T-28C Trojan (N99153) [2W]	Norfolk & Suffolk Avn Museum, Flixton
	150225	WS58 Wessex 60 (G-AWOX) [123]	Privately owned, Lulsgate
	155529	McD F-4J(UK) Phantom II (ZE359) [AJ-114]	American Air Museum, Duxford
	155848	McD F-4S Phantom II [WT-11]	Royal Scottish Mus'm of Flight, E Fortune
	159233	HS AV-8A Harrier [CG-33]	Imperial War Museum North, Salford Quays
	162068	McD AV-8B Harrier II <ff>	Privately owned, Thorpe Wood, N Yorks
	162071	McD AV-8B Harrier II (fuselage)	Rolls-Royce, Filton
	162074	McD AV-8B Harrier II <ff>	Privately owned, South Molton, Devon
	162730	McD AV-8B Harrier II <ff>	Privately owned, Liverpool
	162737	McD AV-8B Harrier II (fuselage) [38]	MoD, Boscombe Down
	162958	McD AV-8B Harrier II <ff>	QinetiQ, Farnborough
	162964	McD AV-8B Harrier II <ff>	Tri Sim Ltd, Peterborough
	162964	McD AV-8B Harrier II <rf>	Privately owned, Charlwood, Surrey
	163205	McD AV-8B Harrier II (fuselage)	Privately owned, Thorpe Wood, N Yorks
	163423	McD AV-8B Harrier II <ff>	QinetiQ, Boscombe Down
	163423	McD AV-8B Harrier II <rf>	Privately owned, Sproughton
	210855	Curtiss P-40M Kittyhawk (43-5802/G-KITT)	Hangar 11 Collection, North Weald
	217786	Boeing-Stearman PT-17 Kaydet (41-8169/CF-EQS) [25]	American Air Museum, Duxford
	224319	Douglas C-47B Skytrain (44-77047/G-AMSN) <ff>	Privately owned, Sussex
	225068	Republic TP-47G Thunderbolt (42-25068/G-CDVX) [WZ-D]	The Fighter Collection, Duxford
	226413	Republic P-47D Thunderbolt (45-49192/N47DD) [ZU-N]	American Air Museum, Duxford
	231983	Boeing B-17G Flying Fortress (44-83735/F-BDRS)[IY-G]	American Air Museum, Duxford
	234539	Fairchild PT-19B Cornell (42-34539/N50429) [63]	Privately owned, Dunkeswell
	236657	Piper L-4A Grasshopper (42-36657/G-BGSJ) [72-D]	Privately owned, Langport
	238410	Piper L-4A Grasshopper (42-38410/G-BHPK) [44-A]	Privately owned, Tibenham
	241079	Waco CG-4A Hadrian <R>	Assault Glider Association, Shawbury
	243809	Waco CG-4A Hadrian (BAPC 185)	Museum of Army Flying, Middle Wallop
	252983	Schweizer TG-3A (42-52983/N66630)	Imperial War Museum, stored Duxford
	298177	Stinson L-5A Sentinel (42-98177/N6438C) [8-R]	Privately owned, Tibenham
	313048	NA AT-6D Texan (44-81506/G-TDJN)	Privately owned, Gloucester
	314887	Fairchild Argus III (43-14887/G-AJPI)	Privately owned, Eelde, The Netherlands
	315509	Douglas C-47A Skytrain (43-15509/G-BHUB) [W7-S]	American Air Museum, Duxford
	319764	Waco CG-4A Hadrian (*237123*/BAPC 157) (fuselage)	Yorkshire Air Museum, Elvington
	329282	Piper J-3C Cub 65 (N46779)	Privately owned, Abbots Bromley
	329405	Piper L-4H Grasshopper (43-29405/G-BCOB) [23-A]	Privately owned, Bicester
	329417	Piper L-4A Grasshopper (42-38400/G-BDHK)	Privately owned, English Bicknor, Glos
	329471	Piper L-4H Grasshopper (43-29471/G-BGXA) [44-F]	Privately owned, Martley, Worcs
	329601	Piper L-4H Grasshopper (43-29601/G-AXHR) [44-D]	Privately owned, Nayland
	329707	Piper L-4H Grasshopper (43-29707/G-BFBY) [44-S]	Privately owned, Old Buckenham

Serial	*Type (code/other identity)*	*Owner/operator location or fate*	*Notes*
329854	Piper L-4H Grasshopper (43-29854/G-BMKC) [44-R]	Privately owned, Biggin Hill	
329934	Piper L-4H Grasshopper (43-29934/G-BCPH) [72-B]	Privately owned, Garford, Oxon	
330238	Piper L-4H Grasshopper (43-30238/G-LIVH) [24-A]	Privately owned, Yarcombe, Devon	
330244	Piper L-4H Grasshopper (43-30244/G-CGIY) [46-C]	Privately owned, Leeds	
330372	Piper L-4H Grasshopper (43-30372/G-AISX)	Privately owned, Booker	
330485	Piper L-4H Grasshopper (43-30485/G-AJES) [44-C]	Privately owned, Shifnal	
411622	NA P-51D Mustang (44-74427/F-AZSB) [G4-C]	Amicale J-B Salis, la Ferté-Alais, France	
413317	NA P-51D Mustang (44-74409/N51RT) [VF-B]	RAF Museum, Hendon	
413521	NA P-51D Mustang (44-13521/G-MRLL) [5Q-B]	Privately owned, Hardwick, Norfolk	
413573	NA P-51D Mustang (44-73415/9133M/N6526D) [B6-V]	RAF Museum, Cosford	
413578	NA P-51D Mustang (44-74923/PH-JAT) [C5-W]	Privately owned, Lelystad, The Netherlands	
413704	NA P-51D Mustang (44-73149/G-BTCD) [B7-H]	The Old Flying Machine Company, Duxford	
414419	NA P-51D Mustang (45-15118/G-MSTG) [LH-F]	Privately owned, Hardwick, Norfolk	
414450	NA P-51D Mustang (44-73877/N167F) [B6-S]	Nordic Warbirds, Västerås, Sweden	
414673	Bonsall Mustang <R> (G-BDWM) [LH-I]	Privately owned, Gamston	
433915	Consolidated PBV-1A Canso A (RCAF 11005/G-PBYA)	Privately owned, Duxford	
434602	Douglas A-26B Invader (44-34602/LN-IVA) [B]	Nordic Warbirds, Västerås, Sweden	
436021	Piper J/3C Cub 65 (G-BWEZ)	Privately owned, Strathaven, Strathclyde	
442268	Noorduyn AT-16 Harvard IIB (KF568/LN-TEX) [TA-268]	Scandinavian Historic Flight, Oslo, Norway	
454467	Piper L-4J Grasshopper (45-4467/G-BILI) [44-J]	Privately owned, White Waltham	
454537	Piper L-4J Grasshopper (45-4537/G-BFDL) [04-J]	Privately owned, Shempston Farm, Lossiemouth	
461748	Boeing B-29A Superfortress (44-61748/G-BHDK) [Y]	American Air Museum, Duxford	
463209	NA P-51D Mustang <R> (BAPC 255) [WZ-S]	American Air Museum, Duxford	
472035	NA P-51D Mustang (44-72035/G-SIJJ)	Hangar 11 Collection, North Weald	
472216	NA P-51D Mustang (44-72216/G-BIXL) [HO-M]	Privately owned, East Garston, Bucks	
472218	NA P-51D Mustang (44-73979) [WZ-I]	Imperial War Museum, Duxford	
472218	Titan T-51 Mustang (G-MUZY) [WZ-I]	Privately owned, Damyns Hall, Essex	
472773	NA P-51D Mustang (44-72773/D-FPSI) [QP-M]	Meier Motors, Bremgarten, Germany	
473871	NA TF-51D Mustang (44-73871/D-FTSI) [TF-871]	Meier Motors, Bremgarten, Germany	
474008	Jurca MJ77 Gnatsum (G-PSIR) [VF-R]	Privately owned, Lewes	
474425	NA P-51D Mustang (44-74425/PH-PSI) [OC-G]	Privately owned, Lelystad, The Netherlands	
479744	Piper L-4H Grasshopper (44-79744/G-BGPD) [49-M]	Privately owned, Marsh, Bucks	
479766	Piper L-4H Grasshopper (44-79766/G-BKHG) [63-D]	Privately owned, Frogland Cross	
479781	Piper L-4H Grasshopper (44-79781/G-AISS)	Privately owned, Insch (under restoration)	
479897	Piper L-4H Grasshopper (44-79897/G-BOXJ) [JD]	Privately owned, Rochester	
480015	Piper L-4H Grasshopper (44-80015/G-AKIB) [44-M]	Privately owned, Perranporth	
480133	Piper L-4J Grasshopper (44-80133/G-BDCD) [44-B]	Privately owned, Slinfold	
480173	Piper L-4J Grasshopper (44-80609/G-RRSR) [57-H]	Privately owned, Wellesbourne Mountford	
480321	Piper L-4J Grasshopper (44-80321/G-FRAN) [44-H]	Privately owned, Rayne, Essex	
480480	Piper L-4J Grasshopper (44-80480/G-BECN) [44-E]	Privately owned, Rayne, Essex	
480551	Piper L-4J Grasshopper (44-80551/LN-KLT) [43-S]	Scandinavian Historic Flight, Oslo, Norway	
480636	Piper L-4J Grasshopper (44-80636/G-AXHP) [58-A]	Privately owned, Spanhoe	

Notes	*Serial*	*Type (code/other identity)*	*Owner/operator location or fate*
	480723	Piper L-4J Grasshopper (44-80723/G-BFZB) [E5-J]	Privately owned, Egginton
	480752	Piper L-4J Grasshopper (44-80752/G-BCXJ) [39-E]	Privately owned, Old Sarum
	483868	Boeing B-17G Flying Fortress (44-83868/N5237V) [A-N]	RAF Museum, Hendon
	493209	NA T-6G Texan (49-3209/G-DDMV/*41*)	Privately owned, Headcorn
	511701A	Beech C-45H (51-11701/G-BSZC) [AF258]	Privately owned, Bryngwyn Bach
	779465	Hiller UH-12C (N5315V)	Privately owned, Lower Upham, Hants
	2100882	Douglas C-47A Skytrain (42-100882/N473DC) [3X-P]	Privately owned, Liverpool
	2100884	Douglas C-47A Skytrain (42-100884/N147DC) [L4-D]	Privately owned, Dunsfold
	2105915	Curtiss P-40N Kittyhawk (42-105915/F-AZKU) [12]	Privately owned, la Ferté-Alais, France
	03-08003	B-V CH-47F Chinook [DT]	RAF Odiham, at main gate
	3-1923	Aeronca O-58B Defender (43-1923/G-BRHP)	Privately owned, Chiseldon
	18-2001	Piper L-18C Super Cub (52-2401/G-BIZV)	Privately owned, Wicklow, Ireland
	39-139	Beech YC-43 Traveler (N295BS)	Duke of Brabant AF, Eindhoven, The Netherlands
	40-2538	Fairchild PT-19A Cornell (N33870)	Privately owned, Mendlesham
	41-19393	Douglas A-20C Havoc (wreck)	WWII Remembrance Museum, Handcross, W Sussex
	41-33275	NA AT-6C Texan (G-BICE) [CE]	Privately owned, Great Oakley, Essex
	42-12417	Noorduyn AT-16 Harvard IIB (KLu. B-163)	Newark Air Museum, Winthorpe
	42-35870	Taylorcraft DCO-65 (G-BWLJ) [129]	Privately owned, Nayland
	42-58678	Taylorcraft DF-65 (G-BRIY) [IY]	Privately owned, Carlisle
	42-78044	Aeronca 11AC Chief (G-BRXL)	Privately owned, Andrewsfield
	42-84555	NA AT-6D Harvard III (FAP.1662/G-ELMH) [EP-H]	Privately owned, Hardwick, Norfolk
	42-93510	Douglas C-47A Skytrain [CM] <ff>	Privately owned, Kew
	43-9628	Douglas A-20G Havoc <ff>	Privately owned, Hinckley, Leics
	43-11137	Bell P-63C Kingcobra (wreck)	WWII Remembrance Museum, Handcross, W Sussex
	43-21664	Douglas A-20G Havoc (wreck)	WWII Remembrance Museum, Handcross, W Sussex
	43-35943	Beech 3N (G-BKRN) [943]	Beech Restorations, Bruntingthorpe
	43-36140	NA B-25J Mitchell <ff>	WWII Remembrance Museum, Handcross, W Sussex
	44-4315	Bell P-63C Kingcobra	WWII Remembrance Museum, Handcross, W Sussex
	44-4368	Bell P-63C Kingcobra	Privately owned, Surrey
	44-13954	NA P-51D Mustang (G-UAKE)	Mustang Restoration Co Ltd, Coventry
	44-14574	NA P-51D Mustang (fuselage)	East Essex Aviation Museum, Clacton
	44-42914	Douglas DC-4 (N31356)	Privately owned, stored North Weald
	44-51228	Consolidated B-24M Liberator [EC-493]	American Air Museum, Duxford
	44-79609	Piper L-4H Grasshopper (G-BHXY) [PR]	Privately owned, Bealbury, Cornwall
	44-80594	Piper L-4J Grasshopper (G-BEDJ)	Privately owned, White Waltham
	44-80647	Piper L-4J Grasshopper (D-EGAF)	The Vintage Aircraft Co, Fürstenwalde, Germany
	44-83184	Fairchild UC-61K Argus III (G-RGUS)	Privately owned, Sibson
	51-9036	Lockheed T-33A Shooting Star	Newark Air Museum, Winthorpe
	51-15319	Piper L-18C Super Cub (G-FUZZ) [A-319]	Privately owned, Elvington
	51-15555	Piper L-18C Super Cub (G-OSPS)	Privately owned, Weston, Eire
	52-8543	CCF T-6J Texan (G-BUKY) [66]	Privately owned, Duxford
	54-005	NA F-100D Super Sabre (54-2163)	Dumfries & Galloway Avn Mus, Dumfries
	54-174	NA F-100D Super Sabre (54-2174) [SM]	Midland Air Museum, Coventry
	54-2223	NA F-100D Super Sabre	Newark Air Museum, Winthorpe
	54-2445	Piper L-21B Super Cub (G-OTAN) [A-445]	Privately owned, Andrewsfield
	54-2447	Piper L-21B Super Cub (G-SCUB)	Privately owned, Anwick
	55-138354	NA T-28B Trojan (138354/N1328B) [TL-354]	Privately owned, Antwerp, Belgium
	62-428	Republic F-105G Thunderchief (62-4428) [WW]	USAF Croughton, Oxon, at gate
	63-699	McD F-4C Phantom II (63-7699) [CG]	Midland Air Museum, Coventry
	64-17657	Douglas B-26K Counter Invader (N99218) <ff>	WWII Remembrance Museum, Handcross, W Sussex
	65-777	McD F-4C Phantom II (63-7419) [SA]	RAF Lakenheath, on display
	65-10450	Northrop AT-38B Talon <rf>	Martin-Baker Ltd, Chalgrove, Fire Section
	67-120	GD F-111E Aardvark (67-0120) [UH]	American Air Museum, Duxford
	68-0060	GD F-111E Aardvark <ff>	Dumfries & Galloway Avn Mus, Dumfries
	68-8284	Sikorsky MH-53M Pave Low IV	RAF Museum, Cosford
	70-0389	GD F-111E Aardvark (68-0011) [LN]	RAF Lakenheath, on display
	72-1447	GD F-111F Aardvark <ff>	American Air Museum, Duxford

Serial	*Type (code/other identity)*	*Owner/operator location or fate*	*Notes*
74-0177	GD F-111F Aardvark [FN]	RAF Museum, Cosford	
76-020	McD F-15A Eagle (76-0020)	American Air Museum, Duxford	
76-124	McD F-15B Eagle (76-0124) [LN]	RAF Lakenheath, instructional use	
77-259	Fairchild A-10A Thunderbolt (77-0259) [AR]	American Air Museum, Duxford	
80-219	Fairchild GA-10A Thunderbolt (80-0219) [AR]	RAF Alconbury, on display	
82-23762	B-V CH-47D Chinook <ff>	RAF Odiham, instructional use	
83-24104	B-V CH-47D Chinook [BN] <ff>	RAF Museum, Hendon	
86-01677	B-V CH-47D Chinook	RAF Odiham, instructional use	
89-00159	B-V CH-47D Chinook	RAF Odiham, instructional use	
92-048	McD F-15A Eagle (74-0131) [LN]	RAF Lakenheath, on display	
108-1601	Stinson 108-1 Voyager (G-CFGE) [H]	Privately owned, Spanhoe	
146-11042	Wolf WII Boredom Fighter (G-BMZX) [7]	Privately owned, Tibenham	
146-11083	Wolf WII Boredom Fighter (G-BNAI) [5]	Privately owned, Haverfordwest	
G-57	Piper L-4A Grasshopper (42-36375/G-AKAZ)	Privately owned, Duxford	
X-17	Curtiss P-40F Warhawk (41-19841/G-CGZP)	The Fighter Collection, Duxford	
CY-D	NA TF-51D Mustang (44-84847/NX251RJ)	The Fighter Collection, Duxford	
CY-G	Titan T-51 Mustang (G-TSIM)	Privately owned, Hereford	
YEMEN			
104	BAC Jet Provost T.52A (G-PROV)	Privately owned, North Weald	
YUGOSLAVIA			
30131	Soko P-2 Kraguj [131]	Aircraft Restoration Group, Thirsk	
30139	Soko P-2 Kraguj [139]	Privately owned, Biggin Hill	
30140	Soko P-2 Kraguj (G-RADA) [140]	Privately owned, Biggin Hill	
30146	Soko P-2 Kraguj (G-BSXD) [146]	Privately owned, Linton-on-Ouse	
30149	Soko P-2 Kraguj (G-SOKO) [149]	Privately owned, Fenland	
30151	Soko P-2 Kraguj [151]	Privately owned, Linton-on-Ouse	

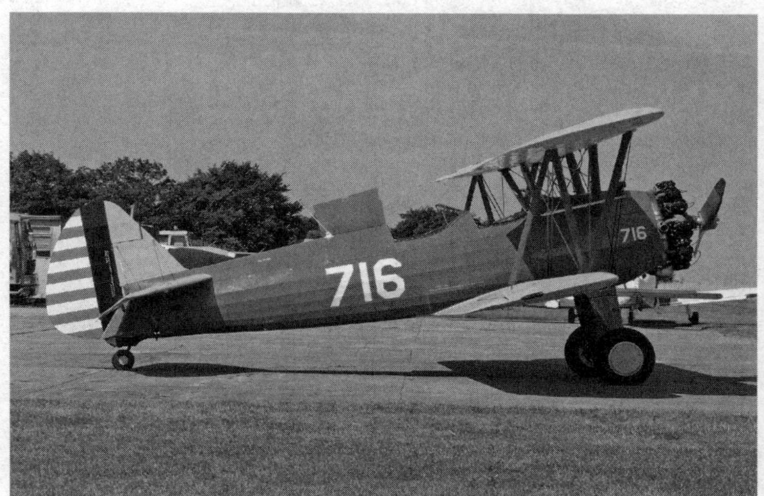

PT-13D Kaydet N1731B wears basic USAAF markings and the code 716. It is based at the beautiful Dorset hilltop airfield at Compton Abbas.

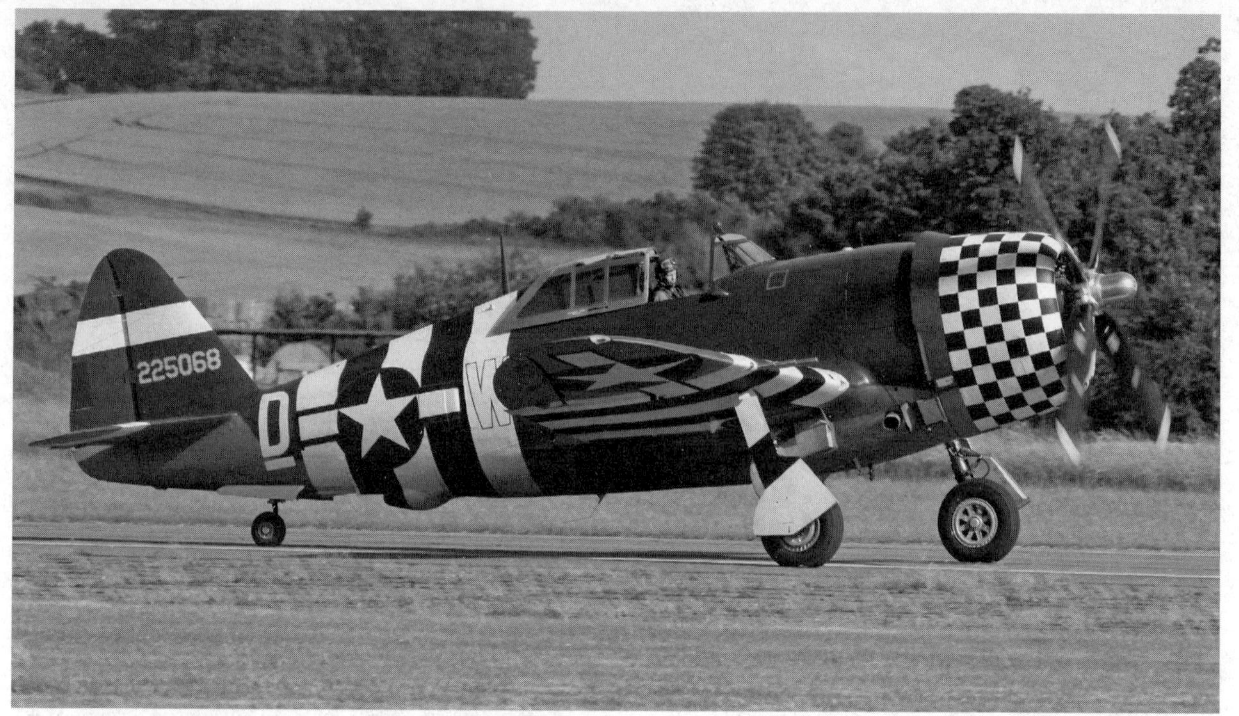

225068 is a Republic TP-47G Thunderbolt, owned by the Fighter Collection at Duxford and registered G-CDVX. One of only two Curtiss-built examples left in the World, she wears the scheme of the 84th Fighter Squadron's P-47D 'Snafu', the mount of Lt Severino B Calderon in late 1944. 2012 saw this magnificent machine take to the skies again.

F-15A Eagle 76-020 now wears the colours of the 5th Fighter Interceptor Squadron USAF which operated the type briefly in the 1980s. It stands guard outside the American Air Museum at Duxford.

Irish Military Aircraft Markings

Notes	Serial	Type (code/other identity)	Owner/operator location or fate
	C7	Avro 631 Cadet (EI-AGO)	IAC, Baldonnel
	34	Miles M14A Magister I (N5392)	National Museum of Ireland, Dublin
	141	Avro 652A Anson C19	IAC Museum, Baldonnel
	164	DHC1 Chipmunk T20	IAC Museum, Baldonnel
	168	DHC1 Chipmunk T20	IAC Museum, Baldonnel
	169	DHC1 Chipmunk 22 (G-ARGG)	Privately owned, Ballyboy
	170	DHC1 Chipmunk 22 (G-BDRJ)	Privately owned, Kilkerran
	172	DHC1 Chipmunk T20	IAC, stored Baldonnel
	173	DHC1 Chipmunk T20	South East Aviation Enthusiasts, Dromod
	176	DH104 Dove 4 (VP-YKF)	South East Aviation Enthusiasts, Waterford
	183	Percival P56 Provost T51	IAC Museum, Baldonnel
	184	Percival P56 Provost T51	South East Aviation Enthusiasts, Dromod
	187	DH115 Vampire T55	South East Aviation Enthusiasts, Dromod
	191	DH115 Vampire T55	IAC Museum, Baldonnel
	192	DH115 Vampire T55	South East Aviation Enthusiasts, Dromod
	195	Sud SA316 Alouette III (F-WJDH)	IAC Museum, Baldonnel
	198	DH115 Vampire T11 (XE977)	National Museum of Ireland, Dublin
	199	DHC1 Chipmunk T22	IAC, stored Baldonnel
	202	Sud SA316 Alouette III	Ulster Aviation Society, Long Kesh
	203	Reims-Cessna FR172H	IAC No 104 Sqn/1 Operations Wing, Baldonnel
	205	Reims-Cessna FR172H	IAC No 104 Sqn/1 Operations Wing, Baldonnel
	206	Reims-Cessna FR172H	IAC No 104 Sqn/1 Operations Wing, Baldonnel
	207	Reims-Cessna FR172H	IAC, stored Waterford
	208	Reims-Cessna FR172H	IAC No 104 Sqn/1 Operations Wing, Baldonnel
	210	Reims-Cessna FR172H	IAC No 104 Sqn/1 Operations Wing, Baldonnel
	215	Fouga CM170R Super Magister	Dublin Institute of Technology
	216	Fouga CM170R Super Magister	IAC Museum, Baldonnel
	218	Fouga CM170R Super Magister	Shannon Aerospace, Shannon Airport
	219	Fouga CM170R Super Magister	IAC Museum, Baldonnel
	220	Fouga CM170R Super Magister	Cork University, instructional use
	221	Fouga CM170R Super Magister [3-KE]	IAC Museum, stored Baldonnel
	231	SIAI SF-260WE Warrior	IAC Museum, stored Baldonnel
	240	Beech Super King Air 200MR	IAC No 102 Sqn/1 Operations Wing, Baldonnel
	251	Grumman G1159C Gulfstream IV (N17584)	IAC No 102 Sqn/1 Operations Wing, Baldonnel
	252	Airtech CN.235 MPA Persuader	IAC No 101 Sqn/1 Operations Wing, Baldonnel
	253	Airtech CN.235 MPA Persuader	IAC No 101 Sqn/1 Operations Wing, Baldonnel
	254	PBN-2T Defender 4000 (G-BWPN)	IAC No 106 Sqn/1 Operations Wing, Baldonnel
	256	Eurocopter EC135T-1 (G-BZRM)	IAC No 106 Sqn/1 Operations Wing, Baldonnel
	258	Gates Learjet 45 (N5009T)	IAC No 102 Sqn/1 Operations Wing, Baldonnel
	260	Pilatus PC-9M (HB-HQS)	IAC Flying Training School, Baldonnel
	261	Pilatus PC-9M (HB-HQT)	IAC Flying Training School, Baldonnel
	262	Pilatus PC-9M (HB-HQU)	IAC Flying Training School, Baldonnel
	263	Pilatus PC-9M (HB-HQV)	IAC Flying Training School, Baldonnel
	264	Pilatus PC-9M (HB-HQW)	IAC Flying Training School, Baldonnel
	266	Pilatus PC-9M (HB-HQY)	IAC Flying Training School, Baldonnel
	267	Pilatus PC-9M (HB-HQZ)	IAC Flying Training School, Baldonnel
	268	Pilatus PC-9M	IAC (option)
	269	Pilatus PC-9M	IAC (option)
	270	Eurocopter EC135P-2	IAC No 302 Sqn/3 Operations Wing, Baldonnel
	271	Eurocopter EC135P-2	IAC No 302 Sqn/3 Operations Wing, Baldonnel
	272	Eurocopter EC135T-2 (G-CECT)	IAC No 106 Sqn/1 Operations Wing, Baldonnel
	273	Eurocopter EC135P-2	IAC, on order
	274	AgustaWestland AW139	IAC No 301 Sqn/3 Operations Wing, Baldonnel
	275	AgustaWestland AW139	IAC No 301 Sqn/3 Operations Wing, Baldonnel
	276	AgustaWestland AW139	IAC No 301 Sqn/3 Operations Wing, Baldonnel
	277	AgustaWestland AW139	IAC No 301 Sqn/3 Operations Wing, Baldonnel
	278	AgustaWestland AW139	IAC No 301 Sqn/3 Operations Wing, Baldonnel
	279	AgustaWestland AW139	IAC No 301 Sqn/3 Operations Wing, Baldonnel

Aircraft included in this section include those likely to be seen visiting UK civil and military airfields on transport flights, exchange visits, exercises and for air shows. It is not a comprehensive list of *all* aircraft operated by the air arms concerned.

ALGERIA
Force Aérienne Algérienne/
Al Quwwat al Jawwiya al Jaza'eriya
Airbus A.340-541
Ministry of Defence, Boufarik
7T-VPP

Ilyushin
Il-76MD/Il-76TD/Il-78
347 Escadron de Transport Strategique, Boufarik;
357 Escadron de Ravitaillement en Vol, Boufarik

7T-WIA	Il-76MD	347 Esc
7T-WIB	Il-76MD	347 Esc
7T-WIC	Il-76MD	347 Esc
7T-WID	Il-76TD	347 Esc
7T-WIE	Il-76TD	347 Esc
7T-WIF	Il-78	357 Esc
7T-WIG	Il-76TD	347 Esc
7T-WIL	Il-78	357 Esc
7T-WIM	Il-76TD	347 Esc
7T-WIN	Il-78	357 Esc
7T-WIP	Il-76TD	347 Esc
7T-WIQ	Il-78	357 Esc
7T-WIR	Il-76TD	347 Esc
7T-WIS	Il-78	357 Esc
7T-WIT	Il-76TD	347 Esc
7T-WIU	Il-76TD	347 Esc
7T-WIV	Il-76TD	347 Esc

Lockheed
C-130H Hercules
2 Escadre de Transport Tactique et Logistique, Boufarik
7T-WHE (4935)
7T-WHF (4934)
7T-WHI (4930)
7T-WHJ (4928)
7T-WHQ (4926)
7T-WHR (4924)
7T-WHS (4912)
7T-WHT (4911)
7T-WHY (4913)
7T-WHZ (4914)

Lockheed
C-130H-30 Hercules
2 Escadre de Transport Tactique et Logistique, Boufarik
7T-WHB (5224)
7T-WHD (4987)
7T-WHL (4989)
7T-WHM (4919)
7T-WHN (4894)
7T-WHO (4897)
7T-WHP (4921)

Grumman
G.1159C Gulfstream IVSP
Ministry of Defence, Boufarik
7T-VPC (1418)
7T-VPM (1421)
7T-VPR (1288)
7T-VPS (1291)

Gulfstream Aerospace
Gulfstream V
Ministry of Defence, Boufarik
7T-VPG (617)

ARMENIA
Armenian Government
Airbus A.319CJ-132
Armenian Government, Yerevan
EK-RA01

AUSTRALIA
Royal Australian Air Force
Airbus A.330-203 MRTT
33 Sqn, Amberley
A39-001 (on order)
A39-002
A39-003
A39-004
A39-005 (on order)

Boeing
737-7DF/-7DT/-7ES AEW&C
34 Sqn, Canberra
A30-001 737-7ES
A30-002 737-7ES
A30-003 737-7ES
A30-004 737-7ES
A30-005 737-7ES
A30-006 737-7ES
A36-001 737-7DT
A36-002 737-7DF

Boeing
C-17A Globemaster III
36 Sqn, Amberley
A41-206
A41-207
A41-208
A41-209
A41-210
A41-211

Canadair
CL.604 Challenger
34 Sqn, Canberra
A37-001
A37-002
A37-003

Lockheed
C-130J-30 Hercules II
37 Sqn, Richmond, NSW
A97-440
A97-441
A97-442
A97-447
A97-448
A97-449
A97-450
A97-464
A97-465
A97-466
A97-467
A97-468

Lockheed
AP-3C Orion
10/11 Sqns, 92 Wing, Edinburgh, NSW
A9-656 10 Sqn
A9-657 11 Sqn
A9-658 10 Sqn
A9-659 11 Sqn
A9-660 11 Sqn
A9-661 10 Sqn
A9-662 11 Sqn
A9-663 11 Sqn
A9-664 11 Sqn
A9-665 10 Sqn
A9-751 11 Sqn
A9-752 10 Sqn
A9-753 10 Sqn
A9-755 10 Sqn
A9-756 11 Sqn
A9-757 10 Sqn
A9-758 10 Sqn
A9-759 10 Sqn
A9-760 10 Sqn

AUSTRIA
Öesterreichische Luftstreitkräfte
Agusta-Bell AB.212/Bell 212*
1. & 2. leichte Transporthubschrauberstaffel, Linz
5D-HB
5D-HC
5D-HD
5D-HF

5D-HG
5D-HH
5D-HI
5D-HJ
5D-HK
5D-HL
5D-HN
5D-HO
5D-HP
5D-HQ
5D-HR
5D-HS
5D-HT
5D-HU
5D-HV
5D-HW
5D-HX
5D-HY*
5D-HZ $

Bell
OH-58B Kiowa
Mehrzweckhubschrauberstaffel, Tulln
3C-OA
3C-OB
3C-OC
3C-OD
3C-OE
3C-OG
3C-OH
3C-OI
3C-OJ
3C-OK $
3C-OL

Eurofighter
EF.2000
Überwachungsgeschwader:
1.Staffel & 2.Staffel, Zeltweg
7L-WA
7L-WB
7L-WC $
7L-WD
7L-WE
7L-WF
7L-WG
7L-WH
7L-WI
7L-WJ
7L-WK
7L-WL
7L-WM
7L-WN
7L-WO

Lockheed
C-130K Hercules
Lufttransportstaffel, Linz
8T-CA
8T-CB
8T-CC

Pilatus
PC-6B/B2-H2 Turbo Porter/
PC-6B/B2-H4 Turbo Porter*
leichte Lufttransportstaffel, Tulln
3G-EB
3G-ED
3G-EE
3G-EF
3G-EG
3G-EH
3G-EL
3G-EN*

Pilatus
PC-7 Turbo Trainer
Lehrabteilung Fläche, Zeltweg
3H-FA
3H-FB
3H-FC
3H-FD
3H-FE
3H-FF
3H-FG $
3H-FH
3H-FJ
3H-FK
3H-FL
3H-FM
3H-FO

SAAB 105ÖE
Überwachungsgeschwader:
Düsentrainerstaffel, Linz
(yellow)
B (105402)
D (105404)
E (105405)
G (105407)
I (105409)
J (105410)
(green)
B (105412)
D (105414)
GF-16 (105416) $
GG-17 (105417)
(red)
B (105422)
C (105423)
D (105424)
E (105425)
RF-26 (105426) $
G (105427)
H (105428)
I (105429)
J (105430)
(blue)
A (105431)
B (105432)
C (105433)
D (105434)
E (105435)
F (105436)
G (105437)
J (105440)

Sikorsky S-70A
mittlere Transporthubschrauberstaffel, Tulln
6M-BA
6M-BB
6M-BC
6M-BD
6M-BE
6M-BF
6M-BG
6M-BH
6M-BI

AZERBAIJAN
Boeing 767-32LER
Azerbaijan Govt, Baku
4K-AI01

BAHRAIN
BAE RJ.85/RJ.100*
Bahrain Defence Force
A9C-AWL*
A9C-BDF*
A9C-HWR

Boeing 747SP-Z5
Bahrain Amiri Flt
A9C-HAK

Boeing 747-4P8
Bahrain Amiri Flt
A9C-HMK

Boeing 767-4SFER
Bahrain Amiri Flt
A9C-HMH

Grumman
G.1159 Gulfstream IITT/
G.1159C Gulfstream IV-SP
Govt of Bahrain
A9C-BAH Gulfstream IV-SP
A9C-BG Gulfstream IITT

Gulfstream Aerospace
G.450
Govt of Bahrain
A9C-BHR

Gulfstream Aerospace
G.550
Govt of Bahrain
A9C-BRN

BELGIUM
Composante Aérienne Belge/
Belgische Luchtcomponent
D-BD Alpha Jet E
11 Smaldeel (1 Wg),

Cazaux, France (ET 02.008)
AT-01
AT-02
AT-03
AT-05
AT-06
AT-08
AT-10
AT-11
AT-12
AT-13
AT-14
AT-15
AT-17
AT-18
AT-19
AT-20
AT-21
AT-22
AT-23
AT-24
AT-25
AT-26
AT-27
AT-28
AT-29
AT-30
AT-31
AT-32$
AT-33

Airbus A.330-321
21 Smaldeel (15 Wg), Melsbroek
CS-TMT

Dassault
Falcon 900B
21 Smaldeel (15 Wg), Melsbroek
CD-01

Embraer
ERJ.135LR/ERJ.145LR*
21 Smaldeel (15 Wg), Melsbroek
CE-01
CE-02
CE-03* $
CE-04*

Lockheed
C-130H Hercules
20 Smaldeel (15 Wg), Melsbroek
CH-01
CH-03
CH-04
CH-05
CH-07 $
CH-08
CH-09
CH-10
CH-11
CH-12
CH-13

Dassault
Falcon 20-5
21 Smaldeel (15 Wg), Melsbroek
CM-01 $
CM-02

General Dynamics
F-16 MLU
1,350 Smaldeel (2 Wg), Florennes [FS];
31,349 Smaldeel, OCU (10 Wg), Kleine-Brogel [BL]

FA-56	F-16A	10 Wg
FA-57	F-16A	2 Wg
FA-67	F-16A	2 Wg
FA-68	F-16A	2 Wg $
FA-69	F-16A	10 Wg
FA-70	F-16A	10 Wg
FA-71	F-16A	2 Wg
FA-72	F-16A	2 Wg
FA-77	F-16A	2 Wg
FA-81	F-16A	10 Wg
FA-82	F-16A	10 Wg
FA-83	F-16A	2 Wg
FA-84	F-16A	2 Wg $
FA-86	F-16A	10 Wg
FA-87	F-16A	10 Wg $
FA-89	F-16A	2 Wg
FA-91	F-16A	2 Wg
FA-92	F-16A	2 Wg
FA-94	F-16A	10 Wg
FA-95	F-16A	10 Wg
FA-97	F-16A	10 Wg
FA-98	F-16A	2 Wg
FA-101	F-16A	2 Wg
FA-102	F-16A	10 Wg
FA-103	F-16A	10 Wg
FA-104	F-16A	10 Wg
FA-106	F-16A	10 Wg
FA-107	F-16A	10 Wg
FA-109	F-16A	2 Wg
FA-110	F-16A	10 Wg $
FA-114	F-16A	10 Wg
FA-116	F-16A	10 Wg
FA-117	F-16A	2 Wg
FA-118	F-16A	10 Wg
FA-119	F-16A	10 Wg
FA-121	F-16A	10 Wg $
FA-123	F-16A	10 Wg
FA-124	F-16A	10 Wg
FA-126	F-16A	2 Wg
FA-127	F-16A	2 Wg
FA-128	F-16A	2 Wg
FA-129	F-16A	2 Wg
FA-130	F-16A	2 Wg
FA-131	F-16A	10 Wg
FA-132	F-16A	10 Wg
FA-133	F-16A	2 Wg
FA-134	F-16A	10 Wg
FA-135	F-16A	10 Wg
FA-136	F-16A	10 Wg
FB-12	F-16B	2 Wg
FB-14	F-16B	10 Wg
FB-15	F-16B	10 Wg
FB-17	F-16B	10 Wg
FB-18	F-16B	10 Wg
FB-20	F-16B	10 Wg
FB-21	F-16B	2 Wg
FB-22	F-16B	2 Wg
FB-23	F-16B	10 Wg
FB-24	F-16B	10 Wg $

Agusta A109HA/HO*
17 Smaldeel MRH (1 Wg), Beauvechain;
18 Smaldeel MRH (1 Wg), Beauvechain;
SLV (1 Wg), Beauvechain

H-01*	SLV
H-05*	18 Sm MRH
H-20	17 Sm MRH
H-21	18 Sm MRH
H-22	17 Sm MRH
H-23	17 Sm MRH
H-24	17 Sm MRH $
H-25	18 Sm MRH
H-26	18 Sm MRH
H-27	18 Sm MRH
H-28	17 Sm MRH
H-29	18 Sm MRH
H-30	17 Sm MRH
H-31	18 Sm MRH
H-33	18 Sm MRH
H-35	18 Sm MRH
H-36	17 Sm MRH
H-38	17 Sm MRH
H-40	18 Sm MRH
H-41	17 Sm MRH
H-42	SLV
H-44	17 Sm MRH
H-45	17 Sm MRH
H-46	17 Sm MRH

Piper L-21B Super Cub
Centre Militaire de Vol à Voile
Bases: Florennes, Goetsenhoeven & Zoersel
LB-01
LB-02
LB-03
LB-05

Sud
SA.316B Alouette III
40 Smaldeel, Koksijde
M-1
M-2
M-3

NH Industries
NH.90-NFH/NH.90-TTH*
40 Smaldeel, Koksijde
RN-01
RN-02 (on order)

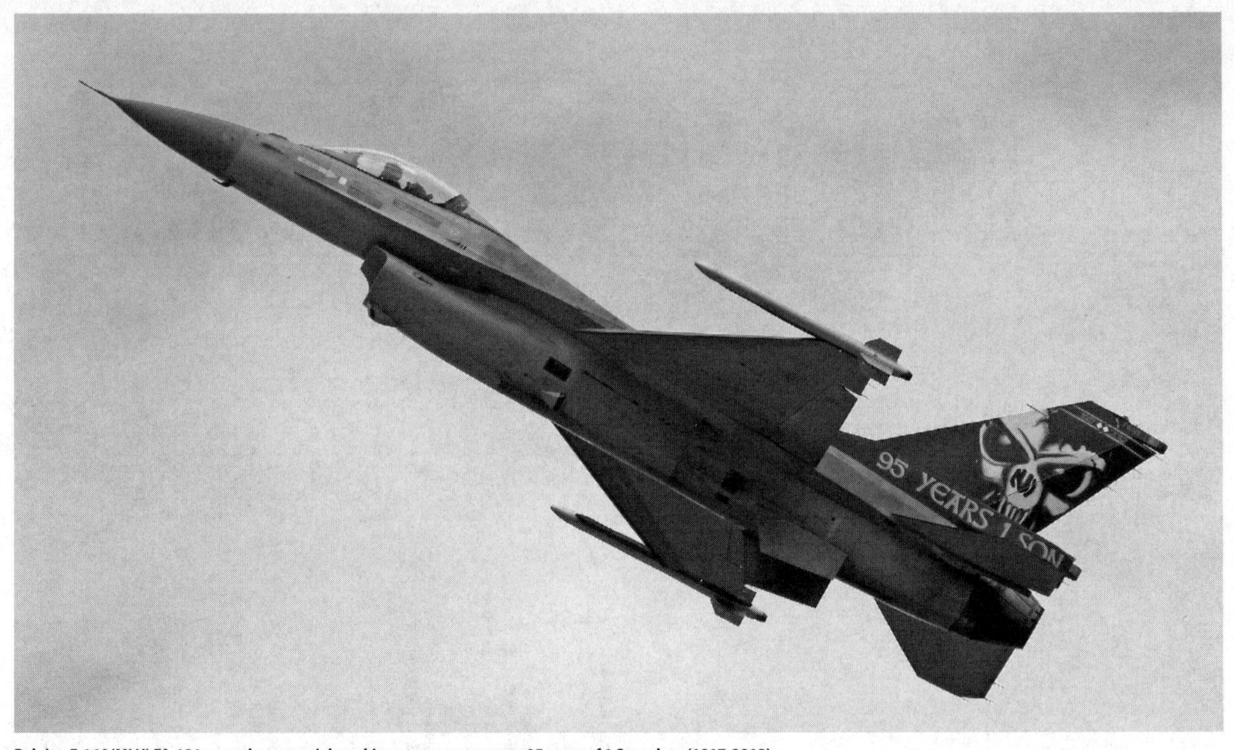

Belgian F-16A(MLU) FA-121 wore these special markings to commemorate 95 years of 1 Squadron (1917-2012).

Agusta 109HA H-24 wore a black dragon design to denote 20 years of flying the A109, making it somewhat distictive in comparison to its drab compatriots.

RN-03 (on order)
RN-04 (on order)
RN-05* (on order)
RN-06* (on order)
RN-07* (on order)
RN-08* (on order)

Westland Sea King Mk48/48A*
40 Smaldeel, Koksijde
RS-02
RS-03*
RS-04
RS-05$

SIAI Marchetti SF260D/SF260M+
Centre of Competence Air, Bevekom (5 Smaldeel & 9 Smaldeel);
Red Devils *
ST-02 SF-260M+ *
ST-03 SF-260M+ *
ST-04 SF-260M+ *
ST-06 SF-260M+
ST-12 SF-260M+
ST-15 SF-260M+ *
ST-16 SF-260M+
ST-17 SF-260M+
ST-18 SF-260M+
ST-19 SF-260M+
ST-20 SF-260M+
ST-22 SF-260M+
ST-23 SF-260M+ *
ST-24 SF-260M+
ST-25 SF-260M+
ST-26 SF-260M+
ST-27 SF-260M+ *
ST-30 SF-260M+ $
ST-31 SF-260M+
ST-32 SF-260M+ *
ST-34 SF-260M+
ST-35 SF-260M+
ST-36 SF-260M+
ST-40 SF-260D $
ST-41 SF-260D *
ST-42 SF-260D
ST-43 SF-260D
ST-44 SF-260D
ST-45 SF-260D
ST-46 SF-260D
ST-47 SF-260D
ST-48 SF-260D $

Police Fédérale/Federal Politie
Cessna 182 Skylane
Luchsteundetachment, Melsbroek
G-01 C.182Q
G-04 C.182R

MDH
MD.520N
Luchsteundetachment, Melsbroek
G-14
G-15

MDH
MD.900/MD.902* Explorer
Luchsteundetachment, Melsbroek
G-10
G-11
G-12
G-16*

BOTSWANA
Botswana Defence Force
Bombardier Global Express
VIP Sqn, Sir Seretse Kharma IAP, Gaborone
OK1

Lockheed C-130B Hercules
Z10 Sqn, Thebephatshwa
OM-1
OM-2
OM-3

BRAZIL
Força Aérea Brasileira
Airbus A.319-133CJ (VC-1A)
1° GT, 1° Esq, Galeão;
2101

Boeing KC-137
2° GT, 2° Esq, Galeão
2401
2402
2403
2404

Embraer EMB.190-190IGW (VC-2)
1° Grupo de Transport Especial, 1° Esq, Brasilia
2590
2591
2592

Lockheed C-130 Hercules
1° GT, 1° Esq, Galeão;
1° GTT, 1° Esq, Afonsos
2451 C-130E 1° GTT
2453 C-130M 1° GTT
2454 C-130E 1° GTT
2456 C-130E 1° GTT
2459 SC-130E 1° GTT
2461 KC-130H 1° GT
2462 KC-130H 1° GT
2463 C-130H 1° GT
2464 C-130H 1° GT
2465 C-130M 1° GT
2466 C-130M 1° GT
2467 C-130H 1° GT
2470 C-130M 1° GT
2472 C-130H 1° GT
2473 C-130H 1° GT
2474 C-130H 1° GT
2475 C-130H 1° GT
2476 C-130M 1° GTT
2479 C-130H 1° GT

BRUNEI
Airbus A.340-212
Brunei Govt, Bandar Seri Bergawan
V8-BKH

Boeing 747-430
Brunei Govt, Bandar Seri Bergawan
V8-ALI

Boeing 767-27GER
Brunei Govt, Bandar Seri Begawan
V8-MHB

BULGARIA
Bulgarsky Voenno-Vazdushni Sily
Aeritalia C-27J Spartan
16 TAB, Sofia/Vrazhdebna
071
072
073

Antonov An-30
16 TAP, Sofia/Dobroslavtzi
055

Pilatus PC.XII/45
16 TAP, Sofia/Dobroslavtzi
020

Bulgarian Govt
Airbus A.319-112
Bulgarian Govt/BH Air, Sofia
LZ-AOA
LZ-AOB

Dassault Falcon 2000
Bulgarian Govt, Sofia
LZ-OOI

Tupolev Tu-154M
Bulgarian Govt, Sofia
LZ-BTZ

BURKINA FASO
Boeing 727-282
Govt of Burkina Faso, Ouagadougou
XT-BFA

CAMEROON
Grumman
G.1159A Gulfstream III
Govt of Cameroon, Yaounde
TJ-AAW

CANADA
Royal Canadian Air Force
Lockheed
CC-130 Hercules
CC-130E/CC-130E(SAR)*
413 Sqn, Greenwood (SAR) (14 Wing);
424 Sqn, Trenton (SAR) (8 Wing);
426 Sqn, Trenton (8 Wing);
435 Sqn, Winnipeg (17 Wing);
436 Sqn, Trenton (8 Wing)
130305* 14 Wing
130308* 8 Wing
130319 8 Wing
130323 8 Wing
130327 8 Wing
130328 8 Wing
CC-130H/CC-130H(SAR)+/ CC-130H(T)*
130332 8 Wing
130333+ 8 Wing
130334+ 14 Wing
130335 8 Wing
130336 8 Wing
130337* 8 Wing
130338* 17 Wing
130339* 17 Wing
130340* 17 Wing
130341* 17 Wing
CC-130H-30
130343 8 Wing
130344 8 Wing
CC-130J Hercules II
130601 8 Wing
130602 8 Wing
130603 8 Wing
130604 8 Wing
130605 8 Wing
130606 8 Wing
130607 8 Wing
130608 8 Wing
130609 8 Wing
130610 8 Wing
130611 8 Wing
130612 8 Wing
130613 8 Wing
130614 8 Wing
130615 8 Wing
130616 8 Wing
130617 8 Wing

Lockheed
CP-140 Aurora
404 Sqn, Greenwood (14 Wing);
405 Sqn, Greenwood (14 Wing);
407 Sqn, Comox (19 Wing)
140101 14 Wing
140102 14 Wing
140103 14 Wing
140104 14 Wing
140105 14 Wing
140106 407 Sqn
140107 407 Sqn
140108 14 Wing
140109 14 Wing
140110 14 Wing
140111 14 Wing
140112 407 Sqn
140113 14 Wing
140114 14 Wing
140115 407 Sqn
140116 14 Wing
140117 407 Sqn
140118 407 Sqn

De Havilland Canada
CT-142
402 Sqn, Winnipeg (17 Wing)
142803 CT-142
142804 CT-142
142805 CT-142
142806 CT-142

Canadair
CC-144 Challenger
412 Sqn, Ottawa (8 Wing)
144601 CC-144A
144614 CC-144B
144615 CC-144B
144616 CC-144B
144617 CC-144C
144618 CC-144C

Airbus
CC-150 Polaris (A310-304/A310-304F*)
437 Sqn, Trenton (8 Wing)
15001 [991]
15002* [992]
15003* [993]
15004* [994]
15005* [995]

Boeing
CC-177 (C-17A Globemaster III)
429 Sqn, Trenton (8 Wing)
177701
177702
177703
177704

CHAD
Boeing 737-74Q
Chad Government, N'djamena
TT-ABD

CHILE
Fuerza Aérea de Chile
Boeing 707
Grupo 10, Santiago
902 707-351C
903 707-330B
904 707-358C

Boeing 737
Grupo 10, Santiago
921 737-58N
922 737-330

Boeing 767-3Y0ER
Grupo 10, Santiago
985

Boeing
KC-135E Stratotanker
Grupo 10, Santiago
981
982
983

Extra EA-300L
Los Halcones
145 [2]
146 [5]
149 [1]
1268 [3]

Grumman
G.1159C Gulfstream IV
Grupo 10, Santiago
911

Lockheed
C-130H Hercules
Grupo 10, Santiago
995
996

CROATIA
Hrvatske Zračne Snage
Pilatus PC-9*/PC-9M
92 ZB, Pula;
93 ZB, Zadar
051* 93 ZB
052* 93 ZB
053* 93 ZB
054 93 ZB
055 93 ZB
056 93 ZB
057 93 ZB
058 93 ZB
059 93 ZB
060 93 ZB
061 93 ZB
062 93 ZB
063 93 ZB
064 93 ZB
065 93 ZB

066 93 ZB
067 92 ZB
068 93 ZB
069 93 ZB
070 93 ZB

Canadair
CL.601 Challenger
Croatian Govt, Zagreb
9A-CRO
9A-CRT

CZECH REPUBLIC
Ceske Vojenske Letectvo
Aero L-39/L-59 Albatros
222.TL/22.zL, Náměšt;
CLV, Pardubice
0103 L-39C CLV
0106 L-39C CLV
0107 L-39C CLV
0108 L-39C CLV
0113 L-39C CLV
0115 L-39C CLV
0441 L-39C CLV
0444 L-39C CLV
0445 L-39C CLV
2344 L-39ZA 222.TL/22.zL
2415 L-39ZA 222.TL/22.zL
2421 L-39ZA 222.TL/22.zL
2433 L-39ZA 222.TL/22.zL $
2436 L-39ZA 222.TL/22.zL
3903 L-39ZA 222.TL/22.zL
5015 L-39ZA 222.TL/22.zL
5017 L-39ZA 222.TL/22.zL
5019 L-39ZA 222.TL/22.zL

Aero
L-159A ALCA/L-159B/L-159T-1
212.TL/21.zTL, Cáslav;
LZO, Praha/Kbely
L-159A
6048 212.TL/21.zTL
6049 212.TL/21.zTL
6050 212.TL/21.zTL
6051 212.TL/21.zTL
6052 212.TL/21.zTL
6053 212.TL/21.zTL
6054 212.TL/21.zTL
6055 212.TL/21.zTL
6057 212.TL/21.zTL
6058 212.TL/21.zTL
6059 212.TL/21.zTL
6060 212.TL/21.zTL
6061 212.TL/21.zTL
6062 212.TL/21.zTL
6063 212.TL/21.zTL
6064 212.TL/21.zTL
6065 212.TL/21.zTL
6066 212.TL/21.zTL $
6068 212.TL/21.zTL
6070 212.TL/21.zTL

L-159B
5831 LZO
5832 LZO
6069 212.TL/21.zTL
6073 212.TL/21.zTL
L-159T-1
6046 212.TL/21.zTL
6047 212.TL/21.zTL
6067 212.TL/21.zTL$
6075 212.TL/21.zTL

Airbus A.319CJ-115X
241.dlt/24.zDL, Praha/Kbely
2801
3085

Canadair
CL.601-3A Challenger
241.dlt/24.zDL, Praha/Kbely
5105

CASA C-295M
242.dl/24.zDL, Praha/Kbely
0452
0453
0454
0455

Evektor
EV-55M Outback
Evektor, Kunovice
0458

LET 410 Turbolet
242.dl/24.zDL, Praha/Kbely;
CLV, Pardubice
0731 L-410UVP-E CLV
0928 L-410UVP-T CLV
1504 L-410UVP 242.dl
1526 L-410FG 242.dl
2601 L-410UVP-E 242.dl
2602 L-410UVP-E 242.dl

Mil Mi-17/
Mi-171Sh*
231.vrl/23.zVrL, Přerov;
CLV, Pardubice
0803 231.vrl/23.zVrL
0811 231.vrl/23.zVrL
0828 231.vrl/23.zVrL
0832 231.vrl/23.zVrL
0834 231.vrl/23.zVrL
0835 231.vrl/23.zVrL
0836 CLV
0837 CLV
0839 231.vrl/23.zVrL
0840 231.vrl/23.zVrL
0848 231.vrl/23.zVrL
0849 231.vrl/23.zVrL
0850 231.vrl/23.zVrL
9767* 231.vrl/23.zVrL
9774* 231.vrl/23.zVrL
9781* 231.vrl/23.zVrL
9799* 231.vrl/23.zVrL
9806* 231.vrl/23.zVrL
9813* 231.vrl/23.zVrL
9825* 231.vrl/23.zVrL
9837* 231.vrl/23.zVrL
9844* 231.vrl/23.zVrL
9868* 231.vrl/23.zVrL
9873* 231.vrl/23.zVrL
9887* 231.vrl/23.zVrL
9892* 231.vrl/23.zVrL
9904* 231.vrl/23.zVrL
9915* 231.vrl/23.zVrL
9926* 231.vrl/23.zVrL

Mil Mi-24/Mi-35
221.lbvr/22.zL, Náměšt
0981 Mi-24V2
3361 Mi-35
3362 Mi-35
3365 Mi-35
3366 Mi-35
3367 Mi-35
3368 Mi-35
3369 Mi-35
3370 Mi-35
3371 Mi-35
7353 Mi-24V $
7354 Mi-24V
7355 Mi-24V
7356 Mi-24V
7357 Mi-24V
7360 Mi-24V

SAAB Gripen
211.TL/21.zTL, Cáslav
JAS 39C
9234
9235
9236
9237
9238
9239
9240
9241
9242
9243
9244
9245
JAS 39D
9819 $
9820 $

Yakovlev Yak-40
241.dlt/24.zDL, Praha/Kbely
0260 Yak-40
1257 Yak-40K

DENMARK
Flyvevåbnet
Lockheed
C-130J-30 Hercules II
Eskadrille 721, Aalborg
B-536
B-537
B-538
B-583

Canadair
CL.604 Challenger
Eskadrille 721, Aalborg
C-080
C-168 $
C-172

General Dynamics
F-16 MLU
Eskadrille 727, Skrydstrup;
Eskadrille 730, Skrydstrup;
416th FTS/412th TW, Edwards AFB, USA
E-004 F-16A Esk 727
E-005 F-16A Esk 727
E-006 F-16A Esk 727
E-007 F-16A Esk 727
E-008 F-16A Esk 727
E-011 F-16A Esk 727
E-016 F-16A Esk 727
E-017 F-16A Esk 727
E-018 F-16A Esk 730
E-024 F-16A Esk 727
E-070 F-16A Esk 727
E-074 F-16A Esk 730
E-075 F-16A Esk 727
E-107 F-16A Esk 727
E-189 F-16A Esk 730
E-190 F-16A Esk 727
E-191 F-16A Esk 730
E-194 F-16A Esk 730 $
E-596 F-16A Esk 730
E-597 F-16A Esk 730
E-598 F-16A Esk 730
E-599 F-16A Esk 727
E-600 F-16A Esk 730
E-601 F-16A Esk 730
E-602 F-16A Esk 730
E-603 F-16A Esk 730
E-604 F-16A Esk 730
E-605 F-16A Esk 727
E-606 F-16A Esk 730
E-607 F-16A Esk 727
E-608 F-16A Esk 730
E-609 F-16A Esk 727
E-610 F-16A Esk 730
E-611 F-16A Esk 727
ET-022 F-16B Esk 730
ET-197 F-16B Esk 727
ET-198 F-16B Esk 730
ET-199 F-16B Esk 730
ET-207 F-16B Esk 727
ET-208 F-16B Esk 730
ET-210 F-16B 412th TW
ET-612 F-16B Esk 727
ET-613 F-16B Esk 727
ET-614 F-16B Esk 727
ET-615 F-16B Esk 727

AgustaWestland
EH.101 Mk.512
Eskadrille 722, Karup
Detachments at:
Aalborg, Roskilde, Ronne, Skrydstrup
M-502
M-504
M-507
M-508
M-510
M-512
M-513
M-514
M-515
M-516
M-517
M-518
M-519
M-520

Aérospatiale
AS.550C-2 Fennec
Eskadrille 724, Karup
P-090
P-234
P-254
P-275
P-276
P-287
P-288
P-319
P-320
P-339
P-352
P-369

Westland Lynx
Mk 90B
Eskadrille 723, Karup
S-134
S-142
S-170
S-175
S-181
S-191
S-256

SAAB
T-17 Supporter
Aalborg Stn Flt;
Eskadrille 721, Aalborg;
Flyveskolen, Karup (FLSK);
Skrydstrup Stn Flt
T-401 FLSK
T-402 FLSK
T-403 FLSK
T-404 FLSK
T-405 Skrydstrup
T-407 Esk 721
T-409 Aalborg
T-410 FLSK
T-411 Skrydstrup
T-412 FLSK
T-413 FLSK
T-414 Esk 721
T-415 FLSK
T-417 FLSK
T-418 Esk 721
T-419 FLSK
T-420 FLSK
T-421 FLSK
T-423 FLSK
T-425 FLSK
T-426 FLSK
T-427 FLSK
T-428 FLSK
T-429 Skrydstrup
T-430 FLSK
T-431 Esk 721
T-432 Skrydstrup

ECUADOR
Fuerza Aérea Ecuatoriana
Embraer
ERJ.135 Legacy 600
Escuadrón de Transporte 1114,
Quito
FAE-051

EGYPT
Al Quwwat al-Jawwiya
il Misriya
Lockheed
C-130H/C-130H-30* Hercules
16 Sqn, Cairo West
1271/SU-BAB
1273/SU-BAD
1274/SU-BAE
1275/SU-BAF
1277/SU-BAI
1278/SU-BAJ
1279/SU-BAK
1280/SU-BAL
1281/SU-BAM
1282/SU-BAN
1283/SU-BAP
1284/SU-BAQ
1285/SU-BAR
1286/SU-BAS
1287/SU-BAT
1288/SU-BAU
1289/SU-BAV
1290/SU-BEW
1291/SU-BEX
1292/SU-BEY
1293/SU-BKS*
1294/SU-BKT*
1295/SU-BKU*

1296/SU-BPJ
1297/SU-BKW
1298/SU-BKX

Egyptian Govt
Airbus A.340-211
Egyptian Govt, Cairo
SU-GGG

Cessna 680
Citation Sovereign
Egyptian Govt, Cairo
SU-BRF
SU-BRG

Grumman
G.1159A Gulfstream III/
G.1159C Gulfstream IV/
G.1159C Gulfstream IV-SP/
Gulfstream 400
Egyptian Air Force/Govt,
Cairo
SU-BGM Gulfstream IV
SU-BGU Gulfstream III
SU-BGV Gulfstream III
SU-BNC Gulfstream IV
SU-BND Gulfstream IV
SU-BNO Gulfstream IV-SP
SU-BNP Gulfstream IV-SP
SU-BPE Gulfstream 400
SU-BPF Gulfstream 400

FINLAND
Suomen Ilmavoimat
CASA C-295M
Tukilentolaivue,
Jyväskylä/Tikkakoski
CC-1
CC-2
CC-3

Fokker
F.27 Friendship
Tukilentolaivue,
Jyväskylä/Tikkakoski
FF-1 F.27-100
FF-3 F.27-400M

McDonnell Douglas
F-18 Hornet
Hävittäjälentolaivue 11,
Roveniemi;
Hävittäjälentolaivue 21,
Tampere/Pirkkala;
Hävittäjälentolaivue 31,
Kuopio/Rissala;
Koelentokeskus,
Halli
F-18C Hornet
HN-401 HavLLv 21
HN-402 HavLLv 11
HN-403 KoeLntk
HN-404 HavLLv 21
HN-405 HavLLv 31
HN-406 HavLLv 11
HN-407 HavLLv 11
HN-408 HavLLv 31
HN-409 HavLLv 11
HN-410 HavLLv 11
HN-411 HavLLv 11
HN-412 HavLLv 21
HN-413 HavLLv 21
HN-414 KoeLntk
HN-415 HavLLv 21
HN-416 HavLLv 11
HN-417 HavLLv 21
HN-418 HavLLv 31
HN-419 HavLLv 31
HN-420 KoeLntk
HN-421 HavLLv 21
HN-422 HavLLv 21
HN-423 HavLLv 11
HN-424 HavLLv 31
HN-425 HavLLv 11
HN-426 HavLLv 31
HN-427 HavLLv 21
HN-428 HavLLv 21
HN-429 HavLLv 21
HN-431 HavLLv 31
HN-432 HavLLv 21
HN-433 HavLLv 31
HN-434 HavLLv 21
HN-435 HavLLv 21
HN-436 HavLLv 31
HN-437 HavLLv 11
HN-438 HavLLv 21
HN-439 HavLLv 31
HN-440 HavLLv 21
HN-441 HavLLv 21
HN-442 HavLLv 21
HN-443 HavLLv 21
HN-444 HavLLv 11
HN-445 HavLLv 31
HN-446 HavLLv 21
HN-447 HavLLv 21
HN-448 HavLLv 31
HN-449 HavLLv 21
HN-450 HavLLv 21
HN-451 HavLLv 21
HN-452 HavLLv 11
HN-453 HavLLv 31
HN-454 HavLLv 31
HN-455 HavLLv 21
HN-456 HavLLv 11
HN-457 HavLLv 31
F-18D Hornet
HN-461 HavLLv 21
HN-462 KoeLntk
HN-463 HavLLv 21
HN-464 HavLLv 21
HN-465 HavLLv 11
HN-466 KoeLntk
HN-467 HavLLv 21

BAe Hawk 51/51A/66
Hävittäjälentolaivue 41,
Kauhava;
Koelentokeskus,
Halli
Hawk 51
HW-301 HavLLv 41
HW-303 HavLLv 41
HW-304 HavLLv 41
HW-306 HavLLv 41
HW-307 HavLLv 41
HW-308 HavLLv 41
HW-309 HavLLv 41
HW-310 HavLLv 41
HW-311 HavLLv 41
HW-312 HavLLv 41
HW-314 HavLLv 41
HW-315 HavLLv 41
HW-316 HavLLv 41
HW-318 HavLLv 41
HW-319 KoeLntk
HW-320 HavLLv 41
HW-321 KoeLntk
HW-322 HavLLv 41
HW-326 HavLLv 41
HW-327 HavLLv 41
HW-328 HavLLv 41
HW-329 HavLLv 41
HW-330 HavLLv 41
HW-331 HavLLv 41
HW-332 HavLLv 41
HW-333 HavLLv 41
HW-334 HavLLv 41
HW-337 HavLLv 41
HW-338 HavLLv 41
HW-339 HavLLv 41
HW-340 HavLLv 41
HW-341 HavLLv 41
HW-342 KoeLntk
HW-343 HavLLv 41
HW-344 HavLLv 41
HW-345 HavLLv 41
HW-346 HavLLv 41
HW-349 HavLLv 41
HW-350 HavLLv 41
Hawk 51A
HW-351 HavLLv 41
HW-352 HavLLv 41
HW-353 HavLLv 41
HW-354 HavLLv 41
HW-355 HavLLv 41
HW-356 HavLLv 41
HW-357 HavLLv 41
Hawk 66
HW-360
HW-361
HW-362
HW-363 HavLLv 41
HW-364
HW-365
HW-366
HW-367

HW-368
HW-369
HW-370
HW-371
HW-372 HavLLv 41
HW-373 HavLLv 41
HW-374 HavLLv 41
HW-375
HW-376 HavLLv 41
HW-377

Gates
Learjet 35A
Tukilentolaivue,
Jyväskylä/Tikkakoski;
Tukilentolaivue (Det.),
Kuopio/Rissala*
LJ-1*
LJ-2
LJ-3

FRANCE
Armée de l'Air
Airbus A.310-304
ET 03.060 *Esterel*,
Paris/Charles de Gaulle
418 F-RADC
421 F-RADA
422 F-RADB

Airbus A.330-223
ETEC 00.065, Evreux
240 (F-RARF)

Airbus A.340-212
ET 03.060 *Esterel*,
Paris/Charles de Gaulle
075 F-RAJA
081 F-RAJB

Airbus Military A.400M
ET 01.061 *Touraine* &
Orléans
... (on order)

Airtech CN-235M-200/-300*
ET 01.062 *Vercours*, Creil;
ET 03.062 *Ventoux*, Creil;
ET 00.052 *La Tontouta*, Noumea;
ET 00.058 *Antilles*, Fort de France;
ET 00.082 *Maine*, Faaa-Tahiti
045 62-IB 01.062
065 82-IC 00.082
066 52-ID 00.052
071 62-IE 01.062
072 62-IF 01.062
105 52-IG 00.052
107 52-IH 00.052
111 62-II 01.062
114 62-IJ 01.062
123 62-IM 01.062
128 62-IK 01.062
129 62-IL 01.062
137 62-IN 01.062
141 62-IO 00.058
152 62-IP 01.062
156 62-IQ 01.062
158 62-IR 01.062
160 62-IS 01.062
165 62-IT 01.062
193* 62-HA 03.062
194* 62-HB 03.062
195* 62-HC 03.062
196* 62-HD 03.062
197* 62-HE 03.062
198* 62-HF 03.062 (on order)
199* 62-HG 03.062 (on order)
200* 62-HH 03.062 (on order)

Boeing C-135 Stratotanker
GRV 02.093 *Bretagne*, Istres
470 C-135FR 93-CA
471 C-135FR 93-CB
472 C-135FR 93-CC
474 C-135FR 93-CE
475 C-135FR 93-CF
497 KC-135R 93-CM$
525 KC-135R 93-CN
574 KC-135R 93-CP
735 C-135FR 93-CG
736 C-135FR 93-CH
737 C-135FR 93-CI
738 C-135FR 93-CJ
739 C-135FR 93-CK
740 C-135FR 93-CL

Boeing E-3F Sentry
EDCA 00.036, Avord (BA 702)
201 702-CA
202 702-CB
203 702-CC
204 702-CD

CASA 212-300 Aviocar
DGA EV, Cazaux & Istres
378 MP
386 MQ

Cessna 310
DGA EV, Cazaux & Istres
190 310N BL
193 310N BG
194 310N BH
513 310N BE
569 310R CS
820 310Q CL
981 310Q BF

D-BD Alpha Jet
AMD-BA, Istres;
CEAM (EC 05.330),
Mont-de-Marsan (BA 118);
DGA EV, Cazaux (BA 120) & Istres (BA 125);
EAC 00.314, Tours (BA 705);
EE 02.002 *Côte d'Or*,
Dijon/Longvic (BA 102);
EPNER, Istres (BA 125);
ETO 01.008 *Saintonge*
& ETO 02.008 *Nice*,
Cazaux (BA 120);
GE 00.312, Salon de
Provence (BA 701);
Patrouille de France (PDF)
(EPAA 20.300),
Salon de Provence (BA 701)
01 F-ZJTS DGA EV
E4 DGA EV
E7 705-TU 00.314
E8 DGA EV
E9 102-LF 02.002
E10 314-UL 00.314
E11 102-UB 02.002
E12 DGA EV
E13 102-MM 02.002
E14 102-FG 02.002
E17 705-AA 00.314
E18 705-AK 00.314
E20 705-MS 00.314
E22 705-LS 00.314
E25 705-TJ 00.314
E26 102-ND 02.008
E28 705-AB 00.314
E29 102-NB 02.008
E30 705-MD 00.314
E31 F-TERK *PDF*
E32 102-FI 02.002
E33 120-FJ 01.008
E35 120-MA 01.008
E37 120-NL 02.008
E38 102-LH 02.002
E41 F-TERA *PDF* [5]
E42 705-TA 00.314
E44 F-UHRE *PDF*
E45 705-TF 00.314
E46 F-UHRF *PDF* [4]
E47 705-AC 00.314
E48 705-MH 00.314
E49 705-LB 00.314
E51 705-AD 00.314
E53 102-LI 02.002
E55
E58 705-TK 00.314
E59 705-LY 00.314
E60 EPNER
E61 102-LQ 02.002
E64 314-TL 00.314
E67 705-TB$ 00.314
E68
E72 705-LA 00.314
E73 120-NE 02.008
E74
E75 705-AE 00.314
E76 102-RJ 02.002
E79 102-NA 02.002
E80 DGA EV
E81 705-FO 00.314

E82 705-LW 00.314
E83 705-TZ 00.314
E85 F-UGFF *PDF* [8]
E86 102-FB 02.002
E87 102-LC 02.002
E88 705-LL 00.314
E89 118-LX CEAM
E90 705-TH 00.314
E91 102-RL 02.002
E93 102-TX 02.002
E94 F-TERH *PDF* [8]
E95 F-TERQ *PDF*
E96 705-TC 00.314
E97 102-MB 02.002
E98 705-MF 00.314
E99 102-AH 02.002
E100
E101 314-TT 00.314
E102 120-LM 01.008
E103 118-UA CEAM
E104 705-TG 00.314
E105 102-FM 02.002
E106
E107 F-TEUD$ 00.314
E108 120-AF 01.008
E109 102-AG 02.002
E110 118-AH CEAM
E112 705-AO 00.314
E113 705-TD 00.314
E114 F-TERR *PDF*
E115 120-MR 01.008
E116 120-FN 01.008
E117 F-RCAI *PDF*
E118 314-LN 00.314
E119 118-FE CEAM
E120 705-LG 00.314
E121 705-LE 00.314
E123 705-RM 00.314
E124 120-RN 01.008
E125 314-LK 00.314
E127 705-FK 00.314
E128 705-TM 00.314
E129 705-LP 00.314
E130 F-TERP *PDF* [3]
E131 120-RO 02.008
E132 705-LZ 00.314
E134 F-TERM *PDF* [0]
E135 102-RX 02.002
E136 120-RP 01.008
E137 705-LJ 00.314
E138 705-RQ 00.314
E139 705-FC 00.314
E140 102-FA 02.002
E141 120-NF 02.008
E142 314-LO 00.314
E143
E144 120-AK 01.008
E145
E146 705-RR 00.314
E147 118-LT CEAM
E148 705-LU 00.314
E149 705-RS 00.314
E151 705-FD 00.314
E152 F-UHRT *PDF* [1]
E153 705-RU 00.314
E154 120-AL 01.008
E155 120-NP 02.008
E156 705-TI 00.314
E157 120-UC 02.008
E158 F-TERF *PDF*
E159
E160 314-UH 00.314
E162 F-TERJ *PDF* [2]
E163 F-TERE *PDF* [9]
E165 F-TERE *PDF* [7]
E166 F-UHRW *PDF* [6]
E167 120-MN 01.008
E168 102-FP 02.002
E170 705-RY 00.314
E171 705-RZ 00.314

Dassault
Falcon 7X
ET 00.065, Villacoublay
68 F-RAFA
86 F-RAFB

Dassault
Falcon 20
DGA EV, Cazaux & Istres
Falcon 20C
79 CT
96 CB
104 CW
138 CR
188 CX
Falcon 20E
252 CA
263 CY
288 CV
Falcon 20F
342 CU
375 CZ

Dassault
Falcon 50
ET 00.065, Villacoublay
27 (F-RAFK)
34 (F-RAFL)
78 F-RAFJ

Dassault
Falcon 900
ET 00.065, Villacoublay
02 (F-RAFP)
004 (F-RAFQ)
... (on order)
... (on order)
... (on order)

Dassault
Falcon 2000LX
ET 00.065, Villacoublay
02 (F-RAFP)
231 F-RAFC
237 F-RAFD

Dassault
Mirage F.1
CEAM (ECE 05.330) *Côte d'Argent*,
Mont-de-Marsan (BA 118);
ER 02.033 *Savoie*,
Mont-de-Marsan (BA 118);
Mirage F.1B
502 118-SW 02.033
504 118-ST 02.033
509 118-SD 02.033
517 118-SC 02.033
Mirage F.1CR
604 118-CF 02.033
605 118-CO 02.033
607 118-ND 02.033
611 118-NM 02.033
616 118-NX 02.033
614 118-NR 02.033
617 118-NE 02.033
620 118-CT 02.033
622 118-FA 02.033
631 118-AA 02.033
632 118-CQ 02.033
638 118-CD 02.033
647 118-CB 02.033
649 118-CR 02.033
654 118-NC 02.033
655 118-FB 02.033
658 118-NQ 02.033
659 118-NT 02.033
660 118-CY 02.033
661 118-NK 02.033
662 118-NF 02.033

Dassault
Mirage 2000B
AMD-BA, Istres;
CEAM (ECE 05.330) *Côte d'Argent*,
Mont-de-Marsan (BA 118);
DGA EV, Cazaux (BA 120) & Istres (BA 125);
EC 02.005 *Ile de France*,
Orange (BA 115)
501 (BX1) DGA EV
506 115-OD 02.005
523 115-KJ 02.005
524 115-OA 02.005
525 115-AM 02.005
526 115-YP 02.005
527 115-OR 02.005
528 115-KS 02.005
529 115-OC 02.005
530 115-OL 02.005

Dassault
Mirage 2000C/2000-5F*

CEAM (ECE 05.330) *Côte d'Argent*, Mont-de-Marsan (BA 118);
DGA EV, Istres (BA 125);
GC 01.002 *Cigognes*, Luxeuil (BA 116);
EC 02.005 *Ile de France*, Orange (BA 115);
EC 03.011 *Corse*, Djibouti (BA 188);
EC 03.030 *Lorraine*, Al Dhafra, UAE (BA 104)

01*		DGA EV
2		DGA EV
38*	116-EI	02.005
40*	116-EX	01.002
41*	116-FZ	01.002
42*	116-EY	01.002
43*	116-EJ	01.002
44*	116-EQ	01.002
45*	188-EF	03.011
46*	116-EN	01.002
47*	188-EP	03.011
48*	116-EW	01.002
49*	116-EA	01.002
51*	118-AS	CEAM
52*	188-EH	03.011
54*	118-EZ	CEAM
55*	116-EU	01.002
56*	116-EG	01.002
57*	116-ET	01.002
58*	116-EL$	01.002
59*	116-EV	01.002
61*	116-ME	01.002
62*	116-ED	01.002
63*	116-EM	01.002
64		
65*	116-MG	01.002
66*	116-EO	01.002
67*	116-MH	01.002
70*	188-AD	03.011
71*	116-EE	01.002
73*	116-ES	01.002
74*	188-EK	03.011
77*	118-AX	CEAM
78*	116-EC	01.002
80	188-LI	03.011
81	115-LB	02.005
82	115-YL	02.005
83	115-YC	02.005
85	103-LK$	
86	115-LL	02.005
88	103-KV$	
89	115-KA	02.005
90	115-YS	02.005
92	118-AW	CEAM
93	115-YA	02.005
94	115-KB	02.005
95	115-KM	02.005
96	115-KI	02.005
97	115-YK	02.005
99	115-YB	02.005
101	115-KE	02.005
102	103-KR	
103	103-YN$	
104	115-KG	02.005
105	115-LJ	02.005
106	115-KL	02.005
107	103-YD	02.005
108	103-LC	
109	115-YH	02.005
111	115-KF	02.005
113	115-YO	02.005
115	115-YM	02.005
117	115-LD	02.005
118	115-YG	02.005
120	115-KC	02.005
121	115-KN	02.005

Dassault
Mirage 2000D

AMD-BA, Istres;
CEAM (ECE 05.330) *Côte d'Argent*, Mont-de-Marsan (BA 118);
DGA EV, Istres (BA 125);
EC 01.003 *Navarre*, EC 02.003 *Champagne* & ETED 02.007 *Argonne*, Nancy (BA 133);
EC 03.003 *Ardennes*, Istres (BA 125);
EC 03.011 *Corse*, Djibouti (BA 188)

601	133-JG	02.003
602	188-XJ	03.011
603	133-XL	03.003
604	133-IP	01.003
605	133-LF	02.003
606	133-JC	02.003
607		DGA EV
609		
610	133-XX	03.003
611	133-JP	02.003
613	133-MO	02.003
614	133-JU	02.003
615	133-JY	02.003
616	118-XH	CEAM
617	133-IS	01.003
618	133-XC	03.003
620	188-IU	03.011
622	133-IL	01.003
623	133-MP	02.003
624	188-IT	03.011
625	133-XG	03.003
626	133-IC	01.003
627	133-JO	02.003
628	133-JL	02.003
629	133-XO	03.003
630	188-XD	03.011
631	133-IH	02.007
632	133-XE	03.003
634	133-JE	01.003
635	133-AS	01.003
636	133-JV	02.003
637	133-XQ	03.003
638	188-IJ	03.011
639		
640	118-IN	CEAM
641	133-JW	02.003
642	133-IE	01.003
643	133-JD	02.003
644		DGA EV
645	133-XP	01.003
646	118-MQ	CEAM
647	133-IO	01.003
648	133-XT	03.003
649	133-XY	03.003
650	133-IA	02.003
651	133-LG	01.003
652	133-XN	03.003
653	118-AU	CEAM
654	133-ID	01.003
655	133-LH	01.003
657	133-JM	03.003
658	133-JN	02.003
659	133-XR	03.003
660	133-JF	01.033
661	133-XI	03.003
662	133-XA	03.003
664	133-IW	01.003
665	133-AF	01.003
666	133-IQ	01.003
667	133-JZ	02.003
668	118-IG	CEAM
669	133-AL	02.007
670	133-XF	03.003
671	133-XK	03.003
672	133-XV	03.003
673		DGA EV
674	133-IR	01.003
675	133-JI	02.003
676		DGA EV
677	133-JT	01.003
678	133-JB	02.003
679	133-JX	01.003
680	133-XM	03.003
681	133-AG	01.003
682	133-JR	02.003
683	133-IV	01.003
685	133-XZ	01.003
686	133-JH	02.003
D02		DGA EV

Dassault
Mirage 2000N

CEAM (ECE 05.330) *Côte d'Argent*, Mont-de-Marsan (BA 118);
DGA EV, Istres (BA 125);
EC 02.004 *Lafayette*, Istres (BA 125)

301		DGA EV
305	116-CS	02.004
306	116-BL	02.004
316	116-AU$	02.004
319		
324	116-CX	
326		

329
330 116-AT
333
334 DGA EV
335 125-CI
337 116-BF
338 125-CG 02.004
340 125-AA 02.004
342 125-BA 02.004
345 125-BU 02.004
348 125-AL 02.004
350 125-AJ 02.004
351 125-AQ 02.004
353 125-AM 02.004
354 125-BJ 02.004
355 125-AE 02.004
356 125-BX 02.004
357 125-CO 02.004
358 116-BQ 02.004
359 125-AK$ 02.004
360 125-CB
361 125-CK 02.004
362 125-CU
364 125-BB 02.004
365 125-AI 02.004
366 125-BC 02.004
367 125-AW 02.004
368 125-AR
369 125-AG 02.004
370 125-CQ
371 125-BD 02.004
372 125-CM 02.004
373 125-CF
374 125-BS 02.004
375 125-CL 02.004

Dassault
Rafale B/Rafale C
AMD-BA, Istres;
CEAM (ECE 05.330) *Côte d'Argent*,
Mont-de-Marsan (BA 118);
DGA EV, Istres (BA 125);
EC 01.007 *Provence*,
EC 01.091 *Gascogne*,
ETR 02.092 *Aquitaine*,
St Dizier (BA 113);
EC 02.030 *Normandie-Niémen*,
Mont-de-Marsan (BA 118);
EC 03.030 *Lorraine*,
Al Dhafra, UAE (BA 104)
Rafale F.2B
301 DGA EV
302 DGA EV
303 118-EA CEAM
304 118-EB 01.007
305 118-EC$ CEAM
306 113-IB 01.091
307 113-IA 01.091
308 113-HA 01.007
309 113-HB 01.007
310 113-HC 02.092
311 104-HD 03.030
312 113-HF 01.007
313 113-HI 01.007
314 104-HP 03.030
315 113-HK 01.091
317 113-HO 01.091
318 113-HM 01.091
319 113-HN 01.007
320 113-HV 01.091
321 113-HQ 01.007
322 113-HU 01.091
323 118-HT CEAM
324 113-HW 01.007
325 113-HX 01.007
326 113-HY 01.007
327 113-HZ 01.007
Rafale F.3B
328 113-IC 01.091
329 113-ID 01.091
330 113-IE 01.091
331 IF CEAM
332 113-IG CEAM
333 113-IH 01.091
334 113-II 02.092
335 113-IJ 01.091
336 113-IK 01.091
337 113-IL 01.091
338 113-IO 01.091
339
340
341
342
343
344
345
Rafale B
B01 DGA EV
Rafale F.2C
101 DGA EV
102 118-EF CEAM
103 113-HR 01.007
104 113-HH$ 01.007
105 113-HE 01.007
106 104-HG 02.092
107 113-HJ 01.007
108 113-HS 01.007
Rafale F.3C
109 118-IM 02.030
110 118-IN 02.030
111 113-IP 01.091
112 113-IQ 01.091
113 118-IR 02.030
114 118-IS 02.030
115 113-IT 01.091
116 113-IU 01.091
117 113-IV 01.007
118 118-IW 02.030
119 118-IX$ 02.030
120 113-IY 01.091
121 113-IZ$ 01.091
122 113-GA 01.007
123 118-GB 02.030
124 104-GC 03.030
125 104-GD 03.030
126 113-GE 01.007
127 113-GF 01.007
128 118-GG 02.030
129 118-GH 02.030
130 113-GI 02.092
131 118-GJ 02.030
132 118-GK 02.030
133 118-GL 02.030
134 118-GM 02.030
135 113-GN 02.092
136 118-GO 02.030
137 118-GP CEAM
138
139 113-GR 01.007
140
141
142
143
144
145
146
147
148
149
150
Rafale C
C01 DGA EV

DHC-6 Twin Otter 200/300*
GAM 00.056 *Vaucluse*, Evreux;
ET 03.061 *Poitou*,
Orléans
292 F-RACC 00.056
298 F-RACD 00.056
300 F-RACE 00.056
730* CA 03.061
745* CV 03.061

Embraer
EMB.121AA/AN* Xingu
EAT 00.319,
Capitaine Dartigues,
Avord (BA 702)
054 YX
055* YZ
064 YY
066* ZA
69*
070* ZC
072 YA
073 YB
075 YC
076 YD
77* ZD
078 YE
082 YG
083* ZE
084 YH
086 YI
089 YJ
090* ZF

091 YK
092 YL
096 YN
098 YO
099 YP
102 YS
103 YT
105 YU
107 YV
108 YW
111 YQ

Eurocopter
AS.332 Super Puma/
AS.532 Cougar/
EC.725AP Cougar/
EC.725R2 Cougar

EH 01.044 *Solenzara*, Solenzara;
EH 01.067 *Pyrénées*, Cazaux;
EH 03.067 *Parisis*, Villacoublay;
EH 05.067 *Alpilles*, Aix-en-Provence;
GAM 00.056 *Vaucluse*, Evreux;
CEAM, Mont-de-Marsan

2014 AS.332C PN 05.067
2057 AS.332C PO 01.044
2093 AS.332L PP 05.067
2233 AS.332L-1 FY 00.056
2235 AS.332L-1 FZ 03.067
2244 AS.332C PM 01.044
2342 AS.532UL FX 00.056
2369 AS.532UL FW 00.056
2375 AS.532UL FV 00.056
2377 AS.332L-1 FU 03.067
2461 EC.725AP SA 01.067
2549 EC.725AP SB 01.067
2552 EC.725AP SE 01.067
2555 EC.725AP SF 01.067
2619 EC.725AP SC 05.067
2626 EC.725AP SD 01.067
2770 EC.725R2 SG 00.056
2772 EC.725R2 SH 00.056
2778 EC.725R2 SI 00.056
2789 EC.725R2 SJ 00.056
2802 EC.725R2 SK 00.056

Eurocopter AS.555AN Fennec

CIEH 00.341, Orange;
EH 03.067 *Parisis*, Villacoublay;
EH 05.067 *Alpilles*, Orange;
EH 06.067 *Solenzara*, Solenzara;
ET 00.068 *Guyane*, Cayenne

5361 UT 05.067
5382 UV 05.067
5386 UX 05.067
5387 UY 05.067
5390 UZ
5391 VA
5392 VB 05.067
5393 VC
5396 VD 05.067
5397 VE 03.067
5398 VF
5399 VG$
5400 VH 05.067
5412 VI 05.067
5427 VJ 03.067
5430 VL 06.067
5431 VM 05.067
5440 VN
5441 VO 05.067
5444 VP
5445 VQ 05.067
5448 VR 03.067
5452 VS 05.067
5455 VT 00.058
5458 VV 05.067
5466 VW 03.067
5468 VX 03.067
5490 VY 05.067
5506 WA 05.067
5509 WB 05.067
5511 WC 05.067
5516 WD 03.067
5520 WE 03.067
5523 WF 05.067
5526 WG 05.067
5530 WH 05.067
5532 WI 05.067
5534 WJ 05.067
5536 WK 05.067
5559 05.067

Extra EA-330LC*/EA-330SC

EVAA, Salon de Provence

03* F-TGCH
04 F-TGCI
05 F-TGCJ

Lockheed
C-130H/C-130H-30* Hercules

ET 02.061 *Franche-Comté*, Orléans

4588 61-PM
4589 61-PN
5114 61-PA
5116 61-PB
5119 61-PC
5140 61-PD
5142* 61-PE
5144* 61-PF$
5150* 61-PG
5151* 61-PH
5152* 61-PI
5153* 61-PJ
5226* 61-PK
5227* 61-PL

SOCATA
TB-30 Epsilon

**Cartouche Dorée*, (EPAA 00.315) Cognac (BA 709);
EPAA 00.315, Cognac (BA 709);
SOCATA, Tarbes

7 315-UF
13 315-UL
26 315-UY
27 315-UZ
30 315-VC
34 315-VG
44 315-VQ
64 315-WG
65 315-WH
66 315-WI
67 315-WJ
69 F-SEWL*
73 315-WP
74 315-WQ
78 315-WU
82 315-WY
83 315-WZ
84 315-XA
87 315-XD
90 F-SEXG*
91 315-XH
92 315-XI
95 315-XL
96 315-XM
97 315-XN
99 315-XP
100 F-SEXP*
101 F-SEXR [1]*
102 F-SEXS [2]*
103 315-XT
104 F-SEXU [3]*
110 315-YA
113 315-YD
116 F-SEYG*
117 315-YH
118 315-YI
121 315-YL
127 315-YR
131 315-YV
133 315-YX
136 315-ZA
141 F-SEZF*
142 315-ZG
144 315-ZI
146 315-ZK
149 315-ZM
150 315-ZN

SOCATA TBM 700A

CEAM (EC 02.330), Mont-de-Marsan;
DGA EV, Cazaux & Istres;
ET 00.041 *Moselle*, Metz;
ET 00.043 *Médoc*,

Bordeaux (BA 106);
ET 00.065, Villacoublay;
EdC 00.070, Chateaudun

33	XA	00.043
35	BW	DGA EV
77	XD	00.041
78	XE	CEAM
80	BY	DGA EV
93	XL	00.065
95	XH	CEAM
103	XI	00.065
104	XJ	00.070
105	XK	00.041
106	MN	DGA EV
110	XP	00.041
111	XM	01.040
115	BQ	DGA EV
117	XN	00.041
125	XO	00.065
131	XQ	00.065
146	XR	00.065
147	XS	00.065

Transall
C-160NG GABRIEL*/
C-160R
CEAM (EET 06.330),
Mont-de-Marsan;
DGA EV, Cazaux & Istres;
EEA 00.054 *Dunkerque*,
Metz;
ET 00.050 *Réunion*,
St Denis;
ET 00.055 *Ouessant*,
Dakar;
ET 00.058 *Guadeloupe*,
Pointe-à-Pitre;
ET 01.061 *Touraine* &
ET 03.061 *Poitou*,
Orléans;
ET 01.064 *Bearn* &
ET 02.064 *Anjou*, Evreux;
ET 00.088 *Larzac*,
Djibouti

R4	C-160R	61-MD	01.061
R51	C-160R	61-MW$	01.061
R54	C-160R	61-MZ	01.061
R55	C-160R	61-ZC	03.061
R86	C-160R	61-ZD	03.061
R87	C-160R	61-ZE	00.050
R89	C-160R	61-ZG	03.061
R90	C-160R	61-ZH	03.061
R91	C-160R	61-ZI	03.061
R93	C-160R	61-ZK	03.061
R94	C-160R	61-ZL	03.061
R96	C-160R	61-ZN	03.061
R97	C-160R	61-ZA	03.061
R153	C-160R	61-ZS	03.061
R154	C-160R	61-ZT	03.061
R157	C-160R	61-ZW	03.061
R158	C-160R	61-ZX	03.061
R159	C-160R	61-ZY	03.061
R160	C-160R	61-ZZ	03.061
R201	C-160R	64-GA	01.064
R202	C-160R	64-GB	02.064
R203	C-160R	64-GC	01.064
R204	C-160R	64-GD	02.064
R205	C-160R	64-GE	01.064
R206	C-160R	64-GF	02.064
R207	C-160R	64-GG	01.064
R208	C-160R	64-GH$	02.064
R210	C-160R	64-GJ	02.064
R211	C-160R	64-GK	01.064
R212	C-160R	64-GL	02.064
R213	C-160R	64-GM	01.064
R214	C-160R	64-GN	02.064
R215	C-160R	64-GO	01.064
F216	C-160NG*	54-GT	00.054
R217	C-160R	64-GQ	01.064
R218	C-160R	64-GR$	02.064
F221	C-160NG*	GS	00.054
R223	C-160R	64-GW	01.064
R224	C-160R	64-GX	02.064
R225	C-160R	64-GY	01.064
R226	C-160R	64-GZ	02.064

Aéronavale/Marine
Dassault-Breguet
Atlantique 2
21 Flottille &
23 Flottille,
Lorient/Lann Bihoué

2	21F
3	21F
4	23F
5	23F
9	23F
11	21F
12	23F
13	21F
14	23F
15	21F
16	21F
17	21F$
18	21F
19	23F
20	23F
21	21F
25	21F
26	21F
28	21F

Dassault
Falcon 10(MER)
ES 57, Landivisiau
32
101
129
133
143
185

Dassault
Falcon 20G Guardian
25 Flottille,
Papeete &
Tontouta
48
65
72
77
80

Dassault
Falcon 50 SURMAR
24 Flottille,
Lorient/Lann Bihoué
5
7
30
36
132

Dassault
Rafale
11 Flottille,
Landivisiau;
12 Flottille,
Landivisiau;
17 Flottille,
Landivisiau;
AMD-BA, Istres;
CEPA, Istres;
DGA EV, Istres;
ETR 02.092 *Aquitaine*,
St Dizier (BA 113)

Rafale F.1

1	DGA EV

Rafale F.2

11	12F
12	12F
13	12F
14	12F
15	12F
16	12F
17	12F
19	12F
20	12F
21	12F
23	12F
26	12F

Rafale F.3

27	CEPA
28	11F
29	02.092
30	11F
31	11F
32	11F
33	11F
34	12F
35	12F
36	11F
37	17F
38	

39
40

Rafale M

M01 DGA EV
M02 DGA EV

Dassault Super Etendard

17 Flottille, Landivisiau;
CEPA, Istres

1	17F
2	17F
4	17F
6	17F
8	17F
10	17F
11	17F
12	17F
13	17F
14	CEPA
16	17F
17	17F
18	17F
19	17F
31	17F
32	17F
33	17F
35	17F
37	17F
39	17F
41	17F
43	17F
44	17F
46	17F
50	17F
51	17F
52	17F
55	17F
57	17F
61	17F
62	17F
65	17F
68	CEPA
69	17F

Embraer EMB.121AN Xingu

24 Flottille,
Lorient/Lann Bihoué;
28 Flottille, Hyères

30	24F
47	24F
65	28F
67	28F$
68	24F
69	24F$
71	28F
74	24F$
77	28F
79	28F
81	24F
85	24F
87	24F

Eurocopter AS.365/AS.565 Panther

35 Flottille, Hyères,
(with detachments at La Rochelle, Le Touquet & Tahiti*)
36 Flottille, Hyères

17	AS.365N	35F
19	AS.365N	35F
24	AS.365N	35F
57	AS.365N	35F
81	AS.365N	35F
91	AS.365N	35F
157	AS.365N	35F
313	AS.365F1	35F
318	AS.365F1	35F
322	AS.365F1	35F
355	AS.565MA	36F
362	AS.565MA	35F
403	AS.565UA	36F
436	AS.565MA	36F
452	AS.565MA	36F
453	AS.565MA	35F
466	AS.565MA	36F
482	AS.565MA	36F
486	AS.565MA	36F
488	AS.565MA	36F
503	AS.565MA	35F
505	AS.565MA	36F
506	AS.565MA	35F
507	AS.565MA	36F
510	AS.365N3	35F
511	AS.565MA	36F
519	AS.565MA	36F
522	AS.565MA	36F$
524	AS.565MA	36F
542	AS.565MA	36F
6872	AS.365N3	35F*
6928	AS.365N3	35F*

Eurocopter EC.225LP Super Puma 2+

32 Flottille,
Lanvéoc/Poulmic & Cherbourg

2741
2752
2851

NH Industries NH.90-NFH/NH.90-NHC* Caiman

31 Flottille, Hyères;
33 Flottille,
Lanvéoc/Poulmic
CEPA, Hyères

1	(F-ZWTO)
2	CEPA
3*	CEPA
4	33F
5	31F
6	33F
7	
8	CEPA
9	
10	
11	
12	

Northrop Grumman E-2C Hawkeye

4 Flottille,
Lorient/Lann Bihoué

1 (165455)
2 (165456)
3 (166417)
4 (on order)

Sud SA.316B/SA.319B/SE.3160 Alouette III

35 Flottille, Hyères;
ES 22/ESHE, Lanvéoc/Poulmic

13	SE.3160	35F
14	SE.3160	22S
18	SE.3160	22S
41	SE.3160	22S
100	SA.319B	22S
114	SA.319B	22S
161	SA.319B	22S
237	SA.319B	35F
244	SE.3160	22S
245	SE.3160	22S
268	SA.319B	22S
279	SE.3160	22S
302	SA.319B	22S
303	SA.319B	22S
309	SA.319B	22S
314	SA.319B	22S
347	SA.319B	22S
358	SA.319B	22S
731	SA.316B	22S
806	SA.316B	22S
809	SA.316B	22S
997	SA.319B	22S

Westland Lynx HAS2(FN)/HAS4(FN)*

34 Flottille, Lanvéoc/Poulmic
(with a detachment at Hyères)
CEPA, Hyères

260
263
264
265
267
270
271
272 $
273
621
623
624
625

627
801*
802*
804*
806*
807*
808*
810*
811*
812*
813*
814*

Aviation Legére de l'Armée de Terre (ALAT)
Aérospatiale
SA.330Ba Puma
1 RHC, Phalsbourg;
3 RHC, Etain;
5 RHC, Pau;
4 RHFS, Pau;
EALAT, Dax & Le Luc;
ESAM, Bourges;
GAM/STAT, Valence;
GIH, Cazaux

1005 DCA ESAM
1006 DAA
1020 DAB 5 RHC
1036 DAC 1 RHC
1037 DAD 5 RHC
1049 DAE 5 RHC
1052 DCB EALAT
1055 DAF GIH
1056 DCC GAM/STAT
1057 DCD EALAT
1069 DAG 1 RHC
1071 DCE EALAT
1073 DCF EALAT
1078 DAH 3 RHC
1092 DAI GAM/STAT
1093 DCG 3 RHC
1100 DAJ 3 RHC
1102 DAK
1107 DAL 1 RHC
1109 DAM 5 RHC
1114 DCH 3 RHC
1122 DCI
1123 DCJ 5 RHC
1128 DAN 1 RHC
1130 DCK 5 RHC
1135 DCL 1 RHC
1136 DCM 1 RHC
1142 DCN
1143 DAO 1 RHC
1145 DCO 3 RHC
1149 DAP 5 RHC
1150 DCP 3 RHC
1155 DCQ 4 RHFS
1156 DAQ 1 RHC
1163 DCR EALAT
1164 DCS 1 RHC
1165 DCT 1 RHC
1171 DCU 1 RHC
1172 DCV 1 RHC
1173 DAR
1176 DAS 3 RHC
1177 DCW 3 RHC
1179 DCX 5 RHC
1182 DCY 1 RHC
1186 DCZ 5 RHC
1189 DAT 3 RHC
1190 DDA 1 RHC
1192 DDB 1 RHC
1196 DDC EALAT
1197 DAU 5 RHC
1198 DDD 1 RHC
1204 DAV 1 RHC
1206 DDE 3 RHC
1211 DAW
1213 DDF 1 RHC
1214 DAX 3 RHC
1217 DAY
1219 DAZ 3 RHC
1222 DDG 1 RHC
1223 DDH EALAT
1228 DDI
1231 DDK 5 RHC
1232 DBA 5 RHC
1235 DDL 5 RHC
1236 DDM EALAT
1239 DDN EALAT
1243 DBB 5 RHC
1244 DDO 5 RHC
1248 DBC 3 RHC
1252 DDP EALAT
1255 DDQ 1 RHC
1256 DDR GAM/STAT
1260 DDS EALAT
1262 DBD 5 RHC
1269 DDT 5 RHC
1277 DBE 1 RHC
1411 DDU 1 RHC
1417 DBF
1419 DDV 1 RHC
1438 DBG GAM/STAT
1447 DDW 1 RHC
1451 DBH 1 RHC
1507 DBI EALAT
1510 DBJ 3 RHC
1512 DBK
1519 DBL 3 RHC
1617 DBM 1 RHC
1632 DBN
1634 DBO 3 RHC
1654 DBP 5 RHC
1662 DDX EALAT
1663 DBQ 4 RHFS
5682 DBR 4 RHFS

Aérospatiale
SA.341/342 Gazelle
1 RHC, Phalsbourg;
3 RHC, Etain;
5 RHC, Pau;
4 RHFS, Pau;
COMALAT, Villacoublay;
EALAT, Dax & Le Luc;
EFA, Le Luc;
EHADT, Etain;
ESAM, Bourges;
GAM/STAT, Valence

SA.341F Gazelle
1119 GHA EALAT
1129 GHB EALAT
1131 GQG
1149 GQH 1 RHC
1171 GQI 1 RHC
1194 GQJ 5 RHC
1198 GHD EALAT
1267 GHE EALAT
1285 GQK 4 RHFS
1291 GQA EALAT
1353 GHF EALAT
1369 GQL 1 RHC
1372 GQM 3 RHC
1383 GQN 5 RHC
1399 GQB EALAT
1416 GQO 3 RHC
1419 GHG EALAT
1420 GQP 3 RHC
1447 GQC
1451 GQQ 1 RHC
1463 GQR 4 RHFS
1467 GHH EALAT
1483 GQS 3 RHC
1487 GQT 4 RHFS
1501 GHI EALAT
1504 GQD EALAT
1508 GQW 1 RHC
1518 GQX 1 RHC
1519 GHJ EALAT
1522 GQU
1523 GQE EALAT
1536 GHK
1540 GHL EALAT
1541 GHM EALAT
1544 GQF EALAT
1562 GQV 1 RHC
1565 GHN EALAT
1593 GQY 3 RHC
1594 GHO EALAT
1597 GHP EALAT
1598 GHQ EALAT
1607 GHR EALAT
1608 GHS EALAT
1611 GHT EALAT
1612 GHU EALAT
1619 GHV EALAT
1657 GHX EALAT
1659 GHY EALAT
1672 GHZ EALAT
1678 GIA EALAT
1690 GIB EALAT
1693 GIC EALAT
1718 GQZ 3 RHC

SA.342L1 Gazelle

4205	GEA	EALAT
4206	GEB	EALAT
4207	GEC	3 RHC
4208	GED	GAM/STAT
4209	GEE	EALAT
4210	GEF	1 RHC
4211	GEG	5 RHC
4212	GEH	ESAM
4214	GEI	EALAT
4215	GEJ	5 RHC
4216	GEK	GAM/STAT
4217	GEL	1 RHC
4218	GEM	1 RHC
4219	GEN	4 RHFS
4220	GEO	1 RHC
4221	GEP	EALAT
4222	GEQ	EALAT
4223	GER	3 RHC
4224	GES	1 RHC
4225	GET	GAM/STAT
4226	GEU	GAM/STAT
4227	GEV	1 RHC
4228	GEW	1 RHC
4229	GEX	4 RHFS
4230	GEY	
4231	GEZ	5 RHC
4232	GFA	EALAT
4233	GFB	3 RHC
4234	GFC	

SA.342M Gazelle

1732	GJA	EALAT
3458	GNA	EALAT
3459	GAA	1 RHC
3476	GAB	4 RHFS
3477	GJB	1 RHC
3511	GJC	EALAT
3512	GAC	1 RHC
3513	GNB	EALAT
3529	GJD	EALAT
3530	GAD	4 RHFS
3531	GJE	EALAT
3546	GJF	EALAT
3547	GJG	EFA
3548	GAE	1 RHC
3549	GNC	EALAT
3564	GAF	3 RHC
3567	GMA	EALAT
3615	GJH	EALAT
3617	GND	GAM/STAT
3848	GAG	5 RHC
3849	GAH	5 RHC
3850	GAI	1 RHC
3851	GJI	EALAT
3852	GNE	1 RHC
3853	GNF	EALAT
3855	GJJ	EALAT
3856	GAJ	5 RHC
3857	GJK	EALAT
3858	GNG	EALAT
3859	GAK	5 RHC
3862	GAL	1 RHC
3863	GAM	3 RHC
3865	GAN	EALAT
3867	GJM	EALAT
3868	GAO	1 RHC
3870	GME	
3896	GNJ	
3911	GAP	1 RHC
3921	GAQ	EALAT
3929	GJN	EALAT
3930	GMF	
3938	GAR	EALAT
3939	GMG	
3947	GAS	5 RHC
3948	GAT	1 RHC
3956	GNK	
3957	GAU	5 RHC
3964	GAV	3 RHC
3965	GJO	EALAT
3992	GNM	EALAT
3996	GAW	5 RHC
4008	GNN	
4014	GJP	GAM/STAT
4018	GAX	3 RHC
4019	GAY	3 RHC
4020	GAZ	1 RHC
4022	GJQ	EALAT
4023	GMH	ESAM
4026	GBA	1 RHC
4032	GNO	EALAT
4034	GBB	1 RHC
4038	GJR	EALAT
4039	GBC	1 RHC
4042	GMB	EALAT
4047	GJS	EALAT
4048	GBD	EALAT
4049	GNP	EALAT
4053	GBE	1 RHC
4059	GBF	1 RHC
4060	GNQ	EALAT
4061	GBG	GAM/STAT
4065	GNR	EALAT
4066	GBH	3 RHC
4067	GJU	EALAT
4071	GNS	EHADT
4072	GBI	1 RHC
4078	GJV	EALAT
4079	GMC	EALAT
4083	GNT	EALAT
4084	GBJ	3 RHC
4095	GBL	5 RHC
4096	GNU	EALAT
4102	GJW	EALAT
4103	GJX	EALAT
4108	GBM	
4109	GBN	5 RHC
4114	GBO	EALAT
4115	GBP	3 RHC
4118	GNV	EALAT
4119	GBQ	1 RHC
4120	GBR	EALAT
4123	GJY	EALAT
4124	GBS	4 RHFS
4135	GNW	
4136	GBT	1 RHC
4140	GBU	1 RHC
4141	GBV	
4142	GBW	5 RHC
4143	GNX	EALAT
4144	GBX	1 RHC
4145	GBY	1 RHC
4146	GNY	EALAT
4151	GBZ	3 RHC
4155	GCA	3 RHC
4159	GNZ	EALAT
4160	GCC	1 RHC
4161	GCD	1 RHC
4162	GCE	5 RHC
4164	GCF	5 RHC
4166	GJZ	EALAT
4168	GCG	5 RHC
4171	GMI	EALAT
4172	GCH	5 RHC
4175	GCI	4 RHFS
4176	GKA	EALAT
4177	GKB	EALAT
4178	GOA	EALAT
4179	GCJ	1 RHC
4180	GCK	GAM/STAT
4181	GCL	3 RHC
4182	GKC	EALAT
4183	GOB	EALAT
4184	GOC	EALAT
4185	GKD	3 RHC
4186	GCM	1 RHC
4187	GKE	EALAT
4189	GCN	4 RHFS
4190	GMJ	EALAT
4191	GCO	4 RHFS
4192	GOD	
4194	GMD	EALAT
4195	GCP	3 RHC
4198	GCQ	3 RHC
4201	GMK	EALAT

Aérospatiale AS.532UL Cougar

1 RHC, Phalsbourg;
4 RHFS, Pau;
GAM/STAT, Valence

2252	CGA	GAM/STAT
2267	CGC	4 RHFS
2271	CGD	4 RHFS
2272	CGE	1 RHC
2273	CGF	1 RHC
2282	CGG	
2285	CGH	
2290	CGI	4 RHFS
2293	CGJ	4 RHFS
2299	CGK	4 RHFS
2300	CGL	1 RHC
2301	CGM	1 RHC
2303	CGN	1 RHC
2316	CGO	4 RHFS

2323 CGQ 4 RHFS
2324 CGR 4 RHFS
2325 CGS
2327 CGT
2331 CGU
2336 CGV 4 RHFS
2443 CGW
2446 CGX 1 RHC

Eurocopter
EC.665 Tigre HAP/Tigre HAD
5 RHC, Pau;
4 RHFS, Pau;
EFA, Le Luc;
Eurocopter, Marseille;
GAM/STAT, Valence

Tigre HAP
2001 BHH EFA
2002 BHI EFA
2003 BHJ EFA
2004 BHK EFA
2006 BHL EFA
2009 BHB EFA
2010 BHA 5 RHC
2011 BHM 5 RHC
2012 BHT GAM/STAT
2013 BHC GAM/STAT
2015 BHD 5 RHC
2016 Eurocopter
2018 BHE 5 RHC
2019 BHF 5 RHC
2021 BHN$ EFA
2022 BHG 5 RHC
2023 BHP 5 RHC
2024 BHO 5 RHC
2025 BHQ 5 RHC
2026 BHR GAM/STAT
2027 BHS 5 RHC
2028 BHU 5 RHC
2029 BHV 5 RHC
2031 BHX EFA
2032 BHW 5 RHC
2033 BHZ 5 RHC
2034 BIB 5 RHC
2035 BIC 4 RHFS
2036 BID EFA
2037 BIE 5 RHC
2038 Eurocopter
2039 BIG
2040 BIH 5 RHC
2041 BII
2042 BIJ 5 RHC
2043 BIK 5 RHC
2044 BIL GAM/STAT
2045 BIM 5 RHC
2046 BIN
2047 BIO
2048 BIP
2049 BIQ
2050 BIR
2051 BIS
2052 BIT

Tigre HAD
6001 (on order)
6002 (on order)
6003 (on order)
6004 (on order)
6005 (on order)

Eurocopter
EC.725AP Cougar
GIH, Cazaux
2611 CAA
2628 CAB
2630 CAC
2631 CAD
2633 CAE
2638 CAF
2640 CAG
2642 CAH

NH Industries
NH.90-TTH
GAM/STAT, Valence
1239 EAA GAM/STAT
1256 EAB GAM/STAT
1271 EAC GAM/STAT

Pilatus
PC-6B/B2-H4 Turbo Porter
1 GSALAT, Montauban
887 MCA
888 MCB
889 MCC
890 MCD
891 MCE

SOCATA
TBM 700A/TBM 700B*
EAAT, Rennes
94 ABZ
99 ABO
100 ABP
136 ABR
139 ABS
156* ABT
159* ABU
160* ABV

French Govt
Aérospatiale
AS.350B Ecureuil
Gendarmerie;
Sécurité Civile*
F-MCSF (2225) AS.350B-1
F-MJCA (1028) AS.350BA
F-MJCB (1574) AS.350B
F-MJCC (1916) AS.350B-1
F-MJCD (1576) AS.350B
F-MJCE (1812) AS.350B
F-MJCF (1691) AS.350BA
F-MJCG (1753) AS.350B
F-MJCH (1756) AS.350B
F-MJCI (2222) AS.350B-1
F-MJCL (1811) AS.350B
F-MJCM (1952) AS.350B
F-MJCN (2044) AS.350BA
F-MJCO (1917) AS.350B-1
F-MJCP (2045) AS.350B
F-MJCQ (2057) AS.350BA
F-MJCR (2088) AS.350B
F-MJCS (1575) AS.350B
F-MJCT (2104) AS.350B
F-MJCU (2117) AS.350B
F-MJCV (2118) AS.350B
F-MJCW (2218) AS.350BA
F-MJCX (2219) AS.350B
F-MJCY (2221) AS.350B
F-MJCZ (1467) AS.350BA $
F-MJEB (1692) AS.350B
F-MJEC (1810) AS.350B
F-ZBBN AS.350B*
F-ZBEA AS.350B
F-ZBFC AS.350B-1*
F-ZBFD AS.350B-1*

Aérospatiale
AS.355 Twin Ecureuil
Douanes Francaises
F-ZBAD AS.355F-2
F-ZBEF AS.355F-1
F-ZBEK AS.355F-1
F-ZBEL AS.355F-1

Beech
Super King Air B200
Sécurité Civile
F-ZBFJ 98
F-ZBFK 96
F-ZBMB 97

Canadair CL-415
Sécurité Civile
F-ZBEG 39
F-ZBEU 42
F-ZBFN 33
F-ZBFP 31
F-ZBFS 32
F-ZBFV 37
F-ZBFW 38
F-ZBFX 34
F-ZBFY 35
F-ZBME 44
F-ZBMF 45
F-ZBMG 48

Cessna F.406 Caravan II
Douanes Francaises
F-ZBAB (0025)
F-ZBBB (0039)
F-ZBCE (0042)
F-ZBCF (0077)
F-ZBCG (0066)
F-ZBCH (0075)

F-ZBCI (0070)
F-ZBCJ (0074)
F-ZBEP (0006)
F-ZBES (0017)
F-ZBGA (0086)
F-ZBGD (0090)
F-ZBGE (0061)

Conair
Turbo Firecat
Sécurité Civile
F-ZBAA 22
F-ZBAP 12
F-ZBAZ 01
F-ZBCZ 23
F-ZBEH 20
F-ZBET 15
F-ZBEW 11
F-ZBEY 07
F-ZBMA 24

De Havilland Canada
DHC-8Q-402MR
Sécurité Civile
F-ZBMC 73
F-ZBMD 74

Eurocopter
EC.135T-2
Douanes Francaises*;
Gendarmerie
F-MJDA (0642)
F-MJDB (0654)
F-MJDC (0717)
F-MJDD (0727)
F-MJDE (0747)
F-MJDF (0757)
F-MJDG (0772)
F-MJDH (0787)
F-MJDI (0797)
F-MJDJ (0806)
F-MJDK (0857)
F-MJDL (0867)
F-MJDM (1055)
F-MJDN (1058)
F-MJDO (1086)
F-ZBGF*
F-ZBGG*
F-ZBGH*
F-ZBGI*
F-ZBGJ*

Eurocopter
EC.145
Gendarmerie;
Sécurité Civile*
F-MJBA (9008) EC.145C-1
F-MJBB (9014) EC.145C-1
F-MJBC (9018) EC.145C-1
F-MJBD (9019) EC.145C-1
F-MJBE (9025) EC.145C-1
F-MJBF (9035) EC.145C-2
F-MJBG (9036) EC.145C-2
F-MJBH (9037) EC.145C-2
F-MJBI (9127) EC.145C-2
F-MJBJ (9140) EC.145C-2
F-MJBK (9162) EC.145C-2
F-MJBM (9113) EC.145C-2
F-MJBN (9173) EC.145C-2
F-MJBO (9124) EC.145C-2
F-MJBR (9169) EC.145C-2
F-MJBT (9173) EC.145C-2
F-ZBPA EC.145C-1*
F-ZBPD EC.145C-1*
F-ZBPE EC.145C-1*
F-ZBPF EC.145C-1*
F-ZBPG EC.145C-1*
F-ZBPH EC.145C-1*
F-ZBPI EC.145C-1*
F-ZBPJ EC.145C-1*
F-ZBPK EC.145C-1*
F-ZBPL EC.145C-1*
F-ZBPM EC.145C-1*
F-ZBPN EC.145C-1*
F-ZBPO EC.145C-1*
F-ZBPP EC.145C-2*
F-ZBPQ EC.145C-2*
F-ZBPS EC.145C-2*
F-ZBPT EC.145C-2*
F-ZBPU EC.145C-2*
F-ZBPV EC.145C-2*
F-ZBPW EC.145C-2*
F-ZBPX EC.145C-2*
F-ZBPY EC.145C-2*
F-ZBPZ EC.145C-2*
F-ZBQA EC.145C-2*
F-ZBQB EC.145C-2*
F-ZBQC EC.145C-2*
F-ZBQD EC.145C-2*
F-ZBQE EC.145C-2*
F-ZBQF EC.145C-2*
F-ZBQG EC.145C-2*
F-ZBQH EC.145C-2*
F-ZBQI EC.145C-2*
F-ZBQJ EC.145C-2*
F-ZBQK EC.145C-2*
F-ZBQL EC.145C-2*

Hawker Beechcraft King Air B350ER
Douanes Francaises
F-ZBGK (FL-682)
F-ZBGL (FL-746)
F-ZBGM (FL-752)
F-ZBGN (FL-781)
F-ZBGO (on order)
F-ZBGP (on order)
F-ZBGQ (on order)
F-ZBGR (on order)

Civil operated aircraft in military use
BAE Jetstream 41
AVDEF, Nimes/Garons
F-HAVD
F-HAVF

Cirrus SR.20/SR.22
EADS Cognac Aviation Training Services/CFAIM 05.312, Salon de Provence
F-HGDU SR.20
F-HKCA SR.20
F-HKCB SR.20
F-HKCD SR.20
F-HKCE SR.20
F-HKCF SR.22
F-HKCG SR.20
F-HKCH SR.20
F-HKCI SR.22
F-HKCJ SR.20
F-HKCK SR.20
F-HKCL SR.22
F-HKCM SR.20
F-HKCN SR.20
F-HKCO SR.22
F-HKCP SR.20
F-HKCQ SR.20
F-HKCR SR.22
F-HKCS SR.22
F-HKCT SR.20
F-HKCU SR.20
F-HKCV SR.20
F-HKCX SR.20

Dassault Falcon 20
AVDEF, Nimes/Garons
F-GJDB Falcon 20C
F-GPAA Falcon 20ECM
F-GPAB Falcon 20E
F-GPAD Falcon 20E

Grob G120A-F
EADS Cognac Aviation Training Services/EPAA 00.315, Cognac
F-GUKA
F-GUKB
F-GUKC
F-GUKD
F-GUKE
F-GUKF
F-GUKG
F-GUKH
F-GUKI
F-GUKJ
F-GUKK
F-GUKL
F-GUKM
F-GUKN
F-GUKO
F-GUKP
F-GUKR
F-GUKS

GABON
Dassault
Falcon 900EX
Gabonese Government, Libreville
TR-LEX

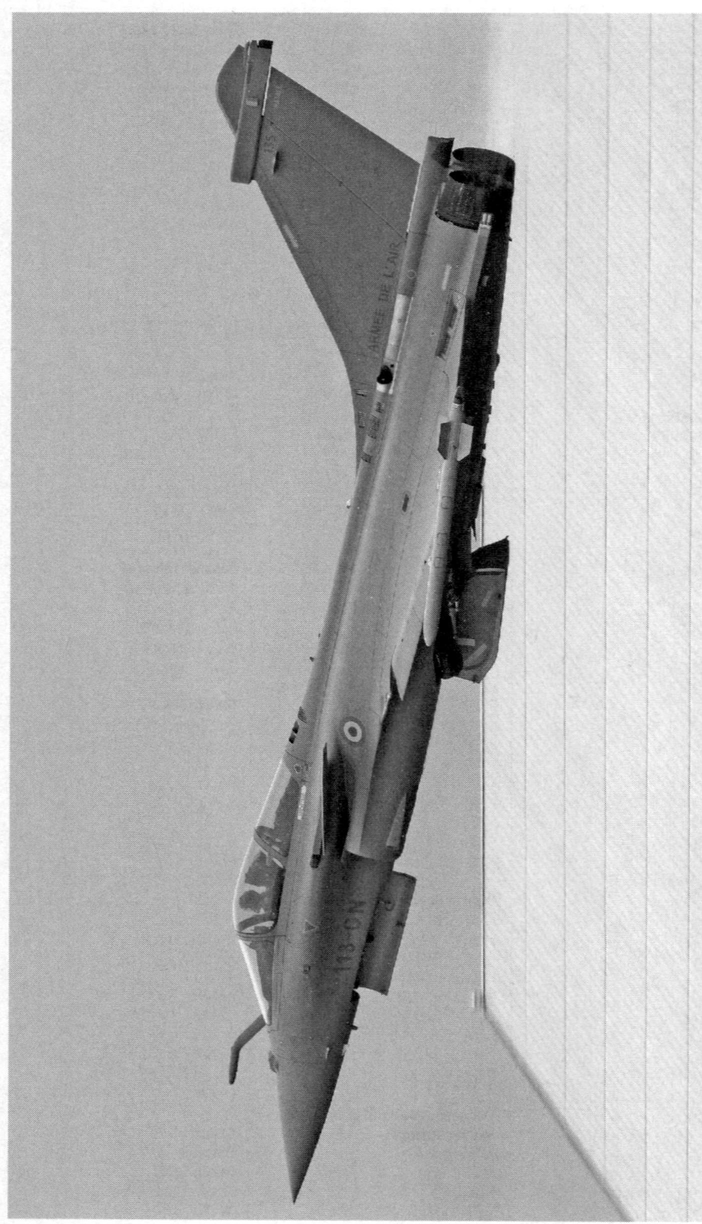

French Air Force Rafale F.3C 135 was newly delivered when this photo was taken at the Royal Internatioanl Air Tattoo, wzich may explain why it only wore the code 113-GN but no other distinguishing markings which revealed it operator, ETR 02.092 Aquitaine, based at St Dizier.

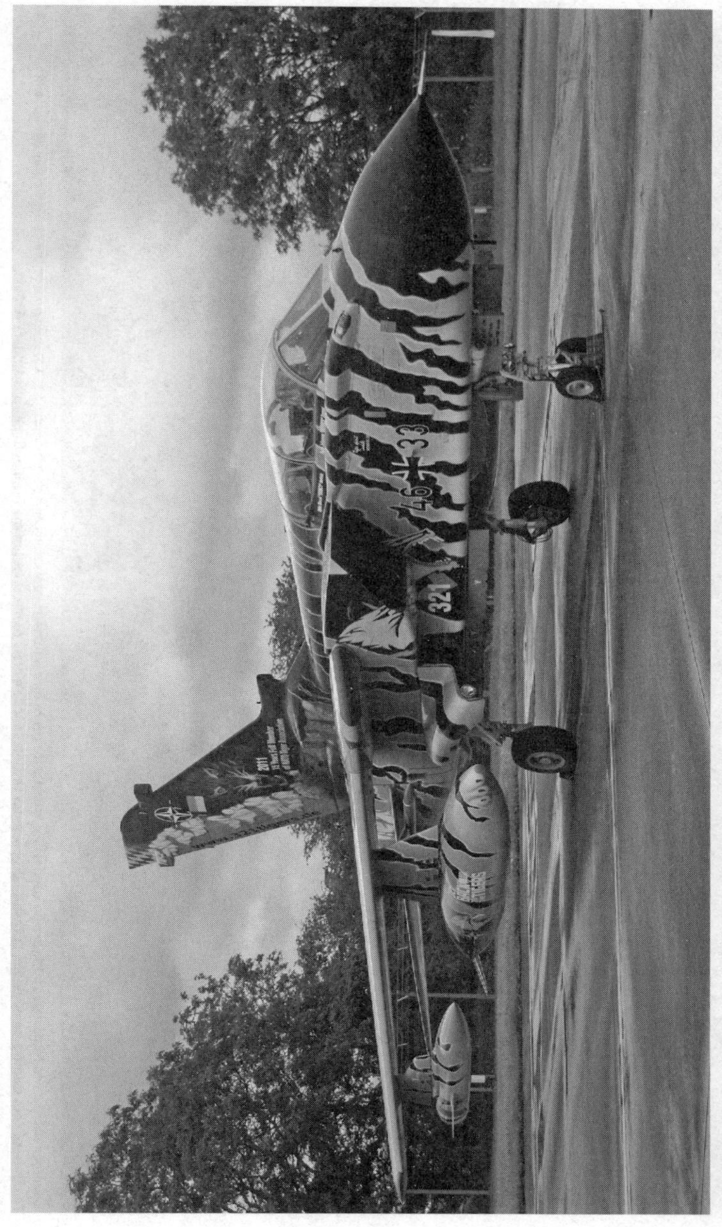

This superbly marked Luftwaffe Tornado ECR, 46+33, belonged to JbG-32 at Lechfeld. 321 Staffel was a member of the Tiger Association until the Staffel was quietly disbanded in late October 2012, which means that we are unlikely to see any further German Tornados marked in the tiger scheme. JbG-32 is due to end Tornado operations in 2013.

A number of Lufwaffe Transall C.160Ds are painted white, usually for UN or humanitarian operations and that includes 51+15, seen here in the static display at Fairford. The Transall fleet soldiers on while the Luftwaffe prepares for the introduction of its replacement in the form of the Airbus Military A400M.

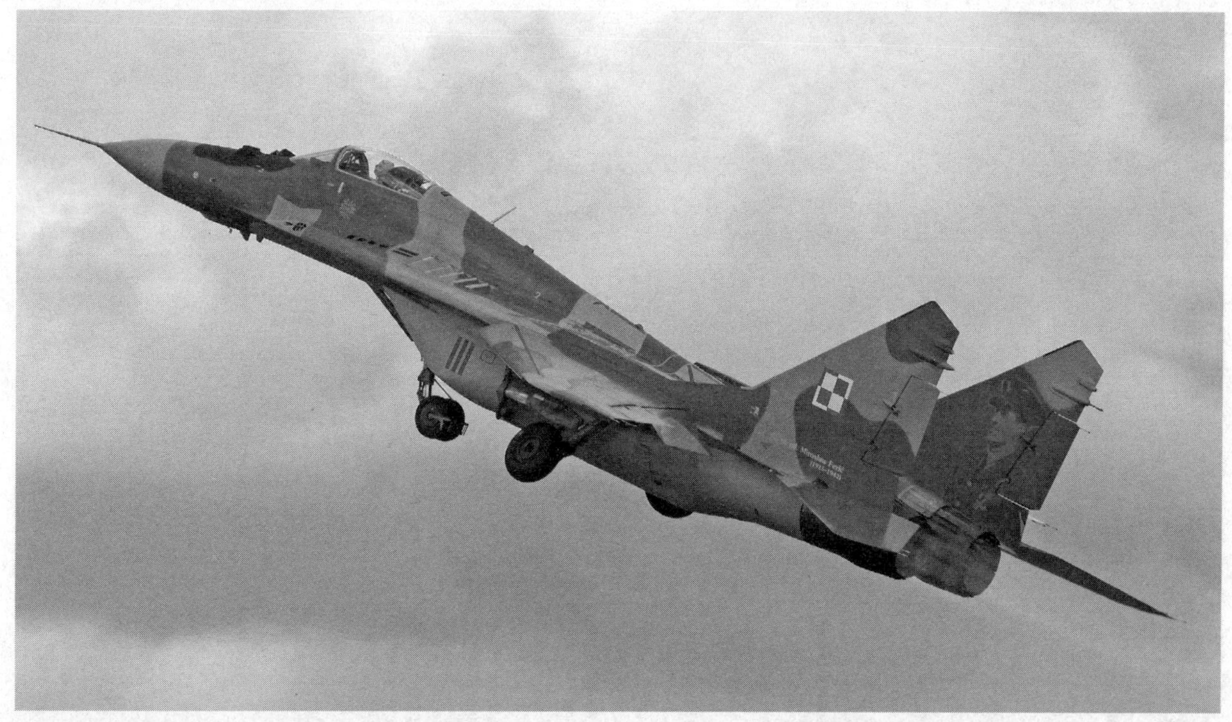

Poland is one of the few European air forces still operating the Mikoyan MiG-29A and this one, 111, bears markings on the tail depicting Flying Officer Miroslaw Feric DFC of No 303 (Polish) Squadron RAF, sadly killed in 1942.

Grumman G.1159C Gulfstream IVSP
Gabonese Government, Libreville
TR-KSP

GERMANY
Please note that German serials do not officially include the '+' part in them but aircraft wearing German markings are often painted with a cross in the middle, which is why it is included here.

Luftwaffe
Airbus A.310-304/MRTT*
1/FBS, Köln-Bonn
10+23
10+24*
10+25*
10+26*
10+27*

Bombardier Global 5000
3/FBS, Köln-Bonn
14+01
14+02
14+03
14+04

Airbus A.319CJ-115X
3/FBS, Köln-Bonn
15+01
15+02

Airbus A.340-313X
3/FBS, Köln-Bonn
16+01
16+02

Eurofighter EF.2000GS/EF.2000GT*
EADS, Manching;
JbG-31 *Boelcke*, Nörvenich;
JG-73 *Steinhoff*, Laage;
JG-74 *Molders*, Neuburg/Donau;
TsLw-1, Kaufbeuren;
WTD-61, Ingolstadt

30+02*	JG-74
30+03*	JG-73
30+04*	JbG-31
30+05*	JG-73
30+06	JG-73
30+07	TsLw-1
30+09	JbG-31
30+10*	JG-73
30+11	JG-74
30+12	JbG-31
30+14*	JG-74
30+15	JbG-31
30+17*	JG-73
30+20*	JG-73
30+22	JbG-31
30+23	JbG-31
30+24*	JG-73
30+25	JG-74
30+26	TsLw-1
30+27*	JG-73
30+28	JG-74
30+29	JG-74
30+30	JG-74
30+31*	JbG-31
30+32	JG-74
30+33	JbG-31
30+35*	JG-74
30+38*	JG-73
30+39	JG-74
30+40	JG-74
30+42*	JbG-31
30+45	JG-73
30+46	JG-73
30+47	JG-73
30+48	JG-74 $
30+49	JG-73
30+50	JG-73
30+51	JG-73
30+52	JG-73
30+53	JG-73
30+54*	JG-73
30+55	JG-73
30+56	JbG-31
30+57	JG-73
30+58	JG-74
30+59*	JG-73
30+60	JG-73
30+61	JG-74
30+62	JG-73
30+63	JG-74
30+64	JbG-31
30+65	JG-74
30+66	JbG-31
30+67*	JG-73
30+68	JG-74
30+69	JG-74
30+70	JG-74
30+71*	EADS
30+72	JbG-31
30+73	JG-73
30+74	JG-74
30+75	JbG-31
30+76	JbG-31
30+77*	JG-73
30+78	JG-74
30+79	JbG-31
30+80	JG-73
30+81	JG-73
30+82	JbG-31
30+83	JbG-31
30+84*	JbG-31
30+85	JbG-31
30+86	JG-74
30+87	JG-74
30+88	JG-74
30+89	JG-74
30+90	JbG-31
30+91	JbG-31
30+92	JbG-31
30+93	JbG-31
30+94	JbG-31
30+95*	JG-74
30+96	EADS
30+97	EADS
30+98	EADS
30+99*	
31+00	EADS
31+01	
31+02	
31+03*	
31+04	
31+05	
31+06	
31+07	
31+08	
31+09	
31+10	
31+11	
31+12	
31+13*	
31+14	JbG-31
31+15	TsLw-1
31+16	JG-73
31+17	JG-73
31+18	JG-73
31+19	JG-73
31+20	JG-73
31+21	JG-73
31+22	JG-73
98+03*	EADS
98+04	EADS
98+07	EADS
98+31*	EADS

McD F-4F Phantom
JG-71 *Richthoven*, Wittmundhaven;
TsLw-1, Kaufbeuren;
WTD-61, Ingolstadt

37+01	JG-71
37+04	TsLw-1
37+15	WTD-61
37+22	JG-71
37+48	JG-71 $
37+63	JG-71
37+65	JG-71
37+77	JG-71
37+79	JG-71
37+81	JG-71
37+85	JG-71
37+89	JG-71
37+92	JG-71
38+00	JG-71
38+01	JG-71
38+02	JG-71
38+10	JG-71 $
38+13	WTD-61
38+16	JG-71
38+26	JG-71
38+28	JG-71 $
38+29	JG-71

38+33 JG-71
38+37 JG-71
38+39 $
38+42 JG-71
38+45 JG-71
38+46 JG-71
38+48 JG-71
38+50 JG-71
38+53 JG-71
38+57 JG-71
38+58 JG-71
38+60 JG-71
38+61 TsLw-1
38+62 JG-71
38+64 JG-71
38+70 JG-71
38+75 JG-71
99+91 WTD-61

Panavia Tornado Strike/ Trainer[1]/ECR[2]

AkG-51 *Immelmann*, Schleswig/Jagel;
EADS, Manching;
GAFFTC, Holloman AFB, USA;
JbG-32, Lechfeld;
JbG-33, Büchel;
TsLw-1, Kaufbeuren;
WTD-61, Ingolstadt

43+01[1] JbG-33
43+02[1] JbG-33
43+07[1] AkG-51
43+10[1] JbG-33
43+23[1] GAFFTC
43+25 JbG-33
43+29[1] GAFFTC
43+31[1] GAFFTC
43+32
43+34 TsLw-1
43+35[1] AkG-51
43+37[1] JbG-32
43+38 JbG-32
43+42[1] GAFFTC
43+45[1] GAFFTC
43+46 AkG-51
43+48 AkG-51
43+50 AkG-51
43+52 JbG-33
43+54 TsLw-1
43+59 TsLw-1
43+71 JbG-32
43+73 AkG-51
43+75 GAFFTC
43+92[1] AkG-51
43+94[1] GAFFTC
43+97[1] AkG-51
43+98 AkG-51
44+00 GAFFTC
44+02 JbG-33
44+06 GAFFTC
44+16[1] JbG-33
44+17 AkG-51
44+21 WTD-61
44+23 JbG-33
44+29 JbG-33
44+30 GAFFTC
44+33 GAFFTC
44+34 AkG-51
44+58 JbG-33
44+61 AkG-51
44+64 AkG-51
44+65 AkG-51
44+69 AkG-51
44+70 JbG-33
44+72[1] GAFFTC
44+73[1] WTD-61
44+75[1] AkG-51
44+78 AkG-51
44+79 JbG-33
44+90 AkG-51
44+92 JbG-33
45+00 JbG-33
45+06 AkG-51 $
45+07 JbG-33
45+08 GAFFTC
45+09 JbG-33
45+13[1] JbG-32
45+14[1] JbG-33
45+15[1] GAFFTC
45+16[1] JbG-33
45+19 JbG-32
45+20 JbG-32
45+22 AkG-51
45+23 JbG-33
45+28 JbG-33
45+35 AkG-51
45+36
45+39 JbG-32
45+40 JbG-33
45+50 AkG-51
45+53 TsLw-1
45+54 GAFFTC
45+57 WTD-61
45+59 JbG-33
45+60[1] AkG-51
45+61[1] AkG-51
45+64 AkG-51
45+66 JbG-33
45+67 WTD-61
45+68 JbG-33
45+69 JbG-33
45+70[1] JbG-33
45+71 AkG-51
45+72 JbG-32
45+74 TsLw-1
45+76 JbG-33
45+77[1] AkG-51
45+84 JbG-33
45+85 AkG-51
45+88 WTD-61
45+90 JbG-33
45+91 JbG-33
45+92 JbG-33
45+93 JbG-32
45+94 JbG-33
46+00[1] GAFFTC
46+01 JbG-33
46+02 JbG-33
46+04[1] GAFFTC
46+05[1] GAFFTC
46+07[1] GAFFTC
46+08[1] JbG-32
46+09[1] GAFFTC
46+10 AkG-51
46+11 JbG-33
46+12 GAFFTC
46+13 AkG-51
46+14 AkG-51
46+15 AkG-51
46+18 JbG-33
46+20 AkG-51
46+21 JbG-33
46+22 AkG-51
46+23[2] JbG-32 $
46+24[2] JbG-32
46+25[2] JbG-32
46+26[2] JbG-32
46+28[2] JbG-32
46+29[2] JbG-32 $
46+30[2] JbG-32
46+31[2] JbG-32
46+32[2] WTD-61
46+33[2] JbG-32 $
46+34[2] JbG-32
46+35[2] JbG-32
46+36[2] JbG-32
46+37[2] JbG-32
46+38[2] JbG-32
46+39[2] WTD-61
46+40[2] WTD-61
46+41[2] JbG-32
46+43[2] JbG-32
46+44[2] JbG-32
46+45[2] JbG-32 $
46+46[2] JbG-32
46+48[2] JbG-32
46+49[2] JbG-32
46+50[2] JbG-32
46+51[2] JbG-32
46+52[2] JbG-32
46+53[2] JbG-32
46+54[2] JbG-32
46+55[2] JbG-32
46+56[2] JbG-32
46+57[2] JbG-32
98+59 WTD-61
98+60 WTD-61
98+77 WTD-61
98+79[2] WTD-61

Transall C-160D

LTG-61 (1.LwDiv), Landsberg;
LTG-62 (1.LwDiv), Wunstorf;

LTG-63 (4.LwDiv),
Hohn;
WTD-61, Ingolstadt

50+08	LTG-61
50+09	LTG-61
50+10	LTG-62
50+17	LTG-63
50+29	LTG-62
50+33	LTG-62
50+34	LTG-63
50+36	LTG-62
50+38	LTG-61
50+40	LTG-63
50+41	LTG-62
50+42	LTG-63
50+44	LTG-61
50+45	LTG-63
50+46	LTG-62
50+47	LTG-61
50+48	LTG-61 $
50+49	LTG-61
50+51	LTG-61
50+53	LTG-61
50+54	LTG-63
50+55	LTG-62
50+57	LTG-62
50+58	LTG-63
50+59	LTG-63
50+60	LTG-62
50+61	LTG-62
50+62	LTG-62
50+64	LTG-61
50+65	LTG-62
50+66	LTG-61
50+67	LTG-63
50+69	LTG-63
50+70	LTG-62
50+71	LTG-63
50+72	LTG-61
50+73	LTG-62
50+74	LTG-61
50+75	LTG-63
50+76	LTG-63
50+77	LTG-62
50+78	LTG-62
50+79	LTG-63
50+81	LTG-62
50+82	LTG-63
50+83	LTG-62
50+84	LTG-61
50+85	LTG-63 $
50+86	LTG-61
50+87	LTG-63
50+88	LTG-61
50+89	LTG-62
50+90	LTG-62
50+91	LTG-62
50+92	LTG-63
50+93	LTG-63
50+95	LTG-63
50+96	LTG-61
50+97	LTG-62
50+98	LTG-61
51+00	LTG-62
51+01	LTG-62
51+02	LTG-63
51+03	LTG-62
51+04	LTG-61
51+05	LTG-62
51+06	LTG-63
51+08	WTD-61
51+09	LTG-63
51+10	LTG-63
51+12	LTG-62
51+13	LTG-61
51+14	LTG-62
51+15	LTG-61

Eurocopter
AS.532U-2 Cougar

3/FBS, Berlin-Tegel

82+01
82+02
82+03

Sikorsky/VFW
CH-53G/CH-53GA/CH-53GE/CH-53GS

HFWS, Bückeburg;
HSG-64, Holzdorf, Laupheim
& Rheine-Bentlage;
TsLw-3, Fassberg;
WTD-61, Ingolstadt

84+05	CH-53G	HFWS
84+06	CH-53G	HSG-64
84+09	CH-53G	TsLw-3
84+10	CH-53G	HFWS
84+12	CH-53G	HSG-64
84+13	CH-53G	HFWS
84+14	CH-53GE	HSG-64
84+15	CH-53GS	HSG-64
84+16	CH-53G	HFWS
84+18	CH-53G	HFWS
84+19	CH-53G	TsLw-3
84+24	CH-53G	HSG-64
84+25	CH-53GS	HSG-64
84+26	CH-53GE	HSG-64
84+27	CH-53G	HFWS
84+28	CH-53G	HSG-64
84+29	CH-53G	HSG-64
84+30	CH-53GS	HSG-64
84+31	CH-53G	HSG-64
84+32	CH-53G	HSG-64
84+34	CH-53G	HSG-64
84+35	CH-53G	HSG-64
84+37	CH-53G	HSG-64
84+38	CH-53G	HSG-64
84+39	CH-53G	HSG-64
84+40	CH-53G	HSG-64
84+41	CH-53G	HFWS
84+42	CH-53GS	HFWS
84+43	CH-53G	HSG-64
84+44	CH-53G	HSG-64
84+45	CH-53GS	HSG-64
84+46	CH-53G	HSG-64
84+47	CH-53G	HSG-64
84+48	CH-53G	HFWS
84+49	CH-53G	HFWS
84+50	CH-53G	HFWS
84+51	CH-53GS	HSG-64
84+52	CH-53GS	HSG-64
84+53	CH-53GE	HSG-64
84+54	CH-53G	HSG-64
84+55	CH-53G	WTD-61
84+57	CH-53G	HFWS
84+58	CH-53G	HSG-64
84+59	CH-53G	HFWS
84+60	CH-53G	HSG-64
84+62	CH-53GS	HSG-64
84+63	CH-53G	HSG-64
84+64	CH-53GS	HSG-64
84+65	CH-53G	HFWS
84+66	CH-53GS	HSG-64
84+67	CH-53GS	HSG-64
84+68	CH-53G	HSG-64
84+70	CH-53G	HSG-64
84+71	CH-53G	HSG-64
84+72	CH-53G	HSG-64
84+73	CH-53GS	HSG-64
84+74	CH-53G	HFWS
84+75	CH-53G	HSG-64
84+76	CH-53G	HFWS
84+77	CH-53G	HSG-64
84+78	CH-53GS	HSG-64
84+79	CH-53GS	HSG-64
84+80	CH-53G	HSG-64
84+82	CH-53GE	HSG-64
84+83	CH-53G	HFWS
84+84	CH-53G	HSG-64
84+85	CH-53GS	HSG-64
84+86	CH-53GA	Eurocopter
84+87	CH-53G	HSG-64
84+88	CH-53G	HSG-64
84+89	CH-53G	HSG-64
84+90	CH-53G	HSG-64
84+91	CH-53GS	HSG-64
84+92	CH-53GE	HSG-64
84+94	CH-53G	
84+95	CH-53G	HSG-64
84+96	CH-53GE	HSG-64
84+97	CH-53G	HSG-64
84+98	CH-53GS	HSG-64
84+99	CH-53GA	HFWS
85+00	CH-53GS	HSG-64
85+01	CH-53GS	HSG-64
85+02	CH-53G	HSG-64
85+03	CH-53G	HSG-64
85+04	CH-53GA	HSG-64
85+05	CH-53GS	HSG-64
85+06	CH-53G	HSG-64
85+07	CH-53GS	HFWS
85+08	CH-53G	HSG-64
85+10	CH-53GS	HSG-64
85+11	CH-53G	HSG-64
85+12	CH-53GS	HSG-64

Northrop Grumman
RQ-4E Euro Hawk
WTD-61, Manching
99+01 WTD-61
..+.. (on order)
..+.. (on order)
..+.. (on order)
..+.. (on order)

Marineflieger
Dornier Do.228LM/Do.228NG*
MFG-3, Nordholz
57+04
98+35*

Lockheed
P-3C Orion
MFG-3, Nordholz
60+01
60+02
60+03
60+04
60+05
60+06
60+07
60+08

Westland
Super Lynx Mk88A
MFG-5, Nordholz;
WTD-61, Ingolstadt

83+02	MFG-3
83+03	MFG-3
83+04	MFG-3
83+05	MFG-3
83+06	MFG-3
83+07	WTD-61
83+09	MFG-3
83+10	MFG-3
83+11$	MFG-3
83+12	MFG-3
83+13	MFG-3
83+15	MFG-3
83+17	MFG-3
83+18	MFG-3
83+19	MFG-3
83+20	MFG-3
83+21	MFG-3
83+22	MFG-3
83+23	MFG-3
83+24	MFG-3
83+25	MFG-3

Westland
Sea King HAS41
MFG-5, Nordholz
89+50
89+51
89+52
89+53
89+54
89+55$
89+56
89+57
89+58$
89+60
89+62
89+63
89+64$
89+65
89+66
89+67
89+68
89+69
89+70
89+71

Heeresfliegertruppe
Eurocopter
EC.665 Tiger UHT
Ecole Franco-Allemande, Le Luc, France;
Eurocopter, Donauwörth;
KHR-36, Fritzlar;
TsLw-3, Fassberg;
WTD-61, Ingolstadt

74+02	Eurocopter
74+03	WTD-61
74+05	EFA
74+06	EFA
74+07	EFA
74+08	EFA
74+09	EFA
74+10	KHR-36
74+11	KHR-36
74+14	KHR-36
74+16	KHR-36
74+17	KHR-36
74+18	KHR-36
74+19	KHR-36
74+20	KHR-36
74+21	KHR-36
74+22	KHR-36
74+23	KHR-36
74+24	
74+26	
74+27	
74+28	
74+29	
74+30	
74+31	
74+32	
74+34	
74+36	
74+37	
74+38	
74+39	
74+40	
74+41	
74+42	
74+43	
74+44	
74+45	
74+46	
74+47	
74+48	
74+49	
74+50	
74+51	
74+52	
74+53	
74+54	
74+55	
74+56	
74+57	
74+58	
74+59	
98+15	
98+16	
98+17	WTD-61
98+18	Eurocopter
98+23	TsLw-3
98+25	TsLw-3
98+26	WTD-61

NH Industries
NH.90-TTH
Eurocopter, Donauwörth;
HFWS, Bückeburg;
HSG-64, Holzdorf;
THR-10, Fassberg;
WTD-61, Ingolstadt

78+01	HFWS
78+02	HFWS
78+03	HFWS
78+04	HFWS
78+05	
78+06	HFWS
78+07	HFWS
78+08	HFWS
78+09	HFWS
78+10	HFWS
78+11	HFWS
78+12	HFWS
78+13	HFWS
78+14	THR-10
78+15	THR-10
78+16	
78+17	
78+18	
78+20	
78+21	
78+22	
78+23	
78+24	
78+25	
78+26	
78+27	
78+28	
78+29	
78+30	
78+31	
78+32	
78+33	
78+34	
78+35	

78+36
78+37
78+38
78+39
78+40
78+41
78+42
78+43
78+44
78+45
78+46
78+47
78+48
78+49
78+50
79+01 HSG-64
79+02 HSG-64
79+03 HSG-64
79+04 HSG-64
79+05 HSG-64
79+06 HSG-64
79+07 HSG-64
79+09
79+10
79+24
79+25
79+26
79+27
79+28
79+29
79+30
98+49 Eurocopter
98+50 Eurocopter
98+90

Eurocopter EC.135P-1
HFWS, Bückeburg
82+51
82+52
82+53
82+54
82+55
82+56
82+57
82+59
82+60
82+61
82+62
82+63
82+64
82+65

MBB Bo.105P
Ecole Franco-Allemande,
 Le Luc, France;
HFUS-1, Holzdorf;
HFUS-7, Mendig;
HFVAS-100, Celle;
HFVAS-300, Mendig;
HFWS, Bückeburg;
KHR-26, Roth;
KHR-36, Fritzlar;
MTHR-25, Laupheim;
THR-30, Niederstetten;
TsLw-3, Fassberg;
WTD-61, Ingolstadt
86+02 KHR-36
86+03 HFWS
86+04 HFWS
86+05 KHR-36
86+06 KHR-36
86+07 HFWS
86+08 HFWS
86+09 HFWS
86+10 KHR-36
86+11
86+12 HFWS
86+13 THR-30
86+14 KHR-36
86+15 MTHR-25
86+16 KHR-36
86+18 HFWS
86+19 HFWS
86+20 HFWS
86+21 HFVAS-100
86+23 TsLw-3
86+24 HFWS
86+25 HFVAS-100
86+26 HFWS
86+27 KHR-26
86+28 HFUS-1 $
86+29 HFWS
86+30 KHR-26
86+31 HFUS-1
86+32 HFWS
86+33 MTHR-25
86+34 HFVAS-100
86+35 KHR-26
86+36 HFVAS-100
86+38 KHR-36
86+39 HFWS
86+40 HFWS
86+41 HFVAS-100
86+44 HFWS
86+45 KHR-36
86+47 HFVAS-100
86+48 HFVAS-100
86+49 KHR-36
86+50 KHR-36
86+51 HFWS
86+52 HFUS-1
86+53 HFVAS-100
86+54 EFA
86+55 KHR-36
86+56 THR-30
86+57 KHR-26
86+58 KHR-36
86+59 HFVAS-100
86+60 HFWS
86+61 KHR-26
86+62 HFWS
86+63 KHR-26
86+64 KHR-26
86+66 KHR-26
86+67 HFVAS-100
86+68 KHR-36
86+69 KHR-26
86+70 HFVAS-100
86+72 TsLw-3
86+73 HFWS
86+74 KHR-36
86+76 KHR-26
86+77 HFWS
86+78 HFVAS-300
86+79 KHR-26
86+80 HFVAS-100
86+83 TsLw-3
86+84 KHR-26
86+85 HFUS-1
86+86 HFVAS-100
86+87 MTHR-25
86+88 HFUS-1
86+89 HFUS-1
86+90 KHR-36
86+92 KHR-36
86+93 HFWS
86+95 HFUS-1
86+96 HFWS
86+97 KHR-36
86+98
86+99 HFWS
87+01 KHR-26
87+02 KHR-26
87+03 KHR-26
87+04 KHR-26
87+06 MTHR-25
87+09 KHR-26
87+10 KHR-26
87+11 KHR-36
87+12 HFWS
87+13 KHR-36
87+15 KHR-36
87+16 HFVAS-100
87+17 KHR-26
87+18 KHR-36
87+19 KHR-36
87+20 KHR-26
87+22
87+23 HFVAS-100
87+24 HFUS-7
87+25 KHR-26
87+26 HFUS-1
87+27 HFWS
87+28 HFUS-1
87+29 HFWS
87+30 KHR-36
87+31 HFWS
87+34 KHR-26
87+35 KHR-26
87+37 HFWS
87+39 KHR-36
87+41 HFWS
87+43 KHR-36
87+44 HFUS-1
87+45 HFUS-1
87+46 KHR-36

87+47 HFWS
87+48 HFVAS-100
87+49 HFWS
87+50 KHR-36
87+51 HFVAS-100
87+52 HFUS-1
87+53 KHR-36
87+55 KHR-36
87+56 TsLw-3
87+58 HFWS
87+59 HFWS
87+60 KHR-36
87+61 HFWS
87+62 HFWS
87+63 HFWS
87+64 HFWS
87+65 KHR-36
87+66 KHR-36
87+67 HFWS
87+68 KHR-36
87+70 KHR-26
87+71 HFWS
87+72 THR-30
87+73 WTD-61
87+75 KHR-26
87+76 KHR-36
87+77
87+78 HFUS-1
87+79
87+82 HFVAS-300
87+83 MTHR-25
87+85 HFWS
87+87 HFVAS-100
87+88 KHR-26
87+89 MTHR-25
87+90 HFWS
87+92 KHR-26
87+97 HFVAS-100
87+98 HFWS
87+99 KHR-36
88+01 HFUS-1
88+02 MTHR-25
88+04 KHR-36
88+06 KHR-36
88+07 HFWS
88+08 HFWS
88+09
88+10 THR-30
88+11 MTHR-25
88+12 HFVAS-100 $

GHANA
Ghana Air Force
Dassault
Falcon 900EASy
VIP Flight, Accra
9G-EXE

GREECE
Ellinikí Polemiki Aeroporía
Aeritalia C-27J Spartan
354 Mira, Elefsís
4117
4118
4120
4121
4122
4123
4124
4125

Dassault Mirage 2000
331 MAPK/114 PM, Tanagra;
332 MAPK/114 PM, Tanagra

Mirage 2000BG
201 332 MAPK
202 332 MAPK

Mirage 2000EG
210 332 MAPK
212 332 MAPK
213 332 MAPK
215 332 MAPK
216 332 MAPK
217 332 MAPK
218 332 MAPK
219 332 MAPK
220 332 MAPK
221 332 MAPK
228 332 MAPK
231 332 MAPK
232 332 MAPK
233 332 MAPK
237 332 MAPK
239 332 MAPK
241 332 MAPK
242 332 MAPK

Mirage 2000-5BG
505 331 MAPK
506 331 MAPK
507 331 MAPK
508 331 MAPK
509 331 MAPK

Mirage 2000-5EG
511 331 MAPK
514 331 MAPK
527 331 MAPK
530 331 MAPK
534 331 MAPK
535 331 MAPK
536 331 MAPK
540 331 MAPK
543 331 MAPK
545 331 MAPK
546 331 MAPK
547 331 MAPK
548 331 MAPK
549 331 MAPK
550 331 MAPK
551 331 MAPK
552 331 MAPK
553 331 MAPK
554 331 MAPK
555 331 MAPK

Embraer
ERJ-135BJ Legacy/ERJ.145H/ ERJ.135LR
352 MMYP/112 PM, Elefsís;
380 Mira/112 PM, Elefsís
135L-484 ERJ-135BJ 352 MMYP
145-209 ERJ-135LR 352 MMYP
145-374 ERJ-145H 380 Mira
145-671 ERJ-145H 380 Mira
145-729 ERJ-145H 380 Mira
145-757 ERJ-145H 380 Mira

Gulfstream Aerospace
Gulfstream V
352 MMYP/112 PM, Elefsís
678

Lockheed
C-130H Hercules
356 MTM/112 PM, Elefsís
**ECM*
741*
742
743
744
745
746
747*
749
751
752$

Lockheed
F-16C/F-16D*
Fighting Falcon
330 Mira/111 PM, Nea Ankhialos;
335 Mira/116 PM, Áraxos;
336 Mira/116 PM, Áraxos;
337 Mira/110 PM, Larissa;
340 Mira/115PM, Souda;
341 Mira/111 PM, Nea Ankhialos;
343 Mira/115PM, Souda;
347 Mira/111 PM, Nea Ankhialos
001 335 Mira
002 335 Mira
003 335 Mira
004 335 Mira
005 335 Mira
006 335 Mira
007 335 Mira
008 335 Mira
009 335 Mira
010 335 Mira
011 335 Mira
012 335 Mira
013 335 Mira
014 335 Mira

015 335 Mira
016 335 Mira
017 335 Mira
018 335 Mira
019 335 Mira
020 335 Mira
021* 335 Mira
022* 335 Mira
023* 335 Mira
024* 335 Mira
025* 335 Mira
026* 335 Mira
027* 335 Mira
028* 335 Mira
029* 335 Mira
030* 335 Mira
046 341 Mira
047 347 Mira
048 341 Mira
049 347 Mira
050 341 Mira
051 347 Mira
052 341 Mira
053 347 Mira
054 341 Mira
055 347 Mira
056 341 Mira
057 347 Mira
058 341 Mira
060 341 Mira
061 347 Mira
062 341 Mira
063 347 Mira
064 341 Mira
065 347 Mira
066 341 Mira
067 347 Mira
068 341 Mira
069 347 Mira
070 341 Mira
071 347 Mira
072 341 Mira
073 347 Mira
074 341 Mira
075 347 Mira
076 341 Mira
077* 341 Mira
078* 347 Mira
079* 347 Mira
080* 341 Mira
081* 347 Mira
082* 341 Mira
083* 347 Mira
084* 341 Mira
110 330 Mira
111 330 Mira
112
113 330 Mira
114
115 330 Mira
116 330 Mira
117 330 Mira
118
119 330 Mira
120
121 330 Mira
122
124
125 330 Mira
126 330 Mira
127 330 Mira
128
129 330 Mira
130
132
133 330 Mira
134
136
138
139 330 Mira
140
141 330 Mira
143 330 Mira
144* 330 Mira
145* 330 Mira
146*
147* 330 Mira
148*
149*
500 343 Mira
501 337 Mira
502 337 Mira
503 343 Mira
504 343 Mira
505 343 Mira
506 340 Mira
507 337 Mira
508 337 Mira
509 343 Mira
510 343 Mira
511 343 Mira
512 343 Mira
513 343 Mira
515 337 Mira
517 347 Mira
518 340 Mira
519 340 Mira
520 343 Mira
521 340 Mira
523 340 Mira
524 337 Mira
525 343 Mira
526 343 Mira
527 343 Mira
528 337 Mira
529 343 Mira
530 337 Mira
531 337 Mira
532 337 Mira
533 340 Mira
534 340 Mira
535 340 Mira
536 340 Mira
537 340 Mira
538 340 Mira
539 337 Mira
600* 343 Mira
601* 340 Mira
602* 340 Mira
603* 340 Mira
605* 340 Mira
606* 337 Mira
607* 343 Mira
608* 340 Mira
609* 337 Mira
610* 340 Mira
611* 337 Mira
612* 337 Mira
613* 343 Mira
614* 343 Mira
615* 343 Mira
616* 343 Mira
617* 343 Mira
618* 343 Mira
619* 337 Mira $

LTV A-7 Corsair II
336 Mira/116 PM,
Áraxos
154404 TA-7C
155424 TA-7C
156747 TA-7C
156750 TA-7C
156753 TA-7C
156767 TA-7C
158825 A-7E $
159263 A-7E
159639 A-7E
159648 A-7E
160552 A-7E
160616 A-7E $
160717 A-7E
160728 A-7E
160736 A-7E
160865 A-7E
160866 A-7E

HUNGARY
Hungarian Defence Forces
Antonov An-26
59 Sz.D.REB, Kecskemét
110
405
406
407
603

Boeing
C-17A Globemaster III
Strategic Airlift Capability (SAC)
Heavy Airlift Wing,
Pápa, Hungary
01 (08-0001)
02 (08-0002)
03 (08-0003)

SAAB 39C/39D* Gripen
59 Sz.D.REB, Kecskemét
30
31
32
33
34
35
36
37
38
39
40
41
42*
43*

ISRAEL
Heyl ha'Avir
Boeing 707
120 Sqn, Nevatim

120	RC-707
128	RC-707
137	RC-707
140	KC-707
248	KC-707
250	KC-707
255	EC-707
260	KC-707
264	KC-707
272	KC-707
275	KC-707
290	KC-707
295	VC-707

Lockheed
C-130 Karnaf
103 Sqn & 131 Sqn, Nevatim

102	C-130H
208	C-130E
305	C-130E
309	C-130E
310	C-130E
314	C-130E
316	C-130E
318	C-130E
420	KC-130H
427	C-130H
428	C-130H
435	C-130H
436	C-130H
522	C-130H
545	KC-130H
...	C-130J-30 (on order)
...	C-130J-30 (on order)
...	C-130J-30 (on order)

ITALY
Aeronautica Militare Italiana
Aeritalia G222/C-27J Spartan
9ª Brigata Aerea,
Pratica di Mare:
14º Stormo/8º Gruppo;
46ª Brigata Aerea, Pisa:
98º Gruppo;
RSV, Pratica di Mare

G222RM (RC-222)
MM62139 14-20 8

G222TCM (C-222)
MM62124 RS-46 RSV
MM62146 14-11 8

C-27J Spartan

CSX62127	Alenia	
MM62214	46-84	98
MM62215	46-80	98
MM62217	46-81	98
MM62218	46-82	98
CSX62219	RS-50	RSV
MM62220	46-83	98
MM62221	46-85	98
MM62222	46-86	98
MM62223	46-88	98
MM62224	46-89	98
MM62225	46-90	98
MM62250	46-91	98

Aeritalia-EMB
AMX (A-11A)/
AMX-ACOL (A-11B)/
AMX-T (TA-11A)/
AMX-T-ACOL (TA-11B)
32º Stormo, Amendola:
13º Gruppo &
101º Gruppo;
51º Stormo, Istrana:
103º Gruppo &
132º Gruppo;
RSV, Pratica di Mare

MM7101	A-11A		
MM7114	A-11B		
MM7115	A-11B	32-23	13
MM7126	A-11B	32-12	13
MM7129	A-11B	32-15	13
MM7143	A-11A	51-21	103
MM7147	A-11A	32-01$	13
MM7148	A-11B	51-61	132
MM7149	A-11B	32-24	13
MM7151	A-11B	51-51	132
CSX7158	A-11A	RS-12	RSV
MM7159	A-11A	51-10$	103
MM7160	A-11B	51-53	132
MM7161	A-11B	51-37	132
MM7162	A-11B		
MM7163	A-11B	32-25	13
MM7164	A-11B	51-40	132
MM7165	A-11B	32-16	13
MM7167	A-11B	51-56	132
MM7168	A-11B	51-55	132
MM7169	A-11B	51-66	132
MM7170	A-11B	32-05	13
MM7171	A-11B	51-52	132
MM7172	A-11B	51-67	132
MM7173	A-11B	51-63	132
MM7174	A-11B	51-60	132
MM7175	A-11A	51-45	132
MM7176	A-11B		
MM7177	A-11B	51-42	132
MM7178	A-11B	51-43	132
MM7179	A-11B	51-64	132
MM7180	A-11B	32-20	13
MM7182	A-11B	51-62	132
MM7183	A-11B	51-41	132
MM7184	A-11B	51-65	132
MM7185	A-11B		
MM7186	A-11B	51-50	132
MM7189	A-11B		
MM7190	A-11B	51-57	132
MM7191	A-11B	51-34	132
MM7192	A-11B	32-02	13
MM7193	A-11B	51-54	132
MM7194	A-11B	32-21	13
CSX7195	A-11A		Alenia
MM7196	A-11A	32-07	13
MM7197	A-11B	51-46	132
MM7198	A-11B	51-44$	132
MM55029	TA-11A	32-50$	101
MM55030	TA-11A	32-41	101
CSX55034	TA-11B	RS-18	RSV
MM55036	TA-11A	32-51	101
MM55037	TA-11A	32-64	101
MM55042	TA-11A	32-56	101
MM55043	TA-11A	32-65	101
MM55044	TA-11A	32-57	101
MM55046	TA-11A	32-47	101
MM55047	TA-11A	32-53	101
MM55049	TA-11A	32-66	101
MM55051	TA-11A	32-42	101

Aermacchi
MB339A (T-339A)/
MB339PAN (AT-339A)/
MB339CD-1 (FT-339B)*/
MB339CD-2 (FT-339C)*/
32º Stormo, Amendola:
632ª SC;
36º Stormo, Gioia del Colle:
12º Gruppo;
51º Stormo, Istrana:
651ª SC;
61º Stormo, Lecce:
212º Gruppo &
213º Gruppo;
Aermacchi, Venegono;
Frecce Tricolori [FT]
(313º Gruppo), Rivolto
(MB339A/PAN);
RSV, Pratica di Mare

MM54443	T-339A	61-50	
MM54446	T-339A	61-01	
MM54452	T-339A		
CSX54453	T-339A	RS-11	RSV
MM54457	T-339A	61-11	
MM54458	T-339A	61-12	
MM54465	T-339A	61-21	
MM54467	T-339A	61-23	
MM54468	T-339A	61-24	

MM54473 AT-339A [FT]
MM54475 AT-339A 0 [FT]
MM54477 AT-339A 3 [FT]
MM54479 AT-339A [FT]
MM54480 AT-339A 8 [FT]
MM54482 AT-339A 2 [FT]
MM54485 AT-339A [FT]
MM54487 AT-339A 5 [FT]
MM54488 T-339A 61-32
MM54492 T-339A
MM54496 T-339A 61-42
MM54500 AT-339A [FT]
MM54505 AT-339A [FT]
MM54507 T-339A 61-55
MM54510 AT-339A 6 [FT]
MM54511 T-339A 61-61
MM54512 T-339A 61-62
MM54514 AT-339A 10 [FT]
MM54515 T-339A 61-65
MM54516 T-339A 61-66
MM54517 AT-339A 1 [FT]
MM54518 AT-339A [FT]
MM54532 T-339A
MM54533 T-339A 61-72
MM54534 AT-339A [FT]
MM54536 T-339A
MM54537 T-339A
MM54538 AT-339A [FT]
MM54539 AT-339A 9 [FT]
MM54542 AT-339A [FT]
CSX54544 FT-339 RS-30 RSV
MM54547 AT-339A [FT]
MM54548 T-339A 61-106
MM54549 T-339A 61-107
MM54551 AT-339A 11 [FT]
MM55052 AT-339A 7 [FT]
MM55053 FT-339 61-114
MM55054 AT-339A 4 [FT]
MM55055 T-339A 61-20
MM55058 T-339A 61-41
MM55059 T-339A 61-26
MM55062 FT-339 61-126
MM55063 FT-339 61-127
MM55064 FT-339 61-130
MM55065 FT-339 61-131
MM55066 FT-339 61-132
MM55067 FT-339 61-133
MM55068 FT-339 RS-33 RSV
MM55069 FT-339 61-135
MM55070 FT-339 61-136
MM55072 FT-339 61-140
MM55073 FT-339 61-141
MM55074 FT-339 36-06
MM55075 FT-339 61-143
MM55076 FT-339 36-04
MM55077 FT-339 61-145
MM55078 FT-339 61-146
MM55079 FT-339 61-147
MM55080 FT-339 61-150
MM55081 FT-339 61-151
MM55082 FT-339 61-152
MM55084 FT-339 61-154
MM55085 FT-339 61-155
MM55086 FT-339 61-156
MM55087 FT-339 61-167
MM55088 FT-339 61-160
MM55089 FT-339 32-161
MM55090 FT-339 61-162
MM55091 FT-339 RS-32 RSV

Aermacchi M311

Aermacchi, Venegono
CPX619

Aermacchi M-346/T-346A Master

Aermacchi, Venegono;
RSV, Pratica di Mare
CPX616 M-346
CPX617 M-346
MM55144 T-346A RSV
MM55145 T-346A RSV
CSX55152 T-346A (on order)
MM55... T-346A (on order)
MM55... T-346A (on order)
MM55... T-346A (on order)
MM55... T-346A (on order)

Aérospatiale ATR.72-600MP (P-72A)

CSX62279 (on order)
CSX62280 Alenia
CSX62281 (on order)
CSX62282 (on order)

Agusta-Sikorsky HH-3F Pelican

15° Stormo:
82° Centro SAR, Trapani/Birgi;
83° Gruppo SAR, Cervia;
84° Centro SAR, Brindisi/Casale;
85° Centro SAR, Pratica di Mare
MM80974 15-01 85
MM80975 15-02$ 85
MM80979 15-06 85
MM80984 15-13 82
MM80985 15-14 83
MM80986 15-15 82
MM80988 15-19 85
MM80992 15-23 83
MM81337 15-25 83
MM81339 15-27 85
MM81341 15-29 83
MM81342 15-30 85
MM81343 15-31 85
MM81344 15-32 82
MM81345 15-33 84
MM81346 15-34 85
MM81347 15-35 84
MM81348 15-36 85
MM81349 15-37 85
MM81350 15-38 85

AgustaWestland AW139

15° Stormo:
81° Centro, Cervia;
82° Centro SAR, Trapani/Birgi;
83° Gruppo SAR, Cervia;
84° Centro SAR, Gioia del Colle;
85° Centro SAR, Pratica di Mare;
31° Stormo, Roma-Ciampino:
93° Gruppo

HH-139A

MM81796 15-40 83
MM81797 15-41 84
CSX81798 15-42
CSX81799 15-43
CSX81800 15-44

VH-139A

MM81806 93
MM81807 93
MM81812 93

Airbus A.319CJ-115X (VC-319A)

31° Stormo, Roma-Ciampino:
306° Gruppo
MM62174
MM62209
MM62243

Boeing 767-2EYER (KC-767A)

14° Stormo, Pratica di Mare:
8° Gruppo
MM62226 14-01
MM62227 14-02
MM62228 14-03
MM62229 14-04

Breguet Br.1150 Atlantic (P-1150A)

41° Stormo, Catania:
88° Gruppo
MM40114 41-76
MM40115 41-77$
MM40116 41-01
MM40117 41-02
MM40121 41-06

Dassault Falcon 50 (VC-50A)

31° Stormo, Roma-Ciampino:
93° Gruppo
MM62026
MM62029

Dassault Falcon 900EX (VC-900A)/

900EX EASy (VC-900B)*

31° Stormo, Roma-Ciampino:
93° Gruppo

MM62171 $	
MM62172	
MM62210	
MM62244*	
MM62245*	

Eurofighter
F-2000A/TF-2000A* Typhoon

4° Stormo, Grosseto:
9° Gruppo & 20° Gruppo;
36° Stormo, Gioia del Colle:
12° Gruppo;
37° Stormo, Trapani/Birgi:
18° Gruppo;
Alenia, Torino/Caselle;
RSV, Pratica di Mare

MMX602	RS-01	Alenia
MMX603	RMV-01	Alenia
MMX614*		RSV
MM7235	36-04	12
MM7270	4-1	9
MM7271	36-03	12
MM7272	36-14	12
MM7273		
MM7274	4-10	9
MM7275	36-11	12
MM7276	4-21	9
MM7277	4-40	20
MM7278	4-44	20
MM7279		
MM7280		
MM7281	4-14	9
MM7282	36-15	12
MM7284	36-10	12
MM7285	4-16	9
MM7286	36-02	12
MM7287	4-3	9
MM7288	4-4	9
MM7289	4-5	9
MM7290	4-7	9
MM7291	4-11	9
MM7292	4-12	9
MM7293	36-33	12
MM7294	4-13	9
MM7295	36-20	12
MM7296	36-22	12
MM7297	36-23	12
MM7298	36-24	12
MM7299	4-41	20
MM7300	36-12	12
MM7301	4-22	9
MM7302	36-25	12
MM7303	4-2	9
MM7304	36-21	12
MM7305		RSV
MM7306	RS-21	RSV
MM7307	37-01	18
MM7308	36-36	12
MM7309	37-03	18
MM7310	36-32	12
MM7311	4-6	9
MM7312	36-34	12
MM7313	36-35	12
MM7314	36-37	12
MM7315	37-02	18
MM7316	4-42	20
MM7317	4-43	20
MM7318		
MM7319		
MM7320		
MM7321		
MM7322		
MM7323		
MM7324		
MM7325		
MM55092*	4-25	20
MM55093*	4-31	20
MM55094*	4-27	20
MM55095*	4-23	20
MM55096*	4-30	20
MM55097*	4-24	20
MM55128*	4-26	20
MM55129*	4-32	20
MM55130*	4-33	20
MM55131*	4-34	20
MM55132*	4-35	20
MM55133*	4-36	20

Lockheed
C-130J/C-130J-30/KC-130J*
Hercules II

46ª Brigata Aerea, Pisa:
2° Gruppo & 50° Gruppo

C-130J

MM62175	46-40
MM62177	46-42
MM62178	46-43
MM62179	46-44
MM62180	46-45
MM62181	46-46
MM62182	46-47
MM62183*	46-48
MM62184	46-49
MM62185	46-50
MM62186	46-51

C-130J-30

MM62187	46-53
MM62188	46-54
MM62189	46-55
MM62190	46-56
MM62191	46-57
MM62192	46-58
MM62193	46-59
MM62194	46-60
MM62195	46-61
MM62196	46-62

Panavia
Tornado IDS (A-200A)/
Tornado IDS[MLU](A-200C)/
Tornado IDS Trainer(TA-200A)/
Tornado IDS Trainer[MLU](TA-200C)/
Tornado ECR(EA-200B)

6° Stormo, Ghedi:
102° Gruppo, 154° Gruppo &
156° Gruppo;
50° Stormo, Piacenza:
155° Gruppo;
RSV, Pratica di Mare

MM7003	A-200C	50-50	155
MM7004	A-200C	6-55	102
CMX7005	A-200A		Alenia
MM7006	A-200C	6-31$	102
MM7007	A-200A	6-01	154
CSX7009	A-200C		Alenia
MM7011	A-200A	6-13	154
MM7013	A-200C	6-75	102
MM7015	A-200C	6-32$	102
MM7016	A-200A	6-20	154
MM7019	EA-200B	50-05	155
MM7020	EA-200B	50-41	155
MM7021	EA-200B	50-01	155
MM7022	A-200C	6-23	154
MM7023	A-200A	36-31	156
MM7024	A-200C	6-50	102
MM7025	A-200A	6-05	154
MM7026	A-200C	6-35	102
MM7027	EA-200B		
MM7028	A-200A	50-52	155
MM7029	A-200A		
MM7030	EA-200B	50-04$	155
MM7031	A-200A	6-61	102
MM7033	A-200A	50-53	155
MM7034	EA-200B		
MM7035	A-200C	6-27	154
MM7036	EA-200B	50-55	155
MM7038	A-200C	6-37	102
CSX7039	A-200C	6-02	154
CSX7041	A-200C	RS-06	RSV
MM7042	A-200A	50-57	155
MM7043	A-200A	6-25	154
MM7044	A-200C	6-76	156
MM7046	EA-200B	6-06	154
CSX7047	EA-200B	RS-05	RSV
MM7048	A-200C		
MM7049	A-200A	6-64	102
MM7051	EA-200B	50-45	155
MM7052	EA-200B	50-02	155
MM7053	EA-200B	50-07	155
MM7054	EA-200B	50-40$	155
MM7055	A-200A	50-42	155
MM7056	A-200A	6-66	102
MM7057	A-200A	6-04	154
MM7058	A-200C	6-11	154
MM7059	A-200A	50-47	155
MM7061	A-200A	6-14	154
MM7062	EA-200B	50-44	155
MM7063	A-200C	6-26	154
MM7065	A-200C	50-56	155
MM7066	A-200A	50-03	155
MM7067	A-200A	6-71	156
MM7068	EA-200B	50-46	155
MM7070	EA-200B	50-06	155

MM7071 A-200C 6-12 154
MM7072 A-200C 6-30 154
MM7073 EA-200B 6-34 102
MM7075 A-200A 6-07 154
MM7078 A-200A
CMX7079 EA-200B Alenia
MM7080 A-200A 6-33$ 102
MM7081 A-200A 6-57 102
MM7082 EA-200B 50-54 155
MM7083 A-200A 6-72 156
MM7084 A-200A 6-03 154
CMX7085 A-200A 36-50 Alenia
MM7086 A-200A 6-60 102
MM7087 A-200C 6-36 102
MM7088 A-200A 6-10 154
MM55000 TA-200A 6-51$ 102
MM55002 TA-200A 6-52$ 102
MM55003 TA-200A
CSX55006 TA-200C Alenia
MM55007 TA-200A 6-56 102
MM55008 TA-200A 6-45 102
MM55009 TA-200A 6-44 102
MM55010 TA-200A 6-42 102

Piaggio
P-180AM Avanti (VC-180A)
14° Stormo, Pratica di Mare:
71° Gruppo;
36° Stormo, Gioia del Colle:
636ª SC;
RSV, Pratica di Mare
MM62159 71
MM62160 71
MM62161 71
MM62162 71
MM62163 71
MM62164 RSV
MM62199 636
MM62201 71
MM62202 71
MM62203 71
MM62204 71
MM62205 71
MM62206 71
MM62207 71

Aviazione dell'Esercito
Dornier Do.228-212 (UC-228)
28° Gruppo Squadrone Cavalleria dell'Aria, Viterbo
MM62156 E.I.101
MM62157 E.I.102
MM62158 E.I.103

Piaggio
P-180AM Avanti (VC-180A)
28° Gruppo Squadrone Det, Cavalleria dell'Aria, Roma/Ciampino
MM62167
MM62168
MM62169

Guardia Costiera
Aérospatiale
ATR.42-400MP (P-42A)/
ATR.42-500MP (P-42B)*
2° Nucleo, Catania;
3° Nucleo, Pescara
MM62170 10-01 3
MM62208 10-02 2
MM62270* 10-03 2

Guardia di Finanza
Aérospatiale
ATR.42-400MP (P-42A)
Gruppo Esplorazione Aeromarittima, Pratica di Mare
MM62165 GF-13
MM62166 GF-14
MM62230 GF-15
MM62251 GF-16

Piaggio
P-180AM Avanti (VC-180A)/
P-180AM Avanti II (VC-180B)*
Gruppo Esplorazione Aeromarittima, Pratica di Mare
MM62248 GF-18
MM62249* GF-19

Marina Militare Italiana
AgustaWestland
EH.101
1° Grupelicot, La Spezia/Luni;
3° Grupelicot, Catania
Mk110 ASW (SH-101A)
MM81480 2-01 3
MM81481 2-02 3
MM81482 2-03 3
MM81483 2-04 3
MM81484 2-05 3
MM81485 2-06 3
MM81486 2-07 3
MM81487 2-08 3
CSX81719 2-22 1
MM81726 2-23 1
Mk112 ASW (EH-101A)
MM81488 2-09 1
MM81489 2-10 1
MM81490 2-11 1
MM81491 2-12 1
Mk410 UTY (UH-101A)
MM81492 2-13 1
MM81493 2-14 1
MM81494 2-15 1
MM81495 2-16 1
MM81633 2-18 1
MM81634 2-19 1
MM81635 2-20 1
MM81636 2-21 1

McDonnell Douglas
AV-8B/TAV-8B Harrier II+
Gruppo Aerei Imbarcarti, Taranto/Grottaglie
AV-8B
MM7199 1-03
MM7200 1-04
MM7201 1-05
MM7212 1-06
MM7213 1-07
MM7214 1-08
MM7215 1-09
MM7217 1-11
MM7218 1-12
MM7219 1-13
MM7220 1-14
MM7222 1-16
MM7223 1-18
MM7224 1-19
TAV-8B
MM55032 1-01
MM55033 1-02

Piaggio
P-180AM Avanti (VC-180A)
9ª Brigata Aerea, AMI, Pratica di Mare:
71° Gruppo
MM62200 9-01
MM62211 9-02
MM62212 9-03
MM62213

Italian Govt
Dassault Falcon 900
Italian Govt/Soc. CAI, Roma/Ciampino
I-CAEX
I-DIES

IVORY COAST
Boeing 727-2Y4
Ivory Coast Govt, Abidjan
TU-VAO
Fokker 100
Ivory Coast Govt, Abidjan
TU-VAA

Grumman
G.1159C Gulfstream IV
Ivory Coast Govt, Abidjan
TU-VAD

JAPAN
Japan Air Self Defence Force
Boeing 747-47C
701st Flight Sqn, Chitose
20-1101
20-1102

JORDAN
Al Quwwat al Jawwiya al Malakiya al Urduniya
Extra EA-300LP

Royal Jordanian Falcons,
Amman
JY-RFA
JY-RFB
JY-RFC
JY-RFD
JY-RFE

Lockheed C-130H Hercules
3 Sqn, Amman/Marka
344
345
346
347

Jordanian Govt
Airbus A.318-112
Jordanian Govt, Amman
VQ-BDD

Airbus A.340-642
Jordanian Govt, Amman
JY-ASX (on order)

Gulfstream Aerospace G.450
Jordanian Govt, Amman
VQ-BCE

KAZAKHSTAN
Airbus A.330-223
Govt of Kazakhstan, Almaty
UP-A3001

Boeing 757-2M6
Govt of Kazakhstan, Almaty
UP-B5701

KENYA
Kenyan Air Force
Fokker 70ER
Kenyan Govt, Nairobi
308

KUWAIT
Al Quwwat al Jawwiya al Kuwaitiya
Boeing C-17A Globemaster III
KAF 3.. (on order)

Lockheed KC-130J Hercules II
KAF 3.. (on order)
KAF 3.. (on order)
KAF 3.. (on order)

Lockheed L100-30 Hercules
41 Sqn, Kuwait International
KAF 323
KAF 324
KAF 325

Kuwaiti Govt
Airbus A.300C4-620
Kuwaiti Govt, Safat
9K-AHI

Airbus A.310-308
Kuwaiti Govt, Safat
9K-ALD

Airbus A.319CJ-115X
Kuwaiti Govt, Safat
9K-GEA

Airbus A.320-212
Kuwaiti Govt, Safat
9K-AKD

Airbus A.340-542
Kuwaiti Govt, Safat
9K-GBA (on order)
9K-GBB (on order)

Boeing 737-9BQER
Kuwaiti Govt, Safat
9K-GCC

Boeing 747-469
Kuwaiti Govt, Safat
9K-ADE

Boeing 747-8JK
Kuwaiti Govt, Safat
9K-GAA

Gulfstream Aerospace G.550
Kuwaiti Govt, Safat
9K-GFA

Gulfstream Aerospace Gulfstream V
Kuwaiti Govt/Kuwait Airways, Safat
9K-AJD
9K-AJE
9K-AJF

KYRGYZSTAN
Tupolev Tu-154M
Govt of Kyrgyzstan, Bishkek
EX-85718

LITHUANIA
Karines Oro Pajegos
Aeritalia C-27J Spartan
Transporto Eskadrile, Siauliai-Zokniai
06
07
08

Antonov An-26RV
Transporto Eskadrile, Siauliai-Zokniai
03
04
05

LET 410UVP Turbolet
Transporto Eskadrile, Siauliai-Zokniai
01

Mil Mi-8
Sraigtasparniu Eskadrile, Panevezys/Pajuostis
02 Mi-8T
09 Mi-8T
10 Mi-8T
11 Mi-8PS
21 Mi-8MTV-1
22 Mi-8MTV-1
28 Mi-8T

LUXEMBOURG
NATO
Boeing 757-28A
NATO, Geilenkirchen, Germany
OO-TFA

Boeing E-3A
NAEW&CF, Geilenkirchen, Germany
LX-N90442
LX-N90443$
LX-N90444
LX-N90445
LX-N90446
LX-N90447
LX-N90448
LX-N90449
LX-N90450
LX-N90451
LX-N90452
LX-N90453
LX-N90454
LX-N90455
LX-N90456
LX-N90458
LX-N90459

MACEDONIA
Macedonian Govt
Bombardier Lear 60
Macedonian Govt, Skopje
Z3-MKD

MALAYSIA
Royal Malaysian Air Force/ Tentera Udara Diraja Malaysia
Boeing 737-7H6
2 Sqn, Simpang
M53–01

Bombardier
BD.700-1A10 Global Express
2 Sqn, Simpang
M48-02

Dassault Falcon 900
2 Sqn, Simpang
M37-01

Lockheed
C-130 Hercules
14 Sqn, Labuan;
20 Sqn, Subang

M30-01	C-130T	20 Sqn
M30-02	C-130H	20 Sqn
M30-03	C-130H	14 Sqn
M30-04	C-130H-30	20 Sqn
M30-05	C-130H-30	14 Sqn
M30-06	C-130H-30	14 Sqn
M30-07	C-130T	20 Sqn
M30-08	C-130H(MP)	20 Sqn
M30-09	C-130H(MP)	20 Sqn
M30-10	C-130H-30	20 Sqn
M30-11	C-130H-30	20 Sqn
M30-12	C-130H-30	20 Sqn
M30-14	C-130H-30	20 Sqn
M30-15	C-130H-30	20 Sqn
M30-16	C-130H-30	20 Sqn

Malaysian Govt
Airbus A.319CJ-115X
9M-NAA

MALTA
Bombardier
Learjet 60
Govt of Malta, Luqa
9H-AFK

MEXICO
Fuerza Aérea Mexicana
Boeing 757-225
8° Grupo Aéreo, Mexico City
TP-01 (XC-UJM)

Armada de Mexico
Gulfstream Aerospace G.450
PRIMESCTRANS, Mexico City
XC-LMF

MOROCCO
Force Aérienne Royaume Marocaine/ Al Quwwat al Jawwiya al Malakiya Marakishiya
Aeritalia
C-27J Spartan
Escadrille de Transport 3,
Kenitra
CN-AMN
CN-AMO
CN-AMP
CN-AMQ

Airtech
CN.235M-100
Escadrille de Transport 3,
Kenitra

023	CNA-MA
024	CNA-MB
025	CNA-MC
026	CNA-MD
027	CN-AME
028	CNA-MF
031	CNA-MG

CAP-232
Marche Verte

28	CN-ABP [2]
29	CN-ABQ [6]
31	CN-ABR [5]
36	CN-ABS [4]
37	CN-ABT [3]
41	CN-ABU [7]
42	CN-ABV [1]
43	CN-ABW
44	CN-ABX [8]

Lockheed
C-130H Hercules
Escadrille de Transport 3,
Kenitra

4535	CNA-OA	C-130H
4551	CNA-OC	C-130H
4575	CNA-OD	C-130H
4581	CNA-OE	C-130H
4583	CNA-OF	C-130H
4713	CNA-OG	C-130H
4733	CNA-OI	C-130H
4738	CNA-OJ	C-130H
4739	CNA-OK	C-130H
4742	CNA-OL	C-130H
4875	CNA-OM	C-130H
4876	CNA-ON	C-130H
4877	CNA-OO	C-130H
4888	CNA-OP	C-130H
4907	CN-AOR	KC-130H
4909	CNA-OS	KC-130H

Govt of Morocco
Boeing 737-8KB
Govt of Morocco, Rabat
CN-MVI

Cessna 560 Citation V
Govt of Morocco, Rabat
CNA-NV
CNA-NW

Cessna
560XLS Citation Excel
Govt of Morocco, Rabat
CN-AMJ
CN-AMK

Dassault Falcon 50
Govt of Morocco, Rabat
CN-ANO

Grumman
G.1159 Gulfstream IITT/
G.1159A Gulfstream III
Govt of Morocco, Rabat
CNA-NL Gulfstream IITT
CN-ANU Gulfstream III

Gulfstream Aerospace G.550
Govt of Morocco, Rabat
CN-AMS

NAMIBIA
Dassault Falcon 7X
Namibian Govt, Windhoek
V5-GON

Dassault Falcon 900B
Namibian Govt, Windhoek
V5-NAM

NETHERLANDS
Koninklijke Luchtmacht
Agusta-Bell AB.412SP
303 Sqn, Leeuwarden
R-01
R-02
R-03

Boeing-Vertol
CH-47 Chinook
298 Sqn, Defence Helicopter Command,
Gilze-Rijen
CH-47D Chinook
D-101
D-102
D-103
D-106
D-661
D-662
D-663
D-664
D-665
D-666
D-667
CH-47F Chinook
D-890
D-891
D-892
D-893
D-894
D-895

Eurocopter
AS.532U-2 Cougar
300 Sqn, Defence Helicopter Command,
Gilze-Rijen
S-419
S-440

S-441
S-445
S-447
S-453
S-454
S-457

General Dynamics
F-16
Now operated on a pool basis. Squadron markings carried do not necessarily reflect the squadron operating.
312/313 Sqns,
Volkel;
322/323 Sqns, Leeuwarden;
148th FS/162th FW, Tucson International Airport, Arizona, USA
J-001 F-16AM 312 Sqn
J-002 F-16AM 312 Sqn
J-003 F-16AM 312 Sqn
J-004 F-16AM 148th FS
J-005 F-16AM 313 Sqn
J-006 F-16AM 322/323 Sqn
J-008 F-16AM 313 Sqn $
J-009 F-16AM 323 Sqn
J-010 F-16AM 148th FS
J-011 F-16AM 312 Sqn
J-013 F-16AM 323 Sqn
J-014 F-16AM 313 Sqn
J-015 F-16AM 312 Sqn $
J-016 F-16AM 312 Sqn
J-017 F-16AM 322 Sqn
J-018 F-16AM 148th FS
J-019 F-16AM 148th FS
J-020 F-16AM 322 Sqn
J-021 F-16AM 312 Sqn
J-055 F-16AM 313 Sqn
J-057 F-16AM 312/313 Sqn
J-060 F-16AM 322 Sqn
J-061 F-16AM 322/323 Sqn
J-062 F-16AM 313 Sqn
J-063 F-16AM 313 Sqn
J-064 F-16BM 148th FS
J-065 F-16BM
J-066 F-16BM 323 Sqn
J-067 F-16BM 148th FS
J-135 F-16AM 322 Sqn
J-136 F-16AM 312 Sqn
J-142 F-16AM 323 Sqn
J-144 F-16AM 323 Sqn
J-145 F-16AM
J-146 F-16AM 323 Sqn
J-193 F-16AM 323 Sqn
J-196 F-16AM 313 Sqn $
J-197 F-16AM 312/313 Sqn
J-199 F-16AM 311 Sqn
J-201 F-16AM 322 Sqn
J-202 F-16AM 323 Sqn
J-208 F-16BM
J-209 F-16BM 148th FS
J-210 F-16BM 148th FS
J-362 F-16AM 323 Sqn
J-366 F-16AM 148th FS
J-367 F-16AM 312 Sqn
J-368 F-16BM 148th FS
J-369 F-16BM 148th FS
J-508 F-16AM 313 Sqn
J-509 F-16AM 322 Sqn
J-510 F-16AM 313 Sqn
J-511 F-16AM 313 Sqn
J-512 F-16AM 313 Sqn
J-513 F-16AM 323 Sqn
J-514 F-16AM 313 Sqn
J-515 F-16AM
J-516 F-16AM 322 Sqn
J-616 F-16AM 323 Sqn
J-623 F-16AM 148th FS
J-624 F-16AM 322 Sqn
J-628 F-16AM 322 Sqn
J-630 F-16AM 312 Sqn
J-631 F-16AM 323 Sqn
J-632 F-16AM 322 Sqn
J-635 F-16AM 312 Sqn
J-637 F-16AM 312 Sqn
J-638 F-16AM 313 Sqn
J-641 F-16AM 312 Sqn
J-642 F-16AM 312 Sqn
J-643 F-16AM 313 Sqn
J-644 F-16AM 313 Sqn
J-646 F-16AM 312 Sqn
J-866 F-16AM 312 Sqn
J-868 F-16AM 323 Sqn
J-870 F-16AM 312/313 Sqn
J-871 F-16AM 323 Sqn
J-872 F-16AM 323 Sqn
J-873 F-16AM 323 Sqn
J-876 F-16AM 322 Sqn
J-877 F-16AM 323 Sqn
J-879 F-16AM 322 Sqn
J-881 F-16AM 323 Sqn
J-882 F-16BM 148th FS

Grumman
G.1159C Gulfstream IV
334 Sqn, Eindhoven
V-11

Lockheed
C-130H/C-130H-30* Hercules
336 Sqn, Eindhoven
G-273*
G-275*
G-781
G-988

Lockheed Martin
F-35A Lightning II
F-001 (on order)
F-002 (on order)

MDH
AH-64D Apache Longbow
301 Sqn, Defence Helicopter Command,
Gilze-Rijen
Q-01
Q-02
Q-03
Q-04
Q-05
Q-06
Q-07
Q-08
Q-09
Q-10
Q-11
Q-12
Q-13
Q-14
Q-15
Q-16
Q-17
Q-18
Q-19
Q-21
Q-22
Q-23
Q-24
Q-25
Q-26
Q-27
Q-28
Q-29
Q-30

NH Industries
NH.90-NFH
860 Sqn, De Kooij
N-088 (on order)
N-102
N-110
N-147 (on order)
N-164
N-175
N-195
N-227
N-228

McDonnell Douglas
DC-10*/KDC-10
334 Sqn, Eindhoven
T-235
T-255*
T-264

Pilatus
PC-7 Turbo Trainer
131 EMVO Sqn,
Woensdrecht
L-01
L-02
L-03
L-04
L-05
L-06
L-07

L-08
L-09
L-10
L-11
L-12
L-13

Sud Alouette III
300 Sqn, Defence Helicopter Command, Gilze-Rijen
A-247
A-275
A-292
A-301

Kustwacht
Dornier Do.228-212
Base: Schiphol
PH-CGC
PH-CGN

Netherlands Govt
Fokker 70
Dutch Royal Flight, Schiphol
PH-KBX

NEW ZEALAND
Royal New Zealand Air Force
Boeing 757-2K2
40 Sqn, Whenuapai
NZ7571
NZ7572

Lockheed
C-130H Hercules
40 Sqn, Whenuapai
NZ7001
NZ7002
NZ7003
NZ7004
NZ7005
Lockheed
P-3K/P-3K2* Orion
5 Sqn, Whenuapai
NZ4201*
NZ4202
NZ4203
NZ4204*
NZ4205
NZ4206

NIGER
Government of Niger
Boeing 737-2N9C
Government of Niger, Niamey
5U-BAG

NIGERIA
Federal Nigerian Air Force
Lockheed
C-130H/C-130H-30* Hercules
88 MAG, Lagos
NAF-910
NAF-912
NAF-913
NAF-917*
NAF-918*

Nigerian Govt
Boeing 737-7N6
Federal Govt of Nigeria, Lagos
5N-FGT [001]

Dassault Falcon 7X
Federal Govt of Nigeria, Lagos
5N-FGU
5N-FGV

Dassault Falcon 900
Federal Govt of Nigeria, Lagos
5N-FGE

Gulfstream Aerospace G.550
Federal Govt of Nigeria, Lagos
5N-FGW

Gulfstream Aerospace
Gulfstream V
Federal Govt of Nigeria, Lagos
5N-FGS

NORWAY
Luftforsvaret
Bell 412HP*/412SP
339 Skv, Bardufoss;
720 Skv, Rygge

139	339 Skv
140	720 Skv
141	720 Skv
142	720 Skv
143	339 Skv
144	339 Skv
145*	720 Skv
146	339 Skv
147	720 Skv
148	339 Skv
149	720 Skv
161	339 Skv
162	339 Skv
163	720 Skv
164*	720 Skv
165	720 Skv
166*	720 Skv
167	720 Skv
194	720 Skv

Dassault
Falcon 20 ECM
717 Skv, Rygge
041
053
0125

General Dynamics
F-16 MLU
331 Skv, Bodø;
332 Skv, Bodø;
338 Skv, Ørland
[All operate from a pool and belong to the FLO]

272	F-16A	$
273	F-16A	
275	F-16A	
276	F-16A	
277	F-16A	
279	F-16A	
281	F-16A	
282	F-16A	
284	F-16A	
285	F-16A	
286	F-16A	
288	F-16A	
289	F-16A	
291	F-16A	
292	F-16A	
293	F-16A	
295	F-16A	
297	F-16A	
298	F-16A	$
299	F-16A	
302	F-16B	
304	F-16B	
305	F-16B	
306	F-16B	
658	F-16A	
659	F-16A	
660	F-16A	
661	F-16A	
662	F-16A	
663	F-16A	
664	F-16A	
665	F-16A	
666	F-16A	
667	F-16A	
668	F-16A	
669	F-16A	
670	F-16A	
671	F-16A	$
672	F-16A	
673	F-16A	
674	F-16A	
675	F-16A	
677	F-16A	
678	F-16A	
680	F-16A	
681	F-16A	
682	F-16A	
683	F-16A	
686	F-16A	
687	F-16A	
688	F-16A	

689 F-16B
690 F-16B
691 F-16B
692 F-16B $
693 F-16B
711 F-16B

Lockheed
C-130J-30 Hercules II
335 Skv, Gardermoen
5601
5607
5629
5699

Lockheed P-3C Orion
333 Skv, Andøya
3296
3297
3298
3299

Lockheed P-3N Orion
333 Skv, Andøya
4576
6603

NH Industries
NH.90-NFH
337 Skv, Bardufoss
013
049
058
171

Westland
Sea King Mk 43/
Mk 43A/Mk 43B
330 Skv:
A Flt, Bodø;
B Flt, Banak;
C Flt, Ørland;
D Flt, Sola
060 Mk 43
062 Mk 43
066 Mk 43
069 Mk 43
070 Mk 43
071 Mk 43B
072 Mk 43
073 Mk 43
074 Mk 43
189 Mk 43A
322 Mk 43B
329 Mk 43B
330 Mk 43B

OMAN
Royal Air Force of Oman
Airbus A.320-214X
4 Sqn, Seeb
554
555
556

Grumman
G.1159C Gulfstream IV
4 Sqn, Seeb
557
558

Lockheed
C-130H Hercules/
C-130J-30 Hercules II
16 Sqn, Seeb
501 C-130H
502 C-130H
503 C-130H
525 C-130J-30
526 C-130J-30 (on order)
527 C-130J-30 (on order)

Omani Govt
Airbus A.319-115CJ
Govt of Oman, Seeb
A4O-AJ

Airbus A.320-233
Govt of Oman, Seeb
A4O-AA

Boeing 747-430
Govt of Oman, Seeb
A4O-OMN

Boeing 747SP-27
Govt of Oman, Seeb
A4O-SO

Gulfstream Aerospace G.550
Govt of Oman, Seeb
A4O-AD
A4O-AE

PAKISTAN
Pakistan Fiza'ya
Boeing 707-340C
12 Sqn, Islamabad
68-19866

Pakistani Govt
Airbus A.310-304
Govt of Pakistan, Karachi
J-757

Boeing 737-33A
Govt of Pakistan, Karachi
AP-BEH

Cessna 560 Citation VI
Govt of Pakistan, Karachi
J-754

Gulfstream Aerospace
G.1159C Gulfstream IV-SP
Govt of Pakistan, Karachi
J-755

Gulfstream Aerospace
G.450
Govt of Pakistan, Karachi
J-756

POLAND
Sily Powietrzne RP
CASA C-295M
13.eltr/8.BLTr, Kraków/Balice
011
012 $
013
014
015
016
017
018
020
021
022
023 (on order)
024 (on order)
025 (on order)
026 (on order)
027 (on order)

Lockheed
C-130E Hercules
14.eltr/33.BLTr, Powidz
1501
1502
1503
1504
1505

Lockheed Martin (GD)
F-16C/F-16D* Fighting Falcon
3.elt/31.BLT, Poznan/Krzesiny;
6.elt/31.BLT, Poznan/Krzesiny;
10.elt/32.BLT, Lask;
412th TW, Edwards AFB, USA
4040 412th TW
4041 6.elt
4042 3.elt
4043 3.elt
4044 3.elt
4045 3.elt
4046 3.elt
4047 3.elt
4048 3.elt
4049 3.elt
4050 3.elt
4051 3.elt
4052 6.elt
4053 6.elt
4054 6.elt
4055 6.elt

4056 6.elt
4057 6.elt
4058 6.elt
4059 6.elt
4060 6.elt
4061 6.elt
4062 6.elt
4063 10.elt
4064 10.elt
4065 10.elt
4066 10.elt
4067 10.elt
4068 10.elt
4069 10.elt
4070 10.elt
4071 10.elt
4072 10.elt
4073 10.elt
4074 10.elt
4075 10.elt
4076* 3.elt
4077* 3.elt
4078* 3.elt
4079* 3.elt
4080* 3.elt
4081* 3.elt
4082* 6.elt
4083* 6.elt
4084* 6.elt
4085* 10.elt
4086* 10.elt
4087* 10.elt

Mikoyan MiG-29A/UB
1.elt/23.BLT, Minsk/Mazowiecki;
41.elt/22.BLT, Malbork
15* 1.elt $
28* 1.elt
38 1.elt
40 1.elt
42* 1.elt
54 1.elt
56 1.elt
59 1.elt
65 41.elt
66 41.elt
67 41.elt
70 41.elt
77 41.elt
83 1.elt
89 1.elt
92 41.elt
105 1.elt
108 1.elt
111 1.elt
114 1.elt
115 1.elt
4101 41.elt
4103 41.elt
4104 41.elt
4105 1.elt
4110* 41.elt
4113 41.elt
4116 41.elt
4120 41.elt
4121 41.elt
4122 41.elt
4123* 41.elt

PZL 130TC-I/TC-II* Orlik
2.OSzL/42.BLSz, Radom
012
014
015
016
017
018
019
020
022
023
024
025
026
027
029
030
031
032
033
035
036
037*
038
040
041
042
043
044
045
046
047*
048
049
050
051
052

PZL M28B Bryza
1.OSzL/41.BLSz, Deblin;
13.eltr/8.BLTr, Kraków/Balice;
14.eltr/33.BLTr, Powidz
0204 M28B-TD 1.OSzL
0205 M28B-TD 1.OSzL
0206 M28B-TD 14.eltr
0207 M28B-TD 13.eltr
0208 M28B-TD 14.eltr
0209 M28B-TD 14.eltr
0210 M28B-TD 14.eltr
0211 M28B-TD 14.eltr
0212 M28B-TD 13.eltr
0213 M28B/PT 13.eltr
0214 M28B/PT 13.eltr
0215 M28B/PT 13.eltr
0216 M28B/PT 13.eltr
0217 M28B/PT 13.eltr
0218 M28B/PT 13.eltr
0219 M28B/PT 13.eltr
0220 M28B/PT 13.eltr
0221 M28B/PT 13.eltr
0222 M28B/PT (on order)
0223 M28B/PT (on order)
0224 M28B/PT (on order)
0225 M28B/PT (on order)

Sukhoi
Su-22UM-3K*/Su-22M-4
8.elt/21.BLT, Swidwin;
40.elt/21.BLT, Swidwin
305* 8.elt
308* 40.elt
310* 40.elt
508* 8.elt
509* 40.elt
707* 8.elt
3201 8.elt
3304 8.elt
3612 40.elt
3713 40.elt $
3715 40.elt
3816 40.elt
3817 40.elt
3819 8.elt
3920 40.elt
7411 40.elt
7412 8.elt
8101 40.elt
8102 8.elt
8103 8.elt
8205 40.elt
8308 8.elt $
8309 40.elt
8310 40.elt
8715 40.elt
8816 40.elt
8818 8.elt $
8919 8.elt $
8920 40.elt
9102 4

Lotnictwo Marynarki Wojennej
Mil Mi-14
29.el/44.BLMW, Darlowo;
1001 Mi-14PL 29.el
1002 Mi-14PL 29.el
1003 Mi-14PL 29.el
1005 Mi-14PL 29.el
1008 Mi-14PL 29.el
1009 Mi-14PL 29.el
1010 Mi-14PL 29.el
1011 Mi-14PL 29.el
1012 Mi-14PL/R 29.el

PZL M28B Bryza
28.el/43.BLMW, Gdynia/Babie Doly;
30.el/44.BLMW, Cewice/Siemirowice

0404	M28B-1E	28.el
0405	M28B-1E	28.el
0810	M28B-1RM	30.el
1003	M28B-TD	28.el
1006	M28B-1R	30.el
1008	M28B-1R	30.el
1017	M28B-1R	30.el
1022	M28B-1R	30.el
1114	M28B-1R	28.el
1115	M28B-1R	30.el
1116	M28B-1R	30.el
1117	M28B-1	28.el
1118	M28B-1	28.el

Straz Graniczna (Polish Border Guard)
PZL M28-05 Skytruck
Base: Gdansk/Rebiechowo
SN-50YG
SN-60YG

Polish Government
Embraer
EMB.175-200LR
Polish Government, Warszawa
SP-LIG
SP-LIH

PORTUGAL
Força Aérea Portuguesa
Aérospatiale
TB-30 Epsilon
Esq 101, Sintra
11401
11402
11403
11404
11405 $
11406
11407
11409
11410
11411
11413
11414
11415
11416
11417
11418

CASA C-295M/
CASA C-295MPA*
Esq 502, Lisbon/Montijo
(with a detachment at Lajes)
16701
16702
16703
16704
16705
16706
16707
16708*
16709*
16710*
16711*
16712*

D-BD Alpha Jet
Esq 103, Beja;
Asas de Portugal, Beja*
15202*
15206*
15208*
15211 $
15220*
15225*
15226
15227*
15230
15231
15232*
15236
15246
15247

Dassault
Falcon 50
Esq 504, Lisbon/Montijo
17401
17402
17403

EHI EH-101
Mk514/Mk515/Mk516
Esq 751, Lisbon/Montijo
Mk514
19601
19602
19603
19604
19605*
19606*
Mk515
19607
19608
Mk516
19609
19610
19611
19612

Lockheed
C-130H/C-130H-30* Hercules
Esq 501, Lisbon/Montijo
16801*
16802*
16803$
16804
16805
16806*

Lockheed Martin (GD)
F-16 Fighting Falcon
(MLU aircraft are marked with a *)
Esq 201, Monte Real;
Esq 301, Monte Real
15101 F-16A*
15102 F-16A*
15103 F-16A*
15104 F-16A*
15105 F-16A*
15106 F-16A $
15107 F-16A*
15108 F-16A*
15109 F-16A*
15110 F-16A
15112 F-16A*
15113 F-16A*
15114 F-16A
15115 F-16A* $
15116 F-16A*
15117 F-16A*
15118 F-16B*
15119 F-16B*
15120 F-16B
15121 F-16A*
15122 F-16A*
15123 F-16A
15124 F-16A*
15125 F-16A*
15126 F-16A*
15127 F-16A*
15128 F-16A*
15129 F-16A*
15130 F-16A*
15131 F-16A
15132 F-16A*
15133 F-16A*
15134 F-16A*
15135 F-16A*
15136 F-16A
15137 F-16B*
15138 F-16A*
15139 F-16B*
15141 F-16A

Lockheed
P-3C Orion
Esq 601, Beja
14807
14808 $
14809
14810
14811

Marinha
Westland
Super Lynx Mk 95
Esq de Helicopteros,
Lisbon/Montijo
19201
19202
19203
19204
19205

QATAR
Qatar Emiri Air Force
Boeing
C-17A Globemaster III
Qatar Emiri Air Force, Al-Udeid
MAA (08-0201)
MAB (08-0202)
MAC (10-0203)
MAE (10-0204)

Lockheed
C-130J-30 Hercules II
Qatar Emiri Air Force, Al-Udeid
MAH (08-0211)
MAI (08-0212)
MAJ (08-0213)
MAK (08-0214)

Qatar Government
Airbus A.310-308
Qatari Govt, Doha
A7-AFE

Airbus A.319-115X/
A.319CJ-133*
Qatari Govt, Doha
A7-HHJ*
A7-MED*
A7-MHH

Airbus A.320-232
Qatari Govt, Doha
A7-AAG
A7-MBK

Airbus A.330-202/-203*
Qatari Govt, Doha
A7-HHM*
A7-HJJ

Airbus A.340-211/-313X/-541
Qatari Govt, Doha
A7-AAH A.340-313X
A7-HHH A.340-541
A7-HHK A.340-211

Boeing 747-8KB/-8KJ*
Qatari Govt, Doha
A7-HHE*
A7-HJA

Bombardier
Global Express
Qatari Govt/Qatar Airways, Doha
A7-AAM

ROMANIA
Fortele Aeriene Romania
Alenia C-27J Spartan
Escadrilla 902,
Bucharest/Otopeni
2701
2702
2703
2704
2705
2706 (on order)
2707 (on order)

Antonov An-26
Escadrilla 902,
Bucharest/Otopeni
801
808
809
810

Lockheed
C-130B/C-130H* Hercules
Escadrilla 901,
Bucharest/Otopeni
5927
5930
6150
6166*
6191*

Romanian Govt
Boeing 707-3K1C
Romanian Govt,
Bucharest/Otopeni
YR-ABB
RUSSIA
Voenno-Vozdushniye Sily Rossioki Federatsii (Russian Air Force)
Antonov An-30B
(Open Skies)
Base: Chkalovskiy
01 black

Antonov An-124
224th Transport Regiment,
Seshcha/Bryansk
RA-82011
RA-82021
RA-82023
RA-82025
RA-82028
RA-82030
RA-82032
RA-82035
RA-82036
RA-82038
RA-82039
RA-82040
RA-82041

Sukhoi Su-27
TsAGI, Gromov Flight
Institute, Zhukhovsky
595 white Su-27P
597 white Su-30
598 white Su-27P

Russian Govt
Ilyushin Il-62M
Russian Govt, Moscow
RA-86466
RA-86467
RA-86468
RA-86539
RA-86540
RA-86559
RA-86561
RA-86712

Ilyushin Il-96-300
Russian Govt, Moscow
RA-96012
RA-96016
RA-96018
RA-96019

Tupolev Tu-134A
Russian Govt, Moscow
RA-65904

Tupolev Tu-154M
Russian Govt, Moscow;
Open Skies*
RA-85041
RA-85155
RA-85631
RA-85655*
RA-85666

Tupolev Tu-214ON
(Open Skies)
Base: Chalovskiy
RA-64519
RA-64520

Tupolev Tu-214SR
Russian Govt, Moscow
RA-64515
RA-64516

SAUDI ARABIA
Al Quwwat al Jawwiya
as Sa'udiya
Airbus A.330-203 MRTT
24 Sqn, Al Kharj
2401 (on order)
2402 (on order)
2403 (on order)

BAe 125-800/-800B*
1 Sqn, Riyadh
HZ-105
HZ-109*
HZ-110*
HZ-130*
BAe Hawk 65/65A
88 Sqn, *Saudi Hawks*, Tabuk
8805 Hawk 65A
8806 Hawk 65A

8807 Hawk 65
8808 Hawk 65
8810 Hawk 65
8811 Hawk 65A
8812 Hawk 65A
8813 Hawk 65
8814 Hawk 65

Boeing 737-7DP/-8DP*
1 Sqn, Riyadh
HZ-101
HZ-102*

Boeing
E-3A/KE-3A/RE-3A/RE-3B Sentry
18 Sqn, Al Kharj;
19 Sqn, Al Kharj;
23 Sqn, Al Kharj

1801	E-3A	18 Sqn
1802	E-3A	18 Sqn
1803	E-3A	18 Sqn
1804	E-3A	18 Sqn
1805	E-3A	18 Sqn
1901	RE-3A	19 Sqn
1902	RE-3B	19 Sqn
2301	KE-3A	23 Sqn
2302	KE-3A	23 Sqn
2303	KE-3A	23 Sqn
2304	KE-3A	23 Sqn
2305	KE-3A	23 Sqn
2306	KE-3A	23 Sqn
2307	KE-3A	23 Sqn

Cessna 550 Citation II
1 Sqn, Riyadh
HZ-133
HZ-134
HZ-135
HZ-136

Grumman
G.1159C Gulfstream IV
1 Sqn, Riyadh
HZ-103

Lockheed
C-130/L.100 Hercules
1 Sqn, Riyadh;
4 Sqn, Jeddah;
16 Sqn, Jeddah;
32 Sqn, Al Kharj

111	VC-130H	1 Sqn
112	VC-130H	1 Sqn
464	C-130H	4 Sqn
465	C-130H	4 Sqn
466	C-130H	4 Sqn
467	C-130H	4 Sqn
468	C-130H	4 Sqn
472	C-130H	4 Sqn
473	C-130H	4 Sqn
474	C-130H	4 Sqn
475	C-130H	4 Sqn
477	C-130H	4 Sqn
478	C-130H	4 Sqn
482	C-130H	4 Sqn
483	C-130H	4 Sqn
484	C-130H	4 Sqn
485	C-130H	4 Sqn
486	C-130H	4 Sqn
1601	C-130H	16 Sqn
1602	C-130H	16 Sqn
1604	C-130H	16 Sqn
1605	C-130H	16 Sqn
1615	C-130H	16 Sqn
1622	C-130H-30	16 Sqn
1623	C-130H	16 Sqn
1624	C-130H	16 Sqn
1625	C-130H	16 Sqn
1626	C-130H	16 Sqn
1627	C-130H	16 Sqn
1628	C-130H	16 Sqn
1629	C-130H	16 Sqn
1630	C-130H-30	16 Sqn
1631	C-130H-30	16 Sqn
1632	L.100-30	16 Sqn
3201	KC-130H	32 Sqn
3202	KC-130H	32 Sqn
3203	KC-130H	32 Sqn
3204	KC-130H	32 Sqn
3205	KC-130H	32 Sqn
3206	KC-130H	32 Sqn
3207	KC-130H	32 Sqn
HZ-117	L.100-30	1 Sqn
HZ-128	L.100-30	1 Sqn
HZ-129	L.100-30	1 Sqn
HZ-132	L.100-30	1 Sqn

Saudi Govt
Boeing 747-3G1/468*
Saudi Royal Flight, Jeddah
HZ-HM1A
HZ-HM1*

Boeing 747SP-68
Saudi Govt, Jeddah;
Saudi Royal Flight, Jeddah
HZ-AIF Govt
HZ-AIJ Royal Flight
HZ-HM1B Royal Flight

Boeing 757-23A
Saudi Govt, Jeddah
HZ-HMED

Boeing MD-11
Saudi Royal Flight, Jeddah
HZ-AFAS
HZ-HM7

Dassault Falcon 900
Saudi Govt, Jeddah
HZ-AFT
HZ-AFZ

Grumman
G.1159A Gulfstream III
Armed Forces Medical Services, Riyadh;
Saudi Govt, Jeddah
HZ-AFN Govt
HZ-AFR Govt
HZ-MS3 AFMS

Grumman
G.1159C Gulfstream IV/ Gulfstream IV-SP*
Armed Forces Medical Services, Riyadh;
Saudi Govt, Jeddah
HZ-AFU Govt
HZ-AFV Govt
HZ-AFW Govt
HZ-AFX Govt
HZ-AFY Govt
HZ-MFL Govt
HZ-MS4* AFMS

Gulfstream Aerospace
Gulfstream V
Armed Forces Medical Services, Riyadh
HZ-MS5A
HZ-MS5B

Lockheed
C-130H/L.100 Hercules
Armed Forces Medical Services, Riyadh

HZ-MS2	C-130H
HZ-MS06	L.100-30
HZ-MS07	C-130H
HZ-MS09	L.100-30

SERBIA
Dassault Falcon 50
Govt of Serbia, Belgrade
YU-BNA

SINGAPORE
Republic of Singapore Air Force
Boeing
KC-135R Stratotanker
112 Sqn, Changi
750
751
752
753

Lockheed
C-130 Hercules
122 Sqn, Paya Lebar

720	KC-130B
721	KC-130B
724	KC-130B
725	KC-130B

730 C-130H
731 C-130H
732 C-130H
733 C-130H
734 KC-130H
735 C-130H

SLOVAKIA
Slovenské Vojenske Letectvo
Aero L-39 Albatros
Zmiešané Letecké Kridlo 'Otta Smika', Sliač:
2 Stíhacia Letka [SL]
1701 L-39ZAM
1730 L-39ZAM
4703 L-39ZAM
5251 L-39CM
5252 L-39CM
5253 L-39CM
5301 L-39CM $
5302 L-39CM

Antonov An-26
Dopravniho Kridlo 'Generála Milana Ratislava Štefánika', Malacky:
1 Dopravná Roj
2506
3208

LET 410 Turbolet
Dopravniho Kridlo 'Generála Milana Ratislava Štefánika', Malacky:
2 Dopravná Roj
1133 L-410T
1521 L-410FG
2311 L-410UVP
2421 L-410UVP
2718 L-401UVP-E
2721 L-401UVP-E

Mikoyan MiG-29AS/UBS
Zmiešané Letecké Kridlo 'Otta Smika', Sliač:
1 Stíhacia Letka [SL]
0619 MiG-29AS
0921 MiG-29AS
1303 MiG-29UBS $
2123 MiG-29AS
3709 MiG-29AS
3911 MiG-29AS
5304 MiG-29UBS
6124 MiG-29AS
6526 MiG-29AS
6627 MiG-29AS
6728 MiG-29AS

Mil M-17/M-17M*
Vrtulnikové Letcecké Kridlo 'Generálplukovníka Jána Ambrusa', Prešov:
2 Bitevná Vrtul'nikova Letka
0807
0808
0812
0820
0821
0823*
0824
0826
0827
0841
0842
0844
0845
0846
0847

Slovak Govt
Yakovlev Yak-40
Slovak Govt, Bratislava/Ivanka
OM-BYE
OM-BYL

SLOVENIA
Slovene Army
LET 410UVP-E
LTO, Brnik
L4-01

Pilatus PC-9/PC-9M*
1/2/3 OSBL, Cerklje
L9-51
L9-53
L9-61*
L9-62*
L9-63*
L9-64*
L9-65*
L9-66*
L9-67*
L9-68*
L9-69*

SOUTH AFRICA
South African Air Force/
Suid Afrikaanse Lugmag
Boeing 737-7ED

21 Sqn, Waterkloof
ZS-RSA

Dassault Falcon 900
21 Sqn, Waterkloof
ZS-NAN

Lockheed
C-130B/C-130BZ* Hercules
28 Sqn, Waterkloof
401
402*
403
404
405*
406*
407*

SPAIN
Ejército del Aire
Airbus A.310-304
Grupo 45, Torrejón
T.22-1 45-50
T.22-2 45-51

Airtech
CN.235M-10 (T.19A)/
CN.235M-100 (T.19B)/
CN.235M-100(MPA) (D.4)/
CN.235M VIGMA (T.19B)*
Grupo Esc, Matacán (74);
801 Esc, Palma/ Son San Juan;
Guardia Civil (09)
D.4-01 (801 Esc)
D.4-02 (801 Esc)
D.4-03 (801 Esc)
D.4-04 (801 Esc)
D.4-05 (801 Esc)
D.4-06 (801 Esc)
D.4-07 (801 Esc)
TR.19A-01 403-01
TR.19A-02 403-02
T.19B-07 74-25
T.19B-11 74-29
T.19B-13 74-31
T.19B-14 74-14
T.19B-16 74-34
T.19B-17 74-17
T.19B-18 74-36
T.19B-19 74-19
T.19B-20 74-38
T.19B-21* 09-501
T.19B-22* 09-502

Boeing 707
47 Grupo Mixto, Torrejón
TK.17-1 331B 47-01
T.17-2 331B 47-02
T.17-3 368C 47-03
TM.17-4 351C 47-04

CASA 101EB Aviojet
Grupo 54, Torrejón;
Grupo de Escuelas de Matacán (74);
AGA, San Javier (79);
Patrulla Aguila, San Javier*
E.25-06 79-06
E.25-08 79-08
E.25-11 79-11
E.25-12 79-12
E.25-13 79-13 [5]*
E.25-14 79-14 [2]*

E.25-15	79-15	
E.25-16	79-16	
E.25-17	74-40	
E.25-19	79-19	
E.25-20	79-20	
E.25-21	79-21	
E.25-22	79-22	[1]*
E.25-23	79-23	
E.25-24	79-24	
E.25-25	79-25	[6]*
E.25-26	79-26	
E.25-27	79-27	
E.25-28	79-28	[7]*
E.25-29	74-45	
E.25-31	79-31	
E.25-34	74-44	
E.25-35	54-20	
E.25-37	79-37	
E.25-38	79-38	
E.25-40	79-40	[3]*
E.25-41	74-41	
E.25-43	74-43	
E.25-44	79-44	
E.25-45	79-45	
E.25-46	79-46	
E.25-47	79-47	
E.25-48	79-48	
E.25-49	79-49	
E.25-50	79-33	
E.25-51	74-07	
E.25-52	79-34	[4]*
E.25-53	74-09	
E.25-54	79-35	
E.25-55	54-21	
E.25-56	74-11	
E.25-57	74-12	
E.25-59	74-13	
E.25-61	54-22	
E.25-62	79-17	[6]*
E.25-63	74-17	
E.25-65	79-95	
E.25-66	74-20	
E.25-67	74-21	
E.25-68	74-22	
E.25-69	79-97	[8]*
E.25-71	74-25	
E.25-72	74-26	
E.25-73	79-98	
E.25-74	74-28	
E.25-76	74-30	
E.25-78	79-02	
E.25-79	79-39	
E.25-80	79-03	
E.25-81	74-34	
E.25-83	74-35	
E.25-84	79-04	
E.25-86	79-32	
E.25-87	79-29$	
E.25-88	74-39	

CASA 212 Aviocar 212A (T.12B)/ 212ECM (TM.12D)/ 212S (D.3A)/ 212S1 (D.3B)

Ala 72, Alcantarilla;
47 Grupo Mixto, Torrejón;
801 Esc, Palma/ Son San Juan;
803 Esc, Cuatro Vientos

D.3A-2	(803 Esc)
D.3B-3	(803 Esc)
D.3B-7	(801 Esc)
T.12B-13	72-01
T.12B-21	72-03
T.12B-37	72-05
T.12B-49	72-07
T.12B-55	72-08
T.12B-63	72-14
T.12B-66	72-09
T.12B-67	72-12
T.12B-69	72-15
T.12B-70	72-17
TM.12D-72	47-12

CASA C-295M

Ala 35, Getafe

T.21-01	35-39
T.21-02	35-40
T.21-03	35-41
T.21-04	35-42
T.21-05	35-43
T.21-06	35-44
T.21-07	35-45
T.21-08	35-46
T.21-09	35-47
T.21-10	35-48
T.21-11	35-49
T.21-12	35-50
T.21-13	35-51

Cessna 560 Citation VI

403 Esc, Getafe

TR.20-01	403-11
TR.20-02	403-12
TR.20-03	403-21

Dassault Falcon 20D/E

47 Grupo Mixto, Torrejón

TM.11-1	20E	47-21
TM.11-2	20D	47-22
TM.11-3	20D	47-23
TM.11-4	20E	47-24

Dassault Falcon 900/900B*

Grupo 45, Torrejón

T.18-1	45-40
T.18-2	45-41
T.18-3*	45-42
T.18-4*	45-43
T.18-5*	45-44

Dassault Mirage F.1BM*/F.1M

Ala 14, Albacete

CE.14-27*	14-70
CE.14-30*	14-76
C.14-37	14-19
C.14-38	14-20
C.14-41	14-22$
C.14-45	14-26
C.14-57	14-32
C.14-63	14-36
C.14-64	14-37$
C.14-68	14-40
C.14-70	14-42
C.14-72	14-44

Eurofighter EF.2000/EF.2000(T)* Tifón

Ala 11, Morón;
Ala 14, Albacete;
CASA, Getafe

CE.16-01*	11-70
CE.16-02*	11-71
CE.16-03*	11-72
CE.16-04*	11-73
CE.16-05*	11-74
CE.16-06*	11-75
CE.16-07*	11-76
CE.16-09*	11-78
CE.16-10*	11-79
CE.16-11*	11-80
CE.16-12*	11-81
CE.16-13*	
CE.16-14*	
CE.16-15*	
CE.16-16*	
CE.16-17*	
CE.16-18*	
CE.16-19*	
C.16-20	11-91
C.16-21	11-01
C.16-22	11-02
C.16-23	11-03
C.16-24	11-04
C.16-25	11-05
C.16-26	11-06
C.16-27	11-07
C.16-28	11-08
C.16-29	11-09
C.16-30	11-10
C.16-31	11-11
C.16-32	11-12
C.16-33	11-13
C.16-34	11-14
C.16-35	11-15
C.16-36	11-16
C.16-37	11-17
C.16-38	11-18
C.16-39	11-19
C.16-40	11-20
C.16-41	11-21
C.16-42	11-22$

C.16-43 11-23
C.16-44 11-24
C.16-45 11-25
C.16-46 11-26
C.16-47 11-27
C.16-48 11-28
C.16-49 11-29
C.16-50 11-30
C.16-51
C.16-52
C.16-53
C.16-54
C.16-55
C.16-56
C.16-57
C.16-58
C.16-59
C.16-60

Fokker
F.27M Friendship 400MPA
802 Esc, Gando, Las Palmas
D.2-01
D.2-02
D.2-03

Lockheed
C-130H/C-130H-30/
KC-130H Hercules
311 Esc/312 Esc (Ala 31),
Zaragoza

TL.10-01	C-130H-30	31-01
T.10-02	C-130H	31-02
T.10-03	C-130H	31-03
T.10-04	C-130H	31-04
TK.10-5	KC-130H	31-50
TK.10-6	KC-130H	31-51
TK.10-07	KC-130H	31-52
T.10-8	C-130H	31-05
T.10-9	C-130H	31-06
T.10-10	C-130H	31-07
TK.10-11	KC-130H	31-53
TK.10-12	KC-130H	31-54

Lockheed
P-3A/P-3M Orion
Grupo 22, Morón

P.3-01	P-3A	22-21
P.3M-08	P-3M	22-31
P.3M-09	P-3M	22-32
P.3M-10	P-3M	22-33
P.3M-12	P-3M	22-35

McDonnell Douglas
F-18 Hornet
Ala 12, Torrejón;
Ala 15, Zaragoza;
Esc 462, Gran Canaria
EF-18B+/EF-18BM Hornet
CE.15-1* 15-70$
CE.15-2* 15-71
CE.15-3 15-72
CE.15-4* 15-73
CE.15-5 15-74
CE.15-6 15-75
CE.15-7* 15-76
CE.15-8* 12-71
CE.15-9 15-77
CE.15-10 12-73
CE.15-11 12-74
CE.15-12* 12-75
EF-18A+/EF-18AM* Hornet
C.15-13* 12-01
C.15-14 15-01
C.15-15 15-02$
C.15-16* 15-03
C.15-18* 15-05
C.15-20 15-07
C.15-21 15-08
C.15-22* 15-09
C.15-23 15-10
C.15-24 15-11
C.15-25 15-12
C.15-26 15-13$
C.15-27 15-14
C.15-28 15-15
C.15-29 15-16
C.15-30 15-17
C.15-31 15-18
C.15-32 15-19
C.15-33 15-20
C.15-34* 12-50$
C.15-35 15-22
C.15-36 15-23
C.15-37 15-24
C.15-38 15-25
C.15-39 15-26
C.15-40 15-27
C.15-41 15-28$
C.15-43* 15-30
C.15-44* 12-02
C.15-45* 12-03
C.15-46* 12-04
C.15-47 15-31
C.15-48* 12-06
C.15-49* 12-07
C.15-50* 12-08
C.15-51* 12-09
C.15-52* 12-10
C.15-53* 12-11
C.15-54* 12-12
C.15-55 12-13
C.15-56 12-14
C.15-57* 12-15
C.15-59* 12-17
C.15-60 12-18
C.15-61 12-19
C.15-62 12-20
C.15-64 15-34
C.15-65* 12-23
C.15-66* 12-24
C.15-67 15-33
C.15-68* 12-26
C.15-69* 12-27
C.15-70* 12-28
C.15-72* 12-30
F/A-18A/EF-18AM* Hornet
C.15-73 46-01$
C.15-75 46-03
C.15-77 46-05
C.15-79 46-07
C.15-80 21-08
C.15-81 46-09
C.15-82 46-10
C.15-83 46-11
C.15-84 46-12
C.15-85 46-13
C.15-86* 46-14
C.15-87 46-15
C.15-88 46-16
C.15-89* 46-17
C.15-90 46-18
C.15-92 46-20
C.15-93* 46-21
C.15-94 46-22
C.15-95 46-23
C.15-96 46-24

Arma Aérea de
l'Armada Española
BAe/McDonnell Douglas
EAV-8B/EAV-8B+/
TAV-8B Harrier II
Esc 009, Rota
EAV-8B
VA.1A-14 01-903
VA.1A-19 01-907
VA.1A-20 01-909
VA.1A-22 01-911
EAV-8B+
VA.1B-24 01-914
VA.1B-25 01-915
VA.1B-26 01-916
VA.1B-27 01-917
VA.1B-28 01-918
VA.1B-29 01-919
VA.1B-30 01-920
VA.1B-35 01-923
VA.1B-36 01-924
VA.1B-37 01-925
VA.1B-38 01-926
VA.1B-39 01-927
TAV-8B
VAE.1A-33 01-922

Cessna 550 Citation II
Esc 004, Rota
U.20-1 01-405
U.20-2 01-406
U.20-3 01-407
Cessna 650 Citation VII
Esc 004, Rota
U.21-01 01-408

SUDAN
Dassault Falcon 50
Sudanese Govt, Khartoum
ST-PSR

Dassault Falcon 900B
Sudanese Govt, Khartoum
ST-PSA

SWEDEN
Svenska Flygvapnet
Grumman
G.1159C Gulfstream 4
(Tp.102A/S.102B Korpen/
Tp.102C)
Flottiljer 17M,
Stockholm/Bromma &
Malmslätt
Tp.102A
102001 021
S.102B Korpen
102002 022
102003 023
Tp.102C
102004 024
Gulfstream Aerospace G.550
(Tp.102D)
Flottiljer 17M,
Stockholm/Bromma &
Malmslätt
102005 025

Lockheed
C-130H Hercules (Tp.84)
Flottiljer 7, Såtenäs
84001 841
84002 842
84003 843
84004 844
84005 845
84006 846
84007 847
84008 848

Rockwell
Sabreliner-40 (Tp.86)
FMV, Malmslätt
86001 861

SAAB JAS 39 Gripen
Flottiljer 4, Östersund/
Frösön;
Flottiljer 7, Såtenäs [G];
Flottiljer 17, Ronneby/
Kallinge;
Flottiljer 21, Luleå/
Kallax
FMV, Malmslätt
JAS 39A
39131 131 $
39132 132
39133 133 FMV
39134 134 FMV
39135 135 F21
39136 136
39138 138
39143 143
39144 44 SAAB
39146 146
39150 150
39151 151
39159 159
39167 167
39168 168
39170 170 F17
39171 171 F17
39172 172
39174 174
39176 176 F17
39179 179 F17
39180 180 F17
39181 181
39182 182
39183 183 F17
39185 185
39188 188 F17
39189 189 F17
39190 190 F17
39191 191 F17
39192 192
39193 193
39194 194
39195 195
39196 196
39198 198
39199 199
39200 200
39201 201
39202 202
39203 203
39204 204
39205 205
39206 206
JAS 39B
39800 58 FMV
39801 801
39802 802 SAAB
39804 804
39805 805
39806 806
39807 807
39808 808
39809 809
39810 810
39811 811
39812 812
39813 813
39814 814
JAS 39C
39-6 6 SAAB
39208 208 F17
39209 209 F17
39210 210 F17
39211 211 F17
39212 212 F17
39213 213 F7
39214 214 F21
39215 215 F21
39216 216 F17
39217 217 F7
39218 218 F21
39219 219 F21
39220 220 F17
39221 221 F17
39222 222 F17
39223 223 F21
39224 224 F21
39225 225 F7
39226 226 F17
39227 227 F7
39228 228 F17
39229 229 F21
39230 230 F17
39231 231 F7
39232 232 F21
39233 233 F17
39246 246 F21
39247 247 F17
39248 248 F21
39249 249 F17
39250 250 F21
39251 251 FMV
39252 252 F17
39253 253 F21
39254 254 F17
39255 255 F17
39256 256 F17
39257 257 F21
39258 258 F21
39260 260 F21
39261 261 F17
39262 262 F17
39263 263 F21
39264 264 F17
39265 265 FMV
39266 266 F17
39267 267 F21
39268 268 F7
39269 269 F17
39270 270 F17
39271 271 F21
39272 272 F7
39273 273 SAAB
39274 274 F17
39275 275 F21
39276 276 F7
39277 277 F7
39278 278 F17
39279 279 F21
39280 280 F7
39281 281 F17
39282 282 F17
39283 283
39284 284 F17
39285
39286

39287
39288
39289
39290
39291
39292
39293
39294

JAS 39D

39815	815	F21
39816	816	F17
39817	817	F21
39818	818	
39821	821	F21
39822	822	SAAB
39823	823	F21
39824	824	F17
39825	825	F7
39826	826	F7
39827	827	F7
39829	829	FMV
39830	830	F17
39831	831	F17
39832	832	
39833	833	F7
39834	834	F7
39835	835	
39836	836	SAAB
39837		
39838		
39839		
39840		
39841		
39842		

JAS 39NG

39-7		SAAB

SAAB
SF.340 (OS.100 & Tp.100C)/
SF.340AEW&C (S.100D)
Argus
Flottiljer 17M, Malmslätt;
TSFE, Malmslätt

OS.100

100001	001	F17M

Tp.100C

100008	008	TSFE

S.100D

100003	003	TSFE
100004	004	TSFE

Förvarsmaktens Helikopterflottilj
Aérospatiale
AS.332M-1 Super Puma
(Hkp.10/Hkp.10B[1]/Hkp.10D[2])
1.HkpSkv, Luleå/Kallax;
3.HkpSkv, Berga, Goteborg/Säve,
& Ronneby/Kallinge

10401	91	3.HkpSkv
10402[2]	92	3.HkpSkv
10403[1]	93	1.HkpSkv
10405	95	3.HkpSkv
10406[1]	96	1.HkpSkv
10407[2]	97	3.HkpSkv
10408[1]	98	1.HkpSkv
10410[1]	90	3.HkpSkv
10411	88	3.HkpSkv
10412	89	3.HkpSkv

Agusta
A109LUH Power (Hkp.15)
2.HkpSkv, Linkoping/Malmen;
3.HkpSkv, Berga & Ronneby/Kallinge

Hkp.15A

15021	21	2.HkpSkv
15022	22	2.HkpSkv
15023	23	2.HkpSkv
15024	24	2.HkpSkv
15025	25	2.HkpSkv
15026	26	2.HkpSkv
15027	27	2.HkpSkv
15028	28	2.HkpSkv
15029	29	2.HkpSkv
15030	30	2.HkpSkv
15031	31	2.HkpSkv
15032	32	2.HkpSkv
15034	34	2.HkpSkv

Hkp.15B

15033	33	3.HkpSkv
15035	35	3.HkpSkv
15036	36	3.HkpSkv
15037	37	3.HkpSkv
15038	38	3.HkpSkv
15039	39	3.HkpSkv
15040	40	3.HkpSkv

MBB Bo.105CBS (Hkp.9A)
2.HkpSkv, Linkoping/Malmen;
3.HkpSkv, Berga & Ronneby/Kallinge

09201	01	2.HkpSkv
09202	02	2.HkpSkv
09203	03	2.HkpSkv
09208	08	3.HkpSkv
09211	11	2.HkpSkv
09212	12	2.HkpSkv
09215	15	2.HkpSkv
09216	16	3.HkpSkv
09217	17	2.HkpSkv
09219	19	2.HkpSkv
09220	20	2.HkpSkv

NH Industries
NH.90
1.HkpSkv, Luleå/Kallax;
3.HkpSkv, Berga & Ronneby/Kallinge;
FMV, Malmslätt

NH.90-HCV (Hkp.14A)

141041	41	
141042	42	1.HkpSkv
141043	43	1.HkpSkv
141046	46	FMV
141047	47	FMV
141048	48	
141049	49	
141050	50	
141051	51	
141052	52	
141053	53	
141054	54	
142044	44	1.HkpSkv
142045	45	1.HkpSkv

NH.90-ASW (Hkp.14B)

142055	55 (on order)	
142056	56 (on order)	
142057	57 (on order)	
142058	58 (on order)	
142059	59 (on order)	

Sikorsky UH-60M
Black Hawk (Hkp.16A)
2.HkpSkv, Linkoping/Malmen;
FMV, Malmslätt

161226	[01]	FMV
161227	[02]	2.HkpSkv
161228	[03]	2.HkpSkv
161229	[04]	2.HkpSkv
161230	[05]	2.HkpSkv
161231	[06]	2.HkpSkv
161232	[07]	2.HkpSkv
161233	[08]	2.HkpSkv
161234	[09]	2.HkpSkv
161235	[10]	2.HkpSkv
161236	[11]	(on order)
161237	[12]	(on order)
161238	[13]	(on order)
161239	[14]	(on order)
161240	[15]	(on order)
161241	[16]	(on order)

Swedish Coast Guard
Bombardier DHC-8Q-311
Base: Nykoping

SE-MAA [501]
SE-MAB [502]
SE-MAC [503]

SWITZERLAND

Schweizerische Flugwaffe
(Most aircraft are pooled centrally. Some carry unit badges but these rarely indicate actual operators.)

Aérospatiale
AS.332M-1/AS.532UL
Super Puma
Lufttransport Staffel 3 (LtSt 3), Dübendorf;
Lufttransport Staffel 5 (LtSt 5), Payerne;
Lufttransport Staffel 6 (LtSt 6), Alpnach;
Lufttransport Staffel 8 (LtSt 8), Alpnach
Detachments at Emmen, Meiringen & Sion

AS.332M-1
T-311

T-312
T-313
T-314
T-315
T-316
T-317
T-318
T-319
T-320
T-321
T-322
T-323
T-324
T-325

AS.532UL

T-331
T-332
T-333
T-334
T-335
T-336
T-337
T-338
T-339
T-340
T-342

Beech 1900D

Lufttransportdienst des Bundes, Dübendorf

T-729

Beech King Air 350C

Lufttransportdienst des Bundes, Dübendorf

T-721

Cessna 560XL Citation Excel

Lufttransportdienst des Bundes, Dübendorf

T-784

Dassault Falcon 50

Lufttransportdienst des Bundes, Dübendorf

T-783

Eurocopter EC.135P-2*/EC.635P-2

Lufttransportdienst des Bundes, Dübendorf (LTDB);
Lufttransport Geschwader 2 (LTG 2), Alpnach;
Lufttransport Staffel 3 (LtSt 3), Dübendorf;
Lufttransport Staffel 5 (LtSt 5), Payerne;
Lufttransport Staffel 6 (LtSt 6), Alpnach;
Lufttransport Staffel 8 (LtSt 8), Alpnach
Detachments at Emmen, Meiringen & Sion

T-351*	LTDB
T-352*	LTDB
T-353	LTG 2
T-354	LTG 2
T-355	LTG 2
T-356	LTG 2
T-357	LTG 2
T-358	LTG 2
T-359	LTG 2
T-360	LTG 2
T-361	LTG 2
T-362	LTG 2
T-363	LTG 2
T-364	LTG 2
T-365	LTG 2
T-366	LTG 2
T-367	LTG 2
T-368	LTG 2
T-369	LTG 2
T-370	LTG 2

McDonnell Douglas F/A-18 Hornet

Flieger Staffel 11 (FlSt 11), Meiringen;
Escadrille d'Aviation 17 (EdAv 17), Payerne;
Flieger Staffel 18 (FlSt 18), Payerne

F/A-18C

J-5001
J-5002
J-5003
J-5004
J-5005
J-5006
J-5007
J-5008
J-5009
J-5010
J-5011$
J-5012
J-5013
J-5014
J-5015
J-5016
J-5017$
J-5018$
J-5019
J-5020
J-5021
J-5022
J-5023
J-5024
J-5025
J-5026

F/A-18D

J-5232
J-5233
J-5234
J-5235
J-5236
J-5237
J-5238

Northrop F-5 Tiger II

Armasuisse, Emmen;
Escadrille d'Aviation 6 (EdAv 6), Sion;
Flieger Staffel 8 (FlSt 8), Meiringen;
Flieger Staffel 19 (FlSt 19), Sion;
Patrouille Suisse, Emmen (*P. Suisse*)

F-5E

J-3004	
J-3005	
J-3014	
J-3015	
J-3030	
J-3033	
J-3036	
J-3038	
J-3041	
J-3044	
J-3056	
J-3057	
J-3062	
J-3063	
J-3065	
J-3067	
J-3068	
J-3069	
J-3070	
J-3072	
J-3073	
J-3074	
J-3076	
J-3077	
J-3079	
J-3080	*P. Suisse*
J-3081	*P. Suisse*
J-3082	*P. Suisse*
J-3083	*P. Suisse*
J-3084	*P. Suisse*
J-3085	*P. Suisse*
J-3086	*P. Suisse*
J-3087	*P. Suisse*
J-3088	*P. Suisse*
J-3089	*P. Suisse*
J-3090	*P. Suisse*
J-3091	*P. Suisse*
J-3092	
J-3093	
J-3094	
J-3095	
J-3097	
J-3098	

F-5F

J-3201
J-3202

J-3203
J-3204
J-3205
J-3206
J-3207
J-3208
J-3209
J-3210
J-3211
J-3212

Pilatus
PC.6B/B2-H2 Turbo Porter
Lufttransport Staffel 7
(LtSt 7), Emmen
V-612
V-613
V-614
V-616
V-617
V-618
V-619
V-620
V-622$
V-623
V-631
V-632
V-633
V-634
V-635

Pilatus NCPC-7
Turbo Trainer
Instrumentation Flieger
Staffel 14 (InstruFISt 14),
Dübendorf;
Pilotenschule, Emmen
A-912
A-913
A-914
A-915
A-916
A-917
A-918
A-919
A-922
A-923
A-924
A-925
A-926
A-927
A-928
A-929
A-930
A-931
A-932
A-933
A-934
A-935
A-936
A-937
A-938
A-939
A-940
A-941

Pilatus PC-9
Zielfligerstaffel 12,
Sion
C-401
C-402
C-403
C-405
C-406
C-407
C-408
C-409
C-410
C-411
C-412

Pilatus PC-21
Pilotenschule, Emmen
A-101
A-102
A-103
A-104
A-105
A-106
A-107 (on order)
A-108 (on order)

Swiss Govt
Pilatus PC-12/45
Swiss Govt, Emmen
HB-FOG

SYRIA
Dassault Falcon 900
Govt of Syria, Damascus
YK-ASC

TANZANIA
Airbus A.340-542
Tanzanian Govt, Dar-es-Salaam
5H-... (on order)

Gulfstream Aerospace G.550
Tanzanian Govt, Dar-es-Salaam
5H-ONE

THAILAND
Airbus A.310-324
Royal Flight, Bangkok
L.13-1/34 (HS-TYQ) [60202]

Boeing 737-448/-4Z6/-8Z6
Royal Flight, Bangkok

HS-CMV	4Z6	[11-111, 90401]
HS-HRH	448	[99-999, 90409]
HS-TYS	8Z6	[55-555]

TUNISIA
Boeing 737-7HJ
Govt of Tunisia, Tunis
TS-IOO

TURKEY
Türk Hava Kuvvetleri
Boeing 737-7FS AEW&C
131 Filo, Konya
06-001 (on order)
06-002 (on order)
06-003 (on order)
06-004 (on order)

Boeing
KC-135R Stratotanker
101 Filo, Incirlik
57-2609
58-0110
60-0325
60-0326
62-3539
62-3563
62-3567

Canadair
NF-5A-2000/NF-5B-2000
Freedom Fighter
134 Filo, *Turkish Stars*, Konya
NF-5A-2000
3004
3025
3027
3032
3036
3039
3046
3048
3052
3058
3066
3072
NF-5B-2000
4005
4009
4020
4021

Cessna 650 Citation VII
212 Filo, Ankara/Etimesgut
004
93-005

Gulfstream Aerospace G.550
212 Filo, Ankara/Etimesgut
09-001
TC-CBK

Grumman
G.1159C Gulfstream IV
211 Filo, Ankara/Etimesgut
91-003
TC-ATA
TC-GAP/001

Lockheed C-130E Hercules

222 Filo, Erkilet

63-3186
63-3187
63-3188
63-3189
65-451
67-455
68-1606
68-1608
68-1609
70-1610
70-1947
71-1468
73-0991 $

Transall C-160D

221 Filo, Erkilet

68-020
68-023
69-019
69-021
69-024
69-026
69-027
69-029
69-031
69-032
69-033 $
69-034
69-035
69-036
69-038
69-040 $

TUSAS-GD F-16C/F-16D* Fighting Falcon

3 AJEÜ, Konya:
 132 Filo;
4 AJÜ, Akinci:
 141 Filo, 142 Filo
 & 143/Öncel Filo;
5 AJÜ, Merzifon:
 151 Filo & 152 Filo;
6 AJÜ, Bandirma:
 161 Filo & 162 Filo;
8 AJÜ, Diyarbakir:
 181 Filo & 182 Filo;
9 AJÜ, Balikesir:
 191 Filo & 192 Filo

07-1001	142 Filo
07-1002	141 Filo
07-1003	141 Filo
07-1004	
07-1005	
07-1006	141 Filo
07-1007	
07-1008	
07-1009	141 Filo
07-1010	
07-1011	
07-1012	
07-1013	
07-1014	
07-1015*	
07-1016*	
07-1017*	
07-1018*	141 Filo
07-1019*	
07-1020*	
07-1021*	
07-1022*	141 Filo
07-1023*	141 Filo
07-1024*	
07-1025*	
07-1026*	
07-1027*	
07-1028*	
07-1029*	
07-1030*	
86-0066	Öncel Filo
86-0068	Öncel Filo
86-0069	Öncel Filo
86-0070	Öncel Filo $
86-0071	Öncel Filo
86-0072	Öncel Filo
86-0192*	Öncel Filo
86-0193*	Öncel Filo
86-0194*	Öncel Filo
86-0195*	Öncel Filo
86-0196*	Öncel Filo
87-0002*	Öncel Filo
87-0003*	Öncel Filo
87-0009	Öncel Filo
87-0010	Öncel Filo
87-0011	Öncel Filo
87-0013	Öncel Filo $
87-0014	Öncel Filo
87-0015	Öncel Filo
87-0016	Öncel Filo
87-0017	Öncel Filo
87-0018	Öncel Filo
87-0019	Öncel Filo
87-0020	Öncel Filo
87-0021	Öncel Filo
88-0013*	Öncel Filo
88-0014*	141 Filo
88-0015*	141 Filo
88-0019	Öncel Filo
88-0020	Öncel Filo
88-0021	142 Filo
88-0024	142 Filo
88-0025	142 Filo
88-0026	142 Filo
88-0027	142 Filo
88-0028	191 Filo
88-0029	142 Filo
88-0030	142 Filo
88-0031	142 Filo
88-0032	142 Filo
88-0033	141 Filo
88-0034	141 Filo
88-0035	141 Filo
88-0036	141 Filo
88-0037	141 Filo
89-0022	141 Filo
89-0023	141 Filo
89-0024	141 Filo
89-0025	141 Filo
89-0026	141 Filo
89-0027	141 Filo
89-0028	141 Filo
89-0030	141 Filo
89-0031	141 Filo
89-0034	162 Filo
89-0035	162 Filo
89-0036	141 Filo
89-0037	162 Filo
89-0038	162 Filo
89-0039	152 Filo
89-0040	162 Filo
89-0041	162 Filo
89-0042*	152 Filo
89-0043*	162 Filo
89-0044*	162 Filo
89-0045*	182 Filo
90-0004	152 Filo
90-0005	162 Filo
90-0006	152 Filo
90-0007	162 Filo
90-0008	162 Filo
90-0009	162 Filo
90-0010	162 Filo
90-0011	162 Filo
90-0012	161 Filo
90-0013	162 Filo
90-0014	162 Filo
90-0016	161 Filo
90-0017	161 Filo
90-0018	161 Filo
90-0019	161 Filo
90-0020	162 Filo
90-0021	161 Filo
90-0022*	161 Filo
90-0023*	161 Filo
90-0024*	161 Filo
91-0001	161 Filo
91-0002	161 Filo
91-0003	161 Filo
91-0004	161 Filo
91-0005	161 Filo
91-0006	162 Filo
91-0007	161 Filo
91-0008	141 Filo
91-0010	141 Filo
91-0011	141 Filo $
91-0012	141 Filo
91-0013	192 Filo
91-0014	141 Filo
91-0015	182 Filo
91-0016	182 Filo
91-0017	182 Filo
91-0018	182 Filo
91-0020	182 Filo
91-0022*	141 Filo

91-0024* 141 Filo
92-0001 182 Filo
92-0002 182 Filo
92-0003 152 Filo
92-0004 182 Filo
92-0005 191 Filo
92-0006 182 Filo
92-0007 182 Filo
92-0008 152 Filo
92-0009 191 Filo
92-0010 182 Filo
92-0011 182 Filo
92-0012 182 Filo
92-0013 182 Filo
92-0014 182 Filo
92-0015 182 Filo
92-0016 152 Filo
92-0017 152 Filo
92-0018 152 Filo
92-0019 181 Filo
92-0020 181 Filo
92-0021 181 Filo
92-0022* 181 Filo
92-0023* 181 Filo
92-0024* 141 Filo
93-0001 181 Filo
93-0003 181 Filo
93-0004 181 Filo
93-0005 181 Filo
93-0006 181 Filo
93-0007 181 Filo
93-0008 181 Filo
93-0009 181 Filo
93-0010 132 Filo
93-0011 181 Filo
93-0012 181 Filo
93-0013 181 Filo
93-0658 151 Filo
93-0659 191 Filo
93-0660 152 Filo
93-0661 151 Filo
93-0663 151 Filo
93-0664 151 Filo
93-0665 152 Filo
93-0667 151 Filo
93-0668 151 Filo
93-0669 151 Filo
93-0670 191 Filo
93-0671 191 Filo
93-0672 152 Filo
93-0673 152 Filo
93-0674 152 Filo
93-0675 191 Filo
93-0676 192 Filo
93-0677 192 Filo $
93-0678 152 Filo
93-0679 192 Filo
93-0680 192 Filo $
93-0681 192 Filo
93-0682 192 Filo $
93-0683 192 Filo
93-0684 192 Filo
93-0685 192 Filo
93-0687 192 Filo
93-0688 151 Filo
93-0689 192 Filo
93-0690 192 Filo
93-0691* 192 Filo
93-0692* 151 Filo $
93-0693* 152 Filo
93-0694* 192 Filo
93-0695* 151 Filo
93-0696* 192 Filo $
94-0071 192 Filo
94-0072 191 Filo
94-0073 191 Filo
94-0074 191 Filo
94-0075 191 Filo
94-0076 191 Filo
94-0077 191 Filo
94-0078 191 Filo
94-0079 191 Filo
94-0080 191 Filo
94-0082 191 Filo
94-0083 191 Filo
94-0084 191 Filo
94-0085 191 Filo
94-0086 191 Filo
94-0088 152 Filo
94-0089 152 Filo
94-0090 192 Filo $
94-0091 152 Filo
94-0092 152 Filo
94-0093 192 Filo
94-0094 152 Filo
94-0095 152 Filo
94-0096 152 Filo
94-0105* 152 Filo
94-0106* 191 Filo
94-0108* 192 Filo $
94-0109* 151 Filo
94-0110* 151 Filo
94-1557* 152 Filo
94-1558* Öncel Filo
94-1559* 152 Filo
94-1560* 151 Filo
94-1561* 191 Filo
94-1562* 192 Filo
94-1563* 192 Filo
94-1564* 191 Filo

Turkish Govt
Airbus A.319CJ-115X
Turkish Govt, Ankara
TC-ANA

Airbus A.330-243
Turkish Govt, Ankara
TC-TUR
Gulfstream Aerospace G.550
Turkish Govt, Ankara
TC-DAP

TURKMENISTAN
BAe 1000B
Govt of Turkmenistan, Ashkhabad
EZ-B021

Boeing 757-23A
Govt of Turkmenistan, Ashkhabad
EZ-A010

Boeing 777-22KLR
Govt of Turkmenistan, Ashkhabad
EZ-A777

UGANDA
Gulfstream Aerospace G.550
Govt of Uganda, Entebbe
5X-UGF

UKRAINE
Ukrainian Air Force
Ilyushin Il-76MD
25 TABR, Melitopol & Zaporozhye
76413 25 TABR
76423 25 TABR
76531 25 TABR
76557 25 TABR
76559
76564 25 TABR
76566
76580 25 TABR
76585 25 TABR
76596 25 TABR
76601 25 TABR
76621 25 TABR
76622 25 TABR
76633 25 TABR
76637 25 TABR
76645 25 TABR
76647 25 TABR
76660 25 TABR
76661 25 TABR
76683 25 TABR
76697 25 TABR
76698 25 TABR
76699 25 TABR
76700 25 TABR
76732 25 TABR
76777 25 TABR
78772 25 TABR
78820 25 TABR
86915

Airbus A.319CJ-115X
Govt of Ukraine, Kiev
UR-ABA

Ilyushin Il-62M
Govt of Ukraine, Kiev
UR-86527
UR-86528

UNITED ARAB EMIRATES
United Arab Emirates Air Force

Aermacchi MB339A*/MB339NAT
Al Fursan, Al Ain
430
431
432
433*
434
435
436*
437
438
439
440

AgustaWestland AW.139
Dubai Air Wing
DU-139
DU-140
DU-141
DU-142
DU-143

Airbus A.330-243 MRTT
.... (on order)
.... (on order)

Boeing C-17A Globemaster III
1223 (10-0401)
1224 (10-0402)
1225 (10-0403)
1226 (10-0404)
1227 (10-0405)
1228 (10-0406)

Lockheed C-130H/L.100-30* Hercules
Abu Dhabi
1211
1212
1213
1214
1215*
1216*
1217*
Dubai
311*
312*

UAE Govt
Airbus A.319CJ-113X
Dubai Air Wing
A6-ESH

Airbus A.320-232
Govt of Abu Dhabi;
Govt of Dubai

A6-DLM	Abu Dhabi
A6-HMS	Dubai

BAE RJ.85/RJ.100*
Govt of Abu Dhabi;
Govt of Dubai

A6-AAB*	Abu Dhabi
A6-RJ1	Dubai
A6-RJ2	Dubai

Boeing 737-7BC/7F0/8AJ/8EC/8EO/8EX
Govt of Abu Dhabi;
Govt of Dubai

A6-AUH	8EX	Dubai
A6-DFR	7BC	Abu Dhabi
A6-HEH	8AJ	Dubai
A6-HRS	7F0	Dubai
A6-MRM	8EC	Dubai
A6-MRS	8EO	Dubai

Boeing 747-412F/422/433/48E/4F6/8Z5
Dubai Air Wing;
Govt of Abu Dhabi

A6-COM	433	Dubai
A6-GGP	412F	Dubai
A6-HRM	422	Dubai
A6-MMM	422	Dubai
A6-PFA	8Z5	(on order)
A6-UAE	48E	Dubai
A6-YAS	4F6	Abu Dhabi

Boeing 747SP-31
Govt of Dubai
A6-SMR

Boeing 777-2ANER/-35RER*
Govt of Abu Dhabi
A6-ALN
A6-SIL*

Grumman G.1159C Gulfstream IV
Dubai Air Wing
A6-HHH

VENEZUELA
Fuerza Aérea Venezolana
Airbus A.319CJ-133X
Esc 41, Caracas
0001

YEMEN
Boeing 747SP-27
Govt of Yemen, Sana'a
7O-YMN

Overseas Military Aircraft Code Decode

This section lists the codes worn by some overseas air forces and, alongside, the serial of the aircraft currently wearing this code. This list will be updated occasionally and those with Internet access can download the latest version via the 'Military Aircraft Markings' Web Site, *www.militaryaircraftmarkings.co.uk* and via the MAM2009 Yahoo! Group.

FRANCE

D-BD Alpha Jet

0 [PDF] E134
1 [PDF] E152
2 [PDF] E162
3 [PDF] E130
4 [PDF] E46
5 [PDF] E41
6 [PDF] E166
7 [PDF] E165
8 [PDF] E85
9 [PDF] E163
102-AG E109
102-AH E99
102-FA E140
102-FB E86
102-FG E14
102-FI E32
102-FM E105
102-FP E168
102-LC E87
102-LF E9
102-LH E38
102-LI E53
102-LQ E61
102-MB E97
102-MM E13
102-NA E79
102-NB E29
102-ND E26
102-RJ E76
102-RL E91
102-UB E11
118-AH E110
118-FE E119
118-LT E147
118-LX E89
118-UA E103
120-AF E108
120-AK E144
120-AL E154
120-FJ E33
120-FN E116
120-LM E102
120-MA E35
120-MN E167
120-MR E115
120-NE E73
120-NF E141
120-NL E37
120-NP E155
120-RE E44
120-RN E124
120-RO E131
120-RP E136
120-UC E157
314-LK E125
314-LN E118
314-LO E142
314-TL E64
314-TT E101
314-UH E160
705-AA E17
705-AB E28
705-AC E47
705-AD E51
705-AE E75
705-AK E18
705-AO E112
705-FC E139
705-FD E151
705-FK E127
705-FO E81
705-LA E72
705-LB E49
705-LE E121
705-LG E120
705-LJ E137
705-LL E88
705-LP E129
705-LS E22
705-LU E148
705-LW E82
705-LY E59
705-LZ E132
705-MD E30
705-MF E98
705-MH E48
705-MS E20
705-RM E123
705-RQ E138
705-RR E146
705-RS E149
705-RT E152
705-RU E153
705-RW E166
705-RX E135
705-RY E170
705-RZ E171
705-TA E42
705-TB E67
705-TC E96
705-TD E113
705-TF E42
705-TG E104
705-TH E90
705-TI E156
705-TJ E25
705-TK E58
705-TM E128
705-TU E7
705-TZ E83
F-RCAI E117
F-TERA E41
F-TERB E163
F-TERD E121
F-TERE E165
F-TERF E158
F-TERH E94
F-TERI E117
F-TERJ E162
F-TERK E31
F-TERM E134
F-TERN E46
F-TERP E130
F-TERQ E95
F-TERR E114
F-TEUD E107
F-UHRE E44
F-UHRF E48

Dassault Mirage F.1

112-CQ 632
112-FA 622
112-NC 654
112-NM 611
118-AA 631
118-CB 647
118-CD 638
118-CF 604
118-CK 634
118-CO 605
118-CR 649
118-CT 620
118-CY 660
118-FB 655
118-NC 654
118-ND 607
118-NE 617
118-NF 662
118-NK 661
118-NQ 658
118-NR 614
118-NT 659
118-NX 616
118-SC 517
118-SD 509
118-ST 504
118-SW 502

Dassault Mirage 2000

103-KR 102
103-KU 114
103-KV 88
103-LA 87
103-LB 81
103-LC 108
103-LK 85
103-YD 107
103-YH 109
103-YN 103
103-YU 98
115-AM 525
115-KA 89

115-KB	94
115-KC	120
115-KE	101
115-KF	111
115-KG	104
115-KI	96
115-KJ	523
115-KL	106
115-KM	95
115-KN	121
115-KS	528
115-LD	117
115-LE	79
115-LJ	105
115-LL	86
115-OA	524
115-OC	529
115-OD	506
115-OL	530
115-OR	527
115-YA	93
115-YB	99
115-YC	85
115-YG	118
115-YK	97
115-YL	82
115-YM	115
115-YO	113
115-YP	526
115-YS	90
116-AT	330
116-AU	306
116-AW	367
116-BL	306
116-BQ	358
116-CS	305
116-EA	49
116-EC	78
116-ED	62
116-EE	71
116-EG	56
116-EI	38
116-EJ	43
116-EL	58
116-EM	63
116-EN	46
116-EO	66
116-EQ	44
116-ER	68
116-ES	73
116-ET	57
116-EU	55
116-EV	59
116-EW	48
116-EX	40
116-EZ	54
116-FZ	41
116-ME	61
116-MG	65
116-MH	67
118-AS	51
118-AU	653
118-AW	92
118-AX	77
118-EB	76
118-EY	42
118-IG	668
118-IN	640
118-IQ	666
118-JK	612
118-KQ	112
118-MQ	646
118-XH	616
125-AA	340
125-AE	355
125-AI	365
125-AL	348
125-AK	359
125-AM	353
125-AQ	351
125-AR	368
125-BA	342
125-BB	364
125-BC	366
125-BD	371
125-BJ	354
125-BS	374
125-BU	345
125-BX	356
125-CF	373
125-CG	338
125-CI	335
125-CL	375
125-CM	372
125-CO	357
125-CQ	370
125-CU	362
133-AF	665
133-AG	681
133-AL	669
133-AS	635
133-IA	650
133-IC	626
133-ID	654
133-IE	642
133-IH	631
133-IJ	638
133-IL	622
133-IO	647
133-IP	604
133-IR	674
133-IS	617
133-IV	683
133-IW	664
133-JB	678
133-JC	606
133-JD	643
133-JE	634
133-JF	660
133-JG	601
133-JH	686
133-JI	675
133-JL	628
133-JM	657
133-JN	658
133-JO	627
133-JP	611
133-JR	682
133-JT	677
133-JU	614
133-JV	636
133-JW	641
133-JX	679
133-JY	615
133-JZ	667
133-LF	605
133-LG	651
133-LH	655
133-MO	613
133-MP	623
133-XA	662
133-XC	618
133-XE	632
133-XF	670
133-XG	625
133-XI	661
133-XK	671
133-XL	603
133-XM	680
133-XN	652
133-XO	629
133-XP	645
133-XQ	637
133-XR	659
133-XT	648
133-XV	672
133-XX	610
133-XY	649
133-XZ	685
188-AD	70
188-EF	45
188-EH	52
188-EP	47
188-IT	624
188-IU	620
188-LI	80
188-MK	74
188-XD	630
188-XJ	602
188-YR	91

Dassault Rafale

104-GC	124
104-GD	125
104-HD	311
104-HG	106
104-HP	314
113-GA	122
113-GE	126
113-GF	127
113-GG	128
113-GI	130
113-GN	135
113-HA	308
113-HB	309
113-HC	310
113-HE	105
113-HF	312
113-HH	104
113-HI	313
113-HJ	107
113-HK	315

113-HM	318
113-HN	319
113-HO	317
113-HQ	321
113-HR	103
113-HS	108
113-HU	322
113-HV	320
113-HX	325
113-HY	326
113-HZ	327
113-IA	307
113-IB	306
113-IC	328
113-IE	330
113-IG	332
113-IH	333
113-II	334
113-IJ	335
113-IK	336
113-IL	337
113-IO	338
113-IP	111
113-IQ	112
113-IR	113
113-IT	115
113-IU	116
113-IV	117
113-IW	118
113-IY	120
113-IZ	121
118-EA	303
118-EB	304
118-EC	305
118-EF	102
118-GB	123
118-GH	129
118-GJ	131
118-GK	132
118-GL	133
118-GM	134
118-GO	136
118-GP	137
118-HT	323
118-IM	109
118-IN	110
118-IR	113
118-IS	114
118-IX	119
IF	331

ITALY

Aeritalia-EMB AMX

32-01	MM7147
32-02	MM7192
32-05	MM7170
32-07	MM7196
32-12	MM7126
32-15	MM7129
32-16	MM7165
32-20	MM7180
32-21	MM7194
32-23	MM7115
32-24	MM7149
32-25	MM7163
32-41	MM55030
32-42	MM55051
32-47	MM55046
32-50	MM55029
32-51	MM55036
32-53	MM55047
32-56	MM55042
32-57	MM55044
32-64	MM55037
32-65	MM55043
32-66	MM55049
51-10	MM7159
51-21	MM7143
51-34	MM7191
51-37	MM7161
51-40	MM7164
51-41	MM7183
51-42	MM7177
51-43	MM7178
51-44	MM7198
51-45	MM7175
51-46	MM7197
51-50	MM7186
51-51	MM7151
51-52	MM7171
51-53	MM7160
51-54	MM7193
51-55	MM7168
51-56	MM7167
51-57	MM7190
51-60	MM7174
51-61	MM7148
51-62	MM7182
51-63	MM7173
51-64	MM7179
51-65	MM7184
51-66	MM7169
51-67	MM7172
RS-12	CSX7158
RS-14	MM7177
RS-18	MM55034

Aermacchi MB339

0 [FT]	MM54475
1 [FT]	MM54517
2 [FT]	MM54482
3 [FT]	MM54477
4 [FT]	MM55054
5 [FT]	MM54487
6 [FT]	MM54510
7 [FT]	MM55052
8 [FT]	MM54480
9 [FT]	MM54539
10 [FT]	MM54514
11 [FT]	MM54551
32-161	MM55089
36-04	MM55076
36-06	MM55074
61-01	MM54446
61-11	MM54457
61-12	MM54458
61-15	MM55054
61-20	MM55055
61-21	MM54465
61-23	MM54467
61-24	MM54468
61-26	MM55059
61-32	MM54488
61-41	MM55058
61-42	MM54496
61-50	MM54443
61-55	MM54507
61-60	MM54510
61-61	MM54511
61-62	MM54512
61-64	MM54514
61-65	MM54515
61-66	MM54516
61-70	MM54518
61-72	MM54533
61-106	MM54548
61-107	MM54549
61-114	MM55053
61-126	MM55062
61-127	MM55063
61-130	MM55064
61-131	MM55065
61-132	MM55066
61-133	MM55067
61-135	MM55069
61-136	MM55070
61-140	MM55072
61-141	MM55073
61-143	MM55075
61-145	MM55077
61-146	MM55078
61-147	MM55079
61-150	MM55080
61-151	MM55081
61-152	MM55082
61-154	MM55084
61-155	MM55085
61-156	MM55086
61-157	MM55087
61-160	MM55088
61-162	MM55090
RS-11	CSX54453
RS-30	CSX54544
RS-32	MM55091
RS-33	MM55068

Eurofighter Typhoon

4-1	MM7270
4-2	MM7303
4-3	MM7287
4-4	MM7288
4-5	MM7289
4-6	MM7311
4-7	MM7290
4-10	MM7274
4-11	MM7291
4-12	MM7292
4-13	MM7294
4-14	MM7281
4-16	MM7285
4-21	MM7276
4-22	MM7301

4-23	MM55095
4-24	MM55097
4-25	MM55092
4-26	MM55128
4-27	MM55094
4-30	MM55096
4-31	MM55093
4-32	MM55129
4-33	MM55130
4-34	MM55131
4-35	MM55132
4-36	MM55133
4-40	MM7277
4-41	MM7299
4-42	MM7316
4-44	MM7278
36-02	MM7286
36-03	MM7271
36-04	MM7235
36-10	MM7284
36-11	MM7275
36-12	MM7300
36-14	MM7272
36-15	MM7282
36-20	MM7295
36-21	MM7304
36-22	MM7296
36-23	MM7297
36-24	MM7298
36-25	MM7302
36-26	MM7294
36-32	MM7310
36-33	MM7293
36-34	MM7312
36-35	MM7313
36-36	MM7308
36-37	MM7314
37-01	MM7307
37-03	MM7309
RMV-01	MMX603
RS-01	MMX602
RS-21	MM7306

Panavia Tornado

6-01	MM7007
6-02	CSX7039
6-04	MM7057
6-05	MM7025
6-06	MM7046
6-07	MM7075
6-10	MM7088
6-11	MM7058
6-12	MM7071
6-13	MM7011
6-14	MM7061
6-20	MM7016
6-23	MM7022
6-25	MM7043
6-26	MM7063
6-27	MM7035
6-30	MM7072
6-31	MM7006
6-32	MM7015
6-33	MM7080
6-34	MM7073
6-35	MM7026
6-36	MM7087
6-37	MM7038
6-42	MM55010
6-44	MM55009
6-45	MM55008
6-50	MM7024
6-51	MM55000
6-52	MM55001
6-55	MM7004
6-56	MM55007
6-57	MM7081
6-60	MM7086
6-61	MM7031
6-64	MM7049
6-66	MM7056
6-71	MM7067
6-72	MM7083
6-75	MM7013
6-76	MM7044
36-31	MM7023
36-50	CSX7085
50-01	MM7021
50-02	MM7052
50-03	MM7066
50-04	MM7030
50-05	MM7019
50-06	MM7070
50-07	MM7053
50-40	MM7054
50-41	MM7020
50-42	MM7055
50-44	MM7062
50-45	MM7051
50-46	MM7068
50-47	MM7059
50-50	MM7003
50-52	MM7028
50-53	MM7033
50-54	MM7082
50-55	MM7036
50-56	MM7065
50-57	MM7042
RS-05	CSX7047
RS-06	CSX7041

SPAIN

CASA 101EB Aviojet

54-20	E.25-35
54-21	E.25-55
54-22	E.25-61
74-07	E.25-51
74-09	E.25-53
74-11	E.25-56
74-12	E.25-57
74-13	E.25-59
74-17	E.25-63
74-20	E.25-66
74-21	E.25-67
74-22	E.25-68
74-25	E.25-71
74-26	E.25-72
74-28	E.25-74
74-30	E.25-76
74-34	E.25-81
74-35	E.25-83
74-39	E.25-88
74-40	E.25-17
74-41	E.25-41
74-42	E.25-18
74-43	E.25-43
74-44	E.25-34
74-45	E.25-29
79-02	E.25-78
79-03	E.25-80
79-04	E.25-84
79-06	E.25-06
79-08	E.25-08
79-11	E.25-11
79-12	E.25-12
79-13	E.25-13
79-14	E.25-14
79-15	E.25-15
79-16	E.25-16
79-17	E.25-62
79-20	E.25-20
79-21	E.25-21
79-22	E.25-22
79-23	E.25-23
79-24	E.25-24
79-25	E.25-25
79-27	E.25-27
79-28	E.25-28
79-29	E.25-87
79-31	E.25-31
79-32	E.25-86
79-33	E.25-50
79-34	E.25-52
79-35	E.25-54
79-37	E.25-37
79-38	E.25-38
79-39	E.25-79
79-40	E.25-40
79-44	E.25-44
79-45	E.25-45
79-46	E.25-46
79-47	E.25-47
79-48	E.25-48
79-49	E.25-49
79-95	E.25-65
79-97	E.25-69
79-98	E.25-73

CASA 212 Aviocar

47-12	TM.12D-72
72-01	T.12B-13
72-03	T.12B-21
72-05	T.12B-37
72-07	T.12B-49
72-08	T.12B-55
72-09	T.12B-66
72-12	T.12B-67
72-14	T.12B-63
72-15	T.12B-69
72-17	T.12B-70

US Military Aircraft Markings

All USAF and US Army aircraft have been allocated a fiscal year (FY) number since 1921. Individual aircraft are given a serial according to the fiscal year in which they are ordered. The numbers commence at 0001 and are prefixed with the year of allocation. For example F-15C Eagle 84-001 (84-0001) was the first aircraft ordered in 1984. The fiscal year (FY) serial is carried on the technical data block which is usually stencilled on the left-hand side of the aircraft just below the cockpit. The number displayed on the fin is a corruption of the FY serial. Most tactical aircraft carry the fiscal year in small figures followed by the last three or four digits of the serial in large figures. Large transport and tanker aircraft such as C-130s and KC-135s sometimes display a five-figure number commencing with the last digit of the appropriate fiscal year and four figures of the production number. An example of this is KC-135R 58-0128 which displays 80128 on its fin.

US Army serials have been allocated in a similar way to USAF serials although in recent years an additional zero has been added so that all US Army serials now have the two-figure fiscal year part followed by five digits. This means that, for example C-20E 70140 is officially 87-00140 although as yet this has not led to any alterations to serials painted on aircraft.

USN and USMC serials follow a straightforward numerical sequence which commenced, for the present series, with the allocation of 00001 to an SB2C Helldiver by the Bureau of Aeronautics in 1940. Numbers in the 168000 series are presently being issued. They are usually carried in full on the rear fuselage of the aircraft.

US Coast Guard serials began with the allocation of the serial 1 to a Loening OL-5 in 1927

UK-based USAF Aircraft

The following aircraft are normally based in the UK. They are listed in numerical order of type with individual aircraft in serial number order, as depicted on the aircraft. The number in brackets is either the alternative presentation of the five-figure number commencing with the last digit of the fiscal year, or the fiscal year where a five-figure serial is presented on the aircraft. Where it is possible to identify the allocation of aircraft to individual squadrons by means of colours carried on fin or cockpit edge, this is also provided.

Type	*Notes*
McDonnell Douglas F-15C Eagle/F-15D Eagle/ F-15E Strike Eagle	
LN: 48th FW, RAF Lakenheath:	
492nd FS *bl*ue/white	
493rd FS black/*y*ellow	
494th FS *r*ed/white	
00-3000 F-15E *r*	
00-3001 F-15E *r*	
00-3002 F-15E *r*	
00-3003 F-15E *r*	
00-3004 F-15E *m* [48th FW]	
01-2000 F-15E *r*	
01-2001 F-15E *m* [48th OG]	
01-2002 F-15E *r* [494th FS]	
01-2003 F-15E *r*	
01-2004 F-15E *m* [48th FW]	
84-0001 F-15C *y*	
84-0010 F-15C *y*	
84-0015 F-15C *y*	
84-0019 F-15C *y*	
84-0027 F-15C *y*	
84-0044 F-15D *y*	
86-0147 F-15C *y*	
86-0154 F-15C *y*	
86-0156 F-15C *y*	
86-0159 F-15C	
86-0160 F-15C *y*	
86-0163 F-15C *y*	
86-0164 F-15C *y*	
86-0165 F-15C *y*	
86-0166 F-15C *y*	
86-0167 F-15C *y*	
86-0171 F-15C	

Type	*Notes*
86-0172 F-15C *y*	
86-0174 F-15C *y*	
86-0175 F-15C *y*	
86-0176 F-15C *y*	
86-0178 F-15C *y*	
86-0182 F-15D *y*	
91-0301 F-15E *bl*	
91-0302 F-15E *bl*	
91-0303 F-15E *bl*	
91-0306 F-15E *bl*	
91-0307 F-15E *bl*	
91-0308 F-15E *bl*	
91-0309 F-15E *r*	
91-0310 F-15E *r*	
91-0311 F-15E *r*	
91-0312 F-15E *bl*	
91-0313 F-15E *r*	
91-0314 F-15E *r*	
91-0315 F-15E *bl*	
91-0316 F-15E *bl*	
91-0317 F-15E *bl*	
91-0318 F-15E *m* [48th OG]	
91-0320 F-15E *r*	
91-0321 F-15E *bl*	
91-0324 F-15E *r*	
91-0326 F-15E *r*	
91-0329 F-15E *r*	
91-0331 F-15E *bl*	
91-0332 F-15E *bl*	
91-0334 F-15E *r*	
91-0335 F-15E *r*	
91-0602 F-15E *r*	
91-0603 F-15E *r*	
91-0604 F-15E *r*	

Type *Notes*

91-0605 F-15E *bl*
92-0364 F-15E *r*
96-0201 F-15E *r*
96-0202 F-15E *bl*
96-0204 F-15E *r*
96-0205 F-15E *bl*
97-0217 F-15E *bl*
97-0218 F-15E *bl*
97-0219 F-15E *bl*
97-0220 F-15E *bl*
97-0221 F-15E *bl* [492nd FS]
97-0222 F-15E *bl*
98-0131 F-15E *bl*
98-0132 F-15E *r*
98-0133 F-15E *bl*
98-0134 F-15E *bl*
98-0135 F-15E *bl*

Sikorsky HH-60G Pave Hawk
56th RQS/48th FW,
RAF Lakenheath [LN]
26109 (FY88)
26205 (FY89)
26206 (FY89)
26208 (FY89)
26212 (FY89)

Lockheed MC-130 Hercules
352nd SOG, RAF Mildenhall:
7th SOS* & 67th SOS,

Type *Notes*

14854 (FY64) MC-130P
50911 (FY65) MC-130P
50992 (FY65) MC-130P
60215 (FY66) MC-130P
60220 (FY66) MC-130P
70023 (FY87) MC-130H*
70024 (FY87) MC-130H*
80195 (FY88) MC-130H*
81803 (FY88) MC-130H*
95822 (FY69) MC-130P

Boeing KC-135R Stratotanker
351st ARS/100th ARW,
RAF Mildenhall [D] (*r/w/bl*)
00353 (FY60)
10295 (FY61)
10304 (FY61)
10306 (FY61)
14830 (FY64)
23499 (FY62)
23540 (FY62)
23551 (FY63)
23565 (FY62)
38008 (FY63)
38884 (FY63)
80001 (FY58)
80034 (FY58)
80100 (FY58)
91492 (FY59)

91-0358 is an F-16CM belonging to the USAF's 480th Fighter Squadron ('Warhawks'), part of the 52nd Fighter Wing at Spangdahlem in Germany. With the withdrawal of the A-10C Thunderbolt II from USAF Europe operations early in 2013, this will be the sole fighter squadron based at Spangdahlem.

European-based USAF Aircraft

These aircraft are normally based in Western Europe with the USAFE. They are shown in numerical order of type designation, with individual aircraft in serial number order as carried on the aircraft. Fiscal year (FY) details are also provided if necessary. The unit allocation and operating bases are given for most aircraft.

Type *Notes*

Fairchild
A-10C Thunderbolt II
SP: 52nd FW, Spangdahlem, Germany:
81st FS *yellow*

81-0945 *y*
81-0948 *y*
81-0952 *y* [81st FS]
81-0960 *y*
81-0962 *y*
81-0963 *y*
81-0966 *y* [52nd OG]
81-0978 *y*
81-0980 *y*
81-0981 *y* [81st FS]
81-0983 *y*
81-0985 *y*
81-0988 *y*
81-0991 *y*
81-0992 *y*
82-0646 *y*
82-0647 *y*
82-0649 *y*
82-0650 *y*
82-0654 *y*
82-0656 *y*

Beech
C-12 Super King Air
US Embassy Flight, Budapest, Hungary

FY83
30495 C-12D
FY76
60168 C-12C

Lockheed (GD)
F-16CM/F-16DM* Fighting Falcon
AV: 31st FW, Aviano, Italy:
510th FS *purple*/white
555th FS *green*/yellow
SP: 52nd FW, Spangdahlem, Germany:
480th FS *red*

87-0350 AV *gn*
87-0351 AV *m* [31st OSS]
87-0355 AV *pr*
87-0359 AV *gn*
88-0413 AV *pr*
88-0425 AV *gn*
88-0435 AV *gn*
88-0443 AV *pr*
88-0444 AV *pr*
88-0446 AV *gn*
88-0491 AV *pr*
88-0510 AV *pr* [510th FS]
88-0516 AV *pr*
88-0525 AV *pr*
88-0526 AV *gn*
88-0532 AV *gn*
88-0535 AV *gn*
88-0541 AV *pr*
89-2001 AV *m* [31st FW]
89-2008 AV *pr*
89-2009 AV *pr*
89-2011 AV *pr*
89-2016 AV *pr*
89-2018 AV *gn*
89-2023 AV *gn*
89-2024 AV *gn*
89-2026 AV *gn*
89-2029 AV *pr*
89-2030 AV *pr*
89-2035 AV *gn* [555th FS]
89-2038 AV *pr*
89-2039 AV *gn*
89-2041 AV *gn*
89-2044 AV *gn*
89-2046 AV *pr*
89-2047 AV *pr*
89-2049 AV *pr* [USAFE]
89-2057 AV *pr*
89-2068 AV *gn*
89-2096 AV *pr*
89-2102 AV *pr*
89-2118 AV *pr*
89-2137 AV *pr* [31st OG]
89-2152 AV
89-2178* AV *gn*
90-0709 AV *pr*
90-0772 AV *gn*
90-0773 AV *gn*
90-0777* AV *pr*
90-0795* AV *gn*
90-0796* AV *gn*
90-0800* AV *gn*
90-0813 SP *r*
90-0818 SP *r*
90-0827 SP *r*
90-0829 SP *r*
90-0833 SP *r*
91-0338 SP *r*
91-0340 SP *r*
91-0342 SP *r*
91-0343 SP *r*
91-0344 SP *r*
91-0351 SP *r*
91-0352 SP *m* [52nd FW]
91-0358 SP *r*
91-0360 SP *r*
91-0361 SP *r*
91-0366 SP *r* [480 FS]
91-0368 SP
91-0402 SP *r*
91-0403 SP *r*
91-0407 SP *r*
91-0412 SP *r*
91-0416 SP *r*

Type | Notes

91-0417 SP *r*
91-0472* SP
91-0481* SP
92-3918 SP *r*
96-0080 SP *r*
96-0083 SP *r*

Grumman
C-20H Gulfstream IV
76th AS/86th AW, Ramstein, Germany
FY90
00300
FY92
20375

Gates C-21A
Learjet
76th AS/86th AW, Ramstein, Germany
FY84
40081
40082
40083
40085
40087
40109
40110
40111

Gulfstream Aerospace
C-37A Gulfstream V
309th AS/86th AW, Chievres, Belgium
FY01
10076
FY99
90402

Boeing C-40B
76th AS/86th AW, Ramstein, Germany
FY02
20042

Lockheed C-130J
Hercules II
37th AS/86th AW, Ramstein, Germany [RS] (*bl/w*)
68610 (FY06)
68611 (FY06)
68612 (FY06)
78608 (FY07)
78609 (FY07)
78613 (FY07)
78614 (FY07)
88601 (FY08) [86th AW]
88602 (FY08) [86th OG]
88603 (FY08) [37th AS]
88604 (FY08)
88605 (FY08)
88607 (FY08)

European-based US Navy Aircraft

Type | Notes

Fairchild C-26D
NAF Naples, Italy;
NAF Sigonella, Italy
900528 Sigonella
900530 Sigonella
900531 Naples
910502 Naples

European-based US Army Aircraft

Type | Notes

Beech
C-12 Huron
'E' Co, 6th Btn, 52nd Avn Reg't, Stuttgart;
'F' Co, 6th Btn, 52nd Avn Reg't, Wiesbaden;
'A' Co, 2nd Btn, 228th Avn Reg't, Heidelberg;
1st Military Intelligence Btn, Wiesbaden;
SHAPE Flight Det, Chievres
FY92
13122 RC-12X 1st MIB
13123 RC-12X 1st MIB
13125 RC-12X 1st MIB
FY93
30699 RC-12X 1st MIB
30701 RC-12X 1st MIB
FY84
40156 C-12U F/6-52nd Avn
40157 C-12U E/6-52nd Avn
40158 C-12U F/6-52nd Avn
40160 C-12U E/6-52nd Avn
40161 C-12U F/6-52nd Avn
40162 C-12U F/6-52nd Avn
40163 C-12U F/6-52nd Avn
40165 C-12U F/6-52nd Avn
40173 C-12U F/6-52nd Avn
40180 C-12U E/6-52nd Avn
FY85
50147 RC-12K 1st MIB
50148 RC-12K 1st MIB

Type	Notes	Type	Notes

50150 RC-12K 1st MIB
50152 RC-12K 1st MIB
50153 RC-12K 1st MIB
FY86
60079 C-12J SHAPE Flt Det
FY89
00273 RC-12X 1st MIB

Grumman
C-20E Gulfstream III
HQ US Army Europe, Ramstein, Germany
FY87
70140

Cessna UC-35A
Citation V
'F' Co, 6th Btn, 52nd Avn Reg't,
Wiesbaden
FY95
50123
50124
FY97
70101
70102
70105
FY99
90102

Boeing-Vertol CH-47F
Chinook
'B' Co, 5th Btn, 158th Avn Reg't,
Ansbach
FY07
08744
08745
08746
08747
08748
FY08
08749
08750
08751
FY09
08070
08071

Sikorsky H-60 Black Hawk
'A' Co, 3rd Btn, 158th Avn Reg't,
Ansbach;
'B' Co, 3rd Btn, 158th Avn Reg't,
Ansbach;
'A' Co, 5th Btn, 158th Avn Reg't,
Ansbach;
'C' Co, 5th Btn, 158th Avn Reg't,
Ansbach;
SHAPE Flight Det, Chievres;
'G' Co, 6th Btn, 52nd Avn Reg't,
Coleman Barracks;
'B' Co, 70th Transportation Reg't,
Coleman Barracks;
'A' Co, 1st Btn, 214th Avn Reg't,
Landstuhl;
'C' Co, 1st Btn, 214th Avn Reg't,
Landstuhl;
6th Avn Co, Vicenza, Italy
FY79
23330 UH-60A C/1-214th Avn
FY82
23750 UH-60A C/1-214th Avn
23754 UH-60A C/1-214th Avn
23755 UH-60A C/1-214th Avn
23756 UH-60A C/1-214th Avn
23757 UH-60A C/1-214th Avn
FY83
23855 UH-60A C/1-214th Avn
23869 UH-60A C/1-214th Avn
23888 UH-60A C/5-158th Avn
FY84
23936 UH-60A C/5-158th Avn
23951 UH-60A C/1-214th Avn
FY85
24397 UH-60A C/5-158th Avn
24422 UH-60A C/1-214th Avn
24437 UH-60A C/1-214th Avn
FY86
24532 UH-60A C/1-214th Avn
24551 UH-60A C/1-214th Avn
24552 UH-60A C/1-214th Avn
FY87
24583 UH-60A SHAPE Flt Det
24584 UH-60A SHAPE Flt Det
24589 UH-60A G/6-52nd Avn
24614 UH-60A C/5-158th Avn
24642 UH-60A G/6-52nd Avn
24644 UH-60A C/1-214th Avn
24645 UH-60A C/1-214th Avn
24656 UH-60A C/5-158th Avn
26004 UH-60A C/5-158th Avn
26005 UH-60A C/5-158th Avn
FY88
26019 UH-60A C/1-214th Avn
26023 UH-60A C/1-214th Avn
26027 UH-60A G/6-52nd Avn
26032 UH-60A C/5-158th Avn
26037 UH-60A A/1-214th Avn
26039 UH-60A C/1-214th Avn
26045 UH-60A C/1-214th Avn
26054 UH-60A C/1-214th Avn
26071 UH-60A G/6-52nd Avn
26075 UH-60A C/5-158th Avn
26080 UH-60A C/1-214th Avn
26082 UH-60A C/5-158th Avn
FY89
26132 UH-60A C/5-158th Avn
26138 UH-60A C/1-214th Avn
26157 UH-60A C/5-158th Avn
26158 UH-60A C/5-158th Avn
26163 UH-60A C/5-158th Avn
FY92
26452 UH-60L A/5-158th Avn
FY94
26551 UH-60L G/6-52nd Avn
26570 UH-60L A/5-158th Avn
26572 UH-60L A/5-158th Avn
26573 UH-60L A/5-158th Avn
26577 UH-60L A/5-158th Avn
FY95
26637 UH-60L A/3-158th Avn
26639 UH-60L A/5-158th Avn

Type	Notes
26641 UH-60L 3-158th Avn	
26642 UH-60L 3-158th Avn	
26643 UH-60L 3-158th Avn	
26645 UH-60L A/3-158th Avn	
26646 UH-60L 3-158th Avn	
26650 UH-60L A/3-158th Avn	
26651 UH-60L B/3-158th Avn	
26652 UH-60L 3-158th Avn	
26654 UH-60L C/3-158th Avn	
26655 UH-60L C/3-158th Avn	
26657 UH-60L 3-158th Avn	
FY96	
26674 UH-60L C/3-158th Avn	
26675 UH-60L A/3-158th Avn	
26676 UH-60L A/3-158th Avn	
26677 UH-60L A/3-158th Avn	
26678 UH-60L A/3-158th Avn	
26679 UH-60L 3-158th Avn	
26680 UH-60L 3-158th Avn	
26682 UH-60L 3-158th Avn	
26683 UH-60L 3-158th Avn	
26684 UH-60L 3-158th Avn	
26685 UH-60L A/3-158th Avn	
26687 UH-60L 3-158th Avn	
26688 UH-60L 3-158th Avn	
26689 UH-60L A/3-158th Avn	
26690 UH-60L 3-158th Avn	
26691 UH-60L 3-158th Avn	
26692 UH-60L A/3-158th Avn	
26696 UH-60L 3-158th Avn	
FY97	
26763 UH-60L A/5-158th Avn	
26766 UH-60L A/5-158th Avn	
26768 UH-60L A/5-158th Avn	
FY05	
27062 UH-60L B/3-158th Avn	
FY06	
27110 UH-60L A/5-158th Avn	

MDH AH-64D Apache

2nd Btn, 159th Avn Reg't, Illesheim;
3rd Btn, 159th Avn Reg't, Illesheim

Type	Notes
FY02	
05294 2-159th Avn	
05297 2-159th Avn	
05299 2-159th Avn	
FY03	
05357 2-159th Avn	
05372 2-159th Avn	
FY04	
05462 2-159th Avn	
05464 2-159th Avn	
05474 2-159th Avn	
05479 2-159th Avn	
FY05	
07005 2-159th Avn	
07007 2-159th Avn	
07008 2-159th Avn	
07009 2-159th Avn	
07011 2-159th Avn	
07012 2-159th Avn	
07013 2-159th Avn	
FY06	
07018 2-159th Avn	
07019 2-159th Avn	
07020 2-159th Avn	
07021 2-159th Avn	
FY07	
05502 2-159th Avn	
05503 2-159th Avn	
05504 2-159th Avn	
05505 2-159th Avn	
05506 2-159th Avn	
05507 2-159th Avn	
05516 2-159th Avn	
FY08	
05540 2-159th Avn	
05541 2-159th Avn	
05542 2-159th Avn	
05544 2-159th Avn	
05545 2-159th Avn	
05546 3-159th Avn	
05549 3-159th Avn	
05552 3-159th Avn	
05553 2-159th Avn	
05554 2-159th Avn	
05555 2-159th Avn	
05556 2-159th Avn	

Eurocopter UH-72A Lakota

Joint Multinational Readiness
Centre, Hohenfels

Type	Notes
FY07	
72029	
FY09	
72095	
72096	
72097	
72098	
72100	
72105	
72106	
72107	
72108	

US-based USAF Aircraft

The following aircraft are normally based in the USA but are likely to be seen visiting the UK from time to time. The presentation is in numerical order of the type, commencing with the B-**1B** and concluding with the C-**135**. The aircraft are listed in numerical progression by the serial actually carried externally. Fiscal year information is provided, together with details of mark variations and in some cases operating units. Where base-code letter information is carried on the aircrafts' tails, this is detailed with the squadron/base data; for example the 7th Wing's B-1B 60105 carries the letters DY on its tail, thus identifying the Wing's home base as Dyess AFB, Texas.

Type	*Notes*

Rockwell B-1B Lancer

7th BW, Dyess AFB, Texas [DY]:
9th BS (*bk/w*), 13th BS (*r*)
& 28th BS (*bl/w*);
28th BW, Ellsworth AFB,
South Dakota [EL]:
34th BS (*bk/r*) & 37th BS (*bk/y*);
337th TES/53rd Wg, Dyess AFB,
Texas [OT] *bk/gy*;
77th WPS/57th Wg, Dyess AFB,
Texas [WA] *y/bk*;
419th FLTS/412th TW, Edwards AFB,
California [ED]

FY85

50059	7th BW	*bk/w* $
50060	28th BW	*bk/r*
50061	7th BW	*bl/w*
50064	7th BW	*bl/w*
50066	28th BW	
50068	412th TW	
50069	7th BW	*bk/w*
50072	7th BW	*bl/w*
50073	7th BW	*bk/w* $
50074	7th BW	*bk/w*
50075	412th TW	
50077	57th Wg	*y/bk*
50079	28th BW	*bk/r*
50080	7th BW	*bk/w* $
50081	28th BW	*bk/r*
50084	28th BW	*bk/r*
50085	28th BW	*bk/y*
50088	7th BW	*bl/w*
50089	7th BW	*bl/w*
50090	7th BW	*bl/w*
50091	28th BW	*bk/r*

FY86

60094	28th BW	*bk/y* $
60095	28th BW	*bk/r*
60097	7th BW	*bl/w*
60098	7th BW	*bk/w*
60099	28th BW	*bk/y* $
60101	7th BW	*bl/w*
60102	28th BW	*bk/y*
60103	7th BW	*bl/w*
60104	28th BW	*bk/y*
60105	7th BW	*bl/w*
60107	7th BW	*bl/w*
60108	7th BW	*bl/w*
60109	7th BW	*bk/w*
60110	7th BW	*bk/w*
60111	28th BW	*bk/r*
60112	7th BW	*bk/w*
60113	28th BW	*bk/y*
60115	28th BW	*bk/r*
60117	7th BW	*bk/w*
60118	28th BW	*bk/y*
60119	7th BW	*bl/w*
60120	53rd Wg	*bk/gy*
60121	28th BW	*bk/y*
60122	53rd Wg	*bk/gy*
60123	7th BW	*bl/w*
60124	7th BW	*bl/w*
60126	7th BW	*bl/w*
60129	28th BW	*bk/r*
60132	53rd Wg	*bk/gy*
60133	7th BW	*bk/w*
60134	28th BW	*bk/r*
60135	7th BW	*bl/w*
60136	7th BW	*bl/w*
60138	7th BW	*y/bk*
60139	28th BW	*bl/y* $
60140	7th BW	*bk/w*

Northrop B-2 Spirit

509th BW, Whiteman AFB,
Missouri [WM]:
13th BS, 393rd BS & 715th BS
(Names are given where known.
Each begins *Spirit of ...*)

FY90

00040 *Alaska*
00041 *Hawaii*

FY92

20700 *Florida*

FY82

21066 *America*
21067 *Arizona*
21068 *New York*
21069 *Indiana*
21070 *Ohio*
21071 *Mississippi*

FY93

31085 *Oklahoma*
31086 *Kitty Hawk*
31087 *Pennsylvania*
31088 *Louisiana*

FY88

80328 *Texas*
80329 *Missouri*
80330 *California*
80331 *South Carolina*
80332 *Washington*

FY89

90128 *Nebraska*
90129 *Georgia*

Lockheed U-2

9th RW, Beale AFB, California [BB]:
1st RS, 5th RS
& 99th RS (*bk/r*);

Type			Notes
Lockheed, Palmdale;			
Warner Robins			
Air Logistics Centre [WR]			
FY68			
68-10329	U-2S	9th RW	
68-10331	U-2S	9th RW	
68-10336	U-2S	9th RW	
68-10337	U-2S	9th RW	
FY80			
80-1064	TU-2S	9th RW	
80-1065	TU-2S	9th RW	
80-1066	U-2S	9th RW	
80-1067	U-2S	Lockheed	
80-1068	U-2S	9th RW	
80-1069	U-2S	9th RW	
80-1070	U-2S	9th RW	
80-1071	U-2S	9th RW	
80-1073	U-2S	9th RW	
80-1074	U-2S	9th RW	
80-1076	U-2S	9th RW	
80-1077	U-2S	9th RW	
80-1078	TU-2S	9th RW	
80-1079	U-2S	9th RW	
80-1080	U-2S	9th RW	
80-1081	U-2S	9th RW	
80-1083	U-2S	9th RW	
80-1084	U-2S	9th RW	
80-1085	U-2S	9th RW	
80-1086	U-2S	9th RW	
80-1087	U-2S	9th RW	
80-1089	U-2S	9th RW	
80-1090	U-2S	9th RW	
80-1091	TU-2S	9th RW	
80-1092	U-2S	9th RWS	
80-1093	U-2S	9th RW	
80-1094	U-2S	9th RW	
80-1096	U-2S	9th RW	
80-1099	U-2S	WR ALC	

Boeing E-3 Sentry

552nd ACW, Tinker AFB,
Oklahoma [OK] (*w*):
960th ACS, 963rd ACS,
964th ACS, 965th ACS
& 966th ACTS;
961st ACS/18th Wg, Kadena AB,
Japan [ZZ] (*or*);
962nd ACS/3rd Wg, Elmendorf AFB,
Alaska [AK] (*gn*)

Type			Notes
FY80			
00137	E-3C	*gn*	
00138	E-3C	*r*	
00139	E-3C	*w*	
FY81			
10004	E-3C	*w*	
10005	E-3C	*or* $	
FY71			
11407	E-3B	*w*	
11408	E-3B	*w*	
FY82			
20006	E-3C	*or*	
20007	E-3C	*r*	
FY83			
30009	E-3C	*w*	
FY73			
31675	E-3B	*w*	
FY75			
50556	E-3B	*w*	
50557	E-3B	*r*	
50558	E-3B	*or* $	
50559	E-3B	*r*	
50560	E-3B	*w*	
FY76			
61604	E-3B	*r*	
61605	E-3B	*w*	
61606	E-3B	*or*	
61607	E-3B	*w*	
FY77			
70351	E-3B	*w*	
70352	E-3B	*w*	
70353	E-3B	*w*	
70355	E-3B	*gn*	
70356	E-3B	*w*	
FY78			
80576	E-3B	*r*	
80577	E-3B	*r*	
80578	E-3B	*w*	
FY79			
90001	E-3B	*w*	
90002	E-3B	*w*	
90003	E-3B	*m*	

Boeing E-4B

1st ACCS/55th Wg, Offutt AFB,
Nebraska [OF]

Type	Notes
FY73	
31676	
31677	
FY74	
40787	
FY75	
50125	

Lockheed
C-5 Galaxy/C-5M Super Galaxy

60th AMW, Travis AFB, California:
21st AS (*bk/gd*) & 22nd AS (*bk/bl*);
105th AW, Stewart AFB,
New York:
137th AS (*bl*);
164th AW, Memphis,
Tennessee ANG:
155th AS (*r*);
167th AW, Martinsburg,
West Virginia ANG [WV]:
167th AS (*r*);
412th TW, Edwards AFB,
California:
418th FLTS;
433rd AW AFRC, Kelly AFB,
Texas:
68th AS;
436th AW, Dover AFB, Delaware:
9th AS (*bl/y*);
439th AW AFRC, Westover
ARB, Massachusetts:
337th AS (*bl/r*)

Type			Notes
FY70			
00448	C-5A	433rd AW	
00451	C-5A	433rd AW	

Type				Notes
00452	C-5A	167th AW	*r*	
00455	C-5A	167th AW	*r*	
00456	C-5A	433rd AW		
00457	C-5A			
00460	C-5A	167th AW	*r*	
00461	C-5A	433rd AW		
00463	C-5A	164th AW	*r*	
FY83				
31285	C-5M	436th AW	*bl/y*	
FY84				
40060	C-5B	60th AMW	*bk/gd*	
40061	C-5M	436th AW	*bl/y*	
40062	C-5B	60th AMW	*bk/gd*	
FY85				
50001	C-5M	436th AW	*bl/y*	
50002	C-5M	436th AW	*bl/y*	
50003	C-5M	436th AW	*bl/y*	
50004	C-5M	LMTAS		
50005	C-5M	436th AW	*bl/y*	
50006	C-5B	439th AW	*bl/r*	
50007	C-5M	436th AW	*bl/y*	
50008	C-5M	LMTAS		
50009	C-5B	439th AW	*bl/r*	
50010	C-5B	LMTAS		
FY86				
60011	C-5B	60th AMW	*bk/bl*	
60012	C-5B	439th AW	*bl/r*	
60013	C-5M	436th AW	*bl/y*	
60014	C-5B	439th AW	*bl/r*	
60015	C-5B	60th AMW	*w*	
60016	C-5B	60th AMW	*bk/bl*	
60017	C-5M	LMTAS		
60018	C-5B	439th AW	*bl/r*	
60019	C-5B	439th AW	*bl/r*	
60020	C-5B			
60021	C-5B	439th AW	*bl/r*	
60022	C-5B	60th AMW	*bk/bl*	
60023	C-5B	439th AW	*bl/r*	
60024	C-5B	60th AMW	*bk/bl*	
60025	C-5M	436th AW	*bl/y*	
60026	C-5B	60th AMW	*bk/gd*	
FY87				
70027	C-5B	439th AW	*bl/r*	
70028	C-5B	60th AMW	*w*	
70029	C-5B			
70030	C-5B	60th AMW	*bk/bl*	
70031	C-5B	439th AW	*bl/r*	
70032	C-5B	60th AMW	*bk/bl*	
70033	C-5B	439th AW	*bl/r*	
70034	C-5B	60th AMW	*bk/bl*	
70035	C-5M	LMTAS		
70036	C-5M	LMTAS		
70037	C-5B	439th AW	*bl/r*	
70038	C-5B	439th AW	*bl/r*	
70039	C-5B	439th AW	*bl/r*	
70040	C-5M	436th AW	*bl/y*	
70041	C-5B	439th AW	*bl/r*	
70042	C-5B	60th AMW	*bk/bl*	
70043	C-5B	439th AW	*bl/r*	
70044	C-5M	LMTAS		
70045	C-5M	436th AW	*bl/y*	
FY68				
80212	C-5A	167th AW	*r*	
80213	C-5C	60th AMW	*bk/gd*	
80214	C-5A	433rd AW		
80216	C-5C	60th AMW	*bk/gd*	
80219	C-5A	433rd AW		
80220	C-5A	433rd AW		
80221	C-5A	433rd AW		
80222	C-5A	167th AW	*r*	
80223	C-5A	433rd AW		
80224	C-5A	167th AW	*r*	
80226	C-5A	433rd AW		
FY69				
90002	C-5A	164th AW	*r*	
90005	C-5A	164th AW	*r*	
90006	C-5A	433rd AW		
90007	C-5A	433rd AW		
90009	C-5A	167th AW	*r*	
90010	C-5A	164th AW	*r*	
90012	C-5A	167th AW	*r*	
90016	C-5A	433rd AW		
90018	C-5A	164th AW	*r*	
90020	C-5A	433rd AW		
90021	C-5A	167th AW	*r*	
90022	C-5A	167th AW	*r*	
90023	C-5A	167th AW	*r*	
90024	C-5M	436th AW	*bl/y*	
90025	C-5A	167th AW	*r*	

Boeing E-8 J-STARS

116th ACW, Robins AFB, Georgia [WR]:
12th ACCS (*gn*), 16th ACCS (*bk*), 128th ACS/Georgia ANG (*r*) & 330th CTS (*y*);
Grumman, Melbourne, Florida [JS]

Type				Notes
FY00				
02000	E-8C	116th ACW		
FY90				
00175	E-8A	Grumman		
FY01				
12005	E-8C	116th ACW		
FY02				
29111	E-8C	116th ACW		
FY92				
23289	E-8C	116th ACW	*m*	
23290	E-8C	116th ACW	*bk*	
FY93				
31097	E-8C	116th ACW	*r*	
FY94				
40284	E-8C	116th ACW	*r*	
40285	E-8C	116th ACW	*bk*	
FY95				
50121	E-8C	116th ACW	*r*	
50122	E-8C	116th ACW	*r*	
FY96				
60042	E-8C	116th ACW	*bk*	
60043	E-8C	116th ACW	*bl*	
FY97				
70100	E-8C	116th ACW	*r*	
70200	E-8C	116th ACW	*bk*	
70201	E-8C	116th ACW	*r*	
FY99				
90006	E-8C	116th ACW	*gn*	

McDonnell Douglas KC-10A Extender

60th AMW, Travis AFB, California:
6th ARS & 9th ARS;

Type			Notes
305th AMW, McGuire AFB, New Jersey: 2nd ARS (*bl/r*) & 32nd ARS (*bl*)			
FY82			
20191	60th AMW		
20192	60th AMW		
20193	60th AMW		
FY83			
30075	60th AMW		
30076	60th AMW		
30077	60th AMW		
30078	60th AMW		
30079	60th AMW		
30080	60th AMW		
30081	305th AMW	*bl*	
30082	305th AMW	*bl*	
FY84			
40185	60th AMW		
40186	305th AMW	*bl/r*	
40187	60th AMW		
40188	305th AMW	*bl/r*	
40189	305th AMW	*bl/r*	
40190	305th AMW	*bl/r*	
40191	60th AMW		
40192	305th AMW	*bl/y*	
FY85			
50027	305th AMW	*bl/r*	
50028	305th AMW	*bl/r*	
50029	60th AMW		
50030	305th AMW	*bl/r*	
50031	305th AMW	*bl/r*	
50032	305th AMW	*bl/y*	
50033	60th AMW		
50034	305th AMW	*bl/y*	
FY86			
60027	305th AMW	*bl*	
60028	305th AMW	*bl/r*	
60029	60th AMW		
60030	305th AMW	*bl/r*	
60031	60th AMW		
60032	305th AMW		
60033	60th AMW		
60034	60th AMW		
60035	305th AMW	*bl*	
60036	305th AMW	*bl*	
60037	60th AMW		
60038	60th AMW		
FY87			
70117	60th AMW		
70118	305th AMW		
70119	60th AMW		
70120	305th AMW	*bl*	
70121	305th AMW	*bl*	
70122	305th AMW	*bl/r*	
70123	60th AMW		
70124	305th AMW	*bl/y*	
FY79			
90433	305th AMW	*bl*	
90434	305th AMW	*bl/r*	
91710	305th AMW	*bl/r*	
91711	305th AMW	*bl*	
91712	305th AMW	*bl/r*	
91713	60th AMW		
91946	60th AMW		
91947	305th AMW	*bl*	
91948	60th AMW		
91949	305th AMW	*bl/r*	
91950	60th AMW		
91951	60th AMW		

Bombardier
E-11A Global Express

653rd ELSG, Hanscom Field

Type	Notes
FY11	
19001	
19355	
19358	
FY12	
29506	

Boeing
C-17 Globemaster III

3rd Wg, Elmendorf AFB, Alaska: 517th AS (*w/bk*);
15th Wg, Hickam AFB, Hawaii: 535th AS (*r/y*);
60th AMW, Travis AFB, California: 21st AS (*bk/w*);
62nd AW, McChord AFB, Washington (*gn*): 4th AS, 7th AS,8th AS & 10th AS;
97th AMW, Altus AFB, Oklahoma: 58th AS(*r/y*);
105th AW, Stewart AFB, New York: 137th AS (*bl*);
172nd AW, Jackson Int'l Airport, Mississippi ANG: 183rd AS (*bl/gd*);
305th AMW, McGuire AFB, New Jersey: 6th AS (*bl*);
412th TW, Edwards AFB, California [ED]: 418th FLTS;
436th AW, Dover AFB, Delaware: 3rd AS (*bl/y*);
437th AW, Charleston AFB, South Carolina (*y/bl*): 14th AS, 15th AS, 16th AS & 17th AS;
445th AW AFRC, Wright-Patterson AFB, Ohio: 89th AS (*r/w*);
452nd AMW AFRC, March ARB, California: 729th AS (*or/y*)

Type				Notes
FY00				
00171	C-17A	3rd Wg	*w/bk*	
00172	C-17A	97th AMW	*r/y*	
00174	C-17A	3rd Wg	*w/bk*	
00175	C-17A	62nd AW	*gn*	
00176	C-17A	62nd AW	*gn*	
00177	C-17A	97th AMW	*r/y*	
00178	C-17A	97th AMW	*r/y*	
00179	C-17A	62nd AW	*gn*	
00180	C-17A	62nd AW	*gn*	

Type				Notes
00181	C-17A	62nd AW	*gn*	
00182	C-17A	62nd AW	*gn*	
00183	C-17A	62nd AW	*gn*	
00184	C-17A	62nd AW	*gn*	
00185	C-17A	3rd Wg	*w/bk*	
FY10				
00213	C-17A	437th AW	*y/bl*	
00214	C-17A	437th AW	*y/bl*	
00215	C-17A	437th AW	*y/bl*	
00216	C-17A	62nd AW	*gn*	
00217	C-17A	62nd AW	*gn*	
00218	C-17A	62nd AW	*gn*	
00219	C-17A	62nd AW	*gn*	
00220	C-17A	62nd AW	*gn*	
00221	C-17A			
00222	C-17A			
00223	C-17A			
FY90				
00532	C-17A	62nd AW	*gn*	
00533	C-17A	15th Wg	*r/y*	
00534	C-17A	437th AW	*y/bl*	
00535	C-17A	445th AW	*r/w*	
FY01				
10186	C-17A	62nd AW	*gn*	
10187	C-17A	62nd AW	*gn*	
10188	C-17A	105th AW	*bl*	
10189	C-17A	437th AW	*y/bl*	
10190	C-17A	97th AMW	*r/y*	
10191	C-17A	437th AW	*y/bl*	
10192	C-17A	97th AMW	*r/y*	
10193	C-17A	437th AW	*y/bl*	
10194	C-17A	97th AMW	*r/y* $	
10195	C-17A	97th AMW	*r/y*	
10196	C-17A	437th AW	*y/bl*	
10197	C-17A	97th AMW	*r/y*	
FY02				
21098	C-17A	437th AW	*y/bl*	
21099	C-17A	97th AMW	*r/y*	
21100	C-17A	437th AW	*y/bl*	
21101	C-17A	437th AW	*y/bl*	
21102	C-17A	62nd AW	*gn*	
21103	C-17A	62nd AW	*gn*	
21104	C-17A	62nd AW	*gn*	
21105	C-17A	62nd AW	*gn*	
21106	C-17A	62nd AW	*gn*	
21107	C-17A	97th AMW	*r/y*	
21108	C-17A	62nd AW	*gn*	
21109	C-17A	62nd AW	*gn*	
21110	C-17A	62nd AW	*gn*	
21111	C-17A	62nd AW	*gn*	
21112	C-17A	172nd AW	*bl/gd*	
FY92				
23291	C-17A	62nd AW	*gn*	
23292	C-17A	437th AW	*y/bl*	
23293	C-17A	437th AW	*y/bl*	
23294	C-17A	62nd AW	*gn*	
FY93				
30599	C-17A	3rd Wg	*w/bk*	
30600	C-17A	62nd AW	*gn*	
30601	C-17A	62nd AW	*gn*	
30602	C-17A	437th AW	*y/bl*	
30603	C-17A	445th AW	*r/w*	
30604	C-17A	445th AW	*r/w*	
FY03				
33113	C-17A	172nd AW	*bl/gd*	

Type				Notes
33114	C-17A	172nd AW	*bl/gd*	
33115	C-17A	172nd AW	*bl/gd*	
33116	C-17A	172nd AW	*bl/gd*	
33117	C-17A	172nd AW	*bl/gd*	
33118	C-17A	172nd AW	*bl/gd*	
33119	C-17A	172nd AW	*bl/gd*	
33120	C-17A	62nd AW	*gn*	
33121	C-17A	412th TW		
33122	C-17A	437th AW	*y/bl*	
33123	C-17A	437th AW	*y/bl*	
33124	C-17A	437th AW	*y/bl*	
33125	C-17A	305th AMW	*bl*	
33126	C-17A	305th AMW	*bl*	
33127	C-17A	305th AMW	*bl*	
FY94				
40065	C-17A	437th AW	*y/bl*	
40066	C-17A	62nd AW	*gn*	
40067	C-17A	105th AW	*bl*	
40068	C-17A	445th AW	*r/w*	
40069	C-17A	437th AW	*y/bl*	
40070	C-17A	437th AW	*y/bl*	
FY04				
44128	C-17A	305th AMW	*bl*	
44129	C-17A	305th AMW	*bl*	
44130	C-17A	305th AMW	*bl*	
44131	C-17A	305th AMW	*bl*	
44132	C-17A	305th AMW	*bl*	
44133	C-17A	305th AMW	*bl*	
44134	C-17A	305th AMW	*bl*	
44135	C-17A	305th AMW	*bl*	
44136	C-17A	305th AMW	*bl*	
44137	C-17A	305th AMW	*bl*	
44138	C-17A	452nd AMW	*or/y*	
FY95				
50102	C-17A	437th AW	*y/bl*	
50103	C-17A	105th AW	*bl*	
50104	C-17A	437th AW	*y/bl*	
50105	C-17A	105th AW	*bl*	
50106	C-17A	62nd AW	*gn*	
50107	C-17A	437th AW	*y/bl*	
FY05				
55139	C-17A	452nd AMW	*or/y*	
55140	C-17A	452nd AMW	*or/y*	
55141	C-17A	452nd AMW	*or/y*	
55142	C-17A	452nd AMW	*or/y*	
55143	C-17A	452nd AMW	*or/y*	
55144	C-17A	452nd AMW	*or/y*	
55145	C-17A	452nd AMW	*or/y*	
55146	C-17A	15th Wg	*r/y*	
55147	C-17A	15th Wg	*r/y*	
55148	C-17A	15th Wg	*r/y*	
55149	C-17A	15th Wg	*r/y*	
55150	C-17A	15th Wg	*r/y*	
55151	C-17A	15th Wg	*r/y*	
55152	C-17A	15th Wg	*r/y*	
55153	C-17A	15th Wg	*r/y*	
FY96				
60001	C-17A	62nd AW	*gn*	
60002	C-17A	437th AW	*y/bl*	
60003	C-17A	62nd AW	*gn*	
60004	C-17A	445th AW	*r/w*	
60005	C-17A	105th AW	*bl*	
60006	C-17A	437th AW	*y/bl*	
60007	C-17A	172nd AW	*bl/gd*	
60008	C-17A	97th AMW	*r/y*	

Type				Notes
FY06				
66154	C-17A	60th AMW	*bk/w*	
66155	C-17A	60th AMW	*bk/w*	
66156	C-17A	60th AMW	*bk/w*	
66157	C-17A	60th AMW	*bk/w*	
66158	C-17A	60th AMW	*bk/w*	
66159	C-17A	60th AMW	*bk/w*	
66160	C-17A	60th AMW	*bk/w*	
66161	C-17A	60th AMW	*bk/w*	
66162	C-17A	60th AMW	*bk/w*	
66163	C-17A	60th AMW	*bk/w*	
66164	C-17A	60th AMW	*bk/w*	
66165	C-17A	436th AW	*bl/y*	
66166	C-17A	436th AW	*bl/y*	
66167	C-17A	436th AW	*bl/y*	
66168	C-17A	436th AW	*bl/y*	
FY97				
70041	C-17A	437th AW	*y/bl*	
70042	C-17A	62nd AW	*gn*	
70043	C-17A	452nd AMW	*or/y*	
70044	C-17A	445th AW	*r/w*	
70045	C-17A	105th AW	*bl*	
70046	C-17A	97th AMW	*r/y*	
70047	C-17A	437th AW	*y/bl*	
70048	C-17A	445th AW	*r/w*	
FY07				
77169	C-17A	436th AW	*bl/y*	
77170	C-17A	436th AW	*bl/y*	
77171	C-17A	436th AW	*bl/y*	
77172	C-17A	60th AMW	*bk/w*	
77173	C-17A	436th AW	*bl/y*	
77174	C-17A	436th AW	*bl/y*	
77175	C-17A	436th AW	*bl/y*	
77176	C-17A	436th AW	*bl/y*	
77177	C-17A	436th AW	*bl/y*	
77178	C-17A	436th AW	*bl/y*	
77179	C-17A	60th AMW	*bk/w*	
77180	C-17A	437th AW	*y/bl*	
77181	C-17A	437th AW	*y/bl*	
77182	C-17A	437th AW	*y/bl*	
77183	C-17A	437th AW	*y/bl*	
77184	C-17A	437th AW	*y/bl*	
77185	C-17A	437th AW	*y/bl*	
77186	C-17A	437th AW	*y/bl*	
77187	C-17A	437th AW	*y/bl*	
77188	C-17A	437th AW	*y/bl*	
77189	C-17A	437th AW	*y/bl*	
FY98				
80049	C-17A	97th AMW	*r/y*	
80050	C-17A	97th AMW	*r/y*	
80051	C-17A	3rd Wg	*w/bk*	
80052	C-17A	62nd AW	*gn*	
80053	C-17A	62nd AW	*gn*	
80054	C-17A	437th AW	*y/bl*	
80055	C-17A	97th AMW	*r/y* $	
80056	C-17A	3rd Wg	*w/bk*	
80057	C-17A	105th AW	*bl*	
FY88				
80265	C-17A	62nd AW	*gn*	
80266	C-17A	437th AW	*y/bl*	
FY08				
88190	C-17A	437th AW	*y/bl*	
88191	C-17A	437th AW	*y/bl*	
88192	C-17A	62nd AW	*gn*	
88193	C-17A	62nd AW	*gn*	
88194	C-17A	62nd AW	*gn*	
88195	C-17A	62nd AW	*gn*	
88196	C-17A	62nd AW	*gn*	
88197	C-17A	62nd AW	*gn*	
88198	C-17A	437th AW	*y/bl*	
88199	C-17A	62nd AW	*gn*	
88200	C-17A	412th TW		
88201	C-17A	62nd AW	*gn*	
88202	C-17A	305th AMW	*bl*	
88203	C-17A	62nd AW	*gn*	
88204	C-17A	437th AW	*y/bl*	
FY99				
90058	C-17A	105th AW	*bl*	
90059	C-17A	62nd AW	*gn*	
90060	C-17A	445th AW	*r/w*	
90061	C-17A	445th AW	*r/w*	
90062	C-17A	437th AMW	*y/bl*	
90063	C-17A	97th AMW	*r/y*	
90064	C-17A	97th AMW	*r/y*	
90165	C-17A	445th AW	*r/w*	
90166	C-17A	62nd AW	*gn*	
90167	C-17A	3rd Wg	*w/bk*	
90168	C-17A	3rd Wg	*w/bk*	
90169	C-17A	437th AMW	*y/bl*	
90170	C-17A	3rd Wg	*w/bk*	
FY89				
91189	C-17A	437th AW	*y/bl*	
91190	C-17A	62nd AW	*gn*	
91191	C-17A	105th AW	*bl*	
91192	C-17A	437th AW	*y/bl*	
FY09				
99205	C-17A	437th AW	*y/bl*	
99206	C-17A	437th AW	*y/bl*	
99207	C-17A	437th AW	*y/bl*	
99208	C-17A	437th AW	*y/bl*	
99209	C-17A	62nd AW	*gn*	
99210	C-17A	62nd AW	*gn*	
99211	C-17A	62nd AW	*gn*	
99212	C-17A	62nd AW	*gn*	

Grumman
C-20 Gulfstream III/IV

89th AW, Andrews AFB, Maryland:
99th AS;
412th FLTS/412th TW Edwards AFB,
California;
OSAC/PAT, US Army, Andrews AFB,
Maryland;
Pacific Flight Detachment,
Hickam AFB, Hawaii

C-20B Gulfstream III

Type		Notes
FY86		
60201	89th AW	
60202	89th AW	
60203	89th AW	
60204	89th AW	
60206	89th AW	

C-20C Gulfstream III

Type		Notes
FY85		
50049	89th AW	
50050	89th AW	
FY86		
60403	89th AW	

Type	Notes

C-20F Gulfstream IV
FY91
10108 OSAC/PAT
C-20K Gulfstream III
FY87
70139 412th TW

Lockheed Martin
F-22A Raptor
1st FW, Langley AFB, Virginia [FF]:
27th FS & 94th FS;
3rd Wg, Elmendorf AFB, Alaska [AK]:
90th FS & 525th FS;
15th Wg, Hickam AFB, Hawaii [HH]:
19th FS;
44th FG AFRES, Holloman AFB, New Mexico [HO]:
301st FS;
49th Wg, Holloman AFB, New Mexico [HO]:
7th FS;
53rd Wg, Nellis AFB, Nevada [OT]:
422nd TES;
57th Wg, Nellis AFB, Nevada [WA]:
433rd WPS;
154th Wg, Hickam AFB, Hawaii ANG [HH]:
199th FS;
192nd FW, Langley AFB, Virginia ANG [FF]:
149th FS;
325th FW, Tyndall AFB, Florida [TY]:
43rd FS;
412nd FW, Edwards AFB, California [ED]:
411th FLTS;
477th FG AFRES, Elmendorf AFB, Alaska [AK]:
302nd FS

FY00
00-4012	TY	43rd FS	
00-4013	TY	43rd FS	
00-4015	TY	43rd FS	
00-4016	TY	43rd FS	
00-4017	TY	43rd FS	
FY01			
01-4018	TY	43rd FS	
01-4019	TY	43rd FS	
01-4020	TY	43rd FS	
01-4021	TY	43rd FS	
01-4022	TY	43rd FS	
01-4023	TY	43rd FS	
01-4024	TY	43rd FS	
01-4025	TY	43rd FS	
01-4026	TY	43rd FS	
01-4027	TY	43rd FS	
FY02			
02-4028	TY	43rd FS	
02-4029	TY	43rd FS	
02-4030	TY	43rd FS	
02-4031	TY	43rd FS	
02-4032	TY	43rd FS	
02-4033	TY	43rd FS	
02-4034	TY	43rd FS	
02-4035	TY	43rd FS	[325 OG]
02-4036	TY	43rd FS	
02-4038	TY	43rd FS	
02-4039	TY	43rd FS	
02-4040	TY	43rd FS	[325 FW]
FY03			
03-4041	TY	43rd FS	
03-4042	TY	43rd FS	
03-4043	TY	43rd FS	
03-4044	TY	43rd FS	
03-4045	HH	199th FS	
03-4046	HH	199th FS	
03-4047	HH	199th FS	
03-4048	HH	199th FS	
03-4049	HH	199th FS	
03-4050	HH	199th FS	
03-4051	FF	27th FS	
03-4052	FF	27th FS	
03-4053	HH	199th FS	
03-4054	HH	199th FS	
03-4055	HH	199th FS	
03-4056	FF	27th FS	
03-4057	FF	27th FS	
03-4058	HH	199th FS	
03-4059	HH	199th FS	
03-4060	HH	199th FS	
03-4061	HH	199th FS	
FY04			
04-4062	HH	199th FS	
04-4063	FF	94th FS	
04-4064	HH	199th FS	
04-4065	FF	27th FS	
04-4066	OT	422nd TES	
04-4067	FF	94th FS	
04-4068	OT	422nd TES	
04-4069	OT	422nd TES	
04-4070	FF	94th FS	
04-4071	WA	433rd WPS	
04-4072	HO	7th FS	
04-4073	FF	94th FS	
04-4074	FF	94th FS	
04-4075	HO	7th FS	
04-4076	HO	7th FS	
04-4077			
04-4078	HO	7th FS	
04-4079	HO	7th FS	
04-4080	HO	7th FS	
04-4081	HO	7th FS	
04-4082	FF	94th FS	[192 FW]
04-4083	HO	7th FS	[301 FS]
FY05			
05-4084	HO	7th FS	
05-4085	FF	94th FS	
05-4086	HO	7th FS	
05-4087	HO	7th FS	
05-4088	HO	7th FS	[49 Wg]
05-4089	HO	7th FS	
05-4090	AK	90th FS	
05-4091	HO	7th FS	
05-4092	HO	7th FS	
05-4093	HO	7th FS	
05-4094	HO	7th FS	
05-4095	HO	7th FS	
05-4096	WA	433rd WPS	
05-4097	HO	7th FS	[49 OG]
05-4098	HO	7th FS	
05-4099	HO	7th FS	
05-4100	HO	7th FS	
05-4101	HO	7th FS	
05-4102	AK	90th FS	[302 FS]
05-4103	AK	90th FS	[3 Wg]

Type			Notes
05-4104	HO	7th FS	
05-4105	HO	7th FS	[44 FG]
05-4106	HO	7th FS	[7 FS]
05-4107	HO	7th FS	
FY06			
06-4108	AK	525th FS	
06-4109	WA	433rd WPS	
06-4110	AK	525th FS	[11 AF]
06-4111	OT	422nd TES	
06-4112	AK	525th FS	
06-4113	AK	525th FS	[3 OG]
06-4114	AK	525th FS	
06-4115	AK	525th FS	[525 FS]
06-4116	WA	433rd WPS	
06-4117	AK	525th FS	
06-4118	AK	525th FS	
06-4119	AK	525th FS	
06-4120	OT	422nd TES	
06-4121	AK	525th FS	
06-4122	AK	525th FS	
06-4123	AK	525th FS	
06-4124	OT	422nd TES	
06-4126	AK	525th FS	
06-4127	AK	525th FS	
06-4128	OT	422nd TES	
06-4129	AK	525th FS	
06-4130	AK	525th FS	
FY07			
07-4131	AK	525th FS	
07-4132	ED	411th FLTS	[411 FLTS]
07-4133	AK	525th FS	
07-4134	AK	525th FS	
07-4135	AK	90th FS	
07-4136	AK	90th FS	
07-4137	AK	90th FS	
07-4138	AK	90th FS	
07-4139	AK	90th FS	
07-4140	AK	90th FS	
07-4141	AK	90th FS	
07-4142	AK	90th FS	
07-4143	AK	90th FS	
07-4144	AK	90th FS	
07-4145	AK	90th FS	
07-4146	AK	90th FS	
07-4147	AK	90th FS	
07-4148	AK	90th FS	
07-4149	AK	90th FS	
07-4150	AK	90th FS	
07-4151	AK	90th FS	
FY08			
08-4152	FF	94th FS	
08-4153	FF	27th FS	
08-4154	FF	94th FS	
08-4155	FF	27th FS	
08-4156	FF	94th FS	
08-4157	FF	27th FS	
08-4158	FF	94th FS	
08-4159	FF	27th FS	
08-4160	FF	94th FS	
08-4161	FF	27th FS	
08-4162	FF	94th FS	
08-4163	FF	27th FS	
08-4164	FF	94th FS	
08-4165	FF	27th FS	

Type			Notes
08-4166	FF	94th FS	
08-4167	FF	27th FS	
08-4168	FF	94th FS	
08-4169	FF	94th FS	
08-4170	FF	27th FS	
08-4171	FF	94th FS	
FY09			
09-4172	FF	27th FS	
09-4173	FF	27th FS	
09-4174	FF	94th FS	
09-4175	FF	94th FS	
09-4176	FF	27th FS	
09-4177	FF	94th FS	
09-4178	FF	27th FS	
09-4179	FF	94th FS	
09-4180	FF	27th FS	
09-4181	FF	94th FS	
09-4182	FF	27th FS	
09-4183	FF	94th FS	
09-4184	FF	27th FS	
09-4185	FF	27th FS	[1 OG]
09-4186	FF	27th FS	
09-4187	FF	94th FS	
09-4188	FF	27th FS	
09-4189	OT	422nd TES	
09-4190	AK	90th FS	
09-4191	FF	94th FS	
FY10			
10-4192	FF	94th FS	[192 FW]
10-4193	AK	525th FS	[3 Wg]
10-4194	FF	94th FS	[94 FS]
10-4195	AK	525th FS	[525 FS]
FY91			
91-4004	ED	411th FLTS	
91-4006	ED	411th FLTS	
91-4007	ED	411th FLTS	[412 TW]
91-4009	ED	411th FLTS	
FY99			
99-4010	OT	422nd TES	[422 TES]
99-4011	WA	433rd WPS	

Boeing VC-25A

Presidential Airlift Sqn/
89th AW, Andrews AFB,
Maryland

FY82
28000
FY92
29000

Aeritalia
C-27J Spartan

175th Wg,
Maryland ANG,
Baltimore:
135th AS;
179th AW,
Ohio ANG,
Mansfield:
164th AS;
186th AW,
Mississippi ANG,
Meridian:
153rd AS;
L3 CIS, Warner-Robins, Georgia

Type		Notes
FY07		
27010	L3 CIS	
27011	L3 CIS	
FY08		
27012	179th AW	
27013	179th AW	
27014	179th AW	
27015	179th AW	
FY09		
27016	175th Wg	
27017	175th Wg	
27018	175th Wg	
27019	L3 CIS	
27020	186th AW	
27021	186th AW	
27022	186th AW	
FY10		
27023		
27024		
27025		
27026		
27027		
27028		
27029		
27030		

Pilatus U-28
1st SOW, Hurlburt Field,
Florida:
34th SOS & 319th SOS;
318th SOS/27th SOW, Cannon AFB,
New Mexico

U-28A

Type		Notes
FY01		
10415	318th SOS	
FY04		
40688	318th SOS	
FY05		
50409	1st SOW	
50419	1st SOW	
50424	1st SOW	
50446	1st SOW	
50447	1st SOW	
50482	1st SOW	
50556	1st SOW	
50573	1st SOW	
50597	318th SOS	
FY07		
70488	1st SOW	
FY08		
80519	1st SOW	

U-28B

Type		Notes
FY04		
40688	1st SOW	
FY06		
60740		
60692	1st SOW	
FY07		
70691	1st SOW	
70711		
70712	1st SOW	
70777	318th SOS	
70779	1st SOW	
70790	1st SOW	
70793	1st SOW	
70808	318th SOS	
70821		
70829	1st SOW	
70838	1st SOW	
70840		
FY08		
80790	1st SOW	
80809	1st SOW	
80822		
80835		
80850	1st SOW	

Boeing C-32
1st AS/89th AW, Andrews AFB,
Maryland;
150th SOS/108th Wg, McGuire AFB,
New Jersey

Type			Notes
FY00			
09001	C-32B	150th SOS	
FY02			
24452	C-32B	150th SOS	
25001	C-32B	150th SOS	
FY98			
80001	C-32A	89th AW	
80002	C-32A	89th AW	
FY99			
90003	C-32A	89th AW	
90004	C-32A	89th AW	
FY09			
90015	C-32A	89th AW	
90016	C-32A	89th AW	
90017	C-32A	89th AW	
FY99			
96143	C-32B	150th SOS	

Gulfstream Aerospace
C-37 Gulfstream V
6th AMW, MacDill AFB, Florida:
310th AS;
15th Wg, Hickam AFB, Hawaii:
65th AS;
89th AW, Andrews AFB, Maryland:
99th AS;
OSAC/PAT, US Army, Andrews AFB,
Maryland

C-37A Gulfstream V

Type		Notes
FY01		
10028	6th AMW	
10029	6th AMW	
10030	6th AMW	
10065	15th Wg	
FY02		
21863	OSAC/PAT	
FY04		
41778	OSAC/PAT	
FY97		
71944	OSAC/PAT	
70400	89th AW	
70401	89th AW	
FY99		
90404	89th AW	

C-37B Gulfstream V

Type		Notes
FY11		
10550	89th AW	

Type			Notes
FY06			
60500	89th AW		
FY09			
90525	89th AW		

IAI C-38A Astra
201st AS/113th FW, DC ANG,
Andrews AFB, Maryland

FY94	
41569	
41570	

Boeing C-40
15th Wg, Hickam AFB, Hawaii:
65th AS;
86th AW, Ramstein,
Germany:
76th AS;
89th AW, Andrews AFB, Maryland:
1st AS;
113th FW, DC ANG,
Andrews AFB, Maryland:
201st AS;
932nd AW AFRC, Scott AFB,
Illinois:
73rd AS

FY01		
10015	C-40B	15th Wg
10040	C-40B	89th AW
10041	C-40B	89th AW
FY02		
20042	C-40B	86th AW
20201	C-40C	201st AS
20202	C-40C	201st AS
20203	C-40C	201st AS
20204	C-40C	201st AS
FY05		
50730	C-40C	932nd AW
50932	C-40C	932nd AW
54613	C-40C	932nd AW
FY09		
90540	C-40C	932nd AW

Boeing B-52H Stratofortress
2nd BW, Barksdale AFB,
Louisiana [LA]:
20th BS (*bl*) & 96th BS (*r*);
5th BW, Minot AFB,
North Dakota [MT]:
23rd BS (*r/y*) & 69th BS (*bk/y*);
53rd TEG, Barksdale AFB,
Louisiana [OT]:
49th TES;
93rd BS/307th BW AFRC,
Barksdale AFB,
Louisiana [BD] (*or/bl*);
419th FLTS/412th TW Edwards AFB,
California [ED]

FY60		
00001	2nd BW	*r*
00002	2nd BW	*gn* $
00003	93rd BS	*or/bl*
00004	5th BW	*r/y*
00005	5th BW	*r/y*
00007	5th BW	*r/y*
00008	2nd BW	*bl* $
00009	5th BW	*bk/y*
00011	93rd BS	*r/y* $
00012	5th BW	*bk/y*
00013	2nd BW	*bl*
00015	93rd BS	*or/bl*
00017	93rd BS	*or/bl*
00018	5th BW	*bk/y*
00021	2nd BW	*r*
00022	2nd BW	*r*
00023	5th BW	*r/y*
00024	2nd BW	*bl*
00025	2nd BW	*bl*
00026	5th BW	*r/y*
00028	2nd BW	*r*
00029	5th BW	*r/y*
00031	93rd BS	*or/bl*
00032	2nd BW	*r*
00033	5th BW	*r/y*
00035	93rd BS	*or/bl*
00036	412th TW	
00037	5th BW	*r/y*
00038	93rd BS	*or/bl*
00041	93rd BS	*or/bl*
00042	93rd BS	*or/bl*
00044	5th BW	*bk/y*
00045	93rd BS	*or/bl*
00047.	2nd BW	
00048	2nd BW	*bl*
00049	53rd TEG	
00050	412th TW	
00051	93rd BS	*or/bl*
00052	2nd BW	*r*
00054	2nd BW	*bl*
00055	5th BW	*or/bk* $
00056	5th BW	*r/y*
00057	93rd BS	*or/bl*
00058	2nd BW	*bl*
00059	2nd BW	*r* $
00060	5th BW	*bk/y*
00061	93rd BS	*or/bl*
00062	2nd BW	*r*
FY61		
10001	5th BW	*bk/y*
10002	2nd BW	*r* $
10003	93rd BS	*or/bl*
10004	2nd BW	*bl*
10005	5th BW	*r/y*
10006	2nd BW	*r*
10008	93rd BS	*or/bl*
10010	2nd BW	*bl*
10011	93rd BS	*or/bl*
10012	2nd BW	*r*
10013	2nd BW	*bl*
10014	5th BW	*bk/y*
10015	2nd BW	*r*
10016	2nd BW	*bl*
10017	93rd BS	*y/bl*
10018	2nd BW	
10019	2nd BW	*r*
10020	2nd BW	*or/bl*
10021	93rd BS	*or/bl*
10028	5th BW	*bk/y*
10029	93rd BS	*or/bl*
10031	93rd BS	*or/bl*

Type			Notes
10032	5th BW	*r/y*	
10034	5th BW	*r/y*	
10035	5th BW	*r/y*	
10036	2nd BW	*r*	
10038	5th BW	*r/bk*	
10039	5th BW	*bk/y*	
10040	5th BW	*r/y*	

Lockheed C-130 Hercules

1st SOS/353rd SOG, Kadena AB, Japan;
4th SOS/1st SOW, Hurlburt Field, Florida;
7th SOS/352nd SOG, RAF Mildenhall, UK;
8th SOS/1st SOW, Duke Field, Florida;
9th SOS/1st OG, Eglin AFB, Florida;
15th SOS/1st SOW, Hurlburt Field, Florida;
16th SOS/27th SOW, Cannon AFB, New Mexico;
17th SOS/353rd SOG, Kadena AB, Japan;
19th AW Little Rock AFB, Arkansas [LK]:
 41st AS (*w*), 50th AS (*r*), 53rd AS (*bk*) & 61st AS (*gn*);
37th AS/86th AW, Ramstein AB, Germany [RS] (*bl/w*);
39th RQS/920th RQW AFRC, Patrick AFB, Florida [FL];
40th FTS/46th TW, Eglin AFB, Florida;
41st RQS/347th Wg, Moody AFB, Georgia [FT];
53rd WRS/403rd AW AFRC, Keesler AFB, Missouri;
55th ECG, Davis-Monthan AFB, Arizona [DM]:
 41st ECS (*bl*) & 43rd ECS (*r*);
58th SOW, Kirtland AFB, New Mexico:
 415th SOS & 550th SOS;
67th SOS/352nd SOG, RAF Mildenhall, UK;
71st RQS/23rd Wg, Moody AFB, Georgia [FT] (*bl*);
73rd SOS/27th SOW, Cannon AFB, New Mexico;
79th RQS/563rd RQG, Davis-Monthan AFB, Arizona [DM];
85th TES/53rd Wg, Eglin AFB, Florida [OT];
95th AS/440th AW AFRC, Pope AFB, North Carolina (*w/r*);
96th AS/934th AW AFRC, Minneapolis/St Paul, Minnesota (*pr*);
102nd RQS/106th RQW, Suffolk Field, New York ANG [LI];
105th AS/118th AW, Nashville, Tennessee ANG (*r*);
109th AS/133rd AW, Minneapolis/St Paul, Minnesota ANG [MN] (*pr/bk*);
115th AS/146th AW, Channel Island ANGS, California ANG [CI] (*gn*);
122nd FS/159th FW, NAS New Orleans, Louisiana ANG [JZ];
130th AS/130th AW, Yeager Int'l Airport, Charleston West Virginia ANG [WV] (*pr/y*);
130th RQS/129th RQW, Moffet Field, California ANG [CA] (*bl*);
136th AS/107th AW, Niagara Falls, New York ANG;
139th AS/109th AW, Schenectady, New York ANG [NY];
142nd AS/166th AW, New Castle County Airport, Delaware ANG [DE] (*bl*);
143rd AS/143rd AW, Quonset, Rhode Island ANG [RI] (*r*);
144th AS/176th CW, Elmendorf AFB, Alaska ANG (*bk/y*);
154th TS/189th AW, Little Rock, Arkansas ANG (*r*);
156th AS/145th AW, Charlotte, North Carolina ANG [NC] (*bl*);
157th FS/169th FW, McEntire ANGS, South Carolina ANG [SC];
158th AS/165th AW, Savannah, Georgia ANG (*r*);
159th FS/125th FW, Jacksonville, Florida ANG;
164th AS/179th AW, Mansfield, Ohio ANG [OH] (*bl*);
165th AS/123rd AW, Standiford Field, Kentucky ANG [KY];
167th AS/167th AW, Martinsburg, West Virginia ANG [WV] (*r*);
169th AS/182nd AW, Peoria, Illinois ANG [IL] (*or*);
180th AS/139th AW, Rosencrans Memorial Airport, Missouri ANG [XP] (*y*);
181st AS/136th AW, NAS Dallas, Texas ANG (*bl/w*);
187th AS/153rd AW, Cheyenne, Wyoming ANG [WY] (*y/bk*);
192nd AS/152nd AW, Reno, Nevada ANG [NV] (*bl/y*);
193rd SOS/193rd SOW, Harrisburg, Pennsylvania ANG [PA];
198th AS/156th AW, San Juan, Puerto Rico ANG;
204th AS/15th Wg, Hickam AFB, Hawaii ANG [HH];
210th RQS/176th CW, Elmendorf AFB, Alaska ANG [AK];
314th AW, Little Rock AFB, Arkansas:
 48th AS (*y*) & 62nd AS (*bl*);
317th AG, Dyess AFB, Texas:
 39th AS (*r*) & 40th AS (*bl*);
327th AS/913th AW AFRC, NAS Willow Grove,

Type	Notes

Pennsylvania (*bk*);
328th AS/914th AW AFRC,
Niagara Falls,
New York [NF] (*bl*);
357th AS/908th AW AFRC,
Maxwell AFB,
Alabama (*bl*);
374th AW, Yokota AB,
Japan [YJ]:
36th AS (*r*);
412th TW Edwards AFB,
California:
452nd FLTS [ED];
522nd SOS/27th SOW, Cannon AFB,
New Mexico;
645th Materiel Sqn, Palmdale,
California [D4];
700th AS/94th AW AFRC,
Dobbins ARB,
Georgia [DB] (*bl*);
711th SOS/919th SOW AFRC,
Duke Field, Florida;
731st AS/302nd AW AFRC,
Peterson AFB,
Colorado (*pr/w*);
757th AS/910th AW AFRC,
Youngstown ARS,
Ohio [YO] (*bl*);
758th AS/911th AW AFRC,
Pittsburgh ARS,
Pennsylvania (*bk/y*);
773rd AS/910th AW AFRC,
Youngstown ARS,
Ohio [YO] (*r*);
815th AS/403rd AW AFRC,
Keesler AFB,
Missouri [KT] (*r*);
LMTAS, Marietta,
Georgia

FY90			
00162	MC-130H	1st SOS	
00163	AC-130U	4th SOS	
00164	AC-130U	4th SOS	
00165	AC-130U	4th SOS	
00166	AC-130U	4th SOS	
00167	AC-130U	4th SOS	
FY80			
00320	C-130H	158th AS	*r*
00321	C-130H	314th AW	*bl*
00322	C-130H	158th AS	*r*
00323	C-130H	158th AS	*r*
00324	C-130H	158th AS	*r*
00325	C-130H	158th AS	*r*
00326	C-130H	158th AS	*r*
00332	C-130H	158th AS	*r*
FY90			
01057	C-130H	142nd AS	*bl*
01058	MC-130W	73rd SOS	
FY90			
01791	C-130H	180th AS	*y*
01792	C-130H	180th AS	*y*
01793	C-130H	180th AS	*y*
01794	C-130H	180th AS	*y*
01795	C-130H	180th AS	*y*
01796	C-130H	180th AS	*y*
01797	C-130H	180th AS	*y*
01798	C-130H	180th AS	*y*
FY00			
01934	EC-130J	193rd SOS	
FY90			
02103	HC-130N	210th RQS	
FY10			
05688	C-130J	317th AG	
05700	C-130J	317th AG	
05701	C-130J	317th AG	
05711	AC-130J		
05716	HC-130J	79th RQS	
05728	C-130J	317th AG	
FY90			
09107	C-130H	757th AS	*bl*
09108	C-130H	757th AS	*bl*
FY81			
10626	C-130H	700th AS	*bl*
10627	C-130H	700th AS	*bl*
10628	C-130H	700th AS	*bl*
10629	C-130H	700th AS	*bl*
10630	C-130H	700th AS	*bl*
10631	C-130H	314th AW	*bl*
FY91			
11231	C-130H	165th AS	
11232	C-130H	165th AS	
11233	C-130H	165th AS	
11234	C-130H	165th AS	
11235	C-130H	165th AS	
11236	C-130H	165th AS	
11237	C-130H	165th AS	
11238	C-130H	165th AS	
11239	C-130H	154th TS	*r*
FY01			
11461	C-130J	115th AS	*gn*
11462	C-130J	115th AS	*gn*
FY91			
11651	C-130H	154th TS	*r*
11652	C-130H	180th AS	*y*
11653	C-130H	187th AS	*y/bk*
FY01			
11935	EC-130J	193rd SOS	
FY64			
14852	HC-130P	71st RQS	*bl*
14853	HC-130P	71st RQS	*bl*
14854	MC-130P	67th SOS	
14855	HC-130P	39th RQS	
14859	EC-130H	55th ECG	
14860	HC-130P	71st RQS	*bl*
14861	C-130H	198th AS	
14862	EC-130H	55th ECG	
14863	HC-130P	71st RQS	*bl*
14864	HC-130P	39th RQS	
14865	HC-130P	58th SOW	
14866	C-130H	198th AS	
FY11			
15717	HC-130J	79th RQS	
15719	HC-130J		
15725	HC-130J		
15727	HC-130J		
15729	MC-130J		
15731	MC-130J		
15732	C-130J	374th AW	*r*
15733	MC-130J		
15734	C-130J	374th AW	*r*

Type				Notes
15735	MC-130J			
15736	C-130J	374th AW	r	
15737	MC-130J			
15738	C-130J	374th AW	r	
FY91				
19141	C-130H	328th AS	bl	
19142	C-130H	328th AS	bl	
19143	C-130H	328th AS	bl	
19144	C-130H	328th AS	bl	
FY82				
20054	C-130H	144th AS	bk/y	
20055	C-130H	19th AW		
20056	C-130H	105th AS	r	
20057	C-130H	144th AS	bk/y	
20058	C-130H	181st AS	bl/w	
20059	C-130H	144th AS	bk/y	
20060	C-130H	144th AS	bk/y	
20061	C-130H	144th AS	bk/y	
FY92				
20253	AC-130U	4th SOS		
FY02				
20314	C-130J	314th AW	y $	
FY92				
20547	C-130H	19th AW	r	
20548	C-130H	19th AW	r	
20549	C-130H	19th AW	m $	
20550	C-130H	19th AW	r	
20551	C-130H	19th AW	r	
20552	C-130H	19th AW	r	
20553	C-130H	19th AW	r	
20554	C-130H	19th AW	r	
21094	LC-130H	139th AS		
21095	LC-130H	139th AS		
FY02				
21434	C-130J	143rd AS	r	
FY92				
21451	C-130H	169th AS	or	
21452	C-130H	169th AS	or	
21454	C-130H	156th AS	bl	
FY02				
21463	C-130J	115th AS	gn	
21464	C-130J	115th AS	gn	
FY92				
21531	C-130H	187th AS	y/bk	
21532	C-130H	187th AS	y/bk	
21533	C-130H	187th AS	y/bk	
21534	C-130H	187th AS	y/bk	
21535	C-130H	187th AS	y/bk	
21536	C-130H	187th AS	y/bk	
21537	C-130H	187th AS	y/bk	
21538	C-130H	187th AS	y/bk	
FY62				
21863	HC-130P	71st RQS	bl	
FY92				
23021	C-130H	773rd AS	r	
23022	C-130H	773rd AS	r	
23023	C-130H	773rd AS	r	
23024	C-130H	757th AS	bl	
23281	C-130H	96th AS	pr	
23282	C-130H	96th AS	pr	
23283	C-130H	96th AS	pr	
23284	C-130H	96th AS	pr	
23285	C-130H	96th AS	pr	
23286	C-130H	96th AS	pr	
23287	C-130H	96th AS	pr	

Type				Notes
23288	C-130H	96th AS	pr	
FY02				
28155	C-130J	815th AS	r	
FY83				
30486	C-130H	139th AS		
30487	C-130H	139th AS		
30488	C-130H	139th AS		
30489	C-130H	139th AS		
30490	LC-130H	139th AS		
30491	LC-130H	139th AS		
30492	LC-130H	139th AS		
30493	LC-130H	139th AS		
FY93				
31036	C-130H	19th AW	r	
31037	C-130H	19th AW	r	
31038	C-130H	19th AW	r	
31039	C-130H	19th AW	r	
31040	C-130H	19th AW	r	
31041	C-130H	19th AW	r	
31096	LC-130H	139th AS		
FY83				
31212	MC-130H	1st SOS		
FY93				
31455	C-130H	156th AS	bl	
31456	C-130H	156th AS	bl	
31457	C-130H	156th AS	bl	
31458	C-130H	156th AS	bl	
31459	C-130H	156th AS	bl	
31561	C-130H	156th AS	bl	
31562	C-130H	156th AS	bl	
31563	C-130H	156th AS	bl	
FY73				
31580	EC-130H	55th ECG	r	
31581	EC-130H	55th ECG	$	
31582	C-130H	19th AW	gn	
31583	EC-130H	55th ECG	r	
31584	EC-130H	55th ECG-		
31585	EC-130H	55th ECG	bl	
31586	EC-130H	55th ECG	bl	
31587	EC-130H	55th ECG		
31588	EC-130H	55th ECG		
31590	EC-130H	55th ECG		
31592	EC-130H	55th ECG	bl	
31594	EC-130H	55th ECG	bl	
31595	EC-130H	55th ECG		
31597	C-130H	19th AW		
31598	C-130H	19th AW		
FY93				
32041	C-130H	169th AS	or	
32042	C-130H	169th AS	or	
32104	HC-130N	210th RQS		
32105	HC-130N	210th RQS		
32106	HC-130N	210th RQS		
FY73				
33300	LC-130H	139th AS		
FY93				
37311	C-130H	187th AS	y/bk	
37312	C-130H	169th AS	or	
37313	C-130H	154th TS	r	
37314	C-130H	187th AS	y/bk	
FY03				
38154	C-130J	815th AS	r	
FY84				
40204	C-130H	700th AS	bl	
40205	C-130H	700th AS	bl	

Type				Notes
40206	C-130H	142nd AS	*bl*	
40207	C-130H	314th AW	*bl*	
40208	C-130H	142nd AS	*bl*	
40209	C-130H	142nd AS	*bl*	
40210	C-130H	142nd AS	*bl*	
40212	C-130H	142nd AS	*bl*	
40213	C-130H	142nd AS	*bl*	
40476	MC-130H	1st SOS		
FY64				
40562	MC-130E	711th SOS		
40565	MC-130E	711th SOS		
40568	MC-130E	711th SOS		
FY74				
41658	C-130H	19th AW	*bk*	
41659	C-130H	374th AW	*r*	
41660	C-130H	374th AW	*r*	
41661	C-130H	374th AW	*r*	
41663	C-130H	374th AW	*r* $	
41664	C-130H	19th AW	*bk*	
41665	C-130H	19th AW	*bk*	
41666	C-130H	374th AW	*r* $	
41667	C-130H	19th AW		
41668	C-130H	374th AW	*r* $	
41669	C-130H	374th AW	*r*	
41670	C-130H	19th AW	*bk*	
41671	C-130H	19th AW		
41674	C-130H	374th AW	*r*	
41675	C-130H			
41677	C-130H	19th AW	*bk*	
41679	C-130H	19th AW	*bk*	
41680	C-130H	19th AW	*bk*	
41682	C-130H	374th AW	*r*	
41684	C-130H	19th AW	*gn*	
41685	C-130H	374th AW	*r*	
41687	C-130H	19th AW	*bk*	
41688	C-130H	19th AW		
41689	C-130H	19th AW	*bk*	
41690	C-130H	19th AW	*bk*	
41691	C-130H	19th AW		
41692	C-130H	374th AW	*r*	
42061	C-130H	374th AW	*r*	
42062	C-130H	19th AW	*bk*	
42063	C-130H	19th AW		
42065	C-130H	374th AW	*r* $	
42066	C-130H	19th AW		
42067	C-130H	374th AW	*r*	
42069	C-130H	19th AW		
42070	C-130H	19th AW	*r*	
42071	C-130H	19th AW	*bk*	
42072	C-130H	19th AW	*gn*	
42131	C-130H	19th AW	*bk*	
42132	C-130H	374th AW	*r*	
42133	C-130H	19th AW	*bk*	
42134	C-130H	19th AW		
FY04				
43142	C-130J	314th AW	*y*	
43143	C-130J	19th AW	*w*	
43144	C-130J	19th AW	*w*	
FY94				
46701	C-130H	169th AS	*or*	
46702	C-130H	167th AS	*r*	
46703	C-130H	169th AS	*or*	
46704	C-130H	154th TS	*r*	
46705	C-130H	167th AS	*r*	
46706	C-130H	167th AS	*r*	

Type				Notes
46707	C-130H	130th AS	*pr/y*	
46708	C-130H	130th AS	*pr/y*	
47310	C-130H	731st AS	*pr/w*	
47315	C-130H	731st AS	*pr/w*	
47316	C-130H	731st AS	*pr/w*	
47317	C-130H	731st AS	*pr/w*	
47318	C-130H	731st AS	*pr/w*	
47319	C-130H	731st AS	*pr/w*	
47320	C-130H	731st AS	*pr/w*	
47321	C-130H	731st AS	*pr/w*	
FY94				
48151	C-130J	19th AW	*w*	
48152	C-130J	815th AS	*r*	
FY04				
48153	C-130J	815th AS	*r*	
FY85				
50011	MC-130H	15th SOS		
50035	C-130H	357th AS	*bl*	
50036	C-130H	357th AS	*bl*	
50037	C-130H	357th AS	*bl*	
50038	C-130H	314th AW	*bl*	
50039	C-130H	357th AS	*bl*	
50040	C-130H	357th AS	*bl*	
50041	C-130H	773rd AS	*r*	
50042	C-130H	357th AS	*bl*	
FY65				
50962	TC-130H	55th ECG		
50963	C-130H	198th AS		
50966	C-130H	198th AS		
50967	HC-130H	122nd FS		
50968	C-130H	198th AS		
50970	HC-130P	39th RQS		
50971	MC-130P	58th SOW		
50973	HC-130P	71st RQS	*bl*	
50974	HC-130P	102nd RQS		
50976	HC-130P	39th RQS		
50977	HC-130H	39th RQS		
50978	HC-130P	102nd RQS		
50980	C-130H	158th AS	*r*	
50981	HC-130P	71st RQS	*bl*	
50982	HC-130P	71st RQS	*bl*	
50983	MC-130P	71st RQS	*bl*	
50984	C-130H	165th AS		
50985	C-130H	198th AS		
50986	HC-130P	71st RQS	*bl*	
50988	HC-130P	71st RQS	*bl*	
50989	EC-130H	55th ECG	*r*	
50991	MC-130P	67th SOS		
50992	MC-130P	67th SOS		
50993	MC-130P	9th SOS		
50994	MC-130P	9th SOS		
FY95				
51001	C-130H	109th AS	*pr/bk*	
51002	C-130H	109th AS	*pr/bk*	
FY85				
51361	C-130H	181st AS	*bl/w*	
51362	C-130H	181st AS	*bl/w*	
51363	C-130H	181st AS	*bl/w*	
51364	C-130H	181st AS	*bl/w*	
51365	C-130H	181st AS	*bl/w*	
51366	C-130H	181st AS	*bl/w*	
51367	C-130H	181st AS	*bl/w*	
51368	C-130H	181st AS	*bl/w*	
FY05				
51435	C-130J	143rd AS	*r*	

Type				Notes
51436	C-130J	143rd AS	*r*	
51465	C-130J	115th AS	*gn*	
51466	C-130J	115th AS	*gn*	
53145	C-130J	19th AW	*w*	
53146	C-130J	314th AW	*y*	
53147	C-130J	19th AW	*w*	
FY95				
56709	C-130H	156th AS	*bl*	
56710	C-130H	130th AS	*pr/y*	
56711	C-130H	156th AS	*bl*	
56712	C-130H	156th AS	*bl*	
FY05				
58152	C-130J	815th AS	*r*	
58156	C-130J	815th AS	*r*	
58157	C-130J	815th AS	*r*	
58158	C-130J	815th AS	*r*	
FY66				
60212	HC-130P	130th RQS	*bl*	
60215	MC-130P	67th SOS		
60216	HC-130P	130th RQS	*bl*	
60217	MC-130P	9th SOS		
60219	HC-130P	130th RQS	*bl*	
60220	MC-130P	67th SOS		
60221	HC-130P	58th SOW		
60222	HC-130P	102nd RQS		
60223	MC-130P	130th RQS	*bl*	
60225	MC-130P	17th SOS		
FY86				
60410	C-130H	95th AS	*w/r*	
60411	C-130H	95th AS	*w/r*	
60413	C-130H	357th AS	*bl*	
60414	C-130H	95th AS	*w/r*	
60415	C-130H	95th AS	*w/r*	
60418	C-130H	95th AS	*w/r*	
60419	C-130H	95th AS	*w/r*	
FY96				
61003	C-130H	109th AS	*pr/bk*	
61004	C-130H	109th AS	*pr/bk*	
61005	C-130H	109th AS	*pr/bk*	
61006	C-130H	109th AS	*pr/bk*	
61007	C-130H	109th AS	*pr/bk*	
61008	C-130H	109th AS	*pr/bk*	
FY86				
61391	C-130H	154th TS	*r*	
61392	C-130H	154th TS	*r*	
61393	C-130H	154th TS	*r*	
61394	C-130H	154th TS	*r*	
61395	C-130H	154th TS	*r*	
61396	C-130H	154th TS	*r*	
61397	C-130H	154th TS	*r*	
61398	C-130H	154th TS	*r*	
FY06				
61437	C-130J	143rd AS	*r*	
61438	C-130J	143rd AS	*r*	
61467	C-130J	115th AS	*gn*	
FY86				
61699	MC-130H	58th SOW		
FY06				
63171	C-130J	317th AG		
FY76				
63301	LC-130H	139th AS		
63302	LC-130H	139th AS		
FY06				
64631	C-130J	19th AW	*w*	
64632	C-130J	19th AW	*w*	

Type				Notes
64633	C-130J	19th AW	*w*	
64634	C-130J	19th AW	*w*	
FY96				
65300	WC-130J	53rd WRS		
65301	WC-130J	53rd WRS		
65302	WC-130J	53rd WRS		
67322	C-130H	731st AS	*pr/w*	
67323	C-130H	731st AS	*pr/w*	
67324	C-130H	731st AS	*pr/w*	
67325	C-130H	731st AS	*pr/w*	
68153	EC-130J	193rd SOS		
68154	EC-130J	193rd SOS		
FY06				
68159	C-130J	815th AS	*r*	
68610	C-130J	37th AS	*bl/w*	
68611	C-130J	37th AS	*bl/w*	
68612	C-130J	37th AS	*bl/w*	
FY87				
70023	MC-130H	7th SOS		
70024	MC-130H	7th SOS		
70125	MC-130H	15th SOS		
70126	MC-130H	15th SOS		
70128	AC-130U	4th SOS		
FY97				
71351	C-130J	314th AW	*y*	
71352	C-130J	314th AW	*y*	
71353	C-130J	314th AW	*y*	
71354	C-130J	314th AW	*y*	
FY07				
71468	C-130J	115th AS	*gn*	
FY97				
71931	EC-130J	193rd SOS		
FY07				
73170	C-130J	317th AG		
74635	C-130J	19th AW	*w*	
74636	C-130J	19th AW	*w*	
74637	C-130J	19th AW	*w*	
74638	C-130J	19th AW	*w*	
74639	C-130J	19th AW	*w*	
FY97				
75303	WC-130J	53rd WRS		
75304	WC-130J	53rd WRS		
75305	WC-130J	53rd WRS		
75306	WC-130J	53rd WRS		
FY07				
76310	C-130J	19th AW	*w*	
76311	C-130J	19th AW	*w*	
76312	C-130J	19th AW	*w*	
78608	C-130J	37th AS	*bl/w*	
78609	C-130J	37th AS	*bl/w*	
78613	C-130J	37th AS	*bl/w*	
78614	C-130J	37th AS	*bl/w*	
FY87				
79281	C-130H	328th AS	*bl*	
79282	C-130H	95th AS	*w/r*	
79283	C-130H	96th AS	*pr*	
79284	C-130H	95th AS	*w/r*	
79285	C-130H	328th AS	*bl*	
79286	MC-130W	73rd SOS		
79287	C-130H	328th AS	*bl*	
79288	MC-130W	73rd SOS		
FY88				
80191	MC-130H	1st SOS		
80192	MC-130H	15th SOS		
80193	MC-130H	16th SOS		

Type				Notes
80194	MC-130H	58th SOW		
80195	MC-130H	7th SOS		
80264	MC-130H	1st SOS		
FY78				
80806	C-130H	758th AS	*bk/y*	
80807	C-130H	758th AS	*bk/y*	
80808	C-130H	758th AS	*bk/y*	
80809	C-130H	758th AS	*bk/y*	
80810	C-130H	758th AS	*bk/y*	
80811	C-130H	758th AS	*bk/y*	
80812	C-130H	758th AS	*bk/y*	
80813	C-130H	758th AS	*bk/y*	
FY88				
81301	MC-130W	73rd SOS		
81302	MC-130W	73rd SOS		
81303	MC-130W	73rd SOS		
81304	MC-130W	73rd SOS		
81305	MC-130W	73rd SOS		
81306	MC-130W	73rd SOS		
81307	MC-130W	73rd SOS		
81308	MC-130W	73rd SOS		
FY98				
81355	C-130J	314th AW	*y*	
81356	C-130J	314th AW	*y*	
81357	C-130J	314th AW	*y*	
81358	C-130J	314th AW	*y*	
FY88				
81803	MC-130H	7th SOS		
FY98				
81932	EC-130J	193rd SOS		
FY88				
82101	HC-130N	102nd RQS		
82102	HC-130N	102nd RQS		
FY08				
83172	C-130J	317th AG		
83173	C-130J	317th AG		
83174	C-130J	317th AG		
83175	C-130J	317th AG		
83176	C-130J	317th AG		
83177	C-130J	317th AG		
83178	C-130J	317th AG		
83179	C-130J	317th AG		
FY88				
84401	C-130H	95th AS	*w/r*	
84402	C-130H	95th AS	*w/r*	
84403	C-130H	95th AS	*w/r*	
84404	C-130H	95th AS	*w/r*	
84405	C-130H	95th AS	*w/r*	
84406	C-130H	95th AS	*w/r*	
84407	C-130H	95th AS	*w/r*	
FY98				
85307	WC-130J	53rd WRS		
85308	WC-130J	53rd WRS		
FY08				
85675	C-130J	317th AG		
85678	C-130J	317th AG		
85679	C-130J	317th AG		
85683	C-130J	317th AG		
85684	C-130J	317th AG		
85685	C-130J	317th AG	*r*	
85686	C-130J	317th AG		
85691	C-130J	317th AG		
85692	C-130J	317th AG		
85693	C-130J	317th AG	*r*	
85697	MC-130J	58th SOW		

Type				Notes
85705	C-130J	317th AG		
85712	C-130J	317th AG		
85715	C-130J	317th AG		
85726	C-130J	317th AG		
86201	MC-130J	522nd SOS		
86202	MC-130J	522nd SOS		
86203	MC-130J	58th SOW		
86204	MC-130J	522nd SOS		
86205	MC-130J	522nd SOS		
86206	MC-130J	522nd SOS		
86207	MC-130J			
88601	C-130J	37th AS	*bl/w* $	
88602	C-130J	37th AS	*bl/w* $	
88603	C-130J	37th AS	*bl/w* $	
88604	C-130J	37th AS	*bl/w*	
88605	C-130J	37th AS	*bl/w*	
88606	C-130J	314th AW	*y*	
88607	C-130J	37th AS	*bl/w*	
FY09				
90108	HC-130J	85th TES		
90109	HC-130J	58th SOW		
FY89				
90280	MC-130H	1st SOS		
90281	MC-130H	15th SOS		
90282	MC-130H	58th SOW		
90283	MC-130H	15th SOS		
FY79				
90473	C-130H	192nd AS	*bl/y*	
90474	C-130H	192nd AS	*bl/y*	
90475	C-130H	192nd AS	*bl/y*	
90476	C-130H	192nd AS	*bl/y*	
90477	C-130H	192nd AS	*bl/y*	
90478	C-130H	192nd AS	*bl/y*	
90479	C-130H	192nd AS	*bl/y*	
90480	C-130H	192nd AS	*bl/y*	
FY89				
90509	AC-130U	4th SOS		
90510	AC-130U	4th SOS		
90511	AC-130U	4th SOS		
90512	AC-130U	4th SOS		
90513	AC-130U	4th SOS		
90514	AC-130U	4th SOS		
91051	MC-130W	73rd SOS		
91052	AC-130U	4th SOS		
91053	AC-130U	4th SOS		
91054	AC-130U	4th SOS		
91055	C-130H	328th AS	*bl*	
91056	AC-130U	4th SOS		
91181	C-130H	154th TS	*r*	
91182	C-130H	144th AS	*bk/y*	
91183	C-130H	144th AS	*bk/y*	
91184	C-130H	144th AS	*bk/y*	
91185	C-130H	144th AS	*bk/y*	
91186	C-130H	328th AS	*bl*	
91187	C-130H	328th AS	*bl*	
91188	C-130H	328th AS	*bl*	
FY99				
91431	C-130J	143rd AS	*r*	
91432	C-130J	143rd AS	*r*	
91433	C-130J	143rd AS	*r*	
91933	EC-130J	193rd SOS		
95309	WC-130J	53rd WRS		
FY09				
95706	HC-130J	58th SOW		
95707	HC-130J	79th RQS		

Type				Notes
95708	HC-130J	79th RQS		
95709	HC-130J	79th RQS		
95710	MC-130J	522nd SOS		
95711	MC-130J	522nd SOS		
95713	MC-130J	522nd SOS		
95714	MC-130J			
FY69				
95819	MC-130P	9th SOS		
95820	MC-130P	9th SOS		
95821	MC-130P	58th SOW		
95822	MC-130P	67th SOS		
95823	MC-130P	9th SOS		
95824	HC-130N	39th RQS		
95825	MC-130P	17th SOS		
95826	MC-130P	17th SOS		
95827	MC-130P	9th SOS		
95828	MC-130P	9th SOS		
95829	HC-130N	58th SOW		
95830	HC-130N	39th RQS		
95831	MC-130P	17th SOS		
95832	MC-130P	17th SOS		
95833	HC-130N	58th SOW		
FY09				
96207	MC-130J	522nd SOS		
96208	MC-130J	58th SOW		
96209	MC-130J	58th SOW		
96210	MC-130J	522nd SOS		
FY69				
96568	AC-130H	16th SOS		
96569	AC-130H	16th SOS		
96570	AC-130H	16th SOS		
96572	AC-130H	16th SOS		
96573	AC-130H	16th SOS		
96574	AC-130H	16th SOS		
96575	AC-130H	16th SOS		
96577	AC-130H	16th SOS		
FY89				
99101	C-130H	154th TS	*bl*	
99102	C-130H	757th AS	*bl*	
99103	C-130H	757th AS	*bl*	
99104	C-130H	757th AS	*bl*	
99105	C-130H	757th AS	*bl*	
99106	C-130H	757th AS	*bl*	

Boeing C-135

6th AMW, MacDill AFB, Florida:
91st ARS (*y/bl*);
15th Wg, Hickam AFB, Hawaii:
65th AS;
18th Wg, Kadena AB,
Japan [ZZ]:
909th ARS (*or/bk*);
22nd ARW, McConnell AFB, Kansas:
344th ARS (*y/bk*), 349th ARS (*y/bl*)
350th ARS (*y/r*) & 384th ARS (*y/pr*);
55th Wg, Offutt AFB, Nebraska [OF]:
38th RS (*gn*), 45th RS (*bk*)
& 343rd RS;
88th ABW, Wright-Patterson AFB, Ohio;
92nd ARW, Fairchild AFB,
Washington:
92nd ARS (*bk*), 93rd ARS (*bl*),
& 97th ARS (*y*);
97th AMW, Altus AFB, Oklahoma:
54th ARS (*y/r*);
100th ARW, RAF Mildenhall,
UK [D]:
351st ARS (*r/w/bl*);
106th ARS/117th ARW, Birmingham,
Alabama ANG (*w/r*);
108th ARS/126th ARW,
Scott AFB, Illinois ANG (*w/bl*);
117th ARS/190th ARW, Forbes Field,
Kansas ANG (*bl/y*);
121st ARW, Rickenbacker ANGB,
Ohio ANG:
145th ARS & 166th ARS (*bl*);
126th ARS/128th ARW, Mitchell Field,
Wisconsin ANG (*w/bl*);
132nd ARS/101st ARW, Bangor,
Maine ANG (*w/gn*);
133rd ARS/157th ARW, Pease ANGB,
New Hampshire ANG (*bl*);
141st ARS/108th ARW, McGuire AFB,
New Jersey ANG (*r*);
151st ARS/134th ARW, Knoxville,
Tennessee ANG (*w/or*);
168th ARS/168th ARW, Eielson AFB,
Alaska ANG [AK] (*bl/y*);
171st ARS/127th Wg, Selfridge ANGB,
Michigan ANG (*bk/y*);
171st ARW, Greater Pittsburgh,
Pennsylvania ANG:
146th ARS (*y/bk*) &
147th ARS (*bk/y*);
173rd ARS/155th ARW, Lincoln,
Nebraska ANG (*r/w*);
174th ARS/185th ARW, Sioux City,
Iowa ANG (*y/bk*);
191st ARS/151st ARW, Salt Lake City,
Utah ANG (*bl/bk*);
196th ARS/163rd ARW, March ARB,
California ANG (*bl/w*);
197th ARS/161st ARW, Phoenix,
Arizona ANG;
203rd ARS/15th Wg, Hickam AFB,
Hawaii ANG [HH] (*y/bk*);
366th Wg, Mountain Home AFB,
Idaho [MO]:
22nd ARS (*y/gn*);
412th TW, Edwards AFB,
California [ED]:
418th FLTS (*or*);
434th ARW AFRC, Grissom AFB,
Indiana:
72nd ARS (*bl*) & 74th ARS (*r/w*);
452nd AMW AFRC, March ARB,
California:
336th ARS (or/*y*);
459th ARW AFRC, Andrews AFB,
Maryland:
756th ARS (*y/bk*);
507th ARW AFRC,
Tinker AFB, Oklahoma:
465th ARS (*bl/y*);
645th Materiel Sqn, Greenville, Texas;
916th ARW AFRC,
Seymour Johnson AFB,
North Carolina:
77th ARS (*gn*);

Type				Notes
927th ARW AFRC, MacDill AFB, Florida:				
63rd ARS (*pr/w*);				
L3 Systems, Greenville, Texas				
FY60				
00313	KC-135R	18th Wg	*or/bk*	
00314	KC-135R	434th ARW	*r/w*	
00315	KC-135R	126th ARS	*w/bl*	
00316	KC-135R	174th ARS	*y/bk*	
00318	KC-135R	203rd ARS	*y/bk*	
00320	KC-135R	97th AMW	*y/r*	
00321	KC-135R	452nd AMW	*or/y*	
00322	KC-135R	434th ARW	*bl*	
00323	KC-135R	203rd ARS	*y/bk*	
00324	KC-135R	22nd ARW		
00328	KC-135R	92nd ARW		
00329	KC-135R	203rd ARS	*y/bk*	
00331	KC-135R	6th AMW	*y/bl*	
00332	KC-135R	168th ARS	*bl/y*	
00333	KC-135R	92nd ARW	*bk*	
00334	KC-135R	168th ARS	*bl/y*	
00335	KC-135T	6th AMW	*y/bl*	
00336	KC-135T	6th AMW	*y/bl*	
00337	KC-135T	92nd ARW	*m*	
00339	KC-135T	6th AMW	*y/bl*	
00341	KC-135R	121st ARW	*bl*	
00342	KC-135T	6th AMW	*y/bl*	
00343	KC-135T	22nd ARW		
00344	KC-135T	6th AMW	*y/bl*	
00345	KC-135T	171st ARS	*bk/y*	
00346	KC-135T	171st ARS	*bk/y*	
00347	KC-135R	121st ARW	*bl*	
00348	KC-135R	97th AMW	*y/r*	
00349	KC-135R	916th ARW	*gn*	
00350	KC-135R	22nd ARW		
00351	KC-135R	97th AMW	*y/r*	
00353	KC-135R	100th ARW	*r/w/bl*	
00355	KC-135R	22nd ARW		
00356	KC-135R	22nd ARW		
00357	KC-135R	22nd ARW		
00358	KC-135R	108th ARS	*w/bl*	
00359	KC-135R	434th ARW	*r/w*	
00360	KC-135R	97th AMW	*y/r*	
00362	KC-135R	22nd ARW		
00363	KC-135R	434th ARW	*bl*	
00364	KC-135R	434th ARW	*r/w*	
00365	KC-135R	117th ARS	*bl/y*	
00366	KC-135R	141st ARS	*r*	
00367	KC-135R	121st ARW	*bl*	
FY61				
10264	KC-135R	121st ARW	*bl*	
10266	KC-135R	117th ARS	*bl/y*	
10267	KC-135R	22nd ARW		
10272	KC-135R	434th ARW	*r/w*	
10275	KC-135R	191st ARS	*bl/bk*	
10276	KC-135R	173rd ARS	*r/w*	
10277	KC-135R	117th ARS	*bl/y*	
10280	KC-135R	452nd AMW	*or/y*	
10284	KC-135R	106th ARS	*w/r*	
10288	KC-135R	18th Wg	*or/bk*	
10290	KC-135R	203rd ARS	*y/bk*	
10292	KC-135R	97th AMW	*y/r*	
10293	KC-135R	22nd ARW		
10294	KC-135R	916th ARW	*gn*	
10295	KC-135R	100th ARW	*r/w/bl*	
10298	KC-135R	126th ARS	*w/bl*	

Type				Notes
10299	KC-135R	97th AMW	*y/r*	
10300	KC-135R	108th ARS	*w/bl*	
10302	KC-135R	203rd ARS	*y/bk*	
10304	KC-135R	100th ARW	*r/w/bl*	
10305	KC-135R	97th AMW	*y/r*	
10306	KC-135R	100th ARW	*r/w/bl*	
10307	KC-135R	459th ARW	*y/bk*	
10308	KC-135R	97th AMW	*y/r*	
10309	KC-135R	126th ARS	*w/bl*	
10310	KC-135R	133rd ARS	*bl*	
10311	KC-135R	22nd ARW	*y*	
10312	KC-135R	97th AMW	*y/r*	
10313	KC-135R	916th ARW	*gn*	
10314	KC-135R	22nd ARW		
10315	KC-135R	18th Wg	*or/bk*	
10317	KC-135R	141st ARS	*r*	
10318	KC-135R	106th ARS	*w/r*	
10320	KC-135R	412th TW	*or*	
10321	KC-135R	97th AMW	*y/r*	
10323	KC-135R	6th AMW	*y/bl*	
10324	KC-135R	452nd AMW	*or/y*	
12662	RC-135S	55th Wg	*bk*	
12663	RC-135S	55th Wg	*bk*	
12666	NC-135W	645th MS		
12667	WC-135W	55th Wg	*bk*	
12670	OC-135B	55th Wg		
12672	OC-135B	55th Wg		
FY64				
14828	KC-135R	191st ARS	*bl/bk*	
14829	KC-135R	117th ARS	*bl/y*	
14830	KC-135R	100th ARW	*r/w/bl*	
14831	KC-135R	197th ARS		
14832	KC-135R	203rd ARS	*y/bk*	
14833	KC-135R	L3 Systems		
14834	KC-135R	434th ARW	*r/w*	
14835	KC-135R	452nd AMW	*or/y*	
14836	KC-135R	133rd ARS	*bl*	
14837	KC-135R	22nd ARW		
14838	KC-135R	6th AMW	*y/bl*	
14839	KC-135R	108th ARS	*w/bl*	
14840	KC-135R	121st ARW	*bl*	
14841	RC-135V	55th Wg	*bl*	
14842	RC-135V	55th Wg	*gn*	
14843	RC-135V	55th Wg	*gn*	
14844	RC-135V	55th Wg	*gn*	
14845	RC-135V	55th Wg	*bl*	
14846	RC-135V	55th Wg	*gn*	
14847	RC-135U	55th Wg	*bk*	
14848	RC-135V	55th Wg	*gn*	
14849	RC-135U	55th Wg	*bk*	
FY62				
23498	KC-135R	22nd ARW		
23499	KC-135R	100th ARW	*r/w/bl*	
23500	KC-135R	126th ARS	*w/bl*	
23502	KC-135R	97th AMW	*y/r*	
23503	KC-135R	507th ARW	*bl/y*	
23504	KC-135R	151st ARS	*w/or*	
23505	KC-135R	97th AMW	*y/r*	
23506	KC-135R	133rd ARS	*bl*	
23507	KC-135R	22nd ARW		
23508	KC-135R	141st ARS	*r*	
23509	KC-135R	916th ARW	*gn*	
23510	KC-135R	434th ARW	*r/w*	
23511	KC-135R	121st ARW	*bl*	
23512	KC-135R	126th ARS	*w/bl*	

Type				*Notes*
23513	KC-135R	132nd ARS	*w/gn*	
23514	KC-135R	141st ARS	*r*	
23515	KC-135R	133rd ARS	*bl*	
23516	KC-135R	197th ARS		
23517	KC-135R	6th AMW	*y/bl*	
23518	KC-135R	434th ARW	*bl*	
23519	KC-135R	92nd ARW		
23520	KC-135R	133rd ARS	*bl*	
23521	KC-135R	434th ARW	*bl*	
23523	KC-135R	22nd ARW		
23524	KC-135R	168th ARS	*bl/y*	
23526	KC-135R	173rd ARS	*r/w*	
23528	KC-135R	916th ARW	*gn*	
23529	KC-135R	6th AMW	*y/bl*	
23530	KC-135R	434th ARW	*bl*	
23531	KC-135R	121st ARW	*bl*	
23533	KC-135R	452nd AMW	*or/y*	
23534	KC-135R	22nd ARW		
23537	KC-135R	916th ARW	*gn*	
23538	KC-135R	22nd ARW		
23540	KC-135R	100th ARW	*r/w/bl*	
23541	KC-135R	22nd ARW		
23542	KC-135R	916th ARW	*gn*	
23543	KC-135R	459th ARW	*y/bk*	
23544	KC-135R	141st ARS	*r*	
23545	KC-135R	22nd ARW		
23546	KC-135R	203rd ARS	*y/bk*	
23547	KC-135R	133rd ARS	*bl*	
23548	KC-135R	18th Wg	*or/bk*	
23549	KC-135R	6th AMW	*y/bl*	
23550	KC-135R	197th ARS		
23551	KC-135R	100th ARW	*r/w/bl*	
23552	KC-135R	22nd ARW		
23553	KC-135R	97th AMW	*y/r*	
23554	KC-135R	22nd ARW		
23556	KC-135R	459th ARW	*y/bk*	
23557	KC-135R	916th ARW	*gn*	
23558	KC-135R	452nd AMW	*or/y*	
23559	KC-135R	6th AMW	*y/bl*	
23561	KC-135R	18th Wg	*or/bk*	
23562	KC-135R	92nd ARW		
23564	KC-135R	22nd ARW		
23565	KC-135R	100th ARW	*r/w/bl*	
23566	KC-135R	174th ARS	*y/bk*	
23568	KC-135R	6th AMW	*y/bl*	
23569	KC-135R	22nd ARW		
23571	KC-135R	168th ARS	*bl/y*	
23572	KC-135R	117th ARS	*bl/y*	
23573	KC-135R	97th AMW	*y/r*	
23575	KC-135R	22nd ARW		
23576	KC-135R	133rd ARS	*bl*	
23577	KC-135R	916th ARW	*gn*	
23578	KC-135R	141st ARS	*r*	
23580	KC-135R	916th ARW	*gn*	
23582	WC-135C	55th Wg	*bk*	
24125	RC-135W	55th Wg	*bk*	
24126	RC-135W	55th Wg	*bl*	
24127	TC-135W	55th Wg	*bl*	
24128	RC-135S	55th Wg		
24129	TC-135W	55th Wg	*gn*	
24130	RC-135W	55th Wg	*gn*	
24131	RC-135W	55th Wg	*gn*	
24132	RC-135W	55th Wg	*gn*	
24133	TC-135S	55th Wg	*bk*	
24134	RC-135W	55th Wg	*bl*	

Type				*Notes*
24135	RC-135W	55th Wg	*bk*	
24138	RC-135W	55th Wg	*gn*	
24139	RC-135W	55th Wg	*gn*	
FY63				
37976	KC-135R	97th AMW	*y/r*	
37977	KC-135R	6th AMW	*y/bl*	
37978	KC-135R	22nd ARW		
37979	KC-135R	100th ARW	*r/w/bl*	
37980	KC-135R	412th TW	*or*	
37981	KC-135R	108th ARS	*w/bl*	
37982	KC-135R	92nd ARW	*bk*	
37984	KC-135R	106th ARS	*w/r*	
37985	KC-135R	507th ARW	*bl/y*	
37987	KC-135R	22nd ARW		
37988	KC-135R	173rd ARS	*r/w*	
37991	KC-135R	173rd ARS	*r/w*	
37992	KC-135R	121st ARW	*bl*	
37993	KC-135R	121st ARW	*m*	
37995	KC-135R	22nd ARW	*gy*	
37996	KC-135R	434th ARW	*bl*	
37997	KC-135R	22nd ARW		
37999	KC-135R	18th Wg	*or/bk*	
38000	KC-135R	6th AMW	*y/bl*	
38002	KC-135R	22nd ARW	*gy/si*	
38003	KC-135R	141st ARS	*r*	
38004	KC-135R	117th ARS	*bl/y*	
38006	KC-135R	6th AMW	*y/bl*	
38007	KC-135R	106th ARS	*w/r*	
38008	KC-135R	100th ARW	*r/w/bl*	
38011	KC-135R	92nd ARW		
38012	KC-135R	22nd ARW		
38013	KC-135R	121st ARW	*bl*	
38014	KC-135R	916th ARW	*gn*	
38015	KC-135R	168th ARS	*bl/y*	
38017	KC-135R	92nd ARW		
38018	KC-135R	173rd ARS	*r/w*	
38019	KC-135R	18th Wg	*or/bk*	
38020	KC-135R	22nd ARW		
38021	KC-135R	22nd ARW		
38022	KC-135R	22nd ARW	*m*	
38023	KC-135R	197th ARS		
38024	KC-135R	452nd AMW	*or/y*	
38025	KC-135R	22nd ARW		
38026	KC-135R	191st ARS	*bl/bk*	
38027	KC-135R	6th AMW	*y/bl*	
38028	KC-135R	168th ARS	*bl/y*	
38029	KC-135R	141st ARS *r*		
38030	KC-135R	203rd ARS	*y/bk*	
38031	KC-135R	97th AMW	*y/r*	
38032	KC-135R	434th ARW	*bl*	
38033	KC-135R	22nd ARW		
38034	KC-135R	22nd ARW		
38035	KC-135R	106th ARS	*w/r*	
38036	KC-135R	197th ARS		
38037	KC-135R	22nd ARW		
38038	KC-135R	197th ARS		
38039	KC-135R	507th ARW	*bl/y*	
38040	KC-135R	141st ARS	*r*	
38041	KC-135R	434th ARW	*bl*	
38043	KC-135R	168th ARS	*bl/y*	
38044	KC-135R	916th ARW	*gn*	
38045	KC-135R	6th AMW	*y/bl*	
38871	KC-135R	22nd ARW		
38872	KC-135R	132nd ARS	*w/gn*	
38873	KC-135R	132nd ARS	*w/gn*	

Type				Notes
38874	KC-135R	18th Wg	*or/bk*	
38875	KC-135R	117th ARS	*bl/y*	
38876	KC-135R	168th ARS	*bl/y*	
38877	KC-135R	22nd ARW		
38878	KC-135R	97th AMW	*y/r*	
38879	KC-135R	92nd ARW		
38880	KC-135R	507th ARW	*bl/y*	
38881	KC-135R	191st ARS	*bl/bk*	
38883	KC-135R	97th AMW	*y/r*	
38884	KC-135R	100th ARW	*r/w/bl*	
38885	KC-135R	92nd ARW		
38887	KC-135R	6th AMW	*y/bl*	
38888	KC-135R	6th AMW	*y/bl*	
39792	RC-135V	55th Wg	*gn $*	
FY57				
71419	KC-135R	117th ARS	*bl/y*	
71427	KC-135R	117th ARS	*bl/y*	
71428	KC-135R	151st ARS	*w/or*	
71430	KC-135R	133rd ARS	*bl*	
71432	KC-135R	191st ARS	*bl/bk*	
71435	KC-135R	191st ARS	*bl/bk*	
71436	KC-135R	151st ARS	*w/or*	
71437	KC-135R	916th ARW		
71438	KC-135R	452nd AMW	*or/y*	
71439	KC-135R	22nd ARW		
71440	KC-135R	22nd ARW		
71441	KC-135R	174th ARS	*y/bk*	
71451	KC-135R	151st ARS	*w/or*	
71453	KC-135R	106th ARS	*w/r*	
71454	KC-135R	22nd ARW		
71456	KC-135R	916th ARW	*gn*	
71459	KC-135R	452nd AMW	*or/y*	
71461	KC-135R	173rd ARS	*r/w*	
71462	KC-135R	121st ARW	*bl*	
71468	KC-135R	452nd AMW	*or/y*	
71469	KC-135R	197th ARS		
71472	KC-135R	434th ARW	*bl*	
71473	KC-135R	106th ARS	*w/r*	
71474	KC-135R	97th AMW	*y/r*	
71483	KC-135R	92nd ARW		
71486	KC-135R	121st ARW	*bl*	
71487	KC-135R	459th ARW	*y/bk*	
71488	KC-135R			
71493	KC-135R	18th Wg	*or/bk*	
71499	KC-135R	18th Wg	*or/bk*	
71502	KC-135R	22nd ARW		
71506	KC-135R	97th AMW	*y/r*	
71508	KC-135R	203rd ARS	*y/bk*	
71512	KC-135R	459th ARW	*y/bk*	
71514	KC-135R	126th ARS	*w/bl*	
72593	KC-135R	121st ARW	*bl*	
72597	KC-135R	151st ARS	*w/or*	
72598	KC-135R	452nd AMW	*or/y*	
72599	KC-135R	916th ARW	*gn*	
72603	KC-135R	452nd AMW	*or/y*	
72605	KC-135R	92nd ARW		
72606	KC-135R	174th ARS	*y/bk*	
FY58				
80001	KC-135R	100th ARW	*r/w/bl*	
80004	KC-135R	106th ARS	*w/r*	
80008	KC-135R	133rd ARS	*bl*	
80009	KC-135R	126th ARS	*w/bl*	
80010	KC-135R	141st ARS	*r*	
80011	KC-135R	22nd ARW		
80015	KC-135R	507th ARW	*bl/y*	

Type				Notes
80016	KC-135R			
80018	KC-135R	22nd ARW		
80021	KC-135R	132nd ARS	*w/gn*	
80023	KC-135R	108th ARS	*w/bl*	
80027	KC-135R	191st ARS	*bl/bk*	
80030	KC-135R	132nd ARS	*w/gn*	
80034	KC-135R	100th ARW	*r/w/bl*	
80035	KC-135R	92nd ARW		
80036	KC-135R	18th Wg	*or/bk*	
80038	KC-135R	916th ARW	*gn*	
80042	KC-135T	22nd ARW		
80045	KC-135T	141st ARS	*r*	
80046	KC-135T	18th Wg	*or/bk*	
80047	KC-135T	22nd ARW		
80049	KC-135T	171st ARS	*bk/y*	
80050	KC-135T	92nd ARW	*bk*	
80051	KC-135R	507th ARW	*bl/y*	
80052	KC-135R	452nd AMW	*or/y*	
80054	KC-135T	171st ARW	*y/bk*	
80055	KC-135T	22nd ARW		
80056	KC-135R	15th Wg		
80057	KC-135R	174th ARS	*y/bk*	
80058	KC-135R	507th ARW	*bl/y*	
80059	KC-135R	117th ARS	*bl/y*	
80060	KC-135T	171st ARW	*y/bk*	
80061	KC-135T	22nd ARW		
80062	KC-135T	171st ARS	*bk/y*	
80063	KC-135R	507th ARW	*bl/y*	
80065	KC-135T	22nd ARW		
80066	KC-135R	507th ARW	*bl/y*	
80067	KC-135R	174th ARS	*y/bk*	
80069	KC-135T	22nd ARW		
80071	KC-135T	22nd ARW		
80072	KC-135T	171st ARW	*y/bk*	
80073	KC-135R	106th ARS	*w/r*	
80074	KC-135T	171st ARW	*y/bk*	
80075	KC-135R	459th ARW	*y/bk*	
80076	KC-135R	434th ARW	*r/w*	
80077	KC-135T	171st ARW	*y/bk*	
80079	KC-135R	507th ARW	*bl/y*	
80083	KC-135R	121st ARW	*bl*	
80084	KC-135T	171st ARW	*y/bk*	
80085	KC-135R	452nd AMW	*or/y*	
80086	KC-135T	6th AMW	*y/bl*	
80088	KC-135T	171st ARS	*bk/y*	
80089	KC-135T	22nd ARW		
80092	KC-135R	92nd ARW		
80093	KC-135R	22nd ARW		
80094	KC-135T	92nd ARW		
80095	KC-135T	92nd ARW		
80098	KC-135R	132nd ARS	*w/gn*	
80099	KC-135T	171st ARW	*y/bk*	
80100	KC-135R	100th ARW	*r/w/bl*	
80102	KC-135R	507th ARW	*bl/y*	
80103	KC-135T	92nd ARW	*bk*	
80104	KC-135R	108th ARS	*w/bl*	
80106	KC-135R	106th ARS	*w/r*	
80107	KC-135R	132nd ARS	*w/gn*	
80109	KC-135R	174th ARS	*y/bk*	
80112	KC-135T	171st ARW	*y/bk*	
80113	KC-135R	18th Wg	*or/bk*	
80114	KC-135R	191st ARS	*bl/bk*	
80117	KC-135T	171st ARW	*y/bk*	
80118	KC-135R	22nd ARW		
80119	KC-135R	151st ARS	*w/or*	

Type				Notes
80120	KC-135R	126th ARS	*w/bl*	
80121	KC-135R	507th ARW	*bl/y*	
80122	KC-135R	117th ARS	*bl/y*	
80123	KC-135R	22nd ARW		
80124	KC-135R	22nd ARW		
80125	KC-135T	22nd ARW		
80126	KC-135R	22nd ARW	*y*	
80128	KC-135R	97th AMW	*y/r*	
80129	KC-135T	171st ARS	*bk/y*	
80130	KC-135R	126th ARS	*w/bl*	
FY59				
91444	KC-135R	121st ARW	*bl*	
91446	KC-135R	132nd ARS	*w/gn*	
91448	KC-135R	151st ARS	*w/or*	
91450	KC-135R	197th ARS		
91453	KC-135R	121st ARW	*bl*	
91455	KC-135R	203rd ARS	*y/bk*	
91458	KC-135R	121st ARW	*bl*	
91459	KC-135R	22nd ARW		
91460	KC-135T	171st ARW	*y/bk*	
91461	KC-135R	168th ARS	*bl/y*	
91462	KC-135T	92nd ARW		
91463	KC-135R	173rd ARS	*r/w*	
91464	KC-135T	22nd ARW		
91466	KC-135R	108th ARS	*w/bl*	
91467	KC-135T	171st ARW	*y/bk*	
91468	KC-135T	171st ARW	*y/bk*	
91469	KC-135R	459th ARW	*y/bk*	
91470	KC-135T	92nd ARW	*gn*	
91471	KC-135T	92nd ARW	*bk*	
91472	KC-135R	203rd ARS	*y/bk*	
91474	KC-135T	97th AMW	*y/r*	
91475	KC-135R	97th AMW	*y/r*	
91476	KC-135R	92nd ARW		
91478	KC-135R	197th ARS		
91480	KC-135T	92nd ARW	*bk*	
91482	KC-135R	452nd AMW	*or/y*	
91483	KC-135R	121st ARW	*bl*	
91486	KC-135R	92nd ARW		
91488	KC-135R	132nd ARS	*w/gn*	
91490	KC-135T	171st ARW	*y/bk*	
91492	KC-135R	100th ARW	*r/w/bl*	
91495	KC-135R	173rd ARS	*r/w*	
91498	KC-135R	132nd ARS	*w/gn*	
91499	KC-135R	151st ARS	*w/or*	
91500	KC-135R	108th ARS	*w/bl*	
91501	KC-135R	97th AMW	*y/r*	
91502	KC-135R	97th AMW	*y/r*	
91504	KC-135T	171st ARW	*y/bk*	
91505	KC-135R	151st ARS	*w/or*	
91506	KC-135R	174th ARS	*y/bk*	
91507	KC-135R	117th ARS	*bl/y*	
91508	KC-135R	22nd ARW		
91509	KC-135R	141st ARS	*r*	
91510	KC-135T	92nd ARW		
91511	KC-135R	22nd ARW		
91512	KC-135T	171st ARS	*bk/y*	
91513	KC-135T	92nd ARW	*bk*	
91515	KC-135R	92nd ARW		
91516	KC-135R	126th ARS	*w/bl*	
91517	KC-135R	151st ARS	*w/or*	
91519	KC-135R	174th ARS	*y/bk*	
91520	KC-135T	6th AMW	*y/bl*	
91521	KC-135R	168th ARS	*bl/y*	
91522	KC-135R	108th ARS	*w/bl*	
91523	KC-135T	171st ARW	*y/bk*	

PZL-Mielec
C-145A Skytruck

6th SOS/1st SOW,
Duke Field, Florida

FY10
00321
00322
00323
00324
FY11
10326
10329
FY12
20331
FY08
80310
FY09
90317
90319
90320

Dornier
C-146A

524th SOS/27th SOW,
Cannon AFB, New Mexico

FY10
03026
03068
03077
03097
FY11
13016
13031
13075
13104
FY12
23040
23060
23085
FY95
53058
FY97
73091
73093
FY99
93106

Type				Notes

Lockheed P-3 Orion

CinCLANT/VP-30, NAS Jacksonville, Florida;
CNO/VP-30, NAS Jacksonville, Florida;
NASC-FS, Point Mugu, California;
USNTPS, NAS Point Mugu, California;
VP-1, NAS Whidbey Island, Washington [YB];
VP-4, MCBH Kaneohe Bay, Hawaii [YD];
VP-5, NAS Jacksonville, Florida [LA];
VP-8, NAS Jacksonville, Florida [LC];
VP-9, MCBH Kaneohe Bay, Hawaii [PD];
VP-10, NAS Jacksonville, Florida [LD];
VP-16, NAS Jacksonville, Florida [LF];
VP-26, NAS Jacksonville, Florida [LK];
VP-30, NAS Jacksonville, Florida [LL];
VP-40, NAS Whidbey Island, Washington [QE];
VP-45, NAS Jacksonville, Florida [LN];
VP-46, NAS Whidbey Island, Washington [RC];
VP-47, MCBH Kaneohe Bay, Hawaii [RD];
VP-62, NAS Jacksonville, Florida [LT];
VP-69, NAS Whidbey Island, Washington [PJ];
VPU-2, MCBH Kaneohe Bay, Hawaii;
VQ-1, NAS Whidbey Island, Washington [PR];
VX-1, NAS Patuxent River, Maryland;
VX-20, Patuxent River, Maryland;
VX-30, NAS Point Mugu, California;
VXS-1, Patuxent River, Maryland [RL]

				Notes
150521	[341]	NP-3D	VX-30	
150522	[340]	NP-3D	VX-30	
153442	[RL-442]	NP-3D	VXS-1	
153443	[302]	NP-3D	VX-30	
154587	[RL-587]	NP-3D	VXS-1	
154589	[RL-589]	NP-3D	VXS-1	
156507	[507]	EP-3E	VQ-1	
156510	[LL-510]	P-3C	VP-30	
156511	[511]	EP-3E	VQ-1	
156514	[514]	EP-3E	VQ-1	
156515	[LL-515]	P-3C	VP-30	
156517	[517]	EP-3E	VQ-1	
156521	[LL-521]	P-3C	VP-30	
156528	[528]	EP-3E	VQ-1	
156529	[529]	EP-3E	VQ-1	
157316	[316]	EP-3E	VQ-1	
157318	[318]	EP-3E	VQ-1	
157319	[PD-319]	P-3C	VP-9	
157325	[325]	EP-3E	VQ-1	
157326	[326]	EP-3E	VQ-1	
157329	[LL-329]	P-3C	VP-30	
157331	[PD-331]	P-3C	VP-9	
158204	[204]	NP-3C	VX-20	
158206	[JQ-21]$	P-3C	VQ-1	
158210	[210]	P-3C	VP-26	
158214	[LN-214]	P-3C	VP-45	
158215	[215]	P-3C	VP-5	
158222	[PD-222]	P-3C	VP-9	
158224	[224]	P-3C	VP-9	
158225	[RD-225]	P-3C	VP-47	
158227	[300]	NP-3D	VX-30	
158563	[YD-563]	P-3C	VP-4	
158564	[564]	P-3C	VP-5	
158567	[567]	P-3C	VP-9	
158570	[LL-570]	P-3C	VP-30	
158571	[LL-571]	P-3C	VP-30	
158573	[LN-573]	P-3C	VP-454	
158912	[912]	P-3C	VX-20	
158914	[914]	P-3C	VP-16	
158915	[915]	P-3C	VP-16	
158916	[LK-916]	P-3C	VP-26	
158917	[917]	P-3C	VP-8	
158918	[918]	P-3C	VP-40	
158919	[RD-919]	P-3C	VP-9	
158921	[LD-921]	P-3C	VP-10	
158922	[LN-922]	P-3C	VP-45	
158923	[YD-923]	P-3C	VP-4	
158924	[RD-924]	P-3C	VP-47	
158925	[925]	P-3C	VP-30	
158926	[926]	P-3C	VP-26	
158927	[927]	P-3C	VP-10	
158928	[LN-928]	P-3C	VP-45	
158929	[LL-929]	P-3C	VP-30	
158934	[LK-934]	P-3C	VP-26	
158935	[LN-935]	P-3C	VP-45	
159318	[318]	P-3C	VP-8	
159320	[320]	P-3C	VP-8	
159322	[PD-322]	P-3C	VP-9	
159323	[323]	P-3C	VP-47	
159326	[326]	P-3C	VP-30	
159327	[327]	P-3C	VP-10	
159329	[LL-329]	P-3C	VP-30	
159503	[LF-503]	P-3C	VP-16	
159504		P-3C	VPU-2	
159507	[PD-507]	P-3C	VP-9	
159885	[LF-885]	P-3C	VP-16	
159887		EP-3E	VQ-1	
159889	[YD-889]	P-3C	VP-4	
159893	[893]	EP-3E	VQ-1	
159894	[LD-894]	P-3C	VP-10	
160283	[283]	P-3C	VP-5	
160285		P-3C	VPU-2	
160287	[287]	P-3C	VP-9	
160290	[290]	P-3C	VX-20	
160291	[291]	EP-3E	VQ-1	
160292	[292]	P-3C	VPU-2	
160293		P-3C	NASC-FS	
160610	[LN-610]	P-3C	VP-45	
160761	[761]	P-3C	VP-16	
160762		P-3C	VPU-2	
160764	[764]	EP-3E	VQ-1	
160770	[PC]$	P-3C	VP-5	
160999	[999]	P-3C	VP-9	
161001	[001]	P-3C	VP-46	
161005	[005]	P-3C	VP-30	
161006	[006]	P-3C	VPU-2	
161010	[LL-010]	P-3C	VP-30	
161011	[011]	P-3C	VP-46	
161012	[012]	P-3C	VP-5	
161121	[121]	P-3C	VP-40	
161122	[226]	P-3C	VPU-2	
161124	[124]	P-3C	VX-20	
161126	[126]	P-3C	VP-8	
161127	[LF-127]	P-3C	VP-16	
161129	[LT-129]	P-3C	VP-62	
161132	[132]	P-3C	VP-1	
161329	[LT-329]	P-3C	VP-62	
161333	[LF-333]	P-3C	VP-16	

Type				Notes
161337	[337]	P-3C	VP-47	
161338	[LF-338]	P-3C	VP-16	
161339	[339]	P-3C	VP-47	
161404	[404]	P-3C	VP-1	
161405	[405]	P-3C	VP-8	
161406	[406]	P-3C	VP-30	
161407	[407]	P-3C	VP-5	
161408	[LC-408]	P-3C	VP-8	
161409	[LT-409]	P-3C	VP-62	
161410	[410]	EP-3E	VQ-1	
161411		P-3C	NASC-FS	
161412	[PJ-412]	P-3C	VP-69	
161413	[413]	P-3C	VX-20	
161414	[414]	P-3C	VP-46	
161415	[LD-415]	P-3C	VP-10	
161586	[QE-586]	P-3C	VP-40	
161587	[RL-587]	P-3C	VXS-1	
161588	[588]	P-3C	VP-10	
161589	[LK-589]	P-3C	VP-26	
161590	[590]	P-3C	VP-1	
161591	[44-P-4]$	P-3C	VP-30	
161593	[593]	P-3C	VP-8	
161594	[LL-594]	P-3C	VP-30	
161595	[LT-595]	P-3C	VP-62	
161596	[596]	P-3C	VP-46	
161763	[763]	P-3C	VP-10	
161764	[764]	P-3C	VP-46	
161765	[LT-765]	P-3C	VP-62	
161766	[YD-766]	P-3C	VP-4	
161767	[PD-767]	P-3C	VP-49	
162314	[LN-314]	P-3C	VP-45	
162315	[RD-315]	P-3C	VP-47	
162316	[316]	P-3C	VP-47	
162318	[LD-318]	P-3C	VP-10	
162770	[770]	P-3C	VP-30	
162771	[771]	P-3C	VP-45	
162772	[772]	P-3C	VP-47	
162773	[773]	P-3C	VP-30	
162774	[774]	P-3C	VX-20	
162775	[775]	P-3C	VP-30	
162776	[LD-776]	P-3C	VP-10	
162778	[PD-778]	P-3C	VP-9	
162998	[998]	P-3C	VP-4	
162999	[LF-999]	P-3C	VP-16	
163000	[000]	P-3C	VP-8	
163001	[001]	P-3C	VP-5	
163002	[LN-002]	P-3C	VP-45	
163003	[LA-003]	P-3C	VP-5	
163004	[004]	P-3C	VP-69	
163006	[006]	P-3C	VP-47	
163289	[289]	P-3C	VP-40	
163290	[290]	P-3C	VP-30	
163291	[291]	P-3C	VP-45	
163292	[292]	P-3C	VP-40	
163293	[LK-293]	P-3C	VP-26	
163294	[LK-294]	P-3C	VP-26	
163295	[295]	P-3C	VP-69	

Boeing E-6B Mercury
Boeing, McConnell AFB, Kansas;
VQ-3 & VQ-4, SCW-1,
Tinker AFB, Oklahoma

162782	VQ-3	
162783	VQ-3	
162784	VQ-4	
163918	VQ-3	
163919	VQ-3	
163920	VQ-3	
164386	VQ-4	
164387	VQ-3	
164388	VQ-4	
164404	VQ-4	
164405	VQ-4	
164406	VQ-3	
164407	VQ-4	
164408	VQ-4	
164409	VQ-4	
164410	VQ-4	

Boeing P-8A Poseidon
Boeing, Seattle;
VP-30, NAS Jacksonville, Florida [LL];
VX-1, NAS Patuxent River, Maryland;
VX-20, Patuxent River, Maryland [JA]

167951		VX-1	
167952	[JA-952]	VX-20	
167953		VX-20	
167954		VX-20	
167955	[JA-955]	VX-1	
167956	[JA-956]	VX-1	
168428	[LF-428]	VP-16	
168429	[LF-429]	VP-16	
168430	[LF-430]	VP-16	
168431	[LF-431]	VP-16	
168432	[LF-432]	VP-16	
168433	[433]	Boeing	
168434	[434]	Boeing	
168435	[435]	Boeing	
168436	[436]	Boeing	
168437		Boeing	
168438		Boeing	
168439		Boeing	
168440		Boeing	

McDonnell Douglas C-9B Skytrain II
VMR-1, Cherry Point MCAS, North Carolina;
VR-46, Atlanta, Georgia [JS];
VR-52, Willow Grove NAS, Pennsylvania [JT];
VR-61, Whidbey Island NAS, Washington [RS];

159113	VR-61	
160046	VMR-1	
160047	VMR-1	
160050	VR-52	
160051	VR-52	
161529	VR-46	
161530	VR-61	

Grumman C-20A/C-20D Gulfstream III/ C-20G Gulfstream IV*
VMR-Det, MCBH Kaneohe Bay, Hawaii;
VR-1, NAF Washington, Maryland;
VR-48, NAF Washington, Maryland [JR];
VR-51, MCBH Kaneohe Bay, Hawaii [RG]

C-20A

830500	VR-1	

C-20D

Type		Notes
163691	VR-1	
163692	VR-1	

C-20G

165093 [JR]	VR-48	
165094	VR-51	
165151	VR-51	
165152	VR-51	
165153	VMR-Det	

Cessna C-35 Citation V

MAW-4, Miramar MCAS, California;
MWHS-1, Futenma MCAS, Japan;
MWHS-4, NAS New Orleans;
VMR-1, Cherry Point MCAS, North Carolina;
VMR-2, NAF Washington, Maryland

165740 [EZ]	UC-35C	MWHS-4
165741 [EZ]	UC-35C	MWHS-4
165939	UC-35D	MWHS-1
166374	UC-35D	MWHS-1
166474	UC-35D	MAW-4
166500	UC-35D	MAW-4
166712	UC-35D	MWHS-1
166713	UC-35D	MWHS-1
166714 [VM]	UC-35D	VMR-2
166715	UC-35D	VMR-1
166766	UC-35D	VMR-2
166767 [VM]	UC-35D	VMR-2

Gulfstream Aerospace C-37B Gulfstream V

CFLSW Det, Hawaii;
VR-1, NAF Washington, Maryland

166375	CFLSW Det
166376	VR-1
166377	VR-1
166378	VR-1
166379	VR-1

Boeing C-40A Clipper

VR-56, NAS Oceana, Virginia;
VR-57, NAS North Island, California;
VR-58, NAS Jacksonville, Florida;
VR-59, NAS Fort Worth JRB, Texas

165829	VR-58
165830	VR-59
165831	VR-59
165832	VR-58
165833	VR-57
165834	VR-58
165835	VR-57
165836	VR-57
166693	VR-57
166694	VR-59
166695	VR-58
166696	VR-57

Lockheed C-130 Hercules

VR-53, NAF Washington, Maryland [AX];
VR-54, NAS New Orleans, Louisiana [CW];
VR-55, NAS Point Mugu, California [RU];
VR-62, NAS Jacksonville, Florida [JW];
VR-64, NAS Willow Grove, Pennsylvania [BD];
VMGR-152, Futenma MCAS, Japan [QD];
VMGR-234, NAS Fort Worth, Texas [QH];
VMGR-252, Cherry Point MCAS, North Carolina [BH];
VMGR-352, MCAS Miramar, California [QB];
VMGR-452, Stewart Field, New York [NY];
VX-20, Patuxent River, Maryland;
VX-30, NAS Point Mugu, California

Type			Notes
148891 [403]	KC-130F	VX-30	
148893 [402]	KC-130F	VX-30	
148897 [400]	KC-130F	VX-30	
160625	KC-130R	VX-20	
160626	KC-130R	VX-20	
160627	KC-130R	VX-20	
162308 [QH]	KC-130T	VMGR-234	
162309 [QH]	KC-130T	VMGR-234	
162310 [QH]	KC-130T	VMGR-234	
162311 [QH]	KC-130T	VMGR-234	
162785 [QH]	KC-130T	VMGR-234	
162786 [QH]	KC-130T	VMGR-234	
163022 [QH]	KC-130T	VMGR-234	
163023 [QH]	KC-130T	VMGR-234	
163310 [QH]	KC-130T	VMGR-234	
163311 [NY]	KC-130T	VMGR-452	
163591 [NY]	KC-130T	VMGR-452	
163592 [NY]	KC-130T	VMGR-452	
164105 [NY]	KC-130T	VMGR-452	
164106 [NY]	KC-130T	VMGR-452	
164180 [NY]	KC-130T	VMGR-452	
164181 [NY]	KC-130T	VMGR-452	
164441 [NY]	KC-130T	VMGR-452	
164442 [NY]	KC-130T	VMGR-452	
164597 [NY]	KC-130T-30	VMGR-452	
164598 [QH]	KC-130T-30	VMGR-234	
164762 [CW]	C-130T	VR-54	
164763	C-130T	*Blue Angels*	
164993 [BD]	C-130T	VR-64	
164994 [AX]	C-130T	VR-53	
164995 [AX]	C-130T	VR-53	
164996 [BD]	C-130T	VR-64	
164997 [AX]	C-130T	VR-53	
164998 [AX]	C-130T	VR-53	
164999 [QH]	KC-130T	VMGR-234	
165000 [QH]	KC-130T	VMGR-234	
165158 [CW]	C-130T	VR-54	
165159 [CW]	C-130T	VR-54	
165160 [JW]	C-130T	VR-62	
165161 [BD]	C-130T	VR-64	
165162 [QH]	KC-130T	VMGR-234	
165163 [QH]	KC-130T	VMGR-234	
165313 [313]	C-130T	VX-20	
165314 [JW]	C-130T	VR-62	
165315 [NY]	KC-130T	VMGR-452	
165316 [NY]	KC-130T	VMGR-452	
165348 [CW]	C-130T	VR-54	
165349 [RU]	C-130T	VR-55	
165350 [RU]	C-130T	VR-55	
165351 [RU]	C-130T	VR-55	
165352 [NY]	KC-130T	VMGR-452	
165353 [NY]	KC-130T	VMGR-452	
165378 [RU]	C-130T	VR-55	
165379 [RU]	C-130T	VR-55	
165735 [QB]	KC-130J	VMGR-352	

Type	Notes
165736 [QB] KC-130J VMGR-352	
165737 [BH] KC-130J VMGR-252	
165738 [BH] KC-130J VMGR-252	
165739 [QB] KC-130J VMGR-352	
165809 [BH] KC-130J VMGR-252	
165810 [BH] KC-130J VMGR-252	
165957 [QD] KC-130J VMGR-152	
166380 [BH] KC-130J VMGR-252	
166381 KC-130J VX-20	
166382 [QB] KC-130J VMGR-352	
166472 [BH] KC-130J VMGR-252	
166473 KC-130J VX-20	
166511 [BH] KC-130J VMGR-252	
166512 [QB] KC-130J VMGR-352	
166513 [BH] KC-130J VMGR-252	
166514 [QD] KC-130J VMGR-152	
166762 [QB] KC-130J VMGR-352	
166763 [QD] KC-130J VMGR-152	
166764 [BH] KC-130J VMGR-252	
166765 [QB] KC-130J VMGR-352	
167108 [BH] KC-130J VMGR-252	
167109 [QB] KC-130J VMGR-352	
167110 [QB] KC-130J VMGR-352	
167111 [QB] KC-130J VMGR-352	
167112 [BH] KC-130J VMGR-252	
167923 [QD] KC-130J VMGR-152	
167924 [QB] KC-130J VMGR-352	
167925 [QD] KC-130J VMGR-152	
167926 [QD] KC-130J VMGR-152	
167927 [QD] KC-130J VMGR-152	
167981 [QD] KC-130J VMGR-152	
167982 [QD] KC-130J VMGR-152	
167983 [QD] KC-130J VMGR-152	
167984 [QB] KC-130J VMGR-352	
167985 [QB] KC-130J VMGR-352	
168065 [QD] KC-130J VMGR-152	
168066 [QD] KC-130J VMGR-152	
168067 [QB] KC-130J VMGR-352	
168068 [QB] KC-130J VMGR-352	
168069 [BH] KC-130J VMGR-252	
168070 [BH] KC-130J VMGR-252	
168071 [BH] KC-130J VMGR-252	
168072 [QB] KC-130J VMGR-352	
168073 KC-130J	
168074 [QD] KC-130J VMGR-152	
168075 [QD] KC-130J VMGR-152	
168096 [BH] KC-130J VMGR-252	

US-based US Coast Guard Aircraft

Type	Notes
Gulfstream Aerospace C-37A Gulfstream V	
USCG, Washington DC	
01	
02	
Lockheed C-130 Hercules	
USCGS Barbers Point, Hawaii; USCGS Clearwater, Florida; USCGS Elizabeth City, North Carolina; USCGS Kodiak, Alaska; USCGS Sacramento, California	
1500 HC-130H Clearwater	
1502 HC-130H Clearwater	
1503 HC-130H Clearwater	
1504 HC-130H Elizabeth City $	
1700 HC-130H Clearwater	
1701 HC-130H Sacramento	
1702 HC-130H Sacramento	
1703 HC-130H Clearwater	
1704 HC-130H Kodiak	
1706 HC-130H Clearwater	
1707 HC-130H Sacramento	
1708 HC-130H Sacramento	
1709 HC-130H Kodiak	
1711 HC-130H Kodiak	
1712 HC-130H Sacramento	
1713 HC-130H Kodiak	
1714 HC-130H Sacramento	
1715 HC-130H Kodiak	
1716 HC-130H Clearwater	
1717 HC-130H Barbers Point	
1718 HC-130H Kodiak	
1719 HC-130H Clearwater	
1720 HC-130H Barbers Point	
1790 HC-130H Kodiak	
2001 HC-130J Elizabeth City	
2002 HC-130J Elizabeth City	
2003 HC-130J Elizabeth City	
2004 HC-130J Elizabeth City	
2005 HC-130J Elizabeth City	
2006 HC-130J Elizabeth City	

Aircraft in US Government or Military Service with Civil Registrations

Type	Notes
Canadair CL.601/CL.604* Challenger	
Federal Aviation Administration, Oklahoma	
N85	
N86	
N87	
N88*	

The yellow 'McGuire' lettering on the blue tailband reveals this USAF KC-1A, 85-0034, to be operated by the 305th Air Mobility Wing fleet. The fleet itself remains fairly static, with few movements between bases but 85-0034 was an exception to the rule, passing ownership to the 60th Air Mobility Wing at Travis Air Force Base some time after this photo was taken in April 2012 at RAF Mildenhall.

Military Aviation Sites on the Internet

The list below is not intended to be a complete list of military aviation sites on the Internet. The sites listed cover Museums, Locations, Air Forces, Companies and Organisations that are mentioned elsewhere in 'Military Aircraft Markings'. Sites listed are in English or contain sufficient English to be reasonably easily understood. Each site address was correct at the time of going to press. Additions are welcome, via the usual address found at the front of the book, or via e-mail to admin@aviation-links.co.uk. An up to date copy of this list is to be found at The 'Military Aircraft Markings' Web Site, http://www.militaryaircraftmarkings.co.uk/.

Name of Site	Web address (All Prefixed 'Http://')
MILITARY SITES-UK	
No 1 Sqn	www.raf.mod.uk/organisation/1squadron.cfm
No 2 Sqn	www.raf.mod.uk/organisation/2squadron.cfm
No 3 Sqn	www.raf.mod.uk/organisation/3squadron.cfm
No 4(R) Sqn	www.raf.mod.uk/organisation/4squadron.cfm
No 5 Sqn	www.raf.mod.uk/organisation/5squadron.cfm
No 6 Sqn	www.raf.mod.uk/organisation/6squadron.cfm
No 7 Sqn	www.raf.mod.uk/organisation/7squadron.cfm
No 8 Sqn	8squadron.co.uk/
No 9 Sqn	www.raf.mod.uk/organisation/9squadron.cfm
No 11 Sqn	www.raf.mod.uk/organisation/11squadron.cfm
No 12 Sqn	www.raf.mod.uk/organisation/12squadron.cfm
No 14 Sqn	www.raf.mod.uk/organisation/12squadron.cfm
No 15(R) Sqn	www.raf.mod.uk/organisation/14squadron.cfm
No 17(R) Sqn	www.raf.mod.uk/organisation/17squadron.cfm
No 18 Sqn	www.raf.mod.uk/organisation/18squadron.cfm
No 19(R) Sqn	www.raf.mod.uk/organisation/19squadron.cfm
No 22 Sqn	www.raf.mod.uk/organisation/22squadron.cfm
No 23 Sqn	www.raf.mod.uk/organisation/23squadron.cfm
No 24 Sqn	www.raf.mod.uk/organisation/24squadron.cfm
No 27 Sqn	www.raf.mod.uk/organisation/27squadron.cfm
No 28 Sqn	www.raf.mod.uk/organisation/28squadron.cfm
No 29(R) Sqn	www.raf.mod.uk/organisation/29squadron.cfm
No 30 Sqn	www.raf.mod.uk/organisation/30squadron.cfm
No 31 Sqn	www.raf.mod.uk/organisation/31squadron.cfm
No 32(The Royal) Sqn	www.raf.mod.uk/organisation/32squadron.cfm
No 33 Sqn	www.raf.mod.uk/organisation/33squadron.cfm
No 39 Sqn	www.raf.mod.uk/organisation/39squadron.cfm
No 41(R) Sqn	www.raf.mod.uk/organisation/41squadron.cfm

INTERNET SITES

Name of Site	Web address (All Prefixed 'Http://')
No 42(R) Sqn	www.raf.mod.uk/squadrons/h42.html
No 45(R) Sqn	www.raf.mod.uk/rafcranwell/aboutus/45sqn.cfm
No 47 Sqn	www.raf.mod.uk/organisation/47squadron.cfm
No 51 Sqn	www.raf.mod.uk/organisation/51squadron.cfm
No 55(R) Sqn	www.raf.mod.uk/rafcranwell/aboutus/55sqn.cfm
No 60(R) Sqn	www.raf.mod.uk/organisation/60squadron.cfm
No 72(R) Sqn	www.raf.mod.uk/organisation/72squadron.cfm
No 76(R) Sqn	www.raf.mod.uk/raflintononouse/aboutus/76rsqn.cfm
No 78 Sqn	www.raf.mod.uk/organisation/78squadron.cfm
No 84 Sqn	www.raf.mod.uk/organisation/84squadron.cfm
No 99 Sqn	www.raf.mod.uk/organisation/99squadron.cfm
No 100 Sqn	www.raf.mod.uk/organisation/100squadron.cfm
No 101 Sqn	www.raf.mod.uk/organisation/101squadron.cfm
No 120 Sqn	www.raf.mod.uk/organisation/120squadron.cfm
No 201 Sqn	www.raf.mod.uk/organisation/201squadron.cfm
No 202 Sqn	www.raf.mod.uk/organisation/202squadron.cfm
No 207(R) Sqn	www.raf.mod.uk/organisation/207squadron.cfm
No 208(R) Sqn	www.raf.mod.uk/organisation/208squadron.cfm
No 216 Sqn	www.raf.mod.uk/organisation/216squadron.cfm
No 230 Sqn	www.raf.mod.uk/organisation/230squadron.cfm
No 617 Sqn	www.raf.mod.uk/organisation/617squadron.cfm
No 702 NAS	www.royalnavy.mod.uk/The-Fleet/Aircraft/Helicopters/Lynx-Mk8/702-Naval-Air-Squadron
No 703 NAS	www.royalnavy.mod.uk/The-Fleet/Shore-Establishments/Aircrew-Training/703-NAS-Elementary-Flying-Training
No 750 NAS	www.royalnavy.mod.uk/The-Fleet/Shore-Establishments/Aircrew-Training/703-NAS-Elementary-Flying-Training
No 771 NAS	www.royalnavy.mod.uk/The-Fleet/Aircraft/Helicopters/Sea-King-Mk5/771-Naval-Air-Squadron
No 814 NAS	www.royalnavy.mod.uk/The-Fleet/Aircraft/Helicopters/Merlin-MK1/814-Naval-Air-Squadron
No 815 NAS	/www.royalnavy.mod.uk/The-Fleet/Aircraft/Helicopters/Lynx-Mk8/815-Naval-Air-Squadron
No 820 NAS	www.royalnavy.mod.uk/The-Fleet/Aircraft/Helicopters/Merlin-MK1/820-Naval-Air-Squadron
No 824 NAS	www.royalnavy.mod.uk/The-Fleet/Aircraft/Helicopters/Merlin-MK1/824-Naval-Air-Squadron
No 829 NAS	www.royalnavy.mod.uk/The-Fleet/Aircraft/Helicopters/Merlin-MK1/829-Naval-Air-Squadron
No 845 NAS	www.royalnavy.mod.uk/The-Fleet/Aircraft/Helicopters/Sea-King-Mk4/845-Naval-Air-Squadron
No 846 NAS	www.royalnavy.mod.uk/The-Fleet/Aircraft/Helicopters/Sea-King-Mk4/846-Naval-Air-Squadron
No 847 NAS	www.royalnavy.mod.uk/The-Fleet/Aircraft/Helicopters/Lynx-Mk9/847-Naval-Air-Squadron
No 848 NAS	www.royalnavy.mod.uk/The-Fleet/Aircraft/Helicopters/Sea-King-Mk4/848-Naval-Air-Squadron
No 849 NAS	www.royalnavy.mod.uk/The-Fleet/Aircraft/Helicopters/Sea-King-ASaC/849-Naval-Air-Squadron
No 854 NAS	www.royalnavy.mod.uk/The-Fleet/Aircraft/Helicopters/Sea-King-ASaC/854-Naval-Air-Squadron
No 857 NAS	www.royalnavy.mod.uk/The-Fleet/Aircraft/Helicopters/Sea-King-ASaC/857-Naval-Air-Squadron
Aberdeen, Dundee and St Andrews UAS	dialspace.dial.pipex.com/town/way/gba87/adstauas/
The Army Air Corps	www.army.mod.uk/aviation/air.aspx
Cambridge University Air Squadron	www.raf.mod.uk/cambridgeuas/
East Midlands UAS	www.raf.mod.uk/eastmidlandsuas/
Fleet Air Arm	www.royalnavy.mod.uk/About-the-Royal-Navy/The-Navy-and-the-Environment/In-the-Air
Liverpool University Air Squadron	www.raf.mod.uk/liverpooluas/
Manchester & Salford Universities Air Sqn	www.raf.mod.uk/manchesterandsalforduas/
Ministry of Defence	www.mod.uk/
Oxford University Air Sqn	www.raf.mod.uk/oxforduas/
QinetiQ	www.qinetiq.com/
RAF Benson	www.raf.mod.uk/rafbenson/

Name of Site	Web address (All Prefixed 'Http://')
RAF Brize Norton	www.raf.mod.uk/rafbrizenorton/
RAF Church Fenton (unofficial)	www.rafchurchfenton.org.uk/
RAF College Cranwell	www.raf.mod.uk/rafcranwell/
RAF Coningsby	www.raf.mod.uk/rafconingsby/
RAF Cosford	www.raf.mod.uk/rafcosford/
RAF Cottesmore	www.raf.mod.uk/rafcottesmore/
RAF Leuchars	www.raf.mod.uk/rafleuchars/
RAF Linton-on-Ouse	www.raf.mod.uk/raflintononouse/
RAF Lossiemouth	www.raf.mod.uk/raflossiemouth/
RAF Lyneham	www.raf.mod.uk/raflyneham/
RAF Marham	www.raf.mod.uk/rafmarham/
RAF Northolt	www.raf.mod.uk/rafnortholt/
RAF Odiham	www.raf.mod.uk/rafodiham/
RAF Shawbury	www.raf.mod.uk/rafshawbury/
RAF Valley	www.raf.mod.uk/rafvalley/
RAF Waddington	www.raf.mod.uk/rafwaddington/
RAF Wittering	www.raf.mod.uk/rafwittering/
Red Arrows	www.raf.mod.uk/reds/
Royal Air Force	www.raf.mod.uk/
Royal Air Force Reserves	www.raf.mod.uk/rafreserves/
University of London Air Sqn	www.ulas.org.uk/
Yorkshire UAS	www.raf.mod.uk/yorkshireuas/
MILITARY SITES-US	
Air Combat Command	www.acc.af.mil/
Air Force Reserve Command	www.afrc.af.mil/
Air National Guard	www.ang.af.mil/
Aviano Air Base	www.aviano.af.mil/
Liberty Wing Home Page (48th FW)	www.lakenheath.af.mil/
NASA	www.nasa.gov/
Mildenhall	www.mildenhall.af.mil/
Ramstein Air Base	www.ramstein.af.mil/
Spangdahlem Air Base	www.spangdahlem.af.mil/
USAF	www.af.mil/
USAF Europe	www.usafe.af.mil/
USAF World Wide Web Sites	www.af.mil/publicwebsites/index.asp
US Army	www.army.mil/
US Marine Corps	www.marines.mil/
US Navy	www.navy.mil/
US Navy Patrol Squadrons (unofficial)	www.vpnavy.com/
MILITARY SITES-ELSEWHERE	
Armée de l'Air	www.defense.gouv.fr/air/
Aeronautica Militare	www.aeronautica.difesa.it
Austrian Armed Forces (in German)	www.bmlv.gv.at/
Belgian Air Component	www.mil.be/aircomp/index.asp?LAN=E
Finnish Defence Force	www.puolustusvoimat.fi/en/
Forca Aerea Portuguesa	www.emfa.pt/
Frecce Tricolori	users.libero.it/gromeo/
German Marine	www.deutschemarine.de/
Greek Air Force	www.haf.gr/en/
Irish Air Corps	www.military.ie/air-corps
Israeli Defence Force/Air Force	www.idf.il/english/
Luftforsvaret	www.mil.no/
Luftwaffe	www.luftwaffe.de/
NATO	www.nato.int/
Royal Australian Air Force	www.airforce.gov.au/
Royal Canadian Air Force	www.airforce.forces.gc.ca/v2/index-eng.asp
Royal Danish Air Force (in Danish)	forsvaret.dk/
Royal Netherlands AF	www.defensie.nl/luchtmacht
Royal New Zealand AF	www.airforce.mil.nz/
Singapore Air Force	www.mindef.gov.sg/rsaf/
South African AF Site (unofficial)	www.saairforce.co.za/
Swedish Air Force	www.forsvarsmakten.se/sv/Forband-och-formagor/Flygvapnet/
Turkish Air Force	www.hvkk.tsk.tr/EN/Index.aspx

INTERNET SITES

Name of Site	Web address (All Prefixed 'Http://')
AIRCRAFT & AERO ENGINE MANUFACTURERS	
AgustaWestland	www.agustawestland.com/
BAE Systems	www.baesystems.com/
Bell Helicopter Textron	www.bellhelicopter.textron.com/
Boeing	www.boeing.com/
Bombardier	www.bombardier.com/
Britten-Norman	www.britten-norman.com/
CFM International	www.cfm56.com/
Dassault	www.dassault-aviation.com/
EADS	www.eads.com/
Embraer	www.embraer.com/
General Electric	www.ge.com/
Gulfstream Aerospace	www.gulfstream.com/
Hawker Beechcraft	www.hawkerbeechcraft.com/
Kaman Aerospace	www.kaman.com/
Lockheed Martin	www.lockheedmartin.com/
Rolls-Royce	www.rolls-royce.com/
Sikorsky	www.sikorsky.com/
UK AVIATION MUSEUMS	
Aeroventure	www.aeroventure.org.uk/
Bournemouth Aviation Museum	www.aviation-museum.co.uk/
Brooklands Museum	www.brooklandsmuseum.com/
City of Norwich Aviation Museum	www.cnam.co.uk/
de Havilland Aircraft Heritage Centre	www.dehavillandmuseum.2ya.com/
Dumfries & Galloway Aviation Museum	www.dumfriesaviationmuseum.com/
Fleet Air Arm Museum	www.fleetairarm.com/
Gatwick Aviation Museum	www.gatwick-aviation-museum.co.uk/
Imperial War Museum, Duxford	www.iwm.org.uk/duxford/
Imperial War Museum, Duxford (unofficial)	dspace.dial.pipex.com/town/square/rcy85/
The Jet Age Museum	www.jetagemuseum.btck.co.uk/
Lincs Aviation Heritage Centre	www.lincsaviation.co.uk/
Midland Air Museum	www.midlandairmuseum.co.uk/
Museum of Army Flying	www.flying-museum.org.uk/
Museum of Berkshire Aviation	www.museumofberkshireaviation.co.uk/
Museum of Flight, East Fortune	www.nms.ac.uk/our_museums/museum_of_flight.aspx
Museum of Science & Industry, Manchester	www.mosi.org.uk/
Newark Air Museum	www.newarkairmuseum.org/
North East Aircraft Museum	www.neam.co.uk/
RAF Museum, Cosford & Hendon	www.rafmuseum.org.uk/
Science Museum, South Kensington	www.sciencemuseum.org.uk/
Yorkshire Air Museum, Elvington	www.yorkshireairmuseum.org/
AVIATION SOCIETIES	
Air Britain	www.air-britain.com/
British Aircraft Preservation Council	www.bapc.org.uk/
Cleveland Aviation Society	homepage.ntlworld.com/phillip.charlton/cashome.html
East London Aviation Society	www.westrowops.co.uk/newsletter/elas.htm
LAAS International	www.laasdata.com/
Lowestoft Aviation Society	www.lowestoftaviationsociety.org/
Royal Aeronautical Society	aerosociety.com/
Scottish Air News	www.scottishairnews.co.uk/
Scramble (Dutch Aviation Society)	www.scramble.nl/
Solent Aviation Society	www.solent-aviation-society.co.uk/
Spitfire Society	www.spitfiresociety.com/
The Aviation Society Manchester	www.tasmanchester.com/
Ulster Aviation Society	www.ulsteraviationsociety.org/
Wolverhampton Aviation Group	www.wolverhamptonaviationgroup.co.uk/
OPERATORS OF HISTORIC AIRCRAFT	
The Aircraft Restoration Company	www.arc-duxford.co.uk/
Battle of Britain Memorial Flight	www.raf.mod.uk/bbmf/
The Catalina Society	www.catalina.org.uk/
Hangar 11 Collection	www.hangar11.co.uk/
Hunter Flying	www.hunterflyingltd.co.uk/